A History of the Parishes of St. Ives, Lelant, Towednack and Zennor: In the County of Cornwall

John Hobson Matthews

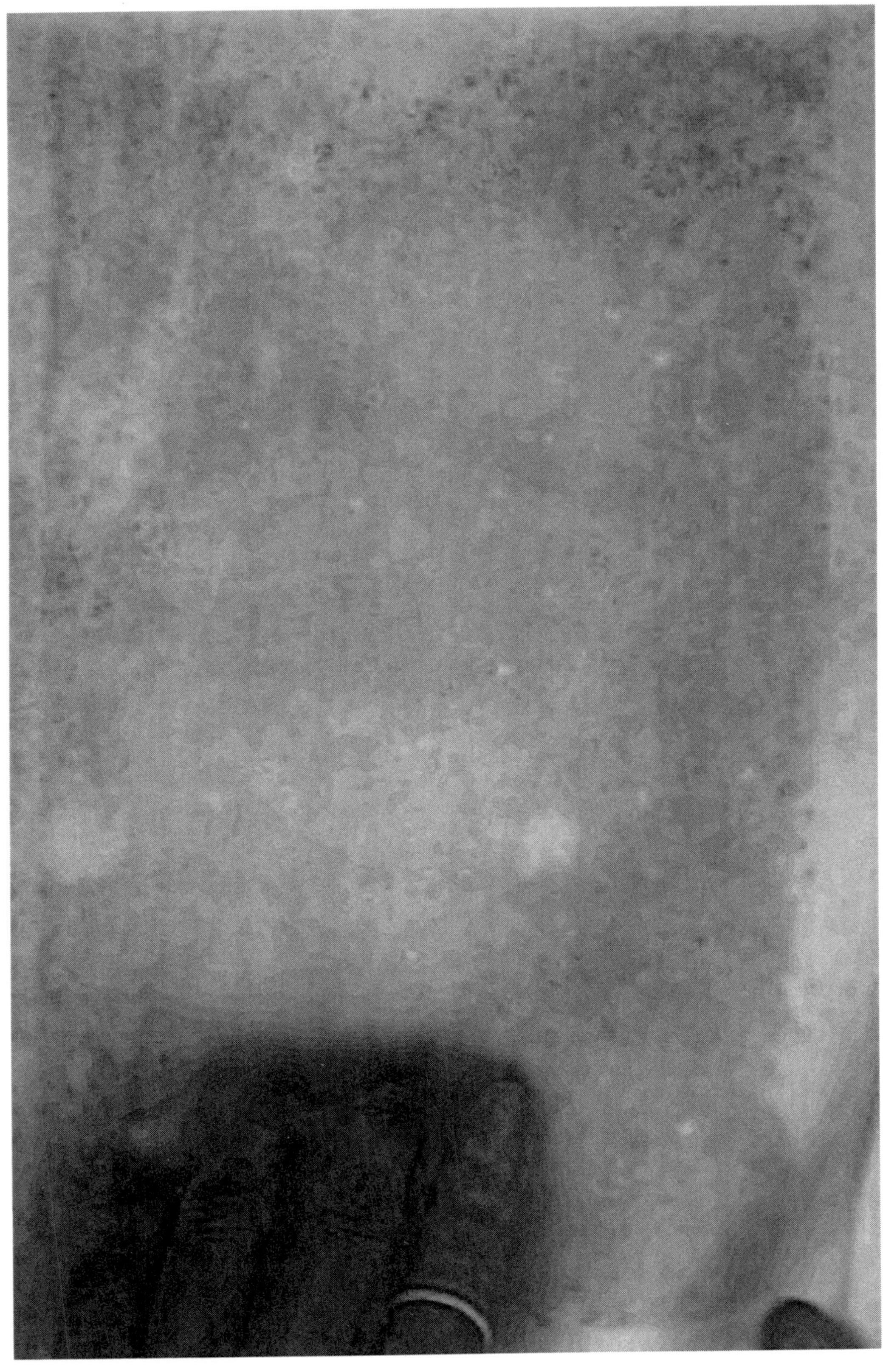

ST. IVES CHURCH, FROM SOUTH-EAST.

A HISTORY

OF THE

PARISHES OF SAINT IVES, LELANT, TOWEDNACK AND ZENNOR,

IN THE COUNTY OF CORNWALL.

BY

JOHN HOBSON MATTHEWS.

LONDON:

ELLIOT STOCK, 62, PATERNOSTER ROW, E.C.

1892.

'I pray you, let us satisfy our eyes
With the memorials, and the things of fame,
That do renown this city.'

TWELFTH-NIGHT.

'Cosi fuggendo, il mondo seco volve;
Nè mai si posa nè s'arresta o torna,
Fin chè v'ha ricondotti in poca polve.'

PETRARCA.

THIS BOOK

IS

DEDICATED TO MY SISTER

HONOR.

LINES ON 'A SCENE IN WEST CORNWALL,'

BY J. M. TINNEY, IN THE 'CORNISHMAN.'

'No leafy crown may poor Cornubia wear,
   Wind-swept from sea to sea her cairns outstand ;
Stranger, away! No charm detaineth here—
   Only brown heath, low wood, and level sand.

'But there between, unseen of passer-by,
   May hidden nook and fairy dell be found,
Lovelier because unlooked for ; gems, they lie
   In summer beauty, consecrated ground.

'So human nature, often poorly shown
   To level eyes, when from the height above
Surveyed, may mirror beauty of its own,
   Kind Heaven will deign to pity and to love.'

TABLE OF CONTENTS.

CHAPTER VI.

THE PARISH CHURCH OF SAINT IVES.

PAGE

CHAPTER VII.

THE CHURCHES OF LELANT, TOWEDNACK AND ZENNOR.

CHAPTER VIII.

THE 'VALOR ECCLESIASTICUS'

CHAPTER IX.

THE REFORMATION PERIOD.

CHAPTER X.

THE ELIZABETHAN PERIOD.

CHAPTER XI.

THE SUBSIDY ROLLS, 1536 TO 1599.

CHAPTER XII.

THE BOROUGH ACCOUNTS, FIRST VOLUME, 1570 TO 1639.

CHAPTER XIII.

SAINT IVES IN THE SEVENTEENTH CENTURY.

CHAPTER XIV.

THE BOROUGH ACCOUNTS, SECOND VOLUME, 1639 TO 1687.

CHAPTER XXII.

SAINT IVES IN THE FIRST HALF OF THE NINETEENTH CENTURY.

CHAPTER XXIII.

SAINT IVES AT THE PRESENT DAY.

CHAPTER XXIV.

THE PILCHARD FISHERY.

CHAPTER XXV.

LEGENDARY LORE.

CHAPTER XXVI.

SURVIVING CUSTOMS.

CHAPTER XXVII.

OLD SAYINGS.

CHAPTER XXVIII.

THE CORNISH LANGUAGE AT SAINT IVES.

CHAPTER XXIX.

PLACE-NAMES IN THE SAINT IVES DISTRICT,

CHAPTER XXX.

LOCAL FAMILIES.

CHAPTER XXXI.

LOCAL NOTABILITIES,

CHAPTER XXXII.

PARLIAMENTARY HISTORY OF THE BOROUGH.

CHAPTER XXXIII.

THE ELECTION OF 1768.

CHAPTER XXXIV.

PUBLIC OFFICERS OF THE BOROUGH AND PARISH OF SAINT IVES.

PREFACE.

WHATEVER be the imperfections of this book, it has at least the distinction of being the first printed history of the parishes which form what we have called the Saint Ives District, save a few brief notices contained in works treating of the entire county of Cornwall. It is true that in the last century Mr. John Hicks, of Saint Ives, wrote a history of his native town, and that many extracts from his work have been handed down to us in the volumes of the county topographers; but Hicks' manuscript, valuable as no doubt it was, was never published, and has long been lost. The author therefore claims from his readers the indulgence which should be readily shown towards the man who is first in the field as the historian of his locality.

To write a history is, in the present day, a very different undertaking from what it was fifty years ago, before the jewel-mines of our public records had been opened up. Time was when a parish church could be dismissed as 'a mediaeval structure in the Gothick style, dedicated to St Mary'; and when a history of England was not so much a record of facts, as an essay on the providential development of our happy constitution in Church and State. But nowadays people read history with the simple desire to obtain accurate information upon all points connected both with the public and private life of their forefathers, and demand rather a digest of authentic records than a literary essay.

Hence this history is to a great extent a compilation. A full and complete history, such as it aspires to be, must embody largely the original records on which it is founded, and also the important results of the study of earlier historians. And it will hardly be denied that a real benefit is conferred upon the reader when the substance of numerous documents (both original and printed) bearing on the bygones of the same locality has been collected into one volume. Nor is the writer willing to resign all claim to originality, for in many chapters of this book will be found, he trusts, things which are at the same time good and new.

Be this as it may, the author is happy to believe that he has, at all events, served in some small degree the cause of historical truth by his persistent practice of checking every statement which he has taken from other books—a practice which has had the effect of revealing no small number of egregious historical blunders which could boast a respectable literary descent. Moreover, he has, he believes, left no likely class of public records unsearched in his endeavour to make his work full and reliable.

Besides his many obligations to those writers a list of whose works will be found at the end of this volume, the author must express his indebtedness to several gentlemen, without whose kindly and willing aid this history of Saint Ives would have been far less complete than it is. Foremost among these friendly coadjutors is the Rev. Prebendary Hingeston-Randolph, who has rendered such invaluable services to the cause of scientific archæology in the West of England. He very kindly lent the aid of his deep and accurate knowledge of matters ecclesiological, and consented to read and correct the proofs of the chapters on the churches of Saint Ives, Lelant, Towednack and Zennor. Mr. Edward Hain, junior, most obligingly lent the recently-discovered volume of Saint Ives Borough Accounts, and several scarce printed books, and permitted the author to overhaul a quantity of old papers in his possession, from which much valuable material has been drawn. Thanks are also due to Mr. W. T. Tresidder for permission to copy a number of municipal records of the last century; to the Rev. J. Balmer Jones, the Rev. R. F. Tyacke and the Rev. S. H. Farwell Roe, vicars of Saint Ives, Lelant and Zennor respectively, who allowed unlimited extracts to be taken from their parish registers; and to Mr. Anthony, postmaster of Saint Ives, who wrote a reliable account of the pilchard fishery. That portion of the first chapter which treats of the fauna and flora of the Saint Ives district was set in order by a learned naturalist, Mr. James Ambrose Story, B.A., of Cardiff. To these gentlemen, and to many others, though not named, the author desires to express his sincere thanks for their kind and highly-valued assistance.

CARDIFF,
Christmas, 1891.

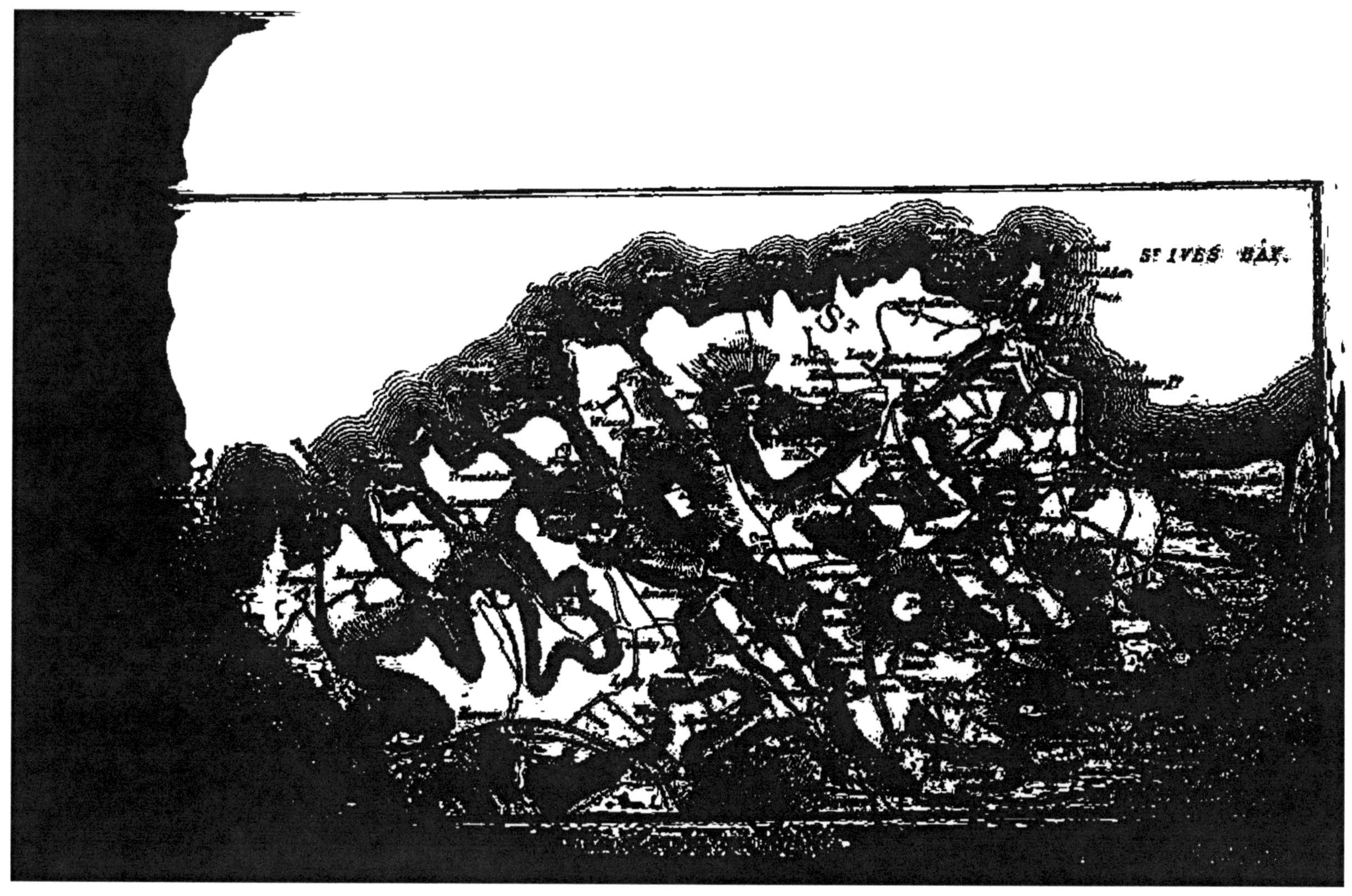
St IVES BAY

A HISTORY OF SAINT IVES, LELANT, TOWEDNACK AND ZENNOR.

CHAPTER I.

A PHYSICAL DESCRIPTION OF THE DISTRICT.

THE town of Saint Ives is situated in the Hundred of West Penwith, on the northern coast of Cornwall, 277 miles south-west of London, and sixteen miles from the Land's End. The older part of the town stands on an isthmus which separates a small peninsula from the mainland. Some centuries ago this peninsula was entirely surrounded by water, and it is still called The Island.

The parish of Saint Ives is bounded on the north and east by the sea; on the south-east by the parish of Lelant; and on the west by the parish of Towednack, which is bounded on the west by the parish of Zennor.

From the highest part of the Island at Saint Ives we have a view which embraces the most prominent natural features of this district. Let us begin by describing the coast line. The farthest points which we can see westward are the jagged headlands of Clodgy and Carthew, between which last and the Island is the cove called Porthmeor. The extreme point of the Island is called Pendinas, or Saint Ives Head. Between this and the town are the cove of Porthgwidden, the rocks of Carn Crowz, and the quay or pier. The shore close to the town is called the Foresand, and is separated by Penolva Point from the sands of Porthminster. Still looking eastward around Saint Ives Bay we trace in succession the headland of Penmester; the small cove of Porthgroynia; the expansive sands of Porthripter, separated by Carrack Gladn Point from those of Porthkitny; Hawk's Point; the sand-hills or *towans* of Lelant, and the mouth of the Hayle

River; and then, on the other side of Saint Ives Bay, the black cliffs and yellow sand-hills of the eastern shore, terminating with the island and lighthouse of Godrevy. Beyond this we see the headland of Saint Agnes, and still farther to the north-east we may dimly discern the far-projecting promontory of Trevose Head. Westward stretches the vast Atlantic.

Inland the district is hilly. Near the town are the eminences called Barnoon and the Stennack, and the hills of Penmester and Tregenna. Further to the south and west are Carn Stabba and Trencrom Hill, the Rocky Downs, Rosewall Hill, Worvas Hill (on which stands Knill's Steeple), Trink, Trendrean and Trevalgan Hills.

The following figures are taken from Wallis' 'Cornwall Register,' 1847:

St. Ives contains statute acres,			1850
Lelant ,,	,,	,,	4240
Towednack	,,	,,	2880
Zennor ,,	,,	,,	4640

The height of the	ground at Lelant Church	is	110	feet.
,, ,,	Trencrom Hill	,,	550	,,
,, ,,	Trink Hill	,,	652	,,
,, ,,	ground at Knill's Steeple	,,	545	,,

From these heights several streams flow into Saint Ives Bay. The Trenwith stream, locally known as the River, rises by Rosewall Hill, in the parish of Towednack, runs down the Stennack through the village of Trenwith, and so into the harbour of Saint Ives. The Tregenna stream rises on the hill of that name, flows through the grounds of Tregenna Castle, and loses itself in the sands of Porthminster, near the foundations of an ancient chapel. Both these streams, but especially the latter, supply good drinking-water.

In the south-eastern end of Saint Ives parish there is another stream (used for tin-streaming) which rises near Knill's Steeple, and flows through Carbis Valley into Carbis Bay.

The Hayle River is the only considerable stream in this part of Cornwall. It gives its name to the manufacturing town of Hayle, and separates the parishes of Lelant and Phillack. This river and the valley of Saint Erth form a continuous, though irregular, depression, stretching from north-west to south-east across the narrowest part of the West Cornwall peninsula, and separating the Land's End district from the rest of the county. Recent geological investigations conclusively demonstrate that this depression was, ages ago, a marine channel, and the island thus formed was probably the chief of the Cassiterides, or tin-bearing islands.

Quaint, laborious old Holinshed found out all about these rivers, and thus describes them:

'The soile also is very hillie here, as for saint Ies towne, it is almost (as I said) a byland, and yet it is well watered with sundrie rilles that come from those hilles unto the same. S. Ies baie is full ten miles from the lands end, & rather more, if you reckon to the fall of the Haile, which lieth in the very middest and highest part of the baie of the same.'

The 'Itinerary' of William of Worcester, written in 1478, has a good deal to say as to the geography of the Saint Ives district:

'Villa Lalant super mare boriale per tria miliaria de Mont-Myghell.' (The town of Lelant is on the northern sea about three miles from St. Michael's Mount.)

'Villa Seynt Hy sup: mare borial: circa 12 milia ab ult° fine occidentalis regni Anglie.' (The town of St. Ives is on the northern sea about 12 miles from the extreme end of the west of the Kingdom of England.)

'Le North sea. Ville pĉipales sup: mare boriale site. Primo Seynt Hyes villa ṽsus orientē ex pte: boriali maris distat a Musholt 8 mil. De S. Hyes usque Lananta 2 miliaria.' (The North Sea. The principal towns situated on the northern sea. First, St. Ives, a town towards the east, on the northern side of the sea, is distant from Mousehole 8 miles. From St. Ives to Lelant 2 miles.)

'Mem. de Seynt Hyves villa, et omnes villæ proxime sequentes sunt scitæ sup: mare boriale ꝟsus orientē preter vill: de Launceston.' (Mem. From St. Ives' town, and all the towns near to it, are situated on the northern sea towards the east, except the town of Lanceston.)

'Mem. from Pensance to Seynt Yves jette 6 myle.'

'Item from Seynt Yves usque Lalant havyn 2 myle.'

Leland's 'Itinerary' (3rd. ed., Oxon., 1769) has these geographical notes:

'Hayle, flu. nunc, ut quidam putant, absorptum a sabulo; it was on the North Se.' (Hayle, a river now, as some think, absorbed by the sand.)

At Lelant there is 'passage at Ebbe over a great Strond: and then over Heyle River.'

'S. Iēs a 2 Miles or more from Lannant. The Place that the chief of the Toun hath and partely dooth stonde yn is a very Peninsula, and is extendid into the Se of Severn as a Cape. This Peninsula to cumpace it by the Rote lakkith litle of a Mile.'

'The Town of S. Iēs is servid with fresch Water of Brokettes that rise in the Hilles therby.'

'The shore from S. Iēs is sore plagued to S. Carantokes [Crantock] with Sandes.'

Holinshed calls Saint Ives a

'Little Byland, Cape or Peninsula, which is not to be counted of in this place. And yet, sith I haue spoken of it, you shall understand, that it is called Pendinas, and beside that the compasse thereof is not aboue a mile, this is to be remembred farder thereof, how there standeth a Pharos or light therein, for ships which saile by those coasts in the night. There is also at the verie point of the said Pendinas, a chappell of saint Nicholas, beside the church of saint Ia, an Irish woman saint. It belonged of late to the Lord Brooke, but now (as I guesse) the Lord Mountioy enioieth it. There is also a blockhouse, and a peere in the eastside thereof, but the peere is sore choked with sand, as is the whole shore furthermore from S. Ies unto S. Carantokes, insomuch that the greatest part of this Byland is now couered with sands, which the sea casteth up, and this calamitie hath indured little aboue fiftie yeares, as the inhabitants doo affirme.' (Edition of 1586.)

Writing of the accumulated sands on the eastern shore of Saint Ives Bay, Halliwell says:

'Their further progress is now retarded by the extensive propagation of the common sea-rush, the *Arundo arenaria* of Linnæus, or, as some have it, *Calamagrostis arenaria.* This rush grows rapidly on the sand, where it mechanically opposes all motion on the surface. The result is that these huge sandy hillocks, instead of being nuisances, are in the process of becoming fine grassy undulating promenades, the reed favouring the growth of turf. Here may also be seen the common eringo, which was cultivated on the sands at Hayle in Elizabeth's time for the sake of its roots, as recorded by Drayton. From the Hayle Towans, note on the right the Godrevy rocks and lighthouse; at low water, the St. Ives fishermen casting their launce-nets for bait; but only at high water turn your eyes in the direction of Penzance, when the wide expanse of the estuary is then a beautiful lake, rendering pretty the rural village of Lelant, with its woods to the water-edge. But above all is from this spot the unique prospect of St. Ives. No one could fancy, as one sees that town as if it absolutely glittered in the sun and ornamented the sea—a sort of minor English Constantinople—of how squalid a character is the mass of buildings there, and how an anticipated romance will be dissipated by a visit.'

In a maritime parish of Cornwall the rocks of the shore are an important feature, and are all the more interesting on account of the ancient names which they bear, names which, for the most part, are now unknown except to the older generation of fishermen. A full list of these coast-rocks will be found in another chapter.

In the ironstone cliffs to the east of Porthminster are several caves. Just under Tregenna is an old house known as the Vow

Cot, meaning 'the cottage by the cave'; and in Carrack Gladn Cove is the cave called Zawn-Abadden.

The piles of rock called 'carns' are exceedingly numerous in the neighbourhood of Saint Ives. They are nearly all composed of granite, but in the immediate neighbourhood of the old town this gives place to a very hard, dark-green slate-rock. This might be expected from the geological formation of the district, the north-east part of Saint Ives parish being, according to Dr. Borlase, composed of compact and slaty felspar rocks, while the other part is granite. Both these rocks, he adds, are traversed metalliferous veins.

Hunt, in his 'Popular Romances of the West of England,' p. 201, thus describes the geological formation of the Island:

'The so-called Island is now a peninsular mass of clay slate-rocks, interpenetrated by very hard trappean masses. Between this and the town of St. Ives is a low neck of land, which consists chiefly of sand and gravel, with some masses of clay slate broken into small angular fragments. On either side of this neck of land are good examples of raised beaches. Everything, therefore, favours the tradition which is preserved in the name. One statement is that the Island was brought in from the sea; another, that it rose out of the sea.'

The mines in the Saint Ives district were formerly many and prosperous; but the general decadence of Cornish mining during the last fifty years has seriously affected them. Wheal Providence, which, a century ago, was one of the most fortunate mines in West Cornwall, has long ceased working. Its remains still cover many acres of ground between Knill's Steeple and the highroad from Saint Ives to Lelant. This mine has given its name to the hamlet of Chy-an-Wheal, *i.e.*, 'Mine House.' Another old, but now disused, mine is that named Saint Ives Consols. It is situated at the top of the Stennack, and the buildings connected with it are very extensive.

'St. Ives Consols tin-mine has been at work some thirty-eight years, and is very rich for tin, and has made large profits. The monthly cost was £2,400, and the number employed was 450 persons; but if tin be at a low price, the mine barely pays expenses. The formation of the tin-ore in this mine is very singular, and is provincially termed *carbona*.' ('Cornwall: its Mines and Miners,' 1855, p. 40.)

Below Saint Ives Consols, on the Stennack, are the Trenwith Stamps, first started about a hundred years ago. On the rocks of Pednolva is seen the engine-house (now an artist's studio) of a mine which was made some thirty years ago, and which proved a failure.

Much tin-mining has been done on the eastern side of Rosewall Hill, which is dotted with engine-houses. The district of Halsetown, near Saint Ives, was built to afford dwellings to the hundreds of miners formerly employed in the neighbourhood.

Saint Ives, as indeed the whole of Land's End, affords a rich field for the botanist. Ferns, mosses, lichens, and flowering plants, rare or unknown in other parts of Great Britain, are here to be found in abundance. Some idea of the riches of this district may be formed from the fact that

'according to the census of distribution given in the "London Catalogue of Mosses and Hepaticæ," published two years ago, every species and variety found in England, south of Lancashire, occurs in West Cornwall, with the single exception of *S. laricinum*, and there is reason to hope it may yet be discovered here.' (Report of the Penzance Nat. Hist. and Antiq. Soc., 1883-84, p. 383.)

The following list contains the names of some of the plants of this district, and the localities in which they may be found:

LICHENS.

Sticta crocata. The moors of Zennor.
Lecanora hæmatomma. St. Ives.
Pycnothelia papillaria. Gurnard's Head.
Petalophyllum Ralfsii. Lelant.

MOSSES.

Hypnum molluscum. Lelant.
H. circinatum. ,,
H. tenellum. ,,
H. commutatum. ,,
Bryium inclinatum. ,,
Entosthodon Templetoni. St. Ives.
Tortula squarrosa. Lelant.
Scapania undulata.
Thuidium abietinum.
Jungermannia Wilsoniana.
J. riparia.
Cephalozia Jackii.
Zieria julacea.
Sphagnum acutifolium purpureum. Gurnard's Head.
S. a. rubellum.
S. fimbriatum. Try Moor.
S. cuspidatum. Gurnard's Head Moor.
var. *plumosum.* Near Zennor cromlech.
,, *falcatum.* Towednack.

MOSSES (*continued*).

S. rigidum. Occurs sparingly on Clodgy Moor.
S. subsecundum.
var. *auriculatum.* Towednack.
S. tenellum. Clodgy Moor.
S. papillosum viride. Gurnard's Head Moor.

FERNS.

The maidenhair fern, *Adiantum capillus veneris.* Between St. Ives and Hayle, in low dripping caves and on rocks by the coast.
The black spleenwort, *Asplenium adiantum nigrum.*
The lanceolate spleenwort, *A. lanceolatum.*
The marine spleenwort, *A. marinum.* On the coast generally.
The rue-leaved spleenwort, or wall-rue, *A. ruta-muraria.* General.
The common spleenwort, *A. trichomanes.*
The lady-fern, *Athyrium filix-fœmina*, var. *convexum.*
The hard fern, *Blechnum spicant.*
The scaly spleenwort, *Ceterach officinarum.*
The hart's tongue, *Scolopendrium vulgare.*
The broad prickly-toothed fern, *Lastrea dilatata.*
The male fern, *L. filix-mas.*
The hay-scented fern, *L. fœnisecii.*
The mountain fern, *L. oreopteris.*
The Tunbridge filmy fern, *Hymenophyllum Tunbridgense.*
Wilson's filmy fern, *H. unilaterale.*
The beech polypody, *Polypodium phegopteris.*
The common prickly fern, *Polystichum aculeatum.*
The common adder's tongue, *Ophioglossum vulgatum.*
The flowering fern, *Osmunda regalis.*
The moonwort, *Botrychium lunaria.*

FLOWERING PLANTS.

The mountain St. John's wort, *Hypericum montanum.*
The stinking iris, *Iris fœtidissima.* Lelant.
The balm-leaved figwort, *Scrophularia scorodonia.* This is a West European plant, found as far south as Madeira; but in Great Britain found only in Jersey, the south-west of Cornwall, and at Tralee in Ireland.
The vernal squill, *Scilla verna.* Common on the cliffs all round the coast of West Penwith. At St. Ives pink and white varieties are mingled with the blue.
The wild columbine, *Aquilegia vulgaris.* The blue, pink, and white varieties are found covering the slopes between Lelant and St. Ives, and also at Hayle Causeway.

FLOWERING PLANTS (*continued*).

The bird's foot fenugreek, *Trigonella ornithopodioides*. On the coast near Gurnard's Head.

The field gentian, *Gentiana campestris*.

The broad-leaved centaury, *Erythræa latifolia*. On the Towans. Also *E. ramosissima*.

The sea-lavender, vars. *Statice Didartii* and *S. spathulata*. At St. Ives Head, etc.

The shore-weed, *Littorella lacustris*.

The common fennel, *Fœniculum vulgare*.

The bearded broom-rape, *Orobanche barbata*.

The wall-mustard, *Sinapis muralis*. St. Ives.

The Portland spurge, *Euphorbia Portlandica*. Between St. Ives and Hayle.

The Cornish money-wort, *Sibthorpia Europæa*. In boggy places.

When, in September, 1882, the Penzance Natural History and Antiquarian Society paid a visit to Towednack church, Mr. Ralfs, one of the members, having summoned the party to the tower, spoke as follows: It was rarely, he said, that a botanist had a chance of saying a word in a church; but here he was able to call their attention to a very rare plant indeed, an alga known under the name of *Oscillatoria cyanea*. Thirty years ago, when he visited the church, it grew all over the walls, and being of a sky-blue colour, it gave a very peculiar appearance to the interior. Shortly afterwards the pews had to be restored on account of dry-rot, and a coat of lime was at the same time put over the walls, destroying the plant. The tower, however, had not been touched, and he was glad to see the oscillatoria still growing there. It was the only place in the West of England where it grew, so far as he was aware. It was remarkable that it was only found in churches, and he left it to others to explain where it was before churches existed. (N.B.—It has since been found elsewhere in the Saint Ives district.)

Grain is produced in the rich level country which lies between the Zennor hills and the sea; but the farms within the four parishes are, for the most part, pastoral and not agricultural. In the first half of the eighteenth century even the pasturage of cattle in Cornwall was restricted by the difficulty of feeding the stock in winter; but about the year 1747 the turnip was introduced into West Cornwall by a Norwich farmer named Mathews, whose son, Thomas Mathews, brought this now well-known root into the Saint Ives district. The first field of turnips ever seen in this locality was grown by him in the parish of Lelant, and old people still speak from tradition of the crowds who went out to see the 'Norfolk whites,' which were to revolutionize the system of farming in West Cornwall. There is an old saying familiar to the elder generation from Truro to the Land's End, that 'Mathews brought in the turnips, and a King brought in the pippins.' The latter part of the phrase is popularly understood to mean that a King of England brought the first apples to Cornwall in his pocket; but the saying, in all probability, arose from the fact that a man of the name of King introduced ribston pippins from Norfolk at the same time that turnips were first made familiar to the Cornish farmer.

Market-gardening is extensively carried on in the parishes of Saint Ives and Lelant. Owing to the mildness of the climate and the fertility of the soil in the low lands, a great trade is done in spring vegetables, especially in potatoes and cauliflowers, which are sent by rail to London. The earliest consignments of English vegetables to be seen in Covent Garden Market are from West Cornwall and Scilly.

Although the neighbourhood of Saint Ives, like the rest of West Cornwall, is somewhat bare of trees, some of the hills and valleys are fairly well wooded. The Stennack shows remains of former orchards, of late encroached upon by building operations. In most parts of the parish of Lelant there is no lack of timber; fine old elms abound near the mouth of the Hayle River, and the estate of Trevetho has been extensively planted within the present century. In the parishes of Towednack and Zennor timber is very scarce; but the bleak moors in these parishes produce large quantities of furze and of peat-turf, which are there used for fuel.

The fauna of the whole district of West Cornwall, like its flora, is very rich, especially in fishes and birds. Many different kinds of fish are caught off the coast; of these, as is well known, pilchards are by far the most important. Of the pilchard-fishery, as a branch of industry, we shall have more to say later on. In birds, perhaps no other part of Great Britain is so rich. Hawks are common among the hills of Zennor, and the peregrine falcon has also been caught there. The merlin has been seen at Zennor in winter, and the ring-ouzel is said to breed there. The rock-dove frequents the cliffs near Bosigran in the same parish. Two specimens of Schinz's stint were shot in the Hayle estuary in October, 1846, and the great snipe was seen at Saint Ives in October, 1855.

The conchologist will find many rarities to reward his researches in this district, both of land and of sea shells. On the Hayle sands, after a strong wind from the west, the *Ianthina communis*, or ocean-snail, is not infrequently found. The Pisan snail, *Helix Pisana*, is found in profusion feeding on the sea-holly (*Eryngium maritimum*), which grows about the coast at Saint Ives, this being the only locality in England in which this species is to be found. The only other localities in the British Isles for this snail are Balbriggan Strand near Dublin, Tenby and Manorbier in South Wales, and Jersey. These snails are said in hot weather to bury themselves some inches deep in the sand, at the roots of *Carex arenaria*. The *Planorbis glaber* (*P. lævis*) is found in Trevetho Pond.

Here is a bit of the natural history of this part of the coast, as observed two centuries ago. The great naturalist Ray was here in 1662, and has left us the following notes:

'Monday, June the 30th, we rode over the sands to St. Ives. We saw here some of the young murres, a bird black on the head and back, white under the breast and belly, and hath a black and sharp bill, black feet, whole-footed. We were assured that the Cornish murre is nothing else but the razor-bill. All along the cliffs, as we rode upon the sand toward St. Ives, grew *Fœniculum vulgare* in great plenty. We saw many of those birds, which they call gannets, flying about on the water. This bird hath long wings and a long neck, and flieth strongly. Possibly it may be the catarractes. He preys upon pilchards, the shoals whereof great multitudes of these fowl constantly pursue.'

In another place he says that

'the gannets were almost of the bigness of a goose, white, the tips only of their wings black. They have a strange way of catching them, by tying a pilchard to a board, and fastening it so that the bird may see it, who comes down with so great swiftness for his prey, that he breaks his neck against the board.'

The same author says of Saint Ives:

'The people of Brittany drive a great trade here for *raiæ*, which they dry in the sun, and then carry away. In exchange for this they bring salt. The inhabitants of this town are of opinion that their fish are better and more daintily tasted than those taken about Penzance.'

Ray also observed near Carrack Du

'a kind of plant, on a moist bank, whose leaf is somewhat like to *Saxifraga aurea*. It runs out in long wires like to *Campanula cymbalariæ fol.* At each leaf it bears one small purplish-coloured flower. We found another plant on a boggy ground, which had small grassy leaves, but very few; it was almost all stalk; it grew not above an hand high, had a yellow flower, but not open in any when we were there, it being a close day. The seed-vessel was somewhat large, round, biggest in the middle, smaller at both ends, like some rolls wherewith they roll corn.'

The climate of this locality is bracing and invigorating, but never very cold. In summer Saint Ives is without the extreme heat and relaxing air which characterize the southern coast of the Land's End district. In going from Saint Ives to places on the opposite coast, an unpleasant change is felt as soon as Saint Michael's Mount comes in sight. Many persons experience lassitude, accompanied by headache, on going from Saint Ives to Penzance, so great is the change produced by the six miles' journey from the north to the south coast of the Land's End district. Courtney's 'Guide to Penzance' (1845) thus illustrates this sharp distinction between the air of the northern and southern coasts, which, moreover, the writer has often personally observed:

'By the old road from Penzance to St. Ives, after leaving Kenegie, the tourist comes upon a sort of tableland. From the foot of the hill, on which is Castel-an-dinas, there is a gradual descent for a considerable distance, until at last a very steep declivity brings him to the village of Nancledrea. On making this descent a very curious atmospheric phenomenon is frequently observable—the clear and cloudless sky becomes suddenly dense and hazy, evidently from the condensation of the warm and rarified air of the Mount's Bay by the colder current which comes from the Bristol Channel.'

Hicks, in his now lost MS. of the History of Saint Ives, after speaking of the plague of 1646, thus proceeds:

'Notwithstanding the plague, in the town lives no doctor, surgeon, nor apothecary, the air being very healthy, and many of the inhabitants now living being above eighty years of age. I have known very few to be blind or troubled with the stone, although the inhabitants of the lower part of the town eat more sand than salt; and seldom or never troubled with the ague, their physic anciently being two-pennyworth of aqua vitæ and a pennyworth of treacle-water, mixed together, which they take, and sweat, and so are cured. I never knew but two persons afflicted with the gout.'

The *Journal of the British Medical Association* of September 23, 1875, says:

'Within ten miles of Penzance is the town of St. Ives, which, from its natural resources and position, should attract convalescents. The climate is bracing, and differs in temperature six or seven degrees from the south. It is hence suitable for lung diseases and debilitated constitutions.'

This is a convenient stage at which to treat of the ethnology of the Saint Ives districts. In the main, of course, the population is Celtic, of the Cymric branch, allied to the Welsh, and still more closely to the Bretons; that is to say, the inhabitants of this district are, like all true Cornishmen, a remnant of the ancient British inhabitants of these islands, aptly and quaintly termed by Holinshed the 'Homelings,' as distinguished from the Teutonic 'Comelings,' the Danish and German foreigners who drove them out of the eastern parts of the country, and cooped them up in Wales and Cornwall. But the best modern writers on the subject, including Professor Rhŷs ('Celtic Britain,' London, 1882), have shown that there yet remain in Cornwall distinct traces of earlier races than the Cymric Celts. The last-named authority points out that vestiges of the earlier Gaelic branch of the Celtic stock, and even of successive pre-Aryan races whom the Celts conquered and absorbed, are to be found in Cornwall, and have materially influenced the racial composition of the Cornish people.

Owing to circumstances which we shall presently recount, the population of Saint Ives has been much mixed with incomers from Ireland, France, and Brittany. The typical Saint Ives man is of medium height, but broad-shouldered, with the Cymric round head and face; he has black hair, black or gray eyes, and swarthy complexion. In character he is warm-hearted and impulsive; quick-tempered, but readily forgiving; of an imagination easily swayed by the spell of music, and influenced by religious feeling; clannish, and hating change.

It is our intention to speak of the Cornish language at a later stage, but we may here remind the reader that this dialect of the British tongue was, until the end of the last century, the spoken language of the poorer folk of the Land's End district. It lingered longer in and around Saint Ives than anywhere else, except perhaps at Mousehole, the home of the renowned Dolly Pentreath—

> 'The last who gabbled Cornish, so says Daines.'

ZENNOR CROMLECH.

CHAPTER II.

PREHISTORIC, BRITISH AND ROMAN PERIODS.

No part of Great Britain can trace its history further back into the past than can West Cornwall. South Wales can indeed point to more remains of classic antiquity, and boast of a more ancient Christian hierarchy; but to Cornwall belongs the prestige of having been the first depot of intercourse with the Eastern world, and the earliest centre of civilization in this island.

In a paper read before a society of savants in 1886 on the then recent discovery of shells in the Saint Erth clay-beds, Professor R. W. Bell remarked that the deposit of clay in the Saint Erth sandpit was one of the most interesting discoveries which had been made in Tertiary geology for some years. His remarks tend to show that the Saint Erth Valley was within historical times an arm of the sea, or, as he terms it, 'a somewhat shallow gulf occupying at least the valley in which St. Erth is placed, and which probably connected the northern and southern seas of Cornwall until a comparatively recent period.' This paper was supplementary to one previously read before the Geological Society of London. The present line of railway between Saint Ives and Penzance runs almost parallel with this valley, and from the carriage window the traveller will see from its general appearance that it was once under water, it being for nearly its whole length a morass. Within comparatively recent times, strong gales have threatened to flood the Saint Erth Valley, and restore the original appearance of the island from which the Phœnicians obtained their tin.

An ancient tradition asserts that the tin used in the construction of Solomon's temple was obtained from the Godolphin Hills. At all events, the Land's End district was certainly the depot which furnished the East with its tin in ancient times. The Saint Ives district is not without architectural remains which may fairly be ascribed to this early period. As in the West of Ireland, and elsewhere in Cornwall, these are generally cyclopean, so called from the massiveness of the stones which compose them.

A relic of this description is still to be seen on the Island at Saint Ives, and is popularly termed the Two Edges. It consists principally of two walls about seven feet high meeting at a right angle, the space between being level with the top of the walls. It is evident that the Island has always been a fortified place; for during the Middle Ages it was defended with dry-stone walls, traces of which still remain, and it is now protected by a small fort for two guns in charge of a corporal of the Royal Artillery. In the absence of violent innovations, the massive rampart of the Ancient Briton will probably long survive the military redoubt of the nineteenth-century engineer. The labour involved in the construction of the Two Edges must have been stupendous, though apparently the materials were obtained in the Island itself. No record is left of the local chieftain to whom the erection of the Two Edges is due, nor of any battles fought upon the Island; but a stone axe or celt was found in 1887 at Saint Ives, which may have been wielded by one of the garrison or besiegers of this prehistoric stronghold. Some Cornish antiquaries are strongly of opinion that such dry-stone forts as this on the Island, which they name Cliff Castles, were erected to be the last refuges of the Stone Men (the 'Giants' of folklore), whom the first Celtic invasion drove to the sea-board.

Traces of another fort, consisting of a vallum of earth and stones running across an isthmus, exist on the promontory called the Gurnard's Head, in the parish of Zennor. The Cornish name of this headland is Treryn Dinas, which signifies a fortified place. The late Davies Gilbert, by the way, purchased this promontory from a desire to possess what is considered one of the most interesting geological formations in the county.

The westernmost headland in the parish of Zennor, near the mouth of the stream which separates Zennor and Morvah, and not far from the villages of Bosigran and Rosemergy, is known as Bosigran Castle. It is fortified on its isthmus by a thick dry-stone vallum. In the centre of the promontory is a large block of granite marked with basins, which is called the Castle Rock; and near this is a large stone scooped, as it were, through the top, known as the Giant's Cradle. A few yards nearer the sea is a logan-rock, over nine yards in circumference, with basins on the top. Norden mentions a fortification called Castle Anowthan, which he describes as 'a craggy rock on the top of a hill near Zennor, some time trenched about and built with stone, as appeareth by the ruins of the walls.'

The most perfect example of a hill-fort in the Saint Ives district is that on the summit of Trencrom. The top of this hill is nearly flat, and around it are the remains of a very extensive circular vallum of earth and stones, upwards of twenty feet in thickness. The entrance on the south-eastern side of the enclosure is about twenty feet wide, and has large upright blocks of granite at the inner corners. Opposite, on the other side, is a similar gateway. The vallum does not form a perfect circle, but is turned out of its regular course in order to unite it with two carns, between which was another entrance nearly opposite Trink Hill. On the largest of these carns are rock basins, known as the Giant's Chair, the Giant's Cradle, and the Giant's Spoon. A serpentine road passes up the hill, through the gateway, and on to the centre of the enclosure. To the right of this road, inside the circle, are traces of a large circular barrow of earth and stones, and nearer the top of the hill are the remains of several circular enclosures, about twenty-five feet in diameter, which seem to be the foundations of similar barrows. Outside the vallum is the Giant's Well, and on the south side of the hill is the Twelve o'Clock Stone, on which the sun's rays fall in such a manner that the country people can tell the hour by the direction of the shadows. (Abridged from Halliwell's 'Rambles in Western Cornwall,' p. 74.) Here also was formerly an ancient granite cross; it was removed about twenty years ago by some person unknown.

Mr. Halliwell mentions a stone on the Church-town Hill, Zennor, called the Giant's Chair, and on the same hill a recess in the rocks known as the Giant's Bed. The reader will observe the frequent use of the term 'Giant' in connection with rude-stone monuments and natural carns. As we shall have more to say about the giants in a later chapter, we will now only remark that they must be taken to represent the popular conception of the Stone Men, who in these rocky fastnesses held their own for some time against the Celtic Aryans. According to an old local chronicle, to which we shall have frequent occasion to refer, a barrow or tumulus known as the Giant's Grave, near the town of Saint Ives, was opened about the year 1690, and in it was found 'a tooth an inch broad.' No doubt some pre-Aryan chieftain was interred there with his horse.

Several cromlechs are to be found in the neighbourhood of Saint Ives, and of these nearly all are in Zennor parish, the most noteworthy being the celebrated Zennor Quoit or Cromlech. The following paragraph appeared in the *Cornish Telegraph* of September 4, 1861:

'Zennor Quoit, one of our local antiquities, has recently had a narrow escape. It consists of seven stones, one of which is a large granite slab which lies in a slanting position against the tallest of the uprights. A farmer had removed a part of one of the upright pillars, and drilled a hole into the slanting quoit in order to erect a cattle-shed, when news of the vandalism reached the ears of the Rev. W. Borlase, vicar of Zennor, and for five shillings the work of destruction was stayed, the Vicar having thus strengthened the legend that the quoit cannot be removed. From Zennor Quoit you see that of Mulfra, and from Mulfra you behold the Chûn and Zennor quoits. The Zennor Quoit or Cromlech is not so often visited as some of the other cromlechs, but it is a remarkable group of stones. There are no other blocks of granite near. It lies directly between Zennor and Towednack churches, about three quarters of a mile from each. The view from the quoit is very extensive. It commands a beautiful prospect of the British Channel, and eastward the county as far as Redruth, with the Bodmin range in the distance.'

In Dr. Borlase's time this cromlech, which is of thin moorstone, was surrounded by a stone barrow; but a mere apronful of the stones now remains. Originally, no doubt, the kistvaen, *i.e.*, massive blocks of the cromlech, merely formed an inner chamber, the whole being a mound of earth and stones. Dr. Borlase ('History of Cornwall,' London, 1769) describes the cromlech as it appeared in his day as being 'quite inclosed and buried, as it were, in the barrow.' His book has an engraving of this cromlech, showing the top-stone in its place, and stones heaped round the base of the structure. He says:

'The kistvaen of the Zennor cromlech is so close that it is with great difficulty any man can get into it' (p. 227).

At p. 231 we read the following further particulars as to this monument:

'On the top of a high hill, about half a mile to the east of Senar Church-town, stands a very large handsome cromlêh; the area inclosed by the supporters is . . . six feet eight inches by four feet, and points . . . east and west (Plate XXI., Fig. III. and IV.). The kistvaen (Fig. IV., No. 5) is neatly formed and fenced every way, and the supporter . . . is eight feet ten inches high, from the surface of the earth in the kistvaen, to the under face of the quoit. . . . The great depth of this kistvaen, which is about eight feet . . . is remarkable . . . the stone barrow, fourteen yards diameter, was heaped round about it, and almost reached the edge of the quoit, but care taken that no stone should get into the repository. This quoit was brought from a karn about a furlong off, which stands a little higher than the spot on which this cromlêh is erected; and near this karn is another cromlêh, not so large as that here described, in other respects not materially different.'

When, in the summer of 1882, the Penzance Natural History and Antiquarian Society paid a visit to Zennor, Mr. Borlase, one of the members, met with a man who had made a find beneath the Zennor Quoit. The man explained that about a year ago, finding that other people were searching about, he and his son thought they would have 'a bit of a speer too.' After removing some of the earth, they came upon a flat stone, which they 'shut' (blasted). Then they removed more earth and came upon another flat stone, which they also 'shut.' Underneath it they found what Mr. Borlase said was an ancient whetstone, which no doubt was buried with the dead, in order that he might have something to sharpen his weapons with in 'the happy hunting grounds' to which he was supposed to have gone. Mr. Borlase had found similar stones, with urns containing the ashes of the dead, in different barrows. Under this quoit he found part of an urn. Mr. Borlase expressed a hope that there would be no more 'shutting' near the quoit, because it ought to be regarded as sacred as the grave of a father—as it was, indeed, the grave of one of our forefathers. Mr. Westlake mentioned that there were remains of an old British village on Zennor Carn, a short distance off.

A few hundred yards to the back of the church at Zennor is a very good specimen of a logan-rock, which visitors may examine without the fatigue of hill-climbing, for (unlike most rocking-stones) it is on a comparatively level plain. No matter how many persons may be sitting on the top, proper pressure in the right direction will set it rocking like a cradle. This is termed by the peasantry the Giant's Rock. It is nineteen feet long, three feet thick, and has on the top several smooth cavities termed by Borlase rock-basins. It has lately been the fashion to laugh at the Doctor's 'rock-basins,' on the ground that his head was too full of the Druids to permit of his seeing that these hollows, instead of having been artificially scooped out, are in reality the result of the action of the weather. But here it seems to me that people err in the opposite direction. After a very careful examination of rocks, principally at Carn Brê, near Redruth, I am convinced that the round, shallow, rough depressions caused by the friction of fragments of the granite, blown around and around on the surface of the boulders in storms of wind and rain, are quite distinct from the deep, smooth, intricate cavities assumed by Borlase to be the handiwork of the Druids. The real rock-basins are as certainly artificial as the Cornish crosses of a later age. There is no doubt that the cromlech was, down to the period of the Roman occupation, the customary style of tomb for prominent chieftains among the Celts; as to the logan-rocks, it appears certain that they are due simply to the gradual wearing away of the soil, leaving the granite thus poised in some few instances.

The moorlands in this neighbourhood can show a great number of rude-stone monuments in various stages of dilapidation, and many more have within the last century been broken up for road-making. There are logan-rocks on Rosewall Hill and Carn Stabba. Between Saint Ives and Zennor, on the lower road over Tregarthen Downs, stood a logan-rock. An old man told Mr. Hunt's informant that he had often logged it, and that it would make a noise which could be heard for miles.

At Balnoon, between Nancledrea and Knill's Steeple, some miners came upon two slabs of granite cemented together, which covered a walled grave three feet square. In it they found an earthenware vessel containing some black earth and a leaden spoon. The spoon was given to Mr. Praed of Trevetho. (Hunt's 'Popular Romances.')

There is a small dismounted cromlech in Zennor parish, four miles and a half north-west by north of Penzance, nearly two furlongs from Bosphrennis, and near the west side of the path leading from Bosphrennis to Bosigran. Around it is a heap of earth and stones, the remains, doubtless, of a barrow which once covered it.

Between this small cromlech and the large one next to be described was another of considerable size in the estate of Trewey, but not a vestige of it now remains. It stood about a furlong south-east of Gundry Cave. The other is a remarkable barrow 110 feet in circumference, raised on a small natural cairn, on an eminence nearly five furlongs south-east by north of Zennor Church and about two furlongs from the east side of the road to Penzance. This barrow is depressed at the centre in the form of a bowl. At the bottom of the hollow was a horizontal slab six or eight feet square, supported by others set upright, all which have since been removed. This singular barrow must therefore have been originally merely a heap covering a cromlech, and the depression in the centre a modern excavation made to ascertain the contents of the barrow. ('Archæologia Cambrensis,' Series III., vol. iii., 1857.)

Dr. Borlase says:

'In the parish of Senor, I met with a remarkable cirque (Plate XV., Fig. IV.), formed by small stones thrown loosely together in a circular ridge. At the entrance A, there is one tall pillar. The dimensions of it may be found by the scale annexed.

I judge this to have been an elective circle; but why this round should consist of such a number of small stones heaped together, and the rest of a few, and so much larger, I cannot guess.'

Halliwell was informed that this circle was situated at the village of Rosemergy. It has long disappeared.

Courtney ('Guide to Penzance,' 1845) says:

'Another small cromlech (unnoticed by Borlase or any other writer) has lately been discovered in a croft near the village of Bosprennis in this parish [Zennor]: it is about five feet in diameter and nearly circular; it is dismounted, and lies on its flat: three of the upright stones on which it rested still remain: the fourth is either under the cromlech or has been taken away. This piece of antiquity is nearly hidden by the furze bushes, but it was no doubt formerly well known, as the croft in which it stands is still called Quoit Croft.'

At a visit paid to Zennor by the Penzance Natural History and Antiquarian Society, in September, 1883, a halt was made at Pennance to visit an ancient barrow known locally as the Giant's House, which, to the disgust of lovers of the picturesque, had in view of the visit of the society been 'shaven and shorn' of its covering of bramble and bracken. Arriving at Trereen, the president led the way down the path to Gurnard's Head, as far as an enclosure with walls in one place twenty feet thick and having an extended entrance, and now used as a sheepfold. It had been in its present state for at least a hundred years. Could anyone tell him what it was? Mr. Cornish proceeded to speak of the Pennance barrow, referring to the peculiar walling of the interior, and the manner in which the slabs were laid on the roof. When he first knew it twenty-one or twenty-two years ago it was used as a calves' house, and they might have detected a faint odour of that use to-day. The barrow was one of many in the district. On the eastern slope of the hill above Trereen were three of precisely the same construction. One was used as a pig's house, and another for storing fern for fuel. A great many barrows had been destroyed in the course of improving land a few years ago. Their use was no doubt sepulchral. When he discovered one of the barrows on the hills above, a man told him he had found an urn in it, and he produced it from a hedge. It was now in the museum of the society. There was a curious superstition that if an urn found in a barrow were taken home, the owner would be sure to come for it; and that the only way of avoiding that was to break the urn and bury it in a hedge.

On Cuckoo Hill, eastward of the village of Nancledrea, there stood about forty years ago two piles of rock some eight feet apart, united by a large flat stone carefully placed upon them, thus forming a doorway which was, as Mr. Hunt's informant told him, large and high enough to drive a horse and cart through. It was formerly the custom to march in procession through this 'doorway' in going to the Twelve o'Clock Stone, on which children were placed to be cured of rickets. ('Popular Romances of the West of England.')

At a point where the four parishes of Zennor, Morvah, Gulval and Madron meet, is a flat stone with a cross cut on it. Seven Saxon kings are said to have dined on this. The same is related of a similar stone near the Land's End.

The following is a list of bronze objects found at Lelant about the year 1802, from Evans' 'Ancient Bronze Implements of Great Britain:'

Knife, with oval socket pierced by two holes to fix handle.
Fragments of swords, regarded as being of copper.
Spear-heads, and broken socketed celts.
Ferrule for end of spear-shaft, tapering to a point near the extremity, then widening into a sphere, with a slight cylindrical projection beyond the spherical part.
Heavy lumps of fine copper.
Circular jet, or waste piece from metal castings, having four irregularly conical runners proceeding from it. (Museum of Society of Antiquaries.)
Pieces of gold in one celt.

(All these are described, and some engraved, in 'Archæologia,' vol. xv., p. 118.)

The Roman conquest of Cornwall was but a nominal one, and left the ancient Cornish in a state of practical independence. Hence our country has little to show in the way of Roman remains. 'In 1702, in the parish of Tawednack, between St. Ies and the Land's End, were found, under a prodigious rock of Moor-stone, called the Giant's Rock, a large flat stone, supported by four pillars of the same, an Urn full of ashes with a round ball of earth by the side of it, and in the said ball fourscore silver Coins, of the latter Emperours, very fair and well preserved. I could not have the sight of more than five of them, of which I got three, of Valentinian I., Gratian, and Arcadius; the rest were seized for the Lord of the Soil.' (Mr. Tonkin's letter to Bishop Gibson, Aug. 4, 1733, M. S. B., p. 224, cited in a footnote in Dr. Borlase's History.)

Gilbert, quoting Hicks, says that in Towednack one Paul Quick dug up a large stone which rested on another placed slopeways, and found thirty small silver Roman coins, two of which he gave to Mr. Hicks. They bore on the obverse a head with the legend '*Valentiniana Cæsar Augustus*'; reverse, Fortune sitting on a wheel: '*Urbs Roma.*' This seems to be the same find as the one referred to above by Tonkin.

On the slope of Carn Ellis, overlooking Saint Ives, is an ancient erection which must be noticed now. It is an ironstone 'crellas,' or British hut-dwelling, of very great antiquity. This relic was examined in 1882, by Mr. William Copeland Borlase (great-grandson of Dr. Borlase, the historian of Cornwall), in presence of the members of the Penzance Natural History and Antiquarian Society. Mr. Borlase said this hut was like the 'Picts' houses' of Scotland, but unlike anything else in Cornwall. The walls are oval in shape, wide at the bottom, narrowing towards the top. On entering, one walks through a narrow passage to an inner door, from which another similar passage leads to the interior of the whole structure.

In a field a little higher than the new cemetery, near the hamlet of Ayr, is what appears to be the remains of another ancient round hut, consisting of a circular mound of earth and stones, about fourteen feet in diameter, with an entrance on the north west. In the middle is a heap of loose smooth local slate-stones, collected from the remains of the crellas.

Near the western extremity of the parish of Zennor, on lands of the farm called Bosphrennis, is a collection of the remains of very ancient hut-dwellings, which have been fully described by the Rev. E. L. Barnwell, in the 'Archæologia Cambrensis.' The best preserved of these huts is figured in several drawings in the Appendix to Blight's 'Churches of West Cornwall.' It consists of two chambers, one circular, the other rectangular, with a communicating doorway. The principal entrance, through the wall of the circular compartment, has a lintel composed of three slabs of granite; a few feet from it, in the same wall, is another very narrow doorway. In the circular chamber each course overlaps that beneath, whereby a perfect dome was formed, but the roof has fallen in. In the end of the rectangular chamber is a small window, which Mr. Barnwell considers almost unique. The entire structure much resembles the ancient oratories of Ireland, and the rude buildings which in Wales are popularly termed 'Gaels' churches.' Blight says:

'This bee-hive hut stands in the angle of a small enclosure, the hedges of which are built of the stones which at one time formed other similar structures, and which were destroyed by a former tenant, but within the remembrance of the person now occupying the estate. In an adjoining field are the remains of the foundations of rectangular chambers, surrounded by a rudely constructed circle; and at a distance of a few hundred yards, among furze and heath, are traces of circular enclosures.'

At a short distance from the hut-dwellings above described is the Bosphrennis cromlech, now fallen. 'It consisted of four supporters, three feet six inches high, forming a complete kistvaen six feet by three; and what is very remarkable, the covering stone is circular, measuring four feet ten inches in diameter and five inches thick. The stone must certainly have been wrought into this form, and it seems to afford the only known instance of the kind.' (Blight.) This seems to be the cromlech referred to by Courtney.

The Bosphrennis huts were visited in 1889 by the Penzance Natural History and Antiquarian Society, when it was remarked that Mr. Arthur Mitchell, who visited the Outer Hebrides in 1866, saw in Lewis and Harris twenty or thirty huts like those of Bosphrennis. 'They were called *bo'h*, or *bothan*, and were used as sheelings or summer residences by the herdsmen on the upper pastures.' Examined in detail, one of the Scottish huts agreed in almost every particular with the Bosphrennis huts, and was at the time inhabited; the smaller apartment being used as a store-room and dairy, the larger and outer as the living-room.

At Bosullow, in Zennor, are the remains of another similar pre-historic British village, the lower courses of the rude walls of the huts being distinctly traceable. These remains were visited by the Penzance Antiquaries in 1883.

LELANT CROSS.

CHAPTER III.

OF THE INTRODUCTION OF CHRISTIANITY TO THE SAINT IVES DISTRICT.

As West Cornwall was the earliest seat of civilization in Britain, so it was one of the first parts of the island to embrace Christianity. East Cornwall was evangelized by Welsh missionaries; West Cornwall is indebted to Ireland for its first knowledge of the Faith. Hence it is that nearly all the parish churches of the Land's End district are dedicated to Irish saints. The churches of Lelant and Saint Ives bear the names of two members of a large company of missionaries who, in the middle of the fifth century, came from Ireland to West Cornwall, and nearly all suffered martyrdom in this neighbourhood. The only remaining records of their history are certain fragments of unknown authorship, and passages in the chronicle of William of Worcester. A manuscript Legendary formerly existed, containing the Acts of Saint Ia (patroness of Saint Ives), which was read in the parish church on her feast-day; but it disappeared at the Reformation.

The ancient authorities do not entirely agree as to some of the details in the history of the first missionary expedition to West Cornwall, but they are unanimous in their enumeration of the principal personages who composed it.

One of the converts of Saint Patrick in Ireland was a certain Fingar, son of a king named Clito. This Fingar, much against the will of his people, renounced his succession to the kingdom, in order to devote himself to preaching the Gospel. With this object he sailed from Ireland, accompanied by a large number of other zealous Christians, among whom were these:

Saint Piala, sister of Saint Fingar, or Finbar.

Saint Ercius, Ertius, or 'Herygh,' as William of Worcester calls him. The church and parish of Saint Erth perpetuate his memory in Cornwall. The same authority says of him that he was brother to Saint Elwinus, that he was a bishop, and that he is buried 'in a certain church situated under the cross of the church of Saint Paul in London.'

Saint Elwin, who, according to this chronicler, 'lies in the parish church of Saint Elwinus near the town of Lalant on the northern sea, about three miles from Saint Michael's Mount.' He is now commemorated in the full title of the same parish, which is Saint Uny Lelant.

Saint Germochus or Germoe.

Saint Breaca, after whom the parish of Breage is named. An unaccountable Cornish tradition asserts that Germo was a king, and Breaga a midwife:

> '*Germo matern,*
> *Breaga lavethes.*'

William of Worcester says that Breaca was born in Ireland, and was a nun in the monastery of Saint Brigit.

Saint Maruanus or Mervyn, monk; also called Mirin and Merran.

Saint Levinus or Levan, bishop.

Saint Sinninus or Sennen, abbot, who was at Rome with Saint Patrick.

Saint Crewenna, patroness of Crowan parish.

Saint Buriana, virgin, of Saint Burian parish.

Saint Ia, virgin martyr, patroness of the town and parish of Saint Ives. There seems to be a tradition that she was sister to Saint Ewinus and Saint Ertius. (Lysons' 'Cornwall.')

The church of Gwinear derives its name from Saint Fingar, or Finguar. (Note that Cymric Gw = Gaelic F.)

William of Worcester, who wrote as a travelling antiquary in the year 1478, had picked up a few traditions of these Cornish saints from 'Thomas Pepderelle of Tavistock, notary public.' Colgan, an Irish priest, whose 'Hyberniæ Sanctorum Acta' was published at Louvain in the year 1645, also mentions Saint Ia, drawing largely from Saint Anselm, whom Dr. Cave ('Historia Literaria') considers [*sed quære*] to be the author of the 'Passio Sancti Guigneri sive Fingari, Pialæ et Sociorum.' To condense these various accounts, the story of the first Christian mission to West Cornwall runs as follows:

'Among the chief virgins of the Sacred Isle was Ia, called by some Iva, a follower of St. Barricius, who was a disciple of St. Patrick. She, leaving her native land, betook herself to Britain and was, indeed, one of that numerous company of 777 bishops, priests, virgins and other clerics who, renouncing worldly honours that they might inherit a heavenly crown, followed St. Fingar into

Britain. St. Ia, being desirous to accompany these holy persons, but having no vessel to travel in, was praying on the shore, when she beheld a slender leaf conveyed by a great miracle to her feet. Embarking upon this frail craft, she reached a British port called Heul, and joined herself to the band of missionaries.

'Being by the shore, at a place where there was a great lack of water for drinking, St. Fingar, full of faith in Jesus Christ, and having prayed, fixed his staff in the earth, and immediately an inexhaustible fountain of purest water burst forth.

'Next the saints came to a town called Conetronia. Here a certain woman, full of the fear of the Lord, showed them no little kindness. For, as her dwellings could not contain them all, and she had no straw for them to lie on, she took down the thatch from the roofs of her houses and with it made a bed for them. This most charitable woman gave them for food her only cow. When it had been killed, and its flesh eaten, Saint Fingar gave thanks, and commanded that the skin should be spread over the bones of the cow. Then he invited his companions to pray, saying "Let us pray, brethren, that God, for the love of whom this woman most kindly provided us with this cow, may restore it to her." And when he had ended his prayer, the cow appeared standing alive before them all, more beautiful than ever it was. Then the saint ordered that milk from this cow should be set before him; which having drunk, he besought God that the cow might thereafter afford thrice as much milk as other cows. This, it is related, was the case not only with that cow, but with all its progeny.

'When morning was come, and the saints would continue their journey, they beheld the houses miraculously roofed anew. And when they had come to a certain wood, the rumour of their coming reached the ears of Theodoric, King of Cornwall, who had his castle at Revyer, on the eastern side of the estuary of Hayle; and he caused them all to be put to death by the sword on one and the same day.'

Such is a compendium of the somewhat vague and involved narratives of the authorities above named. Usher gives 460 as the year of the massacre. Whittaker surmises, with much reason, that Saint Ia is not to be taken to have been among the missionaries then martyred; and William of Worcester says that only 'the greater part' were put to death. Indeed, the later historians, as Leland, distinctly record the tradition that Saint Ia arrived at Cornwall separately from the others:

'The Paroch Chirch is of Ia, a noble Man's Doughter of Ireland, and Disciple of Barricus. Iä and Elwine with many other cam into Cornewaul and landid at Pendinas. This Pendinas is the Peninsula and stony Rok wher now the Town of St. Iës stondith. One Dinan, a Great Lord in Cornewaul, made a Chirch at Pendinas at the Request of Iä, as it is written yn S. Iës Legende. Ther is now at the very Point of Pendinas a Chapel of S. Nicolas.'

applied to the Bishop for licence to have Mass celebrated for a year from June 17, 1398, in the Chapel of the Blessed Virgin

CHAPEL OF ST. NICHOLAS, ST. IVES.

'THE CHAPLE,' ST. IVES, FROM THE N.W.

Mary at 'Breynyon in parochia Sancti Eunii in Cornubia'; but in the margin are the words, 'Non habuit effectum.' In the same manuscript, under the date 1410 or thereabouts, it is called the Chapel of Saint Mary Magdalen.

V. At the farm of Trevarrack, in the parish of Towednack, is a croft known as the Chapel Field, where formerly stood the ruins of an ancient oratory. The site was ploughed up in the year 1840, and the remains of the chapel carted away. A few of the carved stones, including a fragment of the ashlar ogee of a window, are to be seen in the garden of the farmhouse, and into the front of the house an inscribed stone from the chapel has been built, concerning which a few words must be said. It is an oblong block of freestone, about three feet by one foot, and the inscription is in early mediæval Latin characters, lightly incised. The stone is high up in the wall, and, being upside down, the inscription is difficult to make out on a cursory inspection; but the following marks may be distinguished:

Without presuming to hazard a conjecture as to the actual reading of this inscription, we would call attention to the similarity between these characters and the letters marked on the front of the cross at Lanherne Convent, as figured in Blight's 'Cornish Crosses.' It is to be noted also that Blight says the Lanherne cross was removed from an ancient chapel in the parish of Gwinear.

VI. At Higher Tregenna, in 1814, the foundations of a similar old oratory were, according to Lysons, still visible.

VII. The foundations of another chapel of the same kind are to be seen on the narrow part of the small headland called the Gurnard's Head in the parish of Zennor. At its eastern end is a large slab, said by some to be the altar-stone, under which, according to another tradition, certain drowned mariners lie buried. At the beginning of the present century it was still the custom to make a pilgrimage to this spot on the parochial feast-day.

VIII. The MS. collections of Dr. Borlase, quoting from the Exeter Episcopal Registers, mention 'the Chapel of Saint Ante alias Ansa, prope ripam maris,' under the year 1495, at Saint Ives, in which a guild or fraternity was established, and say that it was turned into a smith's shop in June, 1770.

IX. A chapel mentioned by Lysons as having existed at the Chapel Field in the Barton of Kerrow and Cornelloe, Zennor.

X., XI., XII. To these we must add, on the authority of Blight ('Cornish Crosses'), similar chapels at Trewanack, Rose-an-crowz and Chapel Anjou, in Lelant.

These ancient fanes, and others in various parts of Cornwall, bear a strong likeness to each other in their size, shape and mode of construction, and seem to have been built in the earliest Christian period of our country's history.

Crosses.

To the same period are to be ascribed the most ancient of the wayside crosses for which Cornwall is renowned. These are all of granite, and the oldest of them are extremely simple in form. The following are the examples in the Saint Ives district:

I. Penbeagle Cross, at the corner where the Zennor road is joined by the lane from Penbeagle farm (locally 'town'). This cross is badly mutilated, a very large portion being broken off. The face has been marked with a small Latin cross roughly incised, and a reversed B appears on the back. This cross was whitewashed over in September, 1890. Here also are the Prior Field and Park Venton (the 'well-field'). Possibly there was a chapel there. I noticed a holy-water stoup built into a shed at Hellesvean, hard by.

II. A cross at the corner of a hedge (which in Cornwall means a dry-stone wall) bordering the Saint Ives road, in Lelant village. Its round head bears a Latin cross in relief, which some unenlightened restorer has recently marked out with a coating of tar.

III. A tall, round-headed cross in the new Lelant cemetery, close to the churchyard. It bears a rudely-carved crucifix. This venerable monument formerly stood by the side of the highroad to Saint Ives, where it received rough treatment from the Saint Ives fishermen who came to Lelant to paint their boats. Hence its removal to its present position.

IV. A cross pattee fitchee, carved on a round-headed shaft, in Lelant cemetery; on the other side is carved a crucifix.

V. A plain St. Andrew's cross, carved on a round-headed shaft, in Lelant churchyard.

VI. The round head of a cross, on a wall opposite the Praed Arms Inn, in Lelant village.

VII. A cross at Brunnion in Lelant, marking the site of an ancient chapel.

VIII., IX. The round heads of two crosses, now placed upon

the grave of the Rev. William Borlase, the late vicar, in the churchyard of Zennor.

X. A round-headed cross discovered in the wall of a house at Towednack church-town about four years ago; now in the garden at Tredorwin.

XI. Saint Ives Cross, described in our chapter on the church.

XII. A round-headed granite cross built into a hedge on the highroad near Higher Trenoweth, Lelant.

Carn Crowze ('the cross rock'), a spot near the point of the Island, is so called from a cross which formerly stood there. There was also a cross in the ancient earthworks on the top of Carn Trencrom.

Holy Wells.

It is not our place to say more about these in general than that they were probably considered sacred long before they became connected with the traditions of Christianity. It was the policy of the early missionaries to give a Christian character to the ancient stones and springs, by identifying the latter with Christian ideas and surmounting the former with the symbol of our redemption, thus directing to the faith of the Gospel that awe and veneration which had been implanted in the minds of the people by the Druids, and which the Christian priests were unable to eradicate. These wells (in Cornish 'venton') are the following, in the Saint Ives district:

I. Venton Eia (Saint Eia's or Ia's well), on the cliff under the village of Ayr, overlooking Porthmeor. This ancient well, associated with the memory of the patron saint of the town, was formerly held in the highest reverence. Entries occur in the borough records of sums paid for cleansing and repairing it, under 1668-9, 1680-1, and 1692-3. On the last of these occasions the well was covered, faced, and floored with hewn granite blocks in two compartments. It is still known as 'the wishing-well,' from the old custom of divination by crooked pins dropped into the water. For some years past, however, this ancient source of purity has been shamefully outraged by contact with all that is foul. Close to it is a cluster of sties, known as 'Pigs' Town,' and the well has become the receptacle for stinking fish and all kinds of offal. Just above it are the walls of the new cemetery. All veneration for this spot, so dear to countless generations of our forefathers, seems to have departed.

II. Venton Dovey, in the town of Saint Ives. I have not been able to discover who the Dovey is, after whom this well is called; indeed, there is a difficulty even in identifying its site, for although the name occurs in a deed of 1808, I have not met with any person who can remember it. It was perhaps the spring situate at the north side of Shute Street, which, together with the present Dove Street, formed originally one thoroughfare known as Street-an-Poll (Pool Street). Some cottages at the top of the Stennack form a hamlet known as Nanjivvey, or St. Jivvey, perhaps a form of 'Dovey'; and there is a well hard by.

III. Venton Vigean, referred to in a deed of 1808. I cannot explain the name; it was situate at Ayr, where there is a field which is still called Venton Vision.

IV. Venton Uny (the Well of Saint Ewinus, the saint to whom the parish of Uny Lelant owes its name). This well is most picturesquely situated on the cliff at Hawke's Point; its popular appellation is Venton Looly. It is still used by romantic young people as a wishing-well.

Dr. Borlase severely says:

'The vulgar Cornish have a great deal of this folly still remaining; and there is scarce a parish-well, which is not frequented at some particular times for information, whether they shall be fortunate or unfortunate; whether, and how, they shall recover lost goods, and the like; and from several trials they make upon the well-water, they go away fully satisfied for a while; those who are too curious being always too credulous.'

CHAPTER V.

OF THE MANORS AND LORDSHIPS.

THE Saint Ives district has been for many centuries divided into several manors or feudal lordships, namely:

1. The Manor of Ludgvan Lese.
2. " " Dinas Ia and Porthia.
3. " " Saint Ives and Treloyhan.
4. " " Porth Ia Prior.
5. " " and Barton of Trenwith.
6. " " of Lelant and Trevetho.
7. " " Trembethow.
8. " " Amalibria.
9. " " Boswednack.
10. " " Trereen.
11. " " Trewey.
12. " " and Barton of Kerrow and Carnello.

It will perhaps be best if we now proceed to give a brief history of each of these in succession.

1. *The Manor of Ludgvan Lese.*—This was the principal manor in these parts; according to Leland, those who held it were deemed Lords of Saint Ives. Hals tells us that in the Domesday tax of the year 1087, Saint Ives and Towednack were comprised in the Manor of 'Ludduham' (now Ludgvan Lese), which then belonged to the King or Earl of Cornwall, and was privileged with the jurisdiction of a court leet before the Norman Conquest. This manor anciently vested in the family of De Ferrers, whose heiress carried it in marriage to Champernowne, and the heiress of Champernowne brought it to Sir Robert Willoughby, first Lord Broke. After the death of Robert, second baron, this property was divided between his two daughters, married respectively to Lord Mountjoy and Pawlet, Marquess of Winchester, who are described by Leland as 'Lords

TREGENNA CASTLE.

of Saint Ives,' *temp.* Henry VIII. 'This manor still continues,' writes Gilbert, *circa* 1820, 'in the Pawlet family, being vested in the heirs of the late Duke of Bolton.'

2. *The Manor of Dinas Ia and Porthia.*—This manor was sold by John Hele in 1655 to John, Earl of Radnor, of the Robartes family, and descended from him to Vere Hunt, who sold it to John Stevens of Saint Ives, founder of the family of Stephens of Tregenna, *circa* 1750.

3. *The Manor of Saint Ives and Treloyhan* was purchased from Praed of Trevetho by Sir Christopher Hawkins, Bart., about the year 1807.

4. *The Manor of Porth Ia Prior.*—This manor is situated partly in the parish of Saint Ives, and partly in Saint Anthony-in-Menéage and in other places. It belonged to the Benedictine Priory of Tywardreath until the dissolution of monasteries, when Henry VIII. (in 1540) annexed it to the Duchy of Cornwall. The manor was then valued at the annual sum of £7 10s. 10d.

5. *The Manor and Barton of Trenwith.*—Lysons says that this was anciently the name of a district including the whole parish of Lelant. According to Domesday Book, 'Trenwit' was owned, in the time of King Edward the Confessor, by Sitric the Abbot, and before by the Earl (of Cornwall) and his villeins. The following is an extract from that record:

> 'The same Earl (of Moreton) holds Trenwit; Sitric the Abbot held it in the time of King Edward, and it was taxed for 2 hides; but notwithstanding, there are 6 hides; the arable land is 4 carucates; in Domain there are 5 carucates, and 16 bond servants and 30 villeins and 30 borderers, with 12 ploughs; there are 40 acres of wood, and 1,000 acres of pasture; formerly it returned 12 marks of silver; now it returns 25 pounds and 18 shillings and 4 pence.'

In the Exeter Domesday this manor is called 'Trenuwit.' By the Earl of Cornwall Trenwith was granted to John de Beaufort, son of John of Gaunt, and continued in his family till the attainder of Edmund Beaufort, Earl of Somerset, in 1471. Since then the manor seems to have been annihilated; but the barton, some time previous to the reign of Edward IV., became the property of a family called Bailiff, who then took the surname of Trenwith. This ancient house kept possession of Trenwith until the death of Rebecca Trenwith in 1798. A full account of this old stock and their estate will hereafter be given.

6. *The Manor of Lelant and Trevetho.*—These possessions vested of old in the family of Bottreaux or Boterel, which left its original home in Brittany to follow the fortunes of William the Conqueror.

inhabitants to the Pope, through the medium of the lord of the manor, the following passage, giving the reasons urged by the Saint Ives people for their desiring a separate parish church:

'As it had pleased the Almighty God to increase the town inhabitants and to send down temporal blessings most plentifully among them, the people, to show their thankfulness for the same, did resolve to build a chapel in Saint Ives, they having no house in the town, wherein public prayers and Divine service was read, but were forced every Sunday and holy day to go to Lelant church, being three miles distant from Saint Ives, to hear the same, and likewise to carry their children to Lelant to be baptized, their dead to be there buried, to go there to be married, and their women to be churched.'

ST. IVES CHURCH FROM THE N.E.

Accordingly Pope Alexander V., on October 20, 1409, and (after the death of the last-named pontiff) his successor, Pope John XXIII., on November 18, 1410, recommended Bishop Stafford, of Exeter, in whose diocese Cornwall was, to make

'the chapels of S. Tewynnoc and S. Ya parochial, with font and cemetery, but dependent on Lelant.'

The Index to the Ancient Episcopal Registers of the Diocese of Exeter, lately published, with notes and translations, by Prebendary Hingeston-Randolph, supplies us with the following extract from Bishop Stafford's register, under the date September 27, 1409:

'Lelant. Chapels of St. Tewennoc the Confessor, and St. Ya

the Virgin. Peter Pencors, William Stabba, James Tregethes, John Guvan, and other parishioners of the said chapelries, complained that they lived, for the most part, four, three, or (at least) two miles from the Mother-Church of Lelant, the roads being mountainous and rocky, and liable, in winter, to sudden inundations, so that they could not safely attend Divine Service, or send their children to be baptized, their wives to be churched, or their dead to be buried; the children often went unbaptized, and the sick were deprived of the last Sacraments. They stated that they had built the two chapels above-named at their own expense and had enclosed suitable cemeteries, to be sufficiently endowed for two priests to serve therein, and they prayed the Bishop to consecrate the same; who accordingly commissioned Richard Hals and John Gorewyll to meet all the parties (including specially John Clerk, the Vicar of Lelant), and to enquire and report.

'Bulls of Pope Alexander V. and of Pope John XXIII., for the Dedication of the dependent chapels of St. Tewinnoc and St. Ya; presented to the Bishop, in the chapel of his palace at Exeter, 8 Sept. 1411, by two parishioners thereof, viz., Peter Pencors and John Guvan, who asked him to give effect thereto. They told him of the difficulties above recited, complaining that they were obliged to repair to their parish church for the baptism of their children, to receive the Sacraments, and to bury their dead; that occasionally some of them were unable to undertake such a journey, and some were left to die without confession and the last rites of the Church, to the great loss of their souls. Accordingly they desired that fonts might be placed in these chapels and the Sacraments administered therein; also that the cemeteries should be licensed for interments. Inquiry was ordered; the Petition to be granted if the result were satisfactory. Both Bulls are given in full; and in the second, reference is made to a contention between these parishioners and John the vicar of Lelant. The Bishop forthwith directed the Precentor and the Chapter of Crediton (Rectors of Lelant) and the said vicar to appear before him personally, together with any others concerned, in the church of Crediton. But the Bishop shortly afterwards started on a visitation-tour in Cornwall, and, reaching Lelant on the 9th of October, he met the parties there, and granted his license to celebrate Mass in the said Chapels.'

So soon as the requisite authority had thus been obtained, the people of Saint Ives set about building (on the site of the humble oratory, and the chapel which succeeded it) a church which should be worthy of their newly-acquired privilege. In this our common-place age, we can scarcely form a notion of the immense importance with which such an event was then regarded. No pains were thought too great to be undertaken, no expense too heavy to be borne, to make the work a complete success in every respect. In the Middle Ages every capable parishioner was expected to contribute to the undertaking either in work or in money. The mason gave his labour, the artist his skill, and the husbandman lent his beasts of burden.

A local tradition will have it that the granite used in the construction of Saint Ives Church was brought by water from

THE OLD PARSONAGE.

Zennor, and that the boats often had to wait for weeks for weather sufficiently calm. Everything we know bears out this legend; roads at that date West Cornwall could not be said to possess, unless mere bridle-tracks were entitled to the designation. As a natural consequence, wheeled vehicles were unknown, pack-

beautiful example of early fifteenth-century work, was thrown down by the Reformers, and remained half buried in the soil of the churchyard until it was replaced, about the year 1850, at the cost of Robert Hichens, Esq., of Saint Ives and London, a gentleman to whose munificence and taste the parish church of Saint Ives is greatly indebted.

Saint Ives parish church was consecrated by the Bishop of Exeter on February 3, 1434 (Hicks' MS.). We may suppose that the day which united the patronal feast with the consecration of the church was kept with very special solemnity and rejoicings. It was customary in those ages, when a church had been restored or enlarged, or for any other reason reconsecrated, to join another or other saints in a new dedication, in addition to the former patron. This seems to have been done at Saint Ives when the old chapel of Saint Ia gave place to the present parish church. Saints Peter and Andrew were added as the new patrons, and at the present day the church is commonly known only by the name of the latter Apostle; still, the fact that the festival day of Saint Ia (February 3) was chosen for the consecration is sufficient evidence that her name was retained in the dedication. There was no doubt a peculiar fitness in dedicating to God, under the invocation of the Galilean fishermen, the building which was to be used by so many thousands of the toilers of the deep.

The parish festival, locally termed 'feastentide,' being the anniversary of the glorious death of the virgin martyr Ia, the apostle of Saint Ives, has its place in the calendar under February 3; but a long time ago it had become the practice to transfer it to the first Sunday after Candlemas Day, and in quite recent times it has been held on the Monday following the first Sunday after Candlemas Day. Among the sports held on the feastentide is the game of hurling, which ancient Cornish sport is now kept up only at Saint Ives and Saint Columb; and, at Saint Ives, only on Saint Ia's day.

The parish of Saint Ives was anciently under the spiritual charge of the Augustinian canons regular, an order which was very strong in Cornwall, and with which the ancient Celtic monastic foundations had been consolidated. The Ecclesiastical Valuation made by command of King Henry VIII. in 1535 supplies us with particulars as to the church lands and revenues in the Saint Ives district. To these we shall refer later.

The orderly and reverent disposition of Saint Ives church to-day forms a striking contrast to its state during the last century and the first half of the present, and, indeed, gives us a faint notion of what the interior was like at the period which, not without good reason, is called by some the Age of Faith, and by others the Dark Age. It is interesting to reflect upon the various phases through which this parish church has passed, and to contrast the artistic light of the Dark Ages with the, at any rate, æsthetic darkness of the enlightened eighteenth century.

In Catholic times we can imagine the dim interior, its windows storied with angels and saints; the solemn altar of stone, with its crucifix and lights; the beauteous fretwork of the rood-screen, its loft surmounted by the rood or image of the crucified Redeemer, flanked by images of those who 'stood by the cross of Jesus'—the blessed Virgin, and the disciple whom Jesus loved. We may fancy ourselves to be present at high Mass on the feastentide, and see the deacon, in his dalmatic of red velvet bordered with gold, going from the chancel through the little door in the wall of the Trenwith aisle up into the rood-loft, to chant the Gospel of the feast and to read from an illuminated book the Legend of the Acts of Saint Ia. We hear the organ pealing to the chant of 'Gloria tibi Domine,' while the sub-deacon incenses the Book of the Gospels, two surpliced serving-boys standing by, their tapers held aloft; and afterwards the lifting up of the consecrated elements, amid solemn silence, save for the tinkling of the altar-bell, answered by six deep tones from the lofty tower.

Our next picture shall be of the church as it existed under King Edward VI. The rood and its images have been destroyed, and probably burned in the adjacent market-place, along with, let us suppose, a miracle-working image of Saint Ia. The walls have been covered with 'necessarie partes of scryptour and othere wholesome wrytynges' deemed suitable to wean the parishioners from the old religion. Sidesmen parade the aisles, keeping strict watch that none cross themselves, or use rosary-beads in the church.

Next let us peep in at the worship of our great-grandfathers. We shall hardly recognise Saint Ives church. Whitewash reigns supreme; the waggon roof is hidden by a flat ceiling, from which depends a huge brass chandelier of many branches. At the east end of the church towers the good old-fashioned 'three-decker' pulpit, from the top of which the black-gowned parson looks down upon his flock, over the head of the drowsy clerk; both are barricaded by obese cushions, with heavy tassels at the corners. The altar has long ago given place to a Communion-table, on which what remains of the church plate is displayed; and the sculptured or painted reredos has been replaced by the Ten Commandments, or a list of benefactors on a black board. The wall, where perhaps formerly the worshipper beheld the inscription, 'He who looks on Saint Christopher's picture will not suffer sudden death this day,' only cautions the eighteenth-century parishioner against marrying 'his grandmother, grandfather's wife,' etc. At the west end of the church a heavy wooden gallery, locally known as the 'singan-laft,' faced by the lion and the unicorn fighting for the crown, is the arena for the melodious performances of the bass-viol and the clarionet which accompany the singing of the versified Psalms. The floor of the building is rough and uneven; and most of the old seats have been ousted by family boxes by way of pews, some of them additionally fortified by locks and bolts, and sheltered by red curtains on brass rods. The 'storied windows, richly dight,' were smashed a century ago by Major Ceely's Puritans, and have been replaced by round-headed, square-paned lights like those of an engine-house.

Courtney's 'Guide to Penzance,' printed in 1845, and now a scarce book, gives the following somewhat gloomy picture of the state of Saint Ives church in his time:

'The church is a very good old building, and the tower one of the best of its time in the county. The interior of the church has been disfigured by the erection of heavy flat galleries in the north and south aisles; and its original symmetry greatly impaired by the substitution of close pews of various heights and shapes, painted according to the tastes of the owners, for the low and uniform seats of beautifully carved oak, with which it was at first furnished, and a few of which yet remain as a memento of its primitive grandeur. The ceiling is also of carved oak, but by divers coatings of whitewash its beauty has been destroyed.'

From these unlovely surroundings it is refreshing to turn to the present interior of Saint Ives church, which is admirable in its neatness and fitness—save only for the well-meant but incongruous reredos, displaying the Ten Commandments in their usurped position on the east wall of the chancel. A handsome brass eagle lectern, copied from that in Wantage church, Berkshire, was by the present vicar, the Rev. J. B. Jones, presented to the church on its restoration; and a crowd of the Saint Ives Dissenters, who perhaps had never been inside the church before, came to 'hear the great bird sing,' as they said. A modern organ stands at the east end of the north aisle. The new glass is not of the best; but it was given by those who earnestly desired to beautify the parish church, and it is, at least, better than none. That in the chancel window depicts our Lord and

Saints Peter and Andrew. In the south aisle there is a window with paintings of Saint Ia, Saint Levan, and Saint Senan; and an inscription to the effect that it was dedicated in memory of the late John Newman Tremearne and Matilda his wife, by their children John, Matilda and Frances, in 1886. In the spandrels of some of the windows there are fragments of the ancient glass picked up when the church was restored in 1866. At the same date the old flooring of stone was taken up, and encaustic tiles laid down instead. In the centre of the floor of the nave are coloured tiles representing a shield, with the arms of England and France quarterly. The wooden altar-table is covered with a handsome frontal, adorned with artistic needlework; and on the table are a brass cross, and a pair of candlesticks of the same metal. At the back is a small carved wooden reredos of a temporary character.

Saint Ives church has two bells, concerning which we extract the following particulars from Dunkin's 'Church Bells of Cornwall.'

The first bell has a diameter of thirty-six inches at its mouth. It is inscribed:

'Richd Hichens Esqr Mayor. M. M. T. T. Junr & W. H. Church Wardens. Copper House Foundry. Ja^{s} Oatey Maker 9 June 1830.'

The diameter of the second is forty-eight inches. It bears this inscription:

'James Halse Esqr M.P. Matthew Major, Thomas Tremearne Junr & William Hichens Church Wardens. St Ives, June 1830. J^{s} Oatey fecit.'

We learn from a writer in the *St. Ives Weekly Summary* that these bells were cast from the material of five older ones, one of which bore the inscription: 'Thomas Anthony, Mayor, 1721.'

As to the old plate and other belongings of the church, the earliest entry on the subject among the churchwardens' accounts is the one dated 1650, according to which the goods in question were the following:

'2 silver flagons holding above a pottle each.' (The gift of Grace, widow of Lewis Hurley, of Saint Ives, vintner; grandmother of Hicks, the manuscript historian.)

'2 silver cups with covers.' (Described in a list of 1680 as flagons or chalices. One of these was presented by Alice, wife of Thomas Sise, of Saint Ives, merchant, and is inscribed: 'The Guift of Alse Sise to the Church of St Ies. A.D. 1641.' Davies

Gilbert says: 'There is also a silver cup of much greater antiquity,' by which he seems to mean a pre-Reformation chalice. In 1713 the squire of Pendarves gave a communion-plate to this church. It bears the inscription: 'Pendarves de Pendarves Ecclesiæ dedit Anno 1713.')

'2 pewter pottles.
'2 pewter flagons.
'6 font cloths.
'4 table-cloths for the communion table.
'1 stamen carpet for the communion table.
'1 green carpet for the table.
'1 flannel carpet for the table.
'1 scarlet pulpit-cloth and cushion.'

(It is probable that some of these were made out of the old vestments of the priest.)

In the list of 1680 there were in addition:

'1 new bag to hold the plate.
'1 large Bible.
'The works of Bishop Jewel against Harding.' (Thomas Harding, D.D., the famous Jesuit, whose 'Rejoinder to Mr. Jewel's Replie' was printed at Antwerp in 1566 in black letter. Bishop Jewel's book was to be found in many churches; moreover, this was the time of the great 'Popish Plot,' from which a trembling nation was saved by the patriotic Mr. Titus Oates.)

The parish registers commence with the year 1651 (baptisms), the earlier volumes having been lost. Those which remain are long narrow tomes bound in old calf.

Many curious entries of different sorts are to be found upon the fly-leaves, especially of the first volume. We cannot do better than transcribe them in full here:

> 'A Register.
> William Polkinghorne.
> John Keigwin Minister of St Ives, 1726.
> Jo: Bullock minister of St Ives 1669.
> Jonathan Toup lecturer of St Ives, July 4 1721.'

The above are all in the handwritings of these ministers respectively. Under the last is written in another hand:

'Jonathan Toup editor of Longinus &c born at St Ives 1713; sometime lecturer of St Ives, afterwards curate of Sennen & St Levan; afterwards Vicar [*sic*] of St Martins where he died.'

Then follow particulars of restorations in the church fabric:

'The tower of this Burrough of St Ives was Pointed ye Mo^s of 7^ber 8^ber & 9^ber 1727, By one Mr Knott of Devonshire and a Kinsman of his of the same place and one Pharez a St Agnes man. Likewise Two Pinacles ye North East and Northwest

Surely your loss, to me is greatest gain,
For crown'd in Heaven I ever shall remain."
Farewell, dear wife, farewell : to thee I'll haste,
For, till we meet in Heaven, I cannot rest.

In Memory of Ann the wife of John Stevens of Trevalgan, who died 1729, aged 23.'

We will now proceed to give all the tombstone inscriptions in the churchyard, that are by any possibility legible. Probably scores of others are buried beneath the present level of the soil. Some of the following were most difficult to decipher, either through the wearing of the stone, or its being sunk into the ground.

Against the East wall of the church, going from South to North, are these:

'Erected by Hopkin Walters Quick in memory of his grandfather Arnold Walters who circumnavigated the globe with Commodore Lord Anson in H.M.S. "Centurion" and died 1789 aged 74. Also of Mary Walters, daughter of the last named. She died 1811 aged 63.'

'In memory of Mary the wife of John Wall, who died 1825 aged 86. Also her six infant children. Also the above John, died 1831 aged 88. Also Martha their daughter, died 1838 aged 69.'

'In memory of Henry Row, who died 1848 aged 51. Also his twin sons Henry and George, died 1832 aged 4 months.'

'In memory of Catherine youngest daughter of the late Reverend Lewis Morgan; died 1856 aged 61.'

'Sacred to the memory of Thomas Clark late Master Mariner of this parish who departed this life on the 6th September 1829 aged 89 years. Also of Ann his wife who died 1st May 1824 aged 80 years.'

'Sacred to the Memory of Sally daughter of John and Catherine Couch, who died 1st November 1787 aged 1 year. Also of John Couch who died 12th November 1796 aged 49. Also of John son of John and Catherine Couch, who died 11th January 1811 aged 29 years. Also of William son of John and Catherine Couch, who died 27th April 1820 aged 35. Also of John Hodge who died 1824 aged 50.'

'In memory of Mary Berriman, who died 1825 aged 44 years; together with her parents.'

'In memory of Mary the wife of James Berriman, who died 1824 aged 63 years. Also Thomas M[athews] Berriman her infant son. Also Hannah her daughter, died 1825 aged 20.

Lovely innocent, farewell!
  All our pleasing hopes are over;
Formed in person to excel,
  Thee we call our own no more.
Death hath snatched thee from our arms—
Heaven shall give thee brighter charms.'

'In memory of Elizabeth Noall, who died 1827 aged 29.

Farewell! Sweet maid, whom, as black winter sears
The fragrant bud of spring too early blown,
Untimely Death has nipt; here take thy rest,
Inviolable here, while we, than thou
Less favoured, through the irksome vale of life
Toil on in tears without thee; yet not long
Shall Death divide us; rapid is the flight
Of life, more rapid than the turtle's wing;
And soon our bones shall meet; here may we sleep,
Here wake, together, and by His dear might
Who conquered Death for sinful man, ascend
Together hence to an eternal home.'

The next is a vault, with inscriptions:

'In memory of John Paynter, died 1786 aged 70.
Also Mary his wife, died 1791 aged 71.
Also Johanna wife of John Quick and daughter of the above, died 1791 aged 40.
Also Richard son of John and Johanna Quick, died 1819 aged 31.
Also John Quick son of John and Johanna, died 1826 aged 44.

This King of Terrors is the Prince of peace,
Death brings me more than we in Eden lost;
My Body's food for preying worms,
My Soul outrode the stormy blast.
What I am now, thou soon must be;
Reader, prepare to follow me.'

South of the church are the following tombstones:

'In memory of George Henry son of G. and C. Wasley, died 1833 aged 3.
And George Henry also son of the above, died 1842 aged 5.
Also Charlotte daughter of William and Candace Sandow, died 1835 aged 26.'

Then come two small granite headstones thus inscribed:

'W. H. 1812.'

'N. R.
A. C. R.
. . . . R.'

'In memory of Isebellar wife of Thomas Harry, died 1822 aged 29.'

'In memory of Ann Williams, died 1821 aged 19.
Also George Williams, died 1856 aged 52.'

'In memory of Captain Henry Row, died 1831 aged 36.
Also Henry and Joseph Hocking, his infant children.'

'In memory of Margaret Weymouth daughter of John and Mary Stevens, died 1831 aged 3.'

'In memory of Jane wife of Capt. Richard White, died 1855.'

'In memory of William Parker of London, died 1832 aged 48.'

'In memory of John son of Francis and Sarah Bamfield, died 1831 aged 28.

He struggled long to gain relief, physicians was in vain,
Until by Christ he was releasd, and snatched from grief & pain ;
The anchor cast, he rides secure on Canaan's happy shore,
The roaring wind & foaming seas will batter him no more.'

'In memory of Jane daughter of William and Grace Veal, died 1831 aged 5.'

'In memory of Grace Cundy, died 1830 aged 50. She was relict of the late Captain Thomas Cundy who was killed in gallantly defending his vessel in an attack from a French privateer off Dungeness, October the 10th 1819.' Below the soil are verses.

A worn granite headstone, illegible. The footstone is of slate, marked 'B 1701.'

'In memory of John Leggoe, died 1818 aged 31.

Happy the youth who, priviledgd by fate
To shorter labour and a lighter weight,
Leaves a vain world, and does resign his breath
With sweet composure to the hand of Death.'

'In memory of Margery wife of Philip Bennetts, died 1809 aged 44.

Also Philip their son, died 1825 aged 22.

Snatched from his parents in the bloom of youth,
Adorned with virtue, piety, and truth,
Sincere to all and upright in his ways,
And all his actions justly merits praise.'

(Also seven infant children of the first-named.)

Vault surrounded by iron railings, near the churchyard wall; slate slab, bearing this inscription:

'Within this Vault are deposited the Mortal remains of Jasper Williams who died June 5th 1804 aged 71 years.

Also of Mary his wife who died Decr 9th 1793 aged 57 years.

Also of Jasper Williams who died Decr 25th 1809 aged 46 years.

Also of James Eustis Williams who died July 24th 1813 aged 46 years.

Also of Honor Williams who died April 19th 1835 aged 67 years—children of the above named Jasper and Mary Williams.

Also of Mary wife of Jasper Williams, who died Novr 23rd 1833 aged 33 years.

And of Mary their daughter who died Feby 8th 1834 aged 5 months.

Also of William Stevens who died July 24th 1836 aged 3 months, the son of William Stevens and Catherine Williams who were lost at sea 29th July 1837.

Mary Williams Relict of the above Jasper Williams, died 25th October 1841 aged 79 years.

Hannah wife of Jasper Williams died Novr 19th 1844 aged 38 years.

Jasper Williams died 25th July 1849 aged 51 years.'

'In memory of Stephen Jose, died 1788 aged 78.
Also Capt Timothy Jose son of Stephen. Dyed 1808 aged 59.

Corruption, earth and worms
Shall but refine this flesh,
Till my triumphant spirit comes
To put it on afresh.

Also Mary daughter of Timothy, died 1812 aged 13.'

'In memory of Agnes wife of Thomas Grenfell, died 1793 aged 68.'

(This tombstone, a slate one grotesquely ornamented in the style of the period, is nailed to the south wall of the church, near the cross.)

The following are north of the church, a position against which there seems to have been none of that traditional prejudice which is or was common in many other parishes:

'In memory of Mary wife of Thomas Richards, died 1830 aged 44.
Also Edward their son, died 1826.'

'In memory of Henry Curnow, died 1835.'

Vault, the slab inscribed to the memory of:

'Frances wife of James Young, died 1825 aged 29.
Also Frances Maria their daughter, died 1822 aged 2 months.
Also Edward son of the above James by Martha his second wife; died 1835 aged 4.
Also the aforesaid James Young, died 1848 aged 50.'

'In this Repository is layed the mortal remains of William Maine of Bideford, aged 40, lost at sea off this harbour with his dear relation Samuel Spencer aged 14, Decr the Seventh 1807.

Though saild in lower seas and drownd,
That victory and peace the, found
On the celestial shore.'

Obliterated headstone, only this being legible:

' . . . obiit æt. 10.

Oh parents dear! for me do not lament' . . . .

'In memory of Mary widow of Capt W. Christian, died 1819 aged 79.'

'In memory of Phillis wife of Capt S. C. Clark, died 1856 aged 37.'

Vault:

'Edward Stephens esquire died 1776 aged —.
Also Elizabeth his wife, died 1810 aged 86.
Also Francis their son, died 1791 aged 39.
And Susannah his wife, died 1775 aged —.
And Jane his second wife, died 1794 aged —.
Also Hugh Ley Esqre M.D., died 1826 aged 64.
And Elizabeth his wife, died 1848 aged 83.'

Vault:

'Paul Tremearne died 1807 aged 66.
Also Ann Phillipps widow, his daughter, died 1848 aged 71.
And Ann Tremearne Phillipps his granddaughter, died at Nantes 1855 aged 42.
Also three infant grandchildren.'

'In memory of Thomas Quick, died 1811 aged 67; and his four grandchildren and two great-grandchildren.'

'In memory of Eldred Roberts, died 1831. Also Matilda his wife.'

(Also others of the same family.)

'In memory of Richard Jenkyns gen^t, died 1815 aged 66.
Also Elizabeth his wife, died 1823 aged 82.
Also Anna Maria their daughter, relict of Capt. Daniel Sydal, died 1864 aged 83.'

'In memory of Joanna daughter of Uddy' [Bray?] (obliterated).

'M. G.—T. D.'
'T. S. 1812.'

An obliterated headstone.

'In memory of Thomas Rowe, died 1831 aged 65.
Also Nathaniel Hicks Rowe, his son, master of the brig "Importer" of London, died in Jamaica 1825 aged 30.
Also Mary Ann Rowe who is buried in the church.
Also Ann Rowe, died 1806 aged 1 year.
Also Mary Biron his granddaughter, died 1825, aged 2.'

'In memory of Nathaniel Toms, master of the brig "Henry," who died at Giberalter 1827 aged 35.
And Nathl Toms senior, officer of H.M. Customs in this port, who died 1830, aged 72. And Frances his wife, died 1818 aged 56.'

Vault:

'The Family of Stevens lie interred here, 1797.
Martha the wife of John Stevens esquire (Collector of his Majesty's Customs in the Port of St Ives) lies interred here.
John Stevens esquire died 27th March 1807 aged 68.
Also of Page second wife of the above; who departed this life Feby 26th 1835 aged 80 years.
Also of Captain Andrew Thomas of this town, who departed this life Feby 18th 1854 aged 41 years.'

'In memory of Jane daughter of Anthony and Margaret Johns, died 1789 aged 18 months.
Also the above Margaret, died 1813 aged 52.'

'In memory of John Major of Carva, died 1786, aged 47.'

'In memory of Robert Morton, died 1819, aged 37.'

which they gave him during the Civil Wars. Most Cornish churches possess or have possessed similar copies (Saint Ives is a notable exception, owing to its having supported the Parliament). The document reads as follows:

'C. R.

'We are highly sensible of the extraordinary merit of our County of Cornwall, of their zeal for the defence of our Person, and the just rights of our Crown in a time when we could contribute so little to our own defence or to their assistance in a time when not only no reward appeared, but great and probable dangers were threatened to obedience and loyalty; of their great and eminent courage and patience in the indefatigable prosecution of their great work against so potent an enemy, backed with so strong, rich, and powerful cities, and plentifully furnished, and supplied with men, arms, money, ammunition, and provisions of all kinds; and of the wonderful success with which it hath pleased Almighty God, although with the loss of some eminent persons who shall never be forgotten by us, to reward their Loyalty and Patience by many strange Victories over their and our enemies, in despight of all human Probability, and all imaginable Disadvantages; that as we cannot be forgetful of so great Deserts, so we cannot but desire to publish to all the world, and perpetuate to all time, the memory of these their merits, and of our acceptance of them, and to that end, we do hereby render our Royal thanks to that our county in the most publick and lasting manner we can devise, commanding copies hereof to be printed and published; and one of them to be read in every Church and Chapel therein, and to be kept for ever as a Record in the same, that as long as the History of these Times, and of this Nation shall continue, the Memory of how much that County hath merited from us, and our Crown, may be derived with it to posterity.

'Given at our camp at Sudley Castle, the tenth of September, 1643.'

(A Cornish version of this letter is preserved among the Gwavas MSS., at the British Museum.)

A baseless tradition asserts that the name Lelant is derived from Lanent, one of the fifty saintly children of good King Brechan. It is really 'Lan Nant,' the Valley Church.

Other particulars of the history of this church will be found under different chapters of our history.

The parish registers commence thus: 'A Regester of the Names of those that haue Bene Baptized within our Parish of Uny Lelant Begininge in the yeare 1684. John the son of John Hayes was baptized ye 2 February.'

The following are all the names of the pre-Reformation clergy at Lelant, which we have been able to collect:

Andrew de Montibus; succeeded by

A.D. 1261. William de Capella, 'Sub-deacon of our Lord the Pope;' was admitted 'to the whole church [*i.e.* as Rector] . . . . according to the tenour of the Ordination of the Lord John, Cardinal Priest of the Title of San Lorenzo in Lucina, and of the Confirmation of the Lord Pope, on the presentation some time since made by the Prior and Convent of Tywardreath.'

1274. Sir Walter Gascoyn collated vicar.

1281. Sir Amand de Cambron collated vicar.

1306. Thomas 'Presbiter.'

1310. Master Robert le Seneschal.

—— Lucas, 'Sacerdos.'

1311. Master Gilbert de Cornubia (deacon).

1409. John Clerk.

1416. John Bryt.

1520. William Tyrriffe, 'chaplain.'

[1520. John Bretton, 'Chaplain' Towednack.

„ John Hycks, „ Saint Ives.

„ — Pentreth „ „].

The 'Valor Ecclesiasticus' shows that James Gentell was Vicar of Lelant in 1536.

An old man informed the present vicar, that early in this century he had seen Lelant church full of kegs of French brandy, stored there by smugglers, who considered the church as a very safe hiding-place, because no one would ever dream of resorting there on a week-day.

SEPULCHRAL INSCRIPTIONS OF LELANT.

In the church. West wall of South aisle.

Slate tablet: 'Here lieth the bodye of William Praed of Treuethow Gentleman of the adge of five and fiftye yeeres who was Buried the Eight of maye anno dni: 1620 having one sone and three daughters surviving.' In the centre is carved a representation of William Praed, his wife and children, kneeling with clasped hands, on cushions, one behind the other in the order of their respective sizes. Over their heads on scrolls are the names: 'William Praed, Prudence, James, Jane, Alice, Marye.' The father is dressed in a long gown, with a frill round his neck. Prudence, his wife, wears a large round hat with bent brim, a frilled collar, a short jacket kilted below the waist, a girdle, an ample quilted skirt, and a flowing cloak. James wears a frill, doublet, wide trunk breeches, stockings and low shoes. The girls wear caps. Below the figures, in incised Gothic characters, are the words:

'Think gentle friend, that now dost view this tomb,
To-morrow must thou go to thy last home.'

On one side of the tablet is a death's-head and an hour-glass, in renaissance scroll-work; on the other a vase, out of which grows a stiff-looking flower. This tablet, like the others on the same wall, formerly lay on the floor.

Slate tablet: 'Here lyeth the Bodye of Stephen Pawley of this Parish Gentleman who dyed the XIX daye of November in ye yeare of our Lord God 1635.' In the centre are figures carved as in the above example, but in less bold relief, of Stephen Pawley with his wife, five sons and six daughters. Over each head is the baptismal name, thus, beginning with the youngest daughter and reading from left to right: 'J. P.; C. P.; P. P.; G. P.; M. P.; J. P.; C. P.; P. P.; W. P.; S. P.; H. P.; M. P.; 75.' In one corner are two shields of the arms, bearing: Per pale: I. three organ rests (?); on a chief 3 martlets (?) II. Pawley (see post). Also Quarterly: I. and IV., as I. above; II. and III. Pawley; and beneath are the following verses:

'If teares the dead againe to life could calle
Thou hadst not slept within this earthye balle
If holye vertues could a ransome bynn
Soe soone corruption had not rapte thee in
But thou wert ripe for God and God didst crave
So gavst a gladsome welcome to the grave
Assuringe still that thou with God dost dwell
Thy end soe good thy life was lead soe well.'

Slate tablet, fixed in a former doorway. 'Fili Dei, miseris miserere nobis peccatoribus.

Crest: Unicorn's head on a coronet. Squire's helmet and lambrequins.

Arms: Quarterly, I. & IV. a lion rampant, on a chief dancettée three mullets (for Pawley); II. three saws (?) in pale; III. 3 columns, on a chief 3 birds. Inscription:

'This Marble Stone was placed here in the year of our Lord 1713. In Memory of Hugh Pawley of Gunwin Gen^{t} who dyed the 17th day of Septemb^{r} Anno: 1721 & of Judith his wife who dyed ye 30th day of October 1698 by whom were begotten Seaven Children (viz) Prudence, Hugh, Mary, William, George, Peter and Judith.

Virtus post funera Vivit
Vita quasi umbra fugit.'

Slate tablet. At the top a ship sailing. 'In Memory of Elizabeth Cundy, daughter of John and Grace Cundy; died 1799 aged 25. Also of Grace Cundy, died 1799 aged 66; and John Cundy, died 1802 aged 66.

Tho' Boreas Wind and Neptunes Waves
Have toss'd me too and fro
In spite of both by God's decree
I harbour here below
Where now at Anchor I do lie
With many of our fleet
I must one day set sail again
Our Saviour Christ to meet.'

Hatchment. Crest: A unicorn's head argent, armed and crined or, on a coronet. Squire's helmet and lambrequins.

Arms: Quarterly: I. & IV. azure 6 estoiles argent, 3, 2, 1. II. per pale dancettée: 1, sable; 2, ermines, on a bend gules 3 cross crosslets or. III. gules, a bend between 2 martlets or. Over all an escutcheon of pretence, quarterly: I. & IV. argent, on a bend sable 3 spearheads or. II. & III. azure, a saltire argent.

In the churchyard. East side.

Susanna wife of Thomas Treglown, died 1847 aged 81.

John Stevens mine agent, died 1861. Elizabeth his wife, died 1868 aged 69.

'Richard Hichens gent of St Ives, the survivor of the family of Thomas and Mary Hichens.' Born 1782, died 1866.

The wife of the late vicar of Lelant, the Rev. Uriah Tonkin, and the first wife of the present vicar, are buried here.

Matthew Stevens late of St Ives; died 1st January 1795, aged 44. Also Martha his wife, died 1833 aged 84. Also Francis their son, died 1796 aged 7; and Elizabeth Pope their daughter, died 1852 aged 66.

Christiana Banfield, wife of Charles Allen of St Ives; died 1801 aged 42. Also Wilmot Stevens their daughter, died 1810 aged 22. Also the said Charles Allen, died 1825 aged 68. Also Ursula the wife of Charles Allen junior of St Ives, died 1825 aged 46.

'J. H. died 1759 aged 4.
A. H. died 1760 aged 2.
H. H. died 1777 aged 89.
M. H. died 1789 aged 27.
P. H. died 1790 aged 42.
E. H. died 1802 aged 45.
P. H. died 1803 aged 77.
R. H. died 1804 aged 50.
H. H. died 1809 aged 87.
R. H. died 1814 aged 50.
H. H. died 1823 aged 72.
C. H. died 1825 aged 79.
T. H. died 1826 aged 76.
R. H. died 1833 aged 63.
J. H. died 1842 aged 76.
J. H. died 1843 aged 74.'

South of the church.

Sarah the wife of William Osborne of St Hillery, died 1824 aged 66. Also Mary Hosking, died 1846 aged 97.

Mary the daughter of William and Mary Mayn, died 1803 aged 9 months. Sarah, died 1807 aged 10 weeks. Samuel, died 1808 aged 4 years.

Elizabeth, wife of Edward Richards; died 1833 aged 64. (This slab is close to the old cross.)

Thomas, son of Hannibal and Jane Trevorrow, died 1816 aged 21.

Margery Thomas, a native of St Ives; died 1865 aged 87.

Broken and illegible slate near the porch.

James Richards, died 1775 aged 42. (A small freestone slab near the porch.)

Stone sarcophagus surrounded by an iron railing, close to the south wall of the church. In memory of William Praed, Esquire, of Trevetho, died 1833 aged 84. Erected by his children in memory of 'the best of fathers.'

Phillis the widow of Christopher Trewhella; died 1863 aged 84. Also Christopher their son, died 1870 aged 61. Also Martin the son of Matthew and Mary Trewhella, aged 16 months.

Alice Sampson, died 1795 aged 63. Also Richard Sampson, died 1814 aged 85.

Captain Richard Curgenven, of the Royal Navy; died 1784 aged 47. (Fixed against the south wall of the tower.)

John Harry, died 1832 aged 63. Also his wife Cordelia and several children.

Mary the wife of John Bennetts; died 1864 aged 64. Also their children.

Elizabeth the wife of Edward Bennetts, died 1841 aged 64.

Philip Bennetts of St. Ives, died 1841 aged 68. Also Amy his wife.

Benjamin Richards, died 1774 aged 74.

Granite vault with broken slate, of the end of last century. In memory of Elizabeth Kemp and others of the family.

John Cooper, died 1810 aged 84. Also Catherine Kendrick his wife, of Wrexham in Denbighshire, N. Wales, died 1783 aged 50. (There are other tombstones of the Coopers.)

William Hawes, died 1835 aged 70. Also Avice his wife.

Thomas Ninnes, died 1855 aged 47. Also Willmot his daughter, died 1839 aged 8 days.

Christiana, wife of Isaac Wright of Newlyn and daughter of Christopher and Mary Edwards of this parish; died 1827 aged 28.

'This ritual stone thy friend hath laid
O'er thy respected dust,
Only proclaim the mournfull day
When he a Partner lost.
In life to copy thee I'll strive
And, when I that resign,
May some good Christian friend survive
To lay my bones by thine.'

Stone vault with cracked slate. William and Elizabeth Farquharson, 1802.

Johanna wife of John Curnow, died 1851 aged 26.

John Lory, died 1840 aged 48. Also Priscilla his wife.

Clement Uren, died 1849 aged 71. Also Alice his wife.

Charles Richards, died 1864 aged 76. Also Anne his wife.

George Jennings, died 1817 aged 66.

Henry Harris, died 1803 aged 49. Also Caroline his wife.

Hugh Richards master mariner, died 1854 aged 69. Also Sophia his wife.

Richard fifth son of Henry and Blanch Hosking, died 1866 aged 86.

James Williams, died 1864 aged 29.

James Williams of this parish, died 1872 aged 64.

William Bosistow, died 1825 aged 43. Also Margaret his wife.

Thomas Johns, died 1805 aged 29. Also Elizabeth his wife.

Thomas Harry, died 1849 aged 56. Also Elizabeth his wife and their family.

Thomas Uren, died (*circa*) 1850.

West of the church.

Richard Hall, died 1792 aged 4. (Slate on the west wall of the tower.)

North of the church.

Matthew Quick, died 1836 aged 62. Also Elizabeth his wife, died 1868 aged 69.

John Penberthy of St. Ives, died 1845 aged 82. Also Grace Adams Penberthy his granddaughter, died 1839 aged 4. Also Samuel Uren his grandson, died 1844 aged 3.

Richard Uren of Worvas in this parish, died 1816 aged 66.

On the wall by the south gate of the churchyard is a piece of granite bearing the inscription 'J. B.; S. How; 1801.'

In the *Western Antiquary* of March 1884 is an interesting note by Professor Robert Hunt, F.R.S., calling attention to the fact that a burial place had long been known on the Towans of Lelant, near the Hayle ferry and not far from the church, and that in constructing the railway to Saint Ives, this was cut through, and a quantity of skeletons removed. The skulls are said to have been of a pre-Aryan type and similar to some discovered at the Pentuan tin-streams, fifty feet below the surface. There was a tradition, says Professor Hunt, that a shipload of slaves, who were brought to Cornwall to work the tin, perished in a storm on Hayle Bar; but it is questionable whether the interments do not mark the site of an early church-yard, since the skeletons were laid in rough walled graves.

TOWEDNACK CHURCH.

The parish of Towednack is only less wild than Zennor, and its 'church-town' (*i.e.* village round the parish church) consists of two farmhouses and an inn. Towednack church, says Blight, is remarkable as alone possessing a chancel-arch among the churches of West Cornwall; this arch is of the thirteenth century, very acutely pointed, and consists simply of two chamfered orders springing from corbels. The church consists of chancel, nave with western tower, and south aisle and porch; the two latter are [illegible] than the other parts. The tower, of granite, very low [illegible], is altogether unlike every other in the district, and [illegible] constructed without any attempt at ornamentation, proper [illegible] made of the material at hand. The string-course and [illegible] are remarkably bold; the battlemented parapet (walled [illegible] the east and west sides) is of the simplest character. The [illegible] lights are square-headed and chamfered; altogether it is a [illegible]teristic structure, harmonizing well with its site, in the midst of a most wild and dreary region. The tower staircase, on [illegible] unusual plan, is constructed without newel or winders, and [illegible] its entrance direct from the north-west angle of the nave. The tower-arch appears to have been originally, like most others of the same date in Cornwall, a plain soffit-arch; to this responds and a chamfered order have been added. A portion of the old impost-moulding remains, and just inside the arch are two boldly-carved corbels. The springing of the tower-arch is peculiar as being quite a foot back from the face of the columns. The eastern bench in the porch is formed of a block of granite, seven feet long, one foot six inches high and ten inches wide, with an incised double cross. 'This stone evidently does not occupy its original position; it differs from the ordinary types of the Cornish churchyard and wayside cross, and is most probably an early Christian sepulchral monument' (Blight).

On the 27th June, 1542, Bishop Vesey of Exeter directed his suffragan, William of Hippo, to consecrate the cemetery of the parish church of Towednack.*

There are two old bench-ends in this church, each carved with a medallion profile portrait of a man in a hat, with moustachios and beard; on one is inscribed, in letters curiously interlaced, 'Master Mathew Trenwith warden,' and on the other, 'James Trewhela warden.' Both bench-ends, which bear the date 1633, have been worked into a chancel-seat, and are suffering severely from damp. 'The remnant of the chancel-screen is of the same age as the bench-ends,' says Blight.

* I take it that the dedication of this church is to Saint Gwynog, or in English Winnock. According to Rees ('Essay on the Welsh Saints'), Gwynog ab Gildas, a saint of royal British race, lived about the middle of the sixth century, and was a monk of Llancarfan. He is the titular saint of three churches in South Wales, and of Llanwynog, Montgomeryshire. In the chancel window of the latter church he is depicted, in glass of the fourteenth century, in abbatial robes, with a cross in his hand; below are the words '*Sanctus Gwinocus, ora pro nobis.*' Cressy [illegible] he founded the monastery of Saint Vinoc, on the confines of France and [illegible], and that his feast is in Brittany observed on the 6th November. In [illegible] his day is the 26th October. The parish of Landewednack, in the Lisherd [illegible] of Cornwall, and that of Landevenech in Bretagne, likewise bear the [illegible] of this saint. The syllable 'To' is a common prefix to the names of Cymric [illegible] and the 'intrusive d' before 'n' is familiar to students of Cornish.

The font is ancient and simple in form, but was carved in the last century. The upper portion of the bowl is divided into square panels, two of which contain respectively the Latin initials I. R. and W. B.; the other compartments exhibit two quatrefoils, a conventional lily and the date 1720, while another is left blank. The round base of the column and the pedestal meet in a tooth pattern at the joint. On the bowl is an early carving of a face in bold relief.

In the belfry is a mediæval bell, bearing the inscription 'Sancti Spiritus assit nobis gracia' (May the grace of the Holy Spirit be with us). There is a credence on the gospel side of the high-altar space, and a piscina on the epistle side. Also a support for the rood-loft remains, on the south side of the chancel arch.

Over the door of the porch is a small sundial, bearing the following inscription: '1720. Bright Sol and Luna Time and Tide doth hold. Chronodix Humbrale.'

In the north wall is a blocked doorway with a plain and very massive tympanum of granite.

Inside the church, on the south wall, is a marble slab inscribed in memory of Thomas Rosewall of Hellesvear, Saint Ives, Esquire, who died 1841 aged 87. Also of Mary his wife who died 1829 aged 72. Also James, Thomas and Juliana Rosewall, of Talland, Saint Ives.

At a meeting of the Penzance Natural History and Antiquarian Society held in November 1886, Mr. J. B. Cornish mentioned that, during the taking down the chimney of an old house close to Towednack church recently, an ancient cross was discovered in the ruins, and was put up in a garden at Tredorwin about a mile from the church. It is of granite, about three feet high, with rudely cut circular stem and top.

There is an unpleasant and probably erroneous tradition that the bodies in Towednack churchyard, which is very small, after having lain there for twenty years, were disinterred to make way for fresh burials, and stowed away in a charnel-house.

There is an old legend that, 'when the masons were building the tower of this church, the devil came every night and carried off the pinnacles and battlements. Again and again this work was renewed during the day, and as often was it removed during the night, until at length the builders gave up the work in despair.' Associated with this tower is a proverb: 'There are no cuckolds in Towednack, because there are no horns on the church-tower' (See Hunt, 'Popular Romances'). Perhaps this is not unconnected with the celebrated Towednack 'Cuckoo Feast,' noticed in another chapter of our history.

The Parish Registers go back to 1676, if we include a copy

of an early volume, long since lost, which copy was made by Dr. Cardew. One of the first entries is: '1676. Baptised Anne, daughter of Andrew Rosewall.'

Among the peculiar names occurring in this register are those of 'Emlyn Baragwanath,' buried 1684, and 'Duence Battrall,' buried in 1747.

Tombstones in Towednack churchyard. East of the church.

William Rosewall yeoman, of Lower Bussow in this parish; died 1864 aged 50. Also Jane his wife; and William their son who died 1868.

Amy wife of John Chellew and third daughter of John Quick of Chytodden in this parish; died 1874 aged 63.

William Quick of Buzzow in this parish, yeoman; died 1842 aged 81.

'In Memory of the Quick family of Trevalgen, St Ives.' Peter B. Quick, died 1853 aged 71. Richard Quick died 1855 aged 72. William Quick died 1855 aged 67.

Elizabeth Reynolds of Trevessa Wartha in this parish; died 1850 aged 77. And others of the family.

Elizabeth wife of John Green, Clerk of this Parish, died 1843 aged 33.

> 'Weep not, my child and husband dear,
> I am not dead but sleeping here;
> My debt is paid, my grave you see,
> Prepare yourselves to follow me.'

Also John Henry their only child, died 1843 aged 5.

John, Thomasin, Elizabeth and Peter, children of Peter and Mary Quick.

Israel Quick junior, of St Ives, died 1825 aged 36. Also Paul his son.

John and Alice Quick, of St Ives, died 1815 aged 13. (Stone vault with broken slate.)

William Berryman, died 1834 aged 44. Also Wilmot his wife.

Solomon Richards, died 1857 aged 58.

Christopher Edwards, died 1826 aged 68. Also Margery his wife, and their children Thomas, Ann and Mary, the latter of whom died 1871 aged 77.

Stephen Curnow, died 1837 aged 81. Also his sons John and Andrew.

James Quick, died 1859 aged 59.

South of the church.

On the south wall. John Quick of Chytodden in this parish, died 1855 aged 70. Also Elizabeth his wife.

Robert Michell, died 1865 aged 59.

Sampson son of Sampson and Hannah Curnow, died 1865 aged 17.

West of the church.

William Martin of Embla in this parish, died 1865 aged 65. The new cemetery adjoins the churchyard on this side.

North of the church.

3 granite headstones and footstones:

G. S., 1791.
J. J., 1792.
I. O., 1795.

James Quick, died 1839 aged 74. Also Elizabeth his wife.

Lydia Hickes, daughter of Francis and Sarah Hickes of St Ives; died 1804 aged 5.

> 'The Village Maidens to her grave shall bring
> The fragrant Garland each returning spring,
> Selected sweets in enblem of the Maid
> Who underneath the hollow turf is laid.
> Like her they flourish beauteous to ye eye,
> Like her too soon they languish fade and die.'

Margaret wife of Richard James, died 1848 aged 48.

ZENNOR CHURCH.

ZENNOR CHURCH.

Zennor church is dedicated to Saint Sinara, virgin. It consists of chancel, nave, western tower, north aisle, south transept and south porch. The south side of the nave is of the thirteenth century, the transept and chancel decorated and contemporaneous. Originally the church was cruciform, but late in the fifteenth (or early in the sixteenth) century the north transept was removed and a north aisle built, extending the entire length of the nave and chancel, into which it opens by an arcade of six rudely constructed arches of unequal span, supported by plain octagonal granite piers. The tower, of the usual Cornish perpendicular type, is constructed of ashlar granite, and has three stages marked by plain set-offs, and a bold string-course above the plinth. The west window is constructed of catacleuse stone from the neighbourhood of Padstow, which retains its sharpness of angle and outline as freshly as when first inserted, affording a striking contrast to the disintegrated granite. Above this window is an ogee-headed

ZENNOR CHURCH, FROM THE N.W., BEFORE THE RESTORATION.

niche, which formerly contained an image. The south-east portion of the chancel is of Norman date and older than any other part of the building. Westward of the porch-doorway is a single acutely pointed light, three feet high by six inches in breadth, with a wide splay of three feet three inches through a very thick wall. It was mistaken by Blight, writing before the restoration of 1890, for a round-headed Norman one, but on examination it proved to be a very early lancet window of the thirteenth century. It was in his time partially hidden by a gallery, concerning which the following note was made in a private account book of William Borlase, Vicar of Zennor in 1772:

'Memo: April 9th 1794. In the year 1772, when the singing-gallery was erected, and previous to the compass-roofing of that part of the church over the gallery, I observed these figures, on one of the oak sills which supported the south part, 1172 or 1177, which I should take to be the date when the church of Zenor was built, so that about the time of the Lincoln Taxation it was more than one hundred years old.'

But there can be no doubt that the vicar read the figures wrongly; they were, probably, 1472.

The doorway has been so much affected by modern repairs that it is difficult to decide whether it is contemporaneous with the window.

The chancel is raised one step above the nave, and the sacrarium has two steps, all three extending continuously across the aisle, which, in the lower part of the wall to the height of the window-sill, has masonry projecting eight inches, and a rude bracket of granite, for an image, the upper surface of which measures one foot by one foot two inches. The walls of the aisle were rebuilt about fifty years ago.

The transept probably opened into the nave by two arches; but these, except the springing of the westernmost, with the central pillar, have been removed; the space was spanned by a wooden beam until the restoration. The existing piers at the angles of the transept correspond to the second and fourth piers of the nave arcade; they are indeed of the same character and date, and take the places of others of an earlier period. They are in fact an instalment of a new arcade, showing that it had been *intended* to remove the south transept also, and substitute an aisle to correspond with the north aisle. The south wall of the transept has an acutely pointed window, with a plain chamfered scoinson arch. Having lost its tracery, it had been fitted with a wooden sash previous to the restoration, when tracery of a geometrical design was inserted. In the south wall of the chancel is a well-restored two-light decorated window, evidently of the same date as the transept window, and a second window of the same design has been inserted by its side in the blank wall eastward. In all the earlier windows of this building granite was not used, but a finer-grained stone procured from some distant part. The gable-cross on the transept, which was found in the chancel, and the corbel-heads hereinafter referred to, are of this stone. A coarse native sandstone was used in the construction of the Norman piscina in the chancel, and fragments of the same stone were used up elsewhere in later work.

There is a good decorated font, which, before 1890, when it was restored to its pristine beauty, was covered with whitewash, and much mutilated. It had a piece of an iron drain-pipe fixed to it, while an earthenware basin was deposited inside the bowl. Indeed, the whole edifice previous to the restoration was in a very neglected state, with whitewash and green damp and rottenness everywhere. A rickety old kitchen table stood inside the altar-rails, and the floor of the chancel was paved with common red bricks.

Of the three bells, two are mediæval and inscribed 'Sancte Johannes, ora pro nobis,' (Saint John, pray for us) 'Sancta Maria, ora pro nobis' (Saint Mary, pray for us).

ZENNOR FONT.

On the south wall of the tower is a small bronze dial, bearing the figure of a mermaid, and the inscription: 'The Glory of the world Paseth. Paul Quick fecit, 1737.'

Until its restoration, Zennor church, the last in this district to be renovated, preserved for our instruction a sad picture of the surroundings amid which our great-grandfathers were content to worship. The original carved oak seats had all (with one exception) disappeared and been replaced by family boxes. Two old bench-ends only remained, on the south side, near the tower. One of them, known as 'the mermaid of Zennor,' is a great curiosity: it represents a syren with the conventional

Vicaria ibm̄ val. tam in decimis majoribs. qam̄ minoribs. cū agist. glebe ultra cv^s

X^a inde x^s vj^d

Decanat. de Poudre in dict. com. & dioc. Exon.:

Priorat. de Tywardreyth unde Dn̄s Rex est fundator.

Tempālia [inter alia]:

Porthia Prior cū viij^d de pquis. cur.: cxj^s ix^d'

(TRANSLATION OF THE ABOVE.)

Ecclesiastical Valuation of Henry VIII. (1535.) Extract.

'The College of the Church of the Holy Cross of Crediton in the Deanery of Cadbury.

The true annual value of all the possessions as well temporal as spiritual of Richard Errington the Precentor there, and of the Canons of the same College, examined and approved before the aforesaid Commission in the term and year abovesaid.

To wit: The spiritual possessions of the said College: [amongst others] *Lelant* in the Diocese of Exeter in the County of Cornwall.

The value by the year of the entire tithe of the rectory there so demised to Thomas Glyn and others, for the term of ten years, by the indenture in that term commencing on the first day of January in the 21st year of the reign of King Henry VIII.

The College of Saint Thomas of Glasney-by-Penryn, of which Walter Good formerly Bishop of Exeter is the founder, James Gentill being the Superior there [&c.]: £76.

Spiritual possessions. The value of the farm of the tithes of sheaves belonging to the same College, situate and lying in the divers towns and parishes following, namely [amongst others] the parish of Zennor: £8 12s. 2d.

The Deanery of Penwith in the said County of Cornwall and Diocese of the Bishop of Exeter.

Rectories, vicarages, chantries and prebends in the Deanery of Penwith aforesaid, namely in [amongst others]:

Ewny-by-Lelant and Saint Ives:

The profit arising from the rectory there, not rated here for that it is appropriated to the College of Crediton and rated there according to its value: nothing.

The vicarage there is worth, as well in the greater tithes as in the lesser, with the right of pasture of the glebe, beyond 9s. 11d.

For the ancient payment for the synod and proctors £22 11s. 10d.

Tithe thence £2 0s. 2d.

Zennor.

Profits arising from the rectory there, not rated here for that it is appropriated to the College of Saint Thomas in Glasney-by-Penryn and rated there according to its value as appears there: nothing.

The vicarage there is worth, as well in the greater tithes as in the lesser, with the right of pasture of the glebe, beyond £5 5s. 0d.

Tithe thence 10s. 6d.

The Deanery of Powder in the said county and diocese of Exeter:

The Priory of Tywardreath, whereof our lord the King is the founder:

Temporalities [amongst others]:

Porthia Prior, with 8d. of perquisite of the court: £5 11s. 9d.

We have already noticed one Subsidy Roll, that of 1327, the earliest in existence. We will now examine the next of these rolls in order of date; it was made out some time between the years 1509 and 1523.

It begins by stating that the canons of the church of Kyrton were the owners of the rectory of the parish church of Lelant and of the parish church of Saint Ives, and of Towednack, a chapel dependent on the said church of Saint Ives, and that they were worth, in tithes, obits (masses for the dead), and other emoluments pertaining to the said rectory, £54 by the year.

James Gentyll is named as the Vicar of Lelant, Saint Ives and Towednack, who was rated at the annual value of £20 in respect of his tithes, offerings, obits and other emoluments.

Then follows 'the value of the lands within the seid pishe (of Lelant) by the yere,' of which we give a selection:

'The Lady Hastynge is worth in lands and tenements by the yere £24.
Comes Wylsher (the Earl of Wiltshire) £1.
John Arundell Knight £5.
Ricūs Hals £4.
Reginald Mohun £8 10s. od.
Thomas Trevnw[th] (Trenwith) £1 6s. 8d.
John Marys (of the Marsh, or Morris) £1.
The heirs of Edmund Arundell £1.
John Tregian 12s
John Cokyn £1 4s. od.'

(Some years ago an aged woman told the writer that the 'real old Saint Ives names' were:

'Cocking, Perking, Geen, Rosewall,
Hitchens, Couch, and Toman.'

There is still at least one family named Cocking at Saint Ives.)

'John Trewyke (now Treweek) £1 6s. 8d.
The heirs of Calmadye £2.
Roger Arundell £3.
James Trewynnard £1 12s. od.' (This was a family seated at Trewynnard in Saint Erth parish, on Saint Ives Bay; it is long extinct.)
'Dnā de Syon 10s.
Thomas Glynne 10s.
Johēs Payne £1 6s. 8d.
Johēs Bosworveth 12s.
Edwardus Poulaye miles (the Pawley family were seated at Gunwin in Lelant), £2 10s. od.

The value of the goods of the inhānts wthn the seide pishe and their harnes:

Phillippus Walshe (later Wallis) £2.
Willms Plemayne (the Fleming) £2.
Johēs Trewarnaile 200 marks.
Jacob[s] Caskeys £2.
Johēs Wyllms £8.
Johēs Thomas £3.
John and Henry Boshaberthewe £10.
Ricūs Polper —

Johēs Stephyn Thomas £14.
Ricūs Bronyn (of Brunnion), £2
Ric: and Nichūs Trerynke, £9.
Johēs Vyuwyn 10 marks.
Ric. Worves £2.
Johēs Carnynye £3.
Stephūs Jenkyn £2.
Peter & Stephen Goengwyn [of Gunwin] £8.
Will: Thomas £30.
Stephūs Pawlye £20.
Willūs Tyrriffe cappellanus [curate] £4 6s. 8d.

Petytt John de Lanaunt laborer nat in ptibs Brittanñe sub obedienc Regis ffrancor valet in bonis 2s. (Little John of Lelant, labourer, born in the parts of Brittany under the obedience of the King of the French, is worth in goods 2s.)

Michaell Tarcy de ead nat in ptibs Britanñe sub obedienc Regis ffrancor valet in bonis 2s.

Edm̄s servus Johīs Nichūs de ead laborer natus &c. 1s. 8d.

Tudwall servus Harr̄ Hicke de ead laborer nat &c. pauper.

ffranciscus servus Johīs Stephyn de ead lab. nat &c. pauper.

P'ochia de Tewynnak (Towednack).

This is a chapell appendant to Ewny Lanaunt.
The value of the Lands wtñn the seide pysñe by the yere:
Dnā de Hastynge valet in terr̄ et tenement p ann £6.
Katnā Dnā de Broke £10.
heř Brongston £4 13s. 4d.
Johēs Bevyll 10s.
Petr̄ Egecombe miles 19s.
Stephūs Roswall 10s.
Thōs Trevnw^th 6s. 8d.
Thos Tregoos 13s. 4d.
Johēs Porthmer 8s.

The value of Goods of the inñants wtñn the seide pysñe by the yere:
Matheus Nanscludyr 10 marks.
Johēs Embla 10 marks.
David Mathowe £2.
Thos Merthyr 10 marks.
Stephyn Roswall £10.
Johēs Mathowe £2 6s. 8d.
Johēs Bretton, Cappellanus, pauper.

P'ochia de Ya. (St. Ives.)

Rectoria ecclie pōchis ibm̄ ptinet Chauntoř de Kyrton ut antea patet.
Vicaria ibm̄ ptinet Jacobo Jenkyll ut antea patet.
The value of the Lande wtñn the seide pisñe by the yere:
Catinā Dn̄a de Brooke valet in terr̄ &c £15.

Comes Oxonie 4s. 10d. (The Earl of Oxford.)
Joh: Robnett 19s.
Johēs Payne £1 6s. 8d. (Portrieve of Saint Ives in 1549; executed for participation in the Catholic rising of that year.)
Joh: Arundell miles £1 6s. 8d.
Rich: Joh: Huchyns 19s.
Will: Tregenna £1 10s. 0d.
Ric: Bossowsake —
Rog: Arundell £1 17s. 10d.
Thō Glynne 11d.
Thō John Hamblye 10s.
Joh: Tregian £1 4s. 0d.
Hugo Trevanyon 3s. 4d.
Tho: Treunw[th] £10.
Hen: Reskymer 9s.
Hen: Calmadye £2.
her: Carnarthur 18s.
Joh: Nanscothan £1 16s. 0d.
Tho: Tremayne £1.
Por̃ et Cōventus de Tewardreth 3s. 8d. (The Prior and Convent of Tywardreath.)
Joh: Jenkyn £1 6s. 8d.
Joh: Powna £1.
Joh: Barbor £1 5s. 0d.
Joh: Tregoz 11s.
Joh: Hycks capellañ nil.
Regnłds Mohun 5s.
Thom̃ Tregoos 13s.
her: Oth: Wyll[s] Stephyn 2s.
Thom: Treiythall 3s. 4d.
Joh: Wolcok 9s. 4d.
Hen: Thom: Cokyn £3.
Joh̃: An Gayre £1.
Vivian Borthalan 7s. (Borthalan is now called Borallan and Brallan.)
Joh: Syse 3s. 2d.

The value of the Goods of thenhants wthn the seide pishe & theire harnes:

Thomas Glynne £2.
Jenkyn Stephyn and Tho: his son £4.
Thō Harry and James his son £5.
James Pascowe £2.
Joh: Cokyn 20 marks.
Joh: Payne £20.
John Thomas & Robert his son 40 marks.
Cornelius Veane 10[m].
Joh: Bahavela 10 marks.
Joh: Gooda £13.
Tho: Engove £5.
Ric: Thomas £2.
Laurence Goodall 20[m].
Thom̃ Hauke £2.
Joh: Michell 40[m].
Noel Wylliams £3.
tho: Corvagh £3.
Tho: Treunwyth £2.
Tho: Perx £2.
Joh: Wolcok 4[m].
Joh: Bossowe £5.
Tomkyn Trevyssa 11[m].
Vivan[s] Borthalan £4.
— Pentreth capelanus (nil.)

Alieni:

Johes: Britton Taylor de sentt ya na in &c.—

Vivian Britton de ead ffysher 3s. 4d.

(There are 23 foreigners, all Bretons, of whom 4 are tailors, 7 labourers, 9 fishers and 3 smiths.)

P'ochia de Senar. (*Zennor.*)

The prepositus and canons of the collegiate church of Saint Thomas the martyr of Glasney, owners of the rectory of the parish church there, are worth in tithes, obits and other emoluments £8 a year.

Ric: Smyth clerk, vicar of the parish church there, is worth in tithes, oblations, obits and other emoluments 40s. p ann:

Lands:

her: Brongston £2 10s. od.

Johña Tresawall 10s.

Rog: Arundell 10s.

her: Dyngesan 8s.

Will: Tregenna 15s.

Joh: Chykembra 6s. (A village in this parish.)

Johēs Bevyll 12s.

Jenkyn Gotholghan 10s. (Now Godolphin.)

her: Colan 2s. 6d.

Katerina dnā de brooke £6.

Oliuerius Treyaghan 3s. 4d.

Joh: Arundell Talfren £1 4s. od.

Ricūs Pendree £1.

Joh: Reskymer £1.

Johēs Porthmer 10s.

Johēs Trembrace 4s.

Johēs Coisewyn £1.

Reg: Mohune 8s.

her: Gurlyn 10s.

Hugo Trevanyon 7s. 4d.

her Calmodelye 8s.

Prior et conventus de Tewardreth 8s.

Tho: Trevnw[t] 7s.

Joh: Kyllygrewe 7s.

Goods:

Jacob[s] Tregyrthyn £2.

Thomas & John Bosowe 8 marks.

Ricus: Smyth clicūs 10 marks (clerk).

The next Subsidy is dated 1523. Among the persons rated at Lelant we find:

Will[s] Thomas in bonis £20

Johēs Trewarnayle ali Tomkyn in bonis 200[m].

Jacob[s] Caskew in bonis 20[m]

Stephūs Pauly in bonis £20.

Johēs Broncoyse in bonis £6.

Johēs Boshaberthew in bonis £10.

Nichūs Thomas ali Trevorek in bonis £10.

Ricūs Polper in bonis £4.

Ricūs Treffrynk in bonis £9.

Thomas Nanse in bonis £6.

Ricūs Byuwyn in bonis £2.

Johēs Carnyny in bonis . . . .

Robtus Leyty in bonis . . . .

Stephūs Gowndwyn in bonus £8.

Johēs Stephen Thomas in bonis £10.

Will[s] Hayne in bonis £4.

Benedictus [servus] Johannis Thomas ad quem sunt annue £1.

Nichūs Perkyn servus Caskeys habet stipendium £1.

Radūs Stiphō Pawly hēt stipend £1.

Donelus Irishe ad qū sunt ꝑ ann £1.

Johēs Richard Trefrynk ad qū sunt ꝑ ann £1.

Wills Merther het stipend £1.

Johēs Britton etat xvj annoꝛ £8.

P'ochia de Tewynnek. (1523.)

Hugo Bosowe in bonis £2

Pascacius Mathow in bonis £2.

Johēs Embla in bonis 10m.

Dauid Ammell in bonis £3.

Johēs Huchyn in bonis £2.

Thomas Richard ati Merther in bonis 10m.

Stephus Roswall in bonis £2

Matheus Nanscudir in bonis 2m.

Johēs Wills in bonis £4

P'ochia de Seynt Ya.

Leonardus Gowndry in bonis £4.

Petrus Gowndry in bonis £10.

Noelus Willm̄ in bonis £7.

Thoms Corvagh in bonis £3.

Thomas Trevnwt in bonis £40.

Johēs Wolcok in bonis £9.

Alex Gweader [the Weaver] in bonis £2.

Thonkyn Trevissa in bonis £10.

Vivianus Borthalan in bonis 14s.

Thomas Glyn in bonis £2.

Johēs Jenkyn in bonis £16.

Jacobs Pascow in bonis £2.

Johēs Nanscothan in bonis £10.

Thomas Lamiton in bonis £2

Johēs Stephyn [in the next list called Jenkyn Stephyn] in bonis £6.

Johēs Porseny in bonis £10.

Johēs Payn in bonis £16.

Johēs Cokyn in bonis £15.

Simon Willm̄s in bonis £2.

Cornelus Vighan in bonis £5.

Robtūs Remfra in bonis £8.

Johēs Pascow Cockyn in bonis £2.

Johēs Thom̄s Sullouk in bonis £3.

Thomas Engoff [the Smith] in bonis £5.

Lauꝛ Goodall in bonis £10.

Simon Mathew in bonis £5.

Ricūs Vivian in bonis £2.

Johēs Syse in bonis £3.

Johēs Dauy Ambros in bonis £2.

Johēs Trevva in bonis £4.

Jssabella Trevissa in bonis £2.

Johā Treneva in bonis £4.

Johā Herry merc: in bonis £2.

Alien:

Alans servus Thome Trevnwt het stipend £1.

Aliegene super etat' xvj annor' qui hent stipend':

Johēs fm̄ls [familius] Johīs Morsyny 8d.

Johēs Britton Taillor 8d.

Johēs Joce Britton 8d.

Wills Trerany 8d.

Yvo Gylbert 8d.

Oman fm̄ls Radi: Saundry 8d.

Siluest fm̄ls Henrī Radī 8d.

P'ochia de Senar.

Ricūs Baragwaneth in bonis . . . . .

Johēs Trescaw aliͣ Huchyn in bonis 10m.

Johēs Trembath in bonis £6.

Thomas Bosow ali Dauy in bonis £4.

Jacobs Bodener in bonis £4.

Johēs Willm in bonis £4.

Dauid Thomas in bonis £2.

SUBSIDY OF 1524.

P'ochia de Ewny Lanaunt.

Johēs Nealys valet in bonis £2.

Johēs Trewyck in bonis £4.

Ricūs Renawdyn in bonis £2.

Johēs Wyllm in bonis . . . .

Willms Thomas in bonis £20.

Johēs Trewnesarle in bonis 200m.

Jacobs Chynals in bonis £9.

Stephus Pawly in bonis £20.

Johēs Broncorse in bonis £6

Johēs Bossaverthew in bonis £10.

Nichūs Thoms in bonis £10.

Ricūs Polere in bonis £4.

Ricūs Treffrynk in bonis £10.

Thoms Nanse in bonis £6.

Ricūs Vyuwyn in bonis £2.

Johēs Carnynye in bonis £2.

Robtūs Leytye in bonis £4.

Stephūs Gonwyn in bonis £6.

Johēs Stephyn Thomas in bonis £10.

Ricūs Treanowre in bonis £2. (In other lists he is called Treanow, Nowre, and Owre.)

Oto John Stevyn in bonis £10.

Willms Hayne in bonis £4.

Richūs servus Stephī Pawly het stipend £1.

Donelli Yerysch adj' est [has been adjudged] £1.

Dewrdy Downe adj' est £1.

Alieg: pety John Britton etat xvj annor subsid ear 8d.

P'ochia de Tewynnacke.

Hewgo Bosowe valet in bonis £2.

Johēs Guisa valet in bonis 10m.

David Unmellr valet in bonis £3.

Stephūs Roswall valet in bonis 10m.

Matheus Nancludir valet in bonis £2.

Johēs Willms valet in bonis £4.

(The names for St. Ives and Zennor are almost precisely as in the list of 1523.)

There was another Subsidy in 1524, the lists for which were divided into hundreds, but not into parishes. The portion for the Hundred of Penwith consists of fourteen names only, among which are the following:

P. Johē Trenhale £2.

P. Thoma Glyn £2.

P. Thoma Trevnwith £2.

P. Jacobo Trewynnard £2.

P. Thoma Hycke £2.

P. Williño Tregenna 5s 4d.

These are all the names pertaining to our four parishes.

Portion of a Subsidy for Lelant: 1530.

Johēs Trewhela ali in bonis £12.6s. (This is the first entry of this family, which afterwards became seated in Towednack; but Radulph Trewhela and John his son are named in the Subsidy Roll of 1523, at St. Hilary.)

Johēs Tonkyn in bonis £2.
Thomas Ots in bonis £4.
Wills Hoskyn in bonis £2.
Thomas Willms ali: Jamys in bonis £5.
Ricūs Chynowith in bonis £5.
Martins Willms Vighan in bonis £9.
Petrus Bvyune in bonis £3.
Wills Thomas in bonis £18.
Jacobs Trewennard in bonis £40.
Johēs Thomas in bonis £8.
Marcus Trewarnhayle in bonis £4.
Henr Nanspean in bonis £5.
Donelms Irishe, het stipend £1.

Wills Britton etat xvj annor subsid 8d [five other Bretons follow].

CHAPTER IX.

THE REFORMATION PERIOD.

SOME of the chief stages in the change of the national religion probably had but little visible effect upon the aspect of things at Saint Ives. The renunciation by the Government of the Pope's jurisdiction, for instance, in 1534, whether or not it was pleasing to the bulk of the people, caused at least no open manifestation of discontent; and even the suppression of the religious houses, though doubtless involving considerable changes in the order of affairs in our four parishes, where the Benedictine priory of Tywardreath and the Augustinian collegiate church of Glasney had so great an interest, does not seem to have called forth any organized popular protest.

In 1540 the English Bible was ordered to be set up in all churches throughout the land; but, inasmuch as English was then understood by but a small minority of the population of Cornwall, this can have had little result of any sort. On the other hand, the destruction of religious images and pictures, the substitution of the new English prayers for the Latin Mass, and the abolition of the ancient ceremonies and festivals, caused the greatest popular discontent; in fact, provoked an insurrection.

The immediate cause of this revolt in Cornwall was an event which occurred in the summer of 1548, at Helston, where, on the king's commissioner, Mr. Body, attempting to remove the images from the parish church, he was set upon and stabbed by a certain Kilter and others (Carew, 'Survey').

In the following year, 10,000 men of Cornwall and Devonshire, but principally Cornishmen, rose in arms against the innovations, and marched eastwards, headed by Sir Humphrey Arundel of Lanherne, and the Mayor of Bodmin, Henry Boyer. They professed loyalty to the young king, but formulated a set of articles of complaint, which they desired the council to satisfy.

The points insisted on by the malcontents were, that Mass

should be celebrated as theretofore, that the Eucharist should be reserved in the churches, that blessed bread (*pain bénit*) and holy water should be continued, that the celibacy of the clergy should be enforced, that prayers should be offered up for the souls in Purgatory as formerly, and that the abbey lands should be restored.

Those of the Cornishmen who understood only their ancient language, seem to have been the most strenuously opposed to the English service which it was attempted to force upon them:

> 'Item, we will not receyue the new Servyce because it is but lyke a Christmas game, but we wyll have our olde Service of Mattens, masse, evensong and procession in Latten as it was before. And so we the Cornyshe men, whereof certen of us understa'de no Englysh, utterly refuse thys newe English.'

Did they, then, understand the Latin Mass? No, not the words of it; but its outward rites spoke to them plainer than speech itself—their praying they did for themselves, in their venerable mother-tongue.

> 'Ie' we wyl have holy bread and holy water made every Sundaye; Palmes and ashes at the tymes accustomed; Images to be set up again in every church, and all other auncient olde Ceremonyes used heretofore by our Mother the holy Church.'
>
> 'Item we wyll have everye preacher in his sermon and every Pryest at his masse, praye specially by name for the soules in purgatory as owre forefathers dyd'—[the ancient bidding-prayer].

All the authorities, both Catholic and Protestant, are agreed upon the main facts in this revolt; and it will be well for us to note the particulars, as Saint Ives was greatly concerned in the movement, John Payne, portrieve of this town, being among the leaders. Others of the foremost insurgents were Holmes, Winslow and Berry, hanged at Tyburn with Arundel; Pomeroy; John and James Rosogan; William Winslade; Robert Bochym, of Bochym, and his brother; Thomas Underhill; John Salmon, and William Segar; together with several priests, as John Thompson; Roger Barret; John Woolcock (probably a Saint Ives man); William Asa; James Mourton; John Barrow, and Richard Bennet.

The insurgents mustered at Bodmin, 6,000 strong; their banners bore various Catholic emblems, and with them they had a waggon on which was an altar, with a pyx under its canopy, containing the consecrated Host; a crucifix and candles; holy water, and every requisite for the Mass. (See Fox's 'Martyrology,' p. 669.) The rising was inaugurated at Sampford

Courtney, on Dartmoor, by the celebration of Mass, in defiance of the recent command to establish the English Communion Service.

The young King Edward condescended to write a reply to the demands of the Cornish Catholics, which, though it was argumentative, Burnet himself says was 'all penned in a high threatening style.' At all events, the men who constituted this Cornish Pilgrimage of Grace were not satisfied by the royal answer, but proceeded to lay siege to Exeter, they being then 20,000 strong. Here they were defeated by Lord Russell, but not until the greater number of the insurgents had been slain, fighting, as Hals says, with 'inveterate courage, animosity and resolution.' Lord Grey, who fought against the Cornish, said of them, that 'such was the valour and the stoutness of the men, that he never, in all the wars he had been in, did know the like' (Tregellas, 'Cornish Worthies,' vol. i., p. 61). The insurgents lost over 4,000 men in the August of 1549. This Western rising was, in fact, more fierce than any of the many revolts inaugurated by the Catholics of the other counties, during the period of the Reformation. Burnet, 'History of the Reformation,' vol. i., p. 374, says: 'In Devonshire [by which he means South Devon and Cornwall] the insurrection grew to be better formed; for that county was not only far from the court, but it was generally inclined to the former superstition, and many of the old priests ran in among them.'

No sooner had the remnant of the defeated Catholics dispersed to their homes, than Sir Anthony Kingston, the king's commissioner and provost marshal, arrived in Cornwall for the purpose of seeking out and punishing the guilty survivors. Arundel was hanged at Tyburn; Boyer was hanged outside his own door, after the provost had dined with him; Mayow of Clevyan, in Saint Columb Major, was hanged on the signpost of the village inn. 'In like manner the marshal hanged one John Payne, the Mayor or Portreeve of St. Ives, on a gallows erected in the middle of that town, whose arms are still to be seen in one of the foreseats in that church, viz., in a plain field three pine-apples' (Hals). Some historians, we know not why, call this man 'John Payne *alias* Tregenna.'

Local tradition says that the provost marshal dined with the unsuspecting portrieve at the old house which was afterwards called the George and Dragon inn, and hanged his entertainer immediately after dinner, the gallows being set up just in front of the door, on the market-place. No doubt Payne had hoped that his participation in the insurrection had been overlooked by the authorities. Many others were executed in Cornwall. Heywood, in his chronicle, taxes Kingston with extreme cruelty in the infliction of these punishments; and Fuller, in 'Gloucestershire,' says of Kingston that, having been charged with a design to rob the exchequer of Queen Mary, he poisoned himself.

So ended Cornwall's struggle to preserve her ancient creed and rites. After this, the English Bible and Common Prayer had it all their own way, and the old Cornish language began to die out along with the Catholic religion in the duchy.

During the reign of Elizabeth, the 'Recusants' (as those Catholics were called who refused even an occasional conformity with the newly Established Church) were fined, imprisoned and executed in great numbers, in Cornwall as elsewhere; but I have not met with any Saint Ives names in the few Recusant Rolls I have been able to consult.

In 1550 the altars were removed, and were either destroyed or placed on the floor of the porch, while wooden tables for the Communion were set in the centre of the church. I believe that nothing is known as to any altar-stones in the Saint Ives district, so that probably they were broken up there. About this time, too, there was a general demolition of such painted windows as portrayed the old Cornish saints. We are safe in conjecturing that Saint Ia, Saint Ewny, Saint Gwynog and Saint Sinara were formerly represented in the windows of their respective churches.

In 1552 the English Book of Common Prayer was made compulsory in all the churches throughout England, Wales and Ireland; which proceeding had, as is well known, the effect of strongly alienating from the Established Church the Celtic indwellers of the two last-named countries. In Cornwall it had the additional result of ultimately killing the Cornish language. From a philological point of view it is much to be regretted that the Common Prayer was not translated into Cornish; this would not only have prolonged the existence of the language, but would also have preserved a valuable and imperishable memorial of the ancient tongue for the benefit of future generations of Celtic students.

CHAPTER X.

THE ELIZABETHAN PERIOD.

In the fifth year of Queen Mary's reign (1558), Saint Ives was made a Parliamentary borough, to return two members. The borough extended over the whole parish, and all who paid scot and lot were entitled to vote at the election. The first representatives were T. Randolph and W. Champer. At the end of this book will be found a complete list of members returned, down to the present. Writs for electing members of Parliament, or for removing any action at law depending in the Court Leet of Saint Ives, must be directed: 'Prepositis et Burgensibus Burgi sui de St. Ives in Com. Cornub. salutem.'

In the few years following the defeat of the Spanish Armada, great preparations were made throughout Cornwall, to oppose any second attempted invasion; and John Nance, Esq., of an old Saint Ives family, was entrusted with the duty of raising and controlling a body of men in the Saint Ives district. In the *Western Antiquary* magazine, of Plymouth (part ix., vol. viii., p. 169) is a selection of letters relating to John Nance, a few of which shall be given here. The first runs thus:

'Cosen Nance I send you this note whereby y^o^ may perceave what provisyon is made, all wch is shipped and I think wilbe in falmoth wth the fyrst wynd; som litle charge more wilbe in the vnlading, for my part I seek no peny profitt when I shall here of the arivall hereof then I will assemble you and the rest of the Captens to thend ech of you may p'cure vtterance for his portion. Written this x^th^ of Aprill [15]90. Your Loving cosen.

'Fra. Godolphin.

'I pray you ympart the precept for the muster and Treyning to thother ij Captaines this Saturday to thend they may signefy the same on sonday, to ther parishes to be the better p'vided and more redy. You may send the precept to the one send a copy to the other and kepe a note for your selfe.'

On the other side of the document is a list of 'Munycon and powder laden in the grey hound of London: whereof is Mr. Robt. Androwes.'

Endorsed: 'For my cosin Nanse.'

The second letter is dated May 6, 1595, and endorsed:

'To o[r] loving freend, John Nanse esquier, Captayne of the parishes in the midst of the hondred of Penw[th] geve these.'

It contains sundry instructions from the lords of the council, as to precautions to be taken for the greater safety of the land, such as the inspection and careful watching of the beacons in every parish, the guarding of the landing-places, inspection of armoury, drilling and reviewing of the officers and men.—Signed, 'Fra: Godolphin. W[m] Bevyll. Rich: Carew of Antony.'

The next is: 'From the Courte at Greenwiche the 29th of July 1595.'

Lengthy instructions as to precautions for the greater safety of the coast. The opening sentences are:

'After o[r] hartie comendations. This late attempt of the landing of the Spanyards and burninge of dyvers villages & Townes in that countrie aboute Mountes Baye and the want of resistans by the people of the Countrie at the first attempt hathe moved her ma[tie] to enter into further consultation,' &c.—Signed, 'Jo: Pouckeringe. W. Burlye. E. Howard. Hunsdon. Chobam. Ro: Seryll. fforteskewe. W. Wiche. Woolly.'

Endorsed:

'To o[r] verye Lovinge frindes S[r] ffrauncis godolphin and to the rest of the Depute levetenants within the Counteye of Cornewall.'

Also this:

'25 Aug. 1595. To our Lovinge freend John Nance Esquier. These are from three of us her ma[ties] Depute Lieutenantes [of the] Countie of Cornewall to signefy that wee do hereby nom[inate] appoint and authoris you to be Capten and Leader of on[e hundred] and fifty able men w'thin the Towne and parishes of S[t] I[ves], Lelant, Tewednack and Senor,' &c. &c. Then follow long instructions as to 'mylytarye accions.'—'Syned, Fra: Godolphin. W[m] Beyvll. Rich: Carew of Antony.'

Endorsed: 'for M[r] Nance; mylytarye accions.'

Also, a paper of orders for the direction of the trained bands, who were to be at the church, next day, upon the ringing of the bells, with all their weapons in readiness, and their dinners with them.—Signed, 'Fra: Godolphin.'

Endorsed: 'ffor my Cosen Nanst.'

In the year 1590 Richard Ferris, Andrew Hill and William Thomas called at Saint Ives on their way from London to Bristol in a wherry-boat, as we learn from a rare tract of this date.

The neighbourhood of Saint Ives has frequently been the scene of smuggling transactions; we will hope the town never countenanced the more reprehensible pursuit of wrecking. Amongst the documents preserved at the London Record Office is a bundle of parchment rolls containing the depositions of witnesses examined at a commission appointed in the year 1598 to inquire into a smuggling transaction at Saint Ives. The following is an abstract of this document, with its reference heading:

'Record Office, London, Exchequer Special Commissions, No. 562; 44 Elizabeth (1598) Cornwall.

'Examination of Witnesses at Helston. Before S[r] Reginald Mohun knt: Nicholas Hals esqr: & William Hals, collector of the customes & subsidyes in the Portes of Plymouth and ffowey.

'*Richard Smythe* of Ludgvan in the County of Cornwall merchant, aged 52 years, says there were two barques or pynnaces brought into Mountes baye in or aboute November last past, by Captaine Willm̄ Morgan, and that their ladinge was salte and earthen potts; wch this Deponent would not buye nor meddle wth because he understood that the custome to her Ma[tie] was not payed, nor the Tenthes to the Lord Admirall. One near Mornack above Rochell in ffraunce brought a barque into Mountesbaye by way of trade, about August last, laden with salt. Deponent transported the said sault from Mountes baye to Saint Ives, and there landed the same under a Warrant from the Customes to pass the same.

'Peter Newman did yll intreate and abuse Lawrence Birde the deputy customer of St. Ives, and gave the said Lawrence a blowe; the cause of that strikinge was, for that the same deputye customer did staye the landinge of the said salte, untill he might be satisfied that the custome was payed, whereuppon evill wordes increased betweene them.

'*Peter Newman* of Ludgvan, merchaunte, aged 30 years, says that the French barque was named the Pearle of Rochell. The salt was conveyed to S[t] Ives by the direction of Mr. Smythe who bought yt of the frenchmen. This Deponent was factor to the said Richard Smythe, and bestowed yt in Sellars in S[t] Ives for the "used" of the said Richard Smythe.

'This deponent confesses that he called the said Deputy Customer Jack and Knave, and afterwards did strike him, whereuppon the said deputie customer sayd to this Deponent that he would strike him this Deponent againe, whereuppon he this Deponent in his heate vowed that he would be revenged of the said deputie customer, and is hearfore heartilie sourye.

'*William Oates* of S[t] Ives in the said Countie of Cornewall, deputy S . . . . . aged 56 years, says that Charles Cock brought into S[t] Ives in that ffrench Barque xij Buttes of candy Wyne called Muskadell, vj Barbory ffowyl, and had in his said barque the value of v[li] in golde, but he gave onlye about vj peeces thereof. The said Charles Cock had also gold in Brassletts about one of his armes, and another in his hand. One Captaine Georg Hughes paid duty on 161 chests of sugar brought in by him to S[t] Ives. Lawrence Bearde, deputie customer of St. Ives, was contemptuouslye used in words and stricken by Peter Newman for demaunding the Queen's dutyes. This Deponent sawe two butts of the candye Wynes aforesaid rolled into the Sellar of John Stephen for the use of Edward Averye. William Pitts Vynter had one butt, Lewys Hurlye vyntner had another butt, Thomas White Vynter had one butt, and John Naunc Vynter one butt, and one hogshead, and that this Depont: dronke of the same Wynes in everie of the said Vynters houses; ffurther that James Denham had one butt of the same Wyne of Charles Cock for a "geloinge."

'*William Mabbe* of Marka Jewe in the said Countie of Cornewall, aged 44, saith that about September last Captain William Morgan sent in to Mounts-baye two Barques by waye of reprizall, with portingalle salte and earthen potts. Most of the potts were set on lande in Mountesbaie, and about 154 bushells of said salte were landed in S[t] Michaells Iland, and 46 bushells in Marka Jewe.

'This Deponent hath heard some should saye that if the deputie customer should demaund Custome of the said Captaine Morgan, he the said Captain Morgan did not care to cutt off the eares of the deputie customer. Some of the potts were sould to the Inhabitants of the countrey thereabouts, and the rest to Alexander Penrose. 150 bushells of the salt landed in S[t] Michaells Iland came to the possession of John Thomas, for what consideracon this Dpont. knoweth not, and doth yet remayne there in his custodye in his sellar.

'*William Pitt* of St Ives, maryner, aged 28, says that Captayne Hughes brought in a Carvyle with Sugars, and Charles Cock a fflye boate wth wyne since Maye laste, by way of reprizall. Captaine Cockes man of Warr, whereof one Taylor was captaine, brought in fflax and ffishe into S[t] Ives.

'Himself, John Nance of St. Ives &c. bought each of them a butt of the wyne; but what this Deponent payed ffor his Butt, he doth not certainlie knowe.

'There was payed for impost to one Willyam Hutchins for the Butt he bought, after the rate of xl[li] the tonne.

'M[r] Roskarock the viceadmirall did set the Aucher on the two butts of Edward Auerys Wyne in the sellar of John Stephens aforesaid.

'This Depont. sayth that he bought of Captaine George Hughes certeine browne sugars in a chest, of the sugars he brought in to S[t] Ives; what the Weighte thereof was he knoweth not. ffurther this Depont hath heard Anthony Clarke of St. Ives, then Boateson of the said carveill, say to captaine Riddlestone that he the said clark and his companye had seavenhundreth weighte of sugars amongst them.

'Examinations and depositions of dyvers psōns sworen and examyned, taken att St Ives in the Countye of Corne Wall by the forenamed Nichās Hals &c.

'*Bridgett Peter*, the wieff of John Peter of St Ives, aged 40 yeares, sayth that she had of the companye of Capten Cookes fflye aboute two vessells of sweete wynes, for wch wynes dyvers of the same companye had of her meate and drinke.

'*James Denham* of St Ives mrchaunte, aged 37, sayth that Captaine Cock's ship was called the Pynnace of Lubeck, about C tonnes. In it were the following goods:—

'1 butt of candye wyne called by the name of Muscadell; sould to John Nance.

'another of the same; sold to Thomas White.

'½ butt more; divided between John Nance and Thomas White.

'1 butt of the same; sold to Lewys Hurley.

'1 butt delyūed to the use of the Lord Admirall for his Tenthes wch was shipped to his L: use to Plymouth.

'1 butt to William Pitt wch the sd Pitt had from Mr Robert Braggeman of Plymouth.

'1 butt deliūyd to William Oates for the behaulff of William Warde of Peryn, and sould to one Slader a merchaunte of Bristolle.

'Some of the same wyne to one Mr Evens als Peters of St. Ives.

'1 hogshead banded by the Mr of the same shipp called Dyamond, wch was afterwards bestowed in John Stevens his sellar.

'4 Butts to Edward Averye of Barnestable.

'1 Butt was appointed by the captaine to be bestowed on Certeine gentlemen of the cunteye.

'1½ butt full this Depont bought for his owne pvision, and a little barrell of liquor to make aqua vite with.

'(All the above sold at £5 per butt.) Further:

'4 cast of Barbara Hawkes.

'Also this Depont saw the said Cock have in a redd purse barbarie gould wch by the bignes of the purse, remayninge in this Deponts custody, esteemed to be an Cth pounds at the least. And he heard by dyvers of thinhabitants of St Ives that the said Capten Cock had a Bracelett of barbarie gould wch they esteemed to be worth between xx and xxxli.

'Also this Deponent sayth that Thomas Purifie had certeine sugars brought in by Captaine George Hughes. He also sawe in the howse of Richard Goodwyn in St Ives two sackesfull of sugar, thone whereof was white thother muscavades, & one barrell of greene ginger. Mathewe Trenwyth [Trenoweth] of ffowey had a Cth weight of sugar & a Cth weight of cotton wolle and a barrell of greene ginger. James Javelyn of St Ives had also Cth weight of sugars and C weight and upwards of cotton woolle. One Skoper of Thisle of Wight had 200 weighte of Sugar whereof he sould a bristoll barrell full home of Bristolle. Richard Jack of St Ives had cccth weighte in his sellar of the same sugar. Also that John Hamlye of St. Ives had both sugar and cotton.

'*Richard Trenwith* of St Earth gent, aged 40 years, sayth that he bought of one Allyn the Mrs Mate of the shipp wĉh Capten George Hughes brought into St Ives in October last, a peece of loaff sugar of the waighte (as he thinketh) of v^li^ att the moste, wĉh the said Allyn took out of his chest in his hoastes howse, and he payed for it at the rate of xij^d^ by the pound, and ymployed yt for the pivision of his owne house. And he bought allso of the boatesons mate of the said shipp about xij^li^ And he gave pte. thereof awaie to his frindes.

'*Grace Hurlye*, the wieff of Lewys Hurlye of St Ives vynter, aged 28 yeares, sayth that one William Warde of Peryn said in her howse that captaine George Hughes had misused him the said Warde about a chest of sugar wĉh lay on the keye of St Ives, wĉh chest of sugar, as the said Warde reported, one William . . . . had bought.

'*Edward Averie* of Barnestable in the countie of Devon M . . . . . . testified as is before mentioned.

[Great portion of his evidence is torn away.]

'*George Hickes* of St Ives sayler, aged 40, says that he was father in Lawe of Richard Jack, and the latter had about C^th^ waighte of the same sugars in pte of recompence of his pilotship to be pilote to the said carvell for Padstowe, whether they purposed to goe and unlade if the wynde had not byne contrarye. Allyn the Mrs Mate of the said Carvell brought a chest of the sugar into a sellar of Deponents, wĉh sugar (as this Depoñt hath hearde) was afterwards soulde, some pte. to Thomas Edwards, some pte. Arthur, Sr Nichâs Parkers Cooke; and who had the rest of the said sugar he cannot depose.

'To the rest of the Interr^9^ he cannot depose, for that he was sick before & longe after the arrivall of the said carvell of St Ives.

'*Thomas Edwards* of Lelaunte gent. aged 34, beinge sworen and examyned sayth that he bought CC^th^ waighte of sugars and about iiij^li^ more, a barrell of greene ginger and a Jarre of greene ginger of about vj^li^ weighte. He was pŝwaded by the Maryners and some of the men of St Ives that there was always allowed in such cases a chest of sugar to the companie. But did understand by lawrence Beard, the deputie customer in that creeke, that the custome was not paied; and he sent his men to fetch it awaye on his horsback by night, att what tyme (because of a watche sett by the deputie customer) they could not carrye it awaye; and the next day yt was fetched awaye, as he this Deponent remembreth.

'There was also in the same Sellar whereout he had his Sugars another Vessell of greene ginger of the bignes of haulfe a barril, and who had the same Richard Jack can best declare because he the saide Jack had the keye and charge of the said sellar wherein the same sugar and greene ginger was.

'And himself this deponent knoweth that Arthur, Sr Nicholas Parkers cooke, had about C^th^ waighte of the like sugars; Anthonie Rosgreeg and John Chenowth had about C^th^ waighte apeeice. Richard Jack and Thomas Purfrey had the rest of the sugars in the said sellar.

'*Anthonie Clarke* of S[t] Ives maryner, aged 20, sayth that he kept the accompte of the chests sent to lande out of the sayde carvell for one afternoone; and in the eveninge beinge wearye and not having dyned the same daye, he was willing to goe on shoare to eate meate; but before he this Depon̄t went on lande he nayled downe the hatches wth iiij spikes and some pennye nayles, and left the lookinge to the carveille to Richard Goodwyn of S[t] Ives. When he returned he found the hatches broken open and 4 of the said chests of sugar emptyed, the sugars taken out and caryed awaie; and the boards cast into the well of the pumpe, and also dyvers musketts gone and stollen awaye; whereuppon this Depon̄t blamed the said Goodwyn for beinge absent, who made answeare that he onlie went on lande to untrusse his pointes; and since that to his knowledge no hurt was done.

'*Richard Goodwyn* of S[t] Ives, cutler, aged 50 says (inter alia) that M[r] Pitt hired a shipp of Plymouth called the Jack.

'*Ambrose Creed* of St. Ives butcher, aged 30, says that Thomas Rowe of Tregine and Daniell Dundye of Meingisie and Mathew Trenowth of ffowey brought to this Depon̄ts howse certn̄ bags of cotton.

'*John Naunce* of S[t] Ives gent, aged 58 years, sayth that John Preston in the suice of this Depon̄t, James Denhay and John S . . . . . . deputie comptroller of the said creeke, made a seizure of two Butts of the said Wyne being in the sellar of John Stevens of St Ives aforesayd, to the Queens Ma[ts] use.

[*John Cooke* of St. Ives, labourer, aged 60, and *Walter Knight* of St. Ives, also gave evidence, the greater part of which is, however, obliterated.]

'*Honor White*, wieff of Thomas White of St Ives, aged 42.' [Her evidence was very short and contained nothing new.]

'Depositions in the above matter taken at Pengersick in the said County on the 30th January.

'*Richard Haymon* of Market Jewe yeoman, aged 54 years, sayth that John Preston, deputie customer of Mountes baie, demaunded the custome of the sayd salte due to the Queens Ma[tie] whereuppon John Preston sett a locke on the sellars of John Thomas and William Mabbe aforesaid and seized the salt.

'*John Cole* of Market Jew aged 40 yeares sayth that he heard the sayd Captaine Morgan vow to cutt off the eares of the deputie customer.

[Another deponent, illegible.]

'*Arthur Paynter* of St Earth had a wayne-loade of the sayd wyne. He sayth also that one Robert, a pedler of Market Jewe, had of the sayd ffishe about . . . . . and two or three frayles of Reisins brought into the Baye by a Spannishe carvell.

'*Arthur Tanner* of Erisie,

'*Thomas Purefey* of Ludgan,

'*John Thomas* of Market Jewe'

[These also deposed, but their evidence is obliterated.]

9—2

At foot of the fourth and last skin of the depositions is a memorandum that William Mabbe and Peter Newman were 'publicklie punisshed in the counteye for their misdemeanours by authority of the commission and have since demeaned themselves well and have byne of good behaviour and have given bonds for their appearance when called upon.'

Some remarks of our own upon the above document will not be out of place. The examination of the witnesses in this case throws a vivid light upon social life at Saint Ives in the reign of Queen Bess, when, as was the case also for long after, gentle and simple were leagued together to defraud the sovereign of her revenues.

Some of the Saint Ives merchants above mentioned were men of position and influence in the neighbourhood, and, although they were in fact tradesmen, were always considered and styled 'gentlemen'—a condition of things which had its exact counterpart among their cousins in Brittany, where the country noblesse commonly exercised trade without derogation from their quality as gentle families. Of this class were John Stephens, Lewis Hurley and John Nance. The latter, a vintner, was a cousin to the John Nance who seized the casks in Stephens' cellar, and who had taken such a prominent part, ten years previously, in the defence of West Cornwall.

The 'Barbory ffowyl,' alluded to in the depositions, were hawks of a particular and highly valuable breed.

The allusion to the public punishment of the two foremost delinquents would seem to imply that they were put in the stocks.

From the First-Fruits Composition books at the Record Office, we find that in 1547 George Mason, Vicar of Lelant, compounded for the first-fruits of his vicariate, valued at £22 11s. 10d., with 2d. more for the tithe.

In 1549 Gabriel Moreton compounded for the first-fruits of the vicariate of Lelant and Saint Ives, rated at the same amount.

In 1578 Robert Stopford, in 1597 John Bagwell, and in 1603 Thomas Masters, compounded similarly for Lelant and Saint Ives.

In 1606 Robert Challacombe, and in 1611 Nichodemus Pestell, compounded for Lelant.

In 1624 John South, and in 1631 Thomas Cory, compounded for Lelant and Saint Ives.

CHAPTER XI.

SELECTIONS FROM THE SUBSIDY ROLLS, 1536 TO 1599.

We must now make a further selection of names from the various Subsidy Rolls, in chronological order. The next of these rolls that we have to notice is that of 1536, *Hundred de Penwyth*. The following are the names which can be identified as belonging to the Saint Ives district:

P. Willo' Thoms P. bonis, 10s.
Johe' Tomkyn p̃ bonis, £1.
Steph' Pawley p̃ bonis, 10s.
Johe' Thoms harvy p̃ bonis, 10s.
Willmō Trewynnard p̃ terr' suis 10s.
Willmō Chynals p̃ bonis 10s.
Thoma Glyn p̃ terr' suis 10s.
Johe Payne p̃ bonis 10s.
Alexand' Tregennow p̃ bonis 10s.
Robto' Trevose p̃ bonis 10s.
Johe' Noure p̃ bonis 10s.
Martin Pendre p̃ bonis et }
Johe' Richerds } 10s.
Thoma Gorlen p̃ bonis 10s.
Willmō Godale p̃ bonis 10s.
Thoma Plym̃yn p̃ bonis 10s.
Willmo Tregenna p̃ bonis 10s.
Willō Ladaw p̃ bonis 10s.
Johe Clyse p̃ bonis 10s.

SUBSIDY ROLL OF 1541.

(Much damaged by damp.)

St. uny iuxt' Lanant.

Willm̃s Thomas valet in bonis £20.
Stephanus Pauly valet in bonis. . . .
Jacobus Chynals valet in bonis. . . .
Johẽs Thomas hervye valet in bonis. . . .

Alligen :

Willūs Talyn valet in bonis 2s. [' William the Italian '?]
Michael Tarsy —— subsid' 4*d*.
[and 5 other Bretons.]
Johēs Thomas (?) valet in bonis £20.
Johanna Owre via' valet in bonis £20.
Robtūs Trevos valet in bonis £20.
Petrus Saundry valet in bonis £20.
Matheus Treenwith valet in bonis £20.
Odo Lamandy 4*d*.
Oliverus Brytton 4*d*.
Henricus Brytton 4*d*.
Johēs Trescawe valet in bonis £20.
Johēs Willms valet in bonis £20.

87
CORNWALL SUBSIDY. 35 HENRY VIII. (1544). BENEVOLENCE.
172

Cornub. ss. Thees Rollys indented the last daye of ffebruary the xxxvj[th] year of the rayne of our Souvrayn lord Kynge Henry the viij[the] off englonde ffraunce and Irlond kyng defender off the faythe and yn Earthe supreme hede off the church of Inlond and Irlonde bettvene S[r] Willm Godolghan S[r] hughe Trevanyon knyghtte and Thomas Senttawbyn Esquyer comissioner off owr sayde Soverayn lorde the kynge appoyntted for levynge off a benevolence yn the sayde counte to be hade off hys lovynge subiectts disspendynge yn londys ffees and offices to the yerely value of v[li] sterlynge and aboue for the defenc and Sauffe garde off hys lovynge subiectts off the one parttye And John Kellygrewe and Thomas Godolghan Esquiers collectors appoyntted for the resayte off the sayd benevolence accordingly to the Sums entitled upon the namis of the Contributors contayned yn the fore sayd Rolle indenttyd off the other partye Wittnessithe that the sayd Collectors shall make payment off the sayd Benevolens unto S[r] Edmond Peccam knygtht Copherar of owr sayd soverayne lord the kynges most honorabyll howsholde generall resayver off the sayd benevolence appoyndyd afore Ester next commynge In Wytnes here off wee as well the sayd Commissioners as the sayd Collectors thes psēnt Rolles in dentyd haue subscribed wyth owr hondes the daye and yere aboue wrettyn.

Ewny Lenant.

Issebell Wyllm Thomas 6*s*. 8*d*.
Stevyn Powlle 8*s*.

Tewynnacke.

Nil.

Senar.

Nil.

Ya.

John Glyn £1.
Thomas Jenkyn 6s. 8d.
John Stevyn 6s. 8d.
Laurens Goodall 6s. 8d.
John Payne 6s. 8d.
John Thomas 6s. 8d.
Jenet John Owre 6s. 8d.
Robert Trevos 6s. 8d.
Matthew Treenw[th] 6s. 8d.

87/174 CORNWALL SUBSIDY. 35 HENRY VIII. (1544).

Penwyth. Indenture dated 11 January, 35 Henry VIII., witnessing the receipt by Sir John Chamond, Knt., Sheriff of Cornwall, of the sums of money gathered for 'ayde & meyntenance of crysten people' against the Turk, by the churchwardens in the Deanery of Penwith in the County of Cornwall (one sheet of paper much injured, and backed with paper).

SUBSIDY ROLL OF 1546.

This is a very large roll, from which we will select a few names under each of the four parishes:

Uny Lanant.

Symō Nanc valet £5.
John Lawrye valet £1.
Pascow Renold valet £1.
Thomas Brandon [Briant] valet £1.
Jamys Thomas valet £1.
Steuyn Martȳ valet £1.
ux Wllm Thomas valet £10.
Jenken Kelensow valet £1.
Jane ux Chynale valet 6s.
Wyllm̄ Broncose valet £1.
John Thoms̄ valet 7s.
Robert Nenys valet £1.
John Trebethaw valet £6.
Steuyn Sandaw valet £1.
Richard Trernyke valet £6.
Ric Vevēn valet £6.
Wyllm̄ Warvas valet £1.
Stevyn John valet £10.
Wyllym Kelway valet £10.
Richard Leddra valet £10.
John Hawys valet £1.
Otts John valet £10.

Alyanes:

Nowell Bretton, subsid 1d.
[and 6 other Bretons.]

Tewynecke.

John Rossewall valet £6.
Richard Ainell valet £5.
Michell Anbosow valet £4.
Pascaw Mathew valet £6.
Ric: Carbonse valet £2.
Lawrens Myllard valet £4.
Stevyn Thoms̄ valet £4.
Wyllm Thoms̄ valet £3.
Jermā Harry valet £2.
Richard Wyllm̄ valet £2.
Herry Hycka valet . . .

Seynt Iysse.

John Bossowe valet £1.
Amys Toman valet £9.
Thomas Seyse valet £4.
John Angeř valet £2.
Jamys Walls walz' valet £2.
Jermã Denys valet £2.
John Karrallake valet £4.
Jamys Vean valet £2.
Herry Phelyppe valet £6.
John Raw valet £3.
Ric. Clynacke valet £4.
Pascow Angoffe valet. . . .
Robert Cocke valet £2.
Benet Lucke valet £4.
Edwarde Jose valet £2.
John Wyllm̃ valet £2.
Thom̃ Carlaye valet £4.
John Syesse valet £2.
John Bre Vean valet £2.
John Penseu valet £2.
John Wyllm̃ valet £3.
Martyn Trewyn valet £7.
George Benettow valet £3.
Jamys Nansely valet £2.
John Treher valet £5.
John Boskregyn valet £2.
Wyllm̃ Dogowe valet £9.
Bastyn Restomy valet £5.

Alyanes:

Nowell Bretton valet £2.
Olyũ Bretton valet £2.
Harry Bretton subsid. 1*d.*
Rič Bretton 1*d.*
Perye Bretton 1*d*
Antony Bretton 1*d.*
Rawe Bretton 1*d.*
Allen Bretton 1*d.*
Renold Bretton 1*d.*
Udon Bretton 1*d.*
Wyllm̃ Bretton 1*d.*

Sennar.

John Thoms valet £1.
Herry Trewva valet £3.
Thoms Mychell valet £4.
Herry Wicke valet £2.
Jenkyn Wyllm̃ valet £3.
Andrew Vyvya valet £2.
John Bossow valet £4.
John Edwarde valet £4.
John Wyllm̃ valet £8.
Herry Wyllm̃ valet £1.
Davy Thomas valet £2.
John Herry valet £1.

SUBSIDY OF 1547.

Saynt Iyes.

Mathũs Trenwith in lands £3.
Thomas Jenkyn £10.
Jenetta Owre £10.

Unye iuxt' Lanaunt.

Stephũs Pawllye in goods 15*s.*

SUBSIDY OF 1548.

(From the parcel of fragments of subsidies.)

P'ochia de Uney Lanant.

Stephũs Pawley hẽt in bonis £10.
Henr. Angoff £10.
Johẽs Hervey £10.

Alyens :

Phelūs Bretton, subsid. 8*d*.
Ricūs Bretton 8*d*.
Clewde Pykerdy 8*d*.
Niwell Bretton 8*d*.
Olyū Bretton 8*d*.
Willm̄ Pears 8*d*.
Udyn. Bretton 8*d*.

St. Ives.

[Very indistinct.]

Matheus Trenw[th] het in bonis £10.
John Stephyn £10.
Thom̄s Jenkyn £10.
[Then follow five illegible names, the last four aliens.]

SUBSIDY OF 1549.

The following is a selection:

Pōchia de Unye Lanante.

P. Stepho Pawlye 10*s*.
John Willm̄ 8*d*.
Noell Briton 8*d*.
her' Edward 8*d*.
P. Philip Briton 8*d*.
Will[m] Thomas 8*d*.
Oliver Briton 8*d*.

Pōchia de Seint Ies.

P. Matheo Trenwithe 10*s*.
Thomas Jenkyn 10*s*.
Laurence Godale 10*s*.
Robto Trevoes. . . .
Jacobo Normand' 1*s*.
P. Petro Sherman 8*d*.
Reginald Salowe 8*d*.
Richard Haman [Hammond.] 8*d*.
Lewes William brey 8*d*.

Pōchia de Tewynnacke.

P. Thoma Briton 8*d*.
P. Udo Briton 8*d*.

CORNWALL SUBSIDY $\frac{87}{204}$, 3 EDWARD VI. (1549).

(Hundred de Penwith.)

Pōchia de Uny Lelante (almost illegible).

Stephūs Pawlie valet in bonis £10.
Henricus Angoffe valet in bonis £10.
Edward Britton subsid'. 8*d*.

Aligen :

Phūs Britton 8*d*.
Urin[s] Britton 8*d*.
Clowde Britton 8*d*.

Pōchia de Tywynacke.

Thomas Willm̄ allyan valet in bonis nil subsid'. 8*d*.

Pōchia de Senar.

Sum̄ huius pōchie nil.

Pōchia de Seynt Eyes.

[Out of 12 names 8 are aliens. I can only distinguish an alien.]

John Brytton 8*d.*

SUBSIDY, 4 & 5 PHILIP AND MARY (1557).

Pōchia de Seynt Iees.

Matheus Trenwith valet in terris £10.
Georgius Trewynnerd valet in bonis £5.
Thomas Tregena valet in bonis £5.
Laurencius Goodale valet in bonis £5.

Aligen:

Richūs Perse valet in bonis nil subsid. 8*d.*
Udūs Chynowith 8*d.*
Ricūs Oman 8*d.*
Nichūs Brytayne 8*d.*
Johēs Brytayne 8*d.*
Johēs Bryttayne 8*d.*
ffranciscus Alan 8*d.*
Pliberus Bryttayne 8*d.*

Pōchia de Senar.

Johēs Willm̄ valet in bonis £6.
Thom̄s Mychell valet in bonis £5.

Aligen:

Johēs Renold valet in bonis nil subsid'. 8*d.*

Pōchia de Towednack.

Laurencius Thomas valet in bonis £6.

Pōchia de Uny Lelant.

Stephūs Pawly valet in bonis £5.
Johēs Vosse valet in terris £1.
Henricus Ustycke valet in bonis £5.

Aligen:

Johēs Willm̄ valet in bonis nil subsid. 8*d.*
—— Anthony valet in bonis nil subsid. 8*d.*
Petrus Bryttayn valet in bonis nil subs 8*d.*
ffylpott Brytten valet in bonis subs 8*d.*

SUBSIDY, 1 ELIZABETH (1558).

Pōchia de Unye iuxt Lelant.

Stephūs Pawlye val. in bonis £8.
Johēs Udus val. in terr. £10.
Henr. Engove val. in bon. £6.

Aligen:

Johes Wylliā val. in bon. null. subs. 4*d.*
Clowde Breton 4*d.*
Petrus Tristram 4*d.*
Willūs Breton 4*d.*
Phūs Breton 4*d.*

Pōchia de Saint Iees.

Matheus Treunwith val. in terr. £6.
Georgius Trewenard val. in bon. £7.
Thomas Jenkyn valet in bon. £6.
Laurenc. Goodall val. in bon. £7.

Aligen:

Thomas Cehellowe val. in bon. null. 4*d.*
Odo Treunwith 4*d.*
Willūs Alan 4*d.*
Nichūs Perx 4*d.*
ffranciscus Evan 4*d.*

Pōchia de Tewynack.

Laurencius Thoms val. in bon. £5.

Pōchia de Senar.

Johēs Porthmeor val. in bon. 6*s.*
Thoms Michell val. in bon. £5.

Aligen:

Johēs Corhwer val. in bon. null. subs. 4*d.*

SUBSIDY, 1571.

Pōchia de Uny Lelant.

(The amounts are wanting.)

Jacobus Pawley valit in terris.
Johēs Treweke in terris.
Stephūs Pawley in bonis.
Henricus Trevetho in bonis.
Henricus Veuvyn in bonis.
Thoms Stephyn in bonis.
Johanes Rawe in bonis.
Johannes Hawle valit in bonis.
Johannes Willyā allien. a poll.

Pōchia de St. Yves.

Matheus Trenwth valit in terris £6.
Johēs Newman valit in terris £4.
Henrics Trenwth valit in bonis £1.
Thomas Stephyns valit in bonis £1.
Thomas Hicks valit in bonis £1.
Johannes Penhallack valit in bonis £5.
Georgius Gooch valit in bonis £5.
Johannes Williā valit in bonis £8.
Johannes Cockyn valit in bonis £3.
Petrus Noall valit in bonis £3.
Henrics Ots valit in bonis £3.
Johannes Andrew valit in bonis £3.
Udinus Chinowth
Wills Alla
Olius. Treva
Thoms Willya
} allians pols 1*s.* 4*d.*

Pōchia de Sennar.

Johēs Porthmere valit in bonis.
Thomas Michell in bonis.
Radulph Clye in bonis.
David[s] Thomas in bonis.
Alexandrus Harrie in bonis.
Petrus Jeffrye allien a poll'.

SUBSIDY, 1585.

Uny Lelante.

Johēs Trewick in Terris £2.
Jacobus Pawley in Terris £2.
Stephen Pawley in bonis £5.
Johēs Stephens in bonis £3.
Jacobus Trenw[th] in bonis £3.
Willm̄us Stephen in bonis £3.
Willm̄us Edward in bonis £3.

Towynack.

Johēs Roswall in bonis £6.
Benedic. Edwards in bonis £6.
Petrus Harve in bonis £6.
Johēs Hayme in bonis £5.

St. Iues.

Willm̄us Trenwith in Terr. £3.
Johēs Tregenna in Terr £4.
Ottes Mereffyld in Terr. £3.
Henricus Trenw[th] in bonis £4.
Jacob[s] Hickes £3.
Willm̄us Trenw[th] £4.
Johēs Cocken £4.
Thomas James £4.
Henric. Sterry £3.
Stephyn Barbar £3,
Phélipus Sterry £3.
Stephen Barbar £3.
Johes Shaplaine £3.
Phelip Cornall £3.
Thomas Williams in bonis £3.
Willm̄us Wolcock in bonis £3.

Synner.

Johēs Portmor in bonis £8.
Thomas Michaell in bonis £6.
Alexander Harry in bonis £3.
Johēs Thomas in bonis £4.
Pattrick Udie in bonis £3.

SUBSIDY, 1593.

Unie juxta Lelante.

Johnēs Treweeck in terris £2.
Stephin Pawlye in bonis £3.
Willm̄s Stephin als. Powl in bonis £3.
Henrye Lawrye als. Lock in bonis £3.
Willm̄s Otes in bonis £3.
Willm̄s Calesowe in bonis £3.
W[mus] Edward in bonis £3.
Johnēs Thomas in bonis £3.
Johnēs Spurwaye in bonis £3.
Ambrosius Marshfielde in bonis £3
Johnēs Letha in bonis £3.
Johnēs Hoskin in bonis £3.
Henrye Burncoose in bonis £3.

Towidnack.

Johnēs Rosewall in bonis £3.
Pedrus Harry in bonis £2.

St Ives.

Willmūs Trenwithe in terris £3.
Johnēs Tregennowe in terris £4.
Georgius Paine in terris £2.
Wmus Trenwth in bonis £4.
Henrye Trenwth in bonis £3.
Johnēs Cockin in bonis £4.
Thomas Hickes in bonis £4.
Johnēs Stephin in bonis £4.
Thomas William in bonis £4.
Thomas James in bonis £4.
Henricus Hickes in bonis £3.
Wmus Woolcocke in bonis £3.
Thomas Haime in bonis £3.
Johnes Bossowe in bonis —.

Sennar.

Thomas Michill in bonis £4.
Sampson Thomas in bonis £4.
Willm̄s Porthmere in bonis £3.
Ricūs Porthmere in bonis £3.
Johnēs Angeare in bonis £3.

SUBSIDY 1597.

Unye Lelante.

Wmus Praed in ter. £3.
Thomas Edwards in bonis £3.
Johnēs Letha in bonis £5.
Stephanus Pawlie in bonis £3.
Wmus Kalinsowe in bonis £3.
Wmus Edwards in bonis £3.
Johēs Hosken in bonis £3.
Johēs Penberthie in bonis £3.
Johēs Thomas in bonis £3.
Henricus Burnecoose in bonis £3.
Jacobus Stephin in bonis £3.
Johēs Kellwaye in bonis £3.

Tewednacke.

Johēs Rosswall in bonis £3.

St Iues.

Wmus Trenwith ar̃ iñ ter̃. £5.
Johēs Tregiña gt in ter̃. £10.
George Payne gt in ter̃. £3.
Wmus Trenwith de Trevalgan in bon. £5.
Thomas Williams in bonis £6.
Johēs Steephin in bonis £6.
Johēs Cockyne in bonis £5.
Thomas Hicke in bonis £4.
Thomas James in bonis £4.
Wmus Wolcocke in bonis £4.
Elizabetha Taller in bonis £4.
Thomas Taman in bonis £3.

Senar.

Thomas Michell in bonis £5.
Sampson Thomas in bonis £5.
Nicūs Beriman in bonis £3.
Ricūs Porthmere in bonis £3.
Johēs Angeare in bonis £3.

SUBSIDY 1599.

Lelant.

Willūs Prade in ter. £3.
Thomas Edwardes in bonis £3.
Stephen Pawlye in bonis £3.
Willmus Calinsawe in bonis £3.
Willmus Edwards in bonis £3.
Johēs Hoskyne in bonis £3.
Joeēs Penberthie in bonis £3.
Johēs Tomas in bonis £3.
Henricus Burncoose in bonis £3.
Johēs Kellwaye in bonis £3.

Towednacke.

Johēs Baragwanath in bonis £3.

St Ives.

Willmūs Trenwith ar. in ter. £5.
Johēs Tregenna in ter. £10.
Georgius Payne in ter. £3.
Willmūs Trenwithe de Trevalga in ter. £5.
Thomas Williams £6.
Johēs Steevens in bonis £6.
Johēs Cockinge £5.
Thomas Hickes £4.
Jacobus Wolcocke £5.
Elizabetha Tayler in bonis £3.
Thomas Toman in bonis. . . .
Georgius Hicke in bonis. . . .
Henricus Hickes in bonis. . . .

Senar.

Johēs William in bonis £5.
Edwardus Walyshe in bonis £3.

SUBSIDY, 10 JAMES I. (1613).

Lalant.

Willūs Edwards subs 2*s*.

St Ives.

Joane Pokinghorne subs 2*s*. 6*d*.
Johēs Goodale subs 2*s*. 6*d*.

(signed by :)

Wm Godolphin

Nicholas Prideaux.
John Arundell of Trerise.
R. Harrys of Antony.

CHAPTER XII.

THE BOROUGH ACCOUNTS (FIRST VOLUME), 1570-1639.

THE earliest volume of the Borough Accounts of Saint Ives is a paper book, folio size, about half an inch thick. It was lost for a great number of years, and was discovered in 1890 by the Mayor, Mr. Edward Hain junior, amongst the sweepings of a solicitor's office. When it thus came to light, it was in the form of a crumpled and tattered bundle, damp and decayed. Recognising its valuable character at a glance, Mr. Hain sent the documents to a first-rate London binder, who has most skilfully restored and repaired the MSS., and bound them neatly and strongly in vellum. They were afterwards handed to the author, to be transcribed for the purposes of this history.

The work of transcription has been arduous, owing to the ravages which the hand of time had inflicted upon these records; but it has been rendered interesting by the flood of fresh light which this volume pours upon the history and genealogies of the town and parish of Saint Ives.

The title-page commences with a capital letter 'A,' which seems to be a poor copy from some mediæval church-book; indeed, the interlaced pattern of the drawing has a Celtic look. Possibly the copyist had before him the book of the Acts of Saint Ia, which disappeared from the parish church at the Reformation.

Unfortunately, the various writers in this volume of borough records were not careful to carry their entries straight on, from one page to the next. Hence the accounts of the various years are muddled up together in a confused way, which is rendered all the more puzzling by the fact that in a large number of instances the written date has disappeared, owing to the decay of the upper margin of the leaf. We have, therefore, often had to guess at the date of an entry, or to fix it approximately.

[The title-page reads thus :]

INITIAL LETTER TO THE EARLIEST MS. OF ST. IVES BOROUGH ACCOUNTS, 1570.

A booke of Recorde Beloanīge to the parish of Sainte Iues, in Cornewell. Beinge made the xxiiijth Daye of Nouember 1570. And the Thirtenth yeare of the Rayne of Our Sovrayne Ladie Elizabeth, by the grace of god of Englande ffraunce And Ierland Queene Defender of the faith.

[Below is an illegible fragment of writing with the date 1595. It does not appear that the accounts were actually commenced in 1570 ; the earliest dated entries commence in 1573, thus :]

The accompte of thomas hyckes hedwarden in the yeare of o^{r} lorde god 1573.

[Then follow the names of the officials selected for the ensuing year, to wit the Church Wardens, Market-House Wardens and Quay Wardens, the 'Wardens of the Eylde,' or Sidesmen, and the King and Queen of the Summer Games. Of these officials a list will be given in a later chapter. The Account then begins :]

here ffoloweth ye receits

Inpm̄is receiued of m^{r} martine Trewennarde for the halfe yeres anuitie dew at o^{r} Ladie day in marche 1573, viij^{li}.

[We propose to give all such entries in these Accounts as possess historical interest, and the first we will quote, under the year 1573, is this :]

,, receiued of John Clarke for ye enterlude, 1^{li} xj^{d}

[This would seem to mean that the sum in question was paid for a manuscript copy of the miracle-play which was to be performed that year. Many other references to the plays will be met with later. The next two entries refer to the same matter :]

,, receiuyd of Wm Trinwth for sixe score and thre foote of elme bordes in ye playing place, vj^{d}

Item receiuyd of harrie hayne for bordes, 1^s vj^d

,, rec: of the kinge and quene for the somer games. 1^{li} 0^s iv^d

[These officials were annually chosen from among the handsomest lads and lasses of the parish, and the office was considered an important honour. Their duty was probably to preside over the sports at the maypole, on Saint John's Day and at Christmas time.]

,, rec: of thomas stevin & thoms hickes for there full and laste paiment of ye benevolens to wards the churche yearde, vj^s vj^d

[*i.e.* the rate for fortifying the churchyard.]

,, rec: for a shepe that drew harriet doghter gave to the repayringe of the churche, ij^s vj^d

[Meaning a sheep given by Drew, the daughter of Harry Ats, the value whereof was to go towards the cost of repairing the church.]

,, rec: of y^e olde m^r $Trinw^{th}$ for shepe, $xiiij^s$

The charge as ffolwithe :

Item paid to the pishe of Ste Unye for one years rent 1^{li} iij^s $viij^d$

[This was a rent paid annually to the churchwardens of Lelant, apparently in recognition of the supremacy of the mother parish over Saint Ives.]

,, payd to John Cockyn for iij barrels of lyme iij^s

,, payd for a barrell of lyme & vj bundells of lathes for to drese [dress] the churche v^s j^d

,, payd to John W^{ms} for helling stones and lathe nayles for the church v^s

,, payd for thre heliars wages nine daies xj^s iij^d

,, payd to the hyliars for nailes j^s iv^d

,, payd to the glasiar for mendinge ye windows vij^s

,, payd for iij heliars meate & drinke ix daies x^s

,, payd for halfe a barrell of lyme for ye churche j^s

,, payd to the churche of Bathe ij^s [towards its repair.]

,, payd for a sitation for gathering ye pishe dews . . . . .

,, payd for the printed bylle of ye courte . . . . .

,, payd to the prÿter . . . . .

,, payd for the laste preachers charges at John Androwes . . . . .

,, payd to harrie oots & John Androw for y^r charges when the went to lanehearne . . . . .

[Lanhern was the seat of the Arundells, who in various ways possessed influence at Saint Ives.]

,, payd at ye same time for showing [shoeing] of a horse for harrie ots to ryde . . . . .

,, payd to m^r godolphins hinde [farm-servant] for caringe the hurdels to haile . . . . .

,, paid to the vicar at ester . . . . .

Item payd to John Wms for things wch he delyueryd aboute the laste playe . . . . .

„ more paid to mr thomas trinwth to paye coñt of Trewro for lyneclothe [linen] . . . . .

Sm̄ xxiiijli js iijd

So there remaynes dew unto the parishe vs vjd

---

more charges layde owt of the churche Receptys as folowth

It̃ payd for Soppe agynste Crystmas iijd

It̃ payde iiijd

It̃ payde to a man that Gaderyde for a towne burned xvjd

It̃ payd at the vysytacion kepte at pensans vjs viijd

It̃ payd to the bayllyffs for ffees & for the bock iiijd

It̃ payd for a collar for the belle vijd

It̃ payd for a bock to the vickar viijd

It̃ payde the bayllyff for to exñe [examine] us iiijd

It̃ for makyng this Acompts & wreting xijd

Sm̄ xjs vjd

[Penalties for refusing to fill the office of warden, and for not repairing to the council meeting :]

. . . . of novembr ano 1573 yt is agreyed that who so eu' of the xiij men that Reffuyce to be towne warden beyinge Elected that he shalbe chargyd by hys and thyr consent to paye to the towne porte xxs by the next warden chossen to be hade in axcion and for eũy man offycer chossen vs and eũy p'son nat mackynge his Repayr to the halle beynge callyd by the Towne Warden then beyng p'sent the same p'son for his nat comynge shall be charged the sm̄a of xijd beynge eyther of the xij or xxiiij.

The names of the xiij men wherof one of them ys allwas electyd to be towne warden chossen by the xxiiij or most voys of them : whoys names lyckwys dothe folowe :

Añoo 1573.

John lanyon John penhelege towne warden John tregena James trevnwth Rychard Payne harry trevnwth Thomas stephin Willm trevnwth Thomas hicks Jamys trevnwth J. Jamis	preposit :	T. Thomas [?] Renold chenals John Cockin John Willm̄ Geffrye Gooddall harry Ottys harry Alan Richard Rosswall. Willm porthmantr John Anndrew

[1575 ?]

[The churchwardens are to gather *4d.* a year from every householder, for the communion bread and wine :]

Thomas James } Churche wardens: whosse yerely office i . . . d
Pearse Nole } churche dewties and pōfytts of the same for the better māyteynance and all so: the laws of the Reallme dothe alowe and admytt: yt is Inacted: . . . . of the Realme y^t^ ye churge wardens shall yerely gay^r^ of eūy howssolder w[^th^in] townes and pryshes: for the provydinge yerely of bread and wine for the cōmunion the valew of y^r^ churche Loaffe: or iiij^d^ for the same, all grants, all quysts and bequethes: as all so all sylver and lyberty to sell brew for the wch the towne paythe

William Teage } yēlie for y^s^ libert, to the wardons of the
martine Goodall } market house dew vij^s^

Receyts as followith:

Receiued of m^r^ Martine Trewennard for the halfe yeares anuitie dew at our ladye day in marche viij^li^

Itm̄ receiued at Easter for the parishes fine and offringes whiche dothe amounte to ij^li^ xiiij^s^ iij^d^

Itm̄ receiued the firste daye of the playe xij^s^

" receiued the seconde daye wch amounteth to i^li^ xij^s^ ij^d^

" receiued the thirde daye wch amounteth to iiij^li^ x^s^ xj^d^

" receiued the fourth daye wch amōnteth to i^li^ xix^s^ vj^d^

" receiued the 5 daye wch amountethe to iij^li^ ij^s^

" receiued the sixt daye wch amountethe to iij^li^ — j^d^

" more receiued for drincke monye wch am̄ j^s^ ij^d^

" more receiued of william Trinw^th^ in the churche yeard whiche amountethe to j^li^ xvj^s^ ij^d^

" receivyd for drincke monye after the playe ij^s^ viij^d^

Itm̄ receiuyd of the churche wardons to bestowe upon poore people wch Mr Coswarthe gave vij^s^

Itm̄ receiuyd for viij pounde of tithe butter v^s^ x^d^

Itm̄ receiued of James huchine for the somer games xiv^s^ vj^d^

[James Huchine was King of the Summer Games this year, and it was his duty to hand over his receipts for the relief of the poor. Among the payments are these :]

Itm̄ Payd to m^r^ laynyane [Lanyon] for iiij trees, j^s^

" payd to the pypers for there wages,

[Amount torn off.]

" payd to william barreat for xiij pound of hops, ij^s^

" paid to John goman for a barell of drink, iiij^s^

" payd to the vycar for xviij dayes servyce mynistringe the sacrament & other neds, xj^s^

" payd to m^r^ chywone at the vycitacion

[Bishop's visitation. Amount torn off.]

Itm payd for mr trinwthes diñer & myne at the sayd vycitacion . . . .

Itm̄ payd for the Indentures for the plimẽt [Parliament] vjd

Itm̄ payd to a man of earthe [St. Erth parish] for making hurdels iiijs ijd

Itm̄ payd things for the playe, iijs

Itm̄ payd for half a dosin of white lambes skyne ijd

[For making parchment.]

Itm̄ paid to Tregerthar for cutting the trees. iiijd

Itm̄ payd to standlye [Stanley] for a lynge [line] when the . . . . were about the playne, xd

[A cord to keep the people away from the players' arena.]

Itm̄ more payd to mr vose when thomas browne brought the tythine [tithing] chese at harry ats house, ijs viijd

,, payd to wm permanters servant & others for makinge of the leate for the tockyngmyle [tucking-mill.]

,, payd to mr paynter for making ye indentures for the parliament, js

[Then follow entries of money laid out in the purchase of clothes for various parish paupers :]

,, for iiij yeards & a quarter of Canves for harryes sherte & elizabethe argosyas smocke, iiijs

,, payd for ij yeards of Canvas to make dyos doghter a smocke, js vjd

,, ij yeards & a quarter for alye derys smocke, js vjd

,, for threde & making of the same, viijd

[The next item seems to refer to stage scenery put up for the miracle play :]

,, spent upon the carpenters yt made hevin [Heaven] iiijd

,, payd for the vycar when he bargayned to the prishe iiijd

[1576?]

Receyts.

Item recd for the Sommer games of Jo: Holla, xixs iiijd

Paymts Inpmis pd for led to make bollats when the Spanyerds were in Mounts Baye . . . .

Item spent on St Earth men beinge in or towne all night . . . .

Item bestowed on Sr ffrauncis Godolphin a barle of cafeves [barrel of coffee.] . . . .

Item the like bestowed on Mr Tregosse.

Item for my [the Head Warden's] expence being wth Sr Nicholas Parker . . . .

Item pd Mr. Tregosse for dounge [dung] to fill the forte . . . .

Item pd for the pt [part] buyinge of the Bible . . . .

Item p^{d} to Lelant for rent, j^{li} vj^{s} viij^{d}
Item p^{d} for mendinge the midle bell, j^{d}
Item p^{d} for the Subsidye acquytance, ij^{s} iv^{d}
Item p^{d} for making o^{r} platform for o^{r} ordynaunce, ij^{li}
Item p^{d} the collectors of ye maymed souldiers, xiv^{s} iv^{d}

[*i.e.*, of the fund for the relief of the maimed soldiers. We find similar entries almost every year throughout this volume.]

Item p^{d} the drommer at 2 musters, ij^{s}

[The able-bodied males of the parish were assembled for drill as a trained band, at stated intervals, under an officer called the Muster Master and the Sergeant Major.]

Item p^{d} for amending o^{r} kaye [quay] x^{s}
Item p^{d} for croks and other necessaries to o^{r} markett house, 1^{li} vj^{s}
Item p^{d} Mr. Tregosse for the m̄kett house Rent, iv^{s}
Item p^{d} George the mason for his wages ab^{t} the forte, xvij^{s}

[The fort, also spoken of as a platform for ordnance, was perhaps identical with the 'Castle,' the artillery platform opposite the chapel on the quay.]

Item p^{d} m^{r} Praed for drawing o^{r} aunswere in the chauncerye, iv^{s} viij^{d}
Item p^{d} for my horse hyre att the assizes & mending his shoes, v^{s} iv^{d}
Item p^{d} Jo: Steven for his charges to the assizes, j^{li}
Item p^{d} Wm Otes for putting forth the Ireland soldiers, ix^{s} ij^{d}

[*i.e.*, paid the constable for escorting out of the parish certain soldiers who had landed here on their way from Ireland.]

Item for a sworde & other necessaries not p^{d} by the Ireland, xiij^{s} ij^{d}
P^{d} for powder for the Souldiers going to Penryn, xxiv^{s} vj^{d}
P^{d} for 2^{li} mache & 4^{li} of ledd, j^{s} iv^{d}
P^{d} for a kinkerkyn [kilderkin] to hold Butter, j^{s}
P^{d} for horsehyre 2 seūall tymes travayling to Penryn, iv^{s} vj^{d}
P^{d} for bakinge the Biskye, iij^{s}
P^{d} for a Sacke to hold the biskye, j^{s}
P^{d} for cariadg the biskye to the castle, j^{s}
P^{d} for Jo. Taccab^{r} dyett with harry the cutler, j^{s} vij^{d}
P^{d} for mending the furniture, ij^{s} ij^{d}
P^{d} more for horsehyre at Penryn & Clowance, iv^{s}
P^{d} Captayne calffyld at Truro, iij^{s}
P^{d} Sergaunt Maior at marhasewe greene iij^{s}

[The trained bands were mustered on Marketjew Green.]

P^{d} serg^{t} maior at 2 tymes, xiv^{s}
P^{d} for the dyett of 6 poore souldiers com̄ynge from Irland iij^{s}
P^{d} Jo: Stephen for the setting forth of the Irland soldiers j^{li} iv^{s}

P[d] to the pveyor & the acquytance, x[s] iv[d]
P[d] Trery for drawing pleynts, iiij[d]

[The following seems to belong to the year 1577 :]

The Charge as foloweth

Itm̄ payde unto Vny lalante men for there rente dewe, j[s]

Itm̄ payde for breade and drinke the quenes daye to the ryngers, v[s] iiij[d]

[The Queen's Day was her Coronation Day.]

Itm̄ payde ij men for mending of lazerus house, xij[d]

[The Lazarus, or Lazar House, was the house rented by the parish authorities for the lodgment of the paupers.]

Itm̄ payde to Rycharde Watty for nurssing of denys chylde, v[s]

[This child was, it would seem, a foundling. The entries of moneys paid for its nursing occur annually after this.]

Itm̄ payde to the smyth for mending of the bell, v[s]

Itm̄ payde to the hede ballife of the hundrede for sealing our messurs [measures] xij[d]

Itm̄ bestovede one tewenacke men for making the bolwarks, ij[s]

[Bestowed on Towednack men for making the walls of the fort.]

Itm̄ payde to Willm̄ eles the shrifte man for bearing with the prishe, iij[s]

[Paid to William Ellis, the Sheriff's man, for 'squaring' the matter of rates.]

Itm̄ payde to James Kyttawe for mending Jermyn the blinde man house, iij[s]

Itm̄ payde for making the newe church att london, xij[d]

Itm̄ payde to willm̄ eles for the vicare his troble that came uppon the parish from thexcheker [the exchequer] to the shrifte [sheriff] of Cornvell, ...

Itm̄ to John Callame for one dayes worke and halfe upon hys awne mett and drynke . . . . .

Itm̄ for a man to serve him upon hys mett and drinke . . . . .

Itm̄ payde to John bosswage for rede clothe & lasynge to the towne ys use, v[s] ij[d]

Itm̄ for a ponde of candels to the Ryngers quen ys ev iiij[d]

[On the eve of the Queen's Coronation Day.]

Itm̄ for apece of ledar [leather] to mend the coler of the bell iij[d]

Itm̄ payd for the makinge of halfe busshell measure of the corne w[t] a pecke in thend, xviij[d]

Itm̄ for a potell of wyne presented m[r] bevell & m[r] carye x[d]

Itm̄ payd for the helinge Rags in the Markett house window iij[s] ij[d]

[Healing-rags are flat stones.]

Itm̄ for caring [carrying] of them iij[d]

[1577 ?]

Recepts. Inpm̄is Rec^{d} for Rente for the kaye xx^{s}
more Rec^{d} for that was given to the chaple ij^{s}
Paymt^{s} Inpm̄is p^{d} towr̄de the charge of buryinge a poore Woman called crowa^{r} ij^{s} x^{d}
Item p^{d} towr̄de the buryinge of a poore woman of Gvenap, xiij^{d}
Item p^{d} towr̄ds the buryinge her childe, viij^{d}
Item p^{d} for clothes to the pish̄e [parish] child, xij^{d}
Item p^{d} to the parrishe childe for her fyndinge [her keep], xvj^{s}
Item p^{d} Mr Cooke to viewe the towne fforts, x^{s}
Item p^{d} my lord Mounte Joyes Men, xx^{s}

[Then follows the Overseers' Account :]

p^{d} for Rawe Anawgas is shrowde, iij^{s} iiij^{d}
p^{d} for shrowdinge him & bringinge him to his grave, xij^{d}
p^{d} a pore mayde waytinge by the corps all daye at hellesveor, j^{d}
P^{d} Ots Hake to make his grave, ij^{d}
P^{d} for marye Phillippe is shrowde beside xx^{d} gathered, xx^{d}

[The practice of collecting charitable offerings towards the burial of paupers is of ancient date ; according to Catholic doctrine, to bury the dead is one of the 'corporal works of mercy.']

p^{d} Eliz : Rodger to keepe a base childe founde by the prish̄e and for half of a pecke of blye, xviij^{d}
p^{d} for a shrowde to Jenny Drewe & for bread to the woman who shrowded her, iij^{s} iij^{d}
P^{d} Alce caraway who releeveth certaine poore children of the parrishe, vj^{d}
P^{d} a poore man of Morestowe, whoes house was burnte, and his wiefe distracted of her witts, xij^{d}
P^{d} Elizabeth Rodger who keepeth a base childe of the pish̄e, by order of the xij men, viij^{d}
P^{d} for ij kayes & plate of Jron for the pore mens boxe, iij^{s} ix^{d}
P^{d} for a shrowde for Jasp^{r}, a poore man of the towne, iij^{s} vj^{d}
p^{d} another who gathered for englishmen captives under the Spanyerde by like auctoritye, vj^{d}
p^{d} dreamer dewen a poore mā in his sicknes, vj^{d}
Easter Quarter. Inpm̄is p^{d} for two dele boordes to make a newe seate to the vicar, iij^{s}
P^{d} the Joyner to make the viccars newe chaire, iij^{s}
p^{d} to the sheriffs bayliffe beinge arested at m^{r} Tregosse is sute, ij^{s} viij^{d}
p^{d} Sr John Tooker, a minister is wife, her husband beinge blynd, xij^{d}

pd Jasps wife to depte [depart] the towne wth her child, vjd

pd for two ptes of the shrowde of willm a pore man the ropers brother, ijs

Midsommer Quarter. Pd Nicholas Polstronge travaylinge to Truru, beinge pressed for a Pyoner, vjd

Pd the officyallmo beinge psēnted by the churchwardens in defaulte of the books of the churche, iiijs

Pd for the bible beside xjs ijd gathered in the churche, xviijs xd

[Very numerous are the allusions to licensed beggars, such as the following :]

Pd a pore man gatheringe by her Maties lrēs patents 19 Sept. vjd

Pd a pore man gatheringe by the like aucthoritye for a lazar house by launceston, vjd

Pd to Willm Bailye for a halfe yeeres Rente for his house, wherin the poore people dwell, vjs

28 Sept. Pd the glasyer who amendeth yeerlye the church-wyndowes, vjs

Pd for two weks mayntaynaunce of the poore child, viijd

Pd the poore wemen who shrowded diūse [divers] the poore people deceased : abovesaid viijd

---

It paid for the mending of the clocke, xviijd

It paid to John trewennard for stondinge of the treese in the Iland, xijd

It for my charges in trerow [Truro] for the travaill of the comission for settinge the Justice hand ther unto to be cared [carried] to the counsell . . . . . .

It paid to John bowden for byldinge leren [Larren] bridge . . . . .

It paid one which gathered for the pore house att somersetshere . . . . . .

It paid to the younge felow which is our clarke, ijs

It paid for bruten house, vjd

[Breton House, on the Island, as to which see our chapter on the 'Old Houses of Saint Ives.']

[A rate for fitting out Irish soldiers. Their equipments :]

the 22 of June 1578: for the payement of ye pōvision for yrland Sowlldgowrs: as all so for ye furniture of the trayned Sowldiours: the charges for yrland Sowldiowrs amōte to xxxs: the chargs of the trayned Sowldiowrs is a caliū [culiver] flax & tuche boxe a poūd of powdr a pownd of Shott: his maches: moriane: swerd . . . . & girdell: the 12 best men wr sett to iij severall pts . . . . to paye xijd amane: Seavne to paye xd amane & ye 3 to paye viij amane: and ye 24 wr sett to iij severall ptes . . . . t to paye viij^{d} a mane: and ye Seavne: & the 3 to paye vj^{d} . . . . . . & the Rest as it apereth on y^{r} p̃ticuler hedds:

....lenyeyne	W^{m} trenwth	John polkynhorne
...........trenwth	John Cockyn	John Androw
...........tregena	John Carvedris	W^{m} porthmāt^{r}
...........penhelak	harri Alane	harrye otts
		Thoms James
iij^{s}	iij^{s} iiij^{d}	iij^{s} iiij^{d}

together x^{s} viij^{d}

constables only w^{r} exepted: for y^{r} labor to collecte y^{s}

[Against the name of Harry Alane is written 'cōtēpt'; from which it appears that he refused to pay his share. The names of the twenty-four ordinary burgesses follow.]

[*Circa* 1580.]

It paid for the servinge one supine [subpœna] upon w^{m} trenwth att tre valgen ij^{s} vj^{d}

It paid a cord to sett to the drom̄ vj^{d}

It paid to a sowdier which [sic] in lalant vj^{d}

It paid to one m^{r} barry a sowdier of yerland vj^{d}

It paid to cornall stevin for to skins to the drom̄ xij^{d}

It paid to w^{m} trevnwth for goinge to helstone vj^{d}

It paid for both our deners the wensdaie folowinge att pensance xij^{d}

It paid to thomas w^{m} for a springe locke to the stoks iij^{d}

It payed for stocking of John Androwe is sest^{r} [?] ij^{s} vj^{d}

It payed m^{r} harrye Edward for the erecteng of the towence of nantuege, & the Ille of Sent nycolas, att pllemowth xj^{s} & iiij^{d} for a quettaunces.

It payed the plom̄er for mendeng the Leddes of ye towar & churche xij^{s}

It payed for bred & drenke, the quenes daye vj^{s}

[1580 ?]

Md' it is ordered and agreed by The hole xij and xxiiij that no foresteman [stranger] shall lande any apples peson or malte wthin viij daies of there arivall wthin the Key and y^{tt} no townes man shall sett any seller vnto any one of them w^{t} in xv daies of ther arivall upon paine of paymentt of x^{s} to the use of the towne

W^{m} barett vj^{s}	Richard pk'yn . . . .
W^{m} W[olcok ?] vj^{s}	W^{m} bowyer [?] . . . .
Thomas hicks iiij^{s}	James sysse [?] x . . . .
Thomas candrowe iiij^{s}	John Cossynn [?] . . . .
[John ?] payne xviij^{d}	John dayeow vj^{d}
James gyles ij^{s} iiij^{d}	Jermen vj^{d} Julia sterry
harry trenwth [?]	John toman vj^{d}
W^{m} trenwth	peris mychell xij^{d}

[The above regulation was designed to prevent the sale of goods brought into the town, until the townsmen should have had ample opportunity to sell their own goods first. 'Forestman:' compare Italian *forestiere*, a foreigner.]

Anº 158[o ?]

[This is written in a beautiful Chancery text hand, in brown ink.]

The Receppts of Robert luck and Rychard arde churche wrdens for Graves. It recevyd of John polpera vs

It therys owed unto us for mr Thomas treunwth ys grave vs

[There was a payment due to the borough for every interment within the church.]

It Recevyd for one yewe xxijd

It Recevyd at Ester for churche dewtye xjs vjd

It more rec: for a cutte [rate] wch is for the churche, xvjs iiijd

Charges layde owt of thys Receppts of the churche wardens as ffolowth

It furste payde for x horsses to carye morash Russches ffrome connrton gevyn unto the pyshe churche of sent yves yerlye by Sr John Arundell of lannhern knygth & hys awncetors tyme owt of mynde & ther labours that gatheryde the same Rusches, vs viijd

[At this period it was still customary to strew the church with fresh rushes every Christmas; a custom which, indeed, was continued in some remote places in England so late as the end of the last century.]

It for wyne at the comunyon at ester & duyers other tymes thys yer, xijs ijd

It payd for comunyon bred to Candrow xjd

It payd to a poure man that Gaderyd [gathered] in the churche, xijd

[Poor people were often permitted to make a collection in the church for their own necessities.]

The accompte of John Carvoddres hede Warden of the boroughe of sent yves as folowyth.

The Recepts.

It Recevyd of Thomas Eva & Elizabt Amys kynge and Quene of the somer game vijs vjd

It ther remanyth vnpayd for mr Thomas trevnwth ys grave vs

The accompte of monys layd owt in lawe ffor the marcket hows & other chargys.

It payd to the scheffrys [sheriff's] men for ffeys [fees] serving the wrytts vijs vjd

It' payd at Trerowe at the sessyons for coppyes of the wrytts iijs iiijd

It' payd ffor corrye, trevasskes & John carpentr ys dyners at sessyons xiiijd

It' payd for ther sopper that nygth at trerowe xxijd

It' payde the nextt daye for ther dyner xxijd

It payde for owre ij horsses viij^d^
It payde for . . . . vj^d^
It payde for hys bregffaste & hors mett [horse-meat] x^d^
It payde more for the Retorn of the wretys [return of the writs] v^s^
It payde for wrytynge vj^d^

Sm xxiij^s^ ij^d^

More monys layde owt in chargis of the Recepts of the market & pier as ffollow^th^
It payd to my lord Stourton ys man vj^s^ viij^d^
It payde to the vicker of Sydney [Sithney] for prechinge v^s^
It for a quarte of seck [sack] gevin the vyckar of Sydney vj^d^
It payde for brede the Quenys daye gevin to the Ryngars & others iij^s^ iv^d^
It payd for wyne the Quenys daye v^s^ iiij^d^
It payd to the glassyar x^s^
It payde for a holye butte [halibut] gevin to m^r^ ffrauncs Godolphin xviij^d^
It a nother quart of seck gevyne to the vyckar of Sydney vj^d^
It payd for Cadwellys w^c^ was gevyn the dyer when he was kynge [of the summer games] by order gevin me iiij^s^ vj^d^

[Cadwelly must be some garment made of Welsh cloth, from Kidwelly.]

It payd my lorde stourton ys mane xiij^s^

[1584.]

The accounte of ots merifelde hedwarden of the towne made in the yeare of o^r^ lorde 1584.
It Rec of m^r^ tregenna for the standinge of the muster stufe in the markett house xx^s^

[*I.e.*, for the firelocks, swords and other 'stuff' used by the trained-band.]

It Rec of m^r^ tregenna for the bringinge in of the perow shipp x^s^

[This entry is struck through.]

Rec of a fforest man which cam from patcows wth pese iij^s^
It Rec of Andrew Downynge for layinge of his pots a shore x^d^

[Under the foregoing bye-law against landing for sale imported goods before the expiration of a certain time.]

It Rec of James Pormantor for the Roben houde xvj^s^

[The Robin Hood, *i.e.*, the Twelfth Night mummers.]

It Rec of harry stery att twelth efe vj^s^

[1584 ?]

Item paid fòr forelocks for the great Ornance j^s^
Item paid to the Glaser for iij^o^ years stipende xv^s^
Item paid for a Communion book iij^s^
Item paid for a beare to cary the dead ij^s^ vj^d^

Item paid for paper to make a booke to gather y^e^ colection ij^d^
Item paid Steven Coyte for kepinge cleane the harnes x^d^

[Harness = armour.]

Item paid the players of Germal which gathered for y^er^ [their] church ij^s^
Item geven to ij^o^ poore soldiers beinge maymed in the Queens ma^ties^ service j^s^
Item paid for viij^o^ pondes of pouder at the Cominge of the Lord Mouteioye viij^s^
Item paid m^r^ Wisheker for prechinge a sermone vj^s^
Item geven to a poore soldier with the Queen's ma^ties^ brode seale the xix^th^ of Septembre . . . .

Receipts.

Item receyued of the cutt or Collection for the mendinge of the Church hay Wall }—vij^li^ iiij^s^ ix^d^

John James chosen head warden by the consent of the xij & xxiiij sett unto Richard peter the mc̄att & the profets & tole corne aswell thatt wch comythe in the wieke dayes as on the satterday for the yearly rentt of a xj^li^ to be paid quarterly, & he to dischardg all charges for sweping the howse.

John James chosen head-warden by the consentt of the xij & xxiiij sett unto Rychard peter the mc̄att & the pf'ets & tole corne, for the rent of a xj^li^ by the yeare, to be paid quarterly, & he to dischardg the sweping of the howse or makin itt cleane.

[A memorandum of a certain rate levied for mending walls and providing military stores. Of the first paragraph only a fragment is legible ; the second runs thus :]

Md' that y^r^ is a cutte made ye 5 of June 1586 for flaxes h: b 3^li^ . . .^s^ 4^d^ as all so for the skowringe of ye corsletts two flaxes & tuche boxes viij^s^: the whole cutte . . .^li^ . . .^s^ . . .^d^ and above.

The Paymentes and Charges as followeth

Inprimis paid Thomas William for cristopher the mason of his Wages for workinge on the church wal xiiij^d^
Item paid John polkenhorne by the condessente of the Constables, for certayne Iryshemen hosted at his house iij^s^ viij^d^
Item paid the roper for makinge the bels ropes ij^s^

[1587.]

[This account is written in an execrable running Stuart hand.]

P^d^ outt by me as follow^th^

Imprimis paide vnto m^r^ ffysher ffor ij sermons one alhollandaye 1 . . . .

Iteme p^d stephan coite ffor mycaellmas quarter paste ffor cleninge the hareneste [harness, armour] 12*d.*

Iteme p^d henry pawlye ffor chrismas q^r Rente ffor Vny Lelant 6*s.* 8*d.*

Iteme p^d ffor mendinge the churche wall a nother tyme 7*d.*

Iteme ffor 1^lb of gonne pouder and qr' of mache &c vnto the traynyd sodyers the 4 of marche 42*d.*

1588.

Itm̃ Rec: of Thomas Candrowe ffor the ccmpe of younge candrowe beinge the Kinge of the maye games, 4*s.* 4*d.*

Itm̃ paid vnto Sertayne skotts thatt ther barcke was taken awayes, j^s

Itm̃ gave a sodier that came oute of flanders the 24 June 6*d.*

Itm̃ gave the Robin howde of S^t cvllvms the lower [the Robin Hood of St. Colomb Minor] by the apointment of m^r tregena 5*s.*

Itm̃ p^d to ij power menne 1*s.*

Itm̃ p^d to noye the sodier 3*s.*

Itm̃ p^d ffor Reastinge [arresting] poudnance ffor fforstalinge the market 5*d.*

Itm̃ p^d ffor a bucket and a newe sholle [shovel] 1*s.*

Itm̃ p^d ffor mendinge the stocks . . . .

[About this time occurs this entry, at the end of a list of persons rated to some benevolence :]

Thom̃s carpẽt^r for ye intermẽt at Carne stabba xvj^d

[1592.]

[The seats in the church are to be let, and the rents thereof applied to parish requirements :]

It is agreed upon this . . . . daye of mche Anno 1592 by the whole xij men and xxiiij whose names here under are written tuchinge the graunte and settinge of all the chaires wth in o^r churche of S^t yees for the maintayninge and repayringe bothe of ye churche and churche yearde wale, the Key and other nedefull busines wth in the same towne and pishe

In pm̃is we have consented and agreed thatt eũy man and woman shall inioye and use the sayde chaires during there naturall lyves, accordinge to a booke there of made, and rated, where unto o^r hands are subscrybed, and thatt the sayde Rate be of eũy one payde q'rterly, or wth in one monethe of the same, and for defaulte of paymentt to be in the hands of the pishe againe, to be sett att ye moste p'fitt.

Recepts.—The accounte of [Thomas] Williams heade warden An° 1592.

Ite' receiued of a foreste [stranger] barke for the londinge of hir apples 2*s*.

Ite' receiued of Joell hicks for sommer games 18*s*.

Ite' paide William Ots to geue to the soldiour 10*s*.

Ite' paide for a sworde and dagger for him 9*s*. 6*d*.

Ite' paide for makinge speare heads and nailes to naile them 3*s*. 8d.

Ite' paide for mendinge the claper of the bell 2*s*. 8*d*.

Ite' geuen to 2 men taken by the spaniards 1*s*.

Ite' geuē to a man that gathered for men bornte withe powder 1*s*.

Ite' paide for vitall for 5 men taken by the enemies and londed her in a shippe of lyme [Lyme Regis] 3*s*. 4*d*.

Ite' paid to the ringers the carnation [coronation] daie and for candles 6*s*. 10*d*.

Ite paide William Ots for to pay for 2 passengers bounde to Irelande whiche weare hosted at water treweks 3*s*. 4*d*.

Ite' Mr Ots to pay the muster M^r^ [muster-master] and drumer 7*s*. 6*d*.

Ite' paide for oile for the harnes [armour] and oylinge them 6*d*.

Ite' geuen to a man that tooke loste by sea 6*d*.

Ite' geuen to a poore man that tooke loste by fier dwellinge neare bodman 9*d*.

Ite' paide for a hundred and halfe of reede to thacke the lazares houses and for ropes 4*s*. 6*d*.

Ite' paide for butter and spices for Jenny Allen 1*s*. 6*d*.

Ite' paid for furses for hir 1*s*. 4*d*.

Ite' paid william ots for fletcheher our Soldiour 1^{li} 10*s*.

[The following entry possesses a general historical interest :]

Ite' paid George paine ffor his horse to carry campyon to Syr Walter rolie to peryn 2*s*.

Ite' paid for ffoure yeards of dowlis to make fletcher a shorte withe the makinge and thred 4*s*. 9*d*.

['Dowlis,' or 'dowlais,' would seem to be some material of Welsh manufacture.]

Ite' paid william otes for his chargs to cary the soldiours to Markegewe beinge three men 1*s*.

Ite' paid steven quoite ffor makinge the bell ropes and for rushes bread and drinke 2*s*.

Itē paid ffor strawe to heale the ij lazares howses and Vden to thache it 2*s*. 2*d*.

Ite' paid to George mason ffor a dayes worke about the churche and two men one day about S^t^ lenards chappell 3*s*. 2*d*.

Ite' paide to the plommer for xiij^{li} of sowdier [sawder] and ffor his paynes and one man to wayte uppon him ffor mendinge the gutters 14*s*. 6*d*.

Ite' paide Mr Tregenna ffor halfe bushell of Coale 4*d*.

Ite' more paide ffor harde woode to burn amonste the coales 6*d*.

Ite' paide to a man of Irelande that had his barke stollen by pirats 1*s*.

Ite' bestowed in drincke uppon the tynners ffor digginge up the stones wth in the key 1*s*. 10*d*.

Ite' paide ffor a peare of breches ffor John the lasar 1*s*.

Ite' paide to John Kalamey ffor mendinge St nicholas chappell 1*s*. 4*d*.

Ite' paide to another poore man that gathered dwellinge by este bodman havinge syxe Justices hands to his commission 6*d*.

[*I.e.*, having his begging-licence signed by six magistrates.]

Ite' paide to the shrieves men ffor Richard peeter beinge taken wth the shreeues warrants at our lady feare [Our Lady's Fair] 4*s*.

Ite' paide ffor makinge up the lazares Chimly 1*s*. 6*d*.

Ite' paide to Mr nickols the precher 10*s*.

Ite' bestowed uppon Mr trenance the queenes Korroner one gallone of wyne 2*s*. 4*d*.

Ite' paide ffor a Jerkin and a peare of breeches to John the lazare 2*s*. 4*d*.

Ite' paide to James stery to pay the plommer to mende the gutters of the churche . . . .

Ite' paide to mr nicols the precher ffor his sermon 6*s*. 8*d*.

Ite' paide to a man of chester that gathered hauinge a commission ffrom my lorde Admirall 2*s*.

Ite' paide to John Shaplande to make a supplication to mr Chiuertonne ffor the poore children that be in towne 8*d*.

Ite' paide to water hicks to carry the bastarde to burryan 6*d*.

Ite' paide to the Cutler to mende one of the leds of the clocke, 10*d*.

[1594.]

Receipts for the parishe receyued by Henry Hickes heade warden Anno 1594.

monnes taken out of the poore mens box:

It geuen to John the lazar 1*s*.

It to mary the lazer 2*s*.

It to Tregerthen to buie hime asherte and meat 4*s*. 4*d*.

It to buie the poore maide clothes 1*s*. 2*d*.

It to John the lazer for afrise [frieze] breches 2*s*. 8*d*.

It to the wedowe Jenken for apeare of shoes 1*s.* 3*d.*
It to Tregerthen for kandels 2*d.*

00 — 12 — 07

[1594-5.]

It paide to the souldars and a Oman that was taken by the spanniards the 13th of may 2*s.* 6*d.*
Ite' paid the Welsheman for makinge Johan knights house 3*s.* 4*d.*
Ite' paid for Tregirthens, in bringinge downe his stuf and makingh up his beade [bed] 1*s.*
Ite' paid for the redeminge of certayne prisoners 6*d.*
Ite' deliuered the church wardens to buy rushes 6*s.*
Ite' paid for a paire of shoes for Tregirthen 2*s.*
Ite' paid for a gowne for the said tregirthen 2*s.*
Ite' paid the 2 constables and John steuens in goynge to Truro, for vewinge the corne 6*s.*
It paid for lease for tregerthen is kowe 1*s.* 9*d.*
It paide to Jenkine treuingy and philipe for whachinge [watching] of Henry Poter and his sonn in the stokes 2*s.* and for makinge of ther metimas [mittimus] 6*d.*

[1595.]

Pd for a stabell [staple] for the stockes 2*d.*
paid for a shroud for Aly Kreft is cister 2*s.* 6*d.*
paid to mr william trenwith for a poer oman that died in the ten pite [tin-pit] for to healpe to by hier a shroud 1*s.*
paid to a poar man for the aspetall [hospital] house of borfold that had Harry Hex licence to gather the 25 of Aprill 1*s.*
I. payd for fyue haxads [hogsheads] 28*s.* 4*d.*
I. paid the ij day of July to 4 sowdgars that came out of Ierland . . . .
Ite' paid to mr Trevāyon of keryhayes [Trevanion of Caerhays] collector for the mamed soldyares for this yeare of our lord 1595 xiijs
I. paid for mendinge of the koine [coign, corner] of the keaye 8*s.* 6*d.*
I. more dew to John goldsmyth fore casting of shott 2*s.* 6*d.*
I. ther was deliverd the vickar at sent luks daie for Redemyinge of cristians prisoners frō the captivitie of ye turcke xxd to be pd at chapt curte [chapter court] In gwendren churg xxd

M' that ye market plase is set to Rychard Peter for one yere for a leven pound a yere : & to be paid quarterly : & the cōtriefolke yt bringethe corne to ye towne in the myddest of ye weke : by the Request of any of the Townes men for ye maynteynās of yr howssolde & cōmon weale : to be free of tole : payinge nothynge for yt tyme.

[Here follows an almost illegible note to the effect that people begging in the church are in future to receive only *6d.* from the town fund.]

Itm̃ p[d] to mgẽtt bowssow for & yrishe peale [pale, pole] to make a corball for y[e] pentise & a yrishe beame praysed by John stevin & thom[s] candrow & the worke men xvj[d]

M[d] that y[s] is dewe to W[m] smythe for makynge nayles for y[e] gret pyce of ordinãce in y[e] churche yerd & for ij spanges . . . .

[1596.]

[Certain old orders copied out by Mr. Hicks. A rate to be levied for defence of the town against the Spaniards :]

Here folow certaine olde orders, made heretofore by the 12: and 24 men in severalle yeres of the Towne and Parish of S[t] yees throughe out thys booke: I have colle[cted the same y[t] o[r] laws] might y[e] Rather be found out:

The fy . . . . Janiver: [1596 Tho[s] Hicks hed] wardeyne y[tt is] ordred and agreed [by the hed wardein] the 12 men and 24: that cute: whych is dewe [this present] yere: for Resystans of the Enymye [as all soe] for fencynge of the churche and cr[enelling ?] of y[e] churche yerd: All whyche monye [was not received] p' Harrye Hycks: in hys yere: nor be ageine g[h ?] . . . .

John James shall have full pow[r] to collecte and Receve the sayd cute to make up the doores of y[e] churche yard and of the churche: and to take the Lawe against them y[t] refuse [to paye their] dew in that cute.

Thom̃s Hycks ag[?].

[Persons who did not pay their share of the rate for resisting the Spaniards, are to pay it towards the repair of the church :]

It is ordred and agreed by the consent of the 12 men and 24 Thom̃s hicks hed wardeine the 3 day of . . . . 1596 Ano: Elizabethe Regina 38: that the cute and rate made through the hole towne and pry'she of St. Yees in an[o]: 1595 was aftr y[e] attẽpt made by the Spanyards upõ mowsholle newlyn and pẽzans: p[o]vision of ordinãce, shott and powder and other muniments to resyst that Enimy: wh'che at that tyme thredned the distruction of o[r] com̃on weale (the w[c] god en[s] [ensure] keepe ex[t] [exalt] and defend) the which cut and rate is p[d] of many goode, well wyllers to our com̃o wealthe: as by the said boke more largely maye appear: and the reste that hathe not p[d] the rate layd upõ y[t] severall and partycular hedds (in so dangerows a tyme) beynge lafullie sought and demanded to so goode uses as afore said as a token and a syngne that shewethe ther carles [careless] harts and hedds for to resyst that Enymye which thretned the Rewyne of our towne; and for that our churche windowes and churche yard lyethe greatly in decaye at thys instant: therfore all suche as are behynd and have not p^d in that cute muste paye ther monies to ye new hedd warden John James, to repayre the decays afor said: and for the none payment take the lawe, or to distrayn them.

[How the parishioners are to contribute labour, in making up the ramparts for the defence of the town against the Spaniards :]

The 23 daye of m . . . . . . 15[96 ?] ytt was agrede wth the consent of the xij & xxiv thatt the parysshe shall be devydide in to viij pt̃s every pt̃e to be vnder the [command] of some one of the xij men and macke uppe the bollw[orckes at] pormeare apointide by S^r [ffrauncis] godolphin and all soe suche other works as are to be endyde a . . . . one the satterdayes and suche dayes as the hedwarden Do [apointe] and every mane apointide . . . . . . this daye & tyme to worke [?] . . . . . . defalte that any do m . . . . . .

[A new seat to be made for the vicar :]

Vpon the sayings of m^r bagewell ye vickar to have a pew made for hym selfe to sytt in & y't it w^s not cōvenient, y^t ye clarcke shuld syt wythe him: Wm Ots by ye assents of John cockyn, George Hicks, Harrye Hicks, Thomas Candrowe, Thomas James, John James & at the laste [?] came to ye hed wardein Thom̃s Hicks ye v: day of septẽber 1596: to have hys assent to ye makynge of ye said pewe: who all so agreyd; & p^ovyded ye tẽber ye ix^th of septẽber & brought it to Rysse ye Iuner to make it up agenst Sonday next folowinge: we ꝑmised so to do: but dyd not make it y^t weke: be caws of o^r great works in hand.

[The rate levied during Harry Hicks' portrievalty is to be applied to the repair of the church; and in future distraint may be made for non-payment of any rate levied by the Town Council :]

M^d that it is ordred and agreed by the consent of the 12 men the iij daye of october An^o 1596 an^o Elizabethe 38, whose names be here under wretten that ye cut and rate made in harry hycks yere shalbe collected and p^d to the mendinge of the churche wyndowes and churge yard to the new hed Wardeine wch is to be chosen or to take ye lawe for ye none payment therof or to straine them for the same and the lyeke is agreed for any order or rate thatt shalbe hereafter agreed upon by the twelfe men or thee greattyst p^te therof for ye bett̃ maytenãce of any things to be done in our com̃on weale and ye cōstable in any cute made for the quenes maiestie: or her service: throughe towne and p̄rishe to strayne for none payment: being lafully demanded and not ye hedwardeine.

Here folowth ye detts dew to be paid wch̃e Thoms̃ hicke ye warden Receved his yere not answered as folowth 1596:

for halfe a hundred of hadche nailes vj^{d} & all so for chymals to ye great chest in ye churche, xx^{d}

to ye great pice ordinac̃e in ye churche yard: & for the makynge of ye spange for ye trap & churche style vij^{d}

[The churchyard wall was fortified with a great gun, to command the entrance to the harbour.]

Thomas hicks chosen hedwarden an^{o} 1596 an^{o} Regine Elizabethe 38.

The accompt of Thoms̃ Hicks Towne Warden the yere of our lord god 1596: as folowithe

Harry Hendra and Harry Baylye churche wardens: they have not p^{d} nothing thys yere to the hed wardeine nor yet levelled or satysfyed theyr accop̃t Dew towards the parisshe.

here folowithe the Receyptes:

Itm̃ Recevid in the whole for Wyllm̃ Teake is goods: bequethed to the Relyffe of the poore of the tow: and p̃ryshe of S^{t} yees xxvj^{s} iij^{d}

Itm̃ Recevid of margett boussow for a bequethe given by her hosband John boussow to ye stoare of S^{t} yees churge xx^{s}

[*i.e.* to the poor-fund of the church.]

Itm̃ Recevid of harry hendra for spale [spell] of too dayes: about the boulwarke xij^{d}

Itm̃ Recevid by the booke of Rate made in harry hycks is yere by the 12 and 24 for põvicion of ordynances powder shott: for to resyst the spaniards as by the said booke more largely may appear lv^{s}

Charges hereafter followythe 1596:

Itm̃ payd to Eden ye sexton and Job and trewens to gay^{r} [gather] strawe throughe the p̃ishe and to make Roaps to dres and mend ye lazy's howsses and fynd them selfes ij^{s}

Itm̃ p^{d} to a cople of women that shrowded ye lazar John Nyclis: and ther breake faste y^{t} tyme vj^{s}

Itm̃ p^{d} to a pore lame sowldior hurted in the quenes servyce in yrland having a lisens viij^{d}

[*i.e.* a license to beg.]

Itm̃ p^{d} to a poore mã y^{t} hade lysens to gay^{r} for burnỹg of his hows vj^{d}

Itm̃ p^{d} to Joane nyclis for the Kepinge of ye lazar her soñe in the tyme of hys syckenes vj^{d}

Itm̃ p^{d} to the Ryngers and y^{r} meate and drink ye quenes vj^{s} viij^{d}

Itm̃ p^{d} for talowe for the belles y^{t} tyme iij^{d}

Itm̃ p^{d} to mychell tanckyn ptẽ of the paymẽt for the new makynge of the coler for ye bell clapp^{r} xj^{d}

Itm̃ p^{d} to dewen and his wiffe and his wyffes syster at to severall tymes in breade xij^{d}

Itm̃ p^{d} to ye olde vickar stafford to pay at ye chapt^{r} curte [chapter court] at gwendren for redemynge of cristẽ prison^{rs} frō ye turke xx^{d}

[for redeeming of Christian prisoners from the Turk.]

Itm̃ p^{d} for tember nayles and to a laborer to mend the poore is doore by the churge yerd agenst cristm^{s} and aftrward againe broken by men of warre [soldiers] sekin way y^{r} in vij^{d}

Itm̃ p^{d} to Richard is brđth^{r} and fynd him selfe for xvij days and halfe xij^{s}

Itm̃ p^{d} to grygorie is soñe and fynd hym selfe ix^{s}

Itm̃ p^{d} to the too carpenters for viij days worke and a halfe about the pentise and fynd them selves xvij^{s}

['pentise' = penthouse.]

Itm̃ p^{d} to Rysse y^{e} Juner [joiner] for iiij pices of tember for y^{e} style by the porche doore ij^{s} vj^{d}

[*i.e.* the gate by the porch on the south side of the church.]

Itm̃ p^{d} to a laborer to gay^{r} strawe and to make strawen roaps to mend Joane Wats the lazar ys hows the second tyme, broken down w^{t} cattell and fynd hym selfe xij^{d}

Itm̃ p^{d} for W^{m} teake is shrowd and thred iij^{s} v^{d}

Itm̃ p^{d} for hys grave to ye wardeine iij^{s} iiij^{d}

Itm̃ p^{d} to iij wemen to watche ye corps y^{t} night xij^{d}

Itm̃ p^{d} to the olde vickar for candells bread and drincke for ye watchers and other dewtyes dew to y^{t} vycker xvj^{d}

[These were evidently remains of pre-Reformation customs, in connection with burials and the vicar's dues.]

Itm̃ p^{d} to Roger fyssher at cristm^{s} for kepyng a bastard to lew^{s} whorlie is s'vant y^{t} kome in to yrland ij^{s}

Itm̃ p^{d} to Lew^{s} whorlie for iij quarts of wine bestow^{d} upō s^{r} frances godolphin ij^{s}

Itm̃ p^{d} to Elizabethe baylye for kepinge of & oy^{r} [another] whore is bastard one trevorow is daughter ij^{s}

Itm̃ p^{d} to Stevin Jacka is wyfe for ye kepinge of W^{m} teke in his syckenes & for a bequeth y^{t} he gave her vj^{d}

Itm̃ p^{d} to W^{m} hyll and Jenet Jenckyn ye blind woma' y^{t} tyde xij^{d}

Itm̃ p^{d} to ye poore wome' by ye churche yerd that tyme xij^{d}

Itm̃ p^{d} to Annes Hendra & añes boleine to poore widow^{s} xij^{d}

Itm̄ p^{d} for too packs of Russhes agenst cristm^{s} xvj^{d}

[*i.e.* to strew on the floor of the church.]

Itm̄ p^{d} to takabu^{r} is sone to carye ye armor to ye mvster iij^{d}

Itm̄ p^{d} to harry Edward for ye mvste^{r} m^{r} [Muster Master] whiche trained ye soldiors & dromer iiij^{s}

Itm̄ p^{d} to Wm Wolcok for a trusse of strawe for ye clome [earthen] wall of the pentysse xvj^{d}

Itm̄ p^{d} for a pynt of metheklan [metheglin, mead] upō John shapland when he wrote ye townes letter to James Deynam iij^{d}

Itm̄ delyvered to bowyer & W^{m} hyll about shroft tyde to loavs bred iiij^{d}

Itm̄ p^{d} to ye broade seall grāted to gay^{r} for ye m'r shall sea [Marshalsea] for Relyve of prysoners xviij^{d}

Itm̄ p^{d} to a cople of men one owt of camell forth [Camelford] and other out of geran in the presens of Thom^{s} W^{m} w^{o} had lysens xij^{d}

Itm̄ p^{d} to John Trerye for kepinge of borweniks orphāt [orphan] for one quart̃ of ye yere vij^{s}

Itm̄ p^{d} to W^{m} barett about Ester Weke for ye Rate made by the Justices for wheat & other victaylle for ye quenes maiest^{s} flete at Plemowthe iij^{s} iiij^{d}

The Accōpt of George paine Towne Warden for the yeare of our Lorde 1591 as followeth

The Resepts

Reseved of Thom^{s} James his sonn' being Som̄er kinge x^{s}

Reseved of will^{m} Stirrie kinge of the maye game this yere xiij^{s} vij^{d}

Ite' p^{d} to the Ringers the Crownacion Daye viij^{s}

Ite' for making of John Saundrie the Lazer mans house xij^{d}

Ite' for the makinge of dore & dornes xij^{d}

Ite' to the Smyth for ire[iron]worke viij^{d}

Ite' to the mason for settinge the same Dornes vj^{d}

Ite' p^{d} to one to serue him iij^{d}

Ite' for mending the same howse xij^{d}

Ite' for kooping for the same howse iij^{d}

Ite' for iij Irishe bords one poss & naills & for makinge of his Bedsteade xx^{d}

Ite' for a Locke & keye for his howse vij^{d}

Ite' againe for mendinge the same howse iiij^{d}

Ite' p^{d} towards the Byinge of his Shrowde vij^{d}

Ite' p^{d} for makinge of the pore woomans howse at Senner iiij^{s}

Ite' p^{d} Willm barret for tymber for the howse ix^{d}

Ite' p^{d} Towards the healynge of the pore wooman x^{s}
Ite' p^{d} to Rychard woolcock for Bringinge of flecher to the gaille iij^{s} iiij^{d}
Itm̄ p^{d} to Simon Kockwill for tymber to builde Phillip the Lazar mans howse ij^{s} viij^{d}
Ite' for a hundred & halfe of Strowe iiij^{s} vj^{d}
Ite' for kopinge vj^{d}
Ite' for a Clavell for the chimlye viij^{d}
Ite' for ty'bre for the Dornes vj^{d}
Ite' for iij Irishe bords for the dore xij^{d}
Ite' for Ire geare [iron-work] ix^{d}
Ite' for makinge of the howse viij^{s}
Ite' p^{d} to Goite for makinge the dore & dornes xij^{d}
Ite' for a locke & keye vij^{d}
Ite' p^{d} to Currie for appeltre boughes for to laye on the same howse ij^{d}
Ite' for a dossen & halfe of furse to cover the same howse vj^{s}
Ite' for furse for the churchyard walle ij^{s}
Ite' geven to a preacher in the Lent vj^{s} viij^{d}
Ite' geven to Wills when he went in the Queenes Shipp xij^{d}
Ite' for mendinge of the Clocke iiij^{s}
Ite' for a payre of Shoosse for John Kilby xviij^{d}
Itm̄ p^{d} to Wm Otts for ye chargs of ye drom^{r} at ye grene in ye tyme of mowstrigē [mustering] vj^{d}
Itm̄ p^{d} to harry Trenw^{t} for mendinge of ye droome iij^{s} iiij^{d}
It' p^{d} for ye too armed mens supp^{rs} at marhasyow 23 Junij vij^{d}
It' p^{d} to Wm Prade for fees ye fyrst curte: for declaracyons & a destringo to brynge pet' [Peters] in to ye curte iij^{s} iiij^{d}
It' p^{d} to m^{r} Tregosse for hyghe Rent of ye mkētt hows the hole yere iiij^{s}
It' p^{d} for chargs at sent Erthe at ye hundred curte y^{r} holden in harrye baylye is defens agenst tamkyn & for Judgemēt & execucion & the Juries dew y^{t} curte v^{s}
It' p^{d} to ye glaciar for mēdinge ye churge wyndows this yere 1500, v^{s}
It' p^{d} for Evden ye sextōs meate waytyng to dayes upō ye glaziar in bringyng woode & caryng ye lader to & fro vj^{d}
It' p^{d} about Whytsonetyte to ye cutler hardinge for mēdinge y^{r} two picks hedds xv^{d}
It' p^{d} to a laborer for to days to sett posses in ye grownd for ye moryng of shippinge & fynd hīm selfe xij^{d}
It' p^{d} for meate thys quart at mygellm̄s for borweneks child vij^{s}
It' p^{d} to the mehamed [maimed] sowldiors to Mr Vyvian xiij^{s}
It' p^{d} to the Archerye for defawlte in shotynge ij^{s} vj^{d}

It' p^d^ for ye too westkotts ye mazons dener when they came to vew ye churge wyndowe ye 3 of october viij^d^

It' p^d^ to marget boussow for tember to make m^r^ vikar ys new pew or chayre & other more tember iij^s^ iiij^d^

[1597.]

The Accounte of . . . . . hedwarden and of the xij & xxiiij^or^ of the towne & parrishe of St. Yues for one hole yeere ended at the feaste of St. Michaell the Arcke Angle: A^o^ p^d^

Item Rec^d^ of Stephen Barbar for p^te^ of the profitt made by the Sommer games remayninge in his hands vj^s^

Payments. Michaellmas quarter. Inpmis p^d^ two poore men to carrye the coffyn or beare up to Treloighan, and bringinge Willm hill to his grave beinge a poore man of the parrishe ij^d^

Item p^d^ for Reede for the poore lazars housen iiij^d^

Item p^d^ for thatchinge ther housen vj^d^

Item p^d^ for bringinge the Stones of the church wyndowe to hele [to be mended] vj^s^

Item p^d^ 4 men to helpe downe the stones at lalante vj^d^

12 dec: Item p^d^ will^m^ fferys the mason, for hewinge the churchwindowe is Stones, in p^te^ of paymente l^s^

Item p^d^ the Glasyer Affabell Androwe in full paym^te^ for glasynge the churche windowes xxxij^s^ vj^d^

Item p^d^ for neats oyle to anoyle the clocke & bells vj^d^

Item p^d^ Willm Thomas for the Iron Worcke of the churche windowes vij^s^ vj^d^

Item p^d^ for amendinge the stocks vj^d^

P^d^ for bread for the comunyon at xrimas ij^d^

[1599?]

[Burgesses failing to attend the council meetings are to be fined :—]

24 die februarij [1599?]

Rich: . . . . .

It is agreede and ordered by the porthreeve and the [xij and xxiiij] then present, that if any of the xij shoulde refeucse for to com to the markett house, for the makinge of good lawes and orders, and for the common wealthe of this towne and parrishe, either the Quens ma^ties^ Service, or towne occasions, beinge therunto requyed or sum̄oned, in the pishe churche, as heretofore hath bene accustomed, shall forfeyte three Shillings and iiij^d^ for eūy suche defaulte, to be distrained by the portriff, hys Deputie or deputys : except such pson have Sufficient and lawfull cause to be absent, to be levyed to the townes use, by the Porthreeve or his deputy; and the 24or likewies makinge defaulte, upon the like occasyons, to forfeyte xijd for eũye defaulte, to be levyed as before

P.me Ric: Tregosse
Willm Trevnwth
John Cockyns
George hickes

Sign. thomas william
Johis: James
John Ryche Portryffe
John tregenna

[autographs]

[1600 ?]

Mr Willm Trevnwth of Trenwth hath licensyd us the prisheners of Ste yees to fetche upon his land att pripter iij or iiij boetes ladings of stones for the makin of anew penthouse or lenatt aganst the churche wall. Wittnes of henry hickes and John steven henry vune.

['Pripter'=Baripter, or rather Porthripter, a cove south-east of Porthminster.]

[1602.]

James olcoke [Woolcock] portrefe Resevede of the parishe is moneys the some of . . . .

Itm̄ paide the carnasyon Daye to the Ringers vjs viijd

Itm̄ paide whin we weare Ratynge of the sobesedye iijs

Itm̄ paide whin we weare Restede by willm otes xxd

Itm̄ paid whin we did appeare the firste korte ijs

Itm̄ paide when we weare Ratynge of the sopsedye iijs vjd

[No refuse to be deposited above high-water mark. A meeting of all the burgesses called for the 6th of next November :—]

. . . . . ano 1602

James Wolcocke portreeve of this towne and parishe, assemblinge the xij of the same towne and pishe and moste of the xxiiij, by ther mutual agreemt doe order and adiudge that what pson or psons soever shall ꝑmytt and suffer his worcke folcke to carrye or putt Garboyle or gutts or other noysom thinge above full sea marcke shall paye and forfeyte unto the townes behalf vs of good and lawfull monye of England, to be taken and distrayned of ther goods and cattalls.

And also ther order was taken by the said portreeve and his brethren that the said portreeve and the xij and xxiiij shall all holelye meete at the markett house on Saterdaye the sixthe daye of November nexte, by xij of the clocke, at hie noone to confer of other matters concerninge the good estate and welfare of this towne, and who then shall be absent excepte he be in her maties service, or sicke, or have som urgent occasyon to the contrarye, shall likewies paye and forfeyte vs to be levyed as before sd

James wolcocke	sign. Johis James
John cockyns	John Ryche
Thomas hyxte	Richarde candrowe
Tho: william	Thomas James
John steven	

[Any chief burgess presuming to order public affairs independently of his brethren, shall be dismissed from office :—]

27° die Decembris A° Rñi dñe Eliz' xlv [1603].

The xij and xxiiij of this towne and pishe do thes daye order agree and establishe, that ife at any tyme hereafter, anyone of the xij or xxiiij do by himselfe or by or wth any other directlye or Indirectelye procure, abett or counsell, in any manner of wies, or by any meanes, to the preiudice, hurte or hinderaunce of any the Immunityes, freedoms, franchesies or liberties of this towne, or will seeme to swaye and Rule, decree and make lawes, of himselfe, and after his owne private mynde and will wth oute the full and psent assent of other the xij and 24^or as hath in former tymes and ages bene accustomed, agreable to her Maties lawes, such psons, either of the 12 or 24, wth ther confederats, to be exempted, excluded and set oute of the number of the 12 and 24, and others of better knowledge, for reformacon, and better govermn^t in ther roomes, and places appoynted and placed.

W^ch 12 we do nomynate and agree uppon, to be, as follow^the

Richard Tregose gen	John James
Willm Trevnw^the gen	Henrye Hicks
Willm Ceelye gen	John Ryche
	Richard candrowe
John Tregenna gen	Thomas James
John Cockyns	Richarde Hicks
John Steven	Wm Pitt
Thomas Willm	Georgius Payne gen
John Hexte	Peter Jagowe gen
George Hicks	Willm Borthogge gen
Thomas Toman	Willm Hechins

The Accounte of John Ryche portheryve, by and after the deathe of James Wolcocke chosen porthryve at Michās 1592: and dyed nere aboute s^t Nicholas Tyde then Immediatelye followinge, & John Ryche supplyed the Rome vntill Michaellmas then followinge An° doi 1603.

[1603.]

P^d Jenken Trevingye the 18 of mche for pavem^te stones 1s. 6*d*.

Spente uppon Nicholas Bosithiowe & Thomas Brothers 24 of Marche in dryncke, for clensinge the ordynaunce 3*d*.

Pd a soldier of lalant that came owte of Ierland by the consente of the hole 12: 2s. 6d.

Pd Grace lewes [wife of Lewis Hurley vintner] the laste of marche for or capten & his mans dynner when he came to proclayme or king [James I.] . . . .

Pd Grace Hurlye for a pottle of Wyne at her house uppon pclaymynge and publishinge the pclamacion in prynte . . . .

payde then for paper to copye the pclamacion 1d.

pd to carrye a wanderer before Mr harrys 1s.

pd to one when we sente him awaye wth a passe 3d.

Pd sargeant Maior at mchasiewe greene assention daye 5s. 8d.

Pd for tymber to make a cradell for the towre 7s.

Pd John Pawle the 22 of June in pte of paymte for dressinge the towre 3li

pd captayne Jonson wch came owte of Ireld hurte 5s.

pd for two rapyers delived the maryners laste preste 6s. 8d.

pd for a soldiers apparell preste for this towne at mydsommer laste ws 12 monthes 4s. 8d.

d then for dryncke for them 6d.

pd danyell Sprigge for makinge the cuckinge stoole & all things therto belonginge 5s. 5d.

[The ducking-stool for the punishment of scolds]

pd danyell Sprigge for heddinge the drumbe 8s.

pd Jo: cowga for clensinge the parishe corsletts 1s.

[Regulations for prevention of the plague. No inhabitant may receive a stranger coming from an infected district. Persons arriving by sea at Saint Ives from an infected district, are to remain in their ships :—]

. . . . . Septembris [1603].

It is ordered and agreed by the porthreeve and the xij men and others of the better sorte, and the 24 of the said towne and pishe of St. Ies, That for the better prevencion of the plague, wch by the visitacion of almightye god extreamelye raigneth in this or Realme in divers citties, townes, placs and parishes (the lord of his greate mercye spedilye remove and staye it) and in regard divse persons aswell by sea as by land, may hereafter comynge from these places where the Sicknes and plague nowe is, maye by ther accesse and comy'g nye to or towne or pishe of St. Ies, endaunger or estats, and enthrall us in this mortalitye and sicknes, it is therefore ordred and agreed that if any pson or psons with in this towne or pishe shall hereafter in this prest tyme of sicknes lodge, entertayne or receyve into his house any such pson or psons comynge from such infected placs, such ptye or pson so offending, of or Inhabitants, shall paye and forfeyte xiijs iiijd to be levyed and taken of his goods and cattalls, and if any such

Inhabitante chaunce by such his or her entertaynmente to bringe the said sicknes into their housen, ther doares ar to be nayled up, and to be barred from cofnon societye

Also it is farther agreed and ordred, that if any person or persons shall happen to aryve whin or port or Kaye of St. Ies, cofnynge from such placs of sickenes, whin this tyme of daunger of the same, such person or psons so aryvinge, uppon examynacon found of ther directe comynge from such place of sicknes, shall be by the porthreve for the tyme being and such as he shall associate unto himself Entreate such pson or psons so aryving into o[r] said porte or Kaye to staye whin shippe, bark, Boate or vessell wherin he sayled, and if he refuse to staye and remayne therin wth his companye, he shall be enforced herunto, and contynuinge his contumacye herin shall be caryed before o[r] Kings Ma[ties] Justis of the Peace, to be reformed and punnished accordinge to the lawes, and such pson or psons whin o[r] towne or pishe receyvinge them into his or her housen as ther guest, shall forfeyt and paye as before xiij[s] iiij[d] and be debarred as before of comon societye.

Provided nevertheles, that such pson or psons so aryvinge and remayninge in ther vessels by the order abovesaid shall have broughte them what they shall need or wante, that o[r] towne or pishe shall yeld for the supplyinge ther necessities, by the order of the sd. Porth Reve and his brethren.

[Fine for importing beer into the port :—]

It is also agreed and ordered that such person or persons whin o[r] towne as shall hereafter buy, to sell agayne by waye of retayle any barrell of Bristowe beere or any other Beere, brought into o[r] towne, by any manner of shippinge, from and after this o[r] present order, consideringe that o[r] Beere and Ale made whin o[r] towne is by cofnon experience found as good and healthfull to mens Bodyes, and rather more, That such person or psons so buyinge the said Brisowe or other bere, broughte here by shippinge, to be uttred and sold agayne, shall forfeyte and paye ij[s] for eüye Barrell of Beere or pte of such barell, fyrken, or smale quantitye of such beere whatsoeu', by any colorable means whatsoeu' after this notyce and knowledge to them therof given: wch sayde fyne Peanaltye and forfeyture shalbe duelye collected, and accounted for and employed to the use of the poore, of this o[r] towne and pishe

[In the margin is this entry :—]

2º Oct[r] 1603. Thos whyte, for 3 barles of Glocester Beere in mia[r] for the firste offence 18*d*.

[1604-5.]

Paymťs Pd Jo: Stephen for counsell taken in the graunte of the mkett house 5s.

Pd a messenger who carryed a ťre [letter] to London 1s.

paide to John Nance for wyne uppon Mr chiverton 8*d*.

paide Lews hurlie for a pottell of wyne upon mr pker 1s. 4*d*.

paid unto Mr hals men for the maymed souldiours and for their chargis iijs or els they wold have had a barrell of herringe of John stevins if I wold not have paide them iijs more 11s.

Ite' paide John Rawe for stoppinge the holls in the churche wals 6*d*.

paide to a poore souldier that came from Irelande 3*d*.

paide Another soldier that came from Irelande 3*d*.

paide Thomas William for vjc of latte nailes for the churche 1s.

paide to Roger tackaburde to goe to helston 6*d*.

paide to John stevin & mr borthoga to goe to trero 4s.

paide to william launder for goinge to London 4s.

Pd for the copye of marchasiewe charter 1s.

Pd also to Richarde Hockins one of the churche wardens, in full paymte of his demaund, beside he is to take up, for 3 graves to himselfe 13s. 4*d*.—10s. 6*d*.

Pd also unto Wm the goldsmithe, in pte of his wags for kepinge the leds, att michaellms qrter 1s. 9*d*.

Pd unto captn duffild in expence uppon Mr Ed duffild, by the better sorte of the parrishe 5s.

Itm Receved from the king and quene [of the Summer Games] 22s

Itm Receued of harrye sterie for landing of adam Apell 3s 4d

Itm receued of Thomas worte for landing of apell 3s 4d

Receyved of Bersaba hicks besides 10s. pd to George Webber and Saundrye Pencaste for a hogsett of smale wyne given to the parrishe 1li

---

Paymts Paide Mr Praed for a replevyn when Mr Tregosse distrayned a quarter of beiffe from Trevascus 6*d*.

Paid danyell Sprigge to amend the drom 6*d*.

Pd for the Kings Armes in the churche 16s. 4*d*.

Pd catheryn Hake lyinge in the markett house longe sicke 1s. 3*d*.

Pd Mr Praed by commandmte of the Justics to a muster maister one capt: Billings paymte 16s.

Pd for a Poste for the compas in the Iland 4*d*.

Item p^d^ in expence at o^r^ burgeis goinge to London *7d.*
Item p^d^ a messenger for bringinge a L're from o^r^ burgeis *6d.*
Item Bestowed one counsellor Mitchell in monye & Wyne *6s. 10d.*

[1606-7.]

Thomas Willm chosen portrive the 5 of October 1606.
P^d^ Hughe Murfill for kepinge cleane the armor of the pishe . . . .
The Kaye Wardens vzt Teage Jerman and Tho: Kittowe broughte in accounte of 5^li^ *2s. 10d.* they crave allowaunce of 2^li^ *4s.* p^d^ owte aboute the kaye. Remaynes 2^li^ *18s. 10d.* and a bz [barrel] of Salte to be p^d^ by W^m^ hechins. Afterwardes they crave allowaunce as p^d^ George Hicks for lendinge a windles *8d.* And to Henrye Hicks for a hammer a Shever & blocke *6d.* and yett remaynes 2^li^ *17s. 8d.* And yett they take allowaunce of *15d.* wherof the frenchmen deceyved them in frenche monye. rem. 2^li^ *16s. 5d.*

[1608.]

Item p^d^ Perro & Parkin for amendinge the cliffe by my house *2s.*
Item p^d^ for tymber to binde the worke from slydinge *3s.*
Remaynes due to the Portryve *3s. 1d.* wch he acknowledgeth to have receyved in the receyts for the white lyminge the churche *2s. 6d.* more than he paid in.

the 24^the^ of October 1608.

Willm ceelye gen chosen porthryve
Note also ther was charged by Bande [bond] wherein Jo: cokyns & Richarde candrowe were bounde to Jo: Steven aboute Midsommer laste 1607, 24^li^ beinge for m^r^ Masters dett more due to Ric candrowe for the loste of cattall, taken by Jo: Steven p' execucon for masters dett beinge his suertye 9^li^
Payments: Inprimis p^d^ unto m^r^ Tho: Trigges vicar of Gwinnyer for his dynner and for his frindes, wth ther wyne, when he gave us a Sermon grats *4s.*
Item more at his nexte Sermon, for his paynes & dynner *6s. 6d.*.
Item p^d^ Mr Jeffryes & his frindes for ther dynner & wine at a sermon tyme when he preached here *3s. 6d.*
Item p^d^ for the cariadge of the Bell to Gulvall *5s.*
Item p^d^ ffoxe the Apparitor for the discharge of the churchwardens uppon breache of a Canon *2s.*

[They must have had a terrible blowing up!]

Item pd the Bell casters in p̄te of ther labors for castinge the Middle Bell 1li 5*s.* 10*d.*

Item pd an old debet left to paye when Jo: Steven & George Hicks went owte of the constableshipp, for the countye stocke & maymed souldiers 16*s.* 3*d.* & the K. pvisn̄ 4*s.*; to the drommer & the clarck of the bañd at 2 tymes 3*s.* & other paymts in 2 yeres exd

[1612.]

William Pett is chosen Porttriffe in the year 1612 at megelmas by the consent of the her vnder written

Mr William Ceelie	Richard Candrowe
Mr John heckes	Joell hekes
John stevins	Edward Player
George heckes	John barbor
Hendri heckes	hendri bayllefe
William hechins	Thomas watti
Richard Petter	

Willm Borthogge gēn chosen porthryve [1613.] Pd Jo: Sprigge the fee agreed to be paide him heretofore wch was not pd in this 2 yeres paste but this yeere was 4*s.*

of the abovesaide som the said Porth Ryve pd Jo: Stephen the couste to wardes the paymte of the countye stocks & maymed souldiers the laste yere 1li 15*s.* 11*d.*

pd for candles the Kings Ringinge daye 6d

pd when a messenger came wth my L: of Pembroks tre 9*d.* [Lord Pembroke's letter.]

Spent wt̄h consent of the 12 when the towne burges was chosen for & for waxe 3s 9d

---

xxiijo die Octobris anno 1613.

John Barbar Kaye warden, his accounte.

Pd Henrye Bailye for ffyve poles for the kaye . . . .

pd ij laborers for caryinge up of Stones iij . . . .

1613-4.

pd for trusses of ffurces aboute the kaye iij . . . .

pd for cleeringe the sand from the posses xijd

pd Henrye Hickes for his wages 12*d.*, for skikes 12*d.*—ij*s.*

Summa . . . .

and the said John Barber paid in Readye monye iiijli

Summa . . . .

So Mr Borthogge (as appereth) hath Receyved in all xli and is allowed of iijli iiijs: so he is to paye Henrye Hicks the 23the of october 1614 chosen port Ryfe vij[li] who then and ther paide the clarcke

so Remaynes vij[li]

and paide the Nowe porthreeve in the towne hale iiij[li]
and M[r] Borthogge yett oweth to be paide lviij[s]
and the porthryve by the consent of the 12 paid the poore Sexton xij[d]

8° Jan: 1614. Noia xij[cem] cum preposito predco hoc a° Prepositus: Henric[s] Hickes.

Richard Tregosse esqr'
Thomas Trevnwthe de Trevnw[the] esq'
Willms celye gen
Johes Hexte gen
Johes Stevens
Thom[s] Trevnw[the] of Trevalgan gen
George Hicks
George Willm[s]
Willm Borthogge gen
Will[m] huchins
Richard Anne.
Thom[s] Purefoye
John Ryche
W[m] Pitt
James Stearye
Lewes Hurlye.

[1614.]

The Porthrive and the greateste number of the xij above written, wth the goode lykinge of M[r] Pestle our vicar, do agree and give ther consent that the above named M[r] Celye shall have, sitt in and enioye, aswell by himself, his familye and frindes, a fitt and necessarye place to make either pewe or pewes in the sowthe parte of the middle chauncell, where the organs be, so as the said Will[m] [Celye] at his owne coste shall buylde and make up the same.

[1615.]

[From the following note it would appear that in 1615 the Vicar and the Portrieve were allowed to choose the chief councilmen :—]

The names of the xij newlye chosen viz 21 Maij 1615: wth the free and full consent of the most cheifeste Inhabitants then and ther present, who referred the choice of them to the Election and chosing of M[r] Nicodem[s] Pestle o[r] vicar, and Henrye Hicks o[r] present portryve.

[Then follow the names of those appointed.]

At w[ch] meetinge, and after such choice had and made it was then and ther ordered, that if uppon euye laufull sumonaunce or warninge made in the pishe churche or at ther houses by the portryve or his lauful depute for the xij and xxiiij to repayre to the towne hale, for the doinge the Kings service or other townes busynes, who then of the xij shall make defaulte or departe from the towne hale, withowte lawful dimission or iuste excuse of the portryve shall be distrayned and the fyne of iij[s] iiij[d] shall be levied uppon them & either of them for any the causes aforesaid, and any of the 24 for ther like or either such ther defaulte shall be distrayned & xij^d shall be levied of such of them making such defaulte. And it is also ordered that if the Port Ryve for the tyme being shall not levye by himself or his lawfull Deputye such fynes as shall so be due, by such defaulte aforsaid shall wthin xx^ti dayes after such defaulte shall likewies forfeyte vj^s viij^d to be levyed uppon him or his goodes, if he neglecte to collecte & levye the forsaid fynes, uppon such offendors as aforsaid.

[Then follow the signatures.]

John Maye of Bodmyn for 4^li 10*s*. to be p^d him & 12*d*. given him in earnest to New caste o^r bigger Bell: and the townes men to J. . . . molte the Meetall and drye the molde: and uppon this . . . . also newe bolte the middle Bell, taking 10*d*. for ech poundes waighte more then o^r Bell will yelde.

Item p^d for strikinge downe the Bell and hanginge up the same xviij^d

Item p^d the Bell founder when the bargaine was concluded xij^d

Item p^d a captaine for respite of poste horses who came to serche for pirates v^s

Item p^d for drawinge a petition vj^d to Sr Josephe killigrewe for easinge the porte farme and to carrye a ĺre to Mousehole vj^d & to carrye the peticion vj^d to Godolphin xviij^d

More he p^d unto Willm Hechins and Humfrye Anderdon the churchwardens when they concluded and bargayned wth the bell founders for casting the leds of o^r churche xxviij^s

More p^d Mr Paynter the constable for attendaunce aboute the Spanyards by direction of Mr Tregosse & other the chiefe of o^r towne x^s

[Then follows a note of charges :]

P^d owte by Jo: Barber aboute the chaple at the end of the kaye.

[1616.]

[charges for masons' work. The top is worn away :—]

Item paid for vj trusses of furs to burne the worke . . . .

Item paid for a Seaue [sieve] to sifte the lyme . . . .

Item paid Richard Jermon for castinge the sand from the church hay wall and for caryinge the Scaffold tymber ix^d

[At this time the day for the election of the Mayor and Burgesses was the Sunday after Saint Luke's Day, as appears from the following Memorandum. The date was in 1620 shifted to the 1st November :—]

Md' that it was gen̄allye mencioned that the sondaye after S^ct Luke is daye is the daye of election of the Porthrife, wch this yeere was the xx^the of October 1616 wch verye daye was the Porthryfe newe chosen by the moste parte of the xxiiij vzt Thom^s Purfoye.

James Stearye porthrife the laste yere yeldeth in his accounte as followethe: He Receyved xl^s vj^d as appereth in the other Margent.

P^d 3 dartmoth men who loste their ship xij^d

P^d for gravell sett at Treloyhan 18 feby xviij^d

P^d Tho: Poole the xth of Aprill laste for counsell fees for removing Mr Hals is children v^s

P^d Thoms the Welshman for carying poste tres 8 Julij . . . .

P^d for amending the drom 3° Oct^s 1616.

More James Stearye rec^d of Henrye Shapland and Eliz' Taylor lorde & ladye att the Sommer games x^s wherof p^d Henry Shapland to helpe make a maye pole—unto a la . . . . & viij^s to pay sergeaunte maior

[In an account for work done to the quay occurs this :—]

Item for 2 mawnds [shallow baskets] to carrye awaye the gravell xv^d

[1617.]

P^d for making the cover of comunion cup more then Trewyke p^d 5*s*.

P^d to two poore Grecians 4*s*.

P^d for a beame for the pillorye 3*s*. 4*d*.

P^d the organiste 5*s*.

P^d to George Hicks for cleering the posts for the mooringe the shipping 4*s*.

more for pitching downe a poste 4*d*.

[1618.]

P^d daniell Sprig for amending the drom 1*s*.

P^d Ed: Player for amendinge the towne chest 2*s*. 6*d*.

P^d the sexton for 3 weks work ab^t the organs 9*s*.

P^d Ed: Player for nayles & spyks for ye organs 1*s*. 4*d*.

P^d unto Mr Alex^r Harrye the preacher 1*s*.

P^d unto Mr Phippen when he preached 5*s*.

P^d for the marshalls fee to carrye awaye Rogs 1*s*.

P^d towardes the amending of ye organs more then I Rec^d 1^{li} 1*s*. 10*d*.

John Sprigge chosen portryve xxv^o Octob: 1618 contracted wth John Barber to be Warden of ye kaye for this nexte yeere for the rent of iiij^{li} x^s: & if at the yeres ende he uppon his creditt confydentlye do affyrme that he be no gayner he shall satisfye but the 4^{li}

[1619.]

P[d] M[r] Harris the preacher for 2 sermons by order of the xij in Maye 6*s*.

P[d] for hedding the drom & strapping thesame another tyme 4*s*. 6*d*.

P[d] M[r] Morcumbe a preacher 10*s*. & M[r] Harris a nother preacher 6*s*. 8*d*.—16*s*. 8*d*.

Item my Hire this yere for two yeres agreed by the xij men 8*s*.

Primo die Novembris Anno r̄ni dōī nr̄i Jacobi Dei grā regis nunc Angl &c xvij[o] et Scotie liij[o] 1619.

Att this tyme of Meeting, W[m] Trevnw[the] gent the Sondaye sennighte laste paste beinge chosen Porthreve, and John Barber the laste yere kaye warden not cōminge to the towne hale to passe his accounte & nowe this daye at this newe meting the said Jo: Barber came not to the hale but sent x[s] in monye & a note of xvj[s] laid foorth tow[ds] the repayringe the chaple by the kaye, and the viewe and wardenship of thesaid kaye is graunted over to Richard Lynten for v[li] v[s] his yere to begyn from on Sondaye laste was sennighte & so Jo: Barber to be Accounteable for the laste weke to the warden nowe of all profitts receyved.

And it is agreed for all ships & Barcks hencfforth taking Sandes for Ballaste ther Ship or Barcke to paye w[ch] hath a Top ij[s], the barcke w[ch] hath no 3*d*. all straungers w[ch] laye ther hogsetts of fishe or lyme on the peere or kaye to paye for ech tonne ij[d]: no boats to be ther laid wth owte composicion wth the kay warden; All yrishmen landing hencfforth ther loades or Burden of tymber ij[s] ij[d] & ballaste of Sand to be taken at this charge if they liste to take it: And all such Bullocks as ar from owte of yreland here landed to paye for ech bullocke 1*d*. & for ech hors or mare excepte it be one or 2 for private Ryding ij[d]: And no garbage or shels or swepage to be Emted w[thin] the kaye uppon payne of xx[s]: & none w̄thout the kaye uppon payne of x[s] all ballaste of Stones here to be Landed to belonge to the kaye warden.

Richard Amyt. [?] Willm̄ Trevnw[th]. John Steuen. George Hicks. John Ryche. Henry Hicks. John Sprigge.

A rate made the 7 of Maye 1620: for the king's Mat[ies] seruice.

Richard Tregosse 1*s*. 6*d*.
Katheryn Olver 2*d*.
Thom[s] Trerye 2*d*.
Jane Bosseithiowe 2*d*.
Thom[s] Wattie 1*d*.
M[ris] Carlian 1*d*.
Widowe Player 4*d*.
John Thom[s] 1*d*.
Henrye Treweke 1*d*.
George Will[ms] 6*d*.

Ric: Rosemanew[a] 4*d*.
Tho: Benn[t] 2*d*.
M[r] Wm[m] Pytt 9*d*.
M[r] Peers 6*d*.
Martin Bishop 6*d*.
John Gregor 2*d*.
Ric̃ Hockin 3*d*.
Thom[s] Steven 5*d*.
John Steven Jun[r] 2*d*.
M[r] Purifye 1*s*.
W[m] Hechins 6*d*.
M[ris] Lo: Trenw[the] 6*d*.
W[m] Hicks 4*d*.
Jo: Goodale 1*s*.
M[ris] Payne 10*d*.
Ric̃ Goulde 6*d*.
Ste: Barber Juñ 6*d*.
John cockin 8*d*.
Tho: Dayowe 3*d*.
W[m] yolcom̃ 1*d*.
M[r] Anne 1*s*.
Walter knighte 2*d*.
James ffabi[s] 2*d*.
Jo: Nance molkin 1*d*.

John cosen 6*d*.
John Hicks 4*d*.
chesten hockin 4*d*.
Jo: Hockin 3*d*.
M[ris] Harlye 1*s*.
M[ris] Campye 6*d*.
H. hicks constable
St: Luke 4*d*.
Ja: Barber 2*d*.
Jewell Hicks 1*d*.
Thom[s] Toman 6*d*.
marger[t] Toman 6*d*.
John Ryche 9*d*.
Eliz[9] candrowe 3*d*.
Robt foster 3*d*.
Widowe trengoth 1*d*.
Phillip Luke 4*d*.
Ric̃ Lynterne 4*d*.
W[m] cosen 2*d*.
Ric̃ Tregeowe 4*d*.
Jo: Stearye 9*d*.
Daniell Sprigge 3*d*.
M[r] caple 1*d*.

streete Anpoll:

Mr Borthogge 8*d*.
Eliz' Sies 1*d*.
Kate Goodmã 3*d*.
Humfrye Jorye 1*d*.
Agnes Geles 3*d*.
digorye Treweke 2*d*.

Thom[s] Roswall 3*d*.
Chesten Nicãs 1*s*.
Eliz' Thom̃s 2*d*.
Henrye Thom̃s 2*d*.
Johñ Trerye 2*d*.
Henrye James 2*d*.

Westren streete:

Wm Lannton 7*d*.
Jo: Browne constable
James Stearye 8*d*.
Henrye Shapland 2*d*.
John Antonye 1*d*.
M[r] celye 2*s*. 6*d*.

Mr Trewynnard 6*d*.
Wm Thom[s] ye dier 6*d*.
M[r] Jo: Stephen 1*s*. 8*d*.
George Webber 3*d*.
Jane Hicks widowe 1*s*.

streete Angarowe:

Giles Hawke 2*d*.
Richard marten 3*d*.
John R . . . .
W[m] Steven 3*d*.

Phillip Parkin 4*d*.
M[ris] Paynter 2*d*.
Nic̃ Angove 1*d*.

streete towards Are:

Richard Peter 3*d*.
M[ris] Jausling 3*d*.

M[r] Tho: Peers Juñ 3*d*.

The Iland:

Mr Rattenburye 8*d*.
Henrye Bailye 6*d*.
Wm Nance 2*d*.
Tho: Syes 6*d*.
John Kyttowe 2*d*.
John Opye 2*d*.
Jo: Tomā 2*d*.
Jo: Lawnder 3*d*.
Wido Stearye 2*d*.
Ric Tregthen 2*d*.
Tho: Barber 2*d*.
Jo: Keiste 3*d*.
Henrye Tregerthen Jun
Nic Cote 2*d*.
Jo: Lukas 2*d*.
Ric cornwall 1*d*.
Lews Hendra 1*d*.

The Lande:

Thoms who is goodales tenāt 1*d*.
ffrauncs Walker 3*d*.
Mr Hexte 1*s*. 3*d*.
James Philps 4*d*.
Jo: cocke 7*d*.
Timothye Maior 9*d*.
Thoms Trenwthe esqr 2*s*. 8*d*.
Wm Thoms gen & his son 1*s*. 8*d*.
Wm Browne 4*d*.
Wm Davye 4*d*.
Jo: Richard 1*d*.
Tho: Willm 1*d*.
Tho: Braye 6*d*.
Mris Dynham 4*d*.
Lews Rundell 3*d*.
Jo: Bennt 2*d*.
Thoms Nole 3*d*.
Thoms Nole Junr 6*d*.
Tho: Kubert & his son 5*d*.
Wm Bawden 4*d*.
Tho: Berymā 3*d*.
Nic Roswll 1*d*.
Peter harrye 1*d*.
Ric Steven 1*d*.
Nic Allā 2*d*.
Jo: kellihellā 1*d*.
Jo: Sprig 10*d*.
Mic Nolle 3*d*.
Jo: gregor 1*d*.
Jo: Dacey 1*d*.
Mr P . . . .
Ric Pe . . . .

dice——

Marye . . . .
Justi . . . .
chier . . . .
carne . . . .
G. Roswall . . . .
{ a close in helles veor

Sum̄ totalis 2li 17*s*.

xijo die Octobris Anno Rni dōi nri Jacobi dei grā Rege nunc Angl &c xviijo et Scotie liiijo Anno dōi 1620: Mr William Trevnwthe laste yeres porthryve gives in this Accounte

Inprimis receyved by a rate for suppressing the Turcks xli xixs ijd
Wherof payde as hereafter shall appere xli xixs vjd So mr porthrive muste have due to him iiijd

Item recd by him as to the pilchards busynes iijli 3*d*.

Wherof he delivēd mr John Payne to paye mr German Shapcotte ijli xiijs iiijd

[German Shapcotte was a barrister often employed in legal proceedings on behalf of the Borough. His was a Cornish branch of a family originally seated in Devonshire. The author possesses an armorial seal which probably belonged to German Shapcotte. It is of silver, small and oval; the arms, on a rounded Spanish shield, are three dovecotes, one over two; crest, on a knight's helmet (with mantlings) a dovecote as in the arms, flanked by a vol extended. On the shield appear the initials G. N. S., two over one. The second letter most likely stands for the wife's Christian name.]

To the Bellman for Ryngingе this yere iiij^{s}
P^{d} him that broughte the letter aboute the fishing xij^{d}
P^{d} for amending the Drom ij^{s} vj^{d}

[The following note shows the time at which the election day was first shifted from the Sunday after Saint Luke's day to a fixed day early in November.]

Mdm̄ that by an auntient vsage & custom on the Sondaye nexte after St Luke is daye yerlye the porthryfe is chosen & by reason the greateste Number of the xij & xxiiij were the daye of this election absent, the firste daye of November 1620 they have chosen Henrye Hickes porthryfe

P^{d} Sergeant maior is paye 10*s*.
P^{d} Mr Howell by the appoyntm^{te} of the moste of the 12 for the lawe sutes broughte againste m^{r} Trevnw^{the} & others by Mr Tho: Ceelye 10*s*.
P^{d} also vnto John Sprigge for his travayle unto thassizes aboute thesame busynes 8*s*.
P^{d} the Sexton for ringinge from alhollentyde to candlemas 4s.
Spente also one whole nighte in the pi̅shes busynes when Mr Rosecarrocke was here 2*s*.
Spente also when I was att Helston uppon m^{r} Harrys xij^{d} & for Lone of a horse 12*d*.—2s.
also p^{d} a messenger to seke a horse late att nighte 6^{d}
Also I p^{d} for a pynte of Secke when o^{r} burgesse Mr Harrys was chosen 6*d*.
p^{d} m^{r} Howell by the appoyntm^{ts} of the 12 abowte the parishes busynes & trobles of m^{r} celye vz̄t 10*s*. 6*d*. & 30*s*. after, in all xl^{s} vj^{d}
p^{d} for bringinge home the greate beame for [*lege* from] poripp^{r} ij^{s} vj^{d}

[*I.e.* a piece of wreckage brought from Porthripter for the repair of the quay.]

p^{d} for saving up the Kaye that was broken awaye vj^{d}

[1622.]

Item rec̄d of m^{r} Willm ceelye of his rate towardes the flete againste the turcks xiiij^{s}
Item rec^{d} of Mr Trevnw^{the} of Trevalgan in pte' of 10*s*. w̄ch he craved to be respited for the clarcks wags v^{s}
Paym^{te} Inprimis paide m^{r} John Trewynnard in & towardes the paym^{te} to m^{r} ffownes late mayor of Plymothe towardes the chargs he & m^{r} Thomas ceelye charged the pishe for the fleete made owte against the turcks 3^{li}
P^{d} also unto John Stephen for monye borowed for the pi̅shes use to the ppose aforesaide lix^{s} vj^{d}
Item p^{d} a Lawe countrye souldier vj^{d}

It is agreed by genall consent, that hencfforth no owner of Boats or netts shall dryve or sett ther Netts, or owner of Seanes rowe to Steame, the Sondaye nighte, or any tyme before daye of that nighte; who shall herein transgresse, ech owner shall paye for his defaulte x^s^ & ech fisherman iij^s^ iiij^d^ to be levyed of ther goodes to the use of the pishe

John Cockins

John Sterie
William Burthogge
Thomas Purefey
George hickes
W^m^ hechins
John Ryche
henry hicks
James sterry
John Sprigge
Richard Tregeowe

Primo die Novembris a^o^ dōī 1623 Anno rni dōī nri Jacobi regis nunc Angl' &c xxj^mo^ the choice daye beinge deferred untill then wch should have bene the Sondaye after St Luke is daye by reason of som̄ occasyons, was chosen portryfe John Ryche.

J: more payd John Stearye for so much due for a drum due unto him uppon accounte beinge Portreife the yere before 10s.

[1624.]

I: given to Irish Beggars att sundrie tymes 4s.

I: payd m^r^ Jo: Sprigge for his charge beinge Rater for the subsidie . . . .

I: payde for sendinge forth of a souldier 1^li^

I: for two bushells of salte due to the key 9s.

Primo die Novembris 1625 Anno Regni dni nri [Jacobi] charoli Dei grā Regis nūc Anglie &c Primo, the choyse daye beinge deferred untill then which shoulde have benn the Sundaye after S^tt^ Lukes Daye, by reason of some occations, was chosen Portrieve [John Stevens] Thomas Trevnwith gent

[The words printed within square brackets in the above paragraph have been struck out in the original. James I. died in 1625. It would seem that John Stevens refused to fill the office of Porthrieve this year.]

[Millers are not to work on the 'Sabbath:']

Secundo die ffebruarij 1626.

Whereas uppon consideracōn taken of the great abuse comitted by the Millards of our pishe in grindinge of corne uppon the Saboth Daye and carrienge of itt home, wee the

Porthreife and other the xij men of our Towne and pishe of S^tt Ives, for the takinge awaye of this greate abuse Have constituted that yf any Millard within the said Towne and pish shall henceforth grinde any corne uppon the saboth daye, or shall carrie to or from their Mills uppon the saboth daye, That for everie such offence he or they soe offendinge shall paye for everie such offence ij^s vj^d lawfull monie of Englande, to be taken and leavyed uppon their goodes or chattles by the wardens of the poore for the yere beinge, and by them an accompt to be given for the Imployment thereof to the use of the poore.

John Trewinnard Portreeve.
[&c.]

M^9 itt is agreed this present daye by the Portreive and xij men of the Towne and pishe of S^tt Ives, That yf any man hereafter doe refuse to execute the office of a Portreive beinge once chosen by the xxiiij men or the most of them of the same pishe, he that shall soe refuse shall paye to the Portreive that shall then next be chosen the summe of iij^li vj^s viij^d to be levyed by accon or by distrayninge of his or their goodes beasts and chattles.

Thomas trñweth.
[&c.]

[1626.]

I: to a preacher for 2 sermons 10*s.*

I: spent att Trewroe about busines for the Towne beinge the cald [then called] for the shipp by Letters from the councell table 1^li

I: spent att Bodmyn beinge cald about the pishe buisines 16*s.*

I: payd for a broaken barrowe 1*s.* 4*d.*

I: for the lont of 2 barrowes 4*d.*

[Tariff of harbour-dues for the port of Saint Ives, 1626:]

S^ct Ives ss: fforasmuch as itt is chaunced that our Peere or Kaye of St Ives is much decayed the postes wasted and the sandes much annoyeing aboute the porth and the houses and sellers adioyninge, for and towardes the repayringe and remedie whereof wee the Porthryve and moste parte of the xij and cheife inhabitants of the said Towne doe holde it and agree that:

For all English Barques which come with in our Peer for safgard or traffick are to paye to the Key yf without a topp 6*d.*

All Alients without a topp 1*s.*

All English men with one topp 9*d.*

All Alients with one topp 1*s.* 6*d.*

All English yf with two topps 1*s*.

All Alients for the like under 200 tonns 2*s*.

All shipps of greate burden above 200 tonns accordinge to Englishe accompts 2*s*.

All Alients for the like 4*s*.

All Englishe that ballast themselves with sande without a topp to pay for it 8*d*.

All Englishe for ballast of sande with one topp 1*s*. 4*d*.

All such as have two topps, for the like 2*s*.

All Alients Dubble that rate.

All boats, barques and shipps that shall take in ballast of stones within our Peor must buy itt of the wardens of the Key for the yere beinge, except they ffetch itt with their owne boates and companie.

All Townes men that roule ffishe on the Key or sande except for their owne accompt and ventred to sea are to paye as much as any stranger English except herring And all Englishe for roulinge on the sande to paye for the tonn j^{d}

All allients for roulinge on the sande to paye ꝑ tonn ij^{d}

All Englishe on the Key ij^{d}

All allients iiij^{d}

All Herrings to paye that shalbe laden out of our peor by an Englishe man ꝑ barrell j^{d}

By an Allient j^{d}

All beere that shallbe brought from any other place and not brued here, yf landed wheather by Townes man or stranger to paye for everie Kinter Kin to the Key j^{d}, barrell ij^{d}, hogshead iiij^{d}, pipe or butt viij^{d}

All Irishe men landinge their tymber here to paye 2*s*. 1*d*. and they may take in sande for ballast ffree

All bullocks or horses sett on shore out of Irelande to paye for everie bullocke j^{d}

For everie horse or Nagge ij^{d}

No Dead bullocke or horse to be left 24 houres on the sande in payne of three shillings ffower pence to be payd to the Key warden 3*s*. iiij^{d}

And noe garbadge of ffishe or stinkinge ffishe to be cast above full sea marke att neape tide on the sande, on payne of 3*s*. 4*d*. to be payde unto the Key wardens 3*s*. 4*d*.

No kinde of ballast of stones, hells or swepage to be landed within the Key on payne of 20*s*. and none without the Key head on payne of Tenn shillings.

All ballast of stones or otherwise here to be landed to be longe to the Key warden or his ffarmor.

And the bushelledge to be paide to the Key by all straungers Englishe and Alients as to the Lorde of the soyle ; Townsmen only to be ffree.

All ballast of stone shall be landed by the m^r or owner of the Barke or shipp that lande itt, above full sea Marke or on the Key where the Key warden shall appoint, att the cost of the m^r or owner of the said shippe or Barke and not given or soulde to any butt by the Keye warden.

Thomas trevnwith portreive.
George Hicks.
Thomas Purefey.
Jn: Payne.

Keywardens for this yere followinge 1626 and Anno 1627 are } m^r John Payne. and John Cossen.

xix^no Augusti 1627.

John Maye of Bodmyn for 8^li 15s. to be payd him with ffive shillings payd him in Earnest Doth pmise to cast a newe our bigger bell. And he is to ffinde tymber and all other things uppon his owne charge. And to make the same bell tunable to the eere and to contynue the same sounde for one whole yere. And he to stande to the overplus of Mettle that shall be added more then our Bell doth yelde.

sign
p^y Johe + Maye.

---

xxviij^o die Octobris 1627.

John Trewynnard Portreeve received of m^r John Payne for the defaults of such as went to take steame [stem] before daye contrarie to the orders uppon mondaye Morninge ij^s

---

[No driving-nets are to be shot before sunset in neap tides, nor before half-tide in spring tides :]

Primo die Novembris 1627.

ffor the better keepinge of good order in our trade of ffishinge on which the state of our Towne doth depende, Itt is ordered by the genall consent of the Portreeve xij and xxiiij men this present daye, That noe Boate henceforth that goeth a drivinge for herringe ffishinge shall shoote or sett their Nexts before sun sett duringe the neape Tydes. Also itt is further ordered That none of those boates or companie soe goeing a Driving shall in spring tydes shoote or sett their Netts before it be halfe tyde, for the better pfõrmance whereof itt is agreed that one of the Boates that goes soe a Driving shall carrie a candle with him and lighten itt when the tyme is ffitt to shutt the same Netts, that is att halfe Tyde as aforesaid (everie Boate takinge the Beerth before that tyme).

The Masters and companie of everie Boate that shall transgresse against any of the foresaid Orders and agreements shall (for everie such transgression & offence) paye unto the Portreeve for the use of the pishe Tenn shillings ffyne to be leavyed uppon his goods and chattles eyther by accon or waye of distresse.

And itt is also further agreed, That in shootinge of their netts att the ffirste beginning of night they shall not anoye one another by shooting a crosse one over or under another, Butt everie Boate to Keape his place of Birth. And everie one that makes default in this last article shall paye to the Portreeve for there defaults the sume of iij^s^ iiij^d^ to be leavyed for the use of the pishe as aforesaid.

John Browne } constables.	Thomas Purefey Portreife.
Thomas Noale }	Jo : Trewinnard.
John cosen.	John Ryche.
sign.	John Sterie.
Johis + cocke.	John Sprigge.
Edward Hammand.	Henry Hicks.
George Hicks.	Steuen Barbar.
Hector Taylor.	John Hicks.
Arthor wesscott.	

28° die Octobris 1627. Anno Doi charoli dei grā Regis nūc Anglie &c. tertio: the choyse daye beinge deferred till then (which should have benn the sundaye after Stt Lukes Daye) by reason of some occations; chosen Portreeve Thomas Purefey gent.

Mr John Trewynnard Portreefe for this yere 1627 and parte of the last yere 1626 yeldeth upp his account in manner and forme followinge :

his receipts :

from Mr John Paynter for the faults of his servants in shippinge their sayne boates before daye on the Sunday night *2s. 6d.*

I : from Henrie Baylie for his offence and ffive of his companie for drivinge or settinge netts on sundaye nighte before daye 15*s*.

Payments :

I : payd the Bedman for ringing the curfue Bell, 4*s*.

[This is the only notice we have of the curfew bell at Saint Ives. 'Bedman' = Bede-man, *i.e.* prayer-man, and is an old Saxon name for a church clerk or sexton.]

I : payd John Sterrie for Ridinge to Trewroe about the shipp, 6*s*.

[In 1629 occurs another bye-law to prevent burgesses from absenting themselves from the Town Hall after summons :]

It is ordered by the Porthreife, the xij and xxiiij^tie^ men abovesaid That whoe shall be absent from the Towne Hale after Summons given by the Porthreife or some other in his name and behalfe except absentinge Partie cann yeld a iust excuse of such his absence shall pay iij^s^ iiij^d^ and thoes of the 24 to paye ij^s^

[The burgesses will join in resisting the vicar's encroachments in the matter of tithes. This paragraph has been struck out :]

primo Die Maij 1629.

Itt is ordered by the Porthreife and xij men of the same pishe whose names are hereunder written and others, Doe give under their hands And will stande to the tryall of all matters of customes wch heretofore hath not bynn payd accordinge to custome by any pson or psons whosoever within the pishe aforesaid, in matter of Tythes due to the vicar ; And that they will be att the Joynt cost in defending the same custome or customes, or for any other customes within the said pish.

[The market-house is to be let out for a year or more, and the rent applied to defend three parishioners who are prosecuted by the vicar for nonpayment of tithes :].

Septimo Die Maij 1629.

By these presents, the Porthreife and others of the xij then present doe agree and order that whereas there is a suite of Lawe dependinge in the courte of the Archdeconarie of Cornewall betweene mr John South vicar there and Richard Hicks, Thomas Trerie and ffrauncis Walker for the tyth of Kyne and calves, wherein wee labour to Maintaine the auncient custome, to pay iiij^d^ for ech cow and ij^d^ for ech calfe under the number of ffower, wch alreadie amounted and will cost much monies for the defence thereof; wherefore for Raysinge of the meanes for satisfyeinge thereof and repayement of such monies as is alreadie disbursed wee agree that the Marketthouse when and assoone as itt shall fall into the Townes hande, shall be letten out to ffarme for one whole year or more yf neede shall soe require, to satisfie all such charge as aforesaid, for the better confirmacōn herof wee bynde our selves and ech of us to the Porthreife for the tyme beinge, to satisfie and pay to him or his Assignes the sum̃e of iij^{li} vj^{s} viij^{d} Sterlinge, yf he Rather refuse to ffirme to any such act.

John Sprigge porthreeve.
W. Ceely.
Rich : Hext.
Thomas Purefey.
J^{n} Payne.
John Ryche.

Henry Hicks.
Steuen Barbar.
John hicks jnr^{9}
Thomas syse.
Thomas Sprigge.

[The burgesses will resist the vicar's illegal claims for tithes :]

Vicesimo quinto die Maij : 1629 :

Whereas from the tyme (the contrarie whereof) in mans memorie hath not benn knowen, there hath benn, and is an auntient custome, used had and allowed aswell within the precincts of the Mother Church of Unie nere Lalant and the parrishes of S^{tt} Ives and Towednacke, chaples appendant to the saide Mother Church, That all such in habitants to the saide and dwellers within the saide severall parrishes, possessors and owners of Kyne within the saide parrishes under the number of ffower, Have ever benn accustomed and used to pay to the Incumbent and Vicar of the said Mother Church, for the tyme beinge: ffower pence yerelie for the tythe of ech cowe and two pence for ech calfe and not aboue, which auncient custome for our said parrish of S^{tt} Ives we whoes names are subscribed doe here promise to Mayntayne, and to Assiste by our payments, any of our said parrish whoe shall be cyted, sewed or prosequuted in Lawe, for any higher some or rate above the rate of ffower pence for the tythe of eche cowe, and two pence for tithe of eche calfe under the number aforesaid.

Rich : Hext, Port.
W. Ceely.
Thomas Purefey.
John Ryche.
John Sterie. John Sprigge.
James Steary.
Henry Hicks.
John Hicks.

Disbursm^{ts} Imprimis to Mr Hoyle for a serman preached by him 5*s*.

I. to Jo^{n} Plyer for 4 keys & mendinge the locks of the chest that holdes the charter 1*s*. 4*d*.

I. given to Irish mrchants that were taken wth the ffrench & came from London 1s.

I. more to m^r Symons for 4 sermons 10s.

I. to m^r Upcott for a sermon by him preached 5s.

I. to m^r Sherwoode for deliuinge of o^r peticōn to my lord Bishopp 5s.

I. to m^r Trewynnard when he went to exceter about the pishe buisines 17s. 6d.

I. deliued the constables to make puision for the companie of an Irishe barke that came from ffraunce havinge the sicknes abord her 3s. 4d.

I. for bread and drinke to the ffishermen that went abord her being shutt upp 8d.

The keyes of the pishe chest are deliued to Mr Jo^n Sprigge: m^r Richard Hext, m^r John Payne and m^r John Rich.

[In consequence of the scarcity of corn in Saturday's market, it is ordered that the sale of corn on other days of the week shall be subject to a similar toll as that paid on Saturday:]

Decimo Die Octobris 1630.

Whereas wee finde the price of corne is growen to a greate highte, and the Markett dayes are meanelie furnished with corne, for that on some dayes in the weeke diverse bushells of corne are brought to be solde and soe the toll lost, which is much offensive and preiudiciall to the publique weale of this Towne and place, wee order that yf any Inhabitant in any of the weeke dayes buy any corne or graine they give warninge to the farmers of the Markett for the tyme beinge the like accustomed toll as they use to pay in the Markett dayes, or take itt upp to the ffarmers use to be deliued them. And whoe soe shall doe to the contrarie and refuse to yeld or pay the said toll, shall for ech bushell soe bought in the weeke dayes (the said toll not beinge yelded and payd) shall be sued by the Porthreife for the tyme beinge and forfeit for ech bushell soe bought in the weeke dayes xij^d, and for each halfe bushell vj^d and for ech pecke . . . . . As also whoe shall forestale any goods beinge about to be brought to the Markett, as butter, cheese or any of the like comodite, shall forfeit and lost the goods soe to be seized, and the Inhabitant soe offendinge shall be Indited and punished accordinge to the Lawes of this Realme.

Thomas Trñwith.	Henry Hicks.
W^m hechins.	John Sterie.
John Sprigge porthreeve.	Steven Barbar.
Thomas Purefey.	John hicks.
John Ryche.	Jn. Payne Jnr

[No action at law is to be commenced against strangers at Saint Ives, without the assent of the Porthrieve :]

The 28th Day of November 1630.

Whereas there have bin sundrye complaints Made (by straungers) of our Towne, and that the place is by them reported to be a troublesome Towne, wch is a hinderaunce to our trade and trafficke with straungers by whome our place is releeved, and on the trade by sea wee wholye depande, And therefore we have thought good to take itt into our consideracōn to use the best meanes wee may to remove that scandall, and that hereafter wee may have the better reporte of straungers; Wee doe order all Inhabitants of our Towne and pish that doe intende any accōn against anie straunger, that shall come in by sea ffor what cause soever itt be, eyther of trespas or debt or elce, shall before he coīnence his suite or arrest the ptie, Acquaint the Porthreife or his depute in his absence therewith And the Porthreife or his depute will after he understands the Equitie of the cause use meanes for endinge itt, Or Grant Leave to psente; wch yf the Portreife will refuse to doe, whereby the ptie may escape and the other be dampnified, itt shall be lawfull after he be acquainted herewith to psente yf his cause be just. Otherwise yf any of our Towne or pishe shall arrest any straunger soe comming by sea without given the Porthreife knowledge thereof, shall fforfeit for his contempt in that behalfe to be leavyed upon him by accōn or distresse to the use of the poore the sume of tenn shillings for the ffirst offence and for the second the sume of Twentie shillings. To wch order we all agree [as] wittnes our hands.

The keyes of the chest are with Mr Porthreefe, Mr Hext, Mr Henrie Hicks and Mr Thomas Stevens.	Jn : Payne Jnr Rich : Hext. Thomas Purefey. John Sprigge. henry hechins. John hicks jnr

[No fishing for herrings, except by driving, before next All Saints Day :]

Decimo octavo Die Octobris 1631.

It is ordered and agreed by the Porthreife and the rest of his brethren this present day, That noe owner of boates or nets for herringe ffishinge shall sett their netts for the takinge of herrings before the ffeast of All Saints next ensewing but yf they drive with their netts before they may according to the auntient custome. And whoe soever shall offend herein shall pay for his offence (vizt) everie owner tenn shillings and everie one of the companie three shillings and ffower pence to be payd to the Porthreife for and to the use of the Towne and pishe.

Jn : Payne. John Sterie.
Thomas Purefey. John hicks.
Rich : Hext. Edward Hammond.

Primo Die Novembris 1631.

In the Seaventh yere of the Raigne of our souaigne Charles by the grace of god of Englande Scotlande ffraunce and Irelande K : defender of the ffayth m^r^ Henrie Hicks was chosen Porthreife for the yere followinge.

An account of the said Porthreife, for all receipts & disbursements for one whole yere.

Disbursements by him as followeth :
I. to the Bedman for Ringinge 6*s*.
I. for dryncke for the Ringers the 5th of November 3*s*. 6*d*.
I. given by him att Godolphin att Christmas 5*s*.
I. to a poore Northfolke man bounde for Ireland 6*d*.
I. more for a Pynte of sacke 6*d*.
I. spent upon m^r^ Mitch when he preached 1*s*. 4*d*.
I. to a poore man beinge brought captive 6*d*.
I. payd for mendinge the Organs 8^li^
more spent att Hammands when the bargayne was made 5*s*.
I. payd the Organist towards his wages £4 10*s*. 0*d*.
I. payd mylord Bishopps clarke for writinge a letter to m^r^ Currie 5*s*.

1633. William Hechins, Porthrieve.

Itt is agreed by the generall consent of the Porthreife and xij of our Towne, That there shall a Measurer be appointed by the key wardens to measure all salt and other graines as shall be here after sold by Alliants [aliens, foreigners] or any other within the Port of S^tt^ Ives aforesaid.

Wm Hechins portrife. Jñ Payne Jñr.
Rich Hext. John Sprigge.

Anno Doi 1634.

Collected by Jo^n^ the sonn of Henrie Stephens and Margerie the daughter of Edward Hamande be' chosen lord and ladie, the sume of xiiij^s^ and by them delũved to the overseers of the poore for this yere.

Primo die Novembris Anno doi 1635.

Being the day of Election for Porthreeve, James Praed gentleman is chosen Porthreeve, for the yere followinge.

[He declined the office, however, and Edward Hammond was appointed in his stead.]

[Another undertaking to defend those prosecuted for nonpayment of tithes :]

xxix^{no} die Junij 1636.

Whereas there is a suite depending in Lawe betwixt Thomas Corey vicar of Unie lelant and S^{tt} Ives upon tryall of a custome, upon paying unto the said vicar *4d.* a cowe and ij^{d} a calfe for soe manie of the inhabitants as doe milke three kyne or under, wee the Portreeve and other the inhabitants whose names are hereunder written doe pm̄ise to confirme any reasonable rate wch shall be made for to pay all such cost as shall be disbursed in tryall of the said suite.

Edward Hammand Portreeve.	Steven Barbar.
Thomas Purefey.	Thomas Sise.
Henry Hicks.	John hicks.
Charles [+] Steuens.	

[When fishing may begin ; new fishery bye-laws. The first paragraph is struck out.]

The xxijth of Julie 1638.

It is agreed by the generall consent of the Portreeve xij and xxiiij men and other cheefe inhabitants of the Towne of St Ives, That henceforth, That no owners of Boates or netts shall dryve or sett their Netts the Sunday night, nor rowe their Seanes to the steame before sunne risinge on monday morninge or any other day in the weeke untill such tyme as the Huwers be able to deserne ffish.

July xxijth 1638.

Whereas by our auncient custom wee finde itt Nott lawfull to take anie steames before daylight and that euery day, wee doe all agree that none shall goe and take steame on Munday morning untill the sunn rising except the Brush bee upp and that it shalbe lawfull euery other day of the weeke by day light and not keepe steames all night for such as goe away before day & take steame keepe their roape in steame all night shall haue Noe steame att all and shall pay *6s. 8d.* each offender. And the owner of the boate xxvj^{s} viij^{d} to bee leuied on the Boate and netts or other their goode, to the use of the poore.

		John Sterye portreeve.
Jn: Payne.	Rich: Hext.	Thomas Purefey.
Thomas Stevens.		Henry Hicks.
John Player.		John Hicks.
Arthour Wescott.		Edward Hammand.
Ephraim Sise.		John Sprigge.
George Hicks.		Lewes Hendra.
Thomas Goode.		Thomas Sise.

CHAPTER XIII.

SAINT IVES IN THE SEVENTEENTH CENTURY.

In the year 1639 the town of Saint Ives was made a municipality, with a mayor, recorder and town clerk, and a corporation consisting of twelve aldermen and twenty-four burgesses. The same charter which conferred this distinction upon it, confirmed all the privileges granted to the town by previous sovereigns. Thomas Stevens was the last person who held the ancient title of Portrieve of Saint Ives, that office being by this charter superseded by the dignity of mayor, in the person of Richard Hext.

In Charles I.'s charter it is further expressed that the borough and parish of Saint Ives should have a common seal, and that the mayor, senior burgesses and recorder should be justices of the peace, the former during his office and for a year thereafter. It is also provided that the town should have four fairs, viz., May 10, July 20, September 26 and December 3, and a day after each of them; also two markets, on Wednesdays and Saturdays. There was also to be a grammar-school for the instruction of youth, by a master and usher, of which the Bishop of Exeter and the mayor and aldermen for the time being were to be governors. The corporation pays a small fee-farm rent to the lord of the manor, and a small acknowledgment as high rent for the market-house. None of these fairs rose to importance, and Wednesday's market is discontinued. Sir Francis Bassett obtained this charter, with permission to hold magistrates' sessions every three months.

The oldest seal of the corporation now in existence is a round one, about two and a half inches in diameter. The centre is filled by a shield, charged with an ivy-branch overspreading the whole field, and around the edge of the seal is the legend: '*Sigillum Burgi St. Ives in Com: Cornub:* 1690.' The arms of Saint Ives are thus blazoned: Argent, an ivy branch overspreading the whole field, vert.

Davies Gilbert says this charter was forfeited in 1644.

Courtney says: 'The maces, which are of solid silver, were made in 1641, and bear the name of the first mayor of the borough. The seal bears on the back of it this inscription: "Ex dono Jacobi Praed de Trevethoe Armig:"'

We must now glance at matters of high national importance, which were beginning to engross all minds at Saint Ives, as elsewhere throughout the country. But first we will notice the title of a curious chapbook or pamphlet called, 'A True Relation of Certaine Passages which Captaine Bassett brought from the west parts of Cornwall, concerning some shippes which came from Bilbo in Spaine to goe to Ireland, but were driven into an Iland called Saint Ives by reason of tempestuous weather; 1642.' (See *Cornish Telegraph*, October 26, 1864.)

The conflict between King Charles I. and his Parliament excited nowhere more bitter partisanship than in Cornwall. The royal duchy was, in the main, like the other countries inhabited by the Celtic race, warmly attached to the principle of monarchy and to the person of the sovereign; and in the gentry and yeomanry of Cornwall the ill-fated Stuarts had supporters upon whose devotion they could always rely. Very few towns in the westernmost county declared for the Parliament, and, where they did, there was some abnormal condition of things to account for the exception to the rule.

One noteworthy exception is the case of the borough of Saint Ives, which supported the cause of the Commonwealth against the king. This seems to have been partly due to the severities exercised by Sir Richard Grenville upon those of the district who were suspected of being favourably disposed towards the Roundheads, and to his excessive exactions from the whole population of Saint Ives; but it was probably chiefly owing to the fact that the local leaders of opinion at that time happened to be of Puritan proclivities.

Thus Major Peter Ceely was a fierce Puritan and Roundhead, and had demolished the ancient chapel at the holy well of St. Madron; and William Ceely was one of the commissioners appointed, in 1644, to raise money for the maintenance of the Parliament army in Cornwall.

The Stevens family of the Tregarthen branch (later known as Stephens of Tregenna), who had been local supporters of the Reformation, at this time were Independents, and strongly in sympathy with the Revolution. The Sises, too, a wealthy merchant family, were Puritans and Parliament men. These leaders of opinion at Saint Ives lent all their weight to the cause of the new opinions in religion and government, and in the end succeeded in securing the town for the Parliament.

Nevertheless, we learn from Hicks that, during the early part of the war, Saint Ives was rated for the maintenance of the king's Cornish army, and furnished daily 46 lb. of bread, 40 lb. of butter, 30 lb. of cheese, 30 lb. of beef, and 50 lb. of bacon.

Most of the ancient gentle families of the neighbourhood of Saint Ives were understood to sympathize with the Cavaliers, though they seem to have taken no very active part in the stirring politics of their day. Such were the families of Trenwith, Tregenna, Payne, Pawley, etc.

Among the devoted band who held Pendennis Castle for the king were John Matthews (conductor of the train of artillery), Thomas King, Richard Williams, William Williams and Edward Stevens, most, if not all, of whom were, I suspect, from the Saint Ives district. They held out until 1646, and were the last in Cornwall to capitulate.

Sir Ralph Hopton was the Royal Commissioner of Array in Cornwall, and the chief of the king's forces; he commanded the cavalry. In 1645 there was a rising of the Saint Ives Roundheads on Longstone Downs, in Lelant. Sir Richard Grenville came to the west and suppressed the insurrection. He lodged at the house of the mayor, Edward Hammond, and whilst there ordered one Phillipps, a Zennor constable, to be hanged. The day after his departure he had two Saint Ives men hanged at Helston and Truro. Captain Robert Arundell, who, alone among those of his name, supported the Parliament, escaped from Saint Ives to Bridgewater, and there joined the army of Fairfax. (Hicks and Gilbert.) Edward Hammond himself was sent to Lanceston Gaol and fined £400.

In the year 1646-7 Saint Ives was visited by plague and famine. Food was brought from the neighbouring parishes and laid beside the streams which bounded the infected district, and the townspeople placed their money in the streams at Polmantor and Carbis Valley. Each parcel of food was ticketed with the price to be paid, and the purchasers were not to approach the spot for some hours after the money had been placed there. Five hundred and thirty-five persons, being about a third of the population of Saint Ives, are said to have fallen victims to the plague. The market was closed for a considerable time. The Stephens shut themselves up in their country-house at Ayr, a hamlet within the borough, and escaped the contagion. More, says Hicks, would have died of famine than plague, had not a ship belonging to Mr. Opye, of Plymouth, come into the harbour, laden with wheat and some butts of sack, which cargo was purchased for £196, by the mayor and other gentlemen.

In 1647 the Saint Ives merchants fitted out a ship called the *James*, for the West Indies; but on her return she was taken by the Spaniards and carried to Spain.

In 1649 King Charles was beheaded at Whitehall, on January 30. That same day, according to Hicks' MS., a great storm burst over the western coast; the Carreg-an-peul, or Steeple Rock, at the Land's End, was thrown down; and a ship which was riding in Saint Ives Bay, having on board the king's wardrobe and other furniture belonging to the royal family, bound for France, ran ashore on the rocks of Godrevy Island. She had on board about sixty persons, all of whom were drowned, excepting a man and a boy, who, with a wolf-dog, swam to the island, and there for two days subsisted on rainwater and seaweed. As soon as the storm abated they were brought to Saint Ives, and Mr. Hicks conversed with them.

In 1659 a Dutch ship was wrecked in Whitsand Bay. Her cargo, consisting of silver, sugar and other rich goods, was brought to the vice-admiral's house at St. Ives.

Copper mines were first worked, *circa* 1687, hereabouts, by Sir Thomas Clarke and others; and the Duke of Bolton, about the same time, brought hither a German to teach the art of blasting and mining. Also Messrs. Robinson and Bell were instructed in the use of gunpowder by the said German.

SUBSIDY 21 JAMES I. (1624).

Lelant.

Jacobus Prade geñ in terr⁹ £6.
Rator Johēs Thomas geñ in terr⁹ £6.
Rator Greenfreedus Halls geñ in bonis £4.
Thomas Edwards geñ in bonis £4.
Stephanus Pawly in bonis £3.
Leonora Otes in bonis £4.
Willm̄s Edwardes in bonis £3.
Willm̄s Kelwaie in bonis £3.
Johanna Chilcott in bonis £3.

Stt Ives.

Richardus Trenw^th geñ rated at fyve pound in terr' sould all his land died nothinge worth.

Willūs Burthingye rated at two poundes in terr⁹ sould all his land died nothinge worth.

Thomas Treunwith ar. et Laura Trenwith vid. valēt in terris. . . .

Thomas Treunwith ar. in bonis. . . . . .

Thomas Purefoy geñ in bonis. . . . . .

Georgius Hicks in bonis £3.
Willmus Pitt in bonis £3.
Jana Hicks vid. in bonis £3
Johēs Goodall in bonis £3.
Gratia Hurleye in bonis £3.
Johēs Sprigge in bonis £4.
Jacobus Sterrye in bonis £3.
Henricus Hicks in bonis £3.
Georgius Williams [indistinct] in bonis £3.
Thomas Syse in bonis £3.

Sener.

Johnēs Pellamountayne in terris £5.

(The remaining names for this parish are very indistinct, but are almost as in the Subsidy next copied ; the same applies to the names for the parish of Towednack.)

SUBSIDY, 1624.

Uny Iuxta Lelant.

Jacobus Prade gener : valet in terris £6.
Johēs Thomas in terris £6.
Grenfield Haulse in bonis £4.
Thomas Edwards in bonis £4.
Stephanus Pawly in bonis £2.
Honora Oates vid. in bonis £4.
Johēs Lawrye in bonis £4.
Richūs Stephen in bonis £3.
Willmus Edwards in bonis £3.
Sessor Alexander Warren in bonis £3.
Sessor Johēs Richard in bonis £3.
Willmus Penberthye in bonis £3.
Johēs Hoskyn in bonis £3.
Willmus Kellwaye in bonis £3.

Towedneck.

Sessor Johēs Psōns valet in bonis £4.
Mathew Trenwth in bonis £3.
Jacobus Carpenter in bonis £3.
Sessor Thomas Curno in bonis £3.
Willmus Paynter in bonis £3.
Johēs Martyn in bonis £2.
Joanna Nicholas vid. in bonis £3.

St. Ives.

Thomas Trenwth ar. et } valēt in terris £5.
Lora Trenwth vid. }
Christiana Payne vid. in terris £2.
Sessor Johēs Stephens in terris £8.
Willmus. . . . .

Thomas Trenwith in bonis. . . . . .
Johēs Payne in bonis £4.
Sessor Richūs Hext in bonis £4.
Thomas Purefye in bonis £4.
Johēs Rich in bonis £4.
Johēs Sprigg in bonis £4.
Johēs Sterry in bonis £4.
Georgius Hicke in bonis £3.
Willmus Pytt in bonis £3.
Jana Hicke vid. in bonis £3.
Johēs Goodale in bonis £3.
Gracia Hurley vid. in bonis £3.
Jacobus Sterry in bonis £3.
Henricus Hicks in bonis £3.
Edwardus Hamond in bonis £3.
Stephanus Barbar in bonis £3.
Thomas Syes in bonis £3.

Senor.

Johēs Pellamounten valet in bonis £6.
Sessor Thomas Rawe in bonis £3.
Mathias Phillipe in bonis £3.
Elizabeth Richard vid. in bonis £3.
Richūs Davye in bonis £3.
Sessor Johēs Wolcock in bonis £3.
Willms Richard in bonis £3.
Johēs Bossow in bonis £3.
Sampson Thomas in bonis £3.
Johēs Porthmere in bonis £3.
Robertus Michell in bonis £3.

CORNWALL SUBSIDY 1 CHARLES I. (1625).

(Much mutilated.)

Lelant.

Jacobus Prade gen̄ in ter' £6.
Johēs Thomas gen̄ in ter' £6.
Grenfildus Halls gen̄ in bonis £4.
Thomas Edwardes gen̄ in bonis £4.
Stephanus Pawly gen̄ in bonis £3.
Honor Oates vid. in bonis £4.
Johēs Lawrye in bonis £3.
Richūs Stephen in bonis £3.
Rator Willūs Edwardes in bonis £3.
Willūs Kelway in bonis £3.
Rator Alexander Waren in bonis £3.
Johēs Richarde in bonis £3.
Willūs Leonarde in bonis £3.
Johnēs Hoskin in bonis £3.

Towednake.

Johannes Parsons in bonis £4.
Johēs Martin in bonis £3.
Rator Matthew Trenw[th] in bonis £3.
Jacobus Carpenter in bonis £3.
Willūs Painter in bonis £3.
Thomas Curnowe in bonis £3.

St Ives.

Willūs Ceely gen̄ in bonis £6.
Johannes Steuens in bonis £7.
Thomas Trenw[th] in bonis £5.
Johannes Paine in bonis £4.
Johannes Sterry in bonis £3.
Richardus Hexte in bonis £4.
Thomas Purefey gen in bonis £4.
Georgius Hexte in bonis £3.
Willmūs Pit in bonis £3.
Johannes Riche in bonis £4.
Jana Hicks vid. in bonis £3.
Johannes Goodale in bonis £3.
Gratia Hurly vid. in bonis £3.
Rator Johannes Sprigge in bonis £3.
Jacobus Sterrye in bonis £3.
Henricus Hicks in bonis £3.
Rator Eduardus Hamonde in bonis £3.
Stephanus Barbar in bonis £3.
Thomas Syse in bonis £3.
Thom[9] Trenw[th] Ar. et Laura Trenw[th] vid. in ter[9] £5.
Christiana Payne vid. in ter[9] £2.

Senner.

Johannes Pellamountaine in bonis £5.
Johēs Uppcot in bonis £3.
Thomas Crowe in bonis £3.
Matthew Phillip in bonis £3.
Rator Johēs Woolcocke in bonis £3.
Richūs Dauie in bonis £3.
Willūs Richarde in bonis £3.
ffranciscus Maddern in bonis £3.
Richūs Dauie minor in bonis £3.
Johēs Porthmere in bonis £3.
Johēs Bussow in ter[9] in bonis £1.

CORNWALL SUBSIDY, 4 CHARLES I. (1629).

Lelant.

Jacobus Praed gen̄ in terris £6.
Johēs Thomas gen̄ in terris £3.
Stephūs Thomas in terr[9] £1.

Willmūs Hampton in terr⁹ £1.
Grenvilis Hals geñ in bonis £5.
Thom̄s Edwards geñ in bonis £5.
Rator Stephūs Pawlye geñ in bonis £3.
Willm̄s Edwards geñ in bonis £4.
Johēs Lawree geñ in bonis £3.
Richūs Stephen in bonis £3.
Simon Prust in bonis £3.
Willmūs Cellingaye in bonis £3.
Johēs Richard in bonis £3.
Johēs Uryn in bonis £3.

Towednack.

Rator Johēs Parsons in bonis £4.
Willmūs Painter in bonis £4.
Henricus Martin in bonis £4.
Willmūs Trenwithe in bonis £4.
Georgius Roswarne in bonis £4.
Robtūs Pearse in bonis £4.

Saint Ives.

Thom̄s Trenw^th ar. et Laura Trenwith in terr⁹ } £5.
Christiana Payne vid. in terris £2.
Willm̄us Ceely geñ in bonis £6.
Ricūs Hext g: in bonis £4.
Thomas Purefry geñ in bonis £4.
John Stephens geñ in bonis £8.
Thom^s Trenw^th geñ in bonis £3.
Johnēs Payne geñ in bonis £3.
Rator Johēs Sprigge geñ in bonis £4.
Jacobus Sterrye in bonis £3.
Johēs Rich in bonis £3.
Willm̄s Pitt in bonis £3.
Henricus Hicks in bonis £3.
Stephanus Barbar in bonis £3.
Johēs Goodale in bonis £3.
Thom^s Sise in bonis £3.
Henrūs Hamond in bonis £3.
Gracia Hurley vid. in bonis £3.
Jana Hicks vid. in bonis £2.
Honora Oates vid. in bonis £4.

Zennor.

Johēs Pellamounter in bonis £5.
Rator Johēs Upcott in bonis £3.
Thomas Raw in bonis £3.
Jacobus Phillip in bonis £3.
Rator Johnēs Wolcocke in bonis £3.
Willm̄s Richard in bonis £3.
ffranciscus Madderne in bonis £3.

Rogerus Christopher in bonis £3.
Sampson Thomas in bonis £3.
Thomas Wery al^{s} Philip in bonis £3.
Johēs Bosustowe in bonis £2.
Johnēs Phillippes in bonis £3.

CORNWALL SUBSIDY 16 CHARLES I. (1641).

(Hundred de Penwith.)

Crowan.

Johēs Seyntaubyn Arm. valet in terr^{9} £14.

Unye Lelant.

Jacobus Prade geñ in terr.
Grenvile Hals geñ in bon.
Hencūs Edwards geñ in bon.
Margareta Pawleye vid. in bon.
Willm̄us Edwards in bon.
Johēs Lawrey in bon.
Simon Prust in bon.
Willmūs Kelwaye in bon.
Alexander Richard in bon.
Johēs Uren in bon.
Alexander Banfild iñ bon.
Jacobus Morish in bon.
Clement Uren in terr.
Alexander Geene in terr.

Towednacke.

Johēs Parsons valet in bonis £4.
Thomas Wedge in bonis £3.
Petrus Paynter in bonis £3.
Thomas Cornow iuñr in bonis £3.
Jacobus Trewhela in bonis £3.
Georgius Pile in terr^{9} £2.

St. Iues.

Thomas Trenwith arm. in terr^{9} £5.
Thomas Stephens Maior in bonis £4.
Ricūs Hext geñ in bonis £4.
Johēs Paine geñ in bonis £3.
Willmūs Tregose geñ in bonis £3.
Henrūs Hicks in bonis £3.
Stephūs Barber in bonis £3.
Thomas Edwards geñ in bonis £3.
Edrūs Hamond in bonis £3.
Johēs Diggans geñ in bonis £3.
Ephraim Sise in bonis £3.
Alexander James in bonis £3.
Thomas Noale in bonis £3.
Ricūs Couch geñ in bonis £3.
Thomas Sprigg in bonis £4.
Henrūs Stephens in bonis £3.
Johēs Goodale in bonis £3.
Johēs Hetchins in bonis £3.
Ricūs Smith in bonis £3.
Johēs Player in bonis £3.
Andreas Phillips in bonis £3.
Gratia Hurleye vid. in bonis £3.
Anna Purefoye vid. in bonis £3.
Sum. in terr^{9} v^{li}
in bonis lxix^{li}
Sum. soluto xx^{li} viij^{s}

Sennar.

Willm̄us Trenwith in bonis. . . . . .
Georgius Thomas in bonis £1.

Pawle.

Willm̄us Godolphin arm̄ in terr.
Johēs Gwavas gener^{9} in terr.
Johēs Keigwin gen̄ in terr.
Waltūs Burlase in bonis.
Arthūs Berryman in terr.
[et caeteri.]

Burian.

Hugo Levelis gen̄ in terr.
Thomas Tresilian gen.
Hugo Thomas gen.
Thomas Grosse gen.
Humphrūs Noye gener.

Summa totalis huius Hundred^{9} de Penwith in Solutionibus ccc xx viij^{li} v^{s} iiij^{d}

Summa totalis horum Hundred^{9} de Kirrier et Penwith DCLXXII^{li} xiiij^{s} o^{d}.

John Seyntaubyn.
Jo: Trefusis.
John Arundell.
William Pendarves.
William Harris.
Renatus Bellott.

CORNWALL SUBSIDY, 16 CHARLES I. (1641).

Jacobus Praed gen̄ in ter.
Grinvill Halse gen̄ in bon.
Henricus Edwards gen̄ in bon.
Margeria Pawly wid. in bon.
Willm̄us Edwards in bon.
Johēs Lawry in bon.
Symon Prust in bon.
Willm̄us Kelloway in bon.
Alexandrus Richard in ter.
Johēs Urin in ter.
Alexandrus Bondfeild in ter.
Jacob^{s} Morrice in terr.

Towednack.

Johēs Parsons in bon.
Thomas Wedge in bon.
Petrus Painter in bon.
Thomas Cornowe in bon.
Willmūs Russell in bon.
Georgius Nennis in ter.
Warne Roswall in ter.

St Ives.

Thomas Trenwith Ar^{9} in ter.
Thomas Steaven Maior in bon.
Richūs Hext gen̄ in bon.
Johanēs Payne gen̄ in bon.
Willmūs Tregose gen̄ in bon.
Henricus Hicks in bon.
Stephanus Barber in bon.

St Ives.

Edrūs Hamon in bon.
Thomas Edwards gen̄ in bon.
Thomas Hickes in ter.
Johēs Tonkyn in terr.
Effraim Sise in bon.
Alexandrus James in bon.
Thomas Noall in bon.
Richūs Coutch gen̄ in bon.
Thomas Sprigg in bon.
Henricus Steavens in bon.
Johanēs Goodale in bon.
Johanēs Hutchings in terr.
Thomas Dayowe in terr.
Richūs Smith in terr.
Ricūs Hockin in terr.
Johanēs Player in bonis.
Andreas Phillipps in terr.
Johanēs Cossen in terr.
Gracia Hurlye wid. in bonis.
Anna Purefoye wid. in bon.

Zennor.

Johēs Upcott in bon.
Johēs Phillipps in bon.
Jacobus Phillips in bon.
Johēs Woolcocke in bon.
Johēs Bussey in bon.
Richūs Pellamounter in ter.
Georgius Thomas in ter.
Willmūs Richard in ter.
Nicholas Berriman Iu: in terr.
Thomas Sampson in ter
Arthur Beriman in ter.
ffranciscus Maddern in ter.
Robtūs Michell in ter.
Willmūs Trenw^th in ter.
Johēs Andrew in ter.

CORNWALL SUBSIDY, 15 CHARLES II. (1664).

Uny Lelant.

James Prade Esqr. in ter.
Henry Edwards gent. in bonis.
Hugh Pauley g^t in bonis.
John Edwards in bonis.
Wm Kelway in bonis.
Jam^s Morice in terris.
Richard Steephens in terris.
John Steephens in terris.
John Bonfield in terris.
Henry Curnow in ter.
Steephen Uryn in ter.
Richard Thomas in ter.
Hanball Hosken in ter.

Towednack.

Thom^s Painter in bon.
Thos Renawden in ter.
ffrancis Quicke in ter.
Peeter Painter in ter.
Ric: Baragwanath in ter.
James Trewhela in ter.
Zenobia Quicke in ter.
Rob^tt Curnow in terr.
Margrett Russell wid. in terr.
Edmond Uryn in ter.
Thom^s Gyles in ter.

St Ives.

Thomas Trenweth gent. in terris.
Wm Diggens in bonis.
Edward Hamon Mrchtt. in bon.
Tho: & John Noall in bon.
John Hitchens in bon.
George Hamon Mrchtt. in bon.
Th^o: Purefoy et Ed: Stephens in bon.
Thom^s Syse in bon.

Hugh Harris in bon.
Wm Robenson in bon.
Peeter Ceely in bon.
ffrancis Arundell g^t in bon.
Alex : James in bon.
John Player in bon.
Ric : Nance et Pasco Hodge in bon.
Tho : et ffrancis Steephens in bon.
Ric : Polard et Ric : Smith in bon.
Steph : & Tim^o Mayor in bon.
Tho : Hicks & Jo : Thomas in bon.
Wm Pearse et Thos Beryman in bon.
Rich : Hichens in bon.
Nic : Sprigg & Jo : Treweeke in bon.

Zennor.

George Thomas in bon.
Eliz : Upcott in bon.
Wm Steephen in bon.
Mary Usticke in bon.
Robt Michell in bon.
John Wolcock in bon.
Thom^s Phillips in bon.
Arthur Beriman in bon.
John Limbry in bon.
David Udg in bon.
Cornelius Phillips in bon.
Ric : Sleman in ter.

CHAPTER XIV.

BOROUGH ACCOUNTS, 1639-1687.

THE second volume of Borough accounts and memoranda is a quarto paper book bound in calf. Its contents commence thus:

A Register and booke of recorde for the Towne and parrish of St. Ives in the Countie of Cornewall made and written the ffower and twentieth day of October in the viiijth. yere of the raigne of our Soueraigne Lord Kinge Charles; and in the yere of o[r] Lord god: 1638. M[r] John Sterrie then beinge Portreife there.

Primo die Nouembris 1638. The account of M[r] John Sterrie Portreife of y[e] Towne and pīsh of S[t] Ives for all receipts and disbursements of monie for and to y[e] use of y[e] said Towne and pīsh for one whole yere ended y[e] day and yere aforesaid.

Receipts etc:—Imprimis received of y[e] ffarmers of y[e] Market for one yeres rent y[e] sum̄e of £22 10*s*. 0*d*.

y. received of y[e] key wardens for a quarters rent Due y[e] second of ffebruarie £3 2*s*. 6*d*.

y. more received of y[e] key wardens for a quarters due y[e] first of may £3 2*s*. 6*d*.

y. rec' of M[r] Jo[n] Hicks for y[e] pte. of rent due y[e] 25th of Julie 1638. £1 12*s*. 6*d*.

Disbursements, Imprimis y[e] ffifth of November to y[e] Ringers in Candles and drinke 1*s*.

I. payd M[r] Thomas Jackson [the vicar] for y[e] whole yere £14.

I. to Andrew Lawrie for his wages being Towne Clarke 8*s*.

I. to y[e] Organist £2 12*s*. 0*d*.

I. spent at M[r] Hamonds att y[e] tyme he was elected Portreife 14*s*. 6*d*.

[This, of course, refers to conviviality; the amounts expended on such festive occasions increase greatly as time goes on, until, towards the end of the eighteenth century, they absorb a very considerable proportion of the revenues.]

I. spent there when Mr Penuyke payd in ye xvli for ye poore 9*s*.

I. more spent there att Sr. ffrauncis Godolphins being in Towne 7*s*. 6*d*.

y. more at Captaine Bassetts coming to our Towne from Sillye 2*s*. 0*d*.

[The Bassetts of Tehidy are an ancient family, being the head of the Cornish branch of that great baronial house. In the reign of Henry IV., William Bassett held a knight's fee in Tehidy and Trenalga (Carew, 'Survey of Cornwall,' p. 39, b.). In the Civil War they espoused the royal cause, in consequence of which they lost possession of Saint Michael's Mount, which went to the Saint Aubyns, who had taken the side of the Parliament.

y. to certaine English and French Travellors which had passes to travell the countrye 4*s*. 8*d*.

y. payd for sendinge of post Letters to Mr Bassett 1*s*. 6*d*.

y. payd for carrieing of Letters to Mr Bassett about Townes busines 1*s*. 6*d*.

y. payd John Hawke for goinge to Lanceston with a fellon 14*s*.

[The County Gaol was at this time at Lanceston. Hawke was the borough constable.]

Item to ye Masons for their worke about ye Key £1 15*s*. 0*d*.

[The old quay here referred to was situated about 200 yards nearer in towards the church than the present one, and joined the shore right under Carn Glaze. It consequently sheltered a much smaller extent of water.]

y. in expence makinge ye Bargaine and aboute ye worke 2*s*. 4*d*.

[*i.e.*, spent on liquor]

y. ye young Treweeke for Iron wedges 6*s*.

y. pd. for Tymber to make woden wedges £1 10*s*.

y. for a bord of ye keye which was carried away with ye Sea 1*s*. 4*d*.

y. for ye mendinge of a new Hammer with which hee sett upp ye Works 9*s*. 6*d*.

y. more for a peeice of Cable to make slings 3*s*. 4*d*.

y. pd. ye Porters for three tuns of bigge slats 3*s*.

y. for ordinarie stones to fill ye worke and carienge 2 great stones to ye key 3*s*.

y. for two hogsheds of lyme about ye key 10*s*.

[Curious light is thrown upon the treatment of misdemeanants at that period by the following reference to a cage in which offenders were confined. It long stood in the market-place, probably between the market-house and the church tower, along with the whipping-post and the stocks.]

Anno 1638. Disbursements about ye Kaidge and marked howse.

Imprimis for a beame for ye cadge 4*s*.

I. for 13 rafters att js ixd ye rafter £1 2*s*. 9*d*.

I. more for 9 bords att js ivd ye bord 12*s*.

I. more for 3 fresh bords 1*s*.

I. more for a Locke and Key 1*s*. 10*d*.

I. payd for ye culleringe of ye cadge 1*s*. 6*d*.

I. to ye carpenters for making of ye cadge 12*s*.

I. for Nayles spykes and crooks for ye Markett Howse 3*s*.

I. for oile in workinge ye cullers 1*s*.

I. to Jon Anthonie for placinge of a beame in ye wale [wall] for ye cage 1*s*.

I. for 6 deale bords for ye Markett Howse 6*s*. 6*d*.

I. to John Penbeagle for clensinge ye Markett Howse 5*s*.

[Penbeagle is a hamlet in the parish of Saint Ives.]

I. for Nayles aboute ye Markett Howse 5*s*.

Charges about ye Kings Hye Wayes :—

Item payd John Anthonie in anno 1636 for his wages and for stones 8*s*.

I. more in anno 1638 ye same worke beinge broken by violence of waters and newly amended payd ye said John Anthonie 8*s*.

[The streets bordering on the seashore have always been a great source of trouble and expense to the local authorities.]

I. payd ye Porters for stones 2*s*. 6*d*.

I. payd for two peeces of Tymber to bynd ye worke 2*s*. 4*d*.

I. more payd Mr Richard Gould for a newe booke for ye Townes use 12*s*.

[Presumably the original volume containing these writings.]

I. for my [the portrieve's] charge and expence Riding to Mr Bassett for busines concerning ye Pish for my paynes and horse hyre 3*s*. 6*d*.

I. payd for repayring of ye High wayes ye last yere 2*s*. 6*d*.

The whole disbursements with allowance of monie received by Mr Thomas Stevens comes to £32 0*s*. 5*d*.

Disbursements £31 2*s*. 11*d*.

remaynes due — 17*s*. 6*d*. to ye pish

[Above we have given in full the borough accounts of the year 1638-9, during the portrievalty of John Sterrie. In the following year, 1639-40, Thomas Stevens was portrieve, and was the last who held that office at Saint Ives. His account is headed thus :]

Primo Die Novembris 1638. Anno Regni Doī nrī Charoli Dei grā Anglie Scotie ffrauncie e Hibernie fidei defensoris etc. decimo quarto. Mr Thomas Steven is chosen Portreeve.

[Then follow formal lettings of the town revenues to their respective farmers, thus :]

The day and yere above written Peter Goodale hath farmed ye pfitts. of ye Markett Howse for one whole yere and is to pay for ye same ye sume of Twentie two pounds sterlinge to be payd ye Portreife nowe in beinge quarterly by euen portions duringe ye said yere, and for pformance thereof he hath hereunto subscribed his name.

John Diggens. Petter Gooddall.

The day and yere above said Mr Peter Ceely hath farmed ye pfitts. of ye key of St. Ives for one whole yere, and is to pay for ye same ye sume of thirteene pounds sterlinge to be payd ye Portreife nowe in beinge quarterly by euen portions during ye sayd yere, and for pformance thereof he hath hereunto subscribed his name.

Per. Ceely.

Primo die Novembris 1639. The account of Mr Thomas Stevēs late Portreeve for one whole yere ended ye day and yere aforesaid.

I. to ye Organist for halfe a yere and so much left unpayd ye yere before £3 8*s*.

I. for ringinge and candles ye 5th of November 3*s*. 8*d*.

I. payd for a newe chest and 4 lockes and keys for the same 10*s*.

I. spent when he was chosen Portreive 14*s*. 6*d*.

I. to Irish men and Irish women that came here by passes 3*s*. 6*d*.

[At this period, and for long after, destitute persons were sent alone on foot to the parish of their birth, and received passes, also called certificates, entitling them to relief in the various towns through which they journeyed. Those presenting fraudulent passes were severely punished, of which we shall see examples later on.]

I. more to an outlandish man 2*s*. 6*d*.

[*i.e.*, a foreigner.]

I. for a silver Bole [ball] that was brought to Towne 6*s*. 6*d*.

[To be used in hurling-matches.]

I. to Henrie Treweeke for spukes abovt ye key 11*s*. 6*d*.

I. to Robert Bolithowe for work about ye key 6*s*. 8*d*.

I. to John Trerie for working about ye key and chaple £1 1*s*. 0*d*.

I. spent upon ye companie that went to vewe the bounds 4*s*.

[This refers to the ancient custom of 'viewing' or beating the bounds on Ascension Day, which originated in the necessity of keeping up the memory of the precise limits of the parish. In Catholic times this partook of the nature of a religious ceremony, and was accompanied by the blessing of the bounds by the parish priest. See Chambers' 'Book of Days.']

I. for $3\frac{1}{2}$ cwt. hellen stones.

[This is the local pronunciation of 'healing-stones,' the name given to the flat stones used for roofing houses (Carew's 'Survey').]

I. given to 8 distressed ffrenchmen 4*s*.

I. to Ephraim Syse for beames to make y^e postes £1.

I. to Ephraim Syse for quarter beams & a bord for ye Markethouse 11*s*.

I. to Thomas Paynter for making ye Bords and Beames 12*s*.

I. to 2 Irishmen with their wives and child 2*s*.

I. spent att Mr Ham̄onds when ye charter was brought 5*s*. 6*d*.

[That is, the charter of incorporation before mentioned.]

I. to a distressed scholler that came from Scotlande 2*s*. 6*d*.

I. for repayring ye Ilande Chaple 13*s*. 6*d*.

I. more given att Mr Bassetts howse 14*s*. 6*d*.

[Bassett of Tehidy entertained the Corporation every Christmas, and they on those occasions always gave money to his servants.]

[So far we have given the accounts of the two last portreives of Saint Ives, which were entered in the new book provided when the first mayor was appointed. The account of Richard Hext, the first mayor, for the year 1639-40, commences thus :]

Richard Hext gentleman was elected and chosen to be Maior of the Towne and Borrough of St Ives by our souvraigne Lorde Kinge Charles and sworne in the Towne Hall there the first day of November Anno Domini Christi 1639.

Receipts. Imprimis received of Mr Thomas Stevens late Porthreife £7 12*s*. 9*d*.

Received of Mr William Tregosse and Henrie Stevens for ye key 13° Aprilis 1640. £5 19*s*. 6*d*.

I. received of Mr Towne Clarke the vij^th of November p^te of the composition monie that remayned in his hands the sume of £7 12*s*. 8*d*.

Disbursements followeth. Imprimis spent upon Mr Stoan the iudge of the Admiraltie with the consent of Mr John Payne and others of ye xij 16*s*.

I. more given to a poore traveller 1*s*.

I. more given amongst the servants att Tehiddie on Christide 10*s*.

[One seems to see the growing influence of Puritanism in the 'Christ-tide' which was intended to oust the Popish Christ-mass, but never did so.]

I. given to a poor distressed man that lay long in Mr Dale's Prison 2*s*.

I. more spent intertayninge of S^r ffrauncis Godolphin the 23rd of Januarie att his coming from Sillye £1 0*s*. 4*d*.

[The ancient and distinguished family of Godolphin had their ancestral seat at Godolphin in the parish of Breage. They are in many ways connected with the history of Saint Ives.]

I. more given to a poore man that came to the Towne the second of ffebruarie beinge bounde for wales hauinge no monie to pay for his passadge 2*s*.

I. more to William Leonard for carrieinge my Lord Marquis is Letter concerning the Burgesses to Mr Recorder the vij^th^ of ffebruarie 1*s*.

[The marquis referred to is the Marquis of Winchester, then chief landowner here.]

I. for goeinge next day for Mr Townclarke to come to Towne 6*d*.

I. payd Mr Jackson for his whole yeares due £14.

I. payd Andrew Laurie for his whole yeares wages 8*s*.

I. payd Mr Hammand for our expences the 15th of ffebruarie when Mr Recorder pressed o^r^ saylers for his Maties. service £2 3*s*. 0*d*.

I. more given to a poore distressed scholler that came to o^r^ Town from Germanie the 27th of ffebruarie to seeke passadge home from Ireland 2*s*.

I. payd William Lenard for goinge to our Recorder with letters that came from the Princis Commissioners the 27th of ffebruarie 1*s*.

I. payd the post for carridge of o^r^ letters in answere to ye Prince is commissioners 6*d*.

[The Royal Commissioners of Array sate at Truro for the purpose of superintending the movements of the King's forces in Cornwall.]

I. payd Thomas Killington and others of the ffishermen for carrieinge of claye and Rubble from the key to Porthmeor 5*s*.

I. more spent the xvj^th^ of March when Mr Pennicke was in Towne to knowe howe manie would ride to give their voyces for ye knights of ye sheere 7*s*.

[The members returned to Parliament for Saint Ives about this time were, in 1639, W. Dell and Sir H. Martyn; 1640, Francis Godolphin, E. Walker and J. Fielder.]

More Disbursements hereafter followeth. Item spent att our first Sessions att Mr Hammands £2 6*s*. 3*s*.

I. more given to a distressed gent. with his wife that came to looke passadge for Irelande the vij^th^ of May 1*s*.

I. more to two distressed ffrenchmen that were taken by the Dunkarts [Dunkirk privateers] and came to seeke passadge the vth of May 1*s*.

I. more payd for carriadge of a Letter to Mr Recorder to London the second of June 1*s*.

I. more spent att Midsummer Sessions £1 15*s*. 4*d*.

I. more given to Mr Robert Arundle when he brought the cupp given by his Maister to our Towne £2.

[This was the renowned wishing-cup presented to the Borough by Sir Francis Bassett, on which is engraved the following inscription:

'If any discord 'twixt my friends arise,
Within the Borough of beloved Saint Ies,
It is desyred that this my cup of love
To every one a peacemaker may prove;
Then am I blest, to have given a legacie
So like my hearte unto posteritie.

Francis Bassett, A.D. 1640.'

This interesting vessel is of massive silver, about a foot in height. It is kept in the custody of each mayor for the time being. On solemn occasions it was handed round, and its contents sipped by mayor and aldermen, or a draught of mulled wine was presented in it to any distinguished guest. 'Of late years,' says Courtney, in 1845, 'a silver ladle has been placed in the cup, with which the wine is poured into glasses.']

I. more att that tyme att Mr Hammands spent 16*s*.

I. more payd the Gunner for clensinge of the three gunns and for powder to try them £1 13*s*. 4*d*.

I. payd Nicholas Prigge for two loaves of sugar which were presented Mr Recorder £1 10*s*. 0*d*.

[As a parallel to this, the following present was made to the new Recorder of Nottingham, by order of the Hall, in 1603: 'It is agreed that the town shall on Wednesday next present the Recorder Sir Henry Pierrepoint with a sugarloaf 9*s*., lemons 1*s*. 8*d*., white wine one gallon 2*s*. 8*d*., claret one gallon 2*s*. 8*d*., muskadyne one pottle 2*s*. 8*d*., sack one pottle 2*s*.; total 20*s*. 8*d*.' And the year following a present of various kinds of meat was given by the municipality of Nottingham to the Earl of Shrewsbury (Chambers' 'Book of Days,' vol. ii., p. 149).]

I. payd the glaziar for mendinge of the widdowe Spriggs windowes beinge broaken with the sounde of ye Gunns 1*s*.

I. more given a ffooteman that brought my Lord Marques letter the 14th of Qctober 2*s*.

[Powlett, Marquess of Winchester.]

I. payd a footeman that came from Mr Recorder with letters concerning ye Burgesses the xix^th^ of October 6*d*.

[By 'footeman,' in this and the preceding entry, we are to understand a foot messenger.]

I. payd for two hogsheds that beles: [belongs] the Towne store 8*s*.

I. given to them that brought the writs from Mr Recorder for the Election of the Burgesses the xx^th^ of October 6*d*.

I. more given to an Irish gent. and his wife one Mr Makarto [Mac Carthy or Mac Arthur] whoe came to our Towne to seeke passadge being in pouertie 26° octobris 1*s*.

I. more payd Arthur Wescott the 8th of November for carrieinge of the three gūns to the fforte 7*s*. 6*d*.

I. more spent att Mr Hamands All Saints day when Mr Maior was chosen £1 19*s*. 7*d*.

I. payd Mr Christopher Cocke for monie disbursed by him for the Towne and Parrish as by his notes do appeare £10.

[In November, 1640, Thomas Stevens, who had been the last portrieve, was the first to be elected mayor, Richard Hext having been appointed by the King's Charter.]

St Ives. The account of Mr Thomas Stevens merchaunt Maior of the Borough of St. Ives aforesaid for all receipts and disbursements of monie ffor and to the use of the said Borough for one whole yeare ended the ffirst day of November Anno Dõi 1641.

Imprimis. Received of Richard Peter ffarmer of the Markett for one whole yeare reparons: and other charges allowed the sume of £39 4*s*. 4*d*.

I. received of Mr John Payne in pte of payment of a debt of ffifteene pounds eight shillings due to the Towne the sume of £9 13*s*. 4*d*.

I. received of William Phillips for 3 quarters rent for the key the sume of £15.

I. received of Richard Peter for his ffredome 6*s*. 8*d*.

[The freedom of the municipal borough.]

The following also purchased their freedom this year:

William Allan, John Sampson, Richard Pollard, Alexander Penticost and Christopher Morrish.

I. more received from the Lord and Ladie last yeare past 8*s*.

[This is the last mention of the Lord and Lady of the Summer Games. These sports did not survive the Puritan regime.]

Disbursements to balance the former accounte hereafter followeth:

Imprimis. To two Irish men and Irish women the 20th of Nober 1640 beinge distressed 2*s*.

To a man that brought a pclamation to or Towne the xth. of December 1*s*.

I. pd. for a locke and key for the Prison and another for the Stocks 2*s*.

I. payd Mr Jackson for his whole yeares service the sume of £14.

I. payd him for a sermon att the election of a new Maior 10*s*.

I. bestowed att Tehiddie in guifts att Christmas 18*s*.

I. more att Mr Praeds the same tyme 3*s*.

I. given to an Irish man with his wife and 3 children in distresse 5*s*.

I. for ordinaries and expenses att Christmas quarter Sessions £3 1*s*. 9*d*.

I. spent in wyne att the feast of All Saints before when the Maior was elected £1 1*s*. 0*d*.

I. payd for puttinge of Geffrie Nance to Hayle £1 7*s*. 2*d*.

I. payd Henrie Williams for horse hire to carrie him to Hayle 5*s*.

I. given to Mr Bassetts gardner with the consent of the xij men 6*s*.

I. payd Henrie Williams for the countie stocke £1 2*s*. 0*d*.

I. to the Organist for playinge upon the Organs 1*s*.

[The plural form of this word was originally the only one in use; as now in French and Latin: 'Cantantibus organis Caecilia Domino decantabat.']

I. payd for pitch and tarr to putt upon the ornance & carriadges with beere spent 5*s*.

I. payd for sugar and sweet meats presented to our Burgesses £1 3*s*. 6*d*.

I. to an Irish man that came here by passe from the Low Countrie 5*s*.

I. payd Mr Jackson to send to the proctor att Exon. about Mr Treunw^th^ buisiness £1 11*s*. 0*d*.

I. payd to the serjeants att mace for their attendance for half a yeare att May £1.

[This year a new gallery was set up in the parish church. It was erected in the tower arch, at the west end, and used by the singers and musicians down to about 1840. It was highly decorated in front, and bore a painting of the royal arms.]

His receipts towards the building of the gallerie followeth:

Imprimis of John Player in monie pins and a beame iv^s^ the whole is £1.

I. of Matgew [Matthew] Treunwith gent £1.

I. of Mr Thomas Edwards for building the gallerie 5*s*.

I. of the pīshoners by a collection made in the church £20 18*s*. 9*d*. The whole is £23 3*s*. 3*d*.

Disbursements towards the buildinge of ye gallerie the whole is as the pticulars overleafe appeareth £41 2*s*. 0*d*.; from which £41 2*s*. 0*d*. substracted £23 3*s*. 3*d*., rest overpayd £17 18*s*. 9*d*. Which sume by the next Maior was received and counted & he Loweth.

St Ives. 1645. The Accompts of Mr Edward Hamonde late Maior of the Borough of St Ives aforesaid of all Receipts and disbursements of monie for one whole yeare ended the ffirst of November Anno pred:

Receipts

Imprimis received of Richard Hockin wth his disbursements in charges for rent of the Markett House £35 0*s*. 0*d*.

I. received of Peter Gibbs with his charges allowed about the key £14.

The whole sum̄e by him received £49.

Disbursements

I. disburst when Mr Rich: Cowch and Mr Reginald Paynter went to Sr Rich: Grenvill £2 3*s.* o*d.*

[Grenville was a prominent royalist leader in Cornwall.]

I. more when hee and other of the xij went to Bodmin to have the garrison confirmed under the Princes hande with charge for men horses and Equipts. £6 17*s.* 3*d.*

[The mayor and some aldermen seem to have gone to Bodmin in order to declare their devotion to the king, and to receive formal appointments in command of the local militia.]

I. allowed Richard Hockin for charges bestowed about the Markett Howse as by his notes appeares with this allowed by consent of the brethren £4 7*s.* 5*d.*

I. payd men for carrieinge stones that fell from the key to the key againe 4*s.*

I. more for ffurse and tymber to the Match maker 13*s.* 10*d.*

[The man that made fuses for the guns.]

I. spent the day of his election with the xij and xxiiij.

I. more given to some distressed ffrenchmen 4*s.* 6*d.*

I. spent upon Mr John Bassett and Mr Praed with some of the Magistrates 10*s.* 4*d.*

I. spent upon the Earle of Antrim with some of the brethren 8*s.*

I. more given att Mr Bassett's howse att Christmas 13*s.* 4*d.*

I. more when wee did receive the charter and other writings 2*s.* 6*d.*

I. to one that did whipp the mayde that would drowne her self 6*d.*

I. more spent on Mr Bassett a9 many other gents. the brethren being present £3 10*s.* o*d.*

I. more to six distressed Bristoll men their vessell being taken att Sea 4*s.* 6*d.*

I. to men in bread and beere aboute the bulworks 17*s.* 4*d.*

I. more in meate and wyne upon Sr ffrancis Bassett, Sr ffrancis Molsworth and their followers with the brethren £2 2*s.* 9*d.*

I. more wyne upon Sr Rich: Grenvill with the brethren 9*s.*

I. more spent on my Lord Hopton and his followers with consent of the brethren £1 1*s.* 3*d.*

I. more spent on Mr Predeaux the sheriffe and his followers with consent of the brethren 17*s.* 8*d.*

[Probably all these Royalist leaders were then engaged in fixing the rates at which the town was to supply their forces with provisions. Sir Ralph Hopton commanded the cavalry, and was mainly instrumental in retaining all Cornwall for a time in the king's obedience. The ancient family of Prideaux was seated at Place, near Padstow.]

I. more in bolts for the Turne Piks 2*s*. 6*d*.
I. more to distressed men that begged beinge in want 2*s*. 3*d*.
I. disbursed in lawe with Peter Gibbs about the key dues. . . . .
I. for his kitchinge allowance for the whole yeare beinge Maior £12.
I. to the serjeants att Mace for their labour and attendance £2 0*s*. 0*d*.
I. for drawinge and publyshinge this accompt 2*s*. 0*d*.
I. for 18[lbs] of sheete ledd for the guns 3*s*. 0*d*.

The whole disbursements are	£56	8*s*.	4*d*.
From which substract	£49	0*s*.	0*d*.
Resteth due to M[r] Hamonde	£7	8*s*.	4*d*.

Primo die Novembris Anno Dn̄i xp̄i: 1645. Ephraim Sise Mchant: Maior.

Profits of fairs and markets let to John Bosowe and Richard Pollard for £29.
Profits of quay let to M[r] Alexander Bishoppe for £13 10*s*.

Primo die Novembris, Anno Doī 1646. Accounts of M[r] Ephraim Sise, Maior.

I. payd Richard Pollard for candle light for the watch £1 3*s*. 10*d*.
I. payd for bread and beere for y[e] watch men from tyme to tyme £1 1*s*. 9*d*.
I. all[d] for Cockins att his goinge to Helston with the souldiers 10*s*.
I. payd M[r] Cocke for vewinge our charter 10*s*.
I. payd for one hhed: of wyne sent to our Recorder £3 0*s*. 0*d*.
I. payd 7 watch men att the troopers beinge here 17*s*. 6*d*.

[The troopers under Sir Ralph Hopton.]

I. payd for beere att halinge examininge our guñs 4*s*. 2*d*.
I. payd for cleeving the plattforme 1*s*.
I. payd posts for carrieinge of letters att y[e] tyme of the Irishe beinge here 4*s*. 8*d*.

[Probably some of the Irish troops sent over by the Duke of Ormond in 1643, to support the king's cause.]

I. given distressed seamen beinge taken by the Irish 3*s*.
I. p[d] Paynter for 82 scouringe rodds for Musketts 6*s*. 2*d*.
I. p[d] for 2 Deales, workemans wages and nayles for the guard howse & 3 bush: of coles 14*s*. 4*d*.
I. allowed for my charges the whole yeare £12 0*s*. 0*d*.
I. for my expences and other charge on gentlemen att sundrie tymes £2 10*s*. 0*d*.

I. for Mr Ham̄onds boate in bringinge stones to the key 3s.

I. allowed Mr Bishopp for charges layd out about the key £1 2s. 9d.

I. allowed the Serieants att Mace for their attendance £2 0s. 0d.

The whole disbursements are	£47	7s.	4d.
Out of which substract	£42	10s.	0d.
Remaynes due to Mr Sise last Maior	£4	17s.	4d.

St. Ives. The ffifteenth Day of December 1646.

Whereas itt is considered That our Towne of St. Ives aforesaid hath been a verie good place of hooke ffishinge And hath been verie beneficiall and helpfull to the countrie and also to the inhabitants And wee contrarie to our auncient custome have hyred our men for weekly pay And have taken them in att Saint James Tyde in the cheefe tyme of hooke ffishinge wch: is and hath been great dammadge to the Com̄on good and contrarie to the custome of all our ffellow Sayners and neighbours throughout the countie.

We doe therefore constitute and order That no owner of a Sayne or saynes within our Towne of what condition soever shall take or hyer any seamen or ffisherman unto his service for weeklie wages to serve in the sayninge craft; ffor our constitution is That the man that is owner of Sayne or saynes That so doth shall pay unto the Maior of the Borough for his default the sum̄e of twentie pounds to the use of the Towne and Borough To be leavyed on him by way of Action to be expended by the Maior But we constitute and order That itt shall be lawfull for any owner of sayne or saynes to hyer ffishermen for Rewards accordinge to our Auncient costume; And not to give aboue twentie shillings reward for any sayner of what condition soever hee bee eyther directlie or indirectlie And for the confirmation of this constitution wee have subscribed our names

Thomas Sprigge maior.	John Player.	Robert [?] Arundell.
Ephraim Syse.	Rich: Hicks.	Peter Gibbs.
Rich: Hext	Alexander Bishopp.	George Hicks.
Thomas Stevens.	Henry Sterrie.	Thomas Purefoy.
Henry Hickes.	George Hammond.	John Cocking.
Jno: Payne.	Thomas Hicks.	Thomas Painter.
Edward Hammond.	Reignald Paynter.	John Ann.
Alexander James.	Arthour Westcott.	Thomas Dayowe.
John Hichins.	John + Cussens.	John Noall.
Henry Stevens.	Nich: Prigge.	John + Perken.
Thos: Goode.	Andrew + Phillipps.	

Thomas Sprigge mayor 1646.

[This account covers the period of plague and famine; the details will be understood on reference to our description of these visitations in the preceding chapter.]

Profits of fairs and markets let to John Hechins for £40 10s. 0*d*.

—do— quay to Thomas Purefoy & Nicholas Sprigge for £20 0s. 0*d*.

St. Ives Anno Dom: 1646.

& Anno Dom: 1647.

The Account of M[r] Thomas Sprigge maior.

I. Received of Wm: Nance for goods which were John Hawks deceased £4 19*s*. 10*d*.

I. received att seuerall tymes of M[r] George Hicks for Corne monie £142 11*s*. 4*d*.

[Contributions towards the relief fund.]

I. more of Stephen Harris by Georg Hicks order for corne £1 5*s*. 8*d*.

I. more of M[r] George Hicks upon Major Ceelye Tickatts for corne £4 11*s*. 6*d*.

I. more of M[r] Henrie Sterie for a collection in St. Iust pish: £1 17*s*. 8*d*.

I. more sent into by M[r] Sterrie by the Towne post £3 0*s*. 0*d*.

I. received of M[r] Wm: Paynter who hath att London given to the use of y[e] Towne £1.

I. more of M[r] Arthur Westcott for pūision: solde in the Markett £11 0*s*. 0*d*.

I. received of M[r] Richard Pollard for the pīsh: howse £2 9*s*. 10*d*.

I. rec[d] of M[r] Harrison for the Towne upon our agreement for ffish £5.

I. rec[d] of M[r] Hammond for a Butt of the Towne sacke £18.

[From Opye's vessel.]

I. rec[d] of M[rs] Newman for 3 butts of sacke and pte: of a 4th. that shee drew £80 7*s*. 5*d*.

I. rec[d] of Henrie Hutchins for monie by him collected due to the Towne £3 12*s*. 2*d*.

I. more of M[r] Wm̄ Nance for puision: soulde in the Markett howse £2 10*s*. 0*d*.

I. received of the Towne serjeants for puision: by them deliuered £2 4*s*. 6*d*.

The whole sume is £307 19*s*. 9*d*.

Anno pred: Disbursements to ballance the former accont: as followeth:—

Imprimis spent att the settinge of the Markett and key by consent of the brethren 17*s*. 4*d*.

I. more payd the Joyners for takinge downe the Organs and Railings of the church £1 15*s*. 7*d*.

[Here we have a record of the Puritan zeal which demolished the few relics of beauty spared to the parish churches by the Reformation. The Reformers had chastised the church with whips, the Puritans now proceeded to scourge it with scorpions. Men were paid small sums to break all the stained glass which remained, and we now see before us the fate of the beautiful carved oak rood-screen, curtly termed 'Railings,' and the organ.]

I. more to poore Dutchmen that were taken at sea 3*s*.

I. more payd Henrie Treweeke for crooks and Nayles to hang up the sentences and Match 2*s*. 6*d*.

I. more to poore women that came from Ireland 1*s*. 6*d*.

I. more spent upon Mr Saintabyn the 24th of June with some other gent: and some of the brethren 19*s*. 0*d*.

I. more spent on Captaine Cole & other gent: that came with him 8*s*. 3*d*.

I. more to poore distressed sea men that were put on shore in our towne 1*s*. 6*d*.

I. more for canves to make the cartrages for the greate guns 2*s*. 6*d*.

I. payd masons for mendinge and healing of the castle wales 12*s*. 1*d*.

I. more to Ralph Couch for tymber worke in the castle 3*s*. 4*d*.

I. spent att Mr Godolphins beinge in towne with some other gent: that came to Towne the 15th of August 19*s*.

I. payd John Thomas for candles for the guarde 1*s*. 10*d*.

I. more to certaine ffrench men that were taken at sea 1*s*. 4*d*.

I. payd Mr John Payne for bords aboute the castle 13*s*.

I. more bestowed upon Mr Godolphins servants at the tyme he went there with a petition 4*s*. 4*d*.

I. More payd John Hyatt for a little howse to holde the store for one quarter 5*s*.

I. payd to Mr Hughes for a sermon the viij^th day of Oct. 10*s*.

I. payd Mr Veale [the Steward of the Manor] for an accustomed Rent out of the Market howse 4*s*.

1648
1649 St Ives. Alexander James Mayor 1648.

Profits of markets and fairs let to John Bussow for £9 10*s*.

Profits of the quay to Edward Hammond for £19.

Mr Biggs purchased his freedom for 10*s*.

Disbursements. Imprimis. Paid ffor Mendinge the Cause of the great Cupp 3*s*. 6*d*.

[*i.e.*, the case of the silver tankard presented by Sir Francis Bassett.]

I. in allowance for Ciching being Maior for the whole yeare £12.

Primo die Novembris Anno Domini 1647.

M[r] Thomas Noale Maior, elected.

Profits of fairs and markets let to M[r] John Trewinnard for £33.

Profits of the quay to M[r] Edward Hammond for £19 10s.

Anno Domini 1647/1648.

St Ives. The Accompts of M[r] Thomas Noale then Maior of the Towne & Borough of S[t] Ives aforesaid of all Receipts & disbursements of Money for & to the use of the Towne & pisb. for one whole yeare as followeth:—

[The following purchased their freedom:]

Joseph Gubbs, Mathew Adie, and
William Capps, John Jeffries.

I. received of M[r] George Hicks being church warden towards the charge in bringinge downe the Organs Raylinges and other Implements of the church 18*s*.

Disbursements.

Imprimis spent att the ffirst of Nouember being Electiō day £1 19*s*. 10*d*.

Item more to the Ringers the ffiveth day of November and candlelight 3*s*. 9*d*.

I. payed M[r] John Whitworth for a quarter wages at candlemas 3*s*. 10*d*.

I. payd a post to carrie a Letter to the Maior of Pensance 1*s*.

I. payd to carrie a Letter to Justice Thomas 2*s*. 3*d*.

I. payd to preachers for sermons att severall times in our church £7 1*s*. 0*d*.

I. payd for sending of Hazarde to Lanceston Goale £1 4*s*. 0*d*.

I. spent at Markajew to solicit M[r] Saintabin for the Towne 1*s*.

[The St. Aubin family of Clowance, of ancient Norman (or rather Breton) descent, espoused the Parliamentary cause. Soon after this they became possessed of Saint Michael's Mount, which had been held for some generations by the Royalist Bassetts.]

I. to M[r] Cocke for puttinge in the bills against Hazard at the Assises 1*s*.

I. payd the two serjeants for goeinge to Clowance to speake with M[r] Saintabyn 3*s*.

I. more to a post that came from M[r] Saintabyn 1*s*.

I. more spent upon M[r] Saintabyn and other gents that came to our Towne £1 9*s*. 3*d*.

I. more for a post to go to M[r] Paulie at seuerall times 1*s*. 6*d*.

St Ives 1649. John Diggens mayor.

The 6th of January 1650.

Whereas Peter Ceelye gent. had by the consent of this Corporation one peece of ordinance to put aboard his vessell and by accident loosinge his vessell is not able to furnish the towne with the said peece of ordinance agen, itt is therfore ordered by us that the said Peter Ceely shall pay for the said peece of ordinance weighing 5c 2 qr. weight att 6*s*. 8*d*. p.c. the sume of 16*s*. 8*d*. if the said Peter Ceelye cannott ffurnish an other peece.

[Hicks says that Ceely of Saint Ives was 'vice-admiral and commanded a troop of horse.' If so, the 'Horse Marines' were no mere fiction at that date. About this time a Peter Ceely was Maycr of Plymouth.]

The 15th of february 1650.

Wee the Maior & Burgesses of the Burrow of St Ives doe recomend the care of the ffree Grammar Skoole of the said Borrowh to Mr Leonard Welsteede.

Moreover wee agree & consent that Richard ffowler shall be clarke of this pīsh & to have the Allowance of the former clarkes.

And farther wee agree that the Sexton shall have Twelfe shillings ꝑ annum pd him quarterly by the church warden for ringginge of the nine oclock ble. [bell.]

28th May 1650.

Receued of Mr Thomas Stevens & Mr Wm Nance Churchwardens in Anno 1649 Certaine Implements Belonginge unto the Church As followeth

Two Silver fflagons aboue A Pottle each of them.
Two Silluer Cupps with couers each of them.
Two Peuter Pottles & two Peuter fflagons.
Six Font Cloathes.
ffower Table Cloathes for the Cōmunion Table.
One Stamēn Carpet for the Cōmunion Table.

All these goods aboue written are received by us to be Accountable to the Towne for them.

John Player.
George Hammond.

St Ives 1650. Peter Ceely mayor.

Profits of the quay let to Thomas Stevens junior for £18 10*s*. 0*d*.
Profits of the market to John Sprye for £60 0*s*. 0*d*.

A List of things delivered to the new mayor.

Charter and Book containing the same.
The Great Statute Book annotated by Palton.
Daltons Office of a Justice of Peace.
A brazon yard.
The chest of writings.
One Great Gilded Boule with a Couer.

[The gift of Sir Francis Bassett. (See *ante*.)]

Delivered to the new Churchwardens:

2 Silver fflagons.
2 Silver Cupps with covers.
2 Peuter Pottles.
2 Peuter fflagons.
Six font cloathes.
One fflanell carpett for the Comunion Table.
One greene carpett for the Table.
One scarlett pulpitt cloath & cushing.

Alexander James.
Richard Smith.

Xi° Novembr: Anno Dmi: 1650. Att a generall Assembly of the Mayor and Burgesses of St. Ives the day and yeare aforesaid Theis Orders and constitucōns made concluded and agreede uppon as followeth viz: Impr: Whatsoever Seane Boate that hath a Steame [stem, *i.e.*, a right to its place in the bay for catching fish] must come directly home yf hee goe not to helpe his consart in killing of ffishe; for if eyther the Seane Boate or ffollower shall goe from the Steame a ffishing, the Seane Boate shall lose her Steame: And that no Seane-Boate or ffollower roweing to the Eastward or home shall rowe too deepe, but keepe alonge the Shoare, the whch. if they doe they shall paye their fynes [or suffer] imprisonment according to former orders.

John Spenser and John Hocking are to measure all the warp in the seine-boats for the ensuing year. Noe boate shall have aboue Eight Landmen as Blowsers.

[Blowsers are men who stand on the shore and hold the ends of the ropes attached to the seines.]

[Other regulations follow with regard to the fishery.]

Jno Payne.	Peter Ceely maior.
John Treweeke.	John Diggens.
Peter Goodall.	Thos: Stevens.
John Spry.	Henry Hickes.
Christo: Payne.	Edward Hammond.
Effrem Robinson.	Thomas Sprigge.

Wm Pearce.	Thomas Noall.
Jon Thomas.	Alexander James.
Hugh Harris.	Arthour Wescott.
Richard Moris.	George Hicks.
Edward Wescott.	John Player.
Henerey Hitchens.	Tho: Purefoy.
Peter Tonken.	Henry Sterrie.
John Spry.	Thomas Dajowe.
Thom: Beremman.	Nico Prigge.
John Cockins.	Jno: Paine Jr
Peter Gooddall.	Will: Diggens.
Petter Cossenes.	Thomas Stevens Jũr.
Thomas Hicks.	Thomas Painter.
John Tompken.	Rob: Cowch.
Hugh Hickes.	Henry Tryweeke.
Ralfe R. C. Cowch.	Edward Paine.
Alexander Player.	William Nance.
John + Perking.	Rich: Pollard.
William Harriss.	Christo: Morish.
Rob: R. H. Hickes.	Jo. Barber.
Jeffry + Pearce.	John Noall.
Rich: R. M. Morrin.	Richard Smith.

[On November 12, 1650, further bye-laws relating to the fishery were enacted and signed by twenty-one of the above and also by John Bolythowe.]

A Note of such things belonging unto the Towne and corporacõn of St Ives as are delivered over by John Diggens gent. unto Peter Ceely gent. the nowe Mayor 22° November 1650 Impr: The charter of the Towne and the Booke contayneing the same.

The Greate Statue booke collected by Palton.

Daltons office of a Justice of Peace.

A 2 lb weight; 1 lb; ½ lb; ¼ lb of aberdepoize. A 1 lb; ½ lb; ¼ lb; 2 oz; 1 oz; ½ oz Troye weight.

A brazon yeard, The Towne Seale and 2 stamps.

The chest of writings.

The Accounts of Peter Ceely mayor of St. Ives $\frac{1650}{1651}$

Receipts.

Imprimis: Received of seuerall p̄sons for p̄vision delivered them in the tyme of late Contagion £15.

The 1th Aprill 1651.

Item: received of Mr Henrie Hickes & Mr William Hicks for the use & benefitte of the poor of the pish: of St. Ives the sume of £40.

I. John Bolithowe of the pish: of Crowane [presumably of Bolitho in that parish] was admitted a free man of this corporation for the fine of 40*s*. by the consent of the burgesses. Received £2 0*s*. 0*d*.

I. rec: of M[r] William Hickes of Kerris the sume of £10 0*s*. 0*d*.

I. rec[d] for an execution levyed on John Hutchings for Christopher Cocke debt[r] being due unto the towne £3 19*s*. 0*d*.

I. rec[d] of Robert Hickes for puision hee had on the account of the towne in the sicknese yere £1 5*s*. 0*d*.

I. rec[d] of M[r] Diggens last Mayor upon his account for monies due unto the towne £4 0*s*. 0*d*.

Disbursements:

Item: pd: the Ringers for beere the 5th of November 1650 5*s*. 0*d*.

I. for a carpett for the towne haule 12*s*. 0*d*.

I. pd: distressed Irish men 2*s*. 6*d*.

I. pd: distressed English men taken 2*s*. 6*d*.

I. pd: distressed ffrench men 2*s*. 6*d*.

I. for building & errecting of a house for the hewers £1 10*s*. 0*d*.

[The huers are men who shout and signal directions for rowing to the men who are fishing in the bay. The huers watch the movements of the shoal, standing for that purpose on certain hill-tops, where houses or sheds are provided for their shelter.]

I. towards a rate for Poulsew Bridge 3*s*. 6*d*.

I. pd. for a beame for the Markett house to M[r] Cowch 6*s*. 0*d*.

John Diggens.
Nic[o] Prigge.
Geo: Hammond.
Henry Sterries.

St. Ives Thomas Purefoy mayor 1651.

[To the foregoing list of books, weights, etc., the following are this year added as being delivered to the new mayor:]

A brason gallon.
With one ould Towne seale more.
I. a booke called the constables office.
One Great Guilded Boule with a cover.

1st November 1651.

(Town Receiver or Treasurer appointed; the same to be annually chosen for receiving the Town's rents, profits & incomes and for the disbursing thereof for the Town's use.)

3 Itt is agreed on that whereas there is an order formerlye made giving liberty to all ꝑson as well freemen as others Inhabitants of the said Borrough that they should not be

arrested to the Court of the said Burrough unto any mans suite, Butt should be all somoned or warned And on that order or constitution had the priviledge of three courts to make their appearance to any suite in the said court comenced, Wee doe therefore by these presents agree order and constitute that wee make null repeale and utter make voyd the force power and effecte of that constitution. And from hence forth every pson : to be somoned or arrested to the said court and to have loyall p'ceedings accordinge to law.

The xxvth of December 1651.

Burrough of St Ives. Itt is agreed on by a mutuall consent of the mayor, aldermen and burgesses; That the Thirtye ffive pounds due from the Towne to Mr Henrye Sterrye should bee satisfyed.

2 Itt is allsoe agreed on that three pounds bee abated him out of the Tenn pounds due from him to the Towne on accounte in the Sicknesse yere; And this three pounds is allowed him for his paynes then.

3 It is allsoe agreed on that the xv^{lbs} be deducted out of the Thirtye ffive pounds which is due to the poore of the Towne from him for the Legacye given the poore by Mr Goddolphin. And that this be registered on the Towne register and the Towne from hence forthward to be come debitor to the poore for the same. And the Interrest to be payd by the Thresurer for the tyme beinge from tyme to tyme unto the Overseers of the poore.

4 Itt is agreed that Three pounds Twelve shillings due for Interrest be likewise deducted out of the xxxv^{lbs} and that this 3 lbs xij^s bee forth with payd by the Tresurer to the Overseers of the poore.

5 Itt is allsoe agreed on that the vij^{lbs} remayninge of the x^{lbs} above mentioned bee deducted out of the xxxv^{lbs}.

6 Itt is farther agreed on that the Tresurer for the tyme now beinge doe forthwith paye the Nyne pounds eighte shillings to Mr Henrye Sterrye and to deliver upp his bond; takeinge a sufficiente receipte under Mr Sterryes hand to free the Towne of the xxxv^{lbs} above mencyoned.

John Littleton Towne Clarke.
By order.

Burrough of St Ives. The daye and yere abouesaid Itt is agreed on and ordered. That the Tresurer or Collector of the Burrough aforesaid for the tyme beinge from yere to yere duelye paye Three pounds for everye yere unto the Ouerseers of the poore of the burrough aforesaid, allsoe Twentye shillings allsoe yerelye to the minister of the said burrough. And is for the Interest of ffiftye pounds given unto the said uses as a Legacye by the last Will and Testament of M[rs] Chestian Hext widdoe lately deceased which said sume of ffiftye pounds remaynes in the hands of the cheife burgesses for the use of the corporation.

[This charitable lady died in the year 1648. Under the provisions of her will an alms-house for six poor people was founded in the following year. Early in the present century the alms-house was sold by the Corporation, and the proceeds applied to the purchase of a poor-house. On the formation of the district union these latter premises were let as warehouses.]

Item itt is allsoe ordered that the Tresurer allsoe yerely paye unto the Ouerseers of the poore ffower and twentye shillings And is for the Interrest of ffifteene pounds given as a Legacye by S[r] ffrancis Goddolphin unto the poore, which sayd sume remaynes allsoe to the use of the corporation.

St. Ives. 1651. Thomas Purefoye mayor.

Profits of the Keye or Peer to George Hammond for £18.

Ordered by the Mayor & the Burgesses that Richard Hicks shall be Towne Collector for this yere & shall receive such sume or sumes of monye as frō tyme to tyme shall accrewe or belonge unto the towne for this yere And that hee shall receive 20*s*. from the towne towards his labour and expensis.

Burrough of St Ives. Att a general assemblye att the Guild hall of the Burrough aforesaid the 5th day of ffebruarye 1652. John Seyntaubyne Esq[r] was elected Recorder of the said Burrough and sworne the 7th day of ffebruarye aforesaid 1652. Before Nicholas Prigge then Maior att the Guild haule the day and yere aforesaid.

St. Ives. 1652 Account of Thomas Purefoy late Mayor.

Receipts.

Imprimis: Received of M[r] George Hammond for rent of the key £18 0*s*. 0*d*.

Item: Received of ffrancis Arundell Gent. of the pish: of Camborne in the countye of Cornewall to be made free of this corporacōn £3 0*s*. 0*d*.

I. Received of Thomas Purefoy abouesaid Mayor for the use of the corporacōn All the goods beinge lefte of James Shellsens glasier of the said burrough And sould att the seuerall prices as p' a List doth appeare Amountinge to the sume of £6 15*s*. 8*d*.

[Goods forfeited for felony, according to an ancient privilege of the borough. N.B. Dugdale, 'England and Wales,' also mentions a custom at Saint Ives, that every person dying worth £10 should pay 10s. to the curate.]

Disbursements as followeth

Imprimis payd Mr Henrye Sterrye as ꝑ order of the corporacōn £9 8s. 0d.

Item payd Mr William Diggens Ouerseer of the poore, for the Interrest of a sume of monye given as a Legacye by Mr Goddolphin unto the poore; payd him in full of the Interrest of that monie due att Easter last 1652 the sume of £3 12s. 0d.

Item, disbursed: Lost upon portugall monye payd Mr Sterrye 4s. 0d.

I. payd Ralph Cowch for making the Pillorye 3s. 6d.

I. payd Mr Richard Cowch for a beame to make the Pillorye 6s. 0d.

I. Thomas Hickes to mende the Locke and keyes of the castle door 1s. 6d.

I. payd the smiths and the carpenters to mend the prison doore 0s. 6d.

I. payd the men that did sett up the Pillorye 1s. 0d.

I. payd Gerrance Bettye the 11th februarye 1651 for wippinge one 2s. 0d.

I. payd Robert Cowch by order of Mr Maior for a Booke called the Constables office 2s. 0d.

I. payd Ralph Cowch for making a silinge [ceiling] in the Towne Haule 6s. 2d.

I. payd Mr Nichollas Prigge for Boards and Nayles 7s. 4d.

I. lost upon the Portugall monies then payd him 1s. 4d.

I. payd Mr William Diggens Ouerseer of the poore for the Interrest of a Legacye givven unto the poore by Mrs Chestian Hext and is in full of that Interrest due at candlemas last £3 0s. 0d.

I. Lost upon that Portugall monies 3s. 9d.

I. payd Mr Leonard Wellsteed minister one pound and is for the Interrest of a sume of monie given as a Legacye by Mrs Chestian Hext unto the minister of the pish. to be payd for ever for him in full being due att candlemas last £1 0s. 0d.

I. payd Henrye White by Mr Maior's order to goe to Penrin in the states service 1s. 6d.

I. Thomas Tinner to goe to the Mount itt beinge a Towne case, in a Message 1s. 0d.

[This entry is explained by the next.]

I. payd Hugh Harris the constable to carrye the Tacabirds before Justice Seyntaubyne £1 5s. 6d.

I. payd distressed people being quartered at Richard Morrishes 3*s*. o*d*.

I. payd John Bussowe for the like 2*s*. o*d*.

I. payd for the pockett maces 2*s*. 6*d*.

I. lost upon the exchange of some portugall monye by consent 4*s*. 7*d*.

I. Received of Mr Thomas Purefoye for monies disbursed for the Tacabirds £1 5*s*. 6*d*.

[This year the following in addition to those previously mentioned were delivered to the new mayor.]

A Booke of newe Acts of Parliament.

A Booke of Assise of bread & weights & measures.

A payre of brass scales.

The Account of Nicholas Prigge mayor $\frac{1652}{1653}$ St. Ives.

Receipts.

Received of Richard Pollard for a fyne for blooshed [bloodshed] by him 3*s*. 4*d*.

[This does not imply manslaughter, but, as I venture to think, the slaughter of beasts.]

Item Received of John Woolcocke for a fyne for blooshed by him 3*s*. 4*d*.

Disbursements.

[For repairs to the prison and castle.]

Item payd for 2 lockes and keyes for the cubarts [cupboards] in the Towne haule 2*s*. 2*d*.

I. payd for cushings for the Towne's use 5*s*. 10*d*.

I. payd to George Gunner for making cleane the prison o*s*. 4*d*.

I. payd Tho. Hickes for beere and makinge cleane the castle house 3*s*. o*d*.

I. disbursed the 5th februarie 1652, about the markett house this quarter £1 3*s*. o*d*.

I. paid John Spenser the sergeante for a horse to ride to the Recorder 1*s*. o*d*.

I. paid for a locke and keye for the outward castle gate 2*s*. 6*d*.

I. paid Mr John Littleton for the booke of Newe Acts of Parliaments 8*s*.

I. pd. for portage of the booke and letters sent him att London 2*s*.

I. Pd Jon Thomas the constable the 4th May 1653 for a warrant & to carrie the prest men to Truroe 6*s*.

I. paid the constables to carrie the prest men to Penrin the 25th June 1653 £1 0s. 5*d*.

[Two other similar entries occur this year of pressed men sent to Penryn. At the commencement of the year 1653 a fleet of eighty sail was sent against the Dutch, hence this activity. The press-gang was a frequent visitor to Saint Ives down to the end of the first quarter of the present century. To this day the Saint Ives district supplies some of the finest seamen to the British navy. The former custom of forcing men into the service often led to turbulent scenes in the streets of the town, not always without bloodshed. A Saint Ives family named Woolcock has a tradition that a female ancestress of theirs once, with a china bowl, broke the head of a press-gang officer who was attempting to carry off her son.]

I. paid the Hundred constable Mr Rogers for the Countie stocke ended att Michallmas last 1653 16*s*. 6*d*.

I. paid by the constable for the rate to repayre Saint Blazie Bridge 2*s*. 6*d*.

I. paid the constable to paie Major Ceelie for pressing the men monie disbursed by him 12*s*. 0*d*.

I. pd. the 18th 8ber 1653 to colonell Buttler a distressed man taken by the ffrench pyrats 10*s*. 0*d*.

I. paid Mr Land the minister for preachinge two sermons in Mr Wellsteed absence 10*s*. 0*d*.

I. paid Joane Bullie when shee was shutt upp by the Townes order 5*s*. 8*d*.

I. paid for An Assise booke of weights and measures 1*s*. 0*d*.

I. paid for a payre of Brase scales to waite butter and bread 3*s*. 0*d*.

St. Ives 1653. Richard Cowch elected Mayor.

Profits of the Market let to Morrish Diar or Dyer for £40.
Profits of the quay to George Hammond for £15 10s.

Richard Hicks Town Collector.

Arthour Westcott and John Player Overseer of the poor Henry Hicks and Robert Cowch Churchwardens.

1653
——— Mayor's Accounts.
1654

Received ffor a ffyne of bloodshed 3*s*. 4*d*.

I. Received of Peter Ceely Esqr for halfe yeres rent for the Mills ended the 1st of November 1654 £6 13*s*. 4*d*.

Disbursements as followeth

Item, paid William Leonard to putt Chestian Mattie to Lanceston £1 0s. 0*d*.

I. paid Tho: Stevens for a peece of Timber the 1th of december 1653 5*s*. 0*d*.

I. paid J^on^ Rosemewas the 21th Jan. 1653 for a qrs wages for keepinge the clocke 3*s*. 0*d*.

I. Given amonge the souldiers att proclayminge the Lord Protector 10*s*. 0*d*.

[Hicks says that on this occasion blue ribbons were distributed among the soldiers, who, to the number of about one hundred, under the command of Ceely, fired three volleys.]

I. paid Ralph Cowch for makinge the stocks 3*s*. 2*d*.

I. paid the Smith for Iron worke about itt 3*s*. 2*d*.

I. paid for caringe the timber 8*d*.

I. paid for two Bills of Indictemente against Chestian Mattie 4*s*. 8*d*.

I. paid Mr Nicholas Prigge the 15th May 1654 ffor 11^lbs^ of powder for the Guns 13*s*. 9*d*.

I. paid for caringe a poore woman and her childe to Truroe 4*s*. 0*d*.

I. paid the 7th 8^ber^ to J^on^ Spenser for Bread for the Bawde and the whore that were carted 6*d*.

[Whipped through the town at the tail of a cart.]

I. paid Ralph Cowch for makinge the carte to carte the whores for his labour and nayles 2*s*. 2*d*.

The waye wardens for this yere is Lewis Cogar and William Ninnis.

Overseers of the poor Thomas Purefoy, Richard Smith, George Payntеr and William Browne.

[' In 1654, Thomas Purefoy, captain of a small privateer of four guns, belonging to Ceely, captured and brought to Saint Ives two fine Breton barques laden with salt' (Hicks).]

St. Ives 1654. George Hammond elected Mayor.

1654 — His Account. 1655

Received ffor ffynes of bloodshed made by Richard Pollard, Ann his wife and James Pollard 10*s*. 0*d*.

I. Received of Henrye Barbar ffor a ffyne 1*s*. 0*d*.

I. Received of Edward Westcoatt ffor severall fynes 7*s*. 0*d*.

Paid to putt John Tacabird to Lanceston £1 18*s*. 0*d*.

I. paid Rob: Sprigge constable for his charges towards putting Tacabird to Lanceston 2*s*. 6*d*.

I. paid Andrew Job monie layd out in puttinge the said Tacabird to Lanceston 3*s*. 6*d*.

I. paid for whippinge of William Nance his wife and another woman then wipte with her 2*s*. 6*d*.

I. payd Lewes ffoger to goe post to Pendennis 3*s*. 6*d*.

I. paid the 2th June 1655 unto Edward Stevens Collector of the grand Assessement for soe much due being short on the Rate 3s. 6d.

I. paid Rob: Sprigge then constable to go aboard a ffrigett at Pensance 2s. 6d.

I. paid the 18th August 1655 to severall poore distressed ffrench men 14s. od.

I. paid for twoe doz: of Raggs [stones] for the Markett howse and caringe them 6s. 8d.

I. paid Lewis ffoger to goe post to Pensance 1s.

I. paid Math: Gennings carrie Grace the wife of Gerance Bettie to Lanceston Goale being accused for a Witch the 15th of November 1655 the sume of £1 14s. od.

I. paid for a crest ffor the markett house 4d.

I. paid for a hundred of helling stones 10d.

I. paid for a booke for the constitutions 7s. od.

25th October 1655. Another byelaw relating to the seine fishery was passed and signed by

George Hammond mayor.	Edw. Paine.
P. Ceely.	Hugh Harris.
Henry Hicks.	William Pearse.
Edward Hammond.	John Thomas.
Thomas Sprigge.	R. Arundell.
Alexander James.	Renatus Trenwith.
Thomas Noall.	Will: Diggens.
Thomas Purefoy.	Thomas Stevens.
Nic[o]: Prigge.	John Cockin.
Arthour Westcott.	John Tonkin.
George Hicks.	Thomas Painter.
Henry Sterrie.	John Noall.

St. Ives, 1655. Henrie Sterrie elected mayor.

Profits of the Market let to William Ackland and Thomas Painter for £49.

Profits of the Quay let to Peter Ceely for £19 10s.

Renatus Treunwith gent: and M[r] William Pearse collectors for the Porthfarme.

[Renatus was a common baptismal name in these parts; it seems to be a latinized form of Reginald or Reynold.]

1655
—— Account of M[r] Henry Sterrie
1656

Received of John Tacabird ffor his yearlye rent of his house ffor one whole yere ended att Michallmas 1656 the sume of £2 os. od.

Disbursed Item J[on] Noale for horse hiere and Math. Jennings to conveye Grace Bettie to Lanceston 16*s.* 0*d.*

[The alleged witch.]

Item paid Rich. Hichings constable seuerall things being allowed 6*s.* 0*d.*

I. payd Rich. Smith for monies laid out about the prison 3*s.* 0*d.*

I. payd M[r] Littleton towards his London journeye & to doe the Towne business 5*s.* 0*d.*

I. payd then towards the purchase of the Towne in p'te £10 0*s.* 0*d.*

I. payd M[r] Littleton for drawing the deeds of the Towne purchase £1 12*s.* 0*d.*

I. Given M[r] Littleton more for puttinge into the deeds the alms house in the Ilande which wee did not buye 10*s.* 0*d.*

Item: payd Lewis ffoger 3th March 1655 to goe to Hellston to seuerall ministers 1*s.* 6*d.*

Item: paid him to goe with Grace Betties Exaīīon & Recogn' to Lanceston 8*s.* 0*d.*

I. paid Ninnis for keepinge two poore prisoners put here from Lanceston 5*s.* 0*d.*

I. paid ffoger to goe with Letters to seuerall ministers to invite them to preach 2*s.* 0*d.*

28th June 1656. Item payd ffor newe fittinge the cockinge stoole and the carpenters wages 10*s* 6*d.*

I. paid for candles and monis disbursed when Major Ceely's souldiers did watch 6*s.* 4*d.*

I. paid for Residewe of the Towne purchase £14 10*s.* 0*d.*

I. paid M[r] Tucker minister for preaching here on saboath daye 10*s.* 0*d.*

[Mark of the Puritan era, Sunday called the Sabbath.]

I. payd Thomas Steuens for Beniamins John's wages hee beinge clerke £1 10*s.* 0*d.*

I. paid Thomas Clerke, Lewis ffoger and others their fellowes to carrie stones from the keye severall tymes 16*s.* 0*d.*

I. paid Lewis ffoger to goe with post letters in the states service 2*s.* 6*d.*

I. payd for a Locke for the Stocks 1*s.* 0*d.*

I. payd M[r] Vincent the Under Sheriffe for clearinge the Towne from the Assises in Juries 10*s.* 0*d.*

[*i.e.*, for exempting Saint Ives men from sitting on juries at those assizes.]

I. spent on him as ℘ his Rec'pts appeares in sacke 1*s.* 8*d.*

I. payd John Thomas ffor half yere for his clerkes wages ended att Christide next being the yere 1656 £2 0*s.* 0*d.*

St Ives 1656. Richard Hicks elected mayor.

Profits of the Market let to William Truthall *alias* Thomas.

[This Thomas family was often called Trythall or Trethwall from the place where they lived.]

Profits of the Quay let to George Painter.

Collectors of the port farm Richard Hoskings and Edward Wescoatte.

Churchwardens, Alexander James and Robert Cowch.

Overseers of the poor, Nicholas Prigge and Hugh Harris.

1656
—— Account of Mr Richard Hicks.
1657

Payd John Thomas for the former clerks wages being unpayed 4s. 0*d.*

I. payd carpenters ffor mendinge the standings 4s. 6*d.*

[The stalls in the market-house.]

I. payd or given 5 poore distressed taken men 7s. 0*d.*

I. payd Mr Tregosse for his whole yere £14 0s. 0*d.*

I. payd ffor beere to the Ringers the 18th ffeb. 1657 beinge the thanksgivinge Daye 8s. 0*d.*

I. payd ffor wipping a theefe 6*d.*

I. payd a man to goe to Ludgvan for a minister 6*d.*

I. payd ffor makinge a newe stampinge Iron. . . . .

I. payd ffor beere and points in veiwinge the Bounds of the pish: 4s. 0*d.*

I. payd ffor goeing to Lanceston with the Quakers £1 2s. 0*d.*

[One of the offending Friends was no less a personage than John Fox, the founder of the sect. They were imprisoned for distributing tracts at Saint Ives. See Hayden's 'Book of Dates.']

I. payd ffor the ffyne acknowledged by Mr Heale £1 16s. 6*d.*

I. allowed Trithwall for Tacabirds Pentise 4s. 0*d.*

I. payd ffor beere given the Ringers att the P'clayminge the Lord Protector 10s. 0*d.*

I. payd ffor mendinge the Cryers bell 1s. 0*d.*

I. payd towards the repayre of Larren bridge 3s. 0*d.*

I. payd Will: Pearse ffor Tymber 7s. 0*d.*

St Ives 1657 Edward Hammond mayor

Profits of the keye or peere let to George Hammond for £18.

Profits of the Market to William Ackland for £48. 10s.

John Thomas and Thomas Painter collectors of the Port-firme.

1657
—— Account of Mr Edward Hammond.
1658

Item: Received of William Ackland ffor three quarters rent of the markett house the sume of £36 2*s.* 6*d.*

I. received more ffor one quarter rent of the markett house which was levyed out of the goods & chattells of William Ackland after he was sent to the Comon Goale the sume of £12 2*s.* 6*d.*

[We learn from Hicks that, in 1657, William Ackland stabbed John Tackabird, over a game of cards, at a house in Saint Ives, and was hanged. His property was confiscated to the use of the Corporation, 'agreeably to a privilege in the Charter.']

I. received more beinge the overplus of William Acklands goods his charges & expensis in sending him to goale and his quarter rent dew ffor the markett howse out of itt beinge payd the said goods beinge sould by order of the Corporačon £4 5*s.* 3*d.*

I. Received of Jane Tacabird widdow ffor one yeres rent ffor her howse ended att Michallmas 1658 £2 0*s.* 0*d.*

I. payd Mr Thomas Tregosse the minister ffor his yeres salarye the sume of £15 0*s.* 0*d.*

I. payd John Thomas the clerke ffor his yeres salarye then ended allsoe £4 0*s.* 0*d.*

I. payd ffor a post to goe to Pendennis in the states service 3*s.* 0*d.*

I. given to poore distressed sea men being taken 4*s.* 0*d.*

I. payd the 8th maye 1658 ffor lockes, keyes, twists, spukes and nayles ffor the castle gate doore and Lambezoe doore 10*s.* 4*d.*

I. paid Hugh Harris the constable to give unto 34 distressed seamen being taken the sume of £1 11*s.* 6*d.*

I. given the 19th June 1658 to a poore distressed man taken 2*s.* 6*d.*

I given to another poore distressed man taken 2*s.* 0*d.*

I. disbursed by William Ackland the 18th Augt 1658 about the standings and other things in the markett howse as by p'ticulars did appeare 13*s.* 2*d.*

I. payd Geo. Painter ffor Tymber labour and nayles aboute the crookes to hang the musketts in the haule 5*s.* 6*d.*

I. payd Hugh Harris constable for powder match and candles for the guard the sume of 14*s.* 10*d.*

I. payd the 11th 7ber 1658 to the gunners and drumer att the pčlayminge the Lord Richard His Highnesse Lord Protector of the Common Wealth the sume of 3*s.*

[Oliver Cromwell died September 3, 1658.]

I. payd for beere ffor the Ringers and others that daye 12*s.* 0*d.*
I. payd ffor mendinge the Chest 8*d.*
I. allowed William Ackland ffor Tacabirds doore 4*s.* 0*d.*

[This conjunction of the two names is rather a singular coincidence.]

I. payd ffor candles ffor the guard when the cavaliers were here last the sume of 5*d.*
I. payd ffor a brass quarte 2*s.* 6*d.*
I. paid Mr Maior ffor his coroners ffees on the Death of William Grease 13*s.* 4*d.*
I. payd more for a warrante & inquisition on the death of John Tacabird 2*s.* 6*d.*

[Stabbed by Ackland.]

I. payd Richard Smith in earnest ffor his tyme in the Bowling greene 1*s.*

[In Saint Ives and other Cornish towns, including Marazion and Camborne, the bowling-green was Corporation property. Richard seems to have been the man who set up the nine-pins. The Saint Ives bowling-green is now private property, Bowling Green Terrace being built thereupon.]

I. paid ffor the cloath about the chayres in the church the sume of £5 18*s.* 0*d.*

St. Ives 1658. Thomas Sprigge elected mayor.

Market Tolls let to George Hammond for £59.
Quay Tolls let to Edward Stevens for £20.

William Pearse and John Treweeke collectors of the porth-firme.

[Port-farm, *i.e.*, the customs.]

[Here follows a record of the election for the last Commonwealth Parliament, opened on January 29, 1659. St. Aubyn and Ceely were both Republicans.]

Burrough
of
St. Ives Att the Towne Haule there the last day of December In the yere of our Lord 1658. Thomas Sprigge Mayor And the capitall Burgesses of the Burrough aforesaid Haue accordinge to the Tenor of a Writt ffrom Nichollas Cosen Esqr High Sheriffe of this countie of Cornewall received chosen and elected Burgeseses accordinge to their ould and Antiente custome of the Burrough aforesaid in manner & fforme ffollowing in Parliament beinge elected the daye and yere aboue written by the mayor and capitall Burgesses hereunder named viz.

Thomas Sprigge mayor	...	John Seyntaubyne Esqr & Peter Ceely Esqr
Edward Hammond ...	...	do
Peter Ceely Esqr ...	...	do Underwood

(absent) Henrye Hicks ... John Seyntaubyne Esqr & Peter Ceely Esqr
Thomas Noalle ... ... do
Alexander James ... ... do
absent Thomas Purefoye ... do
Nichollas Prigge ... ... do
Richard Cowch ... ... do
George Hamond ... ... do
Henrye Sterrie ... ... Peter Ceely
Richard Hicks ... ... J^on Seyntaubyn—the same
George Hicks ... ... The same—the same

(By voyces elected against everye ones name as is sette downe.)

John Seyntaubyne Esqr Recorder of the Burrough aforesaid And Peter Ceelye Esq of the Burrough aforesaid were elected and chosen by the Mayor and capitall Burgesses of the Borrough aforesaid above named accordinge to their ould and Antiente Custome for electing of Burgesses to serue in Parliament ffor the Burrough aforesaid in manner and fforme above specified the day and yere first above written.

1658/1659 Account of Mr Thomas Sprigge.

Received of Hoskin of Lelant ffor a ffyne ffor bloodshed 3*s*. 4*d*.

I. received of Jane Tacabird widdow for one yeares rent ffor her howse ended michallmas £2 0*s*. 0*d*.

Disbursements Imprimis. Given a poore sea man being taken prisoner by the spaniards 1*s*. 0*d*.

Item. payd J^on Hawkin to lodge the same man one Night 6*d*.

I. given to a poore distressed sea boyes 6*d*.

I. payd Thomas Clarke ffor caring [localism for 'carrying'] the Armes in the castle 1*s*. 0*d*.

I. payd J^on Treweeke then for clensinge them Armes 9*s*. 2*d*.

I. Payd Mr Payne for drawinge the Addresse of the Corporacōn to his highnesse the Lord Protector 2*s*. 6*d*.

[This address to Richard Cromwell is given in full in 'Mercurius Politicus,' No. 549. Extract:

'We are thankfully sensible that whereas the ways of our Zion might be mourning, and judgment been turned backward, we are defended in our Religious and Civil Liberties, sitting under our Vines and Fig-trees, none making of us afraide.'

'Above 90 addresses from the counties and most considerable Corporations, congratulated Richard Cromwell on his accession, in all the terms of dutiful allegiance' ('Student's Hume,' p. 460).]

I. payd Mr Hicks for drawinge the Conveyance betweene the Corporacōn and the minister 4s. od.

I. Payd the post for letters sent Major Ceely 1s. 6d.

I. payd for newe byndinge the statute bookes with other bookes 16s. od.

I. payd for mendinge the waye neere the markett house £10 19s. 9d.

I. payd for mendinge the lower Bridge £1 8s. od.

I. payd for mendinge the keye and the chappell as ꝑ ptīculars appears £1 19s. 10d.

I. payd Lewis ffoger ffor caringe Letters ffor the Cmon Wealth 4d.

I. payd Lewis ffoger ffor goeinge to Pendennis Castell & Pensance 3s. od.

I. payd Hugh Harris for dyett of a ffrenchman which came out of slaverye 1s. 6d.

[He was rescued or ransomed from the Algerines. Compare the note in the parish registers ; see *ante*, page 75.]

I. payd Nichollas Trownsen & Marten Candys to goe to Lanceston 15s. od.

I. payd Nichollas Davye ffor goeinge with a post letter 6d.

I. payd ffor cappinge the poste on the keye head 1s. 6d.

I. payd Henrye Treweeke ffor mendinge the stocks 1s. od.

I. payd John Hawkinge ffor meate and drinke given to prisoners 1s. 6d.

I. payd Edward Stevens for carying of Ruble from ye keye 1s. od.

I. payd ffor horse hire to ride to mairision to the Commissioners 1s. od.

I. payd to carye a letter to Mr Seyntaubyne 8d.

I. payd Rich. Smith for his horse to goe with Lewis ffoger 1s. od.

I. payd Lewis ffoger to goe with a letter to Mr Whitworth 6d.

I. payd Mr Whitworth the 1th Nov. for preaching 10s. od.

I. payd Tho: Syse constable to putt Thomas Bettyė to the howse of correction £1 10s. od.

I. payd the clarke John Thomas his yeres wages £4 os. od.

I. paid John Thomas ffor his paynes aboute the markett house & keye & the bridge & mendinge the waye £1 os. od.

I. payd the Coroners ffees ffor takinge an inquisition on the death of John Tacabird 13s. 4d.

St. Ives 1659. Thomas Noale elected mayor.

A list of such things belonging to the Borough as were delivered to the new mayor this year 1659.

[The Avoirdupois weights as before.]
The Charter and Book containing the same.
The Great Book called Polton.
One brazen gallon.
A Booke called the Constables office.
One iron stamp.
A brazen pynte.

1659
—— The Account of Thomas Noale.
1660

Disbursements Item: pd a poore distressed boy ffrom bristoll 2*s*. 6*d*.

I. pd. a distressed boy of Jersie 1*s*. 0*d*.

I. pd. a post to goe to St. Illarye with a letter 6*d*.

I. pd John Treweeke for a locke ffor the stocks 1*s*. 4*d*.

I. pd. ffor two smale Iron bolts ffor the stocks 10*d*.

I. pd. to constable Cowch when he went to Hellston 5*s*. 6*d*.

I. pd. a distressed sea man taken by the spaniards 3*s*. 0*d*.

I. pd. Morrish Dyer ffor seuerall packetts ffrom Parliament 2*s*. 6*d*.

I. pd. the 11th of June for a letter ffrom Mr Praed 6*d*.

I. pd. Morrish Dyer ffor two letters ffrom Mr Bassett 1*s*. 0*d*.

I. pd. ffor two letters from Mr St Aubyne and Mr Praed 1*s*. 0*d*.

I. pd. to carrye letters to the post att Plymouth 9*d*.

I. pd. ffor two letters sent unto London 6*d*.

[All this correspondence marks the excitement caused by the imminent restoration of the monarchy.]

I. spent when the Newes came that the Kinge and Parliament was agreed By the Maior and brethren £1 10*s*. 0*d*.

I. spent then on the Ringers att John Hawkings house 15*s*. 0*d*.

I. spent when Mr Bassett was in Towne 5*s*. 0*d*.

I. payd Morrish Dyer ffor powder the same day 8*s*. 0*d*.

I. spent att Pollards house the day the Kinge was p'claymed 15*s*. 0*d*.

[Charles II. was proclaimed King on May 8, 1660.]

I. spent then in beere one barrell at 15*s*. 0*d*.

I. spent att John Hawkings the day aforesaid one barrell of beere at 15*s*. 0*d*.

I. spent the same on the Ringers 10*s*. 0*d*.

I. spent att Edward Wescott the same day 3*s*. 0*d*.

I. paid ffor powder spent the same day £2 0*s*. 0*d*.

I. pd. for advice and counsell concerninge Mr Robinsons write [writ] 15*s*. 0*d*.

I. pd. the constable Cowch when he went to Pensance about the Poll monie 3*s*. 0*d*.

I. pd. ffor paper and candles about the Poll monie writinge 1*s*. 0*d*.

I. Pd ffor writinge the Poll Rate 6*s.* o*d.*
I. Pd Player the constable att goeinge to signe the Rate 5*s.* o*d.*
I. Pd the widdow Tacabird one yeres rent ffor her doore 4*s.* o*d.*
I. Pd Mr Bullock ffor his sermon the day of Election 10*s.* o*d.*
I. payd ffor one quarte of sacke when Mr St Aubyne was here att the sermon 2*s.* o*d.*

St. Ives 1660. Francis Robinson elected mayor.

1660
—— His Account is as follows:—
1661

Receipts.

Item received of Mr Peter Ceely for bloudshed 3*s.* 4*d.*
I. received of Thomas Syse for bloudshed 3*s.* 4*d.*
I. received of Richard Smyth ffor bloudshed 3*s.* 4*d.*
I. rec: of Will: Trithall wife ffor bloudshed 3*s.* 4*d.*

Disbursements:

Imprimis pd. the kings coronation day to Cockin to beate the drume 2*s.* 6*d.*
I. pd: Mr Bullock the minister in pte: of his salarye. £5 o*s.* o*d.*
I. pd: the pīsh of Lelant by order £5 o*s.* o*d.*
I. pd: Rich: Pollard ffor beere dranke the coronation day 12*s.* o*d.*
I. pd. Rich: Smith ffor beere the coronation day 5*s.* 4*d.*
I. pd. Symon ffor castinge three dead dogs out of the River 3*d.*
I. pd. ffor cuttinge the Kings Armes in the mace 4*s.* o*d.*
I. pd. by my wife ffor letters while I was in London directed to the Towne 4*s.* o*d.*
I. pd Jon Barbar ffor beere the coronation day 11*s.* 6*d.*
I. pd Edward Payne ffor beere the coronation day 13*s.* o*d.*
I. pd Thomas Hicks ffor beere the coronation day 12*s.* o*d.*
I. pd. ffranc: Hamond ffor beere the coronation day 8*s.* o*d.*
I. pd. ffor beere to Hugh Harris the coronation day 10*s.* 8*d.*
I. pd Edw: Wescoatt ffor beère the coronation day 10*s.* o*d.*
I. pd. ffor beere to Lewis Caple the coronation day 5*s.* o*d.*
I. pd Morrish Dyer the coronation day ffor beere 5*s.* o*d.*
I. spent att his house settinge the markett house & keye 8*s.* o*d.*

[*I.e.*, on the occasion of signing the agreement for farming the tolls.]

I. pd Edward Wescoatt for 1lb of powder spent on the watch 1*s.* 8*d.*
I. pd to him ffor returninge a warrante att Marrasion 2*s.* o*d.*
I. pd Edward Wescoatt constable to goe muster maister att Pensance 12*s.* o*d.*

I. pd by him more ffor returninge the muster bookes 4s. *od.*

I. pd by Mr Diggens then deputie mayor ffor letters ffrom London 7s. 2*d.*

[During Robinson's absence in London.]

I. pd ffor the use of Tacabirds doore 4s. *od.*

I. spent when the Lord St John was here 8s. *od.*

I. spent when Coll: Goddolphin and Mr Robinson was here 8s. *od.*

I. pd the maior towards his Kitchinge £10 os. *od.*

I. pd the constables in sommoninge the Trayned band & writing the muster booke and severall lists 4s. *od.*

I. pd John Lander ffor beere the coronation day 3*s.* 6*d.*

I. pd Will: Ninnis ffor beere the coronation day 8*s.* 4*d.*

I. pd Geo: Painter ffor beere the coronation day 6*s.* *od.*

I. pd Marye Morrish ffor beere the coronation day 5*s.* 6*d.*

St Ives 1661 William Diggens elected Mayor.

1661
—— His Account follows
1662

Item recd of John Rosemenewas for bloudshed 2*s.* *od.*

I. recd of Stephen Harry for bloudshed 2*s.* *od.*

Disbursements Item: payd Mr Bridgwater for a sermon 10s. *od.*

I. pd a footeman to carry a letter to enquire for the muster books 1*s.* 6*d.*

I. pd a Messenger to goe to Mr Recorder about his Maties: busines 1*s.* *od.*

I. pd another Messenger about the p'clamacõn for observing of lent 1*s.* *od.*

I. spent at Mr Hamonds Reioycinge at her Maties Arivall £3 os. *od.*

[Charles II. married Catherine of Braganza May 21, 1662.]

I. pd Edw. Payne for Beere the Musketteers and Ringers had £2 os. *od.*

I. pd the drummer at that tyme 2*s.* 6*d.*

I. to the piper 2*s.* 6*d.*

I. to the ffidlers 1*s.* *od.*

I. pd the drommer the coronation day 2*s.* 6*d.*

I. pd Maurice Dyer for beere the coronation day 7*s.* 8*d.*

I. pd the Smyth for mending holes about Pen Wolva 2*s.* 2*d.*

[Now Penolva Point.]

I. pd Edw. Westcott for beere the coronation day 7*s.* *od.*

I. spent at ffra: Hamonds the coronation daye 13*s.* *od.*

I. for the Art of ffishery 4*d.*

[A book so called, treating of deep-sea fishing.]

I. pd Jo: Hawkings ffor Beere the coronation daye 4*s.* *od.*

I. spent at Mr Hamonds when the Commissioners for Regulating of Corporations sate in Towne £6 3s. 6*d*.

I. p^d^ Mr Bullocke for his salarye this yeare £20 os. o*d*.

I. p^d^ him for his scholinge £5 os. o*d*.

I. p^d^ Sr Charles Vivyans clerk at the signeing of the rate for the comon Amunition of the Towne 1s. o*d*.

St. Ives 1662 Thomas Treunwith elected mayor.

November

A note of the p'ishe goods deliv'ed over the 21th daye of November 1662 by Mr William Diggens Mayor the pre'dent yeare unto Thomas Treunwith Esqr the nowe Mayor viz.

Impr : the Towne Charter and the Coppy thereof in Englishe.
Item. Mr Poultons grand Abridgment.
Item Mr Daltons Justice of Peace.
Item a great guilded boule with the cover thereunto.
Item a payre of brasse scales.
Item a brasse gallon and a brasse pynte.
Item a chest with the Towne Writtings.
Item the Towne seale in Tymber.
Item a brasse yeard.
Brasse weights.

Burrough of St. Ives } The Account of Thomas Treunwith Esquire Late Mayor of the said Burrough for his tearme & tyme ended the first daye of November Anno Dñi 1663 and in the 16th yeare of the raigne of Kinge Charles the second of England &c made as given before Mr Robert Sprigge nowe Mayor of the said Burrough and all the Comon Councell at the Towne hall of the same Borrough the 23th daye of November Anno Dñi 1663 as followeth

Receipts

Impr. rec^d^ of Renatus Treunwith gent. for the p'fitts of the ffayers & marketts for the last yeare £51 os. o*d*.

Disbursements

Impr. paid for drinck for the Ringers the 5th of November 1662 8*s*. o*d*.

Item p^d^ Geo. Paynter for work about the pentises of the m̄ket house 6*s*. o*d*.

[*I.e.*, the pent-house ; the old-fashioned overhanging sheds fixed to the exterior walls of buildings. Excellent examples existed at Saint Ives, in the George and Dragon and the Golden Lion inns, but disappeared in 1887.]

I. p^d^ for mending the markett howse chest 6*d*.

I. p^d^ J^on^ Tonkinge for settinge upp the market howse boards 1s. o*d.*
I. p^d^ Thomas Allan to carry upp the boards 1s. o*d.*
I. to a straunge man that travelled by certificate 2s. 6d.
I. p^d^ to Jane Hitchens mayntaynance in prison 4s. o*d.*
I. p^d^ a poore Irishe man 2s. 6*d.*
I. p^d^ the 29th of Maye for a Barrell of Beere 16s. o*d.*

[Anniversary of the king's restoration.]

I. p^d^ for 7 dosen of Beere brought that day to the m̃ket howse 7s. o*d.*
I. p^d^ for 1 oaken pole 6 crocks & 4 pennard [pennyworth] of nayles 2s. 4*d.*
I. p^d^ 4 distressed Irishe weomen 5s. o*d.*
I. p^d^ for sendinge Katherine Treglohan to Lanceston goale £1 2s. o*d.*
I. p^d^ for hire of Kate Treglohans horse & for shoeing 8s. o*d.*
I. p^d^ for 4 mens q'ters [quarters] at Margaret Morishes 3s. 4*d.*

St Ives. 1663. Robert Spriggs elected Mayor, November.

1663
—— Account of Mr Robert Sprigge.
1664

Receipts. Item received of James Vellenoweth for bloudshed 3s. 4*d.*
Item: received of Henrie Quinall for bloudshed 6s. 8*d.*
Item recd of Mr Bosen of Paule for bloudshed 3s. 4*d.*
Item recd of Richard Giles for his ffreedome 6s. o*d.*
Item recd of Phillipp Carlyan for his ffredome 2s. 6*d.*
Item recd of Richard Cosens for a fyne imposed on him for misdemeanor 10s. o*d.*
Disbursements. Item: paid francis Arundell & Richard Hicks gents towards their expenses & paynes in riding to Sr John Arundell K^t^ about the Towne busines 14s. o*d.*
I. p^d^ the constable for writinge & ridinge to Pensance about the hearth rate 5s. o*d.*

[The Hearth Tax Rolls of this year are the latest documents of the kind to be found at the Record Office.]

I. p^d^ Capt Robert Bawden the 15th of decemb^r^ 1663 beinge here in distresse 2s. 6*d.*
I. the 30th of Januarye 1663 to 2 vagrant p'sons which were stockt and whipt & sent by passe 2s. 10*d.*
I. pd. Mr Coode the schoolmaster for money due to him at Christmas last £5 os. o*d.*
I. pd. John Thomas for his clerks wages for this last yeare £4 os. o*d.*

[*I.e.*, for his wages as town clerk.]

I. p^d for a post letter from London 4*d*.

I. p^d the cofible for ridinge to M'rketiew about ye subsidye 4*s*. o*d*.

I. p^d Cicily Jobe to goe to Lent Assises against Katherine Treglohan 5*s*. o*d*.

[This first baptismal name, a variant of Cecilia, was long continued at Saint Ives, and was often spelled Sisley.]

I. spent when we viewed the p'ish bounds and signed the Church & poore rates 10*s*. o*d*.

I. p^d for bringing home the Drum 29th Maye 1664 2*s*. 6*d*.

I. p^d Jeffry Pearse for beatinge the Drum 30th Maye 2*s*. 6*d*.

I. the 29th of Maye beinge upon the daye of his Maties happy returne for a barrell of beere 14*s*. 6*d*.

I. to the Ringers the same day 8*s*. o*d*.

I. p^d Middleton Thomas for costs about the high wayes 4*s*. 9*d*.

I. given 2 soldiers that came here from Tangeere 2*s*. o*d*.

[*I.e.*, who had been released from slavery there. Tangiers was then a British possession, being part of the queen's dowry.]

I. p^d John Roberts to carry Elizabeth Grenfield to Launceston, in all £1 4*s*. o*d*.

I. sent her when she was sicke in money 3*s*. o*d*.

I. p^d for a smocke for her 3*s*. 4*d*.

I. spent when the Judge sate on her 4*s*. o*d*.

I. p^d Ann Jenkyn to goe to the Assises as a wittnes againster her 10*s*. 6*d*.

I. p^d for meat & drink for her when she was in prison 2*s*. 6*d*.

I. p^d for waterynge of her 5*s*. o*d*.

I. p^d Margery Roswall to goe to the Assises as a wittnes against her 6*s*. o*d*.

I. p^d Cicily Jobe to goethe re as a wittnes ag : Kate Treglohan 8*s*. o*d*.

I. p^d John Thomas to go to thassises then £2 10*s*. o*d*.

I. spent on the men that were first prest for his Maties service 2*s*. 3*d*.

I. payd Jane Tacabird for her dore & way 4*s*. o*d*.

I. p^d Lewis ffoger for himselfe & horse, prest for his Maties service 3*s*. o*d*.

I. p^d Thomas Cubart and his boy to goe to Plymouth with prest men £4 5*s*. o*d*.

St. Ives 1664 John Hichens elected mayor.

November

Market tolls let to George Hammond & Walter Michell. Quay tolls let to Thomas Sise.

1664
—— The Account of Mr John Hichens.
1665

Disbursements. Item: Pd Edward Payne towards pressinge men 15*s*. 6*d*.

I. pd 6 Irish beggars that came here 6*s*. 0*d*.

I. pd for severall tymes sending To Mr Pawley 1*s*. 6*d*.

I. given Capt Connell his wife and child 4*s*. 6*d*.

I. pd the ringers the coronation day 6*s*. 6*d*.

I. pd Kath. Spencer the same day 10*s*. 6*d*.

I. pd Mr Prigg for wine 13*s*. 10*d*.

I. more pd to the ringers 5*s*. 0*d*.

I. pd John Anthony and John Tonkyn for making the pentise and findeinge stuff £10 15*s*. 6*d*.

I. pd Lord Marques high rent 1*s*. 2*d*.

I. pd Coll Trelawnyes man 2*s*. 0*d*.

I. pd Mr ffran. Hamond for the Bulletts £2 3*s*. 6*d*.

I. pd Jeffery Pearse for beatinge the drum 5*s*. 0*d*.

I. pd for the charge in the Spirituall Court Betweene Lake and the Towne 9*s*. 4*d*.

St. Ives 1665 Richard Hichens elected mayor.

November

Profits of the Market let to Thomas Treunwith Esquire.

Profits of the Quay let to Thomas Sise merchant.

1665
—— The Account of Mr Richard Hichens.
1666

Receipts Item Received of Thomas Dayow for stones and pins left of the chapell 4*s*. 0*d*.

I. recd of Thomas Trenwith Esq., for profits of Market h: £41 0*s*. 0*d*.

Disbursements. Item pd for whipping Mary Renoden 1*s*. 0*d*.

I. pd Willyam Hichens for returneing a warrant to Penzance about the Royall ayd 2*s*. 0*d*.

I. pd towards the Sergeants and drum̄ers pay 3*s*. 0*d*.

I. pd Thomas Dayow for returneing a warrt to Penzance about the chimney rate 2*s*. 0*d*.

I. returned to Kate Spenser by consent of the Capitall Burgesses for standing of the powder & match in her house 7 years past, her bill £2 0*s*. 0*d*.

I. pd Thomas Clerke for goeinge to the Recorders 1*s*. 0*d*.

I. pd him to go to Godolphyn. . . . .

I. pd for straw and roapes for the Beacon 1*s.* 9*d.*

[This was lit on the top of the Island.]

I. pd Nich: Prigge for 4 deale boards to close the inner markett house att 20d ℘ board 6*s.* 8*d.*

I. pd for 3 planks to putt over head the markett house to hold the powder and match 8*s.* 3*d.*

I. pd Thomas Trenwith Esqr for his disbursements about the markett house the first quarter £2 1*s.* 6*d.*

I. pd John Hocken for 16c of stones for the chapell 9*s.* 8*d.*

I. pd for one big size barrell of lyme 4*s.* o*d.*

I. pd for lyme and stones for the chapell to carry it upp 2*s.* o*d.*

I. pd for 4 bundells of lafts for the said worke 4*s.* o*d.*

I. for 2 thousand and halfe of pins 10*d.*

I. pd for 8½c 3*d.* nayles 2*s.* 1½*d.*

I. pd for 4 h'hds, staves and nayles for sd worke 8*d.*

I. pd for 2 planks to make a doore 4*s.* 1½*d.*

I. pd for a Locke and nayles for the doore 1*s.* 8*d.*

I. pd: John Tonken to make the doore 1*s.* 6*d.*

I. pd: John Coger & Jno Anthony's man for the worke about the chapell 10*s.* 6*d.*

I. pd: John Hocken for 2 distressed seamens suppers 1*s.* 4*d.*

I. pd: John Treweeke for crooks twists & nayles for the chapell doore 1*s.* 10*d.*

I. pd for a Ladder to come by the match & powder 4*s.* o*d.*

I. paid Thomas Dayow for goeinge to St. Cullombe with prest seamen and for 2 horses and a boy £1 1*s.* 8*d.*

I. pd. the ringers the Kings birth day 3*s.* o*d.*

I. pd. for a barrell of beere 9th June for Joy of a victory over the Dutch 13*s.* o*d.*

[Battle fought in the English Channel between the English fleet under the Duke of Albemarle and Prince Rupert, and the Dutch under De Ruyter. Mist separated the combatants, and in reality the victory was as much that of the Dutch as the English. This sanguinary engagement lasted three days and was terminated on June 4, 1666.]

I. pd for 3 trusses of furse then 1*s.* 9*d.*

I. pd Mr Thomas the Schoolemaster for 1 yr̄s sallery £5 o*s.* o*d.*

I. pd ffran. Hamond & Will. Hichens for goeing to ffalmouth with prest men, and for 4 horses and 2 boyes to goe with them 26th June 1666 £1 8*s.* o*d.*

I. pd for the prest men suppers at Penryn 4*s.* 4*d.*

I. pd Stephen Major for goeing to St Culloms with prest men 2 horses and 1 boy 12*s.* o*d.*

I. pd for drum heads for the Esqr̄s drum 7*s.* o*d.*

I. gave one Lievtenant his wife & 4 children 3*s.* o*d.*

St. Ives 1666 Thomas Sise elected Mayor in November.

1666
—— His Account
1667

Item P[d] M[r] Tremenheere for planks £3 15*s*. 0*d*.
P[d] M[r] Trewren for 3 horses 1 day 5*s*. 0*d*.
P[d] John Coger and Tho. Try for their worke about the prison 3*s*. 0*d*.
P[d] for the cuckingstoole 5*s*. 0*d*.
Spent for carryeing the cuckinge stoole downe and settinge itt upp 1*s*. 0*d*.
P[d] M[r] Peter Thomas for 1 quarter £1 5*s*. 0*d*.
Spent on M[r] Pennell for takinge some Chymnyes of 5*s*. 0*d*.

[*I.e.*, for striking some items off the hearth-tax list.]

P[d] M[r] Bullocke his yeares sallery £10 0*s*. 0*d*.
P[d] John Thomas his sallery £4 0*s*. 0*d*.
P[d] Jeffery Pearse to beate the drum̃ last yeare 10*s*. 0*d*.
P[d] Mary Lerebay for her yeares wages 10*s*. 0*d*.
P[d] Morrish Dyer for the dyett of one man and two women which came from Kettermester 5*s*. 6*d*.

[Kidderminster.]

P[d] for horses and men to carry them away 2*s*. 0*d*.
P[d] Annis Lander for the dyett of a poore man his wife and two chilldren 4*s*. 6*d*.
P[d] Will. Harry to putt a Sylly [Scilly] man to Godolphyn & for meat 3*s*. 0*d*.
P[d] Morrish Dyer John Hocken & John Barber for beere the 29th of May 12*s*. 8*d*.
P[d] M[r] John Hichens for the Townes drum and fraight £1 10*s*. 0*d*.
P[d] him for ½ dozen of bandaleers 11*s*. 0*d*.
The letter brought here and sent on board the victory, the first tyme beere to the men 2*s*. 6*d*.
The next day beere & bread to them 3*s*. 0*d*.
P[d] M[r] ffr: Ham̃ond for beere to the ringers and gunners when peace was proclaymed 12*s*. 0*d*.

[Peace was signed with the Dutch at Breda, July 10, 1667.]

P[d] the Sergeant for deliuering & receaving the Towne armes to the watch 6*s*. 0*d*.
P[d] Willyam Truthwell for bread and drink for Willyam White when hee was in prison 8*s*. 4*d*.
P[d] Richard Cocken for beating the drum £1 0*s*. 0*d*.
P[d] Henry Barber for beating the drum when peace was proclaymed 2*s*. 0*d*.

Spent when I went to Truroe to speake wth M[r] Vincent about the Maypole 5s. o*d*.

St. Ives 1667 Hugh Harris elected Mayor in November

1667
—— His Account
1668

Receaved for an oath 1*s*. o*d*.

Rec[d] of Jasper Willyams for his freedome 10*s*. o*d*.

P[d] M[r] Bullocke [the parson] his yeares sallery £10 os. o*d*.

P[d] John Thomas his sallery & to write the rates [lists of those liable to taxation] £4 9*s*. o*d*.

P[d] M[r] Hoskyn schoolemaster his sallery £5 os. o*d*.

P[d] Will. Diggens overseer of the poore a legacy given them by S[r] ffran: Godolphyn & M[rs] Chesten Hext £4 4*d*. o*d*.

Spent in beere the Kings Birthday 16*s*. 4*d*.

P[d] Rich: Cocken to beat the Drum 2*s*. 6*d*.

P[d] in Candellight and other things watching a ffrench vessell which came from Roan 3*s*. o*d*.

[The Rouen vessel was suspected to be a smuggler, numbers of whom then frequented Saint Ives Bay.]

St: Ives 1668 William Pearse elected Mayor, November.

1668
—— His Account
1669

Rec[d] of John Thomas & Robert Cowch for Interest of £15 18*s*. o*d*.

Rec[d] ℘ bond of John Thomas £10, of M[r] Cowch £5, in all £15 os. o*d*.

Rec[d] ℘ bond from Walter Udy £6 6*s*. 6*d*.

P[d] Ann Dudly a distressed widdow who lost her husband, son and son in law in Portsmouth Engagement 6*s*. 6*d*.

[When the Dutch successfully attacked that harbour, June, 1667.]

The Coroners ffee for Donythorne son 15*s*. 10*d*.

P[d] M[r] Thomas Cockyn for preaching here 10*s*. o*d*.

P[d] ffor carrying the Gun to the Castle from Court Cockyn 12*s*. o*d*.

P[d] ffoger to goe to M[r] Vincent about S[r] John Arundells busines 6*s*. 6*d*.

P[d] ffor post lr̃es: to L[d] S[t] Johns & M[r] Nosworthy 1*s*. 6*d*.

P[d] Timothy Major by order of the Aldermen for money hee p[d] M[r] Prigg for wine about the Sacrament £1 18*s*. 3*d*.

ffor fixing the Towne Armes against the Coronation day 4*s*. 6*d*.

P[d] for bringing the Great Guns from the Iland to the castle the Coronation day with damages of ropes and expenses to the ringers and musketeers with expenses the next day putting the Guns into the castle £2 10s. 0*d*.

P[d] Richard Cockyn the drum̃er the Coronation day 2s. 6*d*.

P[d] M[r] George Ham̃ond for a Tar Barrell 2s. 6*d*.

P[d] for carrynge the Tymber to John Tonkyns sawpitt 1s. 4*d*.

P[d] James Goddyn a distressed seaman and his wife 2s. 6*d*.

P[d] Major Ceely for 1000 of Healingstones 8 bundles Lathes 2000 of nayles with a barrell of Lyme £1 7s. 2*d*.

P[d] for healing pins 1s. 0*d*.

[Pins to fasten the roof slates.]

P[d] M[r] John Hichens & M[r] Pendarves for Lyme £1 5s. 0*d*.

P[d] Coger and Wall masons with his son for working about the pentises, markett house, castle, chaple, Ventan Eia, with Caunseing [localism for 'paving'] the well £3 10s. 0*d*.

P[d] a distressed gent. and his wife with another woman having a patent 5s. 6*d*.

P[d] for a Pumpe for Westcotts well and to bring itt from Trenwith Milpoll 9s. 6*d*.

P[d] for carryeing the stones to Cawse Ventan Eia Well 6s. 6*d*.

St Ives 1669 Francis Hammond elected Mayor November

1669
—— His Account
1670

P[d] 2 distressed gentlewomen 22th November 1669 4s. 0*d*.

P[d] Danniell Seamer his wife and John Holstocke & Robert Michell distressed poor seamen 5s. 0*d*.

Given to the servants at Tehiddy twelft Day last 7s. 6*d*.

P[d] Thomas Clearke when the Esquire Trenwiths Boy was whipt 6*d*.

P[d] John Thomas for coppyinge out of the chimny list 1s. 0*d*.

[The Hearth Rate List, shewing the number of hearths in each house. Each hearth paid so much.]

P[d] by expense on M[r] Henry Sissell for his kindnes 2s. 0*d*.

P[d] by expense on Cap[t] Boucher & them y[t] were with him ......

P[d] by expense when the greate bell was cast 10s. 4*d*.

P[d] Thomas Harris his son and daughter distressed people bound to Ireland 3s. 0*d*.

P[d] towards the County bridge neere Bodmin 5s. 0*d*.

P[d] for swords and one Cuttleax now in the Towne Hale £3 0s. 0*d*.

P[d] M[r] John Hicks for Ingrossinge 7 accompts in the Towne booke 7s. 0*d*.

P[d] John Thomas for writing the Muster Roules & duplicates 1s. 6*d*.

P[d] Henry Barber for Beatinge the Drume at the generall muster 2s. 0*d*.

[Of the militia.]

St. Ives 1670 John Hichings junior elected mayor Novem[r]

His Account for the years $\frac{1670}{1671}$

Rec[d] of Henry Parington for a fine laid on him 3*s.* 4*d.*
Rec[d] by 2 dosen of Creasts 8*s.* o*d.*
Rec[d] from M[r] Thomas Steephens £10; ℘ interest £12; in the hole £10 12*s.* o*d.*
P[d] for one suit for John Sandry 14*s.* 7*d.*
P[d] Andrew Jobe what was due to him for the Sandrys diet before they dyed 13*s.* o*d.*
P[d] a poore distressed man Richard Lawree 3*s.* o*d.*
P[d] Nowell Williams by consent £4 o*s.* o*d.*
P[d] M[r] Boddy by your Consents £1 10*s.* o*d.*
P[d] M[r] Hugh Pawley & John Hicks for cost sewinge [suing] M[r] ffrancis Hammond by consent for M[r] Couch his debt £3 4*s.* 10*d.*

St. Ives 1671 George Hammond elected Mayor in November

The Account of M[r] Hammond $\frac{1671}{1672}$

To three distressed gentlewomen 5*s.* o*d.*
P[d] W[m] Hoskyn for Ringinge & Keepinge the Clocke £1 o*s.* o*d.*
P[d] for mendinge the Dyall in the Churchyeard 3*s.* o*d.*
Spent when the sherrifes man brought the p'clamation & declarations for warr, & at p'clayminge them 8*s.* o*d.*

[England and France declared war against Holland March 17, 1672.]

Spent at three seuerall times on the Vice Admiral £5 1*s.* o*d.*
P[d] for the dyet of prest men being straingers 9*s.* o*d.*
P[d] for horses & men to carry prest mens Cloathes & to them to drinke £1 15*s.* 6*d.*
P[d] for an express 3 times to the Mounts Bay to Acquaint them of men a wars 3*s.* o*d.*

[To inform them that ships of war had been sighted off Saint Ives.]

P[d] for furse carried seuerall times to the Iland 3*s.* o*d.*

[For the beacon fire.]

P[d] for ffillinge the Great Cup & presentinge it to M[r] Bassett 10*s.* o*d.*

[This ceremony is a traditional way of honouring a distinguished visitor to the Borough.]

Spent on M[r] wheare at his 2 preachings here 6*s.* o*d.*
The King's restauration to the ringers & others 6*s.* o*d.*
2 pounds of powder to scald the Guns in the morninge 2*s.* o*d.*

Dammadge of Roapes about the Guns, ten shillings, And to the Drummer 2*s*. 6*d*. both 12*s*. 6*d*.

P[d] for tymber hoops nailes spukes & his worke about the Cucking stoole [to John Tonkyn] 4*s*. 6*d*.

P[d] My Lord Marques rent to Richard Baragwanath 1*s*. 2*d*.

P[d] for 10[c] waight of plaister of pallace [plaster of Paris, Roman cement] for the head of the Key and for carriadge £1 1*s*. 0*d*.

P[d] M[r] John Hichens at his goeing to Lamas sises [Lammas Assizes] being townes busines £2 0*s*. 0*d*.

P[d] a Distressed man & women y[t] Came with a breife 2*s*. 6*d*.

[Another term synonymous with pass, patent, certificate, etc.]

P[d] for expresses to returne seuerall warrants to Justice Jones 6*s*. 0*d*.

St. Ives 1672 Richard Hichens elected Mayor November.
Edward Hammond & John Hockin overseers of the poor.
William Pearse & John Treweeke churchwardens.

1672
—— The Account of M[r] Hichens.
1673

Rec[d] of Jane Tackaberry for one years rent £1 16*s*. 0*d*.
P[d] Thomas Stevens backe his Interest ℘ consent 12*s*. 0*d*.
ffor a Lanthorne for the Markett to John Anthony 2*s*. 0*d*.
Given 4 distressed Scotch men being taken 3*s*. 0*d*.

St. Ives 1673 Thomas Spriggs is elected Mayor.

1673
—— His Accompt
1674

P[d] M[r] Mitchell beinge clerke & schoolmaster £10 0*s*. 0*d*.

Spent & given the ringers & drum̄er when peace was p'claymed by the Dutch 16*s*. 6*d*.

[Which was on February 9, 1674.]

P[d] Rich. Cockyn to head the Towne drum 1*s*. 4*d*.

P[d] Henry Edwards high Con[ble] towards repayre of severall bridges 18*s*. 10*d*.

There is a Barrell of powder in M[rs] Wilmott Hichens Custody which must be p'duced by her or allowed to her husband acc[tt]

St. Ives 1677 William Hichens elected mayor in February.

1677 Feb. to Nov. } His account

22th Nov[r] spent on S[r] George Godollphin £4 15*s*. 0*s*.

Spent on Mr Jackman beinge Chymny man 5*s*. o*d*.

[The man who collected the hearth tax.]

Spent on Sr Charles Osbran survyer for post letters 6*d*.

for expenses goeinge to Trewroe to be sworne £1 3*s*. 6*d*.

Spent on the Ringers 29th May 5*s*. o*d*.

Pd Mr William Robenson for beinge Clarke £8 os. o*d*.

George Hammond	John Hammond	John Treweeke
ffrancis Hammond	Tho : Sprigge Jnr:	Jn Stevens
John Hichens	John Hawking	Alex : Taylor

Edward Nosworthy Mayor

St. Ives 1677 Edward Nosworthy elected mayor November.

Pd John Anthony for mending the Castle and Chappell howse £1 11*s*. o*d*.

Pd Mr Robinson for writing & making a booke 5*s*. 10*d*.

Pd the Lord Marquis of Winchester high rent 1*s*. 2*d*.

Pd for putting in the post att howse end 2*s*. o*d*.

St. Ives 1678 Thomas Purefoy elected mayor in November.

Received of said Edward Nosworthy for his Gift to the towne being wooll and Lamb £7 10*s*. o*d*.

[The tithe on these goods.]

Pd the Sherriffe for allowing the Charter 10*s*. o*d*.

Pd Mr Robinson for binding the towne bookes 4*s*. 6*d*.

Pd for making a new pent house & repayring the market howse £8 4*s*. o*d*.

Pd for Bread & Beare to a poore distracted maid imprisoned 10*d*.

Pd the constables for warrts and Disbursemts about the Key and Cucking stool 17*s*. 6*d*.

St. Ives 1679 November Richard Pollard elected Mayor.

Mr ffrancis Stevens overseer of the poor.

1679
—— The Accompt of Mr Pollard.
1680

Item Received of Richard Nance for the Tyeth of the wooll & lamb being the Guift of Edward Nosworthy Esq. £7 os. o*d*.

Item Pd Mr William Robinson for his sallery £12 os. o*d*.

To Mr Hawking minister, beinge a legacye etc £1 os. o*d*.

To Marjam Body the County Stocke to bury her Bro : 9*s*. o*d*.

To Mr Pawley for a writ a'gt Mr Purefoy, Mr ff: Hamond & Mr Diggens 12*s*. o*d*.

To Mathew Gyles his disbursements about the Marketthowse & his acc'tts for mending the prison 2*s*. 6*d*.

To Mathew Gyles for him & his horse hire to goe to M[r] Vincent about H. Anthony 8*s*. o*d*.

P[d] to carry s[d] Anthony & his children to Lelant 1*s*. o*d*.

P[d] 2 men to goe to Penzance & Penryn to discover a Jesuite 5*s*. o*d*.

[This was the time of the fictitious 'Popish plots,' and of the informers Oates, Bedloe and Dangerfield. Father Whitebread, Provincial of the English Jesuits, with others, was hanged, drawn and quartered.]

Expended on S[r] Joseph Tredinham & the Judge of the Admiralty 10*s*. o*d*.

Spent renewing the Bounds Ascension Day 10*s*. 4*d*.

for Poynts to Whip the Boys 4*s*. o*d*.

[There was an old custom, at the beating of the bounds, to flog the boys who perambulated the boundaries, in order to impress vividly upon them the recollection of the places through which the boundary passed.]

for a Tarr barrell & cost to the drum̄er 2*s*. 6*d*.

Expended the xxix[th] of May by the Aldermen 4*s*. 8*d*.

To the Ringers by their consent 5*s*. 6*d*.

for Powder 5*s*. o*d*.

on the Souldiers then 4*s*. 7*d*.

To ffrancis Jennings for newe Keye for the Charter 2*s*. 6*d*.

[*i.e.*, for the box in which it was preserved.]

For mending the high way on the Cliffe; M[r] Hichens 13*s*. 4*d*.

['The Cliff' is the name given to a part of the old town, in the present Fore Street, close to the shore.]

Expended on the Constables and Guard to put the drum̄er and his children out of Towne 8*s*. o*d*.

[Several French prizes were brought into Saint Ives in 1680.]

Richard Pollard mayor. A note of such plate and other things as belong to the church of this Burrough and delivered over to Thomas Sprig Jun[r] and John Hicks gent', churchwardens, this sixth day of May 1680.

Imps: Two silver ffaggons, two silver chalices with covers, fower pewter pottells, fower table Cloths, two font Cloths, two Carpetts for the Com̄union Table, one new Bag to hold the plate, one Large Bible, the works of Bishop Jewell ag'st Harding [Thomas Harding, D.D., the famous Jesuit, whose 'Rejoinder to Mr. Jewel's Replie' was printed at Antwerp in 1566, in black letter. It should be borne in mind that this was the time of the great No Popery scare.] wc̄h things now have been receuived by us to be accountable to the Towne for them the day and year aforesaid.

Tho. Sprigge Jn[r]
Jo[n] Hicks.

St. Ives 1680 November. Thomas Sprigge junior elected mayor. James Praed Esq. Recorder.

1680
—— The Accompt of M[r] Sprigge
1681

Receipts. Item of Anthony Cowch for leave to build his Barke on the Town Land neere the blew Rocke by the chapell 6*d*.

Disbursements. Item p[d] for mending the launder of the Townes Well 3*s*. 0*d*.

P[d] to put in a post for mooring of shipping and putting of it in 14*s*. 0*d*.

P[d] M[r] W[m] Robinson for one yeare for his Deacon & Clerkeship £12 0*s*. 0*d*.

P[d] Anne Trudgian towards the Releife of Mary Launce 1*s*. 0*d*.

P[d] M[r] John Hawking for building the cage £2 0*s*. 0*d*.

P[d] the Lord Marques of Winton [Winchester] for the Port farme Rent & 1*s*. 2*d*. for the Towne Land 14*s*. 6*d*.

P[d] for drawing Certificats for the poore french Protestants 6*s*. 0*d*.

[The Huguenot refugees, of whom a number came to Saint Ives and were lodged at the expense of the town.]

Given the undersherrifes man when he brought the writ for Electing Burgesses in Parliament 5*s*. 0*d*.

[Parliament was dissolved January 10, 1681, and the new one summoned to meet at Oxford, which it did on March 21.]

to severall distant french people Landed in this Port 10*s*. 0*d*.

p[d] for drawing of writings to discharge a strange woman that had child here 5*s*. 0*d*.

The 30th of october 1681. Rec: of M[r] Richard fowler and M[r] Maddern towards the Releife of the poore destressed protestants which was Landed here in our port of St Ives that did come out of france the sum off 2 pounds.

more rec. of M[r] Robert Beere the sum of 1 pound beinge sent by the quakers of marazion towards the Relife of the aforesaid poore protestants.

more sent by M[r] Rob: beere from M[r] Slade and his family the sum of 15 shillings towards the Relife of the aforesaid poore protestants—

St. Ives 1681 November John Hawking elected Mayor. John Stevens & John Treweek overseers—

1681
—— The Accompt of M[r] Hawking
1682

Receipts. Item Rec[d] of ffower offenders for their breach of the Saboth 4*s*. 0*d*.

ffor a ffine on S[t] Just men for their Riotous assembling in to the Burrough £3 0s. 0*d*.

[There seems to have been a faction fight between Saint Just men and Saint Ives men ; but I have not been able to discover the full particulars of the disturbance.]

Disbursements. Item: to Anthony Creed to goe for a warr[t] for his Sister 1*s*. 0*d*.

Spent on the Pursevant that rec[d] the Port farme 2*s*. 0*d*.

To Counsellor Hoblyn for his ffee and expenses goeing to him 11*s*. 6*d*.

To Edward Spry and John Tonkyn for mending the Stockes 4*s*. 1*d*.

For mending the Towne Cupp 10*s*. 0*d*.

Spent on M[r] Grosvennor 9*s*. 6*d*.

Mary Dunnoes wages clenseing the Markett 18*s*. 0*d*.

P[d] con[bles] to putt St Just men to Lanceston £6 9*s*. 6*d*.

powder candels expens to the guard with their dyett & expens to carry them [the Saint Just men] to Lanceston £5 6*s*. 6*d*.

pd M[r] Robinson to dress their wounds 5*s*. 0*d*.

P[d] Tho. Cubert Ld: Marques port farme rent &c. 14*s*. 6*d*.

P[d] Tho. Try for worke about the kay and chapell 3*s*. 8*d*.

St. Ives 1683 John Stevens elected Mayor in November.

'This and the former mayor had a quo warranto brought against the old Charter by M[r] Thomas Trenwith, the next mayor, elected 1684.'

[Modern side note.]

[In 1682 a writ of Quo Warranto was issued against every corporation in Great Britain. The majority were induced thereby to surrender their charters into the king's hands. Considerable sums were exacted for restoring the charters, and all offices of power and profit were left at the disposal of the crown ('Student's Hume'). 'They took away the Charters as fast as they were able, of all the Corporations in England that would not chuse the Members prescribed them' ('Secret History of Europe,' 1713, Part III., p. 94).]

St. Ives. M[r] Thomas Trenwith elected Mayor in 1684.

His Accompt as follows:—

The Account of Thomas Trenwith Esquire Late Mayor of the sayd Burrough for the yeare ended the ffirst day of November 1685. This account beginning from the 30th day of Aprill last past.

Rec[d] of Hector Taylor the arrears of the Key dutyes £2 10*s*. 0*d*.

I. p[d] for a smale cask of powder 9, 47[lbs] and halfe on the p'clayming King James the Second £2 7*s.* 6*d.*

the charge of a Journey to Saltash to fetch home the charter being out 7 dayes as ꝑ a note of p'ticulars £3 4*s.* 2*d.*

P[d] E[d] Pryor for horsehyre & charge to Stow with the Indenture 14*s.* 0*d.*

P[d] ffor a Tar barrell & 4 bottles of wyne 29th may 1685 4*s.* 6*d.*

P[d] the drum̄er the same day 2*s.* 6*d.*

p[d] for 30[lbs] of powder for the Towne store in tyme of rebellyon £1 10*s.* 0*d.*

[The Duke of Monmouth's rebellion.]

P[d] William Penberthy horsehyre & expence to Helston and Penryn to give the Deputy Leweten[ts] notice of the arrivall of Monmouths ship 5*s.* 0*d.*

[He landed at Lyme in Dorsetshire.]

To a horse and man to goe to Capt[t] Veale on same occasion 1*s.* 0*d.*

Spent on M[r] Sloman who came from the deputy Lewetenants 1*s.* 0*d.*

Spent on the ringers 8th July on newes of the defeat of the rebells 3*s.* 0*d.*

[They were finally routed July 6, 1685.]

p[d] for 6 bottles of wyne then 4*s.* 6*d.*

ffor March beere brought to the churchyard then 3*s.* 6*d.*

Given to the soldiers then 5*s.* 0*d.*

Spent on Capt. Trevanyon & Capt. Ridley 4*s.* 0*d.*

P[d] for the aldermen & assistants att Marazion 2*s.* 6*d.*

Spent att M[r] Pykes and M[r] Uptons on them 3*s.* 0*d.*

P[d] an expres to Justice Jones 1*s.* 0*d.*

P[d] Henry Anthony for new making the Towne drum 2*s.* 6*d.*

P[d] for 3 hoops for the drum and a New Cord 1*s.* 0*d.*

P[d] M[r] Hawkins for a Sermon preached Sessions day on occasion of the Charter 5*s.* 0*d.*

[On the occasion of its return.]

P[d] Henry Barber for beating the drum and severall expresses to Clowance 5*s.* 0*d.*

John Lanyon mayor	John Hawking
Will. Robinson	Thomas Dayow
John Hicks	Tho : Stephens

St Ives 1685 John Lanyon elected Mayor.

St Ives $\frac{1685}{1686}$ His Account

Rec[d] of Gabriell Stanford for the sugar sold him stollen by Teage £1 0s. 0s.

P[d] Thomas Trenwith Esq[re] for his disbursements the last yeare being more than his receipts £17 3s. 1d.

Spent 6th Novemb[r] att Ed. Pryors att a meetinge of the Aldermen to suppres the pilchard driveinge 3s. 6d.

[A practice by which the shoal was unscientifically and illegally plunged into and frightened away.]

Spent by the Aldermen when wee agreed to putt the Towne armes in the constables staves 1s. 0d.

P[d] for 3 staves and paynteing them 7s. 0d.

Spent by M[r] Trenwith, M[r] Robinson, my selfe & M[r] May, att S[t] Earth, Gwynear, Camborne & other places to discover the Sugar stollen ℘ Teage being out two dayes £1 3s. 6d.

[Note the miscellaneous duties undertaken by Robinson the curate. He was able to act as parish clerk in 1677, bookbinder in 1678, surgeon in 1682, and councilman in 1685. He no doubt needed great resources to supplement his meagre salary as a minister.]

P[d] M[r] Robinsons horsehyre for the two dayes 1s. 6d.

P[d] a man to goe to Clowance & Penryn to give notice of the Sessions 2s. 0d.

P[d] 11th Jany: for severall ordinaryes for the Kings wittnesses against Teage & others about the stollen Sugar 4s. 0d.

P[d] expence on 6 men att Ed: Pryors to secure Teage and the rest & for bread & beere for the prisoners 7s. 6d.

P[d] Tho: Quicke as ℘ his acc[tt] appēth for expence & the hyre of 4 horses & 3 men beside the con[ble] to putt Teage and his daughter and Rawlinge to Lanceston £7 2s. 6d.

Spent 6th ffeb. 1685 being the Kings Coronac'on day £1 2s. 6d.

p[d] then for a Tarr barrell 1s. 6d.

p[d] the drum̄er 1s. 0d.

p[d] for mendinge the cover of the Towne cup 6s. 0d.

p[d] for stones, Lyme, Lafts and Masons wages to repayre the chapple in the Top of the Iland 7s. 10d.

p[d] for stones, Lyme, Lafts and Masons wages to repayre the chaple on the Key and Markett house pentises 5s. 7d.

for a payre of shoes for Rawlings wife to goe to Assizes 2s. 6d.

To Gabriell Stanford to goe to the Assizes as an Evidence ag℘ Teage and others by consent 10s. 0d.

p[d] for parchment about the Towne busines 1s. 0d.

p[d] Ephraim Major for 2 horses to goe to Lanceston to carry the wittnesses ag℘ Teage & others 14s.; to Ed. Pryor for his horse 7s.; to Math. Gyles for his horse 7s.; being in all £1 8s. 0d.

Spent by my selfe, M[r] Robinson, Ed. Pryor, and two other wittnesses goeing to Lanceston ag[t] Teage & others and for councells advise £8 15*s.* o*d.*

p[d] for postage of a letter from the sherife with his Ma[ties] pardon 8*d.*

p[d] 13th May 1686 for poynts to whip the boyes veiweinge the pish bounds 1*s.*; p[d] drumer 1*s.*; spent att M[r] Pollards then 6*s.*: 8*s.*

p[d] for postage of another Letter from London with the Kings generall pardon being sent p M[r] Newman 2*s.* o*d.*

spent 29 May att M[r] Pollards 5*s.*, Ed. Pryors 5*s.*, in wyne 4*s.*, att M[r] Morrice Dyers 7*s.*, in a Tar barrell 1*s.*, p[d] drumer 1*s.*, & to the man that brought the small gun 1*s.*, in all £1 4*s.* o*d.*

p[d] to bring the Maypole to Sawpitt 6*d.*

p[d] M[r] Loder for advice about the constituc'ons 10*s.* o*d.*

p[d] M[r] Nicholas Teage of Salt Ash to draw the Constituc'ons and to putt them in a good method 2 ginnyes £2 3*s.* o*d.*

ffor my expences to goe to Penryn about the Bakehouse & to speake with M[r] Newman about other Towne Concernes 5*s.* o*d.*

Spent 14th 8[ber] 1686 being the Kings birth day att M[r] Pollards 3*s.*, att Ed: Pryors 2*s.*, to the drumer 1*s.*, a Tar barrell 1*s.* 6*d.*; in all 7*s.* 6*d.*

P[d] M[r] Robinson for his paynes & endeavors about the new Charter £3 10*s.* o*d.*

Tho: Sprigge mayor	Thomas Dayow
Tho: Trenwith	Rich: Pollard
John Lanyon	Will: Robinson
John Hicks	Jno: Stevens
John Hawking	Tho: Stephens

St. Ives 1686 November Thomas Sprigge elected Mayor.

Borrough of St. Ives } Att the Court of the Burrough aforesaid held the sixteenth day of december in the Second yeare of the Raigne of o[r] Soveraigne Lord James the Second by the Grace of God King of England &c Anno gr: Dñi 1686. Before Thomas Sprige Junr gent' mayor of the said Burrough, John Lanyon gent', William Robinson, John Hicks gent', John Stevens, John Hawkins, Thomas Dayow, Richard Pollard and Thomas Stevens J[nr], Aldermen, being present; James Pollard merchant uppon payment of five shillings to the use of the corporac'on, was admitted and sworne a freeman of the said Burrough. In Testimony whereof the s[d] Mayor & Aldermen have hereunto subscribed their names the day and yeare first above written.

[Signed as above.]

[As above] Zachary Willyams of the Burrough of Helston merchant sworne a freeman upon payment of 6*s*. 8*d*.

[The like] William Snelgrove Junior.

[Without payment.]

Burrough of St. Ives } At the Generall Sessions of the peace held for the sayd Burrough the xiv[th] day of January Anno Dñi 1687 before Thomas Sprigge gent' Mayor of the s[d] Burrough Thomas Trenwith Esq[r], John Lanyon gent. Justices of Peace within the s[d] Burrough all the Aldermen being present, Thomas Diggens cordwayner uppon paym[t] of five shillings to the use ꝑf the corporac'on was admitted and sworne a freeman of the said Burrough. In Testimony whereof the s[d] Mayor & Aldermen have hereunto subscribed their names the day and yeare first aboue written.

[Signed as above.]

1686
—— The Account of M[r] Thomas Sprigge Mayor.
1687

Receipts.

Of Mr James Pollard being sworne a freeman 5*s*. 0*d*.
Of M[r] Thomas Diggens being sworne a freeman 5*s*. 0*d*.
Of M[r] Zachary Willyams being sworne a freeman 6*s*. 8*d*.
Of Henry Hambly for a fyne 1*s*. 0*d*.
of John Tackaberry for a fyne 3*s*. 4*d*.

Disbursements.

P[d] the Cryer 1*s*. 0*d*.
given a poore ffrench man 2*s*. 6*d*.
p[d] for repayring the high way Leading to Are £2 14*s*. 10*d*.
p[d] for clensing the house after the ffrenchpeople 3*s*. 0*d*.

[The house which had accommodated the Huguenot refugees. The revocation of the Edict of Nantes, in 1685, sent its contingent of French Protestant refugees to Saint Ives, though numbers had previously landed here (see *ante*, 1681). The Huguenots were lodged in one house, at the town's expense; and I think this must have been the old house now known as Carn Glaze, situate on the top of the rock of that name. In the earliest known document relating to this house, namelv, a lease of it from John Hicks, gentleman, to Reginald Botterall, sailor, dated January 25, 1699 (and in no other document), it is styled 'Ugnes House,' a name now unknown, and which I am inclined to regard as a corruption of 'Huguenots' House.' This is said to be the oldest dwelling-house in the town. Hard by, on the Island, is 'the Ancient Britons' hut,' a barnlike building where Breton fishermen formerly kept their gear and occasionally resided, and there must have been strong rivalry between the Breton Catholics and the neighbouring Huguenots.]

p[d] for mending the Lover hole of the Markett house 1*s*. 0*d*.

[The lower hold, *i.e.*, the ground floor. The upper floor was used as a petty sessional court room.]

Spent the coronac'on day by consent 7*s.* o*d.*
p[d] drumer 1*s.*, for a Tar barrell 1*s.*; 2*s.* o*d.*
p[d] John Tonkyn to make the Towne Ladder 2*s.* 6*d.*
P[d] Ed: Pryor to goe to Clowance 1*s.* o*d.*
Spent on the Recorder the Sessions day in wyne att dinner 2*s.* o*d.*
pd. for arresting Penzance shoemakers £1 o*s.* o*d.*

[For non-payment of market dues; see *post.*]

pd. M[r] Newman to translate the new Charter into English £2 o*s.* o*d.*

[A new charter was granted by King James II. The translation here referred to is still extant, in Mr. Newman's hand-writing. See p. 270, *post.*]

Spent when M[r] Newman was elected Towne Clerke in wyne 6*s.* o*d.*
Spent when the shoemakers were arrested 4*s.* 6*d.*

J[no] Stevens mayor
Tho: Trenwith
John Hicks
Tho: Stephens
Thomas Dayow

[Saint Ives, September 15, 1687, Enoder Cock and Mathew Gyles undertook to farm the tolls of the markets and fairs for the sum of twenty-nine pounds. These yeomen commenced a suit in the Court of Common Pleas, against Thomas James, *alias* Rosemorran and Hugh Cloake, of Penzance, cordwainers, for the nonpayment of their duties of the said Market. The document now in recital pledges the Corporation to undertake the costs of the said suit provided the case is left entirely in their hands.]

Thomas Hicks.	Enoder Cock.
John Hawkins.	Mathew + Giles.

CHAPTER XV.

ANDREW ROSEWALL AND THE TITHES OF TOWEDNACK, 1681.

THE religious condition of Lelant, Saint Ives, Towednack and Zennor, in the century following the Reformation, seems to have been one of great neglect, though in this particular the neighbourhood was probably no exception. The puritanic zeal of the Reformers having been satisfied by the thorough eradication of Catholicism, religion appears thereupon to have sunk into a more or less apathetic state. At this time, and for long afterwards, the parishes of Lelant, Saint Ives and Towednack were committed to the spiritual charge of one common vicar, who was most frequently an absentee, represented by a curate. The curate, indeed, is in many cases styled 'reader,' showing that he was not in holy orders. The vicar officiated once a week, on Sunday morning or afternoon, at one or other of his three parish churches, and that seems to have been the extent of his ordinary duties. Under these circumstances it is not surprising that a strict demand by the vicar for the full measure of his tithes and dues was sometimes the cause of dissatisfaction amongst his parishioners. An apt illustration of this jealousy between pastor and flock is to be found in the numerous bundles of depositions made before courts of special inquiry held from time to time throughout the country, as occasion demanded.

The following is an abstract of one these, in which tithe is refused to be paid to the vicar by Andrew Rosewall, a member of an ancient Towednack family to which reference is frequently made in these pages:

Record Office; Exchequer Deposition by Commission, 31 Charles II. (1680) Michaelmas, No 6; 32 Charles II. (1681) Easter, No. 29. Depositions of Witnesses taken at the house of Thomas Tonkyn Vintner, scituate within the Village of Newlyn in the parish of Paull within the County of Cornewall, on Monday the first daye of September in the one & thirtieth yeare of the Reigne of our Soveraigne Lord Charles the second by the grace of God of England Scotland ffrance & Ireland Kinge Defender of the faith &c. Before Thomas Hicks Esq. ffrancis Paynter gent. Ezechiell Arundell & ffrancis Arundell Esqrs; by virtue of a Commission issued forth out his Majesties Court of Exchequer to them directed for the Examinacōn of Wittnesses in a cause there dependinge between John Hawkyns clerk Complt. & Andrewe Rosewall Deft. on the behalfe of the said Complt. as followeth :

Arthur Edwardes of the parish of Uni Lelant in the county of Corwall gent. aged ffower and ffifftye yeares or theraboute ꝑduced on the pte. & behalfe of the Complt. to the first ffower, fifth and twentieth Inter. & thereunto Sworne and Examined sayth as followeth :—

Mr John Bullock was Complts. predecessor in the vicariate of Lelant, St Ives & Towednack, and had borrowed money of Mr Edwardes on the security of the smaller tithe. William Robinson of St Ives officiated as a 'Deacen and Clearke' within the said parishes.

William Orchard of St. Hillary, clerke, aged 69. Inducted the complt. into the said vicariate.

James Quicke of Zennor Yeoman aged 48, 'Sayth that the Deft. doth depasture his cattell on the tenemt. called Rosewall and on that pte. of the tenemt. called Boreesa in the possīon of the deft.'; that the deft. 'doth likewise keepe and depasture on the said premisses three or ffower labouringe horses Nagges or Mares which the deft. hath from tyme to tyme and doth usually imploy them in carryinge of tyn stuffe to the stampinge Mill and allsoe to the bloweinge howse.'

Thomas Hodge of Towednack yeoman aged 50, 'doth know a Messuage & Tenemt. called Rosewall scituate in the parish of Towednacke, and that he hath soe known the same from his Childhood, he beinge borne and bred in the same parrish, and hath and doth live neere to the same Tenemt.; that the said Tenemt. called Rosewall is worth yearely to be sett att a Racke Rent the summe of twelve or thirteen poundes.' Deft. also held Bregia Vean or Borisa Veean, worth yearly about £5 10s. 0*d.* Defendant came into possession of said tenements in June 1676. 'And this Deponent further sayth that by the Customes of the said parish every person having above three Cows ought to pay to the Viccar of the said parish of Towednacke for the same tyth in kynd by way of Whitt Sowle, and the calves in kind, and that every person there haveing to the number of three Milch Cowes or under and not exceeding, doe pay to the Viccar of the said parish of Towednack for each of the said Milch Cowes by the custome of the said Parish four pence for every such cow and two pence for every Calfe of such Cow; and that the tyth of Piggs, Geese, Turkeyes, hemp, honey and hay ought by the custom of the said parish to be paid to the Viccar thereof in kinde.'

Phillip Hawkins of Creed gentn. attorney aged 27, proved service of a Writ in the High Court on the Defendant.

Hugh Jones of Sennen Esqre. Justice of Peace aged 50, proved that Complt. had not been before engaged in any law suit.

Thomas Quick of Towednack yeoman aged 34, knew defendant well and heard him say that he had been concerned in three several law-suits and that two thereof went against said Defendant.

James Trewhela of Towednack yeoman aged 65, lived two miles from Rosewall a year and a quarter before. About ¼ part of Rosewall came into possession of Richard Pearse alias Gunne, and Matthew Stevens lately held part of Bregia Vean. Bregia Vean was rated for the poor at £3, and Rosewall at £10. This Deponent lent money to M[r] Bullock on the security of the tithes, 'by a custome for the payment of the tythes within the said parish that if any person of the parish of Towednack hath kept or doth keep above three Milch Cowes within the said parish, such person ought to pay the Vicar thereof white sowle, that is to say butter and cheese in kind, that is made of the milk of such Cowes; which said butter and cheese is to be paid to the Vicar yearly as ffolloweth; to wit nine dayes milk of each cow, which said nine dayes milk is to be made into butter and cheese, 5 days thereof is to be made into five cheeses and to be brought into the parish church for the Viccar the first sunday after Trinity.' Defendant wanted this Deponent to join him in resisting the tithes at Law, but this Deponent refused.

William Andrew of Saint Earth yeoman aged 32, 'sayth that Defendant hath lately prossecuted severall vexatious Law suites against one John Gyles, in one of which said suites the same Gyles beinge under an arrest and in custody of the Bayliffes,' Gyles had assigned to Defendant his interest in Bregia Vean as a security for money lent by the Defendant. 'This Deponant did then propose to the Defendant that there might be an end put to all differences then betwixt them, to which the Defendant replyed that he would make no end with the said Giles but would cast him into prison and allsoe drive his Cattle and other goods that he found upon the lands of the sayd Gyles to pound which Cruell p̄ceedings of the said Deft. to the said Gyles was meerly out of Designe as this Deponent beleiveth to inforce the sayd Gyles to pass over the estate which the sayd Gyles had in some other Lands unto the sayd Defendant.' Defendant also 'was very earnest with one M[r] Hingston of Towednack to prosecute the sayd Gyles at Lawe for a debt,' and said that if he would cast Gyles into prison he, the Deft., would pay Hingston the money owing by Gyles. 'And that one Bottrale and some other poor persons being interrested in a Certayne Tynne work wherein they had given a dole or share to the Defts. Daughter att the Earnest request of the sayd Deft. the sayd Deft. did afterwards cause his sayd Daughter to sue or implead the sayd Bottrall concerninge the said tynn work, as one Quarinn the bailiffe that arrested the sayd Bottrall Informed this Deponent; which sayd cause afterwards came to a Tryall and passed against the sayd Defts. daughter, there being noe cause for the prosecution of the sayd suite but only under the pretence of some sett or grant made to the sayd Rosewall or his daughter by one Stevens or Browne.' Deft. was prosecuted by one Tredinham, a carpenter, for some 'pickhilts.'

William Daniell of Zennor tinner aged 37, was in partnership with the Defendant in mining.

John Baraguanath of Towednack yeoman aged 62, 'sayth that the paper or writing now shewn unto this Deponent purporting a Coppy of the Register book of the Buryall of the sayd M[r] Bullock is a true Coppy of such entry in the register book of the Burrough of S[t] Ives in the County of Cornewall' and was examined therewith by him.

Mary Hodge, aged 48, wife of Thomas Hodge aforesaid, was at the house of Richard Hickes gent[n] at S[t] Ives, with John Baragwanath, when Deft. brought a sum of money in settlement of the tithe, and asked this Depont. to 'tale' it after him.

Paschoe Tresillian of S[t] Levan gent[n] met Deft. at the house of Charles Pike vintner in the town of Penzance, when Deft. said he desired that the question should be settled by arbitration.

Witnesses for the Defendant:—

John Hickes of the Borough of S[t] Ives gent[n] aged 36:— M[r] Bullock's predecessor was M[r] Thomas Corey. M[r] Hawkins lived with his father in law M[r] Tresilian at S[t] Levan, so that the parishioners had to hire Will[m] Robinson to officiate, and pay him £12 a year. Deponent farmed the small tithes of M[r] John Bullock in 1668 and 1669, except the tithes of James Praed Esqr., Hugh Pawly and Henry Edwards gent[n] and another whose name he forgets.

'For the Tyth of each Hen, by the Custome of the sayd parishes of Unylelant and Towednack, the owner thereof ought to pay to the viccar of the sayd pishes yearly one penny or Egs in kind for the same att Easter. And the Tenth young pig and the Tenth young Goose to be payd in kind, as likewise the tyth of Hemp and Hay in kinde; but as for ducks and Turkeyes this Deponent never receaved nor knows not how it was payd.'

It was customary to plough, till and harrow both with horses and with oxen.

Rosewall contained 15 acres of arable land and about 40 acres of furse and heath grouud. Borisa Vean was very 'course' and barren land.

Deponent and Mr George Hamond proposed to Complainant to refer the differences to arbitration, but he refused.

John Hingston of Towednack gentn aged 33, saith that a child of his and children of other parishioners had died unbaptized, owing to the neglect and absence of Complainant, to the great grief of this Deponent; and 'severall psons dyeing wthn the said pish, and haueing noe Preist to bury them according to the Church of England, whereof one of them was left without buryall, which became noysome untill some other minister came to bury him. The Complt. of late since his non residency in the sayd viccaredge very often when hee Comes to officiate Comes very unseasonably, vizt sometymes att Seaven of the Clock in the morninge, sometymes att Eleven of the Clock, sometymes att one of the Clock, and sometymes towards the Eveninge about sun sett. And Imediately on his comeing att church begins prayer although very few of his pishoners are present.'

James Trewhela (this time on behalf of Defendant.)

John Baragwanath (this time on behalf of Defendant.) He was parish clerk of Towednack. Mr Corey's predecessor in the vicariate was Mr John South, and before him was Mr Pestell.

The same cause, 32 Charles II., East. No 29.

Depositions of Wittnesses taken at the house of George Bluett innkeeper in the pish of Maddren, on Saturday the 24th April 1680, before the same Comissioners. On behalf of the Defendant.

John Tonkyn of St. Ives Joyner aged 49, was in the house of John Hawkins innkeeper at St Ives, when Deft. announced his intention of settling with Complt. for the tithes, and asked Deponent for £3 which he owed him, 'which sayd sume of Three pounds the sayd John Hawkins payd the Deft. in Deponts. presence, which sume the sayd Defdt. putt into a purse and tooke a peece of mony called Two pence which hee then receaved from the mayd of the house then present in Exchange for Beere and putt itt into the sayd purse with the sayd Three Pounds.'

This Depont then went with Deft. to the house of one William Truthwell (also spelt Trethall) near to the lodging of the said Complt.

Depositions on adjournment at the house of Morish Dyer Innkeeper at S[t] Ives, on the 28th April 1680.

Willmott Harry wife of Richard Harry of Towednack, aged 47, Says that one John Quick had formerly indifferently divided the lands adjoining those of Deft. between other persons who held the same formerly.

Alexander Odger of Towednack yeoman aged 27, 'sayth that some tyme about Christmas last past this Depont. was present with the said Mary Hodge and Thomas Hodge her husband, att the house of one ffrancis Trewhella in Towidnacke aforesaid, where this Depont. heard the said Thomas Hodge to Complayne and said to his wife Mary Hodge these words ffollowinge I have wronged Andrew Roswall in his Concernes with M[r] Hawkinge, and thou hast wronged him allsoe; to which the said Mary Hodge carelesly replyed to her said Husband and said hold your Tongue, I will sweare any thinge that comes upon my mynd.'

Martha Odger of Towednack Spinster aged 23, says that Complt. rode over to the door of her mother Elizabeth Odgers house and asked to be directed to the house of Mary Hodge. This was one Sunday evening after prayers, last August. Mary Hodge afterwards told this Depont. that Complt. had gone to ask her why she had been from church, and that she had replied that she could not go because she had a sore breast, whereas Complt. had been to tell Mary Hodge not to give evidence against her in this matter. Mary Hodge told Depont. that Complt. was afraid of her, Mary Hodge, 'ffor it lay in her power to cast him or save him in this suite.'

Alse Richards of Towednack Spinster aged 53, says that some time last year, 'Mary Hodge cominge into this Deponents house and sittinge by the ffire there Smoakinge a pipe of tobaccoe,' the said Mary Hodge related to Depont. the incident of the Deft. offering the £3 and *2d.* to Complt. at Saint Ives, and putting the money down on the table in the hall of M[r] Hickes house as aforesaid.

Tobias Odger of Towednack yeoman aged 22 gave evidence, but did not mention any matter of peculiar interest.

William Robinson of St. Ives Clerk aged 34, says that he knew

Thomas Cory Vicar of Uny Lelant and Towednack, and that at that time 'one Mr Lenord Wellsteed Minister was placed in by the present power to officiate as Minister of the Borough of St Ives.' After Mr Cory, one Mr Richard Fowler clerk officiated as Vicar of the same. After Mr Fowler came in one Mr Bridgwater clerk; and after him Mr John Bullocke who died about 15 June 1676. There was service at Towednack once a month on an average.

There was some difference between Mr Bullocke and one Robert Body of St Ives about the payment of tithes, the said Boddy holding certain lands from this Deponts. father within the Borough of St Ives.

Mr Richard Hichens formerly farmed the tithes of Mr Bullock, and, 'being a hard man,' obliged the people to pay him a penny for every pound.

John Hawkinge of St. Ives Merchant (and Innkeeper) aged 59, corroborated the evidence of the aforesaid John Tonkin as to Defendants procuring the three pounds and the twopenny piece at his inn.

Richard Fowler of Gwinear, Clerk, aged 47, says that he was collated in 1660 or 1661 to the vicarage of Lelant with the chapels of St Ives and Towednack thereunto annexed, by John Gawden then Bishop of Exeter.

Issraell Quicke of Morvah, yeoman, aged 36, says Complt. 'lived wthn the said vicaredge some tymes with one Mr Diggens and sometymes with one Mr Richard Hicks. One Robert Curnoe of the pish of Towednack, whose Mother in law dyed about a year and halfe since, was nessitated to gett some other Preist to bury his Mother in law by reason of the Complts. non residence.'

'One Morrice Dyer of the Burrough of S^tt^ Iues holdeth by Lease one stampinge Mill with thappurts pcel of the said Tenement of Roswall.' Mathew Stevens held a moiety of Borissa Vean with Andrew Rosewall.

Complt. 'did allsoe then declare to this Deponent that hee wold be paid tyth for Labor horses and Barren Beasts and Bullocks for ploughinge, for that hee did Carry furse and ffewell to the Burrough of S^tt^ Iues to be sold there and gott money by ploughinge.'

[*i.e.*, Rosewall did so?]

John Browne of St Ives, yeoman, aged 48, says: 'There was a suit commenced for the Tryall of the Right of Certaine Tynn works in which this Depont., Mr Edmond Dauy and the Defendants daughter and others were concerned as Plaintiffs, in which suite one William Botteroll and divers others were Defts.'

Mathew Browne of St. Ives, yeoman, aged 50.

John Bennets of Towednack, yeoman, aged 40, &

Mary Bennets his wife, aged 48.

James Roswall of St. Ives, yeoman, aged 26.

Mathew Stevens of St. Ives, yeoman, aged 35, 'sayth that the writing in the paper now shewne to him is a True Copy of soe much of the Register Book of the Burrough of St. Ives as is conteyned in the said writeing paper and that the same was examined wth the sayd book by this Deponent and more sayth not.' (The witnesses all conclude their answers to each Interrogatory with this formula. The above four witnesses deposed to nothing of sufficient interest to be copied here.)

Richard Stevens of St Erth, yeoman, aged 57, saith: 'The induction of Mr Richard ffowler into the vicariate, under the seal of Archdeacon Cotton, was subscribed by James Praed, Henry Edwards, John Sprig, Benjamin Edwards, Richard Stevens, Thomas Thurleby and John Hampton, as witnesses, and the name Richard Stevens was the signature of this Depont. The induction was performed by Richard Tucker Rector of Ludgvan, and Richard Fowler Vicar of Zennor.

Lowdy Rosewall (Loveday) wife of George Roswall of St Ives aged 45. Her husband had compounded for the tithes due on account of his lands.

Edmond Davy of Ludgvan, gent^{n} aged 55, 'says he hath bynn an adventurer with the sayd Defendant for divers yeares in adventuringe and workinge for Tynn, and that the said Deft. hath bynn Captaine of considerable Tynn works.' The dispute with Tredinham was when Deft. was 'Captaine of a Tynnworke called Hard to Come by.'

Elizabeth, wife of Richard *Pearse*, aged 33 yeares, deposed to nothing of particular interest.

Depositions taken at the house of John Barber Innkeeper at St Ives in the County of Cornwall.

George Hammond of St Ives gent^{n} aged 56 and

Richard Pearse of Towednack yeoman aged 40, deposed to no facts of particular interest.

The following entry, found on a flyleaf of one of the register-books of Zennor parish, shows that the payment of tithe in kind was for long afterwards the subject of disputes between the clergy and their parishioners:

'Be it remembered, That on Sunday the 27th of June 1762,

Thomas Osborn of Trewey, Robert Michell of Tregarthen, Matthew Thomas of Treen, and Elizabeth Phillips of the Church town, brought Butter and Cheese into the Chancel in the Time of Divine Service, imagining, I suppose, it would be accepted instead of their Tithes for Cows and Calves; but not being taken away either by them or any one else before it grew offensive, I ordered the Church Wardens, under pain of being cited to the Spiritual Court, to remove the same as an Indecency and a Nusance to the congregation. I here insert this lest my Successor should be imposed upon by being told that I accepted of that or any other Butter and Cheese instead of Tithes of Cows and Calves, which I assure him I did not, nor of any other sort of Tithe according to the Tenor of the Terrier, dated 1727, and held in the Register of the Consistory Court of Exeter; as Witness my hand this 21st day of July, 1762.

Jacob Bullock, Vicar.

N.B. Samuel Michell, Brother of the said Robert, and John Baragwanath, were church Wardens, and removed the said Butter and Cheese as a Nusance, at my Command.

J. B. Vr.'

and imunities whatsoever which said surrender we have accepted and by these Presents do accept Of our speciall grace certain knowledge and mere instance at the humble request and desire of Our well beloved and most faithfull Kinsman and Counseler John Earle of Bath Groom of Our Stole and Lord Lieutenant of Our County of Cornwall aforesaid We have willed and constituted declared ordained and granted and by these Presents for Us Our heirs and successours We *do will* constitute ordain and Grant That The said Burrough containing the whole Town and Parish of Saint Ives aforesaid Shall for ever hereafter be and remain a Free Borough Incorporate of itself in such and in as ample manner and large bounds circuits and precincts to be bounded and limited as the said Burrough at any time within the space of twenty years now last past was limited and appointed to be known by whatsoever name or whatsoever names which the Mayor and Burgesses thereof have been heretofore incorporated and that they and their successours for ever hereafter shall be and remain by virtue of the Presents one body politique in substance deed and name by the name of the Mayor and Burgesses of the Burrough of Saint Ives one body politique in substance deed and name realy and to the full And for Us Our heirs and successours We *do erect* new make ordain create constitute confirm and Declare by these Presents that by that name they shall have perpetuall succession and that they by the name of the Mayor and Burgesses of the Burrough of Saint Ives shall be and remain in all future times to come persons fitt and capable in the Law to have gett receive and possess lands tenements liberties priviledges jurisdictions franchises and hereditaments of whatsoever kind nature or sort to them and their successours in fee and for ever or for term of lives or years or in any other manner and also goods and chattels and all other things whatsoever of whatsoever kind nature or sort they be And also to *give* grant demise and assigne lands tenements and hereditaments and all other acts and things to do and execute by the name aforesaid And that by the name of the Mayor and Burgesses of the Burrough of Saint Ives they shall and may sue and be sued to answer and to be answered unto defend and be defended in all Courts places and before all Judges and Justices and all other persons and officers whatsoever of Us Our heirs and successours in all suits plaints pleas causes matters and demands reall personall or any as well spirituall as temporall of whatsoever kind nature or sort they be in the same manner and form as other Our leige people of this Our Kingdom of England can or may be fitt and capable in the Law to sue and be sued to answer and to be answered to

The Earl of Bath, Lord Lieutenant of Cornwall, moved for the grant of the new Charter.

Saint Ives to be a Free Borough Incorporate.

Name of the 'Mayor and Burgesses of the Borough of Saint Ives.'

defend and to be defended and to have gett purchase receive possess give grant and demise and that the aforesaid Mayor and Burgesses of the Burrough aforesaid and their successours shall for ever have a Common Seal for demises and grants and for all other causes and business whatsoever to be done And that it shall and may be lawfull to and for the said Mayor and Burgesses and their successours from time to time at their pleasure to break change or new make the said seal as to them shall seem best to be made or done And further We will and by these Presents Do *grant* to the aforesaid Mayor and Burgesses of the said Burrough and their successours that for ever hereafter there shall and may be within the said Burrough one of the most honestest and discreet Aldermen of the Burrough aforesaid in forme hereafter mentioned in these Presents to be elected who shall be and shall be called Mayor of the said Burrough one honest and discreet man learned in the Laws of England who shall be called Recorder of the said Burrough ten other honest and discreet Burgesses of the inhabitants of the Burrough aforesaid in form hereafter in these Presents mentioned to be elected besides the Mayor of the Burrough aforesaid for the time being to witt eleven Capitall Burgesses of the inhabitants of the Burrough aforesaid in the whole who shall be and shall be called Aldermen and Common Councell of the Burrough aforesaid And also that likewise there shall and may be one honest and discreet man learned in the Laws of England who shall and may be called Town Clark or Steward of our Courts within the Burrough aforesaid And We also will and by these Presents for Ourself our heirs and successours Do *grant* to the Mayor and Burgesses aforesaid of the Burrow aforesaid and their successours that the Mayor and Aldermen of the Burrough aforesaid and their successours for the time being or the major part of them of whom the Mayor for the time being we will to be one shall and may have full power and authority of founding constituting ordaining makeing and establishing from time to time such reasonable lawes statutes ordinances and constitutions as to them shall seem good wholesome profitable honest and necessary according to their sound discretions for the good rule and government of the Burgesses trades-men inhabitants and resiants of the Burrough aforesaid and all other persons there from time to time coming and performing their offices ministrations and businesses within the Borrough aforesaid and the limits precincts and liberties of the same who shall well behave carry and use themselves And for the farther good and publick profit and government of the said Burrough and sustenance of the same and also for the better pre-

Common Seal.

Mayor.

Recorder to be a barrister.

Ten Aldermen and Common Councillors.

Town Clerk to be a lawyer.

Power to make constitutions within the Borough.

serving governing disposeing plaining and demising of the lands possessions rents payments and hereditaments goods and chattels to the said Mayor and Burgesses and their successours by these Presents given granted or assigned and all things and causes whatsoever anyway touching or concerning the Borrough aforesaid or the estate right or interest of the said Borrough that they and their successours by the Mayor and his successours for the time being and the Aldermen of the Borrough aforesaid being the Common Councell of the said Borrough or by the major part of them aforesaid as often as they shall please shall and may found make ordain or establish such laws statutes and ordinances to impose and assess such reasonable paines penalties or punishments by fine or imprisonment or amercements against and upon all such offenders against such Laws statutes and ordinances or any or either of them as to them the said Mayor and Councell of the Borrough aforesaid for the time being or the major part of them as aforesaid shall seem reasonable and requisite And also that they shall and may have and leavy the said fines and amercements to the proper use of the said Mayor and Burgesses and their successours without the hindrance of Us Our heirs and successours or any other of Our officers or ministers whatsoever of Us Ours heirs and successours without that any account to Us Our heirs and successours ought to be rendred and made so that such Laws statutes and ordinances fines imprisonments and amercements be reasonable and not repugnant nor against the Laws Statutes Rights and Customs of Our Kingdom of England *And* for the better execution of Our pleasure in this behalf we have assigned nominated constituted and made and by these Presents for Us Our heirs and successours Do assign nominate constitute and make Our well beloved Thomas Trenwith Esquire to be the first and present Alderman and Mayor of the Borrough aforesaid willing that the aforesaid Thomas Trenwith shall continue in the office of Mayor for the Borrough aforesaid from the day of the date of these Presents till the first day of November next comeing and from thenceforth until one other Alderman shall be in due manner elected made and sworn unto the said office of Mayor according to the ordinations and constitutions in these Presents declared if the said Thomas Trenwith shall so long live *And* that every Mayor of the Borrough aforesaid for the time being shall and may be justice of Peace and Coroner and Clarke of the Markett and Keeper of Our Goall and Prison within the said Borrough as of former times he was *Also* We have assigned nominated constituted and made and by these Presents for Us Our heirs and successours Do assign nominate

Power to impose Penalties for breach of the Constitutions.

Fines may be taken to the use of the Corporation.

Mayor, Thomas Trenwith.

Mayor to be a Justice of Peace, *ex officio*, and also Coroner, etc., within the Borough.

Recorder, John, Earl of Bath.

Recorder to be *ex officio* Justice of Peace within the Borough.

Aldermen, Thomas Trenwith, John Lanyon, Thomas Sprigg, sen., Thomas Sprigg, jun., John Stevens, William Robinson, Richard Pollard, Thomas Dayow, John Hicks, John Hawkins, and Thomas Stephens.

Burgesses, Nicholas Prigg, Zachary May, John Hichens, jun., Maurice Dyer, William Penberthy, Edward Spry, John Nance, jun., Edward Pryor, Ephraim Major, William Bussow, and Samuel Noall.

Mayor to have power as a Justice to enforce the Statutes of Artificers and Labourers and Weights and Measures within the Borough.

constitute and make Our said well beloved John Earle of Bath to be the first and present Recorder of the Borrough aforesaid to continue in the same office during his naturall life And that every Recorder of the Borrough aforesaid for the time being is and shall be a justice of Our Peace within the said Borrough *And also* We have assigned constituted nominated and made and by these Presents for Us Our heirs and successours Do assign nominate constitute and make Our well beloved Thomas Trenwith, John Lanyon, Thomas Sprigg senior, Thomas Sprigge junior, John Stevens, William Robinson, Richard Pollard, Thomas Dayow, John Hicks, John Hawkins and Thomas Stephens Gentlemen to be the first and present Aldermen and Capitall Burgesses of the Borrough aforesaid so long as they shall well behave themselves and that they are and shall be the Common Councill of the said Borrough *And also* We have assigned nominated constituted and made And by these Presents for Us Our heirs and successours Assign nominate constitute and make Our well beloved Nicholas Prigg, Zachery May, John Hichens junior, Maurice Dyer, William Penberthy, Edward Spry, John Nance junior, Edward Pryor, Ephraim Major, William Bussow and Samuel Noall to be the first and present Burgesses of the Borrough aforesaid respectively to continue in the said office so long as they shall well behave themselves *And farther* out of Our speciall grace and of Our certain knowledge and mere motion We will and by these Presents for Us Our heirs and successours Do grant to the Mayor of the Borrough aforesaid and to his successours that the Mayor and Recorder of the Borrough aforesaid for the time being and their successours for ever and also every Mayor of the said Borrough for the time being and all times to come shall and may be respectively the justice of Peace of Us Our heirs and successours in the said Borrough of Saint Ives and the liberties and precincts of the same to conserve and keep Our peace therein and also the statutes of Artificers and Labourers and Weights and Measures within the Borrough aforesaid and the liberties and precincts of the same to conserve keep and correct and cause to be kept or corrected *And* that the said Mayor and Recorder for the time being and the said Mayor for the time being dureing one year after he shall go of from the said office of Mayor and the aforesaid first and elder Alderman of the Burrough aforesaid for the time being or any two of them shall and may have power and

Power to hold Quarterly Sessions of the Peace.

authority from henceforth for ever to hold Sessions of the Peace Quarterly within the said Borrough and to enquire hold and determine of all manner of trespasses misprisions and other defaults and articles whatsoever within the Borrough aforesaid and the liberties and precincts of the same done moved and committed which before the Keepers and Justices of Our peace in any County of this Our Kingdom of England by the Laws and Statutes of the same Kingdom may or ought to be enquired heard and determined *And farther* We will and by these Presents for Us Our heirs and successours declare that it shall and may be lawfull to the Mayor of the Borrough aforesaid for the time being if any cause of sickness or necessary and reasonable absence of the said Mayor shall require it from time to time to nominate make and constitute one of the Capitall Burgesses of the Burrough aforesaid to be Deputy of the said Mayor for such and such like times as the same Mayor shall be sick or shall happen to be necessarily absent. And that likewise it shall and may be lawfull for the Recorder of the Burrow aforesaid for the time being likewise if cause require it from time to time to nominate make and constitute one other sufficient and discreet man learned in the laws of England to be Deputy of the said Recorder for such time or times of sickness or absence of such Recorder as aforesaid And that such Deputy Mayor and Deputy Recorder so made nominated and constituted shall and may be Our Justices to keep the peace within the said Burrow and shall and may have like and the same powers and authorities of the Mayor and Recorder of the Burrow aforesaid for the time being by vertue of these Our Letters if personally present or as in any other lawfull mannor he might or could execute the same *And farther* out of Our abundant and speciall grace and of Our certain knowledge and mere motion We have ordained and granted and by these Presents Do grant and confirm to the aforesaid Mayor and Burgesses and their successours for ever hereafter that they shall and may have within the Burrough aforesaid all and singular so many such and the like other officers members and ministers and every of them whatsoever as many and such like as the Mayor and the Burgesses of the Burrow aforesaid and their predecessours at any time within the space of seven years last past have had or are wont to have or might be chosen and nominated by the Common Councell of the Borrough aforesaid and in due manner to be sworn before the Mayor and first or elder Alderman of the said Burrough *Provided always* and We Reserve by these Presents full power and authority to Us Our heirs and successours from time to time and at all times hereafter to remove the Mayor Deputy Mayor Recorder Deputy Recorder and any or either of the Aldermen or Capitall Burgesses and Town Clerke or Steward of Our Court of the Borrough

Power to appoint a Deputy Mayor.

Power to appoint a Deputy Recorder.

Deputy Mayor and Deputy Recorder to be *ex officio* Justices of Peace within the Borough.

Subordinate officers may be appointed by the Common Council.

Reservation to the Crown of power to remove any

dignitary of the Corporation.

aforesaid or any or either of the Common Councell of the said Burrough for the time being att the will and pleasure of Us Our heirs and successours by and Order of Us or Our heirs or successours in Privy Councell made and under the Seal of the Privuy Councell to them signified respectively and to declare him and them to be moved and as often as We Our heirs or successors by any such Order in Privuy Councell made shall declare or shall cause to be declared such Mayor Deputy Mayor Recorder Deputy Recorder or any or either of the Aldermen or Capitall Burgesses and Town Clarke or any or either of the Common Councell of the Borrough aforesaid for the time being to be moved from their respective offices aforesaid then and from thenceforth the Mayor Deputy Mayor Recorder Deputy Recorder or any or either of the Common Councell and Town Clerke of the Burrough aforesaid for the time being so declared or to be declared to be amoved from their severall and respective offices ipso facto without any farther process really to all intents and purposes whatsoever shall be moved and either of them shall be amoved And this so often as the cause shall so happen any Act Statute or Ordinance to the contrary in anywise notwithstanding

Mayor to take the oaths of office before three Aldermen.

And We also will and by these Presence ordaine and firmly command to be enjoyned that the aforesaid Thomas Trenwith in these Presence nominated to be the first and present Alderman and Mayor of the said Burrough before he shall be admitted to the execution of the office of Mayor and office of Justice of Peace Alderman Coroner Clarke of the Markett and Fairs and Keeper of Our Goall or Prison within the Burrough aforesaid respectively shall take the severall Corporall Oaths upon the whole Gospell of God to the said office of Mayor and office of Justice of Peace Alderman Coroner Clerke of the Markett and Fairs and Keeper of Our Goall or Prison within Our said Burrough congruous and also the oaths by the Laws and Statutes of Our Kingdom of England provided and requisite before any three or more of the Capital Burgesses of the Burrough aforesaid in these Presents before named and constituted to which three Capitall Burgesses as aforesaid We Give and Grant by these Presents full power and authority to give and administer such Oaths and without any other Warrant or Commission from Us in that behalf to be procured or obtained

Recorder, Aldermen, Burgesses and Town Clerk to take the oaths before the Mayor and a Special Commissioner.

And farther We will and by these Presents Ordain that the Recorder and Aldermen and Capitall Burgesses and the rest of the Burgesses and the Town Clerke in these Presents named and constituted and all other officers before they shall be admitted to the execution of their respective offices and trusts aforesaid shall respectively and every of them shall take their Corporall Oaths upon the wholly Gospel of God to their said respective offices and trusts congruous and first and also the oaths in that behalf by the Laws and Statutes of this Our Kingdom of England provided and required before the said Thomas Trenwith or Nicholas Courtney Esquire or Thomas Vivyan Esquire and Nicholas Teag Gentleman to which said Thomas Trenwith Nicholas Courtney, Thomas Vivyan and Nicholas Teag joyntly and severally We Give and Grant by these Presents full power and authority to give and administer such oaths and juramenta and to such persons and officers and every of them respectively without any further warrant or commission in that behalfe from Us to be procured or obtayned *And further* We will and by these Presents for Us Our heirs and successors Do grant to the aforesaid Mayor and Burgesses of the Burrough aforesaid and their successours that the Mayor Aldermen and the rest of the Burgesses of the Burrough aforesaid for the time being or the major part of them from time to time and at all times to come shall and may have power and authority yearly and every year in the month of November to witt the first day of November to assemble in the Guild Hall of the Burrough aforesaid or in any other convenient place within the said Burrough according to their discretions in that behalfe to be limited and assigned And so assembled the Mayor and Aldermen of the Burrough aforesaid for the time being or the major part of them shall nominate and in election of the Mayor put two of the Aldermen of the Burrough aforesaid and there together continue or in due manner adjourn themselves within the space of fourteen days then next following untill the Mayor Aldermen and Burgesses of the Burrow aforesaid for the time being or the major part of them then and there assembled shall nominate and chuse one of the same two Aldermen of the Burrow aforesaid so in that behalf by the Mayor and Aldermen of the said Burrough for the time being or the major part of them as aforesaid nominated and in election put to be Mayor and for Mayor of the Burrough aforesaid for one whole year from and after the said first day of November then next following And that he so as aforesaid elected and nominated to be Mayor of the Burrough aforesaid before he shall be admitted to execute the said office shall take his Corporall Oath yearly upon the first day of November or within fourteen days then next following before the last Mayor his predesessour or in his absence before any three Aldermen of the Burrough aforesaid for the time being to execute the said office rightly well and faithfully in all things and by all offices the same concerning

The Mayor and Nicholas Courtenay, Thomas Vivian and Nicholas Teague are appointed Special Commissioners to receive the oaths of Aldermen, the Burgesses, and the Town Clerk.

Rules for the due election of a Mayor of the Borough.

Mayor to be elected on the 1st November at the Town Hall, by a majority of the outgoing Mayor and the Aldermen, from two of the Aldermen.

New Mayor to be sworn before the old Mayor or three Aldermen.

And that after such Oath so taken the office of Mayor of the Burrough aforesaid untill the first day of November then next following he shall and may execute and farther untill one other of the Aldermen of the Burrough aforesaid in due manner and form as aforesaid the Mayor of the Burrough aforesaid shall be elected made choice of and sworne according to the ordination and constitutions in these Presents declared And if it happen the said Thomas Trenwith present Mayor of the Burrough aforesaid before the said first day of November now next comeing or any other Mayor of the Burrough aforesaid for the time being at any time hereafter to the office of Mayor of the Burrough aforesaid as aforesaid elected and chosen do die or from his office be amoved That then and so often it shall and may be lawfull for the Aldermen and Burgesses for the time being or the major part of them to assemble in the Guild Hall of the Burrough aforesaid or in any other convenient place within the said Burrough according to their discretions to be limited and assigned And that they or the major part of them then and there assembled shall nominate elect and make choise of one other of the Aldermen of the Burrough aforesaid to be Mayor of the said Burrough. And that he so elected and chosen to the office of Mayor of the said Burrough shall have and exercise the said office untill one other of the Aldermen of the said Burrough shall in due manner be elected made choise of and sworne to the said office according to the ordination and provision in these Presents declared he so elected the Mayor of the Burrough aforesaid first taking his Corporall Oath before Our Justices of the Peace or any three or more of the Aldermen of the Burrough aforesaid for the time being rightly well and faithfully to execute the said office and so as often as the cause shall so happen And whensoever it shall happen that any or either of the Aldermen of the Burrough aforesaid for the time being do die or from his office be amoved that then it shall and may be lawfull to and for the Mayor Justices of the Peace and the rest of the Aldermen of the Burrough aforesaid for the time being or the greater or major part of them to chuse one other or others of the Burgesses or Inhabitants of the Burrough aforesaid as in these Presents is directed to be advanced and preferred to be Alderman or Aldermen of the Burrough aforesaid in the place or places of him or them which shall so happen to die or be amoved and to elect and make choise of so many and such number of the said Burgesses or inhabitants as may be required to supply the said number of eleven Aldermen of the Burrough aforesaid and that he or they so elected and made choise of in the office or offices of Alderman or Aldermen of the

Rules for the due election of a new Mayor in the event of the Mayor dying in his year of office; viz., by a majority of the Aldermen and Burgesses choosing one Alderman to be the new Mayor until the next regular election day.

Rules for the filling of a vacancy caused by the death of an Alderman. A majority of the Mayor, Justices, and Aldermen are then to elect one of the Burgesses to be the new Alderman.

Burrough aforesaid the said office or offices shall have and exercise so long as they well behave themselves he or they so elected first having taken his Corporall Oath upon the holy Gospell of God before the Mayor Recorder or Deputy Recorder and Aldermen of the Burrough aforesaid for the time being we will to be two his and their offices respectively well and truly to execute in all things to the same appertaining and so when and so often as the cause shall so happen And moreover for Us Our heirs and successours We Grant to the aforesaid Mayor and Burgesses of the Burrough aforesaid and their successors that if any person or persons which shall hereafter in due manner be elected to the severall offices of Mayor Alderman or any other office or any other offices and trusts of the Burrough aforesaid that was usuall in the same by the space of twenty years now last past and he having or they haveing due notice or knowledge of such election or elections he or they shall refuse to exercise and take upon themselves and execute the office and offices and trusts unto which hereafter he or they shall be appointed or elected or shall voluntaryly absent himself in the time or times in which he or they ought to be sworn in manner and form aforesaid unto the said respective offices that then and in every such cause it shall and may be lawfull to the Mayor and Aldermen being the Common Councell of the said Burrough or the major part of them of whom the Mayor and first or elder Alderman for the time being We will to be two And We Give and Grant power and authority to them to put a reasonable fine on every person or officer aforesaid respectively refusing or not accepting or voluntarely absenting himself as aforesaid and also such person or such persons to prosecute to committment untill payment thereof and to elect and name one other or more other persons according to the directions in these Presents mentioned to supply and succeed in the place and office or in the places and offices of him or them so refuseing or voluntarily absenting themselves as aforesaid *And* We also will and by these Presents for Us Our heirs and successors Do grant to the aforesaid Mayor and Burgesses of the Burrough aforesaid and their successours that it shall and may be lawfull to the Mayor Recorder and Aldermen of the Burrough aforesaid for the time being or the major part of them of whom the Mayor Recorder or Deputy Recorder for the time being We will to be two from time to time and at all times hereafter for ever when and so often as it shall seem fitt and necessary to elect and make choise of so many persons only as now to be Burgesses of the Burrough aforesaid and such as they shall please And to the said Burgesses so to be apointed to administer an

New Alderman to be sworn before the Mayor, etc.

Penalties for the refusal to take office; fine, to be enforced by imprisonment.

Rules for the due election of Burgesses, viz., by a majority of the Justices and Aldermen who are to administer the oath of office to the newly-elected Burgesses.

Oath upon the Holy Gospell of God for their fidelity to the Burrough aforesaid and to execute the office faithfully and the things which to the said office of Burgesses appertain to be done And this without any Commission or farther Warrant from Us Our heirs and successours to be procured and obtained And that none other hereafter shall be taken or reputed to be a Burgess of the Burrough aforesaid but the Burgesses by these Presents expresly nominated and he or they which by the suffrage of the Mayor Recorder Deputy Recorder and the rest of the Aldermen or the major part of them in such manner and form as aforesaid shall be elected and sworn by whom the Mayor Recorder or Deputy Recorder We will to be two *And* farther We will and by these Presents for Us Our heirs and successours Do grant to the aforesaid Mayor and Burgesses of the Burrough aforesaid and their successours that the Mayor and Aldermen of the Burrough aforesaid for the time being or the major part of them of which the Mayor for the time being we will to be one in all times to come after the death or removeing of the said Earle of Bath now present Recorder of the Burrough aforesaid that they shall and may have full power and authority to elect nominate and make choise of one other discreet man learned in the Laws of England from time to time and at all times hereafter to be Recorder and Justice of Peace of the Burrough aforesaid and that he so unto the office of Recorder elected and chosen shall or may enjoy and exercise the said office of Justice of Peace as long as he shall in the same well behave himself haveing first taken his Corporall Oath before the Mayor of the Burrough aforesaid for the time being upon the Holy Gospell of God the said offices of Recorder and Justice of Peace of the Burrough aforesaid according to his knowledge in all things touching or concerning the said offices rightly and faithfully to execute *And we also will* and Ordain for Us Our heirs and successours and by these Presents Do grant to the aforesaid Mayor and Burgesses of the Burrough of Saint Ives aforesaid and their successours That there shall and may be in the same Burrough Two Burgesses of Parliament of Us Our heirs and successours as antiently was used to be and that the said Mayor and Burgesses in the said Burrough of Saint Ives for the time being as aforesaid and their successours when and so often as a Parliament of Us Our heires and successours shall be summoned begun or called wheresoever the same shall happen to be holden by virtue of a Writt of Us Our heirs and successours of election of Burgesses in Parliament to them directed or otherwise for their election shall and may have full power authority and faculty of electing and nominating

None to be reputed Burgesses but those so duly admitted.

Rules for the due election of Recorder; viz., by a majority of the Mayor and Aldermen.

New Recorder to be sworn before the Mayor.

Power to return two Burgesses to Parliament.

Parliament-men to be elected by the Mayor and Burgesses.

two discreet and honest men to be Burgesses of Parliament of Us Our heires and successours for the said Burrow which said Burgesses so elected made choise of and nominated We will to be present and stay at such Parliament of Us Our heirs and successours during the time in which such Parliament shall happen to be holden in like manner and form as other Burgess of Parliament for any other Burrows and Towns within Our said Kingdome of England may do or have used or ought to do and which said Burgesses in such Parliament of Us Our heirs and successours shall and may have their voices as well affirmative as negative and do and execute all and singular other things which other Burgesses of Parliament of Us Our heirs and successors of any other Burroughs and Towns may have do and execute or can or may by any ways and means whatsoever have doe or execute *And We* have granted also and by these Presents for Us Our heirs and successours *Do Grant* to the aforesaid Mayor and Burgesses of the Burrough aforesaid and their successours for ever That they and their successours may have hold and keep within the Burrough aforesaid yearly for ever every weeke in the year Two Marketts one to witt on the Wednesday and the other on the Saturday And also Four antient Faires by the year every year for ever the first Fayr of the said four Fairs to begin on the Tenth day of May and from thence to continue by the space of two days the second Faire to begin on the Twentieth day of July and that to continue by the space of two days the third Faire to begin on the twentye sixth day of September and likewise from thence to continue by the space of two days and the fourth Fair to begin on the third day of December and to continue thence by the space of two days Together with the Court of Pypowder att the time of the said Fairs and Marketts to be holden Together with all liberties and free customs to such Courts belonging Together with Tolls stallage pickage and all other profitts of such Marketts and Fairs and Courts of Pypowder or thereunto belonging or appertaining *and we will* and by these Presents for Us Our heirs and successours Do grant to the Mayor and Burgesses of the Burrough of Saint Ives aforesaid and their successors That they and their successours for ever hereafter shall and may have and hold within the said Burrough an antient Court of Record every Thursday from three weeks to three weeks in the year before the Mayor and Aldermen of the said Burrough or before any two of them to be holden And that in that Court they may hold by plaint in the same Court to be levyed all and all manner of pleas actions suits and demands whatsoever in as ample manner and form to all intents and pur-

License to hold two Markets within the Borough on Wednesdays and Saturdays.

License to hold four Fairs within the Borough on the 10th May, the 20th July, the 26th September, and the 3rd December, each for the space of two days.

Power to hold a Court of Piepowder at the Markets and Fairs.

Power to levy Tolls, and Stallage, and Pickage, and to hold the profits thereof, and of the Court of Piepowder at the Markets and Fairs.

Power to hold a Petty Sessions of the Peace within the Borough on Thursdays, every three weeks.

poses as in any other Court of Record in any other Burrough or Town Incorporate within Our said Kingdom of England is used and as in the same Burrough of Saint Ives at any time heretofore was used and accustomed or could or ought to be done and also that the said Mayor and Burgesses and their successours for ever shall have within the Burrough aforesaid a Prison and Goale and the keeping of all Prisoners atached or to be atached or to the said Prison or Goall adjudged so long as and untill according to the Laws and Customs of Our Kingdom of England they shall be delivered And that the Mayor of the Burrough aforesaid for the time being shall and may be Keeper of the said Goalle to all intents and purposes as antiently was used and accustomed in the said Burrough *moreover we* have granted and confirmed and in and by these Presents of Us Our heirs and successours Do Give grant and Confirm unto the said Mayor and Burgesses of the said Burrow and their sucessors of the Burrough aforesaid All Our Commons and Wastes within the precincts of the same Burrough and all and all manner and singular so many such and the same and those Mannors Messuages Lands tenements Rents arrearages of rents Services hereditaments Goods chattles Courts of Record perquisites of Courts Assise of Bread and Beer and Prison within the said Burrough and the keeping of the said Prison Goods and chattles of all fellons fugitives fellons of themselves waved or derelict jurisdiction prescriptions fairs marketts Leets View of Ffrank Pledge return of Writs Fines Mercements Tolls Thealon of tolls and Customes of Marketts for all and all manner of Grain and other commodities within the said Burrough and the liberties and precincts of the same to be brought in or sold only in publick faires and marketts but also every other day of the weeke there to be delivered customs priviledges franchises Treasure Trove and Deodands whatsoever within the Burrough aforesaid happening or coming and also all immunities clearings exemptions offices profits and incomes of Keyadge and Customs and water duties for Tonnage lestage keelage and groundage of all ships and merchandises there comeing and customs or dues for herrings or any other Fish there taken sold or exported and all manner of offices demands or rights whatsoever in as large manner and form and to all intents and purposes whatsoever as many as much such and such like and which the said Mayor and Burgesses of the Burrough aforesaid in any time or times past or which their predecessours or any or either of them have received to be taken for the support and maintainance of the Port Key or Warfe and other charges of the Burrough aforesaid as well of the inhabitants

Power to hold a Gaol attached to the Court of Record, the Mayor to be the Keeper thereof.

Confirmation of the grant of Waste Lands within the Borough to the use of the Corporation.

Confirmation of the grant to the Corporation of their Messuages and hereditaments, and all perquisites thereof.

Power to hold Assize of Bread and Beer, etc.

Grant of the goods of felons, etc.

Grant of Treasure Trove, etc.

Grant of Quay Dues, Tonnage, Lestage, Keelage, and Groundage, etc.

Grant of Tolls of Fish, etc.

of the Burrough aforesaid as of all foreigners and aliens whatsoever And also all such and the like Customs clearings powers and priviledges to the same antiently belonging or appertaining which the Mayor and Burgesses of Saint Ives aforesaid or any or either of them by any name or names whatsoever by any Corporation whatsoever or by colour of any Incorporation heretofore have had exercised or enjoyed or could or ought or were accustomed to have hold exercise use and enjoy to them and their successours for ever by reason or colour of any Charter gift grant or confirmation or of any Letters Pattents to them or any or either of them heretofore made granted or confirmed or by reason or coulouer of any prescription use custom or any other lawfull way right or title heretofore had used or accustomed and which by these Presents are not changed or altered although the same or any or either of them have not or hath not been. used or the same or any or either of them have or hath been forfeited or left *To have hold and enjoy* the Burrough aforesaid and all and singular the premises with the aportinances to the aforesaid Mayor and Burgesses of the Burrough aforesaid and their successours for ever To be held of Us Our heirs and successours as first they were held *And yielding and paying* therefor unto Us Our heirs and successours yearly so many so much such the same and those and the like Rents services sums of money and demands whatsoever as many as much such and which have been accustomed and ought of right to be paid or yielded to Us heretofore for the same Wherefore We will and by these Presents for Us Our heires and successours firmly enjoyn and command that the said Mayor and Burgesses of the said Burrough of Saint Ives and their successours have hold use and enjoy and shall and may fully have hold use and enjoy for ever all and singular the premises with the appurtinances whichsoever Together with all and singular the antient liberties authorities priviledges franchises freedoms immunities jurisdictions lands tenements hereditaments profits and free customs of their predecessours And the same of Our speciall grace to them and their successours We give allow restore and confirm by these Presents as fully freely and wholy as they or their predecessours the same at any time or times heretofore fully and beneficially have had exercised used or enjoyed or ought to have had exercised used or enjoyed without any lett or hinderance of Us Our heirs and successours or the Justices Sheriffs Escheators Bayliffs or other ministers of Us Our heires and successours whatsoever not allowing that the said Mayor and Burgesses of the Burrow aforesaid or their successours or any or either of them by reason of the premises or any of them by Us

Confirmation of all former rights and privileges.

or by Our heires or successours Justices Sheriffs Escheators Bayliffs or other officers or ministers of Us Our heires and successours for the same shall be sued molested grieved or in anything be troubled or vexed *Provided* always that the priviledges freedoms or rights in these Presents above granted be not expounded adjudged or interpreted to the damage or hurt of the Right Honourable and our dear and faithfull cousen Charles Marquesse of Winchester for and concerning his Mannor lands tennements and hereditaments in the Burrough of Saint Ives aforesaid *And We* will henceforward and for Us Our heirs and successours Do Grant to the aforesaid Mayor and Burgesses of the Burrough aforesaid and their successours That these Our Letters Pattents and all and singular liberties franchises priviledges jurisdictions immunities freedoms and all other things herein given granted released and confirmed shall and may be and remain good firm valid sufficient and effectuall in the Law And that this Our present Charter so to them as aforesaid generally made shall and may be of the same strength and effect as it might be if all other the grants privileges and powers above mentioned specified and contained or omitted were more specially legally and particularly in Our said Charter expressed and specifyed And that it may be understood adjudged and determined on the behalf of the said Mayor Aldermen Common Councell and Burgesses of the said Barrow and their successours against Us Our heires and successours for the best advantage and that it may be known or understood against Us Our heires and successours most gratiously and bountifully in favour and benefitt of the aforesaid Mayor and Burgesses of Our Burrough of Saint Ives aforesaid and so from time to time hereafter be expounded adjudged and interpreted in all Our Courts and places whatsoever of Us Our heirs and successours notwithstanding the severall priviledges franchises and other the premises by these Presents granted are not granted by apt and fitt words or any defect omission contradiction or neglect in these Presence contained or any cause matter or thing whatsoever in times past to the contrary thereof had made or provided or any Statute Act Ordinance Proclamation use custom or matter whatsoever to the contrary thereof in any wise notwithstanding *And also* We will and by these Presents Do Grant to the said Mayor Aldermen and Common Councell of the Burrough aforesaid That they shall and may have Our Letters Pattents under Our Great Seal of England in due manner made and sealed without any fine or fee great or small to Us in Our Exchequer or to any other Our officers anywhere else in any manner to be rendred payd or

Saving the just rights of the Right Honourable the Marquess of Winchester, now His Grace the Duke of Bolton, the Lord of the Manor of Dinas Eia and Porthia.

Contrariis quibuscumque non obstantibus.

Remission of the Exchequer on these [illegible]

made express mention of the true yearly value or of the certainty of the premises or any of them or of any gifts or grants by Us or any of Our Progenitors to the aforesaid Mayor and Burgesses of the Burrough aforesaid before this time in these Presents not being any Statute Act Ordinance provision or restriction thereof on the contrary heretofore had done made ordained or provided or any other thing cause or matter whatsoever in any manner notwithstanding *In Witness* whereof these Our Letters We have made Pattents Witness Our Self att Westmester this Eight and Twentieth day of March in the first year of Our Reigne.

Per Ipsum Regem

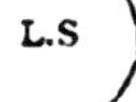

Pardonatus fines Gillford
Pigott.

CHAPTER XVII.

BOROUGH ACCOUNTS, 1689-1776.

St Ives 1689. John Hicks elected mayor.
Quay let to Thomas Collins and William Beriman.
(Signed in presence of Thomas Trenwith.)

1689
—— The Account of Mr Hicks.
1690.

beere bread tobacco and candells to the watch about A suspected ship 4*s.* 0*s.*

5th February 1689.

Disbursed about the Iland Chaple :—

pd for Lyme hellingstons lafts & tymber 8*s.* 0*d.*
pd Try to save the hellingstones blowne of 6*d.*
pd for creases nayls and pins 2*s.* 4*d.*
Masons wages 3*s.* 0*d.*
pd Tonkyn 1*s.* 6*d.*
pd for nayls twists A Lock and Kay for the doore 3*s.* 6*d.*

Disbursements for Chapel Brought forward

Expence on the workemen 1*s.* 0*d.*

Disbursed about the Kay :—

pd for tymber about the kay 10*s.* 0*d.*
pd Ed. Spry for Iron worke 11*s.* 0*d.*
pd Tho : Clarke and 3 other men 3*s.* 0*d.*
pd 8 men more to putt in the posts 3*s.* 0*d.*
pd Tonkyn and his man their wages 2*s.* 6*d.*
Richd Morrish his wages 1*s.* 4*d.*
spent on them for working 2 houres longer than their tyme 1*s.* 6*d.* £1 12*s.* 4*d.*

Expense for me Mr Trenwith & Math : Gyles 3 dayes and nights at Truroe to be sworne £2 5*s.* 0*d.*

pd for swearing us 2*s*. o*d*.
given the cryar 1*s*. o*d*.
pd Math: Gyles and 2 horses to carry 7 mens cloaths to Truro being prest 7*s*. 6*d*.
Spent on Capt: willoby by consent 4*s*. o*d*.
Spent on Capt: Coward at Mr Pollards by consent. . . . . . .
pd William Thomas to goe to Truro & Penzance with Sr Clously Shovells letters 3*s*. 6*d*.

[Sir Cloudesley Shovell.]

pd a man that brought a p'clamacon to apprehend traytors 1*s*. o*d*.

[*I.e.*, suspected Jacobites.]

13 July Spent at Mr Pollards at news of King Williams victory in Ireland £1 os. o*d*.

[The Battle of the Boyne, July 1, 1690.]

pd Mr John Stevens for a Tar Barrell & Syder then 5*s*. 6*d*.
pd Mr Pollard for beere for the boatmen yt went out to Sr Clously Shovell 5*s*. o*d*.
pd Henry Barber to beat the drum 9 weeks to the watch & cleane the Chaple 10*s*. 6*d*.
pd Ld Duke of Boltons rent 14*s*. 6*d*.

St. Ives 1690 November John Lanyon elected mayor

Profits of fairs and markets to Enoder Cock and Thomas Anthony—

Profits of the quay or pier to Richard Couch and Phillip Carlyon—

1690
—— The Account of Mr Lanyon
1691

Given the Ringers the first of November 1*s*. o*d*.
Given ffrancis Browne by consent who brought a Let pas by that name but afterward his name apeared to bee ffr. Jackson 1*s*. o*d*.
pd the Cryer to whip him and for thongs 1*s*. 1*d*.
spent on that occasion 2*s*. 6*d*.
pd the drum̄er to beat the drum to give notice of their Maties p'clamacon about seamen to repayre to their ships 6*d*.
spent on that occasion 1*s*. 6*d*.
spent on William Sutton the Kings messenger at severall tymes who carryed away Mr Hanse 12*s*. 6*d*.
pd a man & two horses to put Mr Hanse to Truro 10*s*. 6*d*.
given the guard to watch 14 men who came in a ship from Lymbrick which was made a prize 2*s*. 6*d*.
spent on that occasion 4*s*. 6*d*.

[Limerick surrendered to William on October 3, 1691.]

Spent on Esq: Praed at Sam Rices house 10s. 0d.

spent on the minister & churchwarden at signing the Certificats 2s. 0d.

[Certificates of having taken the Sacrament, which were necessary previous to accepting any public office, in consequence of the Test Act.]

To Mr Newman to draw a deed to settle pte: of the Towne revenue for my security for the mony due to me from the Towne and for Expence goeing to Penzance & other places 10s. in all £1 0s. 0d.

pd the drumer to read the p'clamation for seamen & spent then 1s. 6d.

19 April 1691 Spent on the news his Matie was returned from Holland, the duke of Boltons steward being then with us, at Mr Pollards 6s., at Sam: Rices 10s., on the Ringers 2s., on the gunners 4s. & brought from Mr Pollards to drink the Kings & Queens health 4s. £1 6s. 0d.

[William went to Holland in the middle of January, 1691, to conduct the campaign against Louis XIV., paid a short visit to England in April, and finally returned in October to open the Parliament.]

23rd July 1691 Spent on the news of the totall defeat of the Irish army 5s. 0d.

to Peter Barber for a tar barrell 1s. 0d.

for furse 4s., ringers 2s. 6s. 0d.

pd Mr Hockyn for a new post put by Mr Stevens doore 5s. and to put in the same with expense 8s. 0d.

Spent on the news of the surrender of Lymbrick [on the 3rd October, 1691] at Tho. Paynters 2s. 4d., to carry a tar barrell 2d., beere in the castle 2s., on the gunners and ringers 5s. Spent at Sam: Rices 5s. 14s. 8d.

Spent on the news of His Maties returne ffrom fflanders at the castle 1s., at Sam. Rices 8s., on the ringers and gunners 4s. 13s. 0d.

St. Ives 1691 Thomas Sprigge elected mayor.

Profits of markets and fairs let to Matthew Gyles and John Stephens for £22.

1691
—— The Account of Mr Sprigge.
1692

Spent by consent the thanksgiving day for his Maties happy returne from fflanders & the reduceing of Ireland £1 7s. 6d.

given a poore distressed soldier landed from Ireland 1s. 6d.

pd a man & horse to ride to Mr Newman about Xpher Willyams who was aprehended for stealing camlett 3s. 0d.

Spent on the men wn: wee did agree to carry Wms to Lanceston 2s. 6*d.*

spent seuerall tymes after hee was imprisoned and in tape to binde him and wn hee ran away in sending hue and cry after him 10s. 6*d.*

pd Wm Thomas to goe to Mr Newman about him 2s. 0*d.*

pd 3 men to watch one night wn the privateere was nigh or head by consent 2s. 0*d.*

pd Mr Bullock for two small pocket maces 4s. 0*d.*

spent on Mr Coleman at the Taverne by consent 4s. 0*d.*

pd Jo: Noale to goe to Penryn about the soldiers 6s. 0*d.*

Pd Ed. Spry to goe to Marazion with a guard of 6 men being required 2s. 0*d.*

26th May 1692. Spent on the good news of the defeat of the ffrench by sea by consent and pd for a tar barrell £1 16s. 6*d.*

[Battle of La Hogue, May 19, 1692.]

pd Mr Hicks his bursements Lamas Assises & bringing a certificate from Sr John Molesworth this Towne and all corporac'ons in Cornewall being presented for not ascertayninge the waights and measures 4s. 6*d.*

ffor parchment for the Towne Roll 6*d.*

29th Oct 1692 Spent then by consent for the good news of his Maties safe arrivall home from fflanders 10s. 6*d.*

St. Ives 1692 John Stevens elected mayor.

1692
—— His Account
1693

To regulating and making new measures & expences 1s. 0*d.*

to caleinge the disorders of the Boyes 2*d.*

[*I.e.*, paid to the town crier for making proclamation of their bad conduct. Gorham seems to have been the ringleader.]

to Mr Hicks drawinge a coppie of the printed teaketts for men Impresed for yr Majesties service 1s. 0*d.*

to Will Clark for the measures making 6s. 4*d.*

to Tauerne Expended fillinge the towne cupp with Sacke on Mr James Praed our Burges 8s. 0*d.*

to Tauerne Expended on the man of warr Keith 2s. 0*d.*

[Treating the officers.]

to Tauerne about Gorems Imprisonment 6*d.*

to Tho: Clark wippinge Gorrem 1s. 0*d.*

to Refittinge to towne Drumb 11s. 0*d.*

to ffillinge the towne cupp on the capt: of the seafeare in company with Mr Bere etc 8s. 0*d.*

to Tho: Burch express from Penzance *6d.*
to fiue men watching by reason of the prіueters *7s. od.*
to Repairinge Venten Eah well *4s. od.*
to meate & drinke duringe Gorrem's imprisonment *11s. 4d.*

St. Ives 1693 John James elected mayor.

Thomas Stephens overseer of the poor—
John Trevaskes and Humphrey Tonkyn constables—
John Hawkins minister—

Mr Hawkins consents to forego arrears of Mrs Chestian Hexts legacy due to him, on account of the present poverty of the Burrough—

[During the last years it has become the custom to consume a quart of brandy, price *2s.*, on setting the profits of the tolls. Also the Cryer now advertises the lease of the said tolls.]

1693
—— The Account of Mr James
1694

Spent setting of the clerkes house *1s.*; to the cryer *3s. 6d.*—— *4s. 6d.*
Spent when Mr John Stephens paid Mr Hawkins clerke the five pounds which was agreed to be paid him *1s. od.*
27th January 1693 pd to William Thomas for his labour to goe to ffalmouth to give an acctt that two ffrench privateers lay in our bay *2s. 6d.*
Given to two distressed souldiers that came from fflaunders *3s. 6d.*
paid for the use of caskes and boardes for the ffaire *2s. 6d.*
[They were used to make standings.]
Given to ffower poor boyes that were taken by a ffrench privateer *2s. 6d.*
To Rich. Cockyn for beating the drum *3s. od.*
Disbursed for Wm Paynter & his sonne while they were prisoners *3s. 6d.*
Allowed to Tho: Anthony for Helstone mens goods. . . . .
For Mr Ceelys boat on the Key *2s. 6d.*

St. Ives 1695 John Hicks elected mayor.

1695
—— His Account :—
1696

Pd Andrew Tyack for fraight of the powder from Plymouth and to carry it aboard, and to ye castle *5s. 7d.*
16th April 1696. Spent thanksgiven day p: consent *14s. od.*

mony to the Guners then 3s. 6d.

p^d^ for postage of severall p'clamacons about the plott and takeing of Rebells 3s. 7d.

[The Jacobites were very active at this time. A conspiracy against the throne and life of William was formed and detected early in 1696. The principal agent in it was Sir George Barclay, who received a commission from James to attempt a general insurrection in his favour. The Dukes of Marlborough and Shrewsbury, Lord Godolphin and Admiral Russell were secretly mixed up in it.]

21st May 1696. pd: Mr Newmans expense att Tho: Anthonyes, Bargwanoes and Mr James, by consent of Mr Lanyon, Mr Hichens, Mr Sprig and Mr Stevens, he being sent for to discorse 8s. od.

pd to amend the chapell on the kay 16s. 10d.

Spent at Assizes on Mr Courtny and Mr Tregena, about the port farme 5s. od.

pd for Saveing 2 greatt peeces of Tymber for the Kay, and to carry them aboue full sea 1s. od.

allowed Vernon Hicks kay duties of Helston goods £1 14s. od.

Spent on Mr Tregena at Taverne by consent 11s. od.

Pd postage of severall p'clamacons about Capt. Eueryes men and other rebells 2s. od.

Disbursed for Coger about the Hext legacy 4s. od.

Allowance for the Kings boat on the Kay 1s. od.

payd for the Cryers Bell 10s. od.

St. Ives 1696 John Lanyon elected mayor.

1696
—— His Account
1697

Given Sr Wm Gordon 2s. 6d.

given 4 Irish Seamen cast away in Whitson Bay 3s. 6d.

[Whitsand Bay, at the Land's End.]

Given a poore Soldier being 8 yeare in his Maties service 1s. od.

Spent signeing the Certificates for receaving the Sacramt 2s. od.

pd for draweinge 4 certificates for sd Concerne 4s. od.

Given five Irish men cast away 3s. 6d.

pd postage of severall letters and books directed to the mayor about the Tyn concerne 4s. 8d.

pd charges to my son attending severall tymes on the duke of Bolton and his Auditor Mr Robinson to goe to Mr Tregenna severall tymes to stop prosecuc'on about the port farme £1 10s. od.

Given Mr Praeds man that brought the venison 5s. od.

[Praed of Trevetho presented venison to the Corporation annually.]

Spent by consent at eating the venison 10s. od.

p[d] Nath. Anthony expence about removeing Symon Peters wife 2s. 6*d*.
postage of severall letters sent to M[r] Hooker & Tregena 1s. 4*d*.
given 9 poore Seamen taken by the ffrench 4s. 6*d*.
postage of 3 letters directed to M[r] Mayor from Mr. Good to know his Age 1s. 0*d*.
To Tho: ffloyd who brought the packett of Letters from the Victory for his Ma[ties] service to help defray his charges to Plymouth 2s. 6*d*.
p[d] William Thomas to carry s[d] packett to Marazion 1*s*. 0*d*.
postage of A Letter with newes of the peace 6*d*.

[The Peace of Ryswick, signed September 10, 1697.]

given A poore woman travelling to get passage to Ireland 1s. 6*d*.
Spent at Sam Rices by consent w[n] peace was proclaymed £1 6s. 0*d*.
To the drumer Rich[d] Cockyn 1s. 6*d*.
To the Ringers p[d] Nath: Anthony 5*s*.; to the Gunners 5*s*.; to beere at the Tar barrell 5*s*. 15*s*. 0*d*.

St. Ives 1697 Thomas Sprigge elected mayor.

1697
—— His Account
1698

23rd Nov 1697 Spent on the good news of his Ma[ties] Safe Arivall from Holland at M[r] Pollards and to the Ringers and Gunners by generall consent £2 6s. 0*d*.
more p[d] for a Tar barrell 1*s*. 6*d*.
given 2 distressed men & their children their houses being burnt 2*s*. 6*d*.
given 2 poore Irish Seamen cast away at Sennor 2*s*. 0*d*.
Spent on M[r] Newman & M[r] Trenwith by consent 14*s*. 0*d*.
26th Jany 1698 spent by consent when the Adres to his Ma[tie] was signed and sent away 6s. 0*d*.
Given A poore Traveller and his wife 2*s*. 0*d*.
given a poor Seaman which lost his hand in the wars 2*s*. 0*d*.
given a poore Capt: haueing Lost all his goods being cast away 2*s*. 6*d*.
given A poore disbanded soldier 1*s*. 0*d*.
given M[r] Praeds servant who brought venison to the corporac'on 2*s*. 6*d*.
given 2 poore soldiers which came from Silly 4*s*. 0*d*.

St. Ives 1698 John Stevens elected Mayor.

1698
—— His Account
1699

Spent att M[r] Pollards rejoycing the Kinges Coming home from Holland £2 0s. 0*d*.

[He came to open the Parliament which assembled in December, 1698.]

Charge of Ringers, Candells, Tarr barrell, Tobacco, and the Dromer 5*s*. o*d*.

Spent att Mr Pollards chuseing the way warners [way-wardens], Mr Sprigg Mr Hickes 1*s*. 6*d*.

Spent on Mr Morgan the singing master 2*s*. o*d*.

Spent wth Mr Sprigg, Mr James, Mr Hockin, Indeauoring to recall the Pettition 1*s*. o*d*.

Given A poore distressed man & woman who buried his Child att Pole 2*s*. o*d*.

Spent att Mr Pollards drinking Mr Praeds health with the venson by Publique consent 8*s*. 8*d*.

Spent att Mr Pollards rejoycing the Kinges Comeing home from Holland 15*s*. 2*d*.

Pd Steuen Rawling to performe the promise for keeping Coggers daughter according to Greement £3 10*s*. o*s*.

[This refers to the taking of a pauper girl as servant.]

St. Ives 1699 John James elected mayor.

1699
—— His Account
1700

Spent att Mr Pollards with Mr Stevens and Mr Hicks when the vagrant Man was whipt 3*s*. 4*d*.

Spent att Mr Pollards in Company of Mr Stevens and Mr Hicks 2*s*. 6*d*.

ffor Expences att Mr Pollards by the Ringers his Maties Coronac'on day 3*s*. 6*d*.

Given 2 poore soldiers that came from fflanders 1*s*. o*d*.

Given to one poore man that his howse was burned 2*s*. o*d*.

Given to a poore woman and son that their house was burned 2*s*. 6*d*.

Spent att Tho: Curnow with Mr Stevens, Mr Sprigg & Mr Hicks 5*s*. o*d*.

given to 4 Duchmen cast away in Ireland and to one Lame soldier 3*s*. 6*d*.

pd to the scavenger for Cleansen the Castell 1*s*. o*d*.

To Wm Thomas for riding to meet the Duke 3*s*. o*d*.

[The Duke of Bolton was coming to be sworn Recorder of the Borough.]

pd for 6 bottles of Sack sent for at Mr Pollards to Treat the Lord Duke 12*s*. o*d*.

pd ffor drinke then att Mr Pollards 4*s*. o*d*.

pd to Mr Pollard when wee did Eate the venson 14*s*. o*d*.

Att Mr Rices the same time in wine with Coll Praed 3*s*. o*d*.

p[d] ffor 3 Horses for the serjeants to Ryde against and with the Lord Duke 1s. 6*d.*

[*I.e.*, as an escort of honour.]

Spent then by the Gunners and Ringers £1 11s. o*d.*
P[d] to John Stevens for 20 lbs. of powder and three pennard of paper 15*s.* 3*d.*
p[d] to Rich[d] Cocken for beating the drum 1*s.* o*d.*
spent att M[r] Pollards & for a Tar barrell when his Ma[tie] returned last from Holland 17*s.* o*d.*
p[d] J[on] Midelton for mending the pentise etc 4*s.* o*d.*
P[d] to John Stevens for one locke for the stockes 6*d.*
Spent att Sam Rices to end the difference with M[r] Pascow 5*s.* o*d.*
Spent when this account was passed 7*s.* o*d.*

13th June 1700. [John, Earl of Bath, resigns the Recordership of St. Ives]

Memorandum that on the Eight day of July Anno Dñi 1700 his Grace Charles Duke of Bolton was personally present at the Guild Hall of the sayd Burrough and was then and there Elected and sworne Recorder of the sayd Burrough in the Roome of the sayd Earll.

St. Ives 1700 John Hawking elected mayor.

Joell Bolitho and Paull Tremearne farmers of the quay.
Jervis Shugg appointed town cryer.

1700
—— Account of M[r] Hawking.
1701

Jan[y] 10th 1701 Spent att the false Report of dissoluing the Parliament 4*s.* 6*d.*
P[d] Henry Hawking for mending the Town Cup 12*s.* 6*d.*
26 Jan[y] 1701 Spent att Tho. Curnows att the News of dissoluing y[e] Parliam[t] 5*s.* o*d.*
Given William Veale of Penzance his house being burnt 2*s.* 6*d.*
P[d] M[r] Hawking for Lewis Thomas & sons cloaths £1 14*s.* 4*d.*
P[d] Tho: Bennatts for making them 6*s.* o*d.*

16th October 1701 William Edwards was admitted and sworn a free man, for five shillings payment.

St. Ives John Hicks elected Mayor 1701.

Profits of the quay let to Thomas Harvy and John Thomas.

[The former witnessed by making his mark.]

Edward Chepman gent and Humphry Pascoe merchant were made free of the Burrough, for ten shillings and two guineas respectively.

1701
—— The Account of Mr Hicks—
1702

Expence of King Williams returne by consent with the guners & ringers charge, powder, oakam & candells 13th Feby £1 14*s*. 11*d*.

[William left Holland in November, 1701, to open Parliament, which met in December and passed a bill for the attainder of the son of King James II. But William met with his death on March 8, 1702.]

Pd to remove a Rock fallen in the Lane 6*d*.

26th Decr Spent by consent when the waywardens were elected, and the Dukes Letter recd 5*s*. 6*d*.

Pd Wm Thomas to goe to Mr Trenwith 3*s*. 0*d*.

[Trenwith was a Justice of the Peace.]

Mr Trenwiths charges coming here 10*s*. 0*d*.

Spent on Capt. Jackson who came here to press Seamen 3*s*. 6*d*.

[On May 4, 1702, war was declared against France and Spain.]

given 2 poore women who came from Ireland 6*d*.

spent by consent proclayming Queene Anne £1 16*s*. 0*d*.

[Anne, Princess of Denmark, was proclaimed Queen on March 8, 1702.]

pd Tho. Hore to cleanse the chaple ......

spent on Col Granvile & gent by consent £4 15*s*. 0*d*.

Rich: Cockyn to beat the drum to the watch 6 weeks 2*s*. 6*d*.

St. Ives 1702 Richard Pollard elected mayor.

1702
—— His Account
1703

Expence Examining the Silly Soldiers 3*s*. 0*d*.

meat & drinke to them whyle in prison 8*s*. 0*d*.

Spent on the Sergeant that came after them 2*s*. 0*d*.

[Apparently they were deserters.]

Being thanksgiven day in powder; 3rd Decr 12*s*. 0*d*.

in beere and brandy then by consent £1 1*s*. 0*d*.

pd Mr Stevens for boards & stuf for the fayre 3*s*. 0*d*.

Spent the fayre day with the Mayor Conbles & Sergeants 1*s*. 0*d*.

Spent wn Mr Hicks returned from London by consent 14*s*. 0*d*.

given the Ringers then 2*s*. 0*d*.

spent the Queens birth day by consent 8*s*. 0*d*.

given the ringers the same day 3*s*. 0*d*.

pd Ed. Spry for a crook for the cage 9*d*.

Mr Trenwiths charge to come here to hold Sessions 11*s*. 6*d*.

pd Mr Stevens mony hee disbursed for the Kay £7 6*s*. 3*d*.

p[d] Emblyn old charge £1 5*s.* o*d.*
p[d] for lock & key for cage and stocks 1*s.* o*d.*
p[d] Con[bles] for powder & ball for the watch 1*s.* 7*d.*
for clearing the sand from the posts of the kay 9*s.* o*d.*
[In 1703 many roads in the borough were widened and improved.]

St. Ives 1703 Richard Hichens elected mayor.

1703
—— His Account
1704

Received for allowance of the ffeaste [the parish festival] being ill and not able to hold it £5 os. o*d.*

To powder from M[r] John Stephens 8th March 1703 & 14th July 1704 for the rejoyceing on the victory obtained by the Duke of Marleburrough at the battle of Bleinhieim. £2 13*s.* 8*d.*

[This powder cannot have been procured for the express purpose of commemorating the victory, as the battle was fought on August 13, 1704.]

for paper and thread for making cartridges 1*s.* o*d.*
To the gunners and ringers then 10*s.* o*d.*
spente then £2 os. o*d.*
Spent on M[r] Praeds man who brought the newes of the battle 2*s.* 6*d.*
p[d] M[r] John Hawking for materialls to repaire the Chapell as by his acc[tt] £4 12*s.* 10*d.*
paid the masons for their worke att the Chaple £1 14*s.* 8*d.*
to the masons to drinke while they were ab[t] the Chaple 1*s.* o*d.*
paid the masons for paveing the high way beetweene M[r] Christopher Harris' and Sam Rices house 9*s.* 4*d.*
Money paid M[r] Veale and expence on M[r] St. Aubyn to prevente a Lawsuite for impairinge his Mill Leate 15*s.* o*d.*
to two poore Jewes and other distressed p̄sons 5*s.* o*d.*
Allowed M[r] Patricke Hawking farmer of the Key for a timber post and putting of it in £1 1*s.* o*d.*
repaire of the musquetts 2*s.* 6*d.*
paid the Drummer 6*s.*; and allsoe p[d] for six thousand of Pinns for the Chaple 2*s.* 8*s.*
p[d] the carpenters for worke about the chaple 6*s.* 6*d.*
p[d] Thomas Hore for cleaneing the Chaple and fitting the benches 1*s.* o*d.*

[It is worth noting that the Chaple was used for purposes of Divine worship at so late a date as this.]

St. Ives 1704 John James elected mayor.
Thomas Mitchell parish clerk.

1704
—— The Account of M[r] James :—
1705

To Thomas Hore for putting the ffrenchmen to Plymouth 16*s.* o*d.*
[Prisoners taken at sea.]

To the Seaven ffrenchmen 9*s*. o*d*.
At John Cockens for beere for the ffrenchmen 1*s*. o*d*.
in meate and drinke for them 3*s*. o*d*.
for watching the ffrenchmen 1*s*. o*d*.
To Euronimus Carne as by his acc[tt] for mending the carriges of the Gunns 8*s*. 6*d*.
for a new Stocke and repairing the stannings & spukes 4*s*. 6*d*.
Spent on the Gunners when the Expedition was driven in 1*s*. o*d*.
[The *Expedition* was a ship so called. I suppose she was a man-of-war driven into the bay by stress of weather, and entitled to a salute of guns.]
for a messenger to goe to Marazion with a petition about the Cruiser 6*d*.
to two Dutch seamen 1*s*. 6*d*.
Rich: Sampson and his man for carrying stones 18*s*. o*d*.
to the Parson £1 o*s*. o*d*.
The Keywardens for M[r] Pawleys salte £1 o*s*. o*d*.

St. Ives 1705 M[r] John Hawking elected mayor.

William Pawley merchant admitted a free man.

1705
—— The Account of M[r] Hawking
1706

To M[r] Tho: Stephens for two quarters rates 11*s*. o*d*.
To two Castaway weomen 2*s*. 6*d*.
To one M[r] Cornish a delirrious man 1*s*. 6*d*.
Expenses on M[r] Jenkyn the Deputy Vice Admirall 3*s*. 8*d*.
To M[r] Robert Davy for the Duke of Boltons rente 1*s*. 2*d*.
To Tho: Hore for beating the Drum 2*s*. o*d*.
ffor a man & Horse to carry Robbert the Cripple to Penzance 2*s*. o*d*.
more in sending a letter to S[r] Bartholomew Gracedieu 2*s*. 6*d*.
expence on the Ringers a rejoyceing day 3*s*. o*d*.
John May for worke about the prison . . . . . .
ffor Carrying of Stones to paue the streete 1*s*. 6*d*.
[The old streets of Saint Ives are still paved with smooth round stones from the shore.]
ffor expences at Tho. Curnows a rejoyceing day 3*s*. o*d*.
allowed the Keywardens for M[r] Jones's Tobaccoe 15*s*. o*d*.
repaireing the Castle house as ℘ ac[tt] £6 17*s*. 4*d*.

St. Ives 1707 John Hicks elected mayor.

1707
—— His Account
1708

Rec[d] by a lease of the Lynny set to Enoder Cock £9 5*s*. o*d*.
[Linney, from lean-hay, a leaning shed. It signifies a small outhouse erected against the wall of a larger building, and having a separate entrance.]
p[d] postage of a proclamac'on about the fast 6*d*.

spent proclaymeing it 6*d*.

[Similar entries relative to nine other proclamations.]

p^d^ to put the gun & carriadges to the Iland 1*s*. 6*d*.

p^d^ for damage of tymber to poss [prop] the towne hall the Elecc'on day 3*s*. 6*d*.

p^d^ Mr John Stevens for repayreing the ladder of the Kay £1 15*s*. 0*d*.

St. Ives 1708 Mr John James elected mayor.

1708
—— His Account :—
1709

To the ringers on the news of the ffrench being routed 2*s*. 6*d*.

17th Feb. 1708 To the gunners in drinke 2*s*. 0*d*.

To the ringers 2*s*. 6*d*.

Spent then att Mr Anthonys 4*s*. 0*d*.

to a poore Souldier comeing from Lisbon and going to Ireland 2*s*. 0*d*.

to the Sherriffe for allowing the Charter and bottle of wine 12*s*. 6*d*.

for clensing the Street by the Bridge 6*d*.

ffor a pumpe for the Shutt 2*s*. 6*d*.

[The 'Shutt' was probably the stream from which Shute Street takes its name.]

p^d^ Mr Polkinhorne £1 0*s*. 0*d*.

St. Ives 1709 Richard Pollard elected mayor.

1709
—— His Account
1710

Gave the seamen that came in here from the Privateer and payd for a pair of shooes for one of the men £1 0*s*. 8*d*.

p^d^ for sending them to Falmouth Spent by the Gentry of the Towne & charge of a man to goe with them 5*s*. 11*d*.

Gave the Ringers the rejoyceing & p^d^ for a Tar barrell 3*s*. 6*d*.

Paid Wm Richards for painting the Con^bles^ staves 11*s*. 0*d*.

Paid a Serjeant that came to the warrs to look for a passage & his sonn 1*s*. 6*d*.

8th March 1710 Spent by myselfe and aldermen and the Gentry of the Towne the Acsession of Queene Anne to the crowne 19*s*. 0*d*.

Putting a woman & child out of Towne that was att Cissells in Helesveor 6*s*. 9*d*.

Spent on Capt Phillips at his first coming to Towne 1*s*. 6*d*.

p^d^ one to watch Mrs Tamelins house and expent then 1*s*. 6*d*.

Paid for writeing the Indenture for putting out the Bastard 4*s*. 0*d*.

[Putting him out to service with someone.]

Paid the charge of putting Jenkin out of Towne & his Familye ꝑ consent 5*s*. 6*d*.
Spent about ffloyds sister 1*s*. 6*d*.
paid the con[bles] to fitt the musquetts 1*s*. 9*d*.

St. Ives 1710 John Hicks elected mayor.

Profits of the market house set to John Thomas cooper, Witness James Tregeare.

1710
—— The Account of M[r] Hicks
1711

p[d] a man to goe to the Recorder about the bastards 1*s*. 0*d*.
Spent on M[r] Recorder when he came to S[t] Ives 3*s*. 0*d*.
p[d] M[r] Recorders & M[r] Veals charges about the Order at Sessions for the Bastards 13*s*. 6*d*.
p[d] M[r] Burlases clerke to write the order 2*s*. 6*d*.
given 4 Seamen taken one being Lame . . . . . .
p[d] M[r] Legoe for a stamp for the flagons 3*s*. 0*d*.
for a proclamac'on about the Post Office & spent to proclaime it. 1*s*. 1*d*.
for a proclamac'on about the Plague etc 1*s*. 1*d*.
P[d] M[r] Samuell Michell to mend the downe high way 2*s*. 6*d*.
Spent on M[r] Harris of Hayne ꝑ consent 8*s*. 0*d*.

Seen and allowed by us

John James, mayor.
Rich. Pollard
Thomas Sprigge
John Stevens

St. Ives 1711 John James elected mayor.

James Tregeare gent, Alexander James gent, John Hichens Junr merch[t], Vyvyan Stevens merch[t], Nathaniel Anthony merch[t], John Hichens mariner, James Westcott and John Quick were Elected assistants for the Burrough.

Memorandum That on the 24th day of June Anno Dñi 1712 James Tregeare gent, Alexander James gent, John Hichens Jun[r] merch[t], Vyvyan Stevens m'rchant and Nathaniell Anthony mrcht were duely Elected Aldermen for the Burrough of S[t] Ives by the Mayor and Aldermen of the s[d] Burrough and did all take the oaths appoynted by the Lawes of this Kingdome and were all severally written on double twelve penny stamp paper.

John James mayor
John Hicks.

1711
—— The Account of Mr James—
1712

Pd Mr Tregeare to write 4 Certificates 6*s*. 6*d*.
more pd him to write 3 accounts in the Towne booke 3*s*. o*d*.
given 3 seamen taken & to sick soldiers from Lisbon 5*s*. o*d*.
pd to put the ffrench men to ffalmouth with a guide 4*s*. 6*d*.
given 4 Seamen & one Soldier Cast away 3*s*. 6*d*.
given A woman & 2 children being taken by ffrench 1*s*. 6*d*.
more when wee agreed with Mr Toupe 7*s*. 6*d*.
given 3 soldiers maymed 2*s*. o*d*.
Spent at Mr Pollards about Sisly & the whore 5*s*. 6*d*.
given Mr Toupe to come here £1 1*s*. 6*d*.
pd Mr Polkinghorne his Legacy £1 o*s*. o*d*.

John Hichens mayor
John Hicks
John Stevens
Rich. Pollard
Vivian Stevens
Nath. Anthony

St. Ives 1712 James Tregeare elected mayor.

St. Ives. The Second day of November Anno Dni 1712. Sett then from and after the first day of November instant by James Tregeare gent, Mayor of the sd Burrough unto John Trevascus the profits of the Kay of the sd Burrough to the first day of November next ensuing the date hereof for the sum of of lawfull money of Great Britain to be paid by quarterly payments; which said sum the said John Trevascus doth hereby promise to pay unto the said James Tregeare as aforesaid. And it is hereby stipulated that no reduction or abatement be made for Helston mens goods. In Wittness whereof the said John Trevascus hath hereunto put his hand the day and yeare aforesaid

John Trevascus

Witness
Jonathan Toup

1712
—— The Account of Mr Tregeare.
1713

[The earliest mention of James Tregeare at Saint Ives occurs in the year 1707, when, according to the parish registers, his daughter Mary was baptized. It would seem, therefore, that he came to Saint Ives at or very shortly before that date. Other children baptized there were Elizabeth in 1708, and John in 1710. In the latter case the father is, by an evident mistake, called John. In 1710 he witnessed a contract for the hiring of the market tolls. In 1712 the Mayor paid 6*s*. 6*d*. to Mr. Tregeare 'to write 4 Certificates,' and 3*s*. 'to write 3. accounts in the Towne booke.' In June the same year James Tregeare, gent., was elected and took the oaths as Alderman of the Borough of Saint Ives, and in the following November he was chosen mayor. In 1718, according to Hicks' MS., James Tregeare, of St Ives, was nominated High Sheriff of Cornwall. 'One Richard Beare of Boyton drinking at a rejoicing at the house of Tregeare on the occasion of his nomination, being drunk fell from his chair and fractured his skull, of which he died.' Mr. Tregeare was indicted for murder, but acquitted.]

Spent at Sessions on Mr Borlase 12*s*. o*d*.

Spent when the peace was proclaymed at Sam Noals, Mr Rices, and Ringers £1 12*s*. o*d*.

[The Peace of Utrecht, signed March 31, 1713.]

Spent at Mr Pollards the thankgiven day 15*s*. o*d*.

Given A man cast away 6*d*.

cost to poss up the Towne hall at Elecc'on 3*s*. 6*d*.

pd Hall to amend the windows 4*s*. 6*d*.

[Broken by the mob.]

pd Nich. Sampson & horse to ryde to Mr Borlase about Mr Sprigs daughter 2*s*. o*d*.

pd Jeronimo Carne and William Richards for wages abt the Kay 16*s*. o*d*.

pd the 2 sergeants and Joseph Lawrence for attendance 3*s*. o*d*.

John Hichens mayor
John Hicks
John Stevens
Rich. Pollard
Vivian Stevens
Nath. Anthony

St. Ives 1713 John Hichens elected mayor.

1713
—— His Account
1714

Treating Mr Harris of Hain and sons by consent £2 o*s*. o*d*.

for a horse and Joseph to goe to Mr Recorder 2*s*. o*d*.

Pd treating Mr Recorder at Mr Anthonys . . . . . .

12 deals of Mr ffrancis Stephens and lending 16 at the faire & other materialls £1 2*s*. o*d*.

Expences on examination of ffrancis Williams and nobles daughter at Mr Pollards 4*s*. o*d*.

Expences treating Mr Painter of Trelissick 5*s*. 6*d*.

apies of timber for a Cucking Stole 4*s*. 6*d*.

A man to sink it in the ground and John May for Iron 10*s*. o*d*.

To William Richards makeing same with Coulering 3*s*. o*d*.

Mr John Stephens gave pole and Chaire

August King George proclaimed powder of Mr Stephens 14*s*. o*d*.

[George did not reach England till September 18, 1714.]

Glasses and wine at the Markett house from Mr Anthony's Cost £1 9*s*. o*d*.

[Glasses had by this time begun to replace cups and flagons as drinking-vessels, just as brandy and rum (punch) had taken the place of sack and nut-brown ale.]

Money to the Gonners and ringers 10*s*. o*d*.

Expences at Mr Rices by consent £1 15*s*. o*d*.

ditto at Mr Pollards and Mr Anthonys 14*s*. o*d*.

Paid Mr Polkinghorne his Leguise £1 o*s*. o*d*.

[The Legacy to the parson *pro tempore*, referred to *ante*.]

att Mr Anthonyes with Aldermen and other gentlemen of the towne signeing an adress to King George £1 6*s*. 6*d*.

[A loyal address on his accession.]

20th Oct. The Kings Coronation day at Mr Anthonys 14*s*. o*d*.

att Mr Rices £1 10*s*. o*d*.

att Mr Pollards, Mr Edwards, Mr Noalls & other houses dancing hayes £1 15*s*. o*d*.

[The old Cornish country-dance.]

money to the Ringers 7*s*. 6*d*.

three tar barrells with some tar put in them 4*s*. o*d*.

12th June 1712 Paid for wine for the Sacrament when the Aldermen and assistance [assistants] were last brought in 10*s*. o*d*.

[In compliance with the Test Act.]

for Causing before Mr Vivyan Stevens doore 2*s*. 6*d*.

[He was an alderman.]

St. Ives 1714 Alexander James elected mayor.

1714
—— His Account from Allhallanday to Allhallanday, viz. :—
1715

Rec^d of Wm Cock for one years rent for his house and garden 4*s*. o*d*.

of Enoder Cock for one years rent for the Coblery shop 1*s*. o*d*.

of James Kingston for the fine of the old wales £1 1*s*. 6*d*.

Given to one Mr Parker 2*s*. o*d*.

Given tŏ one Mr More and wife 3*s*. o*d*.

to Jervas to cry about the Town to forbid the boys to dab stones 8*d*.

['Dab' is a localism for 'throw,' compare the Welsh '*taflu*.']

Spent at Cousin Anthonys makeing warrāt 2*s*. o*d*.

[Signing a warrant at the inn kept by his cousin, Mr. Anthony.]

To Mr Charles ffitzharding a Chyrurgeon [surgeon] 1*s*. 6*d*.

to Jervas to call about the Town for the packers and Talers [tailors] to be sworn 8*s*. o*d*.

Spent at Mr Edwards examining of Honor Colman 8*s*. o*d*.

[Honor is a female Christian name of either Celtic or Roman origin, almost entirely confined to Cornwall and the South of Ireland.]

ffor expences for Stoping the holes in the Town hall 2*s*. o*d*.

Spent examining the boys that threw about the Markett house lime 1*s*. 6*d*.

To Joseph Lawrence to go to Illogan about Norton 2*s*. o*d*.

Expences on Will: Praed Mackworth Esq're 18*s*. o*d*.

Spent at Mr Anthonys being his Maties King Georges birthday 16*s*. o*d*.

ffor a Tarbarrell 5*s*. o*d*.

Ordered then ye next day being the restaurac'on of King Charles 2d to ringers 4*s*. 6*d*.

Spent at Mr Rices and Mr Edwards abt the examinac'on of Mrs Bradshow & Capt. Bullon that lookd to land her & her 9 children 4*s*. o*d*.

To Richard Thomas for makeing the Cawsey [causeway] by Jasper Williams 2*s*. o*d*.

Paid Nicholas Sampson, George Try, their Servants & James Mulfra wages about the Marketthouse £2 o*s*. 6*d*.

To Wm Stabb of Devon having a Certificate of his great Misfortunes by fire 2*s*. 6*d*.

Expences at Mr Edwards when Thomas Hart was taken up & put to prison 2*s*. o*d*.

To watch the prison

Spent at Mr Pollards when Hart was wipt 5*s*. o*d*.

To Job Hodge to whip him 1*s*. o*d*.

August Spent at Mr Anthonys his present Matie that day coming to the Crown £2 3*s*. o*d*.

Ordered to be drunk at the Tarbarrell 3*s*. 6*d*.

ffor expences at Mr Pollards examining Susan Leggoe 2*s*. 6*d*.

Spent at Mr Rices on Mr Bernard Penrose of Helstone 7*s*. 6*d*.

Spent at Mr Pollards in order to take security [recognizances] from Susan Leggoe 2*s*. 6*d*.

Expenses on Liuetennant Pillman looking for a Pilate 7*s*. 6*d*.

ffor expences at Mr Edwards about the Arms £1 o*s*. o*d*.

ffor expences then makeing the Survy of the Town and parish 18*s*. o*d*.

ffor expences severall days makeing up the quotas and lists of the Arms 15*s*. o*d*.

ffor my great pains & labour therein being agreed ꝑ Gent to have at least £3 4*s*. 6*d*.

paid the Sheriffe for allowing the Charter 12*s.* 0*d.*
for a treat on him here 7*s* 6*d.*
for my Kitchen and for the Parson £13 0*s.* 0*d.*

St. Ives 1715 John Hicks elected mayor in November.

Tolls of the Market House and Quay set to Thomas Stephens junior.

John Row of Helstone, Surgeon, and Wm Pawley of Uny Lelant were admitted to the Freedom in 1716.

1715/1716 The Account of Mr Hicks

Expence on the Leftnent & purser of the Bedford gally to gett A pylott 4*s.* 6*d.*

p^d^ ringers when News the rebells were routed in Lancashire 2*s.* 6*d.*

[The Jacobite forces, under MacIntosh and Forster, surrendered to General Carpenter on November 13, 1715. Among the prisoners made on the occasion were Lords Derwentwater, Nithisdale, Wintoun, Kenmure, with many members of old northern families ('Student's Hume').]

p^d^ 2 men to carry downe the stocks from the Constables doore 6*d.*

spent at Mr Anthonys ꝑ consent when the pretender ran away £1 6*s.* 0*d.*

[James embarked for France at Montrose, on the evening of February 4, 1715, on a small French vessel.]

p^d^ masons wages to amend the chaple on the top of Iland £1 10*s.* 0*d.*

p^d^ to pave the Water lane 11*s.* 0*d.*

p^d^ postage of a proclamac'on to take ffoster and spent to proclayme it 1*s.* 6*d.*

given 2 poore soldiers and a poore old man 1*s.* 0*d.*

expence on Surveyor of the windows by consent 6*s.* 0*d.*

[For the purposes of the window tax.]

for a stamp paper to make Safeguard Indentures 1*s.* 7*d.*

[A parish apprentice.]

postage of the p'clamacon against Makentosh 1*s.* 0*d.*

charges about the boy that robed [robbed] Wm Harry 6*d.*

Expence on Sr Humphry Mackworth, Mr Praed and others, beere, wyne, punch etc. 10*s.* 0*d.*

[Rum punch was lately come into use, and along with it the beautiful silver bowls and ladles. The latter were usually made with a new gold or silver coin in the bottom, and were fitted with a long thin wooden handle. See Chambers' 'Book of Days,' vol. ii., page 496, and 'Notes and Queries,' Series 6, vol. xii., 1885.]

payd Cock to mend the Castle door & rayls of ye Markethouse & nails to mend the planching & for his work 12*s.* 2*d.*

['Planching' is a Cornish provincialism for 'floor,' derived, like a large proportion of Cornish-English terms, from the French, viz., '*plancher*.']

St. Ives 1716 Richard Pollard elected Mayor in November.

1716
—— His Account
1717

Spent by the Mayor, Aldermen, & gents, the same day being the Gunpowder Treason by consent £1 2*s*. 9*d*.

To a letter from London 5*d*.

p[d] Leggo to mend the stocks 1*s*. 6*d*.

spent the rejoycing day for King Georges return from Hanover to the ringers & tarr-barrell 6*s*. 8*d*.

[He went to Hanover in the summer of 1717, having named his son 'Lieutenant of the Realm' in his absence.]

Spent when wee went to meet M[rs] Sibella Hichens when brought here to be buried 1*s*. 0*d*.

p[d] to Leggo for mending the stocks for iron work &c̃ broaken by Eliz: Richards 3*s*. 0*d*.

To a Lieutennant his wife & children that came from the Army 4*s*.

Spent on the Hundred Con[ble] which brought a warr[tt] to Seiz our Con̄bles with Justice Hickes &c̃ 3*s*. 6*d*.

Spent on M[r] Borlase after dinner in wine by consent of the Aldermen 8*s*. 0*d*.

Spent by the Corporac̃on on a letter that came from Council about the constables with his advice 6*s*. 0*d*.

John Hicks	Nath. Anthony
John Stevens	Tho[s] Sprigge
Alex. James	Rich. Pollard
Vivian Stevens	John Hichens

St. Ives 1717 John Hichens elected Mayor November

Burrough of St. Ives The 4th day of November 1717 These goods were deliverd over to John Hichens the now present mayor as ffolloweth

Imps: The Charter box with Queen Elizabeth's, King Charles' the first and King James' the Seconds Charters, with the Pop's Bull or license for building the Church or Chappell here, togeather with the Town feoffments, Leases, Certificates and bonds, with several books and records in relation to the s[d] Burrough: Togeather allso with one Silver Gilt Cup and Cover, one Large Statute book from Magna Charta, intituled Poultons Statute book, three Statute books in King Charles the Second's time, Wingate's Abridgm[tt] and two of Washington's Dalton's Country Justice, the Town book of Ano[tts] and the book about the Swaine [seine] and rules of ffishery; The Seal in Silver with a Cristall head, Two Silver Maces, one brass yard, one Copper quart and a pint of the same, one brass Gallon, one pair of brass scales, one box of Troy weight.

[Most of the above documents are lost, charters included. The son of a former mayor cut up a quantity of them to make kites.

Concerning James II.'s Charter the following paragraph appeared in a Cornish paper early in the year 1885:

'An ancient charter of the borough of Saint Ives, which disappeared mysteriously many years ago, has just come to light in a singular manner a few weeks since. Mr. R. H. Bamfield, deputy town clerk, received a letter from Messrs. J. and W. Maude, a firm of London solicitors, informing him that in clearing out their offices they found amongst their papers the Charter of Saint Ives. How it came into their possession they had not the most remote idea, and if the Town Council wished to have it they would be pleased to hand it over. It has now been duly received, and there is no doubt that Mr. Bamfield will take better care of it than did some of his predecessors.'

Curiously, too, Mr. Edward Stevens, of Saint Ives, shortly afterwards found in his house a very old English translation of the charter, which we have transcribed into this History.]

[After 1717 no regular accounts are entered, except during Knill's mayoralty in 1767.]

[The following is an extract from the churchwarden's book of the parish of North Walsham in the County of Norfolk (see the *East Anglian* magazine, First Series, 1864):

'1721. Nov[r] 19th Collected to a Brief for a fire wc'h consumed the Goods and Cloaths of Jinkin Vingoe at S[t] Ives in y[e] County of Cornwall (the damage a Thousand pounds & upwards) 2*s*.'

The name 'Jinkin Vingoe' and 'Jenkyn Trevingy' occurs frequently in the borough accounts and parish registers of Saint Ives.]

1739 Richard Harry elected mayor.

Thomas Kniveton gent' of Uny Lelant received the freedom of the Borough.

1746 William Harry elected Mayor.

Leave granted to James Hingston, cooper, for 99 years to occupy a house on the Island, belonging to the Corporation. Signed by the mayor.

[I suppose this was the 'Briton's Hut,' see *ante*.]

1747 Michael Nicholas elected mayor.

The gold cup was repaired.

9th December 1752.

At a general Meeting of the Mayor, Aldermen, Merchants, and principal Inhabitants of the Burough held in the Guild Hall, it was unanimously agreed upon between them that the Boats undermentioned and none other shall enjoy and be entitled unto the severall Stems hereunder mentioned, and that no other boat shall hold or enjoy any stem until those they now have be lost or new Netts of a sufficient Dimension made. And it is also further agreed that all Netts which have been or shall be made use of as Tuck Netts shall not hold or be entitled to any stem on any account whatsoever.

STEMS AGREED TO.

Carrack Lego.

1. Charles Worth, the Resolution.
2. Mrs Francis Anthony, the Greyhound.

Porthnolver.

1. Mr John Ley, the Ley.
2. Mr Thomas Pascoe, the Nancy.
3. Mr William Harry, the Dolphin.
4. Mr Edward Stephens, the Lyon.

Leigh.

1. Mr John Stephens, the Mayflower.
2. Mrs Elizabeth Stephens, the Tommy.

Porthmester.

1. Mr Richard Holman, the Betty.
2. Mr Nathaniel Hicks, the Ranger.
3. Mr John Stephen, the Southampton.
4. Mr William Hichens, the Saint Ives.

Carrack Gladden:—

1. Mr John Stephens, the Pilchard.
2. ,, —Do— the Good Hope.
3. Mr William Hichens, the John.
4. Mr Jo. Anthony, the Walter.
5. Mr Thomas Pascoe, the Hannah.
6. Mr Edward Stephens, the Neptune.

John Stevens mayor	
William Harry	John Anthony
Edwd Stephen	Wm Hichens
Rd Holman	Fras Wallis
Thos Hichens	Thos Pascoe
Chas Worth	Nathl Hicks

1760 3rd November John Stevens elected Mayor.

Profits of the Quay or Pier set for the sum of Twenty and four pounds for the said year to Thomas Mathews and John Stevens junior.

1764 John Stevens elected mayor. Tolls set to Thomas Mathews inn-keeper and Nicholas Perce, for twenty-five pounds ten shillings.

[Not signed.]

1766 Hugh Edwards elected mayor in November.

Profits of the quay let to Thomas Mathews and Matthew Stevens yeomen, for the sum of Forty five pounds, seven shillings and six pence.

Witness

Hugh Edwards.

St. Ives 1767 [Reference was had to the High Court in London] by reason of the many disputes at Law that have been stirred up in the Borough the Mayor having entertained doubts in what manner he ought to conduct himself at the Election so as to act agreeably to Law as returning officer.

31st day of October 1767

At a general Meeting held in the Guild Hall: It was agreed that if any stem was shot away and the Hearer did not erase the turn from the registry within 24 hours he should pay a penalty of ten pounds to the Churchwardens & Overseers of the Poor within six days after demand, or a distress be levied.

Also any Seine in water with fish, the boat shall not take any stem until the seine is again out of water, under a penalty of ten pounds to be paid for the benefit of the poor, for not erasing the said stem within the term limited, and a distress to be levied if not paid within six days, the said penalty on Seiners and Owners for either using the boat or another net before the seine come with fish out of the water

It was also unanimously agreed that in mooring seines they were at liberty to do so provided they moored with ten anchors on each side of the seines—

Hugh Edwards mayor.	Robert Gray.
Wm Symonds.	Richard Jennings.
John Stevens.	John Wedge.
Edward Stevens.	Edward Richards.
Nathl Hicks.	John Harry.
William Stephens.	John Tregarthen.
Nathl Hicks junr.	Thomas Greenfell.
William Richards.	Collan Pearse.
James Hichens.	Richard Major.
Daniel + Davies.	John Grenfell.
John Thomas.	Thomas Heney.
Samuel Green.	Hugh Mulfra.

St. Ives 1767 Mr John Knill elected Mayor.

[Mr. Knill revived the custom of entering the accounts in the Town Book, which had been discontinued since 1716; and his accounts therein are set out with the greatest neatness and regularity, in a fine bold running-hand, ruled in red ink; but no subsequent mayor followed his example.]

1767
—— Expences of Mr Knill as follows:—
1768.

Paid Mr Mathews for a Dinner for the constables on the Sunday before the Election of a new Mayor and on the Election Day 1768 £1 8*s*. 0*d*.

[This dinner was given at the old George and Dragon Inn on the Market-place.]

P[d] John Greenfell for a padlock for the prison door 6*d*.

P[d] for pulling down the old penthouses at the market 2*s*. 0*d*.

P[d] Rich. Pollard for repairinge the Town Arms 18*s*. 0*d*.

P[d] for wine at M[r] Hickes on the day of Election in entertaining the aldermen, Gentlemen, Constables etc £4 4*s*. 4*d*.

Expences at M[r] Mathews' by the Constables on their being sworn 13*s*. 0*d*.

P[d] for Dinner at the Sessions for the Mayor, Town Clerk and Chaplain 10*s*. 6*d*.

P[d] do. at do. for Constables Sergeants and a Bottle of Wine for Jury £1 8*s*. 11*d*.

P[d] for a cart for whipping Lanyon an Imposter 5*d*.

P[d] M[r] Mathews Subsistance for him 2*s*. 0*d*.

paid Tho[s] Mathews for a dinner for the Constables, it being the first Sunday after the Election of the Mayor 15*s*. 9*d*.

paid Sam[l] and Mar: Daniel a Reward for an Information against Joan Richards for Selling Spirituous Liquors pursuant to the Mayor's proclamation £5 0*s*. 0*d*.

p[d] for wine &c for the gent. Constables &c Xmas day 18*s*. 11*d*.

P[d] M[rs] Hickes for wine &c for gent' [for the aldermen] on the Sunday morning before the election of members £1 6*s*. 10*d*.

P[d] William Williams serjeant at mace one y[rs] salary £1 0*s*. 0*d*.

P[d] do. for years allowance in lieu of Sundays dinners £1 6*s*. 0*d*.

Payd John Paynter for making the serjeants cloaks and lacing their hats 6*s*. 0*d*.

P[d] for a pint of beer at six severall houses by way of tasting 1*s*. 0*d*.

Arthur Beriman for a new window for the Guild Hall as ℘ his contract with the late Mayor £3 10*s*. 0*d*.

Duty for certificate of taking the Sacrament by way of qualification 1*s*. 5*d*.

[In compliance with the Test Act.]

Paid the Clerk and sexton of Towednack church 2*s*. 0*d*.

P[d] Welmot Gear for Lodging &c for John White a poor boy of S[t] Just who was taken ill over and above the acc[tt] of fines which were applied to his relief 3*s*. 0*d*.

Paid the Ringers on being elected mayor 5*s*. 0*d*.

Paid the Sergeants their Fee for bringing the Regalia 5*s*. 0*d*.

[For carrying the mace, town-cup and other paraphernalia to the mayor's house.]

do. ——— do. on swearing the 6 Constables 3*s*. 0*d*.

Expenses on holding a survey on the Market house 6*s*. 10*d*.

[It seems the old building was already in a dangerous condition.]

Paid Constables expenses on the occasion of whipping Lanyon 3*s*. 4*d*.

Pd Mr Ley for cloth & lace for the Sergeants Gowns £5 11s. 7d.

[The Leys were a wealthy family of Saint Ives merchants at this time, and became allied with Stephens of Tregenna.]

Paid for Weights, Scales, & Measures for the Borough £15 9s. 6d.

Paid freight from London and carridge from Penzance 6s. 6d.

Paid Wm Ninnis a witness for attdg. the signing of the Certificate & coming to the Sessions to prove it 6s. 5d.

An appeal to the poor's rate having been made to be heard at the Sessions & the Mayor & Justices having doubts of the manner they ought to act:—

To Mr Thurloe with a case for his opinion how they ought to govern £1 1s. 0d.

To the Solicitor General with a case for his opinion £5 5s. 0d.

Paid John Nance's Bill for painting 46 Constables Poles, additional for Election day.

Pd Mr Symonds for the annual sermon £1 0d. 0d.

Mr Lane in lieu of his Sundays Dinners £2 2s. 0d.

[The above disbursements, with various charges for dinners, wine etc., amounted to £73 6s. 7d.]

In 1770 the old pier was demolished, and a new one built by Smeaton.

In 1776 we find in these accounts a memorandum concerning the *Endeavour* sloop, Henry Pennal master, for the defence of the Port of St Ives. Capt. Cook's first voyage round the world was made in this vessel, in the years 1768-71.

There is preserved at Saint Ives a folio paper book, very much tattered, the heading of which is as follows:

'This Book contains the Records of the several Elections of Mayors &c of & for the Borough of St Ives in the County of Cornwal. Commencing the 31st day of October 1760.

Stevens.

Town Clerk.'

Its chief contents are the 'Form and Appointment of Recorder and Deputy Recorder,' the oaths of the mayor, justice, town sergeant, recorder, and other public officers of the borough, and the records of the various elections of aldermen, etc. The book also contains miscellaneous memoranda connected with the public business. Thus, under date 1723, is recorded the appointment of George Purefoy and Joseph Lawrance as sergeants at mace. There is also, folded within the book, an autograph letter, written in 1723, of the Duke of Bolton, thanking the burgesses for having elected him recorder, regretting his inability to attend and be sworn in to that office, and recommending James Cross, Esq., in his stead.

The following is interesting, as furnishing an explanation of the disappearance of various public records of Saint Ives:

'Burrough of S[t] Ives. Att a Court of the Mayor and Aldermen of the said Burrough met in the Guildhall of the same, the first day of August Anno Domini 1723. Whereas Alexander James Gen[t] one of the Aldermen of the Burrough aforesaid, having for some time before kept and detained in his custody severall books, writings, papers and other memorandums and things belonging to the said Boro' and the said Alexander James having been severall times requested to deliver the said things soe in his custody as aforesaid to the Mayor of the said Burrough, to whom the right of keeping the same does from time to time properly belong, has notwithstanding refused soe to doe, by means whereof the said Alexander James has misbehaved himself in his said office of Alderman and acted contrary to the duty of the same and the oath he took or ought to have taken thereupon. Itt is therefore resolved by this Court, that the said Alexander James be for such his refusal and misbehaviour as aforesaid amoved from his said office of Alderman; and thereupon the Mayor and Aldermen vote as follows:

M[r] Joseph Gubbs, Mayor: ...	That M[r] James be amoved.
M[r] Thomas Anthony, Justice	— do —
M[r] Thomas Sprigge, Justice ...	— do —
M[r] Nathaniel Anthony ...	— do —
M[r] John Stevens	— do —
M[r] Vivian Stevens	— do —
M[r] Alexander James ...	
M[r] John Hichens:	That M[r] James be not amoved.
M[r] Thomas Sprigge junior ...	absent
M[r] John Ceely:	That M[r] James be amoved.
M[r] Richard Harry	— do —

Upon the majority of the votes abovesaid it is resolved by the said Court, that the said Alexander James be and he is accordingly amoved from his office of Alderman.

Per Curiam.
Penrose, Town Clerk.

Done in the presence of
John Vine.
William ffriggens junior.'

There is also a parchment bound Book of Admissions, containing certificates of the admission and election of persons to the offices of Assistant (now called 'Councillor'), Burgess and Alderman of the Borough.

CHAPTER XVIII.

OLD HOUSES IN THE SAINT IVES DISTRICT.

We have now brought down our History to the year 1800, and will take a comprehensive glance at the state of the town during the eighteenth century.

In some respects Saint Ives presented no very different aspect in the last century to what we see to-day. There were the same old narrow, crooked, ill-paved streets which still charm the artistic eye and shock the olfactory nerves. And although a few houses have in recent years disappeared from the sites which they had occupied for centuries, still, in the main, we may see for ourselves, in the course of a ramble through such streets as the Digey, Chy-an-chy, or Street-an-garrow, the kind of homes in which a dozen generations of Saint Ives people grew up and died.

There is a certain type of dwelling-house in the old town which is characteristic of Saint Ives. This typical house is peculiar for the convenient irregularity of its plan of construction, and for the snug solidity of the structure. The principal door is entered either by an upward flight of granite steps, with or without a balustrade, or by a descent of three or four stairs below the level of the street. The thickness of the walls is noteworthy. The ground-floor is in general of stone, though a wooden 'planchen' is also common. As a rule there are but two stories, and the whole building is far more distinguished by length than height. The narrow and infrequent windows admit but little light, though this is in part atoned for by the comfortable deep window-seats, lined with oak. High oak wainscoting surrounds the inner walls, and a few silhouettes and old-world prints, together with the inevitable chest of drawers, covered with old china, add to the antique cosiness of the sitting-room. The fire-place is wide and high, though partly filled by a kitchen stove. Bright brass or pewter trenchers and candlesticks ornament the lofty

called 'Major Ceely's Great House.' It is so named in a deed of 1834, and was the home of that prominent Roundhead leader. In Major Ceely's time the house must have been very pleasantly situated, facing the sea, with only the road between it and the white sands of the beach, the little harbour of that time being far away beyond Court Cocking rock, between Chy-an-chy and Carn Glaze.

In Fore Street, on the side facing the beach, is a red brick house, now occupied by Mr. Woolcock, draper. This was the house of Mr. Knill, the celebrated Mayor of Saint Ives in 1767.

Nearly opposite—now two dwelling-houses, and formerly the Britannia inn, is the house once occupied by the Trenwiths as their town residence.

OLD HOUSES IN LELANT.

In the parish of Lelant the following are the most noteworthy houses:

Trevethoe, the family seat of the Praeds. It is a large but externally plain square structure of the latter part of last century, situated in exquisitely beautiful grounds, with a home-farm adjacent.

Gunwin was for many generations the home of the ancient and now extinct Pawley family, whose heiress married Praed of Trevetho. It has lately been rebuilt as a farmhouse, and is situated near the cliffs, about a mile north-west of the church.

Reviere is a homestead, the name of which perpetuates the title of the ancient palace of Tudor, who was king or chieftain of this district when the Irish saints landed. The word seems to be a Norman-French translation of the Cornish Hêl (Hayle), meaning 'the River.'

To the left of a steep hill in the village of Lelant, on the high road from Hayle to Saint Ives, is a large old house, consisting of two wings at right angles. A third wing, which with the other two blocks formed three sides of a square, was pulled down a good many years ago. This building is called the Abbey, and would seem to have been the clergy-house of Lelant previous to the Reformation. It subsequently became the property of the Edwards family, and in the course of several generations it came into the hands of the Hockings, as representatives of Edwards in the female line. On the outside nothing remains to testify to the antiquity of this house except the remains of mullions, with square hood-mouldings to some of the windows, and a round-headed doorway. Inside, however, the house is quaint in the extreme. A winding stone staircase leads to a tiny room in a remote corner of the building, which is popularly known as 'the confessional,' and looks as though intended for a priest's hiding-chamber. In one of the rooms is preserved an antique wardrobe or cupboard, gaudily painted with flowers in the Elizabethan style, and an old oak chest, elaborately carved, is to be seen on the upper landing.

Nearly opposite the Abbey is a house, over the door of which is a square granite slab inscribed 'M. J. A., 1723.' And in the village, not far from the church, is a cottage with the initials and date, 'E. S., 1745.'

OLD HOUSES IN TOWEDNACK.

The parish of Towednack also affords some interesting examples of old Cornish domestic architecture, as, for instance, the farmstead of Trevegia, or as it is often called, Trevessa (Trevisa), a primitive village in the parish of Towednack, and one of the old homes of the Stevens clan. The farmstead has probably been inhabited, ever since it was built, by a family named Quick. It is of the usual type of Western farmhouse, with a narrow, high-walled court in front, having a wide doorway, through which, in former times, the stock were driven in for the night. On the lintel of this gateway is the inscription: 'P. J. Q., 1702' (Paul and Jane Quick). The windows of the house have formerly been mullioned and diamond-paned, but all the leaden sashes and most of the mullions have been removed. The house is now divided (between two branches of the family) into two separate dwellings. Here one may see the turf-fire in the huge chimney, and the comfortable chimney-seat, from which, on looking upwards, one espies the sky through the top of the shaft overhead. Here and there are mysterious nooks and cupboards, one of which, near the hearth, holds a supply of dried furze. In the window is a broad seat, from which one has a view of the little garden behind. On the mantel-shelf are a variety of old fashioned ornaments, pewter platter, and the lid of a warming-pan, embellished with the figure of a cock surrounded by flowers. In the corner of the sitting-room stands a tall clock, by Vibert, of Penzance. Outside the courtyard we once spoke to an old man, tenant of the adjoining dwelling, and called his attention to the fact that a lot of large stones had fallen from the outer wall. He replied:

'Yes, sir, yes; 't 'es fall'n deown, an no waun don' seem to set et up.'

'But more will fall this winter, if it's not attended to, won't it?'

'Yes, more will fall, come the cold, sure 'nough.'

I considered this a good sample of fatalism.

NAMES OF STREETS, ROADS, LANES, ETC., IN THE TOWN OF SAINT IVES.

Ayr Lane, leading from the bottom of Barnoon to Ayr village.

Bailey's Lane, a narrow street leading from Chy-an-chy up towards Norway. It used to be called Street Petite, a name supposed to have been given to it by French or Breton fishermen.

Bellair Terrace.

The Belliers, a beautiful wooded lane running along the boundary wall of the Tregenna grounds, from the back of the Terrace up towards Higher Tregenna Farm. Its name is supposed to be a corruption of 'Belles Aires,' but hard by is a field called Bellyer's Croft.

Bullan's Lane.

Bunker's Hill, a street or lane running parallel to the Digey; next to it on the eastern side.

Burrow Road.

Carn Crowz, a pile of rocks on the south-eastern shore of the island, near the quay. The immediate neighbourhood of these rocks goes by the same name.

Carn Glaze, a rock-pile and an ancient messuage, on the high ground overlooking the wharf.

Chy-an-chy, a place between Fore Street and the Wharf, on the lowest ground of the isthmus.

The Cliff, that part of Fore Street where Back Lane leads up towards Windypark and Barnoon. Here formerly was a steep open shore on to the beach.

Court Cocking, a narrow lane leading from Fore Street to the Foresand, near the wharf.

Crown Court.

The Digey, a long narrow street in the old part of the town, leading from Fore Street in a northerly direction across the isthmus.

Dixes Hill, or Dick's Hill, in the old part of the town, on the isthmus. It leads from the Wharf to Saint Peter Street.

Dove Street, a continuation of Shute Street, on the opposite or western side of Tregenna Place. Together with Shute Street it formerly bore the name Street-an-Poll.

Fish Street, in the old part of the town.

Flamank's Court.

Fore Street; during the last century this was the principal street in the town. It is a long thoroughfare leading from the Market-place to the wharf.

Green Court, the street leading from the bottom of Tregenna Hill to High Street.

OLD HOUSE AT CARN GLAZE.

Harry's Court.

Hicks' Court, a yard off the west side of the Digey, where the ancient house of the Hicks family is situate.

High Street, the street leading from the Green Court to the Market Place.

Higher Bridge, at the Stennack, over the Trenwith stream.

The Island Wastrel, the waste level land on the south-eastern side of the island.

The Land, a part of the town referred to in a rate-list of 1620.

The Meadow.

The Long Run, a street leading from Island Road to Porthmeor Road.

Market Strand, a lane running parallel with Fore Street, between the latter and the foresand, from the church northward.

FISHERMAN'S DWELLING.

Nanjivvy, or Saint Jivvey, a group of tenements at the top of the Stennack, near Trenwith.

Norway, a street leading from the top of Bunker's Hill into Back Road. It means the 'North Way.' Norway Clear is the name of an open space hard by.

Polkinghorne Lane.

Porthmeor Bank.

Puddingbag Lane, a blind alley leading on to the wharf. Its older designation, Capel Court, was restored by the Corporation in 1890.

Purfle's Plot.

Rose Lane.

Saint Andrew Street, leading from Skidden Hill down to the church, along the shore. This was the principal entrance to the town from this side until early in the present century, when High Street was constructed.

Saint Eia Street (more correctly Saint Ia Street), one of the modern streets of fishermen's houses built on part of the Island Wastrel.

'DOWN-ALONG.'

[*Saint*] *Gabriel Street,* leading from Tregenna Place to the Stennack.

Saint Peter Street, one of the streets on the isthmus, in the old part of the town.

Shute Street, a short straight street leading from Tregenna Place to Saint Andrew Street. It received its name from a wooden 'shoot,' or aqueduct, which formerly stood there, near a pool or well.

Skidden Hill, the steep road leading down from the Terrace to Saint Andrew Street. It was formerly the only approach to the town from this side.

Spriggs' Court.

The Stennack, a road leading by a long ascent from Saint Ives up to Penbeagle and Hellesvean.

Street-an-Bollar, a street named in the Tregenna rent-roll.

Street-an-Garrow, a quaint thoroughfare leading from the back of the Manor House up towards the Stennack.

Street-an-Poll, the name formerly given to Shute Street and Dove Street. It is now confined to the former.

The Terrace, a road with dwelling-houses overlooking Porthminster and Penolver. Near the town end of the Terrace is a bastion or boulevard called the Malakoff, constructed in Crimean times. The Terrace was made by Sir Christopher Hawkins, about 1820, but did not become a highway until a good many years later.

Tregenna Place, another name for the Green Court.

Tregenna Terrace, a short road which overlooks the town from the north.

Virgin Street, in the old part of the town.

The Warren, a street just above the shore, between Penolver and Westcott's Quay.

Water Lane, a short street of old houses close to the Wharf.

Westcott's Quay, that part of Saint Andrew Street which abuts on the shore, between the Warren and the churchyard.

Westren Street, a street named in a rate-list of 1620.

The Wharf borders the harbour, from Chy-an-chy to the Quay.

Windypark, a late Georgian house on the eastern slope of Barnoon.

CHAPTER XIX.

ST. IVES IN THE LAST CENTURY.

If in these days of easy and rapid communication between places far distant, Saint Ives is still its own little world, holding but slight intercourse with the rest of humanity, isolated indeed must the town-life have been in an age when Cornwall was almost as much cut off from the rest of Britain as the island of Saint Kilda, and when, all in all to itself, and independent of aught beyond its narrow limits, the little westernmost borough lived its own life in its own way, and preserved its individuality unimpaired.

In 1705 Saint Ives contained only 240 houses. Dr. Davy has furnished us with a graphic description of this part of the country as it existed about the year 1780. 'Cornwall,' he observes, 'was then without great roads. Those which traversed the county were rather bridle-paths than carriage-roads; carriages were almost unknown, and even carts were very little used. I have heard my mother relate that when she was a girl there was only one cart in Penzance, and if a carriage occasionally appeared in the streets it attracted universal attention. Pack-mules were then in general use for conveying merchandize, and the prevailing manner of travelling was on horseback. At that period the luxuries of furniture and living now enjoyed by people of the middle class were confined almost entirely to the great and wealthy, and in Penzance, where the population was about two thousand persons, there was only one carpet; the floors of rooms were sprinkled over with sea-sand; and there was not a single silver fork. The only newspaper which then circulated in the West of England was the *Sherbourne Mercury*, and it was carried through the country, not by the post, but by a man on horseback specially employed in distributing it.'

In the year 1761, the turnpike road only reached as far as Falmouth. The last team of mules in the Saint Ives district was kept at Helles-vean.

CHAPTER XX.

WESLEY AT SAINT IVES.

BOTH Wesley and his followers were subjected to much abominable ill-treatment in Cornwall, and particularly at Saint Ives. A society had been formed at this town by Charles Wesley, in the face of fierce opposition. So unpopular were the 'Canorums,' as the Cornish people nicknamed the Methodists, that when the news reached Saint Ives of Admiral Matthews' victory over the Spaniards, the mob pulled down the meeting-house for joy, being under the impression that the Methodists, as disaffected and disorderly persons, must necessarily be in sympathy with Jacobitism and foreign invasions. The most usual way of persecuting Wesley and his adherents at Saint Ives was for the magistrates to issue warrants to have them taken by the press-gang, as 'able-bodied men, who had no lawful calling or sufficient maintenance.'

John Wesley went to Saint Ives in 1748; he found the inhabitants more tractable than before, but still inhospitable. He was detained here for some time by the illness of one of his companions. 'All that time,' says John Nelson, 'Mr. Wesley and I lay on the floor; he had my greatcoat for his pillow, and I had Burkitt's "Notes on the New Testament" for mine. After being here near three weeks, one morning, about three o'clock, Mr Wesley turned over, and finding me awake, clapped me on the side, saying, "Brother Nelson, let us be of good cheer; I have one whole side yet, for the skin is off but on one side."'

In his last Journal, Wesley notices the meeting-house of the Methodists at Hayle being 'unlike any other in England, both as to its form and materials. It is exactly round, and composed wholly of brazen slags, which, I suppose, will last as long as the earth.'

The present Wesleyan chapel at Saint Ives is a very large plain building, at the bottom of the Stennack. It was built about the year 1820. Close by are the schools, disused since the board schools were opened; and in the rear, in Street-an-Garrow, are the ruined remains of an old house where Wesley stayed during his later visits to Saint Ives, when the house was the home of the Uren family. The house next to this, which is still entire, was the home of John Nance, of whom mention is made in Wesley's journal. From this interesting book we glean the following particulars of Wesley's doings in the Saint Ives district:

Wesley first visited Saint Ives August 30, 1743. 'All were quiet and attentive.' The Society were about 120. 'As we were going to church at eleven, a large company at the market-place welcomed us with a loud huzza; wit as harmless as the ditty sung under my window (composed, one assured me, by a gentlewoman of their *own* town),

'"Charles Wesley is come to town,
To try if he can pull the churches down."'

In the evening, after preaching, many began to be turbulent; but John Nelson went into the midst of them, spoke a little to the loudest, who answered not again, but went quietly away.

7 September, Wesley preached to two or three hundred people at Zennor; he 'found much good-will in them, but no life.'

13 Sept[r] Wesley sailed from S[t] Ives for Scilly with John Nelson, M[r] Shepherd, three men and a pilot, in a fishing-boat; they returned to S[t] Ives in the same boat.

'16 Sept[r] In the evening, as I was preaching at S[t] Ives, Satan began to fight for his kingdom. The mob of the town burst into the room, and created much disturbance; roaring and striking those that stood in their way, as though Legion himself possessed them. I would fain have persuaded our people to stand still; but the zeal of some, and the fears of others, had no ears: so that, finding the uproar increase, I went into the midst, and brought the head of the mob up with me to the desk. I received but one blow on the side of the head, after which we reasoned the case, till he grew milder and milder and at length undertook to quiet his companions.'

'19 Sept[r] at S[t] Ives; We were informed, the rabble had designed to make their general assault in the evening. But one of the Aldermen came, at the request of the Mayor, and stayed with us the whole time of the service.'

Wesley visited S[t] Ives a second time on 3 April, 1744. He says 'I was a little surprised at entering John Nance's house;

being received by many, who were waiting for me there, with a loud (though not bitter) cry.' 'As soon as we went out, we were saluted, as usual, with a huzza, and a few stones, or pieces of dirt. But in the evening none opened his mouth, while I proclaimed, "I will love thee, O Lord, my strength; I will call upon the Lord, who is worthy to be praised; so shall I be delivered from my enemies."'

'Thurs. 5.—I took a view of the ruins of the house which the mob had pulled down a little before, for joy that Admiral Matthews had beat the Spaniards. Such is the Cornish method of thanksgiving. I suppose if Admiral Lestock had fought too, they would have knocked all the Methodists on the head.' (The Methodists, it will be understood, were most unjustly suspected of sympathising with the Pope and the Pretender.)

On this occasion the Methodists encountered much persecution, which Wesley says 'was owing in great measure, to the indefatigable labours of Mr Hoblin and Mr Simmons [Hoblin the vicar, and Symonds the curate]; gentlemen worthy to he had in everlasting remembrance, for their unwearied endeavours to destroy heresy.'

On the 7th April he writes: 'I took down part of the account of the late riot; which (to show the deep regard of the actors herein for His Majesty) was on the self-same day on which His Majesty's Proclamation against rioters was read. Yet I see much good has been brought out of it already; particularly the great peace we now enjoy.'

Wesley went with John Nance to 'Rosemargay' in Zennor, where he found there had been a 'shaking' among the brethren 'occasioned by the confident assertions of some that they had seen Mr. Wesley a week or two ago with the Pretender in France.'

At Rosemergy Wesley had prepared for him 'a little chamber, and set for him there a bed, and a table, and a stool, and a candlestick.' This was called 'Mr Wesley's Room,' and some of the furniture, with his inkstand, was long preserved there.

Dr. Borlase, the renowned vicar of Ludgvan, had, complains Wesley, spoken evil of the Methodists, in spite of the evident change for good which the Society had effected among his parishioners. The Doctor asked Jonathan Reeves to tell him who of them had been improved by Wesley's teaching; to whom when Reeves named one John Daniel, the doctor answered, 'Get along, you are a parcel of mad, crazy-headed fellows,' and thrust him to the door.

On April 10 Wesley records in his journal that he walked over to Zennor, and after preaching, 'settled the infant Society.'

April 11. 'Being the Public Fast, the church of S[t] Ives was well filled. After reading those strong words, "If they have called the master of the house Beelzebub, how much more them of his household," M[r] Hoblin fulfilled them, by vehemently declaiming against *the new sect*, as enemies of the church, Jacobites, Papists, and what not. This sermon had such an effect, that next day, as James Wheatley, one of Wesley's companions, was walking through the town, he was assailed with a shower of stones. 'He stepped into a house; but the master of it followed him like a lion, to drag him out. Yet after a few words his mind was changed, and he swore nobody should hurt him. Meantime one went for a Justice of Peace, who came and promised to see him safe home. The mob followed, hallooing and shouting amain. Near John Paynter's house the Justice left him: they quickly beset the house. But a messenger came from the Mayor, forbidding any to touch M[r] Wheatley, at his peril. He then went home. But between seven and eight the mob came and beset John Nance's house. John Nance and John Paynter went out, and stood before the door; though they were quickly covered with dirt. The cry was "Bring out the Preacher! Pull down the house!" And they began to pull down the boards which were nailed against the windows. But the Mayor, hearing it, came without delay, and read the Proclamation against riots: upon which, after many oaths and imprecations they thought proper to disperse.' The principal accusation against John Wesley was that he had brought the Pretender secretly to Saint Ives the previous autumn, under the name of John Downes.

In September, 1744, one of Wesley's co-evangelists, Henry Millward, wrote to him from Cornwall, informing him that in that county 'the devil rages horribly. Even at S[t] Ives, we cannot shut the doors of John Nance's house, to meet the society, but the mob immediately threaten to break them open. They now triumph over us more and more, saying it is plain nothing can be done against them.' He also complains that Dr. Borlase had committed his companion, Mr. Westall, to Bodmin goal as a vagrant, but he was soon set at liberty.

John Wesley was at Saint Ives for the third time on June 22, 1745, and again suffered much vexatious treatment at the hands of that irreconcileable antiquary, Dr. Borlase. On the 23rd, which was a Sunday, 'as we returned from church at noon, a famous man of the town attacked us, for the entertainment of his masters. I turned back and spoke to him, and he was ashamed.

We expected a visit in the evening from some of the devil's drunken champions, who swarm here on a holy-day, so called; but none appeared; so after a confortable hour, we praised God, and parted in peace.'

'On Sunday, 30, about six in the evening, I began preaching at S[t] Ives, in the street, near John Nance's door. A multitude of people were quickly assembled, both high and low, rich and poor, and I observed not any creature to laugh or smile, or hardly move hand or foot.' But one Mr. Edwards came from the mayor, with a man whom he ordered to read the proclamation, whereupon Wesley concluded his discourse.

So great had been the famous preacher's influence on the inhabitants of the westernmost borough, that, on July 8, 1745, scarcely two years since his first arrival there, Wesley calls Saint Ives 'the most still and honourable post (so are the times changed) which we have in Cornwall.'

On the 11th he writes, 'I found some life, even at *Zennor*,' and next day he met the stewards of all the societies, at Saint Ives.

From Cornwall it was Wesley's usual practice to proceed to South Wales, making Cardiff his head-quarters.

He arrived at Saint Ives for the fourth time on September 5, 1746, and preached in the Green Court next day. Afterwards he rode to *Zennor*, before the church service began, and preached near the churchyard ('and surely never was it more wanted') upon the text, 'Whom ye ignorantly worship, Him declare I unto you.' 'I preached,' he says, 'at S[t] Ives about five, to a more understanding people, on "Thou art not far from the kingdom of God."'

A fifth visit to Saint Ives was made on June 30, 1747. 'We came to Saint Ives before Morning Prayers, and walked to church without so much as one huzza. How strangely has one year changed the scene in Cornwall! This is now a peaceable, nay, honourable station.'

Next day John Wesley spoke severally to all those who had votes in the ensuing election, and prevailed upon them to accept no bribes. 'Five guineas had been given to W. C., but he returned them immediately. T. M. positively refused to accept anything. And when he heard that his mother had received money privately, he could not rest till she gave him the three guineas, which he instantly sent back.' Among Wesley's 'Exhorters' at this date are those indicated by the initials J. B., A. L., and J. W.

On August 19, 1750, Wesley visited Saint Ives for the sixth

time, and next day held a quarterly meeting and the first watch-night service that had ever been held in Cornwall.

23rd August. 'Having first sent to the mayor [John Edwards] to inquire if it would be offensive to him, I preached in the evening, not far from the market-place. There was a vast concourse of people, very few of the adult inhabitants of the town being wanting. I had gone through two-thirds of my discourse, to which the whole audience was deeply attentive, when Mr S. sent his man to ride his horse to and fro through the midst of the congregation. Some of the chief men in the town bade me go on; and said no man should hinder me, but I judged it better to retire to the room.'

A seventh visit to Saint Ives was paid on September 19, 1751, but nothing special is recorded of it.

For the eighth time Wesley came to the town on July 26, 1753, when, upon his examination of the society, 'I found an accursed thing among them; well-nigh one and all bought or sold uncustomed goods. I told them plain, either they must put this abomination away, or they would see my face no more. They severally promised to do so. So I trust this plague is stayed.'

He was at Saint Ives again on September 7, 1755, for the ninth time. Mr. K., a young attorney, who had attended the meetings, was seized with a kind of possession. Wesley set aside a day of fasting and prayer on his behalf, after which his condition improved.

On September 12, 1757, Wesley was for the tenth time in the Saint Ives district, and preached in a field at Lelant.

John Wesley visited Saint Ives for the eleventh time on the September 10, 1760, and preached in a field to an immense congregation. He says 'the clear sky, the setting sun, the smooth, still water, all agreed with the state of the audience.' Inquiring about the great storm of March 9, 1759, he was informed that 'it began near the Land's End, between nine and ten at night, and went eastward, not above a mile broad, over St Just, Morva, Zennor, St Ives, and Gwinear, whence it turned northward over the sea. It uncovered all the houses in its way, and was accompanied with impetuous rain. About a mile south-east from Saint Ives, it tore up a rock, twelve or fourteen ton weight, from the top of a rising ground, and whirled it down upon another, which it split through, and at the same time dashed itself in pieces. It broke down the pinnacles of Gwinear church, which forced their way through the roof. And it was remarkable the rain which attended it was as salt as any sea-water.'

On the 21st Wesley preached at Cubert, where James

Roberts, a tinner, of Saint Ives, gave a thrilling account of his conversion.

The great preacher's twelfth visit to Saint Ives occurred on September 14, 1762, when he preached near the quay. 'Two or three pretty butterflies came, and looked, and smiled, and went away; but all the rest of the numerous congregation behaved with the utmost seriousness.'

For the thirteenth time Wesley was preaching at Saint Ives, on September 13, 1765, before an immense congregation assembled in the open air.

His fourteenth visit was paid on September 9, 1766, when he called on Alice Daniel, of Rosemergy, in Zennor, with whom he had formerly lodged. At Saint Ives the rain compelled him to preach in the house.

For the sixteenth time Wesley came to Saint Ives, on August 21, 1770, concerning which visit he writes: 'Here God has made all our enemies to be at peace with us, so that I might have preached in any part of the town. But I rather chose a meadow, where such as would might sit down, either on the grass or on the hedges,—so the Cornish term their broad stone walls, which are usually covered with grass.'

Next day, Sunday, 'being desired to preach in the town, for the sake of some who could not come up the hill [the Stennack] I began near the market-place at eight, on "Without holiness no man shall see the Lord?" We had an useful sermon at church. At five I preached again. Well-nigh all the town were present, and thousands from all parts of the country.'

Curious is the following passage: 'At nine I renewed the meeting of the children, which had also been given up for a long season. But so dead a company have I seldom seen. I found scarce one spark of even the fear of God among them.'

On August 20, 1773, a seventeenth visit was paid to Saint Ives. On the evening of that day Wesley preached in the Market-place, to the largest congregation he had ever seen in Cornwall.

An eighteenth visit was paid on September 2, 1774, when Wesley preached, in Saint Ives Market-place, to nearly the whole of the inhabitants of the town.

On September 4, 1775, John Wesley again went to Saint Ives, and 'preached in the little meadow above the town.' He writes that 'the people in general here (excepting the rich) seem almost persuaded to be Christians. Perhaps the prayer of their old Pastor, Mr Tregoss, is answered even to the fourth generation.' This was Wesley's nineteenth visit.

The next, the twentieth, of which nothing particular remains on record, was on September 24, 1776.

At his twenty-first visit, on October 23, 1777, Wesley preached on the Cliff, at St. Ives.

On August 28, 1778, John Wesley visited Saint Ives for the twenty-second time, and 'rejoiced to find that peace and love prevailed through the whole circuit. Those who styled themselves My Lady's Preachers, who screamed, and railed, and threatened to swallow us up, are vanished away. I cannot learn that they have made one convert—a plain proof that God did not send them.'

A twenty-third visit was paid on August 25, 1780, when Wesley writes, 'Here is no opposer now.'

On August 31, 1781, he was preaching for the twenty-fourth time at Saint Ives, in the market-place.

Concerning his twenty-fifth visit, on August 26, 1785, Wesley writes: 'In the evening I preached in the market-place at St. Ives, to almost the whole town. This was the first place in Cornwall where we preached, and where Satan fought fiercely for his kingdom; but now all is peace. I found old John Nance had rested from his labours. Some months since, sitting behind the preacher, in the pulpit, he sunk down, was carried out, and fell asleep.'

On September 8, 1787, Wesley was once more at Saint Ives, for the twenty-sixth time. Being market-day, he preached in a convenient field at the end of the town to a very numerous and serious congregation.

For the twenty-seventh and last time, on August 25, 1789, Wesley 'went to St. Ives, and preached, as usual, on one side of the market-place. Wellnigh all the town attended, and with all possible seriousness. Surely forty years labour has not been in vain here.'

Such is the account, written by his own hand, of the labours of John Wesley at Saint Ives, which, commencing in the teeth of the most dead-headed opposition, produced in the result an effect so deep and so lasting.

It would be impossible to overrate the results of Wesley's preaching in Cornwall, the inhabitants of which, from a careless people whose only religion was a curious mixture of the remains of Catholicism with the yet more ancient vestiges of Celtic paganism, became a sober, Bible-reading folk, only less strongly Protestant and matter-of-fact than their Welsh cousins, who received Calvinism from Whitfield at the same date. The rise of

Methodism was the signal for the final disappearance of the old Celtic beliefs in witchcraft, fairies, and other relics of Druidism, and will be admitted, by both the friends and foes of Puritanism, to have been the crowning of the movement commenced by the Reformers in the sixteenth century. To Methodism, undoubtedly, we owe it that, along with the poetic and lovable forms of old-world misbeliefs and practices, Cornwall has thrown off those formerly universal evils—smuggling, wrecking, and drunkenness.

CHAPTER XXI.

A SAINT IVES MAN PRISONER OF WAR IN FRANCE.

At the beginning of this century, when an invasion by Buonaparte began to be feared, active preparations were commenced at Saint Ives for resisting any French landing in the neighbourhood. A corps was formed, under the title of the Royal Cornwall Volunteer Militia. It was an artillery force, largely composed of sailors and miners; the year of its formation was 1815. Squire Stephens, of Tregenna, subscribed largely to the expenses, as will be found on reference to our extracts from his account-book.

From the same account-book of Squire Stephens we gather that several Saint Ives men were languishing in French prisons at this time. Two Saint Ives men were then confined in the prison of Charleville in French Flanders. Their names were Thomas Williams and John Short. They had the most surprising adventures during their captivity of ten years. There are in the possession of their descendants manuscripts in the handwriting of both Thomas Williams and John Short, giving accounts of their adventures in France. The following abridgement may not be inappropriate to our History:

'NARRATIVE OF THE ADVENTURES OF THOMAS WILLIAMS, OF ST. IVES, IN THE COUNTY OF CORNWALL, WHO WAS THIRTEEN YEARS A PRISONER OF WAR IN FRANCE.

'I was taken prisoner of war by the French on the 28th of March, 1804, on board the brig *Friendship*, of London, Josias Sincock, master, bound from London with copper and flour for the Devonport dockyard. We weighed anchor in the Downs, and sailed down the Channel with a fair wind, under convoy of the *Spider* (or *Speedy*) gun-brig; but not being a fast sailer, and having waited too long at the Downs, to take on board a new long-boat, we were rather astern of the fleet when night came on.

I was on the forecastle looking out (being then a lad of 13 years of age) when we espied a lugger coming towards the shore upon a wind. We lost sight of her for some time, but at length we saw her coming up close astern of us. We hailed her, but got no reply. At last she sheared up under our quarter, and hove a grapnel on board; and very soon a great number of her crew came onto our deck well armed, and took possession of our ship, driving all our ship's company below, except myself, whom they kept on deck to show them the leading ropes. They soon altered our course for the coast of France, the lugger keeping us company the whole night. In the morning early we were close into Dieppe harbour, not having seen an English cruiser during the whole time. When the tide suited, we were put into the harbour, and were the same day sent on shore to a round castle, where they kept us three days. When we landed they took away all our clothes, excepting what we had on, and had the audacity to come and see us in the prison, with some of our men's clothes on them.

'On the 1st of April we began our march towards Givêt. I believe we were a fortnight in getting there, having travelled between two and three hundred miles. When we arrived at Givêt we found several other ships' companies: H.M.S. *La Minerve's*, which was lost at Cherbourg, several of the men of the Harwich packet, which had been detained in the country, and the crew of H.M.S. *Hussar*, which was lost on the Saints Rocks near Brest. The prison was a very large horse-barrack, divided off into corridors, each corridor containing eight rooms, and each room sixteen persons, and at night the doors were all locked. In the mornings we had liberty to go into a long, narrow yard close to the river Meuse. Three times a day we were mustered, and the yard would then scarcely contain our numbers. The provisions allowed us were as follows: 1 lb. of brown bread, ½ lb. of so-called "meat," consisting of heads, livers, lights, and offal of a bullock's carcase. We were paid three farthings a day, from which they kept back a portion towards keeping the prison in repair. We were so reduced that we could scarcely fetch our own food from the town, as we were obliged to do every fourth day. The truth of this can be known from a small book published by the Rev. Robert Barber Woolfe, acting chaplain of the depôt, who came there from Verdun some time after the depôt was established. You can easily imagine the state of society in such a place, without any kind of restraint. Capt. Joel Brenton, of the *La Minerve*, laid down certain rules for the commandant with respect to spirits, etc., which he rigidly adhered to as far as he could in a direct way. But the old navy men found out many dodges and inventions whereby smuggling was carried on in every possible way, and you'll easily guess the consequence.

'However, in the midst of much confusion I did all I could to improve my learning; but not having many books, and for want of means to buy paper, pens and ink, my progress was not very rapid. But I did with much pains and self-denial get on pretty well in arithmetic. I then began to learn navigation: but we having only one old Hamilton Moore amongst us, I was obliged to copy out all the tables in that book, before I could proceed with my studies. I then began in right earnest, and soon made myself master of that science. Before long I became a teacher of navigation to many others, and by that means made myself more perfect, and earned many a sol to help out my own necessities.

'Some three or four years, I think, after we arrived at the depôt, we were allowed 1d. a day from the English; it was said to be from Lloyd's. By that supply, although very small, we were kept from starvation.

'After being confined at Givêt for seven years, and seeing no hopes of an exchange of prisoners, myself and two others made up our minds to get away. This could only be at the risk of life and limb, for they would not scruple to fire upon you at the least alarm. Several prisoners attempted to escape; but all were taken in the act and were cut down and beaten most severely. Two midshipmen, Haywood and Tyrell, started from the town and concealed themselves in a cave until night. But their own servant, a marine named Wilson, belonging to the frigate *La Minerve*, informed the authorities. They fired into the cave, and killed Haywood, afterwards cutting Tyrell very badly with the sword; so that it was difficult to escape. I made two or three attempts before I succeeded, as the prisons are so well guarded day and night.

'About this time Buonaparte's army was in Spain and badly in need of recruits. They sent officers to each depôt of prisoners to recruit men for an Irish Brigade. Accordingly Captain Mackey and Lieutenant Devereaux, two Irishmen, who I believe left their country at the time of the Rebellion, came to the depôt of Givêt for that purpose.

'In March, 1811, I escaped from Givêt with my two companions. But in four days we were recaptured, tried by Military Court Martial, and sentenced to six years in irons. We were then sent to the county jail at Meziers, to wait for orders from Paris to send us to our place of destination. But whilst we were there, Napoleon the Second was born, and we received orders to march back to Givêt, to be pardoned, as we supposed, and we were free of irons. When we reached Givêt they put us in close confinement at Charlemont, until further orders from Paris. Before the further orders arrived, we broke out again with two others who were under sentence for misdemeanours in the prison, and in eleven nights we reached the sea-coast between Ostend and Nieueport. Finding we could not do anything at Newport, we went along the coast from there to Boulogne, but could not find a boat anywhere on the coast. Being arrived near Dunkirk about daybreak, we reached a certain house. The host came down and was very savage with us. We asked him for a drink ot water and a bit of bread, and begged him to sell us some milk. After a while he consented to open the door and take us in. He then lit a good fire, and we had some boiled milk and bread, which was very acceptable.

'During this journey we obtained food by getting near a house a little before dark, as we were then sure that there would not be many men about. It was my duty to enter and make my best terms with the family, while the others kept sentry outside. If I found the family ill-disposed, I summoned my companions, and then they were forced to comply with our demands.

'We slept at the above-mentioned house in a loft nearly full of onions. Our host proved to be a very fine fellow. When we left him, on the second night, he very pointedly asked us what we were and where we were going to; in reply to which we said we were Englishmen trying to get to our own country. He told us there were 400 or 500 English vessels then in the harbour, and advised us to go into the town. This, however, we were unwilling to do, as we still wore our prison dress, and so feared the sentries at the draw-bridges. Our host then agreed to take a letter for us to one of the English ship-masters. Accordingly I sat down and wrote a long epistle describing our situation. Our host put on his best clothes and carried the letter into the town. When he arrived at the quay he gave our letter to an English sailor, who thereupon conducted him to a public house. At this place a long conference was held, between several English captains, on the subject of the letter; but our host, understanding no English, could not guess the purport of their conversation. However, it appeared that the Englishmen would not help us nor even come to see us, which put our kind entertainer in a bitter temper against them. He then said to me, "If you will come with me in the morning I will show you a breach in the ramparts through which you can get to the harbour. I know the Englishmen will then take you." But I refused to have anything to do with such a bad set of fellows. We then set out, our host accompanying us for several miles along the coast from Dunkirk to Boulogne, but could not obtain a boat anywhere.

'We reached Boulogne about midnight, intending to join some American ship at Havre. But being challenged by two sentries in succession we decided to go no further until daylight. When day dawned, to our great mortification we found ourselves in the French camp, with ten thousand troops. Escape was impossible; but observing some soldiers go into the town over a breach in the ramparts, we took courage and followed them. Strange to say, nobody accosted us, so we reached the quay, where there were some small men-of-war, and went into a wine-shop. Whilst we were having a glass of brandy and some bread and butter, the mistress of the house questioned us as to who we were. We told her we were Americans, and wanted to get a vessel. She said she would go and fetch some of the owners who lived near there, as soon as they would be out of bed. By-and-by she left the house, but soon returned with two gensdarmes with their swords in their hands, who came to us and demanded our passports. We were then handcuffed and marched off to the Civil Gaol. Here we found an old Welshman named Powel, in a most wretched state, covered with vermin. He had come over to France in the Peace, to teach them about their coal-mines, and when he got old he wished to be sent home. As the authorities refused to send him back to England, he made a canvas boat, but found himself unable to carry it to the water-side. He then hired a woman to assist him; but they were both taken by the gensdarmes and put into prison, where I found him. Next day they brought to the gaol three Englishmen prisoners of war from Valenciennes. The day after our apprehension I was taken before the Prefêt and strictly examined by his secretary. After taking my deposition, the Prefêt asked me which was the last place we ran from? I said Thilt. He asked where that was. I replied "Please give me a chart and I will show you." He then said "How did you get away from there?" I said in French "We made a hole in the wall, Sir." He then said in English "You were like one little mouse," and we all laughed heartily. I was then taken back to the Civil Gaol, and after being there four days we were transferred to the Military Gaol in the Castle—a large cell 25 steps underground. Here we had a guard-bed to lie on, but no straw. We found here hundreds of very large rats.

'Before proceeding further with my narrative, I will mention another very narrow escape we had after leaving Givêt not far from Valenciennes. We were travelling through a wood, and came in sight of a house. Thinking it to be a farmhouse we knocked at the door. When it was opened, to our great astonishment we found it to be the house of a Garde Champêtre, with all his arms arranged round the walls of the room. The Garde was a rough-looking fellow, but we took possession and made him boil us some milk and bread, of which we then ate our fill. We left there before daylight, and in the morning came to a small village, where we were very kindly treated by one of the inhabitants. Our host told us that that village had been the Duke of York's head-quarters at the siege of Valenciennes. At night he went with us for some distance, to put us on the right road. We steered principally by the comet, which appeared in the N.W. quarter, and by the North Star, so that we made a pretty direct route towards the coast. Great was our joy at once more seeing the sea, and hearing the billows breaking on the shore. It now rained incessantly for hours, and we had no shelter but stalks of barley-corn which was nearly ripe. One of our number, Thomas Eyles, caught a severe cold, and was very ill with the shingles; nevertheless he kept up bravely, until taken near Newport, when we seized a boat in the river.

'We were eleven nights in getting to the coast. We were not able to travel in the daytime, for fear of being seen. We generally contrived to hide ourselves in some wood or corn-field. On one occasion while lying in a field of corn we were suddenly surrounded by women who had come to reap. We jumped up and ran, whereat they screamed out, being more frightened than we were.

'One night we came to a deep river, and as I could not swim my companions advised me to mount a horse which was standing near, and make him swim across, but I was afraid to venture. We then unshipped a gate from the field, took a harrow and put it on the gate, and on this I floated across the river, my two comrades swimming alongside and pushing me along. Soon afterwards we came to a farmhouse, the occupant of which put us into his barn. We had not been long there before some gensdarmes came in search of us; for, seeing what had been done at the river, they supposed we were conscript deserters from the army. However, our good host would not betray us, so we passed the day in safety and were well supplied with soup and bread by the mistress of the house. I might have stayed there for good, if I had liked, but I had my native land in view.

'To return to my prison at Boulogne: whilst being confined

in this underground cell we had served out to us each day 1lb of brown bread and soup. The jailor would bring down to the cell a large kettle of soup made with a few potatoes, some cabbage and a little bread. Around this kettle stood ten men, each having a wooden spoon, and everyone took his turn to dip in his spoon. If by chance he got a potato, he was sure to lose his chance to dip in turn, as the potato would be too hot to eat all at once. We only had meat once all the ten days I was there. There were over a hundred prisoners in that gaol, army and navy deserters and we English. The serving out of the meat ended in a general scramble, in which I got considerably less than my fair share. We had scarcely an hour's sleep all the time we were there, because the soldiers and sailors kept bantering and singing songs against each other constantly. We were very glad to leave that horrible place.'

The MS. is so confused and defective, that for the subsequent adventures of Thomas Williams we must rely upon a brief note found amongst his papers, from which it appears that he was court-martialed and sentenced to six years in irons, after having escaped three times from prison; that he was then confined in the citadel of Briançon, in the Alps, in a bomb-proof room, and one month in a dark underground cell, from which he dug his way out in fifteen days, and got away on the mountains not very far from Mont Blanc. He was recaptured and had to march, chained to other prisoners, with Napoleon's army across the Alps. After the general pardon he was sent to Cornwall, and put ashore at Mousehole, from which place he walked to Saint Ives, and finally reached his home on May 14, 1814. His own mother did not know him at first. He set up as a schoolmaster at Saint Ives, and became the parish clerk. He died in 1862. His descendants still possess, in addition to the relics previously mentioned, a cockade of white silk with a black centre, stitched on to a knave card, which was made for him by some French girls on his release. Thomas Williams's representatives preserve also, besides the above manuscript, a water-colour drawing of the prison at Givêt, and the original parchment certificate of the Emperor's pardon, signed by Buonaparte himself; translated it runs as follows:

'Napoleon, by the grace of God and the Constitution of the Empire, Emperor of the French, King of Italy, Protector of the Confederation of the Rhine, Mediator of the Swiss Confederation &c &c &c To the First President, Presidents and Councillors composing our Imperial Court at Grenoble: We have received the demand which has been made to us in the name of Thomas

Williams, apprentice seaman, English prisoner of war, condemned, by a military court-martial sitting at Givêt on the 16 March 1811, to the punishment of six years in irons for having eloped from the depôt of Givêt, and detained at Briançon in order to obtain our Pardon; and having observed that divers circumstances might incline us to make him sensible of the effects of our clemency, we have assembled in a Privy Council in our Palace of Saint Cloud, the 4th day of August, 1811, our Cousin the Prince Arch-Chancellor of the Empire, the Prince Governor General of the Departments beyond, our cousin the Prince Vice Grand Elector, and the Prince Vice Constable, the Duke of Massa, Great Judge, Minister of Justice, and de Feltre, Minister of War, Count Decrès, Minister of Marines, & Count Lacépède, Minister of State, President of the Senate, Count Garnier, Senator, the Councillors of State, Count Boulay, President of the Legislative Body, and Deformon Minister of State, President of the Section of Finances, Count Muraire, First President of the Court of Abrogation, and Count Merlin, Councillor of State, our chief Solicitor in the same Court, and after having heard the Duke of Massa's report and the advice of the other members of the Privy Council, everything seen and examined, being willing to prefer mercy to the rigour of the law, we have declared and do declare full mercy and entire Pardon to the said Thomas Williams, And command and order that these presents, sealed with the seal of the Empire, be presented to him by our chief Solicitor in the said Court, in public audience, whither the offender will be conducted to hear it read, standing, and his head uncovered, in the presence of the officer commanding the Gendarmerie at Grenoble, and that the said presents be afterwards transcribed on your registers by the request of the same Solicitor, with the annotation of this margin from the moment of pronouncing his condemnation.

'Given in the palace of the Tuileries, under the seal of the Empire, on the 15th day of August in the year one thousand eight hundred and eleven.

'Napoleon.

'Seen by us Arch Chancellors of the Empire, Armling, Great Judge, Minister of Justice, Duke of Massa.

'By the Emperor, the Minister Secretary of State.

'C. Nernez.'

[The *General Foix* was the most valuable prize ever brought into port by the St. Ives pilots and hobblers, no less than a thousand guineas being paid for the services rendered. There are men still living in St. Ives who took part in the salvage of this valuable ship and cargo. She was seen from St. Ives the previous evening, and the pilot-boat *Dolphin* went out in search, but, taking a wrong direction, failed to find the abandoned vessel. Meanwhile, she was again descried from St. Ives, and the boat *Caesar*, the only boat in the pier having ballast on board, was manned, and eventually succeeded in bringing the prize safely into port.]

March 2. The *General Foix* began to discharge.

1838. September 8. Last evening at 8 o'clock a great concourse of people paraded the streets with an effigy of 'Rover,' which they burned in front of Richard Penrose's house, and at the same time a great many panes of glass were broken. It is conjectured that this affair took place on account of Richard Penrose bringing a number of miners to clear up an old mine, called Wheal Ayr. By so doing it is thought that the present supply of water at Ventenear Well would be cut off, which happened at the previous working of the mine, and the well, which formerly gave an abundant supply, is now greatly diminished.

1839. November 1. This day being the day, by Act, to elect the Councilmen, four in number, and one in the room of D. Bamfield, Esq., he being elected Alderman. State of the poll:

Mr. John Newman Tremearne	118
Samuel Hocking	101
Vivian Stevens	98
Thomas Rosewall	91
John Chellew	89
Matthew Trewhella	82
Anthony Rosewall	44
Richard Williams	42
James Berriman	22
Robert Bennetts	20
Francis Stevens	16
Thomas Bryant	13

In the year 1831 there were eight convictions for smuggling on foreign vessels at Saint Ives, such vessels being in each case of Breton or French nationality:

At the same date, too, the practice of wrecking, though shorn of its ancient horrors, was not yet extinct. Persons yet living can remember going down to the shore at Saint Ives, on news of the wreck of some ship, and returning home laden with spoil cast up by the waves.

We give *in extenso* one of the convictions for smuggling above referred to. It runs thus:

'BOROUGH OF SAINT IVES IN THE COUNTY OF CORNWALL TO WIT.

'Be it remembered that on the thirteenth day of December in the Year of Our Lord One thousand eight hundred and thirty-one at the Borough of Saint Ives in the County of Cornwall an Information was exhibited before us Walter Yonge and James Halse Esquires Two of his Majestys Justices of the Peace in and for the said Borough of Saint Ives in the County of Cornwall aforesaid against Jean Marie Yves Creach by Augustus Stephens Esquire an officer of Customs who was directed by the Commissioners of his Majestys Customs to prefer the same which said information Charged that Jean Marie Yves Creach not then and there being a Subject of his Majesty and being liable to be stopped arrested and detained for the offence therein mentioned within six Months then last past that is to say on the fourth day of December in the Year of our Lord One thousand eight hundred and thirty-one was discovered to have been before that time that is to say on the thirtieth day of November in the Year aforesaid within One league of the Coast of the United Kingdom to wit within one league of the Coast of Cornwall on the High Seas on board a certain Vessel liable to forfeiture under the provisions of a certain Act of Parliament relating to the revenue of Customs For that the said Vessel being a foreign Vessel not being square rigged and in which there were then and there one or more Subjects of his Majesty was on the said fourth day of December discovered to have been before that time that is to say on the said thirtieth day of November on the high Seas aforesaid within eight Leagues of that part of the Coast of the United Kingdom which is not between the North Foreland on the Coast of Kent and Beachy Head on the Coast of Sussex to wit within Eight leagues of the Coast of Cornwall and not proceeding in her Voyage Wind and Weather permitting the said Vessel then and there having on board divers Spirits to wit Five Hundred Gallons of Brandy and One Hundred Gallons of other Spirits called Geneva in divers Casks to wit Three hundred and thirty nine Casks of less size and Content than forty Gallons each the said Brandy and the said Geneva not being then and there for the use of the Seamen then belonging to and on board the said Vessel not exceeding two Gallons for each such Seaman Contrary to the form of the Statute in that case made and provided And the said Jean Marie Yves Creach being found on board the said Vessel at the time of her becoming and being so subject and liable to forfeiture and the said Jean Marie Yves Creach having been afterwards to wit on the said fourth day of December in the year last aforesaid for the offence aforesaid stopped arrested and detained by one Moses Martin he the said Moses Martin being then and there an officer of Customs and having been by him taken brought and carried into a certain place on land in the United Kingdom to wit into the Borough of Saint Ives in the County of Cornwall aforesaid and within the Jurisdiction of us the said Justices which offence hath been duly proved before us the said Justices. We the said Justices do therefore convict the said Jean Marie Yves Creach of the said offence and do adjudge that the said Jean Marie Yves Creach hath forfeited for his said offence the sum of One Hundred pounds. Given under our hands and Seals at the Borough of Saint Ives aforesaid this thirteenth day of December in the Year of our Lord One thousand eight hundred and thirty one.

'W. YONGE—Mayor.
'JAS. HALSE.'

CHAPTER XXIII.

ST. IVES AT THE PRESENT DAY.

THINGS had, perhaps, reached the lowest stage at Saint Ives about the year 1877, at which period mining was at a standstill, owing to the importation of cheap tin from the Colonies, and the pilchards had for several years seemed to shun the bay of Saint Ives. On May 24, 1877, the new railway from St. Erth on the main line, to Saint Ives, was opened, and the town soon began to receive the advance-guard of the host of London visitors which has since invaded it. It is upon these visitors, the majority of whom belong to a wealthy class, that Saint Ives mainly depends for the support of its inhabitants. Great contrasts are observable in the condition of the town at present as compared with its state 'before the railway.' Previous to 1877 Saint Ives was hardly ever visited by tourists, and held but little communication with the outer world. Travellers drove from the junction, then called Saint Ives Road Station, on a bus, which took a considerable time to perform the journey. The advent of this bus was looked forward to as a daily treat, the greatest interest being taken in the arrival of any stranger from 'foreign parts.' But now the many trains come in and go away without exciting much notice. Such goods as fish and early vegetables are now sent direct to the metropolis, greatly to the advantage of the town's-people; nor could the neighbourhood dispense with the large number of visitors who now come every year to circulate money in this remote watering-place. On the other hand, the fishermen and gardeners of the neighbourhood have not been benefited by the railway to the extent that they anticipated, owing to the reluctance of the Great Western Railway Company to moderate their charges.

The season at Saint Ives is a short one, extending only over August and September, but during those two months the private lodging-houses are full and the tradespeople busy. Foremost among the visitors are the artists, of the renowned 'Newlyn and Saint Ives school,' who have made the scenery of our four parishes so familiar to the frequenters of West End galleries, that the Island at Saint Ives bids fair soon to cover as much canvas as Saint Michael's Mount itself.

The following are some of the pictures of local subjects produced by the Saint Ives school:

Field-path to the Stennack, Saint Ives. E. A. Waterlow.

Breakers, Saint Ives. W. A. Ingram, R.B.A.

Saint Ives Seine-boats. Louis Monro Grier.

Carthew. William Eadie.

Their Daily Bread. Stanhope A. Forbes. (An exquisite picture of homely life in the old streets of Saint Ives.)

View of Saint Ives. Helena Sherfbeck.

The Vicar of Saint Ives. William Eadie.

Porthmeor, Saint Ives. William Eadie.

In the Valley, Saint Ives. Percy R. Craft.

A Village Street. Louis Monro Grier.

From the Foresand, Saint Ives. Adrian Stokes.

Among the Old Seine-boats, Saint Ives. Percy R. Craft.

Saint Ives Bay, from above Tregenna. G. H. Fortt.

Porthmeor, from Carthew. G. H. Fortt.

On the Wharf, Saint Ives. G. H. Fortt.

Godrevy, from Saint Ives. T. Backhouse.

Mr. William Eadie has been specially successful with his Saint Ives interiors. One of these represents a little girl trying on her great-great-grandmother's wedding-dress. Another gives us a view of the interior of Saint Ives church during the service-time, with several portraits of well-known members of the congregation.

Mr. Walter Titcombe has also painted a wonderfully true picture of the inside of the Saint Ives Primitive Methodist Chapel during the service, with a portrait of a fine old fisherman.

To enumerate all the pictures, or even all the painters, who are making Saint Ives famous in the world of art, would be beyond the scope of this work; the above list must, therefore, be taken as simply furnishing examples of the work done by the Saint Ives school. We must not conclude these brief notes on our artists without recalling the well-known names of Mr. Leonard Stokes, Mr. Edward E. Simmons and Mrs. Vesta Simmons, Mr. E. Wyly Grier, and Mr. Bloomfield.

In painting scenes of the life and manners of our forebears, we have to rely upon musty records and dim traditions. But to preserve for our descendants a picture of the social surroundings of our own time, we have but to turn observant eyes upon the men and things in whose midst we find ourselves, and faithfully record what we see. And there can be no doubt that the details of our daily life will be to our posterity as interesting as the doings of our ancestors are to us.

The writer of this history holds at Saint Ives a kind of amphibious position, being neither native resident nor foreign visitor, but a mixture of both. Hence he is, perhaps, better qualified to judge of the peculiar features of Saint Ives society than either a person born in the neighbourhood or one who has but spent a summer holiday there.

Speaking, then, as an outsider, we should say that Saint Ives is still, in spite of the railway, a little world to itself, and, in many respects, a peculiar little world, too. In the first place, your Saint Ives man is one of two things; either he is of those who go down to the sea in ships—in which case he is not often seen at his native town—or else he has in earlier life done business in great waters, and is living at home in comfortable retirement. In the latter case the typical Ivesian passes his time in a very regular and systematic manner. In the forenoon he will, perhaps, go 'down along,' and have a little talk with various seafaring acquaintances on the wharf and the quay. After dinner he will have a look in at the reading-room, study *Lloyd's List* and the *Western Mercury*, and have a furtive chat with some other quondam ship-master. These two will then probably proceed together to the 'Malakoff,' where they will pace up and down, backwards and forwards, along a track of some eight or ten yards in length, discoursing deeply of freights and shares. If our type dwells in a house which commands a view of the sea, he will spend many an hour at an open window, scanning the horizon through a goodly telescope.

Let us pass to the typical young woman of the place. She dresses well for her station in life, which is that of a draper's assistant. Her demeanour is frank and unaffected, even towards persons of the opposite sex. She can pull an oar in seamanlike style, and understands a good deal about sailing a boat. See her with her friends, walking up the Terrace, after chapel on a Sunday evening. She knows that her bonnet is well up to date, and that her gloves and boots are good and fit her well; therefore she feels that she is as good as anybody in the crowd, and she steps out with a free and independent gait and an air of honest self-satisfaction.

The visitor from London thinks to himself, as he surveys the lovely bay of Saint Ives, that the natives of the place must enjoy their surroundings immensely. They must, he imagines, revel in the bracing sea-breezes and bask in the genial rays of the western sun; they must glory in their heather-clad hills and pure-sanded porths. He is quite mistaken. The genuine unsophisticated native cares for none of these things, and will declare to you that Saint Ives is 'a dead-and-alive old place,' devoid of any interest to a cultured mind. He (the native) thinks things would be tolerable if a nice new marine parade were built around the shore of the harbour, and the island turned into public gardens like they have at Penzance. But in default of these and other similar advantages of a ripe civilisation, your Ivesian sighs for the more artificial charms of a popular watering-place. He has never been onto Porthminster beach in his life, and would as soon think of swimming to Cardiff as of walking to Zennor. Do not blame the native for this, Mr. Smith, of London. Who of us consistently admires his daily surroundings? You are enthusiastic about Saint Ives because you spend your Augusts and Septembers here. But stay here through the winter; hear the western wind howling round your house at night, and try to round the corner of the Terrace in a March gale, and you will find that Saint Ives weather has its surly moods. Besides, are you really thrown into ecstasies every time you pass under the shadow of Saint Paul's? and do you often avail yourself of the unrivalled advantages of the British Museum?

We have hinted that the women of Saint Ives are well abreast of the age in the matter of dress, and this is true. Yet there still lingers some remnant of the quaint picturesqueness of costume which we might have expected in the elder generation inhabiting so rural a neighbourhood. In the farms of our four parishes the visitor will see knee-breeches and blue woollen stockings which will remind him of Ireland; in Saint Ives town he will meet with short homespun dresses and chequered aprons which will carry his thoughts to Wales. Beyond this there is nothing to say on the subject of local costumes. But we may add that the heart-shaped, long-handled spade of Wales and Ireland is equally in vogue in Cornwall. A few years ago an ironmonger of Redruth ordered a quantity of spades from a Sheffield manufacturer. The consignment duly arrived, but the ironmonger sent them all back because they were the square, short-handled spades commonly used throughout England proper; and in the law-suit which arose out of this transaction, the conduct of the Redruth shopkeeper was triumphantly justified. Indeed, it was shown that it was impossible to sell any but the long-handled spade in Cornwall.

An interesting volume might be written about nicknames. They are a relic of a primitive state of society, and flourish only where primitive ideas still prevail. At Malta we knew a man who was called 'Manetta.' It was not until a couple of years after we first made his acquaintance, that we discovered that 'Manetta' (*i.e.*, 'Little-hand') was not his real name, and that he owed the designation to the fact of his grandfather's being born with a withered hand. The practice of calling people by nicknames has always obtained at Saint Ives, as is abundantly proved by ancient records; nor is it yet by any means obsolete. Some of these names cling to a family through many generations, and some are considered by their bearers highly offensive. Nicknames are an important feature of Saint Ives society, and many of them are interesting from their history; but for obvious reasons we cannot give any examples.

BOARD SCHOOLS, ST. IVES.

CHAPTER XXIV.

THE PILCHARD FISHERY.

SAINT IVES is the headquarters of the Pilchard fishery, and this industry, therefore, claims especial notice in our History. 'The least fish in bigness, greatest for gain, and most in number is the pilchard,' says Carew. As to the history of this fishery, we glean from Lord de Dunstanville's edition of the 'Survey' that, previous to the reign of Henry II., no one was allowed to salt, dry or pack fish in Cornwall, without the licence of the Duchy Officers. An unsuccessful attempt to revive this restriction was made by Queen Elizabeth. Local custom or private arrangement decides questions concerning the pilchard fishery out of St. Ives; but the bye-laws passed at different times by the Corporation of Saint Ives were embodied in an Act of Parliament in the year 1776. This Act was repealed and replaced by another in 1841. The custom of counting the fish is obsolete, the hogsheads being now weighed. The Government bounty is discontinued, and the duty on salt abolished.

The largest shoal of pilchards ever enclosed was taken in a seine of Mr. Roger Wearne, at Saint Ives, on November 25, 1834.

The arrival of the pilchard-shoals in Saint Ives Bay coincides to a day with that of the herrings at Yarmouth; so that the Yarmouth men are always anxious to know when the pilchards have been descried by the Saint Ives huers.

The following is the concise and graphic account of the older methods of seine-fishing, as given in Carew's 'Survey':

'The sein is a net of about forty fathom in length, with which they encompass a part of the sea, and draw the same on land, by two ropes fastened at his ends, together with such fish as lighteth within his precinct. To each of these there commonly belong three or four boats, carrying about six men apiece, with which, when the season of the year, and weather serveth, they lie hovering upon the coast and are directed in their work by a balker or huer, who standeth on the cliff side and from thence best discerneth the quantity and course of the pilchards, according whereunto he cundeth (as they call it) the master of each boat (who hath his eye still fixed upon him) by crying with a loud voice, whistling through his fingers, and wheazing certain diversified and significant signs with a bush which he holdeth in his hand. At his appointment they cast out their net, draw it to either hand, as the shoal lieth or fareth, beat with their oars to keep in the fish, and at last, either close and tuck it up in the sea, or draw the same on land, with more certain profit if the ground be not rough of rocks. After one company have thus shot their net, another beginneth behind them, and so a third as opportunity serveth. Being so taken, some, the country people, who attend with their horses and panniers at the cliff's side in great numbers, do buy and carry home, the larger remainder is by the merchant greedily and speedily seized upon.

'They are saued three maner of wayes: by fuming, pressing, or pickelling. For euery of which, they are first salted and piled vp row by row in square heapes on the ground in some cellar, which they terme, Bulking, where they so remaine for some ten daies, vntil the superfluous moysture of the bloud and salt be soked from them: which accomplished, they rip the bulk and saue the residue of the salt for another like seruice. Then those which are to be ventred for Fraunce, they pack in staunch hogsheads, to keepe them in their pickle. Those that serue for the hotter Countries of Spaine and Italie, they vsed at first to fume, by hanging them vp on long sticks one by one, in a house built for the nonce, & there drying them with the smoake of a soft and continuall fire, from whence they purchased the name of Fumados: but now, though the terme still remaine, that trade is giuen ouer: and after they haue bene ripped out of the bulk, reffed vpon sticks, & washed, they pack them orderly in hogsheads made purposely leake, which afterward they presse with great waights, to the end the traine may soke from into a vessell placed in the ground to receyue it.

'In packing, they keepe a iust tale of the number that euery hogshead contayneth, which otherwise may turne to the Marchants preiudice: for I haue heard, that when they are brought to the place of sale, the buyer openeth one hogs-head at aduentures, and if hee finde the same not to answere the number figured on the outside, hee abateth a like proportion in euery other, as there wanted in that. The trayne is well solde, is imployed to diurs vses, and welneere acquiteth the cost in sauing, and the sauing setteth almost an infinite number of women and children on worke, to their great aduantage: for they are allowed a peny for euery lasts carriage [a last is ten thousand] and as much for bulking, washing, and packing them, whereby a lusty huswife may earne three shillings in a night, for towards the euenings they are mostly killed.

'This commodite at first carried a very lowe price, and serued for the inhabitants cheapest prouision; but of late times, the deare sale beyond the seas hath so encreased the number of takers, and the takers iarring and brawling one with another, and forsaking the fishes taking their kind within harbour, so decreased the number of the taken, as the price daily extendeth to an higher rate, equalling the proportion of other fish: a matter which yet I reckon not preiudiciall to the Commonwealth, seeing there is store sufficient of other victuals, and that of these a twentieth part will serue the Countries need, and the other nineteene passe into forraine Realmes with a gainefull vtterance.

'The Sayners profit in this trade is vncertayne, as depending upon the seas fortune, which he long attendeth, and often with a bootlesse trauaile: but the Pilcherd Marchant, may reape a speedy, large, and assured benefit, by dispatching the buying, sauing and selling to the transporters, within little more then three moneths space. Howbeit, diuers of them, snatching at wealth ouer-hastily, take mony beforehand, and bind themselues for the same, to deliuer Pilcherd ready saued to the transporter, at an vnder-rate, and so cut their fingers. This venting of Pilcherd enhanced greatly the price of cask, whereon all other sorts of wood were conuerted to that vse: and yet this scantly supplying a remedie, there was a statute made 35. Eliz. that from the last of June 1594 no stranger should transport beyond the seas any Pilcherd or other fish in cask, unlesse he did bring into the Realme, for euery sixe tunnes, two hundred of clapboord fit to make cask, and so rateably, vpon payne of forfeyting the sayd Pilcherd or fish. This Act to continue before the next Parliament, which hath reuiued the same, vntill his (yet not knowne) succeeder.

'The Pilcherd are pursued and deuoured by a bigger kinde of fish, called a Plusher, being somewhat like the Dog-fish, who leapeth now and then aboue water, and therethrough bewrayeth them to the Balker; so are they likewise persecuted by the Tonny, and he (though not verie often) taken with them damage faisant. And that they may no lesse in fortune, than in fashion, resemble the Flying fish, certaine birds called Gannets, soare ouer, and stoup to prey vpon them. Lastly they are persecuted by the Hakes, who (not long sithence) haunted the coast in great abundance; but now being depriued of their wonted baite, are much diminished, verifying the proverb, What we lose in Hake we shall haue in Herring.'

With regard to the seines, Davies Gilbert says: 'It seems that these nets must have been originally introduced from Dungarvon in Ireland, since they are still said to be braided according to the Dungarvon mesh; but no similar fishery is remembered at that place.'

For the following lucid and reliable account of the fisheries of Saint Ives, as conducted at the present day, I am indebted to Mr. Anthony, of Saint Ives, whose words are here copied as they stand:

'In the main there are two methods of taking fish, by the Sean and by the Drift net. By the Sean the fish are enclosed and then "tucked," or dipped into the boats by baskets. In the drift nets,

little Skillywidden,' took it away in great haste. This is believed to have occurred so late as the year 1869.

As might have been expected, legends of mermaids are very prevalent along the sea-board of the four parishes. Bottrell tells, in his inimitable style, the typical story of the 'Mermaid of Zennor.' The people of the parish of Zennor were long renowned for their beautiful singing. Mathey Terweela (Matthew Trewhella), a young man belonging to a family well known in the parish, was the sweetest singer of them all, and exercised his vocal talent in the church choir on Sundays. Zennor church was occasionally visited by a richly-dressed lady, whose marvellously sweet voice charmed even that musical congregation. Nobody knew whence she came, nor where she went after the service; but she so fascinated young Trewhella, that he one day went in search of her, and was never seen again. Zennor folks would never have known who she was but for the following occurrence. One Sunday morning the captain of a ship which lay at anchor near Pendower Cove was hailed by a beautiful mermaid, who begged him to trip his anchor, as the fluke of it rested on the door of her dwelling, so that she could not enter to dress in time for church. Her request was politely complied with. We have noticed this tradition in our description of the mermaid carved on the bench-end in Zennor church.

If we may be excused for ascribing a matter-of-fact origin to such poetical legends, we would hazard a surmise that the first mermaids were nothing more nor less than the harmless and graceful seals which disport themselves on the rocks of the sequestered porths of this coast. Anyone who has seen them, with their earnest, half-human eyes and their curious cry, will own that our theory is not far-fetched.

Students of Celtic folk-lore know the important place held by traditions of submerged lands. We have in a former chapter noticed the stories about the sea-devoured and sand-covered tracts on the coast of Lelant and St. Ives. Mr. Hunt records a popular belief that the 'towans' (in his work misprinted 'towns') were all meadow-land, which was covered by sand in a single night; nor is the story at all improbable. According to his account of the traditions, 'The site of the ancient church and village of Lelant was somewhere seaward of the Black Rock; the ancient burial-ground has been long washed away,' and human teeth are still sometimes found on the shore; further, he says that where the sand has been cleared away, between the church and the sea, ancient plough-furrows have been found. In these accounts it is often difficult to separate fact from fancy, but it cannot be doubted that, either suddenly or gradually, the coast-line has been enormously affected by the forces of nature.

Coming to the wide subject of ghostly apparitions, we find a wealth of local lore. James Berryman, of Lelant, told Mr. Hunt about a 'half-face' which used to appear in a house rented by his father at that town, and which was believed to be the ghost of a poor man who died there in a fit, on receiving notice of eviction from his tyrannical landlord.

Mr. Bottrell tells us of the ghost of a certain An' Katty, at Trewey, in Zennor, which haunted a family because a shawl which she had bequeathed to a little girl had not been given to the child. The youthful legatee was one evening mysteriously borne through the air and set down upon the old woman's grave at Ludgvan, where one of the child's shoes was found next day.

One of the greatest heroes of Western ghost-stories is Parson Polkinghorne, who was Vicar of Lelant, Saint Ives and Towednack, as appears by a note on a fly-leaf of the Saint Ives Parish Registers. He was the most powerful ghost-layer, or exorcist, of his time in West Cornwall, and had such complete dominion over unruly spirits that at his first approach they would take to flight, crying, 'Polkinghorne has come, I must begone!' Bottrell gives instances of the vicar's ghost-quelling skill, as when he laid the Harris ghosts at Kenegie, which had long troubled that ancient mansion. The same writer informs us that Polkinghorne was the boldest fox-hunter of those parts, but would never chase a hare. He kept many of these innocent animals running about his house like cats; foolish people said they were his familiar spirits. He was a capital hurler, and encouraged all kinds of manly games. The parson had a wonderful horse, called Hector, and used to ride about the country accompanied always by his dog. He made long journeys with his steed walking alongside or behind him, and, if the vicar called at a house on his way, Hector never required to be held, but would quietly wait for his master's reappearance. Polkinghorne's exorcising formula commenced with 'In Nommy Dommy!' (*In nomine Domini*), and was Latin throughout.

The following yarn, entitled 'The Pilot's Ghost Story,' is so peculiar to Saint Ives, that we must set it down almost in full. It is from Mr. Hunt's 'Romances,' p. 357:

'Just seventeen years since,' said Mr. Hunt's informant, 'I went down on the wharf from my house one night about twelve and one in the morning, and found a sloop, the *Sally*, of St. Ives (she was wrecked at St. Ives in 1862) in the bay, bound for Hayle. When I got by the White Hart public-house, I saw a man leaning against a post on the wharf. I spoke to him, wished him good-morning, and asked him what o'clock it was, but to no purpose. Finding I got no answer to my repeated inquiries, I approached close to him and said, "Thee'rt a queer sort of fellow not to speak. Who art 'a at all? Thee'st needn't think to frighten me; that thee wasn't do, if thou wert twice so ugly." He turned his great ugly face on me, glared abroad his great eyes, opened his mouth—and it was a mouth sure nuff. Then I saw pieces of sea-weed and bits of sticks in his whiskers; the flesh of his face and hands were parboiled, just like a woman's hands after a good day's washing. Well, I did not like his looks a bit, and sheered off; but he followed close by my side, and I could hear the water squashing in his shoes every step he took. I stopped a bit, and thought to be a little bit civil to him, and spoke to him again, but no answer. I then thought I would go to seek for another of our crew, and knock him up to get the vessel, and had got about fifty or sixty yards, when I turned to see if he was following me, but saw him where I left him. Fearing he would come after me, I ran for my life the few steps that I had to go. But when I got to the door, to my horror there stood the man in the door grinning horribly. I shook like an aspen leaf; my hat lifted from my head. What to do I didn't know, and in the house there was such a row, as if everybody was breaking up everything. After a bit I went in, for the door was on the latch, and called the captain of the boat; but everything was all right, nor had he heard any noise. We went out aboard of the *Sally*, and I put her into Hayle, but I felt ill enough to be in bed. I left the vessel to come home as soon as I could, but it took me four hours to walk two miles, and I had to lie down in the road, and was taken home to Saint Ives in a cart, as far as the Terrace; from there I was carried home by my brothers, and put to bed. Three days afterwards all my hair fell off as if I had had my head shaved, the roots, and for about half an inch from the roots, being quite white. I was ill six months, and the doctor's bill was £4 17s. 6d. for attendance and medicine.'

Mr. Hunt was told that to whistle by night was by the fishermen of St. Ives accounted highly unlucky. His informant added: 'I would no more dare go among a party of fishermen at night, whistling a popular air, than into a den of untamed tigers.' Mr. Thomas Cornish, in the *West of England Magazine*, of October, 1887, writes: 'The occurrence at night of whistling noises in the air is the terror of West Country people. It is known as "The Seven Whistlers," and presages death or dire misfortune to the hearer, or disaster to the district if it is repeated several nights

Some years ago some of the inhabitants of Saint Ives, in Cornwall, were greatly perturbed by the occurrence, night after night, of the Seven Whistlers.' The scepticism of the present age attributes these nightly whistlings to flocks of birds of a kind which migrate by night.

It is, perhaps, not surprising that numerous superstitions and sayings are connected with the pilchard-fishery, that industry which enters so largely into the town-life of Saint Ives. Thus it is considered unlucky to eat the fish from the head downwards; the legitimate process is to eat it from the tail towards the head. 'This brings the fish to our shores, and secures good luck to the fishermen' (Hunt).

The squeaking noise produced by the bursting of the air-bladders of the pilchards, when they are 'put in bulk,' *i.e.* salted and packed, is called 'crying for more,' and is regarded as an omen that more fish may soon be expected to be brought to the same cellar.

The 'pressing-stones' are round boulders of granite, weighing about a hundredweight, with an iron hook fixed into them for the convenience of moving; these stones are used for placing on the fish when packed in the barrels, in order to squeeze out the remaining oil. When not in use, the pressing-stones are piled on the floors of the cellars, or in corners of the streets. It is a common superstition at Saint Ives that the advent of a good shoal of pilchards is presaged by a supernatural commotion among these stones, which are then supposed to roll about spontaneously. Mr. Hunt tells a story of how one Jem Tregose and his family, who lived in a room over one of the fish-cellars at Saint Ives, heard the pressing-stones rolling tremendously. There had been a long dearth of fish, but the stones proved true prophets, and unusually heavy catches of pilchards ensued.

Another of Mr. Hunt's Saint Ives sailor-yarns is entitled 'The Phantom Ship,' and narrates how a pilot attempted to board a ghostly schooner in the bay, but fell into the water. Next morning the *Neptune*, of London, Captain Richard Grant, was wrecked at Gwithian, and all the crew perished.

The next story in the same book tells of the sea phantasms called 'Jack Harry's Lights,' because he was the first man who was fooled by them. They are generally observed before a gale, and the ship seen is like the ship which is sure to be wrecked. An old Saint Ives pilot told Mr. Hunt how one Sunday night their big boat, the *Ark*, vainly chased this delusive apparition.

'The Lady with the Lantern' is another of the quaint folk-tales picked up at Saint Ives by Mr. Hunt. Years ago a ship struck on a sunken rock off the Island. Many of her company perished at once; but a lady was observed on the deck with a child in her arms, imploring aid from the shore. Some hardy salts launched a boat in the teeth of the storm, and took the woman safely off the wreck. The lady had fainted and lost her child; and, on recovering consciousness and finding that the babe was not with her, she speedily closed her eyes in death, and was buried in the churchyard. Shortly afterwards a lady was often seen to pass at night over the wall of the churchyard on to the beach, and walk towards the island. There she would spend hours in looking for her child, and not finding it, she would sigh deeply and return to her grave. On dark and stormy nights she was frequently seen, carrying a lantern, and the apparition has ever been regarded as presaging disaster on this shore.

Mr. Bottrell (2nd series) tells a quaint legend about a Zennor sailor who received directions from the spirit of a deceased messmate how to recover certain prize-money left by the dead man in a chest at a Plymouth publichouse.

No country, however enlightened, is free from superstition of the kind represented by the belief in witchcraft. Sorcery, indeed, seems to have had its votaries in every age. Mr. Hunt quotes from Cornish newspapers of a very recent date, showing how one, James Thomas, of Illogan, a notorious 'pellar,' or 'white witch,' duped a great number of supposed bewitched persons at Saint Ives, Hayle and elsewhere. He had been in the habit of receiving money annually for keeping witchcraft from vessels sailing out of Hayle.

One way of becoming a witch was to get on the Giant's Rock, a very sensitive logan-stone at Zennor church-town, nine times without shaking it.

Treva, or Trewey, a hamlet near the same village, is said to have been the place where, at midsummer, all the witches of the West met. Amidst the myriad granite boulders which strew the place was one very large pile of square blocks, known as the Witches' Rock. Anyone touching this rock nine times at midnight was insured against ill-luck. The rock has been removed, and the last of the Zennor witches is supposed to have died about fifty years ago. The most celebrated of the sorceresses of this parish was an old woman known to tradition as the Witch of Trewey, whose spells made her the terror of the neighbourhood. She is said to have assumed the form of a hare when engaged in her supernatural work. She once made her husband a dinner of cooked meat without any visible material for the preparation of a meal of any sort. 'She was borne to the grave,' says Mr. Hunt, by six aged men, and was carried, as is the custom, underhand. When they were half-way between the house and the church, a hare started from the roadside and leaped over the coffin. The terrified bearers let the corpse fall to the ground and ran away. Another lot of men took up the coffin and proceeded. They had not gone far when puss was suddenly seen seated on the coffin, and again the coffin was abandoned. After long consultation, and being persuaded by the parson to carry the old woman very quickly into the churchyard, while he walked before, six others made the attempt, and as the parson never ceased to repeat the Lord's Prayer all went on quietly. Arrived at the church stile they rested the corpse; the parson paused to commence the ordinary burial-service, and there stood the hare, which, as soon as the clergyman began 'I am the resurrection and the life,' uttered a diabolical howl, changed into a black, unshapen creature, and disappeared.

Bottrell tells how Sir Rose Price's hounds chased a hare into a cottage at Kerrow, in Zennor. When the huntsman came up and opened the door, he saw an aged crone sitting on the chimney-stool, bleeding about the head and face, with her hair hanging loose; then the sportsmen saw they had hunted a witch.

The above legends have all been taken from the admirable collections of Hunt and Bottrell. But the writer has himself picked up a few waifs of folk-lore which have never before been printed; they follow on here without classification. In our chapter on the parish church we noticed the ancient house opposite the south porch. This has the reputation of being haunted by the ghost of a young man who was 'shot underground' (*i.e.*, perished in a mine explosion) and afterwards appeared, pale and bleeding, at his father's bedside. Only a few years ago a respectable woman, who then kept the shop next door, was annoyed at night by mysterious laughs and whisperings, which proceeded from the deserted and ghostly tenement. She also frequently saw lights moving about in the haunted chamber, which was the one on the upper story, overlooking the church porch. The house has since been repaired and re-occupied, and it does not appear that its present occupants are troubled by the ghost.

The following story is told of Mary Stevens *née* Bryant, whose father had a large interest in the pilchard fishery toward the close of the last century. On one occasion his women were packing the fish for curing, in the cellars near the old Market-house. It was Saturday night, and if left until Monday the fish must have spoiled. Mary therefore went down to the women and told them to prolong their work into the Sunday morning. On her way home, as she passed by the open window of the Market-house, facing the George and Dragon, she was startled by seeing the form of a man lying upon the Market House floor, on which he appeared to be writing with his finger, his head supported by the other hand. She stopped to watch the writing, and by a great light which proceeded from the man's side, she was enabled to trace these words: 'Remember the Sabbath Day, to keep it Holy.' The narration of this vision caused a great sensation in the town, and did much toward securing that strict observance of the Sunday which the rise of Methodism was then gradually bringing about.

The old house called Carn Glaze, described in a former chapter, was said to be visited by the spirit of Reginald Bottrell, a sea-captain who lived in the reign of Charles II. The old salt's ghost appeared to a fisherman named Tom P., who has described the apparition most minutely to the writer. Tom was born at Carn Glaze about the year 1820. One Sunday evening, when he was about twelve years of age, he and his elder brother, 'Ephrim,' were lying in front of the fire in the big room, awaiting the return of the rest of the family. The only light was that of the glowing turves under the broad chimney, and of a flickering rush. Happening to look up, Tom saw, on the steps which led down into the room from a side-door, 'a ruddy-faced, pleasant-looking, stout little gentleman,' dressed in a long cut-away coat, long black velvet waistcoat, black breeches of the same material, black ribbed stockings, and pump shoes tied with a bow ribbon. His head was bald, save for a small bit of hair at the back, and he had no hat. 'His belly was round and as tight as a drum.' (!) Brass or gold buttons adorned his coat and waistcoat, on the latter two rows. The buttons of his coat were embossed in the centre in the shape of flowers. He was 'most pleasant-looking in his features.' This prepossessing ghost held Tom spell-bound for a minute, then vanished. Tom roused his brother, and told him of the little gentleman. Ephraim thereupon suggested that they should leave the house, which they did. Ephraim would never mention the apparition from that moment to the present; but when his friends came home Tom told them of the unearthly visitor, and described him, but was only laughed at. He said: 'I was not wise enough to thenk 't was a sperat, but I knaw now.'

An old man who was born and reared near Carn Glaze, says that children used to be afraid to pass the north-east corner of the old house after dark. Four streets meet at this corner, and the old Celtic superstitions as to cross-roads may have something to do with the 'hauntedness' of the spot.

The old Market House, erected in the fifteenth century, was a picturesque old building, with a penthouse around the wall on the outside. There were no windows on the side facing the church; but right opposite the George and Dragon Inn was a deep window possessing very weird associations. It was through this window that Mary Bryant beheld the supernatural vision above related, and it was to this window that the professional ghost-layers used to banish the unruly sprites which they exorcised. And there, after dark, they shrieked and jabbered in their prison, in a manner that was perfectly shocking. A gentleman who died quite recently informed the writer that his father, when a boy, one night saw Mr. James Wallis, a renowned ghost-layer, exorcising spirits in the Market-place, with a candle, a book, and a bell, which was rung by a boy in attendance. My informant's father took to his heels with fright, and did not wait to watch the ceremony.

This James Wallis, who was the last of the professed ghost-layers, was also a renowned will-maker, though not a lawyer. He was also a maker of sun-dials; one which bears his name, and the date 1790, may be seen on the wall of an old house, facing the spectator as he ascends Barnoon from the Market-place.

In 1832 the old Market House disappeared, and the restless ghosts along with it.

On the west side of Fore Street, near the church, is an old house with a small square courtyard of quaint aspect. The quadrangular messuage which encloses this yard was, in the last century, an inn, known as the Globe, and, still later, as 'The Tap-house.' When first built this house was the residence of the Edwards family, one of whom, Hugh Edwards, had the misfortune to ride down Trevegia mine-shaft one dark night. His body was recovered and buried inside the church, near the chancel-rails, with his clothes on. About fifty years ago, the Edwards family vault being opened, the remains of the unfortunate Hugh were found; but of his clothes nothing remained except the yellow tops of his riding-boots, which were as good as new. An old woman recently residing at Cardiff said that when quite a child she once slept at 'The Tap-house,' and at dead of night heard heavy footsteps ascend the stairs, and three smart blows struck on the door of one of the bedrooms, as if with the handle of a riding-whip. Several other persons have related similar experiences of the nocturnal visits of Hugh Edwards to his old home.

Between Chy-an-gweal and Lelant village the high-road leads to a group of three or four old houses, and just beyond is bordered by two rows of fine elms, forming a dark lane. This lane is said to be haunted at night by a phantom coach, furiously driven by the ghost of a lady.

Another part of the same road, between Carbis and Lelant, was supposed to be haunted. There is now living in the village of Carbis one who still tells, with genuine agitation, of a ghostly experience that befell her there. She was going home to Carbis from Lelant, one starry summer night, some forty years ago, when she noticed, on the right-hand side of the road, between Longstone and Boskerris Lane, what she at first took to be a prominent furze-bush. As she came nearer to it, she saw that it was a man in a tall hat, standing on the hedge. She came opposite to him, and was expecting the usual 'Good evening,' when, to her horror, she saw that he had no face. She could see the hat plainly enough, and the coat and collar, but not a single feature—only blank space where the man's face should have been. A feeling of terror crept over her, and she stood as though rooted to the spot. How long she remained so she could not tell; but gradually the paralyzing horror left her limbs, she gave a leap forward, ran all the rest of the way home, and fainted as soon as she got into safety. Of course she told her friends all about the ghost; but she only got laughed at, until an old local-preacher declared that he had seen a similar apparition near the same place.

'The Zennor charmers' was a name commonly accorded, not only to the women, but also to the men of this parish. It originated in a traditional belief that the inhabitants of Zennor were largely possessed of magical powers. A Zennor man assured Mr. Hunt that, so great was their power of stopping a flow of blood, that 'Even should a pig be sticked, if a charmer was present and simply *thought* of his charm, the pig would not bleed.' The charm used was most commonly thus worded:

'Christ was born in Bethlehem,
Baptised in the Jordan;
The river stood—
So shall thy blood,
Mary Jane Polgrain [or whatever the person may be called]
In the name of the Father, and of the Son, and of the
Holy Ghost. Amen.'

Mr. Hunt gives a curious instance of a test resorted to by a Towednack farmer to discover the thief of certain stolen property. Acting in accordance with the traditions of the 'old people,' he invited his neighbours into his kitchen, and placed a cock under the 'brandice' (an iron vessel formerly employed in baking over a fire of furze and ferns). Every one had to touch the brandice with his third finger, and say: 'In the name of the Father, and of the Son, and of the Holy Ghost, speak.' The only person who shewed any reluctance to submit to the test was a woman who worked in the fields. She was forced up to the brandice, and had no sooner touched it than the cock crew; whereupon she confessed her guilt and restored the stolen property.

CHAPTER XXVI.

SURVIVING CUSTOMS.

THE flood of innovations which in the last few years has poured into Saint Ives from the outer world, has well-nigh swept away the last lingering vestiges of the many quaint old customs which were peculiar to this town.

From time immemorial the practice has obtained of 'throwing the silver ball' at Saint Ives on the feastentide. This is one of the last relics of the ancient Cornish sport of hurling, the best account of which is to be found in Carew's 'Survey of Cornwall,' and which still prevails in Brittany. Some days before the parish festival the boys used to make a money collection from door to door, and then take the silver to Jasper Williams or some other silversmith, who beat it out and put it round a globe of cork about the size of an orange. In ancient times this ball bore the Cornish inscription, 'Guare teag yu guare wheag'—'Fair play is good play.' The ball is taken onto Porthminster beach, where it is thrown about for a short time. The old rhyme, 'Toms, Wills and Jans take off all on the sands,' refers to the custom by which persons of the names of Thomas, William and John were pitted against all others, as a fairly equal division. But this arrangement would not hold good now that Methodism has introduced so many Old Testament names.

One of Mr. Hunt's correspondents wrote to him thus, from Saint Ives:

'*Hurling the Silver Ball.*—This old custom is still observed at St. Ives. The custom is also kept up at St. Columb and St. Blazey on the anniversary of the dedication of the church. St. Ives Feast is governed by Candlemas-day, it being the nearest Sunday next before that day. On the Monday after, the inhabitants assemble on the beach, when the ball, which is left in the custody of the mayor for the time being, is thrown from the churchyard to the crowd. The sides are formed in this way:

> "Toms, Wills, and Jans,
> Take off all on the sands"—

that is, all those of the name of Thomas, John, or William, are ranged on one side, those of any other Christian name on the other; of late years the odd names outnumbered the Toms, Wills, and Jans. There is a pole erected on the beach, and each side strives to get the oftenest at the "goold," *i.e.*, the pole; the other side as manfully striving to keep them out, and to send their opponents as great a distance from the pole as possible. The tradition is, that the contest used to be between the parishes of Ludgvan, Lelant, and St. Ives—St. Ives then being part of the *living* of Ludgvan—and that they used to have a friendly hurling at Ludgvan, and that afterwards the contest was between Lelant and St. Ives. A stone near to Captain Perry's house is shown where the two parishes used to meet at the feast, and the struggle was to throw the ball into the parish church, the successful party keeping the ball, the unsuccessful buying a new one. St. Ives is said to have outnumbered the Lelant folks, so that they gave up the contest, and the ball was left with St. Ives. This much is certain, that the feasts of St. Ives, Lelant and Ludgvan fall properly on one Sunday; though a misunderstanding has arisen Lelant claiming to be governed by the day before Candlemas-day, which will alter the three every seven years.'

Mr. Hunt adds: 'The game of hurling is now rarely played, and the Sabbath is never broken by that or by any other game.'

Wrestling, the twin sport of hurling, is also practically obsolete. A note in the manuscript diary of Captain John Tregerthen Short, of Saint Ives, runs as follows:

'1820. July 24. A grand Wrestling Match on Longstone Downs. James Halse, Esq., and other gentlemen contributed to the same. July 25. The wrestling ended at a late hour in the evening. The St. Just men carried the day.'

The village of Treloyhan was a favourite rendezvous for wrestlers, and their meetings were often attended by the squire's son, the late Mr. John Augustus Stephens, of Tregenna Castle, a great friend of the sport, and himself a wrestler of no mean prowess.

A correspondent, whose letter Mr. Hunt prints in full, gives particulars of the ancient custom of 'guise-dancing,' as observed at Saint Ives at Christmas time. For weeks previous the boys were busy preparing the most carnavalesque costumes they could devise. The various choirs practiced their carols, and general preparations were made for the approaching estival. Cottages were smartened up with a good touch of the limebrush outside, and inside with 'Prickly Christmas,' as the holly is here called. On Christmas Day the mayor, aldermen, and councillors, walk in procession from the mayor's house to the church. The guise-dancing time is from Christmas Day to Twelfth Day. 'The maidens are dressed up for young men, and the young men for maidens; and, thus disguised, they visit their neighbours in companies, where they dance and make jokes upon what has happened during the year, and everyone is humorously "told their own," without offence being taken. The music and dancing done, they are treated with liquor, and then they go to the next house and carry on the same sport.' The disguises represented Father Christmas, Saint George, a Turkish Knight, Maid Marian, etc.

The 'Popular Romances' contains the following paragraph as to Shrove Tuesday at Saint Ives:

'Formerly it was customary for the boys to tie stones to cords, and with these parade the town, slinging these stones against the doors, shouting aloud:

'"Give me a pancake, now, now, now,
Or I'll souse in your door with a row, tow, tow."'

May-Day at Saint Ives is at the present day almost without any of its traditional observances; but the boys are accustomed to rob the gardens of their choicest flowers in the early morning of that day. It was at one time no uncommon thing for persons to sit up all night at their windows to protect their plants from these nocturnal raids. The children of Saint Ives rise early on May morning and go out to gather 'may,' which they bring back in triumph to the sound of horn-blowing.

At Saint Ives the custom still prevails of giving children a large apple on All Hallows Eve, or 'Allan-day,' as it is there called. These apples the children place under their pillows, and eat next morning. A quantity of large apples are thus disposed of at what is termed the Allan Market.

'Shallals' were bands of infernal music, of the 'marrow-bone and cleaver' type, which used to play at night outside the houses of newly-married couples whom, for any particular reason, the town roughs had a grudge against. The shallals got so bad at Saint Ives that a special bye-law was passed by the Town Council to suppress them. The principal instruments of sound used by the performers in the shallals were the long speaking-trumpets with which fishermen hail boats from Porthminster.

A funny story is told at Saint Ives to the effect that an elderly lady, one of the most respected inhabitants of the town, was awakened one night, about Christmas time, by a loud knocking at the street-door. She looked out of her window and asked who was there, and what they wanted. 'Mr. Jones, Esquire!' answered a voice in the darkness. 'Ah, well,' replied the lady, 'he doesn't live here, so please go away.' In a short time, however, the knocking was repeated, while a sound as of voices in concert was borne on the midnight air. Again the disturbed lady asked, 'Who are you?' and again came the vague reply, 'Mr. Jones, Esquire!' Indignantly she rejoined that Mr. Jones, Esquire, would receive the contents of her water-jug unless he quickly took himself off. She was no more disturbed, nor was it till a later day that the good lady learned that her rest had been troubled by 'Mr. Jones' choir' from the parish church, singing carols to honour the approach of Christmas.

The Towednack feastentide, or parish festival, occurs on the nearest Sunday to April 28. According to local tradition, this parish at one time had no feastentide. It is said that a certain inhabitant of the parish, one springtime, invited some friends to a merry-making at his house. A large log of wood was placed on the hearth, and no sooner did it begin to crackle and blaze, than a cuckoo flew out from a hole in the log. The host caught the bird and kept it, and he and his guests resolved to renew their festive gathering every year in the future, which afterwards became the parochial festival, under the name of the Cuckoo Feast. It is also sometimes called the Crowder Feast, *i.e.*, the fiddler's feast, because the fiddler formed a procession at the church-door and led the people through the village to some lively tune. But in connection with the derivation of the name of this feast, it will be well to record the old tradition mentioned by Mr. Hunt at p. 427 of his book: 'When the masons were building the tower of Towednack Church, the devil came every night and carried off the pinnacles. Again and again the work was renewed by day, and as often removed during the night, until at length the builders gave up in despair, feeling that it was of no use to contend with the evil one. Thus it is that Towednack Church stands lonely, with its squat and odd-looking tower, associated with which is the proverb, "There are no cuckolds in Towednack, because there are no horns on the church-tower."'

The following is an extract from the *Western Antiquary* of 1883:

'A Dissenting minister bequeathed a sum of money to his chapel at St. Ives, Cornwall, to provide six bibles every year, for which six men and six women were to throw dice on Whit

Tuesday after morning service, the minister kneeling the while at the south end of the communion-table, and praying God to direct the luck to his glory' ('Curiosities of the Search Room,' p. 49). 'Who was this minister, and what phase of religion did he represent, or to what denomination did he belong?—E. Parfitt, Exeter.'

This query did not receive an answer.

We must not conclude our account of the old customs of Saint Ives without alluding to the 'Fairy-mow,' a fair held on November 30, the Feast of Saint Andrew, to whom the parish church is dedicated. This ancient fair is still kept up to some extent, with stalls in the streets, music and merry-making. Its name, which correctly written is Fêr-a'-Moh, is nothing more nor less than the Cornish words for 'Pig Fair.'

CHAPTER XXVII.

OLD SAYINGS.

THAT department of legendary lore which consists in the smart ironical sayings levelled at the inhabitants of one parish by those of another, and which we may term 'parish taunts,' is familiar to students of folk-lore. Cornwall is particularly rich in these sayings.

The people of Saint Ives appear to have held in Cornwall a position analogous to that occupied in the Midlands by the villagers of Gotham, near Nottingham—that is to say, the men of Saint Ives were credited with less of worldly wisdom than was possessed by their neighbours, and the taunts hurled at their parish all insinuate a lack of common-sense at Saint Ives. Thus the most common taunt applied to a native of this town is, 'Who whipped the hake?' This sarcasm has reference to a legend that the fishermen of Saint Ives once flogged a hake round the town to deter its voracious brethren from making havoc among the pilchard shoals. It has been alleged in defence of the fishermen that the Hake flogged was a man of that name, who had done some injury to the fishery.

Another story tells how some Saint Ives boatmen eagerly manned a boat, and put out into the Bay for the purpose of picking up a 'floating millstone,' which they believed had been left by some wreck. One of the crew stood up in the bow of the boat, and, in his haste to secure the prize, leaped on to the supposed millstone, which proved to be only the stave of a cask enclosing a lot of sea-foam. Mr. Tregellas has immortalised this legend in his dialect story, 'The Swemming Grending-Stone.'

For a bit of genuine Saint Ives humour, we would recommend a perusal of Fortescue Hitchins' rhyme, entitled 'The Saint Ives Mutton Feast' (Bottrell, 3rd Series, p. 89). It describes how a flock of sheep was driven by a mighty wind from Gwithian Downs into Saint Ives Bay, and how, with cries of 'Heva!' the fishing population rushed to bring the sheep ashore. The fisherman's cry of 'heva!' is a word of great antiquity, and is supposed to be derived from a Cornish word meaning to find, to get. The common rhyme is, 'Heva to the lea, the boats are gone to sea!'

In a former chapter we have noticed the origin commonly assigned to the Towednack Cuckoo-feast. Closely connected with this is the parish taunt, 'Who built a hedge round the cuckoo to keep the spring back?' applied to persons of that parish. The men of Towednack are reported to have said on that memorable occasion, 'If we had only put one more course on the walls, we should have kept him in.'

'Nancledrea all your own' is a saying well known to a genuine Saint Ives man. It signifies that a man is 'monarch of all he surveys'; that he is 'all alone in his glory,' or 'in clover.' The few inhabitants of this remote hamlet were nicknamed 'Nancledrea Rats,' a designation which they seem to have owed to their mill.

'Towednack quay-head, where the Towednack people christen their calves,' is a venerable witticism, the origin of which is wrapped in obscurity.

'Like Pudding-bag Lane, in one way and out the same,' is a Saint Ives phrase which explains itself.

'Saint Ives Hakes,' 'Towednack Cuckoos,' and 'Zennor Goats,' are terms of contempt applied to inhabitants of these parishes respectively.

Zennor is called 'the place where the cow ate the bell-rope,' a saying which probably alludes to the barrenness of the hills in that parish.

Just as egregious folly is the amiable quality popularly ascribed to the in-dwellers of Saint Ives and Towednack, so a mean parsimony is the attribute fixed upon the natives of Zennor. The old droll-tellers had a large stock of stories illustrating the supposed poverty and meanness of Zennor people. These were, it is true, credited with great musical and vocal talents; but even this good trait was generally united, in the popular tales, with the less admirable characteristics of parsimony and squalour. The people of this parish, be it observed, were once so renowned for their beautiful singing, that no 'wedding, funeral, or other merry-making,' was considered perfect unless a Zennor man was present to raise his tuneful voice. Like the bards of old, the Zenorians at length became so over-bearing in the pride of their musical powers, that their ancient fame sank into a joke, and they became a byword and a reproach among the western parishes. They expected to be invited to every occasion of festivity, and thought that they made ample return for their gluttony by giving a few staves of their church-music before going home. Such, at least, is the amusing and exaggerated picture of a former generation of Zenorians, given us in the pages of Bottrell. It was said that Zennor people would contrive, by their thrifty habits, to live like goats. Hence the nickname 'Zennor Goats.' 'As careful as Zennor people' was a common saying in the neighbouring parishes.

In the second series of Bottrell's work is the following wonderful will made by a Zennor man:

'I'll make my will while I am well. I will bestow my riches. I'll give to Ellek, my eldest son, my best coat, jacket and breeches. As for my watch, it is in pawn, else Elexander should have that. Neckey shall have the courage horse, and Jan the little sprat. Mary shall have the milking cow, and Lystria the heifer; Phillis shall have the flock of sheep, and what can I do better? Old Polly shall have the purse of gold, and that will most maintain her. Sally shall have the old brass pan, the bucket and the strainer. Signed in the presence of Cousin Matthew Hollow, Uncle Philip Eddy and John Quick the schoolmaster.'

'A healthy man can ate a mackerl, but Jan Nance can ate tin' (eat ten), is a Saint Ives saying which doubtless owes its origin to some long-forgotten incident.

CHAPTER XXVIII.

THE CORNISH LANGUAGE AT SAINT IVES.

It would be going beyond the scope of this work to pretend to give a philological account of the Cornish language; but the reader may be reminded that Cornish is a High Cymric division of the Celtic family of speech, and that it died out as a spoken language at the close of the last century. It is expressly recorded that Saint Ives was one of the very last strongholds of the ancient tongue. A woman called Cheston Marchant, who could speak nothing but Cornish, died at Gwithian, on the eastern shore of Saint Ives Bay, in 1676, aged 164 (Borlase, MS. Coll.). Indeed, the fishermen of the Saint Ives district, who are exceptionally conservative in their habits, may still be said to retain something of the old language, since they alone (or the oldest of them) are familiar with the ancient names of all the rocks and caves along the coast, of which a collection will be found in our list of proper names. Mr. Hicks of Saint Ives, writing in 1722, says: 'This language within the last fifty years is almost forgotten, being seldom used by any of the inhabitants excepting fishermen and tinners.'

The following curious Cornish folk-rhyme, or children's ditty, was published, for the first time, in the *Journal of the Royal Institution of Cornwall*, vol. ii., p. 7. The heading is, 'Unpublished Cornish Proverbs. A Fisherman's Catch. Given by Capt. Noel Cater, of St Agnes, to T. Tonkin, Esq., 1698':

'A mi a moaz, a mî a moaz, a mî a moaz in gûn glaze,
Mî a clowaz, a clowaz, a clowaz a Troz, a Troz, a Troz, an Pusgaz miniz.
Bez mî a trouviaz un Pysg brawze, naw Losia,
Oll a poble en Porthia, ha Maraz-Jowan,
Nevra ni ór dho gan zingy.'

The translation, given in the same magazine, is as follows:

'As I was walking, was walking, was walking on the sea [*lit.* green plain]
I heard, I heard, I heard, a noise, a noise, a noise, of small fishes;
But I found it to be a great fish with nine tails,
All the people in St Ives, and Market-Jew,
Were not able to draw it in.'

On a careful study of this late Cornish fragment, I feel certain that it is a Saint Ives ditty, and would be fully appreciated only in that neighbourhood. Both the original and the translation above cited contain errors. Thus, 'goon glaze,' which is rightly translated 'green downs,' is, I feel sure, a mistake for 'Garn Glaze,' the feminine mutation of Carn Glaze ('the Grey Rock-heap'), which is the name of a spot in the old part of that town, overlooking the harbour. 'Troz an Puscaz miniz' should be rendered, not 'the noise of little fishes,' but 'the feet of the fishes walking,' I think. True, the sentence is curiously ambiguous, and the other version is possibly correct, but my amendment makes the humours of the ditty hang together better. 'Naw losia' should be 'naw lostia,' which means, not 'nine yards,' but 'nine tails.'

I would suggest the following rendering:

'A me a moaz, a me a moaz, a me a moaz en Garn Gleaz,
Me a clowas, a clowas, a clowas a' troz a' troz, a' troz an puscas mynez:
Mez me a welys un pysg brâz, naw lostya,
Oll a' pobl en Porth Ia ha Maradzhawan,
Nevra ni ôr dho gan zingy.'

To be translated thus: 'As I was going, was going, was going on Carn Glaze, I heard, I heard, I heard, the feet, the feet, the feet of fishes walking; but I saw one big fish, (with) nine tails—all the people of Saint Ives and Marazion were not able to pull it (ashore).'

The only other mention of Saint Ives which I am aware of as occurring in Cornish composition is a late fragment, written when the language was almost in its final stage of decay, and giving an account of the geographical limits within which it then still lingered. It has been printed in the *Journal of the Royal Institution of Cornwall*, 1879, No. xxi., p. 182, from a MS. of Dr. Borlase. The author is believed to be John Boson, of Newlyn.

The piece is as follows:

'Nebbas Gerriau dro tho Carnoack.

'Gun Tavaz Carnoack ew mar pu guadn hez, uz na ellen skant quatiez tho ewellaz crefhe arta; rag car dreeg an Sausen e thanen en pow idden ma an Kensa, an delna ema stella teggo warno tha, hep garra tho tha telhar veeth buz dro tho aulz ha an more, el eu a va clappiez lebben oggastigh en durt Pedn an Wollaz tho an Karrack Cooez, ha tuah Poreeah ha Redruth, ha arta durt an Lizard tua Helles ha Falmouth.'

Translation:

'A few Words about Cornish.

'Our Cornish tongue hath been so long in the wane that we can hardly hope to see it increase again; for, as the English confined it into this narrow country first, so it presseth on still, leaving it no place but about the cliffs and sea, it being almost only spoken from the Land's End to the Mount, and towards St Ives and Redruth, and again from the Lizard towards Helston and Falmouth.'

The above is a very correct and elegant bit of Cornish, though we would suggest a few slight improvements in the spelling, viz., *Cernoek* for 'Carnoack,' *drîg* for 'dreeg,' *vîth* for 'veeth,' *môr* for 'more,' *Porth Ia* for 'Poreeah,' and *Lezherd* for 'Lizard.' The true Cornish for 'Falmouth,' moreover, is *Pen-a'-cûm-guic*.

It will easily be understood that Cornish public archives contain nothing of the ancient language of the Duchy except, indeed, proper names, personal and local, including a few nicknames. Such isolated words are often very valuable, however, as supplying expressions not to be met with elsewhere. The following is a list of the most curious Cornish words which occur in documents relating to the Saint Ives district.

Subsidy of 1327.

'Johannes Moyl.' (Welsh *moel*, 'bald.')
'Johannes Bydewy' = Bo Dewy, 'David's abode (?).'
'Thomas de Pendrelan.' The latter word means 'The end of the church town.'

Subsidy of 1523.

'Alexander Gweader,' *i.e.*, 'The weaver.'
'John Thomas, 'Sullouk' (the Scillonian ?).
'Thomas Engoff,' *i.e.*, 'an gov,' 'the smith.'

Borough Accounts.

1620. John Nance, 'Molkin'; Welsh *Maelgwyn*.

Parish Registers.

Stevens *alias* Gonew (Welsh *guineu*, 'brown' ?).
Stevens, 'Trevalgen' (Maelgwyn's town).
Williams *alias* Porthmere.
Williams, 'Shoorin.'
Thomas *alias* Trewal or Trythwall (Ithwal's town).
Thomas *alias* Daddoe.
Thomas *alias* Midleton.
Thomas *alias* Tregenhowe.
John Thomas, 'Welsh.'
Wm Thomas, *alias* 'Kyow [?] Angove' (1615).
Richards *alias* Carway.

Of course, many of the above additional surnames are simply

the names of country residences of those who bear them. Of this class are 'Gonew' (?), 'Trevalgen,' 'Porthmere,' 'Trythwall,' 'Midleton,' 'Tregenhowe,' and 'Carway'; but I cannot identify 'Sullouk,' 'Shoorin,' or 'Daddoe' as place-names. The appellation 'Welsh' no doubt indicates that that particular Thomas family originated in Wales, like many others in this neighbourhood. In our transcript of the evidence given before the Commission which inquired into the fish-tithe dispute at Saint Ives in 1711, the reader will find it stated that, when the tenth basket of fish was delivered to the agent, the fishermen called out 'Deka, deka!' This, of course, is the pure Cornish word for 'ten,' and also for 'tithe,' or 'tenth.'

The names of some streets in Saint Ives are Cornish, as:

Street-an-garrow = Rough Street.
Street-an-bollar.
Chy-an-chy = The house by the house.
Nanjivvy = St. David's Valley (?).
The Digey (derivation uncertain).
The Stennack = 'the tin-place.'
Skidden Hill.

All the other place-names of the district will be found in a complete list in the next chapter.

It is a somewhat curious fact that a decaying language lingers longest, not in remote rural places, but in small towns. Nevertheless, the wild uplands of Towednack and Zennor were no doubt very late in exchanging the Celtic speech of their inhabitants for the all-conquering idiom of the Saxon. The families of Stevens and Trewhella were among the last to keep up the Cornish language in the parish of Towednack. The late Dr. Stevens of Saint Ives told the writer that his great-grandfather, Andrew Stevens of Trevegia, used to take his (Dr. Stevens's) grandfather on his knee, and say, 'Come here, my little *kennack* [rush-light], and say, "Wonnen, deau, tri, pedar, pemp,"' etc. He would then make the youngster count after him in Cornish. He also habitually used the exclamation, '*Scavel angow!*' which Jago says is equivalent to 'A pack of lies!' (Or is it equivalent to the Welsh words *ysgafael angau?*)

In the year 1890 there was still living at Boswednack, in Zennor, an old man named John Davy, who had some hereditary knowledge of Cornish. He knew the meanings of the place-names round about, and could converse on a few simple topics in the ancient language. He recited the following rhymes, which he said he had learned from his father:

'**A grankan, a grankan,
A mean a gowaz o vean;
Ondez parc an venton,
Dub trelowza vean.
Far Penzans a Maragow,
Githack mackwee,
A githack macrow,
A mac trelowza varrack.**'

This seems, however, to be a mere jumble of place-names.

As regards the local dialect of English, the Saint Ives speech is in a great measure different from that of the rest of Cornwall. This is what we might have expected, seeing that almost every parish has its own peculiarities of dialect. It used, indeed, to be said that a Saint Ives man could tell a Treloyhan man by his accent!

Mr. J. T. Tregellas gives specimens of many local varieties of the Cornish dialect in his delightful little book, 'Peeps into the Haunts and Homes of the Rural Population of Cornwall.' From this work we select the following as an illustration of the Saint Ives brogue:

'They had a wreck there some years "agone," and, "weth other things washed ashore, was a thing," said he, "maade of tember, and in pieces nailed up all of a raw: every waun of es said he thoft 'pon somethin' that it must be; at laest Josha Wearne settled ut. "I knaw what ut es," says he, "'t es a horgan weth the inside of un waashed out." And so we all agreed ut was, and they agreed to put un up in my laarge room, and there a was for nigh a year, when a gentleman seed un, and said 'twas nothan but a hin coop."'

Other Saint Ives dialect stories by the same author are 'The Squire's Tame Conger,' and the 'Swemming Grendingstone,' in his 'Cornish Tales.' These show a strong local colouring, as well as genuine Cornish humour.

CHAPTER XXIX.

PLACE-NAMES IN THE PARISHES OF SAINT IVES, LELANT, TOWEDNACK AND ZENNOR (WITH THEIR MEANINGS IN ENGLISH WHENEVER THESE CAN BE ASCERTAINED WITH TOLERABLE CERTAINTY).

Alleluia Rock, in Saint Ives Bay, east of the Eastern Carrack. The name was given by some fishermen, who accidently discovered it, in the present century.

Amălèbra, in old deeds Amalibria, a hamlet in Towednack; formerly a manor.

Amălvèor, a hamlet in Towednack; Welsh *ymyl fawr*, 'great slope, edge, or boundary.' (But *ymyl* is of the masculine gender in Welsh.)

Amălwìdn, a hamlet in Towednack; Welsh *ymyl wen* (or, rather, *ymyl gwyn*), 'white slope, edge, or boundary.'

Anjèwăn, a hamlet in Saint Ives.

Ayr, in old deeds Arthia, a hamlet in Saint Ives; Welsh *yr ardd Ia*. 'Saint Ia's garden or enclosure.'

Bàhăvèlă, a hamlet in Saint Ives.

Balcunnow, a tenement in this district; named in a deed of 1751.

Bălnoòn, Bal-an-ûn ('the mine on the down'), in Saint Ives.

Bămbălùz, a rock off the head between Porthgwidn and the wooden pier, Saint Ives.

Bărnòon, in old deeds Bar-an-wûn ('the top of the down'); it is a hill just over Saint Ives town, on the north-west.

Bayelea, a hamlet in the Saint Ives district.

Beăgletùbm, a hamlet in Towednack. Welsh *bugail twyn*, 'shepherd's hillock.'

Beersheba, a hamlet in Lelant; corrupted from Cornish words.

Belliers, The; land along the western outskirts of the grounds of Tregenna Castle, and especially the beautiful wooded lane so well known to visitors. A received derivation of the name is from Belles Aires, but it is to be noted that hard-by is a field called the Bellyer's Croft, *i.e.*, 'the bell-ringer's allotment'

Blynam, The, a rock in Zennor, between Gurnard's Head and the Western Carrack; Welsh *blaenaf*, 'most prominent.'

Bolenna, a hamlet in Towednack; Welsh *bŏd llynau*, 'the abode by the pools.'

Borallan, in old deeds Borthallan, a hamlet in Saint Ives.

Borough Green, The, a piece of land at Saint Ives.

Borough Rock, or Burry Rock, The, a rock on the Island Wastrel, Saint Ives.

Bŏscùbm, a hamlet in Zennor; from words equivalent to Welsh *bŏd* and *cwm*, 'the abode in the valley or coombe.'

Bose, a tenement in this district named in a deed of 1751.

Bŏshàber, a property in the Saint Ives district named in a deed of 1751. It also occurs in Subsidy Rolls *temp.* Henry VIII., as Boshaberthew.

Bosìgrăn, a hamlet in Zennor.

Boskerris, a hamlet in Lelant ('the habitation by the cherry-trees')—Welsh *ceiroes*.

Bosphrennis, in old deeds Bosporthennis, a hamlet in Zennor. The name would seem to mean 'the abode on the marsh-island,' using *porth* in the sense in which *port* is used in the South of Ireland, to signify a bog.

Bŏssòw, or Bŭssòw, the name of two hamlets in Zennor and Saint Ives, with the addition of 'Higher' and 'Lower' respectively. 'Bossow' is simply the plural of 'bos,' an abode.

Bosùllow, a hamlet in Zennor.

Boswèdnack, or Boswednan, a hamlet in Zennor. ('The abode of Wenoc.') This Wenoc, Gwynog, or Winnoc, is the saint whose name is preserved in the word Towednack.

Bothen, a field in Saint Ives.

Bowl Cove, is in Towednack parish.

Bowns, or Bounds, The, a rock between the old breakwater and the wooden pier at Saint Ives.

Brace Teag, a field in Saint Ives; *brăs tèg*, 'the big, fine' (field).

Brègiă, or Boregia, a corruption of Boher Isa, 'the lower road.' It is a hamlet in Towednack.

Browthin (*th* soft), a big rock a little to the south-east and seawards of Clodgy Point, in Saint Ives.

Brunnian, in ancient documents Breynion, a hamlet in Lelant.

Burnt Downs, a hill on the boundary between the parishes of Saint Ives and Zennor. Halliwell calls it the Burning Mountain.

Bŭrnvòire, a hamlet.

Bùzzăck, a rock in the eastern part of Saint Ives Bay.

Căgwèneth (Welsh *cae gwenith*, 'the wheat field'); a tenement in this district named in a deed of 1751.

Càrbĭs, a district in Lelant containing Carbis Valley and Carbis Water.

Càrlŏw Rocks, off the Zennor coast.

Carn (Farm), in Lelant.

Càrnăbillan, a range of rocks on a hill west of Gurnard's Head.

Carnăvèrth, on the cliffs of Towednack.

Carn Crowz ('cross rocks'), over the shore between Bamalûz Point and the wooden pier at Saint Ives. Probably there was a cross here formerly.

Carnèllŏ, or Cornellow, a hamlet, formerly a barton, in Zennor. The same place is also called Chy-an-dowr.

Carnèvrăs, a rock in the sea to the north-west of Saint Ives Head.

Carn Galva, a hill in Zennor.

Carn Glaze ('grey or blue rock'), an eminence near the shore of Saint Ives harbour.

Carn Gloose, a rock-pile on the Zennor coast. The 'gloose' seems to be a variant of 'glaze,' grey or blue, but used in the sense of 'hoary'; Welsh *llwyd*.

Carninny, a hamlet in Lelant.

Carn Mên ('stone carn'), a rock-pile on the Towednack coast.

Carn Stabba, a hill in Saint Ives.

Carn-tisco, a hamlet in Lelant.

Carn Watch, a hill in Towednack; a famous beacon to the fishermen.

Carrack Carn-ēthen (*th* soft) ('the bird's rocks'), on the Towednack coast.

Carrack Du ('black rock'), also shortly 'Carthew' (*th* soft), a headland west of Saint Ives, between the latter and Clodgy Point.

Carrack Gladn ('the rocks on the brink'), on the Lelant coast.

Carrack Leggo, a fishing-stem at Saint Ives mentioned in a document of 1752.

Chapel Anjou, in Lelant.

Charlestown, a hamlet in Lelant.

Chy-an-chy ('the house by the house'), a place in the old town of Saint Ives.

Chy-an-dowr, 'the house by the water,' another name for Carnello, a hamlet in Zennor.

Chy-an-drea ('the house of the townplace') corruptly 'Chern Dray,' a field at Talland, in Saint Ives.

Chy-an-gweal ('mine-house'), a village in Lelant, which sprang up around Wheal Providence, in the last century.

Chyarton, Chiarton or Chivarton ('barton house'), a tenement of the manor of Ludgvan Lese.

Chykèmbra (' Welshman's House'), a hamlet in Zennor.
Chyldson, a hamlet in Towednack.
Chy̆pòns (' bridge house'), a hamlet in Towednack.
Chytòdn (' house on a hillock'), a hamlet in Towednack.
Clègăr Bank, a quarter of a mile northwards off Saint Ives Head. 'Clegar' means a cliff-like rock; Welsh *clegyr*.
Clòdgy Point, a headland on the north coast of Saint Ives parish. The word would seem to be related to Welsh *clogau*, large stones.
Cock Hill is on the Tregenna estate in Saint Ives.
Cocking's Hole, the sand-vent constructed by Smeaton at the shore end of the quay. At the date of the new extension of the quay, in 1889, this hole had become entirely choked up with the sand.
Coldharbour, a hamlet in Towednack. The prevalence of this name throughout the British Isles is very remarkable. Its derivation has long been a puzzle to philologists.
Coom (' the valley, combe'), a tenement in Lelant.
Còrvăh, or Corvagh, a hamlet in Saint Ives.
Couch's Cove, another name for Zawn-abadden, a tiny cove just south-east of Penmester Point, Saint Ives. The name was given early in the present century, when a fisherman called Daniel Couch lost his boat there, on which occasion his son was drowned.
Court Cocking, a street in the old town, Saint Ives.
Court Cocking Rock, in Saint Ives harbour.
Crab Rock, off Pednolva Point, Saint Ives.
Crànkăn Vean, a field in Zennor.
Creeg Awze, *Creeg Vean*, and *Creeg Voaze*, little hummocks of hills west of Zennor church-town, used as landmarks by fishermen; the two last mean 'little' and 'great hillocks' respectively.
Croft Shĕwàmĕă, a field at Carninny in Lelant.
Crow's Nest, The, a fishing-ground off the Eastern Carrack, Saint Ives.
Cuckoo Hill, in Towednack.
Culver House, in Towednack parish.
Dìgĕy, The, a street in the old town of Saint Ives. The origin of the name has never been ascertained. Considerable discussion of the question will be found in the *Saint Ives Weekly Summary* of the spring of 1890. The second syllable is a mutation of *chy*, 'house'; the difficulty is in the meaning of the particle 'Di.'
Dìnŭs Iă (pronounce 'Dinnus Eea'), 'Saint Ia's fortified town,

an ancient name of Saint Ives, and still used in designating the 'Manor of Dinas Ia and Porth Ia.'

Drone Field, The, at Penbeagle in Saint Ives.

Doremoor, a field in Saint Ives.

Dove Street, an old street at Saint Ives. The name is probably connected with Venton Dovey and Nanjivvey (q.v.).

Eastern Carrack,, another name of Carrack Gladn, on the Lelant coast.

Ebŏl, The (pronounced 'Hebble'), a rock in the sea off the Gurnard's Head. The word signifies 'a colt.'

Emblă, a hamlet in Towednack.

Estòver, a farm on the Tregenna estate, Saint Ives.

Featherbeds, The, a range of rocks off the old breakwater, Saint Ives Head.

Feneder, a tenement in this district, named in a deed of 1751.

Fōag, or Fogue, a hamlet in Zennor. The word is a variant of Fuggoe, Hugo, and Vow, meaning 'a cave.'

Folly, The, a tenement in Saint Ives parish.

Fowe Wartha, a field in Saint Ives. The second word means 'upper or highest'; the first is probably connected with Fogue, Vow, etc. (q.v.).

Fuggoe ('the cave'), a tenement at Chy-an-gweal in Lelant.

Garden Garrow ('the rough garden'), a field in St. Ives.

Gear ('the fortified enclosure'), a hamlet in Zennor. The Cornish name 'Care' (Welsh *caer*) is the same word without the feminine mutation after the definite article.

Gŏllăstreà ('the town in the bottom'), a tenement in the manor of Lelant and Trevetho.

Gŏnnèw ('High Downs'), a hamlet in Lelant.

Goonwin, or Gûn-win ('the white downs'), a farm in Lelant, formerly the seat of the now extinct Pawley family.

Gowna, a big rock off Carrack Du, on the north coast of Saint Ives.

Great Downs, a hill on the Tregenna estate, Saint Ives.

Grigs, a hamlet in Lelant; 'grig' is the heath-plant.

Gundry Cave, in Zennor.

Gurnard's Head, a bold and picturesque promontory on the Zennor coast, much frequented by tourists. Its Cornish name is Treryn Dinas (q.v.).

Halsetown, a mining village in Saint Ives, built in the present century by a gentleman named Halse.

Harva, a rock in Saint Ives Bay, west of the Stones, Godrevy.

Hawk's Point, on the steep cliffs west of Carrack Gladn, in Lelant.

Hayle River separates the parishes of Lelant and Phillack. The Cornish word 'Hêl' signifies a river.

Helles-vean ('the little slope'; Welsh *yr allt fychan*), a hamlet in Saint Ives.

Helles-veor ('the great slope'; Welsh *yr allt fawr*), a hamlet in Saint Ives just west of Helles-vean.

Hendra (Welsh *hên-drê*, 'old hamlet'), a farm in Saint Ives on the Tregenna estate.

Hoe, The, a little rock just under Tom May's Rock off Saint Ives Head. A rowing-boat can pass between them.

Hor Point, a promontory on Helles-veor cliff, Saint Ives.

Kèrrŏw, a hamlet in Zennor, formerly a barton (Welsh *caerau*, 'an encampment').

Kẹrvis-town, a hamlet in Towednack.

Lady Downs, in Zennor. 'Lady' is 'Leath-dy' (Welsh *llaeth-dy*, 'a milkhouse,' 'dairy').

Laity ('the dairy'), a hamlet in Saint Ives and another in Lelant bear this name.

Lămbèzo ('the enclosure of the birch-tree.' Welsh *llan-fedw*), a place referred to in the Saint Ives borough accounts.

Lăngwèth ('the enclosure of trees.' Welsh *llan-gwŷdd*) a tenement in Lelant.

Lapurrian, or Laporian, a tenement in Lelant.

Lea Hole, or Leigh Hole, The, a little cave at Penmester Point, Saint Ives.

Lèbmăs, a fishing-ground east of Carrack Gladn, on the Lelant coast. Its other name is Skil-vean.

Leigh Point, a small promontory south-west of Penmester, Saint Ives.

Lĕlànt, the mother parish of Saint Ives and Towednack. An older form of the name is Lan Nant—*i.e.*, 'the valley church.' The full name of the parish is Saint Uny Lelant, from Saint Euinus, the patron of the church.

Lĕthùggă, a rock in Portreath Bay.

Longstone, a district in Lelant, including Longstone Downs. Probably so called from a *mên-hîr* or ancient sepulchral monument.

Lùdgvăn Lese, or Leas, an ancient and extensive manor, which included a great portion of the Saint Ives district. 'Greystone Meadows' would seem to be the English equivalent of these words; Welsh *llwyd-faen*, 'a grey stone.'

Lump Rock, near the extremity of Saint Ives Head.

Man-o'-War Rock, a big rock just off Pednolva Point, at Saint Ives. The name is a corruption of *mên-ar-warh*, 'the stone on high,' *i.e.*, the 'high stone.'

Mên Dèrrăns, a rock off the northern extremity of Saint Ives Head.

Mên Fleming ('the Fleming's stone'), at Saint Ives, between Smeaton's quay and the wooden pier; it is now covered with sand.

Mên Ionas, a rock off Carrack Gladn.

Mên Lānder, a rock in Saint Ives Bay north-west of Godrevy.

Mennor, a hamlet in Lelant.

Merra Hill, a high moorland hill in Towednack.

Merryn Rock, The, a big rock in the sea off Porth Gwidn, Saint Ives Head. The fishermen believed that, if they sailed inside the Merryn on putting to sea, they would catch no fish that day. This tradition almost certainly points to some ancient religious observance in connection with the Merryn Rock. In the south transept of Paisley abbey there is a chapel of Saint Mirin, in whose name the church of Marshfield, Monmouthshire, is also dedicated, as well as the parish of Saint Merryn in Cornwall. It would almost seem that there was anciently an image of this saint on the rock, though the superstition above referred to probably originated in pre-Christian times. A little rock at the extremity of the Merryn is known as 'the Beak of Merryn.'

Mount Tyack, a tenement in Lelant. Tyack (Welsh *taeog*) means 'a farmer.'

Mun House, a fishing-ground in the Bay, off Saint Ives. The word 'mun' ordinarily means fish kept for manure.

Nance, properly Nans ('the valley'), a hamlet in Lelant.

Nancemeor ('the great valley'), a tenement in this district, named in a deed of 1751.

Nănclèdrĕa, a hamlet in Towednack. In the Subsidy Roll of 1327 it is called Nanscludry (Welsh *Nant-clyd-dre*), 'the valley of the sheltered habitation.'

Nănjìvvĕy ('Saint Dovey's valley'), a place at the top of the Stennack, Saint Ives. It is sometimes called 'Saint Jivvey.'

Nănkèrvis, a hamlet in this district.

Ninnis, or Ninnes, a hamlet in Lelant. The name is derived from *an enys*, 'the island,' and is a common surname in the Saint Ives district.

Noŏnbèllas, a hamlet in Zennor.

Norway ('the north way'), a street in the old town, Saint Ives.

Parc-an-carn ('the cairn field'), at Ayr, in Saint Ives.

Parc-an-creet, at the Stennack, St. Ives.

Parc-an-down ('the downs field'), at Ayr, in Saint Ives.

Parc-an-drean ('the thorn-tree field'), a field in this district.

Parc-an-garrow ('the rough field'), at Carthew, Saint Ives. It is also called King's Field.

Parc Angell, a field in Saint Ives.

Parc-an-growz ('the cross field'), in Saint Ives, also called Parc Arthia.

Parc-an-rack (Welsh *parc-y-wraig*, 'the wife's field'), at Ayr, Saint Ives.

Parc-an-roper ('the roper's field'), just west of Saint Ives town.

Parc-an-skebbar (Welsh *parc-yr-ysgubor*, 'the barn field'), in Lelant.

Parc-an-woon ('the downs field'), in Lelant.

Parc Arthĭa ('the field of Saint Ia's garden or enclosure'), in Saint Ives; also called Parc-an-growz.

Parc Bean Ayr ('little Ayr field'), in Saint Ives.

Parc Noweth ('the new field'), at Helles-vean, in Saint Ives.

Parc Owles, properly Parc Als ('the field with a slope'), at Chyangweal, in Lelant.

Parc Pedn-an-drea ('the field at the end of the town'), in Lelant.

Parc Shaftoes, at Vorvas Vean, in Lelant.

Parc Towans ('the field of sand-hillocks'), Chyangweal, Lelant.

Parc Tron ('the round field'), at Trenwith, in Saint Ives.

Parc Troon ('the round field'), a field in this district.

Parc Venton ('the well-field'), at Penbeagle, in Saint Ives.

Parc Vorn, at Vorvas Vean, Lelant.

Pedn-an-drea ('the town end'), a hamlet in Lelant. Perhaps identical with Pendrelan in the Subsidy Roll of 1327.

Pedn-a-vounder, a hamlet in Saint Ives.

Pedn-olva, a headland half-way between Saint Ives Head and Penmester Point (Welsh *olchfa*, a washing-place ?).

Penbeagle ('the shepherd's hill'), a hamlet in Saint Ives.

Pĕndĕrleàth ('the moist hill'), a hamlet in Towednack.

Pendinnas ('the fortified headland'), the old name of Saint Ives Head, and still sometimes used for the extreme point thereof.

Pĕndòwr, ('the hill by the water'), a point on the Zennor coast.

Peninnis ('the island headland'), a point on the north coast of Saint Ives.

Pĕnmu̍ster, a headland a mile south-east of Saint Ives town. The name is apparently a corruption of Porthminster, and is used indifferently for the headland and the adjacent cove; but in recent years there has been a tendency, founded on very reasonable grounds, to distinguish between the two by calling the headland Penmester, and the cove Porthminster. The name means 'the headland by the church.'

Pĕnnànce ('the head of the valley'), a hamlet in Zennor.

Pĕnpòl ('the head of the pool'), a tenement in this district, named in a deed of 1751.

Pitpry, a hamlet in Zennor.

Plain-an-gwarry ('the playing plain'). The place, at the top of the Stennack, Saint Ives, where the miracle-plays were performed. The name occurs as that of an orchard, in a deed of 1808, but is now forgotten.

Pŏldìce, a hamlet in Lelant.

Pŏlmànter, anciently Pellamounter and Pellamountayne; a stream and a hamlet on the boundary between Saint Ives and Towednack. ('Elisha Pallamounter' was buried at Lelant in 1797.)

Pŏlmèar ('the great pool'), a hamlet in Zennor.

Pŏlpèar, a hamlet in Lelant; once the residence of an ancient family of this name, now extinct.

Ponion, a hamlet in Zennor.

Pŏrthcòcking ('Cocking's Cove'), another name for the Foresand, the beach of Saint Ives harbour. It is to be noted that the term 'porth' is applied only to a bay in which there is sand at high tide; a bay the beach of which is composed of stones or rocks, is termed a 'pool.'

Pŏrthglàze ('the blue, green, or gray cove'), in Zennor.

Porthgroynia ('the cove of seals'), a little cove west of Penmester Point.

Porthgwidn ('the white cove'), on the east side of Saint Ives Head; it was formerly a harbour for the fishing-boats, which were hauled up here as they now are at Porthminster.

Porth Ia ('Saint Ia's port'), the Cornish name for Saint Ives. It was commonly pronounced 'Poreea.' Porth Ia Prior was a manor comprising part of Saint Ives parish; it belonged to the Benedictine Abbot of Tywardreath.

Porthkitny, The big cove to the south-east of Carrack Gladn, in Lelant.

Pŏrthmèor ('the big cove'), west of the island, Saint Ives.

Pŏrthmìnster ('the church cove'), the big cove between Pednolva and Penmester points. So called from an ancient chapel which formerly stood on the rocks just above the beach. In the fifteenth century there was a village of Porthminster. These are the sands chiefly frequented by visitors.

Porthmoina ('the cove of mines'), Zennor. Hard by are the Morvah and Zennor mines.

Porthripter, the big cove between Penmester and Carrack Gladn points, on the coast of Saint Ives and Lelant.

Porthzawzen ('the Saxons' or Englishmen's cove'), between Hor Point and Peninnis, in Saint Ives parish.

Porthzennor ('Saint Sinara's cove'), on the Zennor coast, near the boundary of Saint Ives parish.

Pull, The ('the pool'), a fishing-ground in the Bay, off Saint Ives.

Purfle's Plot, i.e., Purefoy's Plot, a piece of land at Saint Ives.

Rabal, a field in Saint Ives.

Rĕjàrn, a hamlet in Lelant. *Tre-dzharn* ('the habitation in a garden).'

River Cove, in Towednack.

Riviere, a tenement in Lelant; also called Rovier.

Rocky Downs, a hill in Lelant.

Rose-an-growz ('the cross heath'), in Lelant.

Rose-an-hale, properly Rôz-an-hêl ('the river heath'), on the Zennor coast.

Rŏsemèrgy (the *g* hard), a hamlet in Zennor. In old deeds Rosemargay.

Rŏsewàll, Rôz-whal ('the high heath'), a high hill and a hamlet at its foot, in Towednack.

Saint Ives, the westernmost borough town in England; so called after Saint Ia, who introduced Christianity here. Previous to her arrival the place was called Pendinas. Its later Cornish name was Porth Ia. Saint Ies became Saint Ives *temp.* Elizabeth.

Scavel-an-gow ('the smith's bench,' Welsh *ysgafell y gôf*), a field in Saint Ives. Curiously, these words were used as an exclamation of incredulity: '*Scavel-an-gow*' ('a pack of lies!), *gow* meaning a lie, as well as a smith.

Scuddy Mên, a deep-water fishing-ground for bait, half a mile north of Saint Ives Head.

Shoaler Stone, The, a rock near Saint Ives.

Skidden Hill, the steep hill leading from Tregenna down into the town of Saint Ives.

Skillywàdn (Welsh *ysgîl y wadn* 'the nook at the base' of the hill), a hamlet in Towednack.

Skil-vean ('the little nook'), a fishing-ground to the east of Carrack Gladn, in Saint Ives Bay. Its other name is Lebmas.

Spaniard, The, a fishing-ground in the Bay, off Saint Ives. Probably so called because some Spanish vessel was lost there.

Splat-an-redden ('the fern splot'), in Lelant. A splot is a small piece of land in a flat region.

Stennack, The ('the tin-bearing place'), a hill just west of Saint Ives town. Here is the mine called St. Ives Consols.

Street-an-bollar, a street in Saint Ives town. (Tregenna Rent Roll.)

Street-an-garrow ('rough street'), Saint Ives town.

Street-an-pol ('pool street'). Saint Ives town.

Street Pĕtìte ('little street'), a name given by the French or Breton fishermen to what is now called Bailey's Lane, in Saint Ives town.

Tàlăvòna, a creek at the east end of Porthmeor, near the Island, Saint Ives.

Tàllănd, a dwelling-house on an ancient site at Porthminster Hill, Saint Ives.

Three Brothers, The, rocks on the western shore of the Island, Saint Ives.

Three Humps of Meg, The, hills west of Zennor, a landmark to the fishermen.

Tom May's Rock, on the eastern shore of Saint Ives Head. So called after a man who used to sit on it to fish.

Tonkin's Stone, a rock between Gurnard's Head and the Western Carrack.

Tors, The, rocks at sea a quarter of a mile west of Saint Ives Head.

Tŏwèdnăck, a church-town and parish west of Saint Ives, between the latter parish and Lelant on the east, and Zennor on the west. Named after Saint Wennoc, or Gwynog.

Trĕdrèath ('the dwelling by the sands'), a tenement in this district, named in a deed of 1751.

Trĕgàrthĕn, or Tregerthen ('the habitation in the enclosure'), a hamlet in Towednack.

Tregenna ('the dwelling at the mouth or entrance'), an ancient residence a mile south-east of Saint Ives.

Tregoos, Tregôz ('the habitation in the wood'), a field at Chyangweal in Lelant.

Trehidy Downs, on the boundary between Towednack and Zennor.

Trĕlòyhăn, a village in Saint Ives, a mile east from the town ('the habitation in the grove'; Welsh *tre lluyn*). The village is now corruptly called 'Trelyon,' 'Trelion,' and even 'Treline.'

Trĕmbèthŏw ('the habitation by the graves'; Welsh, *tre beddau*), probably in allusion to some prehistoric place of sepulture.

Tremeddar, or Tremeddo, a hamlet in Zennor.

Tremellyn ('the mill-dwelling'), a tenement in the manor of Dinas Eia and Porth Ia.

Trencrom, in old writings 'Trecrobben' ('the crooked, concave habitation'), a hamlet and high hill in Lelant.

Trendraen, pronounced 'Tendrine' ('the habitation of thorn-trees'; so in Welsh), a hamlet and high hill in Towednack.

Trendreath ('the habitation by the sands'), a tenement in Lelant.

Trĕnòwĕth (Welsh, *Trenewydd*, 'Newtown'), a hamlet in Lelant.

Trènwĭth ('the habitation by the trees'; *Tre-an-guŷdh*), a homestead in Saint Ives, the residence of an ancient family which took its name from this place. The early form of the name was 'Treunwyth.'

Trerŷn Dinas ('the habitation on the fortified headland'; the Cornish name for Gurnard's Head), a promontory in Zennor.

Trĕrŷnk Hill, a hamlet and high hill in Lelant. The name was originally 'Trefrenk' and 'Trefrynk' ('the Frank's habitation'), which was softened into 'Trerynk' and 'Trink.'

Trèvă (Welsh, *trigfa*, 'a place of habitation'), a hamlet in Zennor. The name is now pronounced 'Trewey.'

Trevalgen (the *g* hard; now usually written 'Trevalgan'), a hamlet and hill in Saint Ives. The most probable meaning is 'Maelgwyn's or Malkin's dwelling.'

Trevarrack, a village in Lelant. If we are warranted in regarding this name as a variant of 'Tregarrack,' the meaning is 'the habitation by the rock,' in allusion to the huge boulder in the highroad by the stream. But perhaps it is 'Tre-war-ic' ('the habitation on the brook').

Treveal, or Trevail, Trev-hêl ('the habitation by the river'), a hamlet in Towednack, on a stream near the sea. This derivation assumes that the pronunciation 'Treveel' is incorrect.

Trĕvèthŏ (Welsh, *Trefedw*, 'the habitation by the birch-tree'), the ancient seat of the Praed family, in Lelant.

Trevorrow ('the habitation by the roads'), a hamlet in Lelant.

Trewanack, a hamlet in Lelant.

Trewartha ('the upper town'), a hamlet in Lelant.

Trowan, in old documents 'Trewoen,' 'Trevowen,' and 'Trewoon' (Welsh, *tre yr waun*, 'the habitation in the meadow'), a village in Saint Ives.

Try Moor, in Zennor parish.

Two Guns, The, a rock on which they formerly stood, on the western slope of the Island, Saint Ives.

Vĕnàyr, a tenement in Saint Ives.

Venton Dovey ('St. Dovey's or David's Well'), a spring at Saint Ives town. Welsh, *Ffynon Dewi*.

Venton Eia, or Venton Ia ('the Well of St. Ia'), a spring at Saint Ives.

Venton Uny, pronounced 'Venton Oony,' corruptly 'Venton Loony' and 'Venton Looly' ('the Well of St. Euinus'), a spring in Lelant.

Venton Vigean (corruptly 'Venton Vision'), a spring at Ayr, Saint Ives. The name occurs in a deed of 1808, but is now forgotten.

Venven, a hamlet in Lelant.

Vinny Gonner, a field at Carninny in Lelant.

Vorvas (or Worvas) *Hill*, that which is now called 'Knill's Steeple,' from the monument which stands on it, on the boundary between Saint Ives and Lelant.

Vorvas, and Vorvas Vean, hamlets in Lelant. Worvas, being a feminine noun, becomes 'An Vorvas' with the definite article, and imposes a corresponding initial mutation on the adjective 'Bean.'

Vow Cot ('the cave cottage'), a house near the shore at Porthminster, Saint Ives.

Westaway ('the western way'; cf. 'Norway,' *ante*), a hamlet in Lelant.

Western Carrack, The (another name for 'Carrack Du'), a big rock on the north coast of Saint Ives.

Wheal Ayr, a disused tin-mine at Ayr in Saint Ives.

Wheal Dream, a spot on the east shore of the Island, Saint Ives. The words *huel*, a 'mine,' and *gwel*, a 'field,' are both now 'wheal.'

Wheal Reeth ('the red mine'), in Lelant.

Wheal Snuff, an ancient adit at the east end of Porthmeor, Saint Ives.

Wheal Sperris ('the spirit mine, the haunted mine'), on the boundary between Towednack and Zennor.

Wheal Widn ('the white field'), at Chyangweal, Lelant.

White Rock, The (anciently 'Carrack Widn'), a picturesque, ivy-grown carn on Porthminster Hill, Saint Ives.

Wicka, or Wicca ('the village'), in Towednack. The house so-called, situate near Wicka Pool on the coast, is now in ruins. It was the old home of a family called Quick, who perhaps took their name from this tenement.

Windypark, a place on Barnoon Hill, Saint Ives town.

Withen (*an wethen*, 'the tree'; from *gwethen*), a hamlet in Lelant.

Zawn-abadden, a cave under Penmester Point, Saint Ives. It is now better known as Couch's Cove (q.v.). A 'zawn' is a little cove, or opening in the cliffs, usually with a cavern.

Zawn-avilia, a cove just west of Hor Point in Saint Ives.

Zennor, a parish and church-town bounding Towednack on the west. So called after St. Sinara, the patron. This name is the last on the alphabetical list of the parishes of the United Kingdom.

CHAPTER XXX.

LOCAL FAMILIES.

Bossowsack.

RICHARD BOSSOWSAKE of Saint Ives figures as a landowner in the Subsidy of 1520—the only mention of such a surname in these Rolls.

According to the Visitation of 1620, Ralph Bosawsack of that ilk married 'a Westmoreland gentlewoman wch was an inherytrix & had a part of the Bartyn called Tregenha nere St Ives.' Their son, Richard Bosawsack, married a Westmoreland heiress, who brought him part of Tremedo' and Boswednock in Zennor. (By 'Westmoreland' is meant the parishes of Towednack and Zennor.)

Bottrell.

One of the most powerful and widely-established of the baronial houses founded by the followers of the Conqueror was the family of the Boterels, who, soon after leaving their original home in Brittany, became possessed of the estate and seat named after them, Bottreaux, on the north coast of Cornwall.

In the fortieth year of the reign of Henry III., William and Reginald de Botriaux were registered as owning fifteen *libratæ* ot land, or more, in Cornwall; and, under Edward William I., de Boteraus and Reginald de Bottreaus held land or rents to the total of twenty *libratæ*, or over (Rolls transcribed in Carew's 'Survey').

In our chapter on the Manors and Lordships we have seen that the manor of Lelant and Trevetho belonged to this family, and that in 1295 William Bottreaux was the lord of that manor.

On March 1, 1395, Bishop Stafford, of Exeter, granted a license to Elizabeth Bottreaux, 'mulieri,' to have Mass celebrated in her private chapel of St. Mary Magdalen at Boswithguy. This license was renewed July 20, 1398, the chapel being described as

'Boswythgy infra parochiam Sancti Ercii in Cornubia' (*i.e.*, St. Erth). This is probably the estate now called Bosworgey. On November 24, 1399, a similar license was granted to William, son of Sir William Botreaux, Knt., and to Sir Ralph Botreaux, Knt., etc.; and again, June 27, 1410, to William, Lord of Botraux, and his family, also again, July 15, 1411, to John Botreaux and Elizabeth his wife, for all their mansions in the diocese.

From the Calendar of Inquisitiones Post Mortem, Cornwall, 2 Edw. IV., No. 15, at the Record Office, we learn that in 1463 inquisition was held on the death of 'Willūs Botreaux miles,' possessed of lands in Lelant Manor. This appears to mark the decline of the family, and henceforward none of the records to which I have been able to refer give any particulars about them until we come to the period of parish registers. Strange to say, the family is not named in any of the Subsidy Rolls, not even in that of 1327. This family bore arms: Chequy or and gules, on a chevron azure 3 horseshoes of the first.

By the middle of the seventeenth century this branch of the family, though still existing, had fallen from its high estate, and was represented by Reginald Botterall, of Saint Ives, who in 1661 married Christian Rosewall. Of their issue William died young, and Reginald was the only son who married; his wife was Elizabeth Murth, married in the year 1689, with issue Christiana, and Samson, who died unmarried.

Christiana Botterall was married in 1709 to Jean Lemal or Lamalle, a French or Breton mariner, to whom she bore eight daughters. (See Lemal.)

Ceely.

According to the Visitation of Cornwall, this family traced their descent from Thomas Ceely, of Comesberie, in Somersetshire, whose eldest son, Christopher Ceely, of Plymouth, married Avis Marchant. Their second son, Peter Ceely, was born in 1580, and removed to Saint Ives. He married Anne Penrose, of Penrose, and had issue (*inter alios*), Peter, of whom later; Priscilla, married to William Tregosse, of Saint Ives, with male issue; and Jane, married to Henry Williams, of the same place, with issue Jane, Epharem, Margaret, and another.

The last-named Peter Ceely, born *circa* 1618, married Joan, daughter of Thomas Purefoy, of Saint Ives, with issue, William, born 1643; Thomas, born 1644; Peter, born 1645.

This account does not appear to tally accurately with the municipal records, which show that so early as the year 1603

William Ceelye, gent, was one of the capital burgesses of Saint Ives; also in 1612 and 1613.

In 1620 'Mr Celye' was rated for the royal subsidy, he being at the time a resident in 'Westren Streete.'

In 1621 occurs this entry: 'Pd Mr Howell by the appoyntmte of the moste of the 12 for the lawe sutes broughte againste mr Trevnwthe & others by Mr Tho. Ceelye, 10s.'

In 1629 we find William Ceely, gen., one of the 12 principal burgesses, in which capacity he took part in signing a mutual agreement by the burgesses to join in resisting the vicar's encroachments in the matter of tithes. In 1631 he was still a capital burgess.

In 1638 Peter Ceely farmed the profits of the quay of Saint Ives. The next extract refers to him:

1647. Received 'of Mr George Hicks upon Major Ceelye Tickatts for corne.' (This was in the famine time.)

'I: payd to Major Ceelye to wards the corne for Mr Opie £135. (In payment for the corn taken from Opie's ship.)

In 1650 we find a memorandum that Peter Ceelye, gent., borrowed a piece of ordnance from the Corporation to put on board his ship. The ship having foundered, Ceely is ordered to pay for the lost cannon. (See *ante*, Extracts from the Municipal Accounts.)

In the autumn of 1650 Peter Ceely was chosen Mayor.

1653. 'Paid the constable to paie Major Ceelie for pressing the men, monie disbursed by him, 12*s*.'

1654. 'Received of Peter Ceely, Esqr, for halfe years rent for the Mills ended the 1st of November 1654, £6 13*s*. 4*d*.'

1656. 'Payd for candles and monis disbursed when Major Ceelys souldiers did watch, 6*s*. 4*d*.'

1658. Peter Ceelye Esqr and John Seyntaubyne Esqr were elected to Parliament by the Capital Burgesses. (See the chapter on the Members for Saint Ives.)

1669. 'Paid Major Ceely for 1000 of Healingstones, 8 bundles Lathes, 2000 of nayles with a barrell of Lyme £1 7*s*. 2*d*.'

1694. 'For Mr Ceelys boat on the Key, 2*s*. 6*d*. in all.'

In 1723 and 1733 John Ceely was mayor of the borough.

The following entries in the Parish Registers carry on the genealogy from the Visitation period:

1651. Baptised John son of Peter Ceely gent:
1654. Buried John s. of Peter Ceely Esq:
1654. Baptised Peeter s. of Peter Ceely Esq:
1655. Buried Joan wife of Peter Ceely Esq:

1656. Married Peter Ceely Esq: and Honor Pridieux.
1658. Baptised (and born) Honor d. of Peter Ceely Esq:
1660. Baptised Ann d. of Peter Ceely Esq:
1663. Baptised Kathern d. of Peter Ceely gent:
1667. Baptised Ann d. of Peter Ceely gent:
1688. Married M[r] Rob[t] Beere & M[rs] Honour Ceely.
1705. Married M[r] W[m] Busvargus & M[rs] Anne Ceely.
1709. Married M[r] John Ceely & M[rs] Honour Penrose.
1711. Baptised Anne d. of John Ceely.
1712. Baptised Peter s. of M[r] John Ceely.
1713. Baptised John s. of M[r] John Ceely.
1716. Baptised Honor d. of M[r] John Ceely & Honor his wife.
1719. Baptised Peter s. of Mr. John Ceely & Honor his wife.
1720. Baptised Allis d. of John Ceely & Honor his wife.
1721. Baptised Honor d. of M[r] John & Honor Ceely.
1726. Baptised Jane, d. of Richard & Jane Ceelly.
1726. Baptised Bridgett d. of M[r] John & Honor Ceely.
1728. Baptised Elizabeth d. of Jn[o] & Honor Ceely.
1739. Baptised Peter s. of M[r] John Ceely.
1741. Baptised Anne d. of M[r] John & Ann Ceely.
1773. Married Richard Bosence & Elizabeth Ceely, sojourner & spinster; in the presence of W. Harry & Ann Harry. [The contracting parties both made their marks.]

Davies Gilbert says Peter Ceely, of Saint Ives, is buried in the north aisle of Saint Andrew's church, Plymouth, a monument marking the place of his interment; *sed quaere* whether he is not confounding two namesakes. Peter Ceely, of Plymouth, was mayor of that town, and cousin to Ceely of Saint Ives.

Lyson gives the arms of Ceely as: Azure, a chevron or between 3 mullets argent; quartering Fulneby, Graunt and Angeville.

This family rose to importance in Cornwall during the Civil War, at which time they sided strongly with the Parliament. Some account of their doings will be found in our chapter on the Civil War.

In a Saint Ives deed of the year 1808, reference is made to a messuage called 'Major Ceely's Great House,' which was situated in the heart of the town, close to the river. This would appear to have been built by the Puritan leader, Peter Ceely. Various buildings, in particular a tenement known as the 'Shoot Cellar,' were built upon the ruins of the old house towards the close of the last century. Before its final demolition, Major Ceely's house was named the 'Smelting House.'

The *Coram Rege* Rolls, Trin., 31 Car. II. (1679), contain a memorandum to the effect that Johanna Gregory, of Truro, widow, George Hamond, of Saint Ives, merchant, and Jane Praed, of Saint Ives, spinster, did, on the 19th day of February, 1678, with force and weapons, at the parish of Saint Ives aforesaid, unlawfully and riotously assemble, to the disturbance of the peace of our lord the King, at the mansion house of Peter Ceely, gent., and did then and there insult and maltreat the said Peter Ceely, he being then in the King's peace, to the evil example of others in the like case offending, and against the peace of our lord the King, his crown and dignity. Wherefore the King's attorney prays for judgment against the said offenders. But the defendants, through William Tyre, their attorney, say that they are not guilty; and concerning this they put themselves upon their country (in other words, they elect to be tried by a jury).

This memorandum is in the usual roundabout Law-Latin of the period, which, abbreviated as almost every word of it is, covers a goodly skin of vellum. There is nothing to show either the precise origin of this dispute, or its result.

Cocking.

This family is notable as having been connected with Saint Ives from time immemorial, being the first of the seven named in the old saw which we quoted in a former chapter. It may, indeed, be regarded as a typical Saint Ives family of the yeoman class. In the course of the long period during which the history of the Cocking family may be traced in public records, it has, of course, seen many ups and downs; and if at present it occupies a humble position, it can boast of having, at one period of its history, been among the foremost families of the place.

Circa 1520 John Cokyn was rated at £1 4*s*. for lands in the parish of Lelant, and Hen. Thom. Cokyn at £3 for lands in Saint Ives. In the same subsidy, John Cokyn is charged 20 marks in respect of goods at Saint Ives.

In 1523 and 1524 the goods of John Cokyn, of Saint Ives, were valued at £15.

In 1571 John Cockyn, of Saint Ives, was valued at £3 in goods, in 1585 and 1593 at £4, and in 1597 and 1599 at £5.

In 1573 John Cockyn was a capital burgess of Saint Ives, and farmed the profits of the quay. In 1578 he was again a capital burgess, and also in 1580 and 1583.

In the municipal accounts for the year 1584 is this singular item: 'Payde to John Cockyn for nurssing of denys chylde v^s^.'

In 1585 Elyzabeth Cockyn was Queen of the Summer Games.

In 1592 we again find John cockens a capital burgess, and in 1593 he was chosen head warden. In 1594 he farmed the profits of the market.

1594-5. 'It: paid John Cockens that hee forgate in his akownte by henry hickes 2*s.* 9*d.*'

1595. 'I: paid to gyles hawke by consentt of John cockin for the redemyng of the prisoners outt of Turkie the some of iiij^{s}.'

In 1596 John Cockyns and Thomas Cocken were capital burgesses, and in 1597 John Cocken paid 5*s.* to a local rate. In 1602 he was again a capital burgess.

In 1603 John Cockyns was chosen porthrieve, and his son, John Cockins, junior, became a burgess.

In 1608 we find this entry: 'Smā 33^{li}. Wherof Jo: cokyns muste paye 2^{li} wc̄h he was allowed of in his fathers yeres and beinge porthryve and paide it not by Jo: Stevens reporte.'

In 1620 John Cockin, of Saint Ives, paid 8*d.* to a rate for the King, and in 1622 he was one of those who signed an agreement not to permit fishing on Sundays.

In 1646 John Cocking was a burgess, and in 1650 and 1655 he signed consent to bye-laws relating to the fishery.

Somewhat later we find Richard Cocking occupying the position of town drummer. As such, in 1660, he received 2*s.* 6*d.* 'to beate the drume' on the King's Coronation Day. In 1667 and 1668 similar payments were made to him, and in 1673 he received 1*s.* 4*d.* to head the town drum. In 1693 Richard Cockyn had 3*s.* for beating the drum, and in 1696 is the entry: 'To the drumer Richd Cockyn, 1*s.* 6*d.*' Similar entries are found under the years 1699 and 1701; the latter runs thus: 'Rich: Cockyn to beat the drum to the watch 6 weeks, 2*s.* 6*d.*'

In 1704 one of the family was an innkeeper at Saint Ives, as witness this item: 'At John Cockens for beere for the ffrench-men 1*s.*'

The harbour of Saint Ives has from ancient times borne the name 'Porthcocking.' An old street which leads down to the Foresand is called 'Court Cocking'; and the sand-vent under the quay is known as 'Cocking's Hole.'

Edwards.

This ancient family was seated at Lelant in 1549, when the 'heirs of Edwards' paid 8*d.* to a subsidy.

In 1585 and 1593 William Edward was rated at £3 for goods in the parish of Lelant.

Circa 1593 Mr. Henry Edwards was receiving a high rent of 1s. a year from the town of Saint Ives for lands in the parish.

1594. 'Item, paid henry Edwards for hir ma^ties^ purueighers, 4s.'

Circa 1595. 'It. payed m^r^ harry Edward for the erecteng of the towence of nantuege, & the Ille of Sent nycolas, att pllemowth, xj^s^, & iiij^d^ for a quettaunces.'

1597. 'Item p^d^ Henrye Edwards for bringinge of ꝑcepts, xij^d^.'

In 1597 and 1599 Thomas Edwards' goods in Lelant were valued at £3.

In 1598 Thomas Edwards, of Lelant, gent., born 1564, was a witness before the Special Commission which was held to inquire into a case of smuggling at Saint Ives. (See *ante*, p. 130.)

In 1613 William Edwards, of Lelant, paid 2s. to a royal subsidy.

In 1620, when the heraldic and genealogical visitation of Cornwall was made, the pedigree was deduced from Henry Edwardes, of Lelant, whose third wife was Margaret Gavrigan of that ilk in Cornwall. By her he had issue a second son, Thomas Edwards, of Lelant, who married Jane Roscruge, of Roscruge, with issue *inter alias*, Henry Edwards, born 1600.

In 1624 and 1625 Thomas Edwards, gent., was rated at £4, and William Edwards at £3, for goods in Lelant, the latter being one of the rators in 1625.

In 1629 Thomas Edwards, gent., was rated at £5, and William Edwards, gent., at £4, in respect of their goods.

Thomas Edwards, gent., was a burgess of Saint Ives *circa* 1632.

In 1641 Henry Edwards, gent., and William Edwards, paid to a subsidy for their goods in Lelant; and Thomas Edwards, gent., paid £3 for his goods at Saint Ives, and contributed 5s. towards the building of the church gallery.

In 1664 Henry Edwards, gent., and John Edwards, were rated in respect of goods in the parish of Lelant.

In 1680 Arthur Edwards, of Lelant, gentleman, born 1526, was a witness before the Commission held to inquire into a dispute as to the tithe in the parish of Towednack. Henry Edwards is also mentioned therein. (See *ante*.) The former of these two gentlemen was a county magistrate, and the latter appears to have been High Constable of the Hundred of Penwith.

In 1740 John Edwards, gent., and others, purchased lands at Carn Stabba and Trowen in Saint Ives.

In 1749 John Edwards was Mayor of Saint Ives; he was again chosen to that office in 1758.

In 1766, 1768, and 1779, the Mayor of Saint Ives was Hugh

Edwards, attorney-at-law. In 1769 he appeared in the list of subscribers to Carew's 'Survey of Cornwall.' He possessed large property in the town of Saint Ives.

In 1771 and 1785 Hugh Edwards was a borough justice.

In 1780 Thomas Edwards and Ann, his wife, and another, purchased lands at Nenis in Saint Ives.

In 1786 John Edwards, gent., and another, purchased lands parcel of the Manor of Lelant and Trevetho.

In 1810 the name of Hugh Edwards appears in the list of subscribers to Fortescue Hitchins' 'Sea-shore, and other Poems.' This gentleman, who was eldest son of Hugh Edwards, the justice, was a clerk in the War Office.

Parish Registers.

1707. Married Hugh Edwards of St Just in Penwith & Catherine Pryor.

1708. Baptised Elizabeth daughter of Hugh Edwards.

1710. Baptised Grace daughter of Hugh Edwards.

1713. Baptised James son of Hugh Edwards and Catherine his Wife.

1729. Married William Hichens and Grace Edwards.

1735. Baptised John son of Mr John & Ann Edwards.

1736. Baptised Elizabeth daughter of Mr John Edwards & Ann his wife.

1739. Baptised Hugh son of Mr John and Ann Edwards.

1739. Baptised Elizabeth daughter of Mr John and Ann Edwards.

1741. Baptised Edmond son of Mr John and Ann Edwards.

1767. Mr Thomas Slade of the Parish and Town of Namptwich in the County of Cheshire and Miss Mary Hichens of this parish spinster were married in this church by License in the presence of Hugh Edwards and Edward Hichens.

Soon after the Reformation, this family were in possession of the old church-house, called 'The Abbey,' at Lelant, where they continued to reside for several generations, and where the Hosking family, who represent Edwards in the female line, still live.

Arms: Ermines, an antelope rampant or. Crest: an antelope rampant sable bezantee, attired or.

Glynne.

In the Subsidy Roll made in about the year 1520, Thomas Glynne's lands in Lelant are stated to be worth ten shillings, and his lands in Saint Ives elevenpence, annually, while his goods in the latter parish are valued at £2.

In 1523 his lands in Saint Ives are valued at the very high sum of £40, which seems to mark the date when, as we are told by Hicks, Thomas Glynne married the heiress of Nicholas, a large landed proprietor of Saint Ives.

In 1524 the goods of Thomas Glyn at Saint Ives are again valued at £2, which amount he paid to two subsidies that year. In a Penwith Subsidy List of 1536 he is rated to pay ten shillings for his goods.

In the 'Valor Ecclesiasticus' of 1535 it is recorded that the rectorial tithe of Lelant had been demised by the college of the Church of the Holy Cross, at Crediton, in the deaconry of Cadbury, to Thomas Glynne and others for the term of ten years.

In 1544 John Glyn of Saint Ives was rated at £1 for a subsidy, to which the other eight persons there paid only 6*s*. 8*d*.

In 1583 the Mayor and Burgesses of Saint Ives granted to John Tregose, esquire, all the pews and chairs in the church and chancel of Saint Ives, which had been formerly possessed by Thomas Glynne, esquire, deceased. Thomas, who appears to have been the last of his race, probably died between 1550 and 1580. Leland, who wrote in the reign of Elizabeth, says, 'There dwellith a Gentilman of a 50 Markes Land by Yere caullid Glynne yn S. Ies̃.' Arms: Argent, 3 salmon-spears sable; with the Cornish motto: '*Dre weres agan Dew ny*'—'A sure city is our God.'

Hals.

This family is said to have descended from John Hals, Justice of the Common Pleas in 1423, who sold the manor of Trembethow in Lelant to Godolphin.

In the Subsidy Roll of 1327 we find the name of John Halse, who was rated at 10d. for property in Saint Ives.

In that of *circa* 1520 Richard Hals' lands in the parish of Lelant are valued at £4 by the year.

After that the subsidies make no mention of this family until 1624, when 'Greenfreedus Halls, gen.,' was a rator, and contributed £4 in respect of goods in Lelant.

In another list of the same year he is styled 'Grenfield Haulse.' A similar entry occurs in 1625.

In 1629 'Grenvilis Hals, gen.,' paid £5 for goods at Lelant. He was rated again in 1641 as 'Grinvill Halse,' gent.

The borough records make mention of 'Mr Hals' in 1604 and 1616. The latter entry runs thus: 'P^d^ Tho: Poole the xth of Aprill laste for counsell fees for removing Mr Hals is children vs.'

Early in the present century the representati was Mr. James Halse, solicitor, who was mayor 1813, and an alderman in 1834. He was co local mining industry, and built the once po almost deserted, industrial suburb called after h

The arms of this family, as given by Bur fesse, between 3 griffins' heads erased, sable.

Sir Nicholas Hals, living at Fentongollan in Hals, the historian, represented other branches

Hext.

This family is first found at Saint Ives sixteenth century. The surname would seem 'Hicks,' especially as the armorial bearings are very similar. According to Burke, 'Ge of Trenarren and Hicks of Trevithick bea tower triple-towered, between 3 battle-axes

The following is the documentary hist Saint Ives:

Borough Records.

In 1597 John Hexte, gent., contributed

In 1603 John Hext was a capital burg lands within the parish of Saint Ives.

In 1614 he was again a capital bur Hexte, living at a part of the town called to a royal subsidy.

In 1624 Richard Hexte paid 4d. for to a subsidy of which he was one of t similar payments in the years 1625, 162

In 1629 Richard Hext was a capital porthrieve of Saint Ives. He was a 1630, 1631, 1633 (in which year he fa 1635.

In 1639 Richard Hext became the by appointment in the charter of Ki alderman in 1645.

Circa 1650, Mrs. Chesten (*i.e.*, Ch the interest of which was to be paid Ives for the benefit of the poor of the name Hext no more appears in the

Hichens.

In or about the year 1520 Richa had lands valued at 19s. a year in th

In 1523 the goods of John Huchyn at Towednack were rated at £2, and in 1524 at £3.

There is no further mention of Hichens or Huchins until 1641, when John Hetchins' goods at Saint Ives were valued at £3 by the year. In another subsidy list of the same date he was charged for lands in the parish as 'Johanes Hutchings.'

In 1664 John Hitchens was rated for goods at Saint Ives, as was also Richard Hichens. Thus far the Subsidy Rolls.

Borough Records.

In 1578 James hychen of Saint Ives contributed *2d.* to a local rate, and in 1584 he was a quay warden.

William Hechins was a capital burgess of the borough in 1603 and 1607. In the latter year he paid his cousin, John Tregenna, five pounds at Bristol, on behalf of the town of Saint Ives, and in 1607 he was chosen porthrieve. He held again the office of capital burgess in the years 1612, 1615 (when he was also churchwarden), 1622, 1629, 1630, and 1633 (when he was a second time porthrieve). In 1620 he paid *6d.* to the royal subsidy.

In 1630 Henry Hechins was a capital burgess.

In 1634 John Hechins was an overseer of the poor, and he was a waywarden in 1636.

In 1646 John Hichins was an alderman of Saint Ives, and farmed the profits of the markets and fairs held within the borough.

In 1650 'Henery Hitchens' agreed to and signed a bye-law relating to the pilchard fishery.

In 1655 Richard Hichings was the borough constable.

In 1664 John Hichens was chosen mayor.

In 1665 Richard Hichens was elected to that dignity; and two shillings was 'pd. Willyam Hichens for returneing a warrant to Penzance about the Royall ayd.'

1667. 'P[d] M[r] John Hichens for the Townes drum & fraight, £1 10*s.* 0*d.* P[d] him for ½ dozen of bandaleers, 11*s.*'

1668. 'P[d] M[r] John Hichens & M[r] Pendarves for Lyme, £1 5*s.* 0*d.*'

In 1670 John Hichings, junior, became mayor.

1671. 'P[d] M[r] John Hichens at his goeing to Lamas sises being townes busines, £2.'

In 1672 Richard Hichens was elected mayor.

Under the year 1673 occurs this memorandum: 'There is a Barell of powder in M[rs] Wilmott Hichens Custody which must be ꝑduced by her or allowed to her husbands acc[tt].'

In 1677 William Hichens was chosen mayor of Saint Ives, and John Hichens signed the accounts as an alderman.

In 1680, when the Commission was inquiring into the Towednack tithe dispute, it appeared from the evidence of one of the witnesses that Mr. Richard Hichens of Saint Ives formerly farmed the tithes, and 'being a hard man' obliged the people to pay him a penny for every pound.

In 1682 John Hichens became mayor.

In 1694 Richard Hichens was raised to that office, and he was again chosen mayor in 1703.

In 1711 John Hichens, junior, merchant, was elected an alderman of the borough, and was a witness before the Commission of inquiry into a disputed fish-tithe at Saint Ives. John Hichens, mariner, was one of those elected 'assistants for the Burrough' this year.

In 1713 John Hichens again became mayor.

In 1717 Mrs. Sibella Hichens died, and her body was brought to Saint Ives to be buried. The corporation went in procession to escort her remains into the town. From this it would appear that she was a near relative of John Hichens, who was mayor again in 1717.

John Hichens was elected mayor in 1726, and John Hichens, senior, in 1728.

In 1737 and 1748 we again find a John Hichens mayor of Saint Ives.

In 1752 William Hichens was owner of a fishing-boat called the *Saint Ives*, having a stem at Leigh, and the *John* with a stem at Carrack Gladden.

In 1767 James Hichens signed a fishery bye-law.

Thomas Hichens was mayor in 1772, 1781, and 1785.

(Richard Hichens, who was chosen to be mayor in 1831, appointed town steward at a salary of £2, and an alderman in 1834, was of another family, that of the Hichens of Penzance, as was also Mr. Robert Snaith Hichens, mayor of Saint Ives in 1867 and 1868.)

It will be seen how closely this family has been connected with the public history of Saint Ives during the last 250 years. It has given to the town one Porthrieve, whilst fifteen times has a Hichens been elected mayor of the borough.

Parish Registers.

1651. Baptised Marie daughter of John Hichens.
1688. Baptised Lewis son of Robert Hichens.
1689. Baptised Robert son of Robert Hichens.

1869. Baptised Henry, son of Mr Richard Hichens.
1691. Baptised John son of Robert Hichens.
" Baptised Wilmott daughter of Mr John Hichens.
1695. Married Henry Hichens and Zenobia Quicke.
" Baptised Welmot daughter of Henry Hichens.
1703. Married John Hichens and Mary Thomas.
1705. Married John Hichens 3^ius and Mrs Jane Lanyon.
1706. Baptised John son of John Hichens Jun. Merchant.
1709. Baptised Margery daughter of John Hichens Mariner.
1710. Baptised Honor daughter of Henry Hichens.
1711. Baptised William son of Mr John Hichens jun^r
1712. Baptised John son of Mr John Hichens.
1714. Baptised Richard son of Mr Richard Hichens.
1716. Married Mr. John Hicks mayor, and Mrs Ann Hichens.
1728. Baptised John son of John and Phillip Hichens.
1729. Married Wm Hichens and Grace Edwards.
1730. Baptised John son of William and Grace Hichens.
1735. Baptised John son of Mr William and Grace Hichens.
1738. Married Mr William Hichens (Roper) and Mary Williams.
1740. Married Thomas, son of William and Grace Hichens, Marriner.
1741. Baptised Hector son of John and Elizabeth Hichens.
1760. Married Jasper Williams, mariner, and Mary Eustis, spinster, both of this parish, by William Symonds, vicar, in the presence of John Hichens and John Williams.
1767. Mr Thomas Slade, of the Parish and Town of Namptwich, in the County of Cheshire, and Miss Mary Hichens of this parish, spinster, were married in this church by License in the presence of Hugh Edwards and Edward Hichens.

From entries on the flyleaves of the registers, which we have copied in our chapter on the parish church, it appears that John Hichens was churchwarden in 1730. The same extracts show the useful part which the late Mr. Robert Hichens, of London, took in the restoration of the church in the year 1850.

Hicks.

This family, like that of Hichens, has from time immemorial been associated with the public history of Saint Ives. C. S. Gilbert tells us that: 'John Hicks, of the town of St. Ives, in the year 1400, received by grant and deed from John Hele, of St. Ives, one tenement situate within the said town, and to remain to him and his heirs for ever. Mr. Hicks, of St. Ives, the immediate descendant of John Hicks, inherited the said tenement in

1722, and was the author of a valuable manuscript history of his native town.'

Lysons says: 'We have not been able to discover who is the present possessor of a MS. history of the borough town of Saint Ives, written by Mr. Hicks, some time an attorney at St. Ives, before the year 1756, mentioned in Dr. Borlase's parochial collections.'

Edward Hain, Esq., jun., of Saint Ives, has recently made great efforts to recover the missing manuscript, but his praiseworthy attempt has not been successful. The present representatives of the Hicks' family are in complete ignorance as to its whereabouts.

None of the Cornish historians give the Christian name of the writer of the manuscript history of Saint Ives. We had therefore better state at once that the author was John Hicks, who, as we shall show in this chapter, was for many years an alderman, and several times mayor of the borough.

Gilbert's account of the manuscript is as follows:

'The best account given of this place is now in MS., written by Mr. Hicks, a native, and finished 1722, at which time the author appears to have been very aged. Mr. Hicks was for some time coroner of St. Ives, and we believe served the office of chief magistrate, as did several others of his family. In consequence of his free access to the records, his book abounds with curious anecdotes and particulars not to be found in any other work; and, although replete with tautology, and rendered thereby in some parts perplexing and tiresome to the reader, yet it is evidently the production of an inquisitive mind and the fruit of much labour and industry. The loan of this document has been kindly granted to us by Nicholas Harris Nicholas, Esq., in order that such extracts might be made from it as should tend to the improvement of what we had before collected relative to the early history of St. Ives.'

It will be understood that the 'records' to which Hicks had access were simply the borough accounts; the treasures of the London Record Office were in his day inaccessible and almost unknown.

But to return to the early history of the family. In connection with Gilbert's statement, quoted at the commencement of this chapter, it is curious to notice the following entry in the Borough Accounts of 1658:

'I: payd Jo^{n} Hicks ffor a post ffyne ffor land bought of Mr Heale, 5s.'

Mr. Heale was steward of the Lord of the Manor. Is this a

mere coincidence, or is it another gross piece of bungling on the part of a county historian?

In the parochial valuation of *circa* 1520, mention is made of 'Joh: Will[s] Hicka,' whose lands in Saint Ives were of the annual value of 13s. 6d. Also of John Hycks, chaplain, and Davyd: Joh: Hicks, the latter of whom had goods at Saint Ives of the annual value of five marks.

In 1523 and 1524 David John Hicks' goods were valued at £3, and in the latter year Thomas Hycke had goods to the value of £2 in the Hundred of Penwith.

In 1536 Nicholas Hycka's goods at Saint Ives were valued at 10s. by the year.

In 1571 Thomas Hicks' goods at Saint Ives were found to be of the annual value of £1; and James Hicks' effects were set down at £3 in 1585.

In 1593 Thomas Hicks had goods worth £4, and Henry Hicks £3 per annum.

In 1597 and 1599 Thomas Hicks' goods were again valued at £4, and those of Henry Hicks and George Hicks at £3 each.

In 1624 George Hickes, Jane Hicks, widow, and Henry Hicks, had goods to the value of £3 a year each.

In 1641 Henry Hicks was again rated at £3 for goods at Saint Ives, and Thomas Hicks had lands in the parish.

In 1664 Thomas Hicks and John Thomas were rated together for their goods.

Borough Accounts.

In 1572 Thomas Hicks was chosen head warden of Saint Ives. He was a capital burgess in 1573, 1580 and 1592. In 1595 he was again head warden, and copied out some old bye-laws into the volume then newly purchased to hold the records. In 1597 he figures among those who paid a local rate, and in 1603 he was a capital burgess again.

In 1580 George Hicks was a capital burgess, which office he held also in the years 1603, 1612, 1614, 1615, 1619, 1622, 1625, 1626, 1627 and 1638. He was an ordinary burgess in 1592, 1629 and 1631; a borough constable in 1604; a churchwarden in 1636; paid the local rate of 1597; was a quay-warden in 1585, and held the office of porthrieve in 1611 and 1624.

Joel, or Jewell Hicks, was king of the summer games in 1592, quay warden in 1596, an ordinary burgess in 1603, a capital burgess in 1612, and paid 1d. to the royal rate of 1620.

Nicholas Hicks was lord of the summer games in 1596.

Henry, or Harry Hicks, was king of summer games in 1585; quay-warden in 1590; burgess in 1592; head warden in 1594;

paid the local rate of 1597; was a capital burgess in 1603 and 1612; and porthrieve in 1614 and 1615. Henry Hicks, junior, was burgess in 1615, and capital burgess in 1619, 1622, 1625, 1626, 1627, 1629, (also quay-warden) 1635, 1636 (also churchwarden), 1638; porthrieve in 1631.

Richard Hicks was burgess of Saint Ives in 1603, 1629, 1631.

Mr. John Hicks was a capital burgess in 1612, and an ordinary burgess in 1615. In 1620 he paid *4d.* to the royal rate; and he was quay-warden in 1625. He was again a capital burgess in 1627, and a burgess in 1629.

John Hicks, junior, was a capital burgess in 1630 and 1631, in which latter year he was also quay-warden and churchwarden. He became porthrieve in 1632, was capital burgess in 1635 and 1636; again quay-warden in 1637, and capital burgess in 1638.

In 1620 William Hicks paid *4d.* to the royal rate.

Jane Hicks, widow, paid *1s.* to the same rate.

Ann Hicks, widow, owed *6d.* to the county stock in 1629.

Henry Hickes was mayor of Saint Ives in 1641.

In 1646 Henry and Richard Hicks were aldermen of the borough; and in the same year Thomas and George Hicks were burgesses. In 1647 John Hicks caught the plague, which then raged in the parish. In 1647-8 George Hicks was churchwarden.

In 1650 Thomas, Hugh, Robert, Henry and George Hicks, signed the new fishery regulations.

In 1651, the year of famine, Mr. Henry Hickes and Mr. William Hicks gave together £40 to the poor of Saint Ives, and Mr. William Hickes, of Kerris, gave £10. Robert Hickes that year paid £1 *5s.* for provisions which he had supplied to the sick at Saint Ives in the year of the plague.

In 1656 Richard Hicks was chosen mayor of Saint Ives.

In 1658 John Hicks, attorney, was employed by the Corporation to draw a conveyance between the town and the vicar, and about other legal business.

In 1663 ffrancis Arundel and Richard Hicks, gentlemen, received *14s.* towards their expenses in riding to Sir John Arundel about town business.

In 1674 Thomas Hicks was elected mayor.

In 1680 John Hicks, gen[t], was a churchwarden. In the same year Thomas Hicks, Esq., was a justice of the peace, and one of the commissioners who held the inquiry in the Towednack tithe dispute. Among the witnesses and persons mentioned by the witnesses, we find Richard Hicks, of Saint Ives, gent: and John Hickes, of Saint Ives, gent:, born 1644, who farmed the small tithes of Towednack in 1668 and 1669. John Hicks, gen^t, was an alderman in 1685, 1686, 1687, 1712 and 1716, and was chosen mayor in 1689, 1695, 1701, 1707, 1710 and 1715. In 1687 Thomas Hicks was an alderman. John Hickes, of Saint Ives, gen^t, born 1644, was a witness before the Saint Ives Fish-tithe Commission in 1711.

In 1696 Vernon Hicks was allowed £1 14*s*. 0*d*. for quay duties of Helston goods. John Hicks was an alderman in 1712 and 1716, and was again chosen mayor in 1715.

In 1752 Mr. Nathaniel Hicks owned a seine-boat called the *Ranger*. Nathaniel Hicks, senior, and Nathaniel Hicks, junior, signed new fishery regulations in 1767. One of these two gentlemen figures in the list of subscribers to Carew's 'Survey of Cornwall,' in 1769. Nathaniel Hicks was elected mayor in 1784, 1795 and 1803.

To sum up, the Hicks family has given a mayor to the borough of Saint Ives no fewer than twelve times, besides at least nine headwardens or porthrieves.

Parish Registers.

1666. Married Edward Hicks and Jane Boaz.
1671. Married John Hicks and Elizabeth the daughter of Mr Vernon Brown gen^t.
1680. Married George Hicks Junr and Margery Dyer.
1693. [Zennor] Married Robert Robins of Blisland gen^t and Anne daughter of John Hicks of St Ives gen^t.
1702. Married ffrancis Stephens jun^r and Marjery Hickes.
1716. Married Mr John Hicks mayor and Mrs Ann Hichens.
1728. Baptised Mary daughter of John and Elizabeth Hicks.
1737. [Zennor] Married George Hickes of St Ives and Sibella Thomas.

In our chapter on the old houses of Saint Ives will be found a description of the family mansion at the Digey, built by George Hicks, and referred to in the quotation at the beginning of this chapter.

Hickes bears: Argent, a tower triple-towered between three battle axes sable.

Lemal.

This family, whose name we find also sometimes spelt Lamalle, was of French origin, descended from Jean Lemal, who appears to have been one of the Huguenot refugees who came to Saint Ives about the year 1680 (see *ante* our chapter on the Old Houses of Saint Ives). As we have there shown, there had been from time immemorial a constant traffic between Saint Ives and France (especially Brittany), and a French colony in the town. In 1680 a number of poor French Protestants settled here, and were assisted out of the public money and by private charity (see the borough accounts for that year). It would seem that the Huguenots, or some of them, were lodged at the old Carn Glase House, which we have described in a former chapter, and which was known in 1699 by the name 'Ugnes House' (Huguenots' House?). In 1699 Ugnes House was let by John Hicks, of Saint Ives, gent, to Reginald Botterall, of the same town, sailor, for ninety-nine years, or for the lives of the said Reginald, Elizabeth his wife, and Christian their daughter, 'at the yearly rent of ffower shillings by quarterly payments And two good cod fishes yearly at the feast of St James theappostle dureing the sayd terme or twelve pence for the same and one good dry ling yearly for every yeare dureing the said terme at the feast of the Birth of our Lord God or twelve pence for the same.'

Christian Bottrell, daughter of Reginald, married Jean Lemal in 1709, and in 1712 Reginald Bottrell assigned to his son-in-law and daughter a ground room and a chamber over the same in Carn Glase House.

The following were the issue of Jean and Christian Lemal or Lamalle:

Elizabeth, born 1711; d. unm. 1754.
Christian, born 1714; m. Leonard Humphreys 1754.
Mary, born 1716; m. to Richard Bryant 1737.
Margeret, born 1719; m. to William Williams 1744.
Thamsyn, born 1721; d. unm. *circa* 1773.
Marcella [?], born 1723.
Agnes, born 1726; d. unm. 1743.
Ann, born 1728; m. to John Green; living in 1768.

Jean Lemal was drowned in Saint Ives Bay. His widow 'Kit,' or 'Kitty Lemal,' with her eight daughters, were known as 'the nine Lemals.' A game played by boys with marbles, in which the marbles are aimed to run through nine holes or arches carved in a plane of wood, was (and perhaps still is) called at Saint Ives 'Kit Lemal,' that name being given specially to the central arch of the board.

Christian, or 'Kitty' Lemal long occupied an important place in the inner social history of Saint Ives, nor is her name yet quite forgotten by the oldest generation of the townspeople. It is far from easy to discover fully the events which made her name a household word in her native town for generations. There are confused traditions of her having figured prominently in the electioneering contest of 1768, in which Dr. John Stevens, a native of Trowan, was the popular candidate. Stevens was one day haranguing the people near Carn Glase, when Kitty Lemal came out of her house with 'a stocking full of guineas,' which she poured into the hands of the favourite candidate, who was by her timely aid enabled to carry on the contest. John Knill, the mayor, however, took such proceedings as resulted in Stevens' defeat. The doctor afterwards went abroad and married the wealthy daughter of Bishop Ellis, of Bower Hall, Sussex. A certain Colan Pearse seems to have endeavoured to get some of Kitty Lemal's money in the same way as Dr. Stevens had done, but without success. All these events were embodied in a rhyme by the local bard of that day, and the song was for long afterwards sung about the town by the boys on the occasion of elections. (For a full history of the political matters in question, the reader is referred to our account of the election of 1768.)

Christian Lemal inherited her father's property, and was considered to be very wealthy. It is said of her that she used to lend money out on interest; that she measured it in a quart pot; also that she kept it in a blue stocking. She and her daughters were noted for their beauty.

In our chapter on the old houses of the district, we have described Kitty Lemal's room in the old house at Carn Glase. The surname Lemal became extinct in this parish on the death of Thamsyn or Thomasine Lemal about the year 1773.

There is at Saint Ives, in the possession of a descendant of this family, a beautiful bowl of beaten silver, elaborately chased, bearing the initials M.K. and E.L., the latter of which stand for 'Elizabeth Lemal.' The bowl is apparently of the seventeenth century.

Matthews.

This family settled at Saint Ives in the middle of the last century. An ancestor seems to have been a Walloon, who, about the year 1565, migrated from Brabant to Norwich, to escape the sword of the ferocious Alva, and introduced into East Anglia many important fruits and flowers previously strangers to English soil. In 1697 Peter Mathies or Mathews held lands in the parishes of Saint Julian and Saint Etheldred in the city of Norwich. Thomas Mathews, of Norwich, yeoman, settled *circa* 1730 at Truro, and in 1772 purchased the small estate of

Pithenlew near that town. His son, Thomas Mathews, married Mary Branwell, of Penzance, and came to Saint Ives in 1757. He acquired several parcels of land in the town of Saint Ives and the parish of Lelant, and his name appears on the list of subscribers to the edition of Carew's 'Survey of Cornwall' which was published in 1769. His signature, and various entries relating to him and his son Thomas, are to be found in the Borough Accounts. Since 1757 this family has been constantly connected with Saint Ives.

Nance.

This is one of the original Saint Ives families. The name, which is a misspelling of the Cornish word 'Nans,' a valley, indicates that the ancestor who first assumed this cognomen was a dweller in some inland dale of the neighbourhood.

'Luca de Nans,' of Lelant, paid one shilling towards the subsidy of 1327.

In 1523 Thomas Nanse had goods at Lelant valued at £6 by the year.

In 1573 'John Nanste' was a burgess of Saint Ives, and in 1578 contributed to the equipment of the trained band fitted out against the Spaniards.

In 1580 John Nans was again a burgess. In 1585 he purchased from Martin Trewinnard land in the manor of Connerton.

As we have shown in our chapter on the Elizabethan period, John Nance, gen^t, had command of a trained band, which he had raised in the parishes of Saint Ives, Lelant, Towednack and Zennor—a position which he held from 1590 to 1595, at least.

In 1592 we again find John Nanse a burgess.

From the commission of inquiry into the smuggling transactions at Saint Ives in 1598, we learn that John Nance, of Saint Ives, vintner, bought some of the contraband wine, and that John Nance, of Saint Ives, gen^t, born 1540, seized the wine on behalf of the Queen.

In 1604 we have in the borough accounts this entry relating to the aforesaid vintner: 'Paide to John Nance for wyne uppon M^r chiverton, 8*d.*'

In 1620 'John Nance molkin,' of Saint Ives, paid 1*d.* to the Royal Rate, while William Nance, who lived on 'The Iland,' contributed 2*d.*

In 1629 Richard and William Nance, of Saint Ives, were rated at 6*d.* for the county stock.

In 1631 William Nance was overseer of the poor for the

parish of Saint Ives, and he was holding some similar position in 1646, during the famine. In 1650 he was a churchwarden, and he signed the fishery regulations of that year.

In 1664 Richard Nance figures in a Subsidy Roll, in respect of his goods at Saint Ives.

After this we find no further mention of the family until the year 1768, when John Nance sends in an account for painting forty-six constables' poles for the election day.

The following are entries in the parish registers relating to this family:

1652. Baptised Mary daughter of Mr William Nance.
1657. Buried John Nance gent.
1667. Married John Nance junior and Elizabeth Stevens.
1701. Married Alien Nance and Welmott Thomas.
1711. Married Mr Thomas Kempthorne and Elizabeth Nance.
1729. Married Richard Eustis and Margery Nance.

Paulet.

This distinguished house, which was originally seated at Legh Powlet, in Devonshire, became associated with Saint Ives when, about the year 1580, William Paulet, Marquis of Winchester, became possessed of a moiety of the manor of Ludgvan Lese, by his marriage with one of the two daughters and co-heirs of Robert Willoughby, second Lord Broke.

In 1620 John, Lord Paulet, was one of the two members of Parliament for the Borough of Saint Ives.

The Dukedom of Bolton, which was afterwards conferred upon the head of the house, became extinct in 1794.

In the later volume of borough accounts are several references to visits paid by the lords of the manor of Ludgvan Lese to Saint Ives, and to other transactions with them. See *sub dato* 1640, 1641, as to correspondence between the Marquess of Winchester and the Corporation about the royal army. The Corporation paid annually to the lord 1*s*. 2*d*. for rent of the 'Town Land,' and 13*s*. 4*d*. for the 'Portfarm Rent.'

In 1700 Charles, Duke of Bolton, was personally sworn as Recorder of the Borough of Saint Ives, at the Town Hall, on the resignation of the Earl of Bath. His Grace was on that occasion treated with six bottles of sack at the inn kept by Richard Pollard.

In 1710 the sum of three shillings was 'spent on Mr Recorder when he came to St Ives.' Again, in 1713 there was a charge for 'treating Mr Recorder at Mr Anthony's.'

Arms of Paulet: 'Sable, three swords in pile, argent, points to the base, hilts or.' The seal with these bearings is affixed to several Saint Ives deeds of the last century in the author's possession, signed 'Bolton.'

Pawley.

This family was anciently seated at Gunwin in Lelant. In the subsidy of 1327 'Johannes Paly' is rated at 2*s.* at Saint Ives.

In the subsidy of *circa* 1520 we find the name of 'Edwardus Poulaye, miles,' whose lands in Lelant were valued at £2 10*s.* 0*d.* by the year. In the same roll 'Stephanus Pawlye' is named as possessing goods at Lelant of the annual value of £20.

In 1523 Stephen Pauly's goods at Lelant were worth £20 a year; and Radulph, the servant of Stephen Pawly, was in receipt of £1 annual wages.

The following are the other entries in the subsidy roll for Lelant parish:

1524. Stephen Pawly worth in goods £20. Richard, his servant, wages £1.
1536. Stephen Pawley, goods worth £10.
1541. Stephanus Pauly.
1544. Stevyn Powlle rated at 8*s.*
1546. Thomas Pollye, worth £4 a year.
1547. Stephen Pawllye, rated at 15*s.*
1548. Stephen Pawley, in goods, £10.
1549. Stephen Pawlye, rated at 10s.
1549. Stephen Pawlie, worth in goods £10 a year.
1557. Stephen Pawly " " £5 "
1558. Stephen Pawlye " " £8 "
1571. James Pawley, in lands.
1571. Stephen Pawley, in goods.
1585. James Pawley, in lands, £2.
1585. Stephen Pawley, in goods, £5.
1593. Stephin Pawlye, in goods, £3.
1597. Stephen Pawlie, in goods, £3.
1599. Stephen Pawlie, in goods, £3.
1624. Stephen Pawlie, in goods, £3.
1624. Stephen Pawly, in goods, £2.
1625. Stephen Pawly gen[t], in goods, £3.
1629. Stephen Pawly gen[t], in goods, £3.
1641. Margaret Pawleye, widow, in goods.
1641. Margery Pawly, widow, in goods.
1664. Hugh Pauley, gen[t], in goods.

Borough Accounts.

1671. 'P[d] M[r] Hugh Pawley & John Hicks for cost sewinge [suing] M[r] francis Hammond by consent for M[r] Couch his debt, £3 4*s.* 10*d.*

(Hugh Pawley held the office of Town Clerk of Saint Ives from 1675 till 1683.)

1704. Paid 'the Keywardens for M[r] Pawleys salte, £1.'

The Pawley family became extinct in the eldest male line on the death, in 1724, of Hugh Pawley of Gunwin, gentleman. Junior branches survived, as will be seen by our extracts from the parish registers, but the representation is now in the Thomas family.

In Lelant church, on the wall of the south aisle, are two monumental slabs to the memory of members of this family. The first is a black slate tablet, commemorating Stephen Pawley and his wife and children; it was set up in 1635, and bears a 'black-letter' inscription, under the effigies of Dame Pawley, her five sons and six daughters, together with the arms of Pawley—argent, a lion rampant sable; on a chief dancettee of the last, three mullets of the field—quartered. (See our account of Lelant church.)

The other tablet, also of black slate, but with an inscription in Latin letters, commemorates Hugh Pawley, gen[t], of Gunwin, who died in 1721, and bears his arms quarterly.

Parish Registers.

Lelant:

1718. Baptised Jane daughter of Hugh Pawley.

1724. M[r] Hugh Paly was buried the 20th September.

Saint Ives:

1735. Baptised Elizabeth the daughter of M[r] William and Elizabeth Pawley.

Lelant:

1762. M[r] William Pawley of this parish Roper and Mary Blackwell of Crowen Spinster, were married by license. Present, Charles Penberthy and Elizabeth Pawley.

1767. Married William Ninnis and Mary Pawley.

Payne.

This was one of the original families of the Saint Ives district. The name of Walter Payn occurs in the Subsidy Roll of 1327, in which he is rated at a shilling for Lelant parish. Late in the fifteenth century John Payne married the heiress of Polpear, a man who owned much landed property at Saint Ives.

In the subsidies of a later period the family of Payne figures largely. The following are particulars of these entries:

1520. John Payne, Lelant, lands valued at £1 6*s*. 8*d*. per annum.
1520. John Payne, St Ives, lands valued at £1 6*s*. 8*d*.
1520. John Payne, St Ives, goods valued at 20 marks.
1523. John Payn, St Ives, goods valued at £16.
1524. John Payne, St Ives, goods valued at 10*s*.
1536. John Payne, Penwith, rated at 10*s*. for goods.
1544. John Payne, St Ives, rated at 6*s*. 8*d*.

He was porthrieve of the town in 1549, and was executed for his participation in the Catholic revolt of that year. (See our chapter on the Reformation period.)

1593. George Paine, St Ives, rated at £2 for lands.
1597. George Payne gent, St Ives, rated at £3 for lands.
1599. — The like —
1624. Christiana Payne widow, St Ives, rated at £2 for lands.
1624. John Payne, St Ives, rated at £4 for goods.
1625. John Paine — The like —
1629. Christiana Payne, St Ives, widow, rated at £2 for lands.
1629. John Payne gent St Ives, rated at £3 for goods.
1641. John Paine gent — The like —
1664. [The name does not occur.]

Borough Accounts.

In 1573 Richard Payne was a capital burgess of Saint Ives.

In 1585 George Payne was a capital burgess, and in 1591 porthrieve. In 1592 occurs this entry: 'Itẽ paid George paine ffor his horse to cary campyon to Syr Walter rolie to peryn, 2*s*.' (This is the only mention of Sir Walter Raleigh in the borough records.) In 1597 George Payne contributed a small sum towards a town rate. In 1603 he was again a capital burgess, and *circa* 1605 he was a market-warden. In 1605 he was again chosen porthrieve.

In 1615 John Payne, gent., was a capital burgess; and in 1620 'Mistress Payne' paid 10*d*. to the royal rate, though the name of John Payne, who was again a capital burgess in that year, does not appear in the rate-list. In 1625 John Payne was still a capital burgess, and quay-warden in 1626. In 1627 we have this entry: 'Recd from Mr John Payne for the faults of his servants in shippinge their sayne boates before daye on the Sunday night, 2*s*. 6*d*.' John Payne was a capital burgess again in 1629 and 1631; in the latter year he was chosen porthrieve.

His son John Payne was a capital burgess in 1630, 1633 (and overseer), and 1638.

In 1639 John Payne was a capital burgess, and in 1641 the Corporation received from him an instalment of a debt of £15 8s. due to the town. In 1646 he was an alderman of the municipal borough of Saint Ives, and his signature as such appears in the accounts for that year. In 1642 he was chosen mayor.

In 1649 we find this entry in the town accounts: 'I: payd Mr John Payne for bords aboute the castle, 13s.'

In 1650 John and Christopher Payne were aldermen, and signed new fishery constitutions. So did John Paine, junior, and Edward Payne, who this year figure among the burgesses.

Edward Payne signed another fishery bye-law in 1655, and received 13s. in 1661 'ffor beere the coronation day.' In 1662 he was paid £2 'for Beere the Musketteers and Ringers had,' so that he seems to have been an innkeeper. He may have been a descendant of a younger branch of the ancient family of Payne; in any case, the above is the last entry of the surname in the borough accounts, and it does not appear in the parish registers.

The Paynes resided at Place Polmear, below Barnoon.

The arms, as represented on a choir-stall at Saint Ives church, are three pears, which, however, are probably intended to represent pines.

Praed.

The family of Praed, though of very ancient residence in the Saint Ives district, did not attain to public importance until the middle of the seventeenth century. Early in the eighteenth it died out in the male line, and became merged by the marriage of the heiress with the Mackworths. Trevetho in Lelant is the family seat.

The Lelant Subsidy List of 1597 commences with the name of William Praed, who was rated at £3 in respect of lands in that parish. In 1599 'Willūs Prade' was again rated for the same amount at Lelant.

In a Pes Finis of 13 Jac. I., Mich., Cornub., William Praed, gent., had of Thomas Tresaher, knight, and George Williams, gent., lands in Saint Ives, Lelant and Illogan.

In 1624 James Prade, gent., was rated at £6 for his lands in the parish of Lelant, and the same again in 1625 and 1629. He was also rated for lands in Lelant in the years 1641 (*bis*) and 1664, in which last year he is described as esquire. James Praed, Esq., whose estate was valued at £600 per annum, was one of the knights of the Royal Oak, an Order created in 1660.

Particulars of the Parliamentary history of this family will be found in another chapter. From the borough accounts we gather that the Praeds of Trevetho increased their influence on the restoration of the monarchy after the Civil War. They possessed the manor of Saint Ives and Treloyhan for several generations, and then sold it to Sir Christopher Hawkins.

Borough Accounts.

1595 (*circa*). 'Item pd mr Praed for drawing or aunswere in the Chauncerye, 4*s*. 8*d*.'

1597. 'It: pd to Wm Praed for fees ye fyrst curte: for declaracyons & a destringo to brynge pēt [Peters] in to ye curte, iijs. iiij*d*.'

1604. 'Paid Mr Praed for a replevyn when Mr Tregosse distrayned a quarter of beiffe from Trevascus, 6*d*.'

1604. 'Pd Mr Praed by commandmte of the Justics to a muster maister one capt Billings paymte 16*s*.'

In 1629, 1635 and 1636, James Praed was a capital burgess of Saint Ives; in 1635 he was mayor.

In 1659, as we learn from a Roll of the Manors belonging to Sir John Arundell of Lanhearne, James Prade, Esq., held land in 'Buswirgy' with two other persons, each of whom 'doth the office of a tything man when it cometh to his turn.'

In 1691 we find the entry: 'Spent on Esq: Praed at Sam Rice's house, 10*s*.;' and, in 1693, 'To Tauerne Expended fillinge the towne cupp with Sacke on Mr James Praed our Burges, 8*s*.'

About this time it began to be the custom of Squire Praed to make an annual gift of venison to the aldermen, who, on their part, were in the habit of making a present of money to the servants at Trevetho at Christmas time. In 1697 occur these entries: 'Given Mr Praed's man that brought the venison, 10*s*. Spent by consent at eating the venison, 10*s*.' And in 1698: 'Given Mr Praeds servant who brought venison to the Corporācon, 2*s*. 6*d*.' 'Spent att Mr Pollards drinking Mr Praeds health with the venson by Publique consent, 8*s*. 8*d*.' Another convivial memorandum is the following in 1699: 'Att Mr. Rices the same time in wine with Coll Praed, 3*s*.' In 1704 the mayor gave half-a-crown to Mr. Praed's man who brought the news of the victory of Blenheim.

1715. 'Expences on Will: Praed Mackworth Esqre, 18*s*.' (By this time the Praed family had become extinct in the male line, and was represented by Mackworth.)

1716. 'Expence on S[r] Humphrey Mackworth, M[r] Praed and others beere wyne punch etc., 10s.'

In 1717 died John Praed, M.P. for Saint Ives, the last male representative of Praed of Trevetho. His daughter and heir Martha was married to William Mackworth of Glamorganshire.

The arms of Praed are: 'Azure, 6 mullets argent. Crest: Out of a ducal coronet, an unicorn's head argent, maned and horned gold.'

In the list of subscribers to the new edition of Carew's 'Survey of Cornwall,' published in 1769, appears the name of 'Herbert Mackworth, Esq., Exon.'

In 1770 Humphrey Mackworth Praed was elected mayor of Saint Ives.

Parish Registers.

Lelant:

1709. Baptised William son of Rodger Praed.

1715. Baptised Roger son of Roger Praed.

1717. M[r] Praed was buried the 7th November.

1719. Homphry y[e] son of William Mackworth Praed Esq. Bap: y[e] 16th of febuary.

1721. Bockly y[e] son of William Mackworth Praed Esq. Bap: y[e] 2 day of december.

1789. Buried the Rev. Herbert Praed late Rector of Ludgvan.

Purefoy.

This family seems to have been an offshoot from the Purefoys of the Midlands, who were seated at Misterton in Leicestershire as early as 1277. They first appear in West Cornwall in the year 1598, when Thomas Purefoy, of Ludgvan, is mentioned by a witness at a Special Commission, whose proceedings we transcribe elsewhere.

In 1603, 1614, 1615, 1616, 1622, 1625, 1626, 1627, 1629, 1631, 1635, 1636 and 1638, Thomas Purefoy was a capital burgess of Saint Ives; in 1616 and 1627 he was chosen porthrieve. In 1620 he paid 1s. to the royal rate; and in the subsidy rolls of 1624, 1625 and 1629, he was rated at £4 in respect of his goods at Saint Ives. He was a quay-warden in 1625 and 1629, and a churchwarden in 1633.

He seems to have died soon after 1638, for in 1641 'Anna Purefoye widow' was rated to pay £3 to a subsidy, for her goods at Saint Ives.

In 1664 Thomas Purefoy, presumably a son of Thomas and Anna, was, together with Edward Stevens, rated for goods at Saint Ives. He was as closely associated with the municipal life of the town as his father, for in 1646 he was a burgess, and signed a new constitution anent the fishery. In the same year he farmed the profits of the quay. In 1651 he was chosen mayor. In 1653 he was an overseer of the poor. In 1655 he was an alderman; also in 1658, in which year, however, he was marked 'absent' from the meeting which elected Saint Aubyn and Ceely to Parliament. In 1678 either he or his son was chosen mayor.

In 1687 Thomas Purefoy, junior, probably son of the above, farmed the quay tolls. He was agent to Edward Nosworthy, sometime M.P. for Saint Ives.

Parish Registers.

1652. Baptised Joan daughter of Thomas Purefoy gent:
1654. Bapt[d] Jane d. of John Purefoy.
1654. Bapt[d] John son of John Purefoy.
1657. Bapt[d] Margaret d. of Thomas Purefoy.
1657. Baptd: Grenville s. of John Purefoy.
1660. Baptd. Michael s. of Thomas Purefoy.
1663. Baptd. George s. of Thomas Purefoy.
1671. Married John Paddon of Sinnoth to Mary d. of M[r] Thomas Purefoy.
1680. Married Thomas Purefoy gent. & Deborah Morrish.
1681. Baptd. Thomas s. of Thomas Purefoy gen[t]
1683. Baptd. Mary d. of Thomas Purefoy.
1685. Baptd. Richard s. of Thomas Purefoy.
1689. Baptd. Michael s. of Thomas Purefoy.
1691. Baptd. William s. of Thomas Purefoy.
1691. Baptd. Frances d. of George Purefoy.
1692. Baptd. John s. of Thomas Purefoy.
1695. Baptd. Anne d. of Thomas Purefoy.
1697. Baptd. Anne d. of Thomas Purefoy.
1700. Married Jeronimo Carn and Avis Purefoy.
1700. Baptd. Joan d. of George Purefoy.
1702. Baptd. Matilda d. of George Purefoy.
1703. Baptd. Elizabeth d. of Thomas Purefoy.
1707. Married Thomas Purefoy and Mary Pearse.
1709. Baptd. John s. of Thomas Purefoy gent:
1716. Baptd. Ann d. of Richard Purefoy.
1717. Baptd. Thomas s. of John Purefoy gent. & Ann his wife.
1719. Baptd. John s. of John & Ann Purefoy.
1721. Baptd. Richard s. of John & Ann Purefoy.
1723. Baptd. William s. of John & Ann Purefoy.
1727. Baptd. George s. of John & Ann Purefoy.
1735. Baptd. John s. of John & Mary Purefoy.

1737. Baptd. John s. of John & Mary Purefoy.
1740. Married James Eddy & Deborah Purefoy.
1740. Baptised Mary d. of John & Mary Purefoy.
1743. Baptd. Richard and William twin sons of John & Mary Purefoy.
1763. [John Purefoy witnessed a marriage.]
1765. Married William Purefoy and Ann Watty.

The descendants of this last marriage have long since removed from Cornwall; but the local pronunciation of the family name was until recent times commemorated by a piece of land at Chy-an-chy, now built over, which was known as 'Purfle's Plot.'

In 1786 there was a John Purefoy, mariner, living at Saint Ives.

The arms of Purefoy of Caldecote, Warwickshire, confirmed by Camden, Clarenceux, are: Sable: six armed hands in pairs embracing, two and one, argent. Crest: In a dexter gauntlet argent, a broken tilting-spear or. The motto of a younger branch is 'En bonne foy.'

Rosewall.

Few Cornish families can vie with this one in point of antiquity. Though apparently never entitled to bear arms, the Rosewalls for countless generations occupied an ancient homestead called 'Rosewall,' on the eastern slope of Rosewall Hill, in the parish of Towednack.

The Subsidy Roll of 1327 shows the name of John de Ryswal and Noal de Ryswal of Towednack, who paid 2*s*. each towards the royal aid.

In the roll of *circa* 1520 we find the name of Stephanus Roswal, having lands in Towednack of the annual value of 10*s*. Again in 1523 he is rated—this time at 10 marks; and the same in 1524. In the Penwith Subsidy of 1536, 'Stephyn Rosewarn' [*lege* 'Rosewall'] is rated at 10 marks.

In 1523 and 1524 Pascacius (Pasco) Roswall had goods value £2 at Saint Ives.

In 1546 'John Rossewall' was rated at £6 for his lands in 'Tewynecke.'

In 1585 Johannes Roswall was rated at £6, but in 1593 at £3, for goods at Towednack, and again at £3 in 1597.

In 1629 Georgius Roswarne ['Rosewall'] paid £4 to the subsidy for his goods at Towednack.

In 1641 'Willmūs Russell' (*i.e.*, 'Rosewall') was rated for goods, and Warne Roswall for lands, in Towednack parish.

In 1664 'Margrett Russell widow' was rated for lands in the same parish.

Borough Accounts.

In 1573 Richard Rossewall was a capital burgess; in 1578 he paid 4*d.* to a town rate.

Circa 1590 Thomas Roswall paid 2*d.* to a town rate.

In 1620 Thomas Roswall, who resided in Westren Street, paid 3*d.* to a royal rate levied in Saint Ives. In the same list with the last name occur those of Nicholas Roswall, living on 'The Lande,' and George Roswall.

In 1636 James Rosewall was an overseer of the poor, and in 1638 he was a sidesman.

The only entry in the later volume of accounts of persons of this name is to the effect that Margery Roswall was paid 6*s.* for going to Lanceston Assizes as a witness against one Elizabeth Grenfield in 1664.

In another chapter will be found a full transcript of the proceedings connected with the tithe dispute between Andrew Rosewall and the Vicar of Towednack in 1680.

Parish Registers.

Saint Ives:

1661. Married Andrew Rosewall & Mary Steuens.
1661. (Novr 18.) Married Regnald Botterall and Christian Rosewall.
1661. Baptised Chesten daughter of Andrew Rosewall.
1663. Married George Rosewall & Lidia Hollman.
1666. Buried Thomas son of Tiberias Rosewall.
1675. Married Hugh Rosemenewas and Mary Rosewall.

Towednack:

1676. Baptised Anne d. of Andrew Rosewall.
1681. Married Thomas Major and Chesten Rosewall.
1689. Married Michael Curnow and Margery Rosewall.

Saint Ives:

1691. Baptised Margaret d. of Thomas Rosewall.

Towednack:

1693. Married Robert Curnow and Wilmot Rosewall.

Saint Ives:

1696. Married John Mathews and Anne Rosewall.
1706. Married Henry Major and Elizabeth Rosewall.
1707. Married Paul Stevens *alias* Gonew and Elizabeth Rosewall.
1708. Married Thomas Rosewall and Mary Ninnes.
1709. Baptd. Mary d. of Thomas Rosewall.
1713. Married Wm Harry of Penzance & Mary Rosewall.
1723. Married Robert Simons & Margaret Rosewall.
1723. Married James Rosewall & Sibella Robins.

Towednack :

1744. Married John Couch and Zenobia Rosewall.

Saint Ives :

1746. Married Thomas Rosewall & Elizabeth Rosewall.

1752. Married William Kitto and Earthy Rosewall.

1754. Baptised Thomas s. of Thomas & Elizabeth Rosewall.

1775. Married William Stephens mariner & Mary Rosewall spinster.

Towednack :

1778. Buried Elisabeth Rosewall.

1784. Baptised William son of William and Margaret Rosewall.

1784. Buried Mary daughter of Thomas and Mary Rosewall. The house was rebuilt about the year 1888.

In the last century the fee of Rosewall was made over to the Praeds; but the old homestead remained in the occupation of the Rosewalls until the termination of the last 'life' in the year 1883. ~~The house~~ was rebuilt about the year 1888.

Sise.

This merchant family, long extinct, occupied an important position in the town of Saint Ives, and were at the height of their wealth and influence in the reign of James I. and Charles I. During the Civil War they seem to have espoused the cause of the Parliament, and the then head of the family was apparently an ardent Puritan.

The first mention of the family in our public archives occurs in the Subsidy Roll of *circa* 1520, wherein John Syse has his lands in Saint Ives valued at 3s. 2d. by the year. In 1523 his goods were valued at £3. In 1524 'Johēs Seise' was similarly rated.

In 1546 Thomas Seyse, of Saint Ives, had his lands valued at £4 a year, while those of John Syesse were stated to be worth £2.

In 1624 Thomas Syse's Saint Ives goods were valued at £3, and in 1625 and 1629 at the same sum.

In the year 1641 we meet with the name of Ephraim Sise, of whom we have many memorials remaining. In our chapters on the church and old houses of Saint Ives respectively, will be found a description of the sepulchral monument and the family residence of the Sises, on both of which the name or initials of Ephraim Sise appear. He would seem to have professed the Puritan religion and politics, which were probably adopted by his father. In 1641 his goods at Saint Ives were valued at £3 per annum.

In 1664 Thomas Syse appears in the subsidy rate-list.

Borough Accounts.

In 1573 Thomas Syes was a capital burgess of Saint Ives, and contributed to a local rate *circa* 1580.

In 1578 John Sysse contributed towards a local rate, and again *circa* 1590.

In 1592 James Syse was a burgess.

In 1596 Lawrens Sysse was a burgess, and James Sysse a capital burgess. In 1597 James Syse paid towards a local rate; *circa* 1605 James Syes was a capital burgess and quay-warden.

About the year 1616 Thomas Syes was a capital burgess, and in 1620 he paid 6d. towards the royal rate; his residence was on the Island. Elizabeth Sies, residing in Street-an-Poll, paid 1d. towards the same rate. Thomas Syse was again a capital burgess in 1629, 1631 (and overseer), 1635, 1636 (and portrieve), 1637 (and quay-warden) and 1638.

Ephraim Syse was a burgess in 1631, and a capital burgess in 1638.

In 1639 we find this entry: 'I: to Ephraim Syse for quarter beames and a bord for ye Markethouse, 11s.'

In 1645 Ephraim Sise, merchant, was elected mayor of Saint Ives, and in the following year he was still an alderman of the borough.

In 1659 occurs the item: 'Payd Tho: Syse constable to putt Thomas Bettye to the howse of correction, £1 10s. 0d.' In 1664 Thomas Sise farmed the market dues, and in the following year those of the quay were let to 'Thomas Sise merchant.' In 1666 Thomas Sise was chosen mayor.

Parish Registers.

1657. Married Mr Thomas Sise and Mrs Eliz: ffleming.
1659. Baptised Ann daughter of Mr Thomas Sise.
1660. Baptised Ephraim son of Mr Thomas Sise.
1662. Bapt^{d} Elizabeth d. of Mr Thomas Sise.
1663. Bapt^{d} Alice d. of Mr Thomas Sise.
1663. Bapt^{d} Blanch d. of Mr Thomas Sise.
1666. Bapt^{d} Catherine d. of Mr Thomas Sise.
1669. Buried John s. of Mr Thomas Sise.
1671. Bapt. John son [*sic*] of Mr Thomas Sise.

Stephens.

The whole of this now numerous clan is said to be descended from an Irish farmer (probably from Dungarvan) who, about the year 1470, was shipwrecked (so says tradition) at Wicka Pool in the parish of Zennor. He was bringing over a cargo of cattle, with two other men named Quick and Mitchell. The Quicks and Mitchells, who are also now very numerous about Saint Ives, aver that Stephens was only a subordinate to their own ancestors. Their ancestors, they say, owned the cattle, and Stephens was the drover. These adventurers are also credited with having introduced the seine-fishery; and to this day Saint Ives fishermen call the netting of which the seans are made, 'Dungarvan.' These families first settled in the villages and hamlets of the parishes of Zennor and Towednack, where many of their descendants still remain. Their chief colonies were the farm-hamlets of 'Tregarthen and Bregia, Trevalgen and Trevegia.' Members of these various branches of the Stephens or Stevens family eventually settled at Saint Ives. A Stevens of Tregarthen became the ancestor of Stephens of Tregenna Castle; while a Stevens of Bregia was ancestor to the second house, who spell the name 'Stevens.' The Stevens of Trevalgen were ancestors to John à Court, *alias* John Stevens, of Trevalgen, of whom we have written in a former chapter.

The Stevens, or Stephens, of Tregarthen, claimed direct descent from John Stephyn, the shipwrecked Irishman, and to be considered chiefs of the clan. However, they were, on first settling at Saint Ives, earning a living by the trade of bakers, at which time their home was the present Victory inn, a quaint old tenement at the corner of the Digey and Fore Street. By dint of industry and economy they soon acquired importance in the borough. Thomas Steven, or Stevens, was elected the last portrieve of Saint Ives, 1638, and was the second mayor, in 1640. John Stevens was fined for refusing to attend the coronation of James I. The original receipt for the fine reads as follows:

'xxii° die Octobris
'Año Domi 1603.

'Received of John Stephens of the burrough of St. Ives in the Hundred of Penwith within the county of Cornwall Gent. for his composition with his Maies Commissioners for his not appearing at the coronation of our said Souvraigne Lord the King, for to receive the Order of Knighthood according to His Highness proclaymasion in that behalfe, the sum of sixteen pounds. I saye received xvjli

'Fra. Godolphin; Coll.'

The substance of the Stephenses increasing still more, it was darkly whispered that they had discovered beneath their house a crock of gold. They next built the Manor House in Green Court, to be the 'dower house,' or residence for the elderly spinsters of the family, at the commencement of the eighteenth century. This interesting old building is described in our chapter on the old houses of the town. About the year 1683 this branch revived the form Stephens, which spelling has since continued to mark the senior house of the clan, all others remaining Stevens.

It would be impossible for us to give even a sketch of the history of all the branches of this extended family, or rather, clan; we must perforce content ourselves with briefly noticing the gradual rise of its most important branch, that which was first known as Stevens of Tregarthen, but, for several generations past, as Stephens of Tregenna.

Circa 1520 Jenkyn Stephyn had goods at Saint Ives valued at £4 by the year; and in 1523 and 1524 John Stephyn (evidently the same person as Jenkyn Stephyn) had goods there valued at £6.

In 1548 John Stephyn had goods at Saint Ives worth £10 a year.

In 1571 Thomas Styphens of Saint Ives was reported to be worth in goods £1 by the year.

In 1593 John Stephin had goods at Saint Ives of the annual value of £4; and in 1597 £6 was given as their worth. In 1599 John Steevins' was worth £6 in goods at Saint Ives; and in 1624, in which year he was one of the assessors of the subsidy, we find him possessed of lands in that parish of the yearly value of £8. The following year he was again assessed at £7 for goods; and in 1629 their value had risen to £8, while 'John Stephens' has the title 'generosus' affixed to his name in the subsidy roll. In 1603 he was fined for refusing the honour of knighthood, as we have already seen.

In 1641 'Thomas Stephens, Mayor,' is reported to be worth £4, and Henry Stephens £3, in goods at Saint Ives.

In the subsidy list of 1664 the names of Edward, Thomas, and Francis Steephens occur among those of persons taxed at Saint Ives.

The borough accounts show clearly the gradual rise of this family in wealth and importance. The Stephenses seem to have lent money on interest, both to the borough and to private persons, as will be seen from three out of the following extracts:

1573. Thomas Stephin, Capital Burgess.
'Rec: of thomas stevin & thoms hickes for there full and laste paiment of ye benevolens to wards the churche yearde, 6*s*. 6*d*.'

1578. John Stevin paid towards another local rate.

1586. John Steuen, Churchwarden.

1590. John Steeven, Head Warden.
John Steuen paid 6*d*. to a local rate.
Thomas Stevyns paid 3*s*. 4*d*. to a local rate.

1591. John Steeven, Quay Warden.

1592. John Steuens, Capital Burgess.

1595. 'Itē paid the 2 constables and John steuens in goynge to Truro, for vewinge the corne, 6*s*.'

1596. John Stevin, Capital Burgess.

1597. John Stephen paid 2*s*. to a local rate.
'Item Recd of John Stephen wch he collected towrds the Repayringe of the churchewindowes, 21*s*.'

1602. John Steven, Capital Burgess.

1603. John Steven, Capital Burgess.

1604. 'paide John stevins for the lone of his money, £2.'

1605. John Stephen, Capital Burgess.
'Item pd Jo: Steven for his charges to the assizes, £1.'
'Pd Jo: Stephen for the setting forth of the Irland soldiers, £1 4*s*. 0*d*.'
'Paymts Pd Jo: Stephen for counsell taken in the graunte of the m̄kett house, 5*s*.'

1608. 'Note also ther was charged by Bande wherin Jo: cokyns & Richarde candrowe were bounde to Jo: Steven aboute Midsommer laste 1607, 24*li*. beinge for mr Masters dett more due to Rič candrowe for the loste of cattall, taken by Jo: Steven ꝑ execucōn for masters dett beinge his suertye, 9*li*.'

1613. John Stevens, Capital Burgess.

1615. John Stevens, Capital Burgess.
Thomas Stephen, Burgess.

1619. John Steuen, Capital Burgess.

1620. Royal rate. Payments *inter alios*:
Thomas Steven 5*d*.
John Steven Junr 2*d*.
Mr Jo: Stephen, Westren Streete, 1*s*. 8*d*.

1622. 'Pd also unto John Stephen for monye borowed for the ꝑishes use to the ꝓpose aforesaide £2 19*s*. 6*d*.'

1625. It appears that John Stephens refused the office of Porthrieve this year, whereupon the Burgesses imposed a penalty for such a refusal in future.

1629. Thomas Stephen, Burgess, keeps the keys of the archive-chest.
1630. Thomas Stephen, Burgess.
1631. Thomas Stephen, Capital Burgess.
1633. Henry Stevens, Overseer of the Poor.
1634. Henry Steephen, Sideman.
Thomas Stevens, Overseer of the poor.
John the son of Henry Stephens was Lord of the Summer Games this year.
1635. Mr Thomas Stevens, Capital Burgess.
1638. Thomas Stevens, Capital Burgess.
Thomas Stevens, Porthrieve. (The last who held this ancient dignity at Saint Ives.)
1639. Henry Stevens, Quay Warden.
1640. Mr Thomas Stevens, Mayor. (The second who held this office, and the first who was elected to it—Mr Hext having been appointed by the King.)
1646. Thomas Stevens and Henry Stevens, Aldermen, signed new fishery constitutions.
1650. Thomas Stevens and Thomas Stevens Junior signed new fishery constitutions.
1653. 'I: paid Thomas Stevens for apeece of Timber, 5*s*.'
1655. Thomas Stevens, Burgess, signed fishing bye-laws.
1656. 'I: payd Thomas Steuens for Beniamin Johns wages hee beinge clerke £1 10*s*. 0*d*.'
1658. Edward Stevens farmed the quay tolls.
'I: payd Edward Steuens for carying of Ruble from ye Keye, 1*s*.'
1670. 'Recd from Mr Thomas Steephens £10; ꝑ interest 12*s*.; in the hole £10 12*s*. 0*d*.'
1677. John Stevens, Alderman.
1679. Mr Francis Stevens, Overseer of the Poor.
1681. John Stevens, Overseer of the Poor.
1683. John Stevens, Mayor.
1685. Thomas Stephens and John Stevens, Aldermen.
1687. John Stevens, Mayor.
Thomas Stephens, Alderman.
1690. The Corporation paid 5*s*. 6*d*. to Mr John Stevens for a tar-barrel and cider, to celebrate King William's victory in Ireland.
1691. 'pd Mr Hockyn for a new post put by Mr Stevens doore 5*s*.'
John Stevens farmed the market tolls.
1692. John Stevens, Mayor.
1693. Thomas Stephens, Overseer of the Poor.

1693. 'Spent when Mr John Stephens paid Mr Hawkins clerke the five pounds wch was agreed to be paid him, 1s.

1698. John Stevens, Mayor.

1699. 'Pd to Mr John Stevens for 20lbs of powder and three pennard of paper, 15s. 3*d*.'

'Pd to Mr John Stevens for one locke for the stockes, 6*d*.'

1702. 'pd Mr Stevens for boards & stuf for the fayre, 3s.'

'pd Mr Stevens money hee disbursed for the Kay, £7 6s. 3*d*.'

1704. 'To powder from Mr John Stephens, 8th March 1703 & 14th July 1704, for the rejoyceing on the victory obtained by the Duke of Marleburrough at the battle of Bleinhieim, £2 13s. 8*d*.'

1705. 'To Mr Tho: Stephens for two quarters rates, 11s.'

1707. 'pd Mr John Stevens for repayreing the ladder of the Kay, £1 15s. 0*d*.'

1710. John Stevens, Alderman.

1711. John Stephens of Saint Ives, merchant, aged 60, and John Stevens of Saint Ives, merchant, aged 40, gave evidence before the Commission which held an enquiry into the fish-tithe dispute.

1712. John Stevens, Alderman.

1713. '12 deals of M^r ffrancis Stephens' were paid for by the Corporation.

'Mr John Stephens gave pole and Chaire' for the new cucking-stool.

'August, King George proclaimed powder of Mr Stephens, 14s.'

1715. Tolls of the market and quay set to Thomas Stephens Junior.

1716. John Stevens, Alderman.

1726. Francis Stephens junior signed an account in the Town Book.

1727. John Stevens, Mayor.

John Stevens junior, signed an account.

1742. John Stephens gent Mayor.

John Stephens junior signed an account.

1743. John Stevens, Mayor.

1744. Francis Stevens, Mayor.

John Stevens signed an account.

1750. Edward Stephens, Mayor.

1751. John Stephens, Mayor.

1752. John Stevens, Mayor.

Mr. John Stephens owned the ***Mayflower***, the ***Southamp-***

ton, and the *Pilchard*, seine-boats. Mr. Edward Stephens owned the *Lyon* and the *Neptune*, and Mrs. Elizabeth Stephens the *Tommy*.

1753. John Stephens, Mayor.
1754. Edward Stephens, Mayor.
1760. John Stevens, Mayor.
John Stevens junior and Thomas Mathews farmed the quay-dues.
1761. Samuel Stephens, Mayor.
1762. John Stevens, Mayor.
John Stevens junior, Town Clerk.
1763. Samuel Stephens, Mayor.
1764. John Stevens, Mayor.
1765. Samuel Stephens, Mayor.
1767. John Stevens, Edward Stevens and William Stephens, Aldermen.
1769. John Stevens, Mayor.
[Edward and William Stevens, and Miss Sarah Stephens, of Saint Ives, subscribed to the new edition of Carew's 'Survey,' published this year.]
1771. John Stevens, Mayor.
1773. Edward Stevens, Mayor.
1776. William Stephens, Mayor.
William Stevens of Trevalgen, Constable.
1777. John Stevens, Mayor.
1780. John Stevens, notary, signed an account.
1783. William Stephens, Mayor.
1786. John Stevens junior, Mayor.
1788. John Stevens junior, Mayor.
1789. Francis Stephens, Mayor.
1796. John Stevens, Mayor.
1804. John Stevens, Mayor.
1806. John Stevens, Town Clerk.
1816. Augustus Stephens, Mayor
1828. Augustus Stephens, Mayor.

Having thus traced the public history of this family through the Borough Accounts, we will now give a selection of extracts from the Parish Registers relating to the same branch of the Stevens clan:

1651. Bapt[d] Ann d. of John Stevens.
1654. Buried M[r] Thomas Steuens elder.
1654. Buried M[rs] Jane Steuens widdowe.

1657. Bapt[d] Willmett d. of Thomas Stephens alias Gonew.
1665. Bapt[d] Thomas s. of John Stephens alias Gonew.
1665. Married ffrancis Stevens alias Gonew and Alse Coga.
1665. Bapt[d] John s. of M[r] ffrancis Steuens.
1666. Buried John Steuens the yonger.
1666. Married M[r] Edward Steuens and Grace d. of W[m] Diggens gen[t].
1667. Bapt[d] Prudence d. of M[r] Edward Stevens.
1669. Buried Uncle John Stevens.
1669. Bapt[d] Honor d. of M[r] Edward Stevens.
1670. Buried Honor d. of M[r] Edward Stevens.
1670. Buried Grace wife of M[r] Edward Stevens.
1674. Bapt[d] Susanna d. of M[r] Francis Stevens.
1688. Married M[r] John Stephens junior and Susanna Dyer.
1689. Bapt[d] Elizabeth d. of M[r] John Stephens.
1692. Bapt[d] John s. of M[r] John Stephens junior.
1696. Bapt[d] Jane d. of M[r] John Stevens.
1699. Bapt[d] Mary d. of John Stevens jun[r] merchant.
1717. Bapt[d] John s. of M[r] John Stephens jun[r] & Mary his wife.
1719. Bapt[d] Sarah d. of M[r] John Stephens & Mary his wife.
1721. Bapt[d] John s. of M[r] John Stephens jun[r] & Mary his wife.
1722. Bapt[d] Susanna d. of M[r] John Stephens jun[r] & Mary his wife.
1723. Married M[r] Francis Ley & M[rs] Jane Stephens.
1724. Bapt[d] Thomas and Frances s. & d. of M[r] John Stephens jun[r] merchant & Mary his wife.
1726. Bapt[d] Susanna d. of M[r] John Stephens jun[r] merchant and Mary his wife.
1728. Bapt[d] Samuel s. of M[r] Jnō & Mary Stephens jun[r].
1728. Bapt[d] Elizabeth d. of M[r] Francis & Elizabeth Stephens.
1728. Bapt[d] Thomas s. of M[r] John Stephens junior & Mary his wife.
1730. Bapt[d] Francis s. of M[r] John Stephens junior & Mary his wife.
1730. Bapt[d] Francis s. of M[r] Francis Stephens and Elizabeth his wife.
1731. Bapt[d] Mary d. of M[r] Francis & Elizabeth Stevens att meet: house.
1731. Bapt[d] Elizabeth d. of M[r] John & Mary Stephens jun[r] at meeting house.
1735. Bapt[d] Thomas s. of M[r] Francis & Elizabeth Stephens att the meeting.
1739. Bapt[d] William s. of M[r] Francis & Elizabeth Stevens at meeting.
1740. Bapt[d] John s. of M[r] Francis & Elizabeth Stephens (at the meeting).

1775. Buried Mr Edward Stephens gent.

1775. Buried Susanna wife of Mr Francis Stephens.

1803. John Augustus the son of Samuel and Betty Stephens was baptised the 29 Novr 1803.

1806. Francis Hearle the son of Samuel and Betty Stephens was baptised 1806, November 29.

1810. Henry Lewis the son of Samuel and Betty Stephens was baptised 1810, November 29.

1810. Buried Elizabeth wife of Edward Stephens, aged 86 years.

From the records relating to the Stephens family we deduce the following pedigree:

John Stephyn of Dungarvan came to West Cornwall *circa* 1470, and died *post* 1524.

John Stephyn, son of the above; living in 1548.

Thomas Stephyns, son of the last-named; living 1571—1590.

John Stephin, son of the last-named; living 1578—1629.

Thomas Stephyns, son of the last named. Died 1654.

ffrancis Stevens (alias Gonew) M. in 1665 Alse Cogar.

John Stephens, son of the last-named; b. 1665. M. in 1688 Susanna Dyer, with issue Elizabeth, John (of whom presently), & Jane.

John Stephens or Stevens (called 'the Old Greek'), born 1692, died 1764. Married in 1716 Mary, eldest daughter of Samuel Phillips esq. of Pendrea in Cornwall, and had the following issue:

John, born 1717; died in infancy.
Sarah, b. 1719.
John, b. 1721. Went to Holland as a merchant for his father.
Susannah, b. 1722; died in infancy.
Frances, b. 1723.
Thomas, b. 1724; died in infancy.
Susannah, b. 1726.
Samuel, b. 1728, of whom presently.
Thomas, b. 1728.
Francis, b. 1730.
Elizabeth, b. 1731.

Hals says, 'John Stephens was very successful in his various concerns of merchandise and fisheries, as he added largely to his landed property in the neighbourhood of St Ives, and in the parishes of Newlyn and St Enoder. He acted for many years as the agent of the Earl of Buckinghamshire in managing the political concerns of the town; but at last broke off the connection by getting his son Samuel Stephens returned on a vacancy.'

To this account we are able to add the following facts: John Stephens was locally known as 'the old Greek with his calves in front,' from his crooked limbs and foreign trading. He made voyages to Italy in his own ships with pilchards for Lent. The 'Old Greek' had two brothers, both fine, handsome young men, and both military officers. One was killed in active service and the other in a duel, both dying without issue. John was the 'ugly duckling' of the family, and was harshly treated by his father, yet he came into possession of the property.

Samuel Stephens, born 1728, son of the above, married (says Hals) Anne Seaborn of Bristol, and '(his eldest brother having died) on the decease of his father in 1764, disposed of everything connected with the trade and fishery of this place, and having abandoned the Presbyterians, to which sect all his family and relations had been strongly attached, he went so far as to pull down the meeting-house, and to withdraw his support from its minister; proceedings well remembered to his disadvantage subsequently. About 1774 Mr Stephens commenced building his new house at Tregenna, and in that year he unsuccessfully contested the borough. He died March 1794.' His children were:

John, rector of Ludgvan.

Samuel, of whom presently.

Augustus, collector of Customs at Saint Ives.

All three died in the year 1834.

Samuel Stephens, Esq., of Tregenna Castle, son of Samuel and Anne, was a student of Trinity College, Cambridge. He became member of Parliament for Saint Ives, justice of the peace, barrister-at-law, and high sheriff of Cornwall in 1805. On November 29, 1796, he married Betty, only child and heiress of Captain Samuel Wallis, R.N., of Tremaine, Cornwall (the celebrated circumnavigator who was the precursor of Captain Cook), by his wife Betty, daughter and heiress of John Hearle, Esq., of Penryn, Cornwall. Much property was brought into the Stephens' family through this match. A portrait of Betty Wallis formerly hung over the staircase at Tregenna, and one of 'the Old Greek' over the door in the library.

The issue of Samuel and Betty Stephens were:

John Augustus, b. 1803; d.s.p. 1888.

Francis Hearle, b. 1806; Major 1st Royal Dragoons; d.s.p. 1852.

Henry Lewis, b. 1810; d. 1867.

Somuel Wallis, died at Toulouse in 1835.

Ferdinand Thomas, Rector of St. Mawgan; d.s.p.

Sarah Maria, m. to the Rev. Charles William Davy, with issue two daughters, both married into the Richardson family, in whom the representation now rests.

The will of Samuel Stephens, Esq., provided that he was to be succeeded in his estates in West Cornwall by his sons Henry, Francis, and John, in that order. John left the castle immediately after hearing the will read, and never again set foot west of Truro. In the course of time the whole property devolved upon John, as the surviving son, but he sold the estate of Tregenna and the lands in Zennor, retaining no part of his father's possessions except Killigrew.

During the lifetime of Henry Lewis Stephens, Esq., of Tregenna, the fortunes of this family reached their highest point. This gentleman's income amounted to £20,000 a year, derived principally from real estate in Cornwall, Hampshire, etc. Tregenna Castle had, when first built, only twelve bedrooms; to these Henry Stephens added ten more.

Mr. John Augustus Stephens died at his London house, 29, Baker Street, Portman Square, on April 21, 1888, aged 84 years. He was a fine, robust man, and sometimes engaged in wrestling and boxing with the Treloyhan men. He was first articled to a Devonport solicitor, and then spent five years at Malta. He never married, and was the last lineal descendant of this house. Thus ended a family which had been gradually raised, by successive generations of thrift, enterprise and wealthy marriages, to a position of the highest importance in the county.

The following are a few extracts from an account-book in the handwriting of Samuel Stephens, of Tregenna, 1798-1812:

1799, Novr 13. 'Pd. the Fine for not serving in the supplementary Militia for Middlesex, £10 10*s*. 0*d*.'

1799, Decr 7. 'P^d Messrs. Riley and Fowler (Undertakers) their Bill for the Funeral of little Mary Stephens, £7 14*s*. 0*d*.'

1800, June 28. 'Rec^d of Mrs Wallis, due April 1st last, £25.'

1800, June 6. 'P^d Mr W. Medlycott for Sorrel Mare, £17 17*s*. 0*d*.'

1800, Sept. 20. 'P^d Swann for Armorial Tax, 10*s*. 6*d*.'

1803, March 2^d. 'P^d Geo. Arden (Exeter) for cloth for blue Coat, £2 7*s*. 0*d*.'

1803, March 4. 'P^d for Hay & Corn at ye Seven Stars Exeter sundry times, ostler and Gates, 7*s*. 6*d*.'

1803, March 21. 'Sexton at Teingrave church, 1*s*. 6*d*.'

1803, Novr 29. 'P^d Parson Arthur for baptising John Augustus, 10*s*. 6*d*.'
1803, Novr 29. 'P^d the nurse, £1 6*s*. 0*d*.'
1805, Feby 2. 'Journey from Tregenna to Town, £48 12*s*. 6d.'
1805, Nov. 25. 'Volunteer Band [St Ives,] £1 1*s*. 0*d*.'
1805, Dec. 10. 'St Ives Subscription (Nelson) £2 2*s*. 0*d*.'
1805, Dec. 10. 'Charities there, £1 11*s*. 6d.'
1805, Dec. 31. 'Female Club (St Ives), £5 5*s*. 0*d*.'
1806, Feby. 13. 'Charity to ye widows &c of ye persons drowned in St Ives Bay, £3 3*s*. 0*d*.'
1806, March 8. 'P^d for ye mare's keep at Tattersall's, 3*s*. 6*d*.'
1806, Oct. 16. 'P^d Property Tax for Tregenna, £2 12*s*. 0*d*.'
1807, May 30. 'P^d House acct. at Tregenna Castle, £12 11*s*. 3½*d*.'
1807, June 15. 'P^d Wedgewood & Co their bills, £7 4*s*. 10*d*.'
1807, June 25. 'Powder &c & Hair Dresser, 5*s*.'
1807, July 11. 'P^d all arrears & demands to ye Society of Lincolns Inn on withdrawing my name, £55 15*s*. 4*d*.'
1807, July 20. 'Journey from London to Tregenna Castle, £49 13*s*. 9*d*.'
'Carriage of Trunk from London to Truro, £1 17*s*. 9*d*.'
'Servants Fees and Ringers, £5 5*s*. 0*d*.'
'Horse shoeing on ye road & at Scorrier, 14*s*. 8*d*.'
" Sept. 26. 'Present to ye old Lady at Bath, £25.'
1808, Feb. 20. Our posting to London & road expenses, £29 15*s*. 6*d*.
The children & Horses expenses with our own carriage, £18 14*s*. 1½*d*.
Three mens Board & Wages on ye road, £4 15*s*. 6*d*.
Shoeing on do., 8*s*. 6*d*.
P^d the Bill at Bedford for horses & children, £1 6*s*. 4*d*.
" March 2. Porter at ye door of the Ho: of Commons, *i.e.*, ye Door-Keeper of ye House itself, £1 1*s*. 0*d*.
" April 16. By a present to Mrs Anne Stephens, £25.
" May 24. Dancing Master six Lessons, £1.
Teas at ye Ho: of Commons 6*s*., Gloves 5*s*., 11*s*.
1809, Mch. 8. P^d at the Vote office for sending the votes of this present Session, £2 2*s*. 0*d*.
" Oct. 1. A present to ye Poor of St Ives, £10.
1810, May 19. Mr Courquain (French Master), £2 2*s*.
Present to the St Ives men Prisoners in France.

Arms of Stephen of Tregenna: Per pale gules and vert, a fess indented argent guttee de sang, between three eagles displayed or. Crest: A lion rampant argent, guttee de sang. Motto: 'Virtutis amore.'

Burke's 'General Armory' says that these arms were granted temp. Henry VIII. to 'Henry Stephens, the immediate ancestor of the family.' This is almost certainly erroneous; they would seem to have been granted *circa* 1628 to John Stephens, the first of the family who is styled 'gentleman' in the Subsidy Rolls. (See *ante*.)

Stevens.

As we have already shown, the great clan of Stephens, or Stevens, has long been divided into a number of different families, all of them descending from a common stock. Having given a history of the Stevenses of Tregarthen, who afterwards became known to fame as Stephens of Tregenna, we must now give some account of the second house, Stevens of Bregia, or more correctly 'Bôrissa,' in the parish of Towednack, that being the next, both in point of genealogy and importance, to the Stevenses of Tregarthen. Just as the Stephens of Tregenna were distinguished by the Christian names John, Francis and Sarah, so the Stevens of Bregia affected the baptismal names Andrew, Vivian and Christian.

Without attempting to disentangle the intricate relationships between the various branches at an earlier period, we will commence with Vivian Stevens, who in 1711 married Ann Sprigg at Saint Ives, and by her had numerous issue. In 1711, also, 'Vyvyan Stevens mercht,' was elected an assistant for the borough, and in the following year an alderman.

In 1713 we have this entry in the 'Borough Accounts': 'for Causing before Mr Vivyan Stevens doore, 2*s*. 6*d*.'

Vivian Stevens was an alderman again in 1716, 1718, 1719, 1720 (and mayor), 1733, 1734. (Another Vivian Stevens was mayor in 1802.)

John Stevens, of the Bregia branch, was mayor of Saint Ives in 1752 and 1762; and in the latter year his son, John Stevens, junior, notary, was town clerk.

The following are the principal entries in the Parish Registers relative to the Bregia Stevenses:

1690. Married William Stephens & St noby Quick. [*Zennor.*]
1693. Baptd William s. of William Stevens.
1695. Baptd John s. of William Stevens.
1697. Baptd Jobe son of William Stevens.
1698. Baptd Mathew s. of William Stevens.
1701. Baptd Andrew s. of William Stevens.
1702. Baptd Jane d. of William Stevens.
1704. Baptd James s. of William Stevens.

1706. Bapt[d] Zenobia d. of William Stevens.
1711. Married Vivian Stevens & Anne Sprigg.
1711. Bapt[d] Richard s. of William Stevens.
1712. Bapt[d] Elizabeth d. of M[r] Vivian Stevens.
1714. Bapt[d] John s. of M[r] Vivian Stevens.
1717. Bapt[d] Andrew s. of M[r] Vivian Stevens & Ann his wife.
1720. Bapt[d] Ann d. of M[r] Vivian Stevens Mayor and Anne his wife.
1721. Married William Stevens and Elizabeth Thomas.
1721. Baptised Thamsin d. of Thomas & Elizabeth Stevens.
1722. Married John Stevens & Elizabeth Jennings.
1722. Bapt[d] Elizabeth d. of William & Elizabeth Stevens.
1722. Bapt[d] John s. of John & Elizabeth Stevens.
1723. Baptised Catherine d. of M[r] Vivian Stevens & Ann his wife.
1724. Bapt[d] Matthew s. of William and Elizabeth Stevens.
1726. Bapt[d] William s. of William and Elizabeth Stevens.
1727. Bapt[d] Zenobia d. of Matthew & Jane Stevens.
1728. Bapt[d] Margery d. of William & Elizabeth Stevens.
1729. Bapt[d] John s. of William & Elizabeth Stevens.
1731. Bapt[d] Phillis d. of William & Elizabeth Stevens.
1733. Bapt[d] Andrew s. of W[m] Stevens officer & Elizabeth his wife.
1735. [Bapt[d] Tho[s] s. of John & Christian Stevens Trevalgen.]
1735. Bapt[d] Vivian s. of William & Elizabeth Stevens.
1737. Bapt[d] Richard s. of Will[m] Stevens officer & Elizabeth his wife.
1738. Bapt[d] John s. of M[r] John Stevens lawyer [and Eleanor his wife].
1740. Bapt[d] Edward and James twin sons of William and Eliz: Stevens officer.
1759. Married Andrew Stevens and Mary Bryan[t]. (She died aged about 90, and was borne to the grave by her great-grandsons.)
1760. Married Vivian Stevens mariner and Margaret Tregerthen.
1762. Married John Stevens jun[r] of this parish attorney and Martha Nicolls, by license.
1770. Buried Vivian Stevens.
1769. Buried Vivian s. of Vivian & Catherine Stevens.
1772. Buried Andrew Stevens.

The name *Zenobia*, which has often been appealed to as favouring the theory of the Phœnicians coming to Cornwall for tin, in reality commemorates Saint Sinara, the patron of Zennor, where this baptismal name chiefly prevails. The first extract which we have made from the parish registers relating to the Stevenses of Bregia, shows the form, 'St Noby.' It was also written 'Sinoby' and 'Sinobia.'

The most famous bearer of the name *Zenobia* in West Cornwall was *Zenobia* Stevens, of Trevegia-Wartha in Towednack.

The following description of her is extracted from the 'Autobiography of a Cornish Rector,' by the Rev. James Hamley Tregenna, who, it will be observed, has changed the old lady's name and locale:

'Soon after our settlement at Truro we were surprised by a visit from old Mrs Matthews, a tenant of my mother's, who came to request that her lease of 99 years, which had just run out, might be renewed. Leases were granted in those days subject to the condition that after the death of 3 persons, whom the lessee was allowed to nominate on payment of a sum down, the estate should revert to the proprietor, whether the term of 99 years had expired or not. I suppose such an instance as this had hardly ever occurred before, of one of the lives coming, at the expiration of the term, to petition for a renewal. Supposing Mrs. Matthews' life to have been put on the estate, as the phrase was, the very day of her birth, she must have been entering now on her 100th year. Yet there she stood as upright as my mother, and much more robust. She was dressed in what was called a Joseph, which might have been coeval with herself, for any remains of colour that it had; but the quaint riding-dress was perfectly whole and nicely brushed, and so were the silver-buckled shoes that peeped from under it. Her head-dress, like the lady in "Christabel," was "a thing to dream of, not to tell," it was so marvellously and inexplicably put together. What it was made of none but a milliner of those days could hope to explain; but it looked very grand, especially by the side of my mother's modest little cap. From the waist downwards she wore what she called, I think, a "safeguard," a coarse garment of camlet or serge, which served to protect her Joseph, as well as to cover her feet when she was in the saddle. The long skirt of this garment was now drawn through her pocket-hole. Her hair was twisted behind into what was then called a "club," a sort of overgrown pig-tail, as it seemed to us. In her hand she carried a riding-whip with a heavy silver knob.'

The story given by Mrs. Piozzi, in her Letters, written in 1773, concerning the same old body, is as follows (see Chambers' 'Book of Days'):

'I must tell you a story of a Cornish gentlewoman hard by here [Penzance], *Zenobia* Stevens, who held a lease under the Duke of Bolton by her own life only ninety-nine years—and going at the term's end ten miles to give it up, she obtained permission to continue in the house as long as she lived, and was asked of course to drink a glass of wine. She did take one, but declined a second, saying she had to ride home in the twilight upon a young colt, and was afraid to make herself giddy-headed.'

Dr. Daniel Freeman Stevens, of Saint Ives, a member of the same family as the heroine of the story, related it thus:

'Zenobia Stevens *alias* Baragwanath, of Trevisa-wartha in Towednack [these words form a local Cornish shibboleth], lived to the age of one hundred and three. Her life-lease expiring at ninety nine, she went to the landlord's meeting to have it renewed. The lawyer or agent put her mind at rest by saying kindly: "Go thee wayst home, An *Z*'noby, and live so long as thee cust." (Go home, Aunt Zenobia, and live as long as thou canst.)'

From the information of her great-nephew, communicated to Lysons by the curate of Saint Ives, it appeared that Zenobia Stevens, of Skilly-Waddon, in Towednack, was born in the year 1661, and was buried at Zennor in 1763, aged 102 years. Her daughter Zenobia Baragwanath died aged ninety-eight or ninety-nine.

Thomas.

In the case of the Stevenses we had to deal with the various sections of one great clan. But the families of the name of Thomas are so numerous and so interlaced, that all it is possible for us to do is to say a little as to the most distinguished of them, namely, the Thomas family of Lelant. This, then, is the pedigree registered in the Visitation of Cornwall:

'Rich. Thomas gent. of Wales, dealing in merchandise between Wales & Cornwall, m. at Lelant with the d. & h. of John Hickes of Lelant.

'Henry Thomas, s. of Richard, m. the heire of Pawly. From them descended

'William Thoms of Lelant, m. d. of Rosewarne.

'John Thoms of Lelant m. the h. of Rosmell of Bodmin.

'John Thoms of Lelant m. the h. of John Godolphin of Gwennap.

'Wm Thomas of Cury viv. 1620 m. (1.) Jane d. & h. of Nic. Penticost. (2.) Mary d. of John Pendarveis. By (1.) he had John s. & h. æt. 22. By (2.) he had Hester, Grace, Willm, Bartho: Lowday, Samwell, Ellinor, Jane, Mary, Edmond.'

Colonel Vivian's edition of the Visitation gives the pedigree of another branch thus:

'1. John Thomas of Crowan m. Margerie.
'2. John Thomas of Crowan m.
'3. John Thomas of Crowan m. Ellinor d. of William Paynter of St Erth.
'4. John Thomas of Lanant viv. 1620. m. Phillipa d. of William Reskemer of Merthen.

'5. John Thomas son & heir of the latter, æt. 4 in 1620.
(William, 2nd sonne.)
(Ellinor, eldest da.)
(Katherine, 2nd daughter.)

Subsidy Rolls (Lelant).

1520. (c.) Johēs Thomas (lands) £3.
Willmūs Thomas (goods) £30.
1523. Willmūs Thomas (goods) £20.
Ricūs famulus Witti Thomas hēt stipend⁹ £1.
1524. Willims Thomas in bonis £20.
1530. Willms Thomas in bonis £18.
1536. De Willō Thoms ꝑ bonis £10.
1541. Willms Thomas valet in bonis £20.
1544. Jssebell Wyllm Thomas, 6*s*. 8*d*.
1546. ux Willi Thomas valet £10.
1549. P: Willmō Thomas 8*d*.
1593. Johnēs Thomas in bonis £3.
1597. Johēs Thomas in bonis £3.
1599. Johēs Tōmas in bonis £3.
1624. Rator, Johēs Thomas gēn in terr £6.
1625. Johēs Thomas gēn in terr £6.
1629. Johēs Thomas gēn in terr £3.
1664. Richard Thomas in ter —.

Borough Accounts.

1620. William Thomas, gent., and his son, paid 1*s*. 8*d*. to the royal rate.

In the later volume there are several allusions to 'Justice Thomas,' who was of this family, and resided at Lelant.

Of the less-known families of Thomas there are a large number in all the four parishes. One of these, distinguished by the baptismal name Hannibal, was originally of Zennor, and a daughter was married into the Hicks family, as recorded in the Zennor registers: '1737. Married George Hickes of St Ives & Sibella Thomas.' The representation of Pawley of Gunwin is claimed by this branch of the Thomas family.

William Thomas, '*alias* Kyow an Gove,' was a burgess of Saint Ives in 1615, 1629, 1631, and 1636.

Deep in the sands of Hayle Bar there lies a sunken ship, in which, after the sand has been shifted by a heavy gale, the fishermen sometimes entangle their nets. This is known as 'Thomas' Wreck,' from James Thomas, captain of the ill-fated vessel which went down with all hands in the first half of the last century. A Saint Ives ship, commanded by a master named James Thomas, was also lost with all hands in the year 1819.

John Thomas is a name which, coming down constantly through the pages of the Borough Accounts and Parish Registers, marks the descent of a third family of this surname. The three families are so difficult to distinguish, in the records, from each other, and from others of the same cognomen, that to attempt to set down their genealogies would be to run great risk of inaccuracy and confusion.

Arms of Thomas of Lelant: Per pale nebulee argent and azure. (Thus in the 'General Armory'; *sed quaere* whether the arms are not: Gules, a chevron and canton ermine.)

Tregenna.

The beautiful estate of Tregenna, so well known to visitors to Saint Ives, was long ago the seat of an ancient gentle-family which derived its name from the place of their abode. The only mention which has been made of this family by historians is the meagre memorandum of Lysons to the effect that the Tregennas, of Tregenna in Saint Ives, were not extinct in the elder branch till after the reign of James I., and that a younger line settled at Polgreen in Saint Columb.

The name does not appear in the Subsidy Roll of 1327; but in that of *circa* 1520 William Tregenna was rated in respect of lands in Saint Ives and Zennor, and for lands in Saint Ives in those of 1524 and 1536.

In 1557 Thomas Tregenna was rated at £5 for his goods at Saint Ives.

In 1573 John Tregenna was a capital burgess, and again in 1578 and 1583. In 1585 he contributed £4 for his lands in Saint Ives, and the like for lands and goods in 1593, 1597, and 1599. I have a note to the effect that he was Bailiff of Penwith in 1581.

The following are entries concerning members of this family in the Municipal Records of Saint Ives:

1584. 'Rec: of m^r^ tregenna for the standinge of the muster stufe in the markett house, xx^s^.

'It: Rec: of m^r^ tregenna for the bringinge in of the perow shipp, x^s^.' (The ship belonging to a man named Perro.)

1588. 'Itm: gave the Robin howde [Robin Hood] of S^t^ colloms the lower by the apointment of m^r^ tregena, 5s.'

In 1592 John Tregenna appears to have lent money to the parish on a bond, and in the same year he received 4*d.* for half a bushel of coal.

In 1594 mention is made of a Henry Tregenna.

In 1596 John Tregenna was one of the capital burgesses, and it would seem [*sed quaere*] that he was head warden in the year following.

In 1603 John Tregenna, gent., was a capital burgess, and he is mentioned again in the Mayor's Account of 1604.

In the reign of Elizabeth, Mr. Richard Tregosse tried to prevent the huers from entering upon his land on Porthminster Hill, and went to law about it. John Tregenna went to London on behalf of the town; the inhabitants paid his expenses, £141, and afterwards out of gratitude returned him to Parliament, 1603. The following extract from the earlier MS. of Municipal Records bears upon this matter:

'27° Jan: 1603. It is agreede uppon, by the geñall agreement of the 12 & 24 of or towne this ꝑsent daye, that whereas the laste fishinge season & in som few seasons now latelye paste, Mr Richard Tregosse & Jno Hexte geñ, as in the possession of ther lands here at Porthminster & Tregenna hills, have molested diũse ꝑsōns inhabitants of or towne & p̃ishe, as the Baulkers & blowsers, followinge ther crafte of fishinge, as the custome hath bene, from the contrarye whereof mans memorye hath not bene, & have threatned som others, & latelye served lawe uppon others, & som in expectation to be served wth other processes, That the p̃ties, & eũye of them, so served wth processes, to be borne & defended by the stocke & charge of or parrishe, if the trespasses & offences layde to ther charge be for the cause of fishinge, & for no other cause, And it is moreover agreed, that all and eũye of the pties so to be sewed & served wth processes, the accion of lawe once attempted, or dependinge not to release, frustreate, discontynue or compound wth the ꝑties who so attempte processes & suts of lawe, w̃thowte the order and composicōn also of the 12 & 24 or the moste number of them, in defence of this or p̃sent righte herein, And likewies no one pson or psons of the townesmen or prishñers ioyninge in lawe againste the said mr Richd Tregosse & Jno Hexte geñ or either of them, or any ther children or servaunts by the counsell, meanes, & at the chargs of the pishe, not to release unto them, or any of them, any offence of thers, ther children or servaunts, who have taken or shall hereafter take any fishe owte of the townes mens netts at the fishinge tyme & seasons, And what pson or psons soever shall herein doe to the contrarye shall forfeyte to the townes behalfe xls, to be distrayned levyed & taken by waye of distres of the goods beasts & cattalls of all & eũye such offendor. [Signed:] John tregenna. John cokyns. George hicks. Richard hicks. William hechins. William Pitt. Walter Knight. lewes hurley. peter + cloke. James Stearye. Willm + cocke. John steven. Jo: + James. Nich: + Boseithiowe. Willm + Baylye. Joh: + hamblye. Rich: + Peter. Jo: + Stirrye. Thomas James. Tho: + Toman. Richard Candrowe. Peeter lenyon [?]. stev: + Barber. Jo: + hocken. Mich: + Nuttell.

In 1605 are entries of payments of money by the town to Mr Tregenna; and again, in 1607, is this: 'Pd Wm hechins wch he pd Mr Tregenna in Bristowe, 5*li.*'; and, 'Pd my cosen Tregenna for so much due to him from ye pishe, 11*li.* 3*s.* Item pd for the use of his moneye 7 Monethes, 6*s.*'

By John Tregenna's death, soon after 1607, this ancient family became extinct in the male line. I have not been able to learn who represents Tregenna in the female line, but, as it appears that the 'cosen' who made the last-extracted entry in the town accounts was William Hichens, it is probable that the representation of Tregenna is in the Hichens family.

Some of the Cornish historians, I know not on what authority, call the head warden who took part in the rising of 1549, 'John Payne, *alias* Tregenna.' Certainly Payne's arms, as given on the stall-end in the chancel, are entirely different from those of Tregenna, which are: Or, a chevron azure, between 3 Moors' heads proper, filleted argent.

The following entries in the Mayoral Accounts for 1696 and 1697 no doubt refer to a member of the younger branch, Tregenna of Saint Columb:

'Spent at Assizes on Mr Courtney and Mr Tregena, about the port farme, 5*s.*'

'Spent on Mr Tregena at Taverne by consent, 11*s.*'

'Pd charges to my son attending severall tymes on the duke of Bolton to goe to Mr Tregenna severall tymes to stop prosecuc̃on about the port farme, £1 10*s.*'

'Postage of severall letters sent to Mr Hooker & Tregena, 1*s.* 4*d.*'

Tregosse.

This family is one of the oldest in the neighbourhood of Saint Ives. The Subsidy Roll of 1327 gives the names of Clement and John Tregoce, of Saint Ives, rated at 2*s.* and 1*s.* respectively.

In the list of *circa* 1520, Thomas Tregoos' lands in Towednack are assessed at the yearly value of 13*s.* 4*d.*, and those of John Tregoz in the parish of Saint Ives at 11*s.* Thomas Tregoos also had lands in Saint Ives valued at 11*s.*

In 1641 William Tregose, gent, had at Saint Ives goods to the annual value of £3.

Borough Accounts.

In 1583 the authorities of the borough granted 'unto John Tregose esquire, all suche pewes & chayres in the churche &

chansell of S^{tt} yees as were in tymes paste possessed by Thomas Glynne esquire decessed.'

1584. 'Itm̃ payde maister John Tregose at maye for the marckate house rent, 2*s*.'

Similar entries occur yearly about this time, when he was receiving a shilling a quarter in rent. 'Mr John Tregoosse' paid about this date towards a rate for mending the church.

From an entry of *circa* 1595 it appears that the town presented a barrel of coffee to 'Mr Tregosse.'

In 1603 Richard Tregose, gen^t, was a capital burgess; and in this year he had the famous dispute with the town concerning the huers' right to cross his land on Porthminster Hill. (For an account of this controversy see *ante*, p. 468.)

1604. 'Paide Mr Praed for a replevyn when Mr Tregosse distrayned a quarter of beiffe from Trevascus, 6*d*.'

In 1613 Richard Tregosse, esq^e, became once more a capital burgess, from which it would appear that he had by this time made his peace with the town.

1615. 'More p^d Mr Paynter the constable for attendaunce aboute the Spanyards by direction of Mr Tregosse & other the chiefe of o^r towne, 10*s*.'

In 1620 Richard Tregosse's name is the first on the list of those who paid to the royal rate; his share—1*s*. 6*d*.—was above the average.

In 1633 William Tregosse witnessed a contract for the letting of the quay dues.

In 1638 we have a mutilated document in the Borough Accounts, setting forth that whereas one James Thomas, the son of Thomas James deceased, was left an infant dependent on the care of the public, 'and for that the sayde towne and pishe is att this instantt surcharged with [divers paupers] and impotentt psons, therefore we the [burgesses] of the same towne & pishe whose names are here under written, have deliuivryd the same orphantt unto John Tregosse esqẽ and Wilmott his wief, and to there assignes, to dwell and serve after the manner of [an apprentice] for the terme and tyme of eightene yeares ensuinge the date here of, to be broughte [upp] to worcke and husbandrye laboure, or any other sũice that they shall thincke moste beste for th[emselues]. In witnes where of we haue here unto putt our hands the daie & yeare aboue written.

Thomas Hicks hedwardeine.'

In 1640 William Tregosse and Henry Stevens farmed the tolls of the quay.

1658. 'I: payd Mr Thomas Tregosse the minister ffor his yeres salarye the sum̃e of £15.

The following extract from C. S. Gilbert's 'History of Cornwall' may appropriately be inserted here:

'In 16— was born in St Ives Thomas Tregosse, of an ancient family in Cornwall. He was bred a sojourner in Exeter College in July, 1655. Quitting the University he took holy orders, and was a constant preacher in his native place for two years. He afterwards removed to the vicarage of Mylor and Mabe, where he remained until 1662, when he was silenced for nonconformity. After this he preached privately, chiefly in St Ives and Penryn, at which latter place he died in January, 1672.'

It may be added that Mr Tregosse was on more than one occasion committed to Lanceston Gaol, where he was in confinement more than twelve months altogether. A century later, we find Wesley bestowing high praise upon the Rev. Thomas Tregosse. (See *ante*, p. 347.)

Parish Registers.

1658. Married Mr Thomas Tregosse minister of this burrough & Margt Sparnon of Gwynier.'

Burke ('General Armory') assigns the following arms to Tregosse of Cornwall: Or, three bars azure, on a chief of the last a lion passant of the first.

In the *Western Antiquary* of Plymouth, for September, 1882, vol. ii., No. 6, p. 93, appear the following notes as to the ejected minister:

'REV. THOMAS TREGOSS.—In the issues of the Cornish papers, accounts are given of the Congregational Sunday School, Falmouth. It is stated that the first congregation was gathered by the Rev. Thomas Tregoss, who was one of the 2,000 ministers evicted by the passing of the Uniformity Act, 1662. Was it not James Tregoss who held the livings of Mylor and Mabe at the time of the passing of the Act? In the *Christian Miscellany* for 1877 an interesting account is given of the Rev. James Tregoss, son of Thomas Tregoss.

'Perhaps a few facts from the account in the *Miscellany* may be of interest:

'"James Tregoss was born at St. Ives, Cornwall. The family must have been one of influence in the county in its early history, but wealth and power seem to have departed from it by the beginning of the seventeenth century. Thomas Tregoss appears to have lived at St. Ives in the reign of Charles I. James went to Oxford, and in 1657 returned to his birthplace. He became the pastor of the church, and remained there until 1659, when he took charge of the livings of Mylor and Mabe. It is related during his St. Ives pastorate that the fishing during one season had been a complete blank. No pilchards had come; he proposed 'Let us have a day of humiliation and prayer!' The next day the bay was alive with shoals of fish. During the next season a great quantity was captured on a Saturday, and on Sunday the men dried their nets. Tregoss solemnly reproved them. 'You have provoked the Lord to withdraw His blessing,' said he. The rest of the season was a failure.

'"From the peaceful retreat at Mylor, Tregoss often passed through Penryn and Falmouth, the latter in its infancy, to Mabe. In 1662, we read of his being homeless. Soon three months of imprisonment awaited him for preaching. He afterwards ministered at Kegillick near Budock, and people came from a distance to listen to his discourses. Tregoss resolved to visit his former congregation at Mabe, and there incurred the persecution of one Robinson, a Justice of the Peace, a great landowner in the west, and a 'Fanatic hunter.' The Justice used his influence and Tregoss was lodged in Launceston Jail. At liberty, he returned to Mabe to be again imprisoned.

'"Once more freed from prison he preached at Mabe, and then visited Devonshire. Returning to Mabe, in 1666, he was heard once again in the old church. Then he was found in Bodmin Prison until 1667 (September). Released by Royal order, he set up a Monday Lecture at Penryn. Still hunted and persecuted, Tregoss visited Devon, was put into Exeter Jail, went to Torrington, and returned to Penryn. Here he died January 18, 1671. Amongst his last utterances we read: 'And now, Lord God, Thy servant must away to holy angels, and to the spirits of the just made perfect. Keep them that do believe in Thee.'"

'Query, Is there any earlier mention of the family?

'H. H.

'Porthleven.'

'REV. THOMAS TREGOSS.—The ejected vicar of Mylor and Mabe was Thomas Tregosse, son of William (of *Western Antiquary*, vol. i., 215; Bib: Cornub: ii., 759).

'J. I. DREDGE.

'Buckland Brewer.'

Trenwith.

This family is said to have formerly been called Bayliffe, a name which, indeed, appears in the town records of Elizabeth's reign. Hals says that the change of name took place in the reign of Henry VIII., and that the family in question then entered into possession of the Trenwith estate; but he evidently mistakes here, although Lysons seems to have accepted this account. Lysons himself says that Trenwith of Trenwith traced back to the time of Edward IV., though he does not notice the brass in the church commemorating Otho Trenwith, who died in the second year of that reign. Lysons gives these further particulars as to the family and its alliances:

'The elder branch in consequence of a match with the heiress of Tredenzy of Burian, removed thither. The posterity of the second son of Peter Trenwith by the heiress of Vincent, continued at Trenwith and became extinct before the middle of the 17th century; the heiress married Burgess. This branch married the heiress of Vincent Tredenzy & Caskayes, and a coheiress of Militon [of Pengerswick]. At a later period Trenwith appears to have reverted to the elder branch, which became extinct by the death of Mr Thomas Trenwith in 1796. This branch is represented by Lander.'

The Manor and Barton of Trenwith is said by Lysons to have anciently included the whole parish of Lelant, and to have continued in the Beauforts till the attainder of the Earl of Somerset in 1471.

In the earliest Cornish Subsidy Roll, that of 1327, we find a Thomas de Trenewyth rated in Lelant parish; but it is probable that we have here the name Trenoweth, not Trenwith. Nor does such a name appear under the heading of Saint Ives in this roll.

A note in Lieut.-Col. Vivian's 'Visitation of Cornwall' is as follows:

'Ped. fin. Cornub., 34 Hen. VI. No 3. Otonem Treunwyth qu. Joh: Velour def., Porthya, lananta, Carnesuwe et Helston.'

That is to say, that in the year 1456 Otho Trenwith purchased of John Velour the manors and lands of Porthia (Saint Ives), Lelant, Carnsew, and Helston.

And that the family was of consequence even before that date appears from the preceding note, which shows that in the fifteenth year of Richard II. (1392) Henry Treunwith purchased of Hugh Canas, and Emma his wife, the lands called 'Carbons' and 'Carnyny' (Carbis and Carninny), both in the Saint Ives district.

From these particulars it will be seen how erroneous is the statement of Hals and Lysons that the Trenwiths took that estate and name in Henry VIII.'s reign.

C. S. Gilbert says:

'Thomas Baillie was living at Tregenna, 45 Edw. III., 1371. His son, Henry Baillie, got possession of Trenwith, and changed the name. Otho Trenwith was buried under [*lege* before] the high altar of Saint Ives church.'

The following are the instances of mention made of this family in the Subsidy Rolls:

1520 (*circa*). Thomas Trenwith, rated at £1 6*s.* 8*d.*, 6*s.* 8*d.*, £10, and 7*s.*, for lands in Lelant, Towednack, Saint Ives and Zennor respectively.

1523, 1524. Thomas Trenwith, lands in Saint Ives.

1541, 1544, 1547, 1548, 1549, 1557. Mathew Trenwith, lands in Saint Ives.

1558. Mathew Trenwith, £6 for lands in Saint Ives.

1571. Mathew and Henry Trenwith, lands and goods in Saint Ives respectively.

1585. William Trenwith, £3 for lands in Saint Ives; Henry Trenwith, £4 for goods at Saint Ives; James Trenwith, £3 for goods at Lelant.

1593. William Trenwith, £3 for lands in Saint Ives; Henry Trenwith, £3 for goods at Saint Ives.

1597. William and John Trenwith, lands in Saint Ives; William Trenwith de Trevalgan, goods at Saint Ives.

1599. William and John Trenwith, lands in Saint Ives.

1624. 'Richardus Trenw^th^ gen: rated at fyve pound in terr: sould all his land died nothing worth.'

'Thomas Treunwith ar: et Laura Trenwith vid: valent in terris.' [The amount is illegible.]

1624. Mathew Trenwith, £3 for goods at Towednack. Thomas and Laura Trenwith, widow, £5 for lands in Saint Ives.

1629. William Trenwith, £4 for goods at Towednack. Thomas and Laura Trenwith, widow, £5 for lands in Saint Ives.

1641. Thomas Trenwith, 'armiger,' £5 for lands in Saint Ives. William Trenwith, lands in Zennor.

1664. Thomas Trenwith, lands in Saint Ives.

In 1598 Richard Trenwith, of Saint Erth, gent., was a witness before the Commission whose minutes we have elsewhere recorded. He was born 1558. He was the Richard Trenwith who 'died nothing worth' just before 1624. In him the second house or line of Trenwith became extinct, his daughter marrying Burgess, as mentioned by Lysons.

The pedigree, as given in the 'Visitation of Cornwall,' compiled in 1624, commences with Henry Trenwith of Trenwith, who married Elinor Rosmadres of Saint Burian, with issue Peter and Otes. Peter Trenwith married Elizabeth Vincent, and had issue William and Henry. William Trenwith married Jane Predeney of Saint Burian, and had issue Thomas Trenwith, who married Margery Erisey. Mathew Trenwith of Trenwith married Elizabeth Caskayes. (Their son William, together with his son Thomas, was named in the will of John Bosustow of Saint

Levan, dated 1604.) Thomas Trenwith of Trenwith married Elizabeth Myllyton of Pengerswick, by whom he had issue Richard Trenwith of Saint Erth, who married Ann Merritt of Probus, and whose only child Ann was married to Humphry Burgis of Saint Erth.

To turn to the Borough Records, William and Harry Trenwith are mentioned *circa* 1572; and in 1573 William Trenwith paid for some elm boards in the playing-place, while Thomas, 'the olde M[r] Trenwithe,' paid for some parish sheep and other things.

In 1573 James, Harry and William Trenwith signed the resolution to impose a penalty on those who should refuse to fill the office of warden. This seems to have been resolved on in consequence of the refusal of William Trenwith to officiate; for in the same year 'was elected Will[m] Trevnw[th] pposite or hed warden,' but John Penhellack was the person actually raised to that dignity.

As will be seen by our copy of the document, a Trenwith, whose baptismal name is illegible, was one of those who, on June 22, 1578, were rated to pay towards fitting out Irish soldiers.

In 1580 there is a note that 5*s.* were owing to the town for Thomas Trenwith's grave.

Circa 1580 we have a list of people who seem to have been rated toward the expense of resisting the Spaniards. Among them we have entries of four members of the Trenwith family, one being styled 'of Trenwith,' and the other 'Trenwith the elder,' but their Christian names are worn off.

Somewhere about the same date, too (for these dates are extremely difficult to fix), there was a benevolence towards the mending of the church, to which Mr. William Trenwith of Trenwith, another Trenwith of Trenwith, and Mistress Elizabeth Trenwith, contributed.

In 1580 Henry and William Trenwith the elder were elected burgesses, William Trenwith, junior, taking his father's place a few years later. The younger William is again mentioned in a year which I take to be 1587, when he paid £3 7*s.* 2*d.* in full satisfaction of his poll moneys.

In 1583 we find the following agreement:

'A trewe copie of the grantt unto m[r] tregose & m[r] w[m] trenw[th] sentt to the courte by m[r] stowforde.

'Memorand: that we whose names are here under written, beinge of the xij of the towne and pishe of S[t] yees, the xxvj[th] of June 1583 do demyse & graunt vnto John Tregose esquire, all such pewes & chayres in the churche and chansell of St[t] yees as were in tymes paste possessed by Thomas Glynne esquire decessed; and we demyse & graunt vnto Wm Trinwth gent: sonn & heire vnto thomas trinwth decessed the pewe nextt adioyninge to the litle dore in the s[ide nexte ?] the new yewe, wherein mathew trinwth de[cessed, grand-]father to the sayde Wm trinwth did sitt in the tyme of the sayde thomas glynne. In witnes,

harrye Stirye portrive

Ots merifeld	John penhelege
John carvedris	John Tregenna
John cockins	John Androw
harrye Oots	thoms hicks
	Wm Wolcocke'

In 1592 (?) 'Mr Trenwithe of Trevalgin' was paid 1s. 3*d*. for his charges in going to Helston.

In 1595 a shilling was paid to Mr. William Trenwith 'for a poer oman that died in the ten pite [tin-pit] to healpe to by hier [her] a shroud.'

About the same date occurs the following memorandum:

'Mr Willm Trenwth of Trenwth hath licensyd us the prisheners of Ste yees to fetche upon his land att pripter [Porthrepter] iij or iiij boetes ladings of stones for the makin of anew penthowse or lenatt aganst the churche wall. Wittnes of henry hicks & John Steven, henry vune.

In 1596 or 7 Mr. William Trenwith was paid £4 4*s*. 0*d*. 'for James Dinham is sute, for chargs of lawe'; and at the same date we have William Trenwith esq., William Trenwith gent: and Henry Trenwith on the roll of burgesses.

In 1603 William Treunwithe gen: signed, as one of the twelve principal burgesses, a resolution to the effect that any chief burgess presuming to order public affairs independently of his brethren, should be dismissed from office.

In 1605, apparently, Mr. William Trenwith was one of the rators appointed for rating to a Subsidy.

In 1607, William Trenwith gen: was chosen porthrieve; but, he preferring to be fined, William Hichens was chosen in his place.

In 1614 Thomas Treunwithe of Trenwith Esq.: and Thomas Treunwithe of Trevalgen gen: were among the capital burgesses; and William Trenwith was a burgess in the following year.

In 1619 William Trenwith gen: was chosen porthrieve. In the following year Mistress Lora Trenwithe was rated at 6*d*. for the subsidy and Thomas Trenwith esq: at 2*s*. 8*d*.

In 1622 the town 'recd of Mr Trevnwthe of Trevalgan in pte of 10*s*. wch he craved to be respited for the clarcks wags: vs.'

In 1625 Thomas Treunwith gent: was chosen portrieve, as it seems, on the refusal of John Stevens to take that office. It was thereupon resolved that such a refusal should in the future entail a fine of £3 6s 8*d*.

In 1629 Thomas Treunwith gent: was a capital burgess; and in the same year, among those who had not paid the rate for the county stock and maimed soldiers, we find the names of Thomas Trenwith esq: rated at 3s., and Thomas Trenwith gent: at 1s. 8*d*.

In 1641 Mathew Treunwith gent: gave £1 towards the erection of a west gallery in the church.

In 1655 Renatus Trenwith was a burgess of Saint Ives, and a collector for the Porthfarm.

In 1662 Thomas Trenwith Esq. was elected Mayor of the Borough, and in 1665 he farmed the profits of the market.

In the first year of James II.'s reign, 1684, Thomas Trenwith Esquire became Mayor of Saint Ives by the royal appointment under the renewed charter.

Parish Registers.

1634, Nov[r] 10. William Trenewith gent: and Mary Pellamounter were married at Zennor. (Bishop of Exeter's Transcripts.) All the following extracts are from the Saint Ives Registers.

1654. Married Ezechiell Trenwith gent:, son of Thomas Trenwith Esq:, to Elizabeth daughter of William Lanion gent.

1654. Baptised William son of Edward Trenwith gent:

1654. Baptised Renatus son of Renatus Trenwith gent:

1656. Buried William s. of Renatus Trenwith.

1656. Baptised Joane, d. of Edward Trenwith gent:

1656. Baptised William s. of Renatus Trenwith.

1657. Baptised Henry s. of Renatus Trenwith.

1657. Buried Thomas Trenwith gent:

1659. Baptised Elizabeth d. of Ezechiell Trenwith gent:

1659. Buried M[rs] Elizabeth Trenwith widow.

1661. Baptised Joane d. of Renatus Trenwith gent.

1663. Buried M[rs] Jane Trenwith.

1665. Buried Joan wife of Thomas Treunwith Esq:

1666. Married Thomas Trenwith Esq: and Jane Richards *alias* Carway.

1667. Buried Thomas Trenwith Esq:

1675. Married Thomas Trenwith gent: and M[rs] Revena Lanyon.

1677. Baptised Renatus s. of Thomas Trenwith gent:

1678. Baptised John s. of Thomas Trenwith gent:
1681. Baptised Rebekah d. of Thomas Trenwith gent:
1682. Baptised Jone d. of Thomas Trenwith gent:
1684. Baptised Renatus s. of Thomas Trenwith Esq:
1686. Baptised Thomas s. of Thomas Trenwith Esq:
1688. Married Mr Thomas Leach of Devon to Mrs Lore Trenwith.
1689. Baptised Mary d. of Thomas Trenwith gent:
1708. Baptised Elizabeth d. of Renatus Trenwith gent:
1771. [George Trenwith witnessed a marriage contract.]
1772. Married Henry Trenwith mariner and Margaret Stephens widow; witness Alexander James and John Grenfell.

The arms of Trenwith: Argent, on a bend cotised sable three cinquefoils of the field.

We have treated in other chapters of the seat and estate of Trenwith.

In 1769 Thomas Trenwith, Esq., of Saint Ives, is named in the list of subscribers prefixed to the new edition of Carew's 'Survey of Cornwall,' published in that year. This gentleman, who was a lieutenant in the Royal Navy and the last male of his ancient house (being the heir of his uncle, Renatus Trenwith, who was the heir of his father, Thomas Trenwith), in 1760 barred the entail of 'All that capital messuage Barton farm and demesne Lands of in or called Trenwith situate lying and being in the Borough and Parish of Saint Ives in the County of Cornwall then in the tenure of him the said Thomas Trenwith.' Shortly afterwards he devised the same lands by will to Rebecca Trenwith, and died in the year 1796.

Rebecca Trenwith died in 1798, after having by will devised the fee simple and inheritance of Trenwith unto the heir or heirs of her great-uncle, Henry Trenwith deceased, provided they could be found, and subject to pecuniary legacies to her servants, Jennipher Leggoe and Bridget Quick, spinsters. If a direct male heir could not be discovered, the estate was to go to her cousin, 'William Lander's son of Plymouth Dock.' In 1803 the heir of Trenwith was advertised for; it was stated that the said Henry Trenwith was captain of an East Indiaman, and died in India *circa* 1790. No heir appeared, however, and William Lander took possession, and afterwards sold to divers persons.

Treweeke.

This is one of the original families of the district, more particularly of Lelant.

John Trewyke had lands in the parish of Lelant, which were

valued *circa* 1520 at £1 6*s.* 8*d.* per annum, and in 1523 and 1524 his goods were valued at £4.

John Treweke had lands in Lelant in 1571 and 1585, valued at £2 a year. In the latter instance the surname is spelt 'Trewick.' In 1593 John 'Treweeck's' lands there were again valued at £2.

Borough Accounts.

1592. 'Ite paide to Walter Treweeke ffor a qr̄ rente ffor duen and others, 3*s.*

1592. 'Walter treweke geveth his consent' as Burgess, to some resolution the purport of which does not plainly appear.

1594. 'Itē Receued of Jonno Treweeke for aburiall, 3*s.*'

1595. 'Itē paide Jone treweage for cresmas qr̄, 3*s.*'

1620. Digorye Treweeke of Street-an-Poll pays 2*d.* to a royal rate levied at Saint Ives.

1634. Henrie Treweeke was chosen Sidesman of the parish church.

1638. 'I: ye younge Treweeke for Iron wedges, 6*s.*'

1640. 'I: to Henrie Treweeke for spukes about ye Key, 11*s.* 6*d.*'

1649. 'I: paid John Treweeke for 2 twists for the guard gate, 2s.' In 1650 John Treweeke was one of the Burgesses who signed the new Fishery Constitutions. So did Henry Tryweeke in 1650.

1659. 'I: payd Henrye Treweeke ffor mendinge the stocks, 1*s.*' He also received a shilling for cleaning the town muskets.

1660. 'I: pd John Treweeke for a locke ffor the stocks, 1*s.* 4*d.*'

1665. 'I: pd John Treweeke for crooks twists & nayles for the chapell doore, 1*s.* 10*d.*

John Treweeke was appointed collector of the port-farm in 1658, was chosen churchwarden in 1672, and was an alderman in 1677. In 1681 he was chosen overseer of the poor.

In 1769 'George Treweeke, Surgeon, of Penzance,' figures among the subscribers to Carew's 'Survey.'

Parish Registers.

1657. Married Allexander Richards & Joane Treweeke.

1728. Married Henry Thomas widdower & Catherine Treweek.

Trewynnard.

Though seated at Trewinnard, in the neighbouring parish of Saint Erth, before the Norman conquest, this now extinct family was long intimately connected with the Saint Ives district. Their ancestral home, called in Domesday 'Trewinider,' was anciently the most important residence in Saint Erth. Burke ('General Armory') says that one of them represented the county in Parliament, *temp.* Edward III. William of Worcester says that Michael Trewynnard, a native of Saint Ives, died on Maunday Thursday, 1471, Provost of the Collegiate Church of Saint Thomas of Glasney.

James Trewynnard had lands in Lelant parish, *circa* 1520, valued at £1 12*s.* by the year, and paid £2 to the subsidy of 1524, apparently for lands or goods at Saint Ives. In a subsidy list of about the year 1530, he is recorded to have had goods to the value of £40 at Lelant.

In 1536 William Trewynnard paid 10*s.* for lands in the parish of Lelant.

In 1557 William Trewynnerd had goods at Saint Ives valued at £5, and in 1558 their value was £7.

At the end of the reign of Henry VIII. John Trewynnard, member of Parliament for I know not what borough, was arrested for debt during the prorogation.

Deiphobus Trewynnard, grandson of the above, in his anger killed an innocent man and buried him secretly in Trewinnard oratory. The murder being discovered, Trewynnard was sentenced to death and imprisoned in Lanceston Castle. He made a compact with Sir Reginald Mohun, knight, one of the favourites of Queen Elizabeth, whereby that courtier was to procure a pardon for the condemned man, in exchange for a grant of the Barton and Manor of Trewinnard. This compact was carried out by both parties, and Deiphobus afterwards lived on a small pittance allowed him by Mohun. The Trewynnards seem then, or soon afterwards, to have removed to Saint Ives, where they dwelt until they became extinct in the male line, which happened about the middle of the seventeenth century. The last male was John Trewynnard, of Saint Ives, as we gather from the records hereunder cited.

The following are the entries in the Borough Accounts relative to members of this ancient family:

1573. 'Receuived of m^r^ Martine Trewennarde for the halfe yeres anuitie dew at o^r^ ladye day in marche 1573, £8.'

Similar entries occur quarterly about this time.

1605 (c) John Trewynnard paid to a local rate.
1615. Mr John Trewynnard was a Capital Burgess.
1620. 'Mr Trewynnard, Westren Streete,' paid 6*d.* to the royal rate.

1622. 'Paym[ts] Imprimis paide m[r] John Trewynnard in & towardes the paym[te] to m[r] ffownes late mayor of Plymothe towardes the chargs he & m[r] Thomas ceelye charged the pishe for the fleete made owte againste the turcks, 3[li].'

1626. John Trewynnard gen[t] was chosen Porthrieve.

1627. John Trewynnard, Capital Burgess.

Parish Registers.

1623. [Towednack.] Married John Trewinnard of S[t] Ives gen[t] & Margaret daughter of Humphrye Yorke of Gwinnear gen[t].

1653. An Intention of marriage betweene m[r] Leonard Welsted minister of this Towne and Grace one of the daurs of Jo[n] Trewynard gen[t] was published y[e] 8th Jan : y[e] 15th & y[e] 22th of the same three lords dayes. [They were married on February 1.]

In 1585 Martin Trewinnard sold to John Nance certain land in the manor of Connerton. (See the Penzance Natural History and Antiquarian Society's Transactions, 1887-8, p. 346.)

Arms: Argent, a fess azure between three Cornish choughs sable, two in chief pecking and one in base rising.

Vivian.

The great herald and genealogist, Sir Bernard Burke, has said that this is probably the most ancient surname in Britain. It is purely Celtic, and not Latin as is generally supposed. The name has undergone many changes, as will be seen from the following history of it.

In 1327, Galfridus Bieuyen, of Lelant, paid six pence to the subsidy.

In 1520, *circa*, Johannes Vyuwyn, of Lelant, with another person, had goods at Lelant of the annual value of ten marks.

In 1523, Ricardus Byuwyn of Lelant had goods there valued at £2 yearly.

In the Subsidy Roll of 1524 is the same record as the last, but the name is spelt Vyuwyn.

In 1524 Richard Vyvyan of Saint Ives had goods there of the value of £2 by the year.

Circa 1530 Peter Bvyune, of Lelant, was rated at £3 for goods in that parish.

In 1546 Richard Vevien, of Lelant, was stated to be worth £6, and Andrew Vyvyan of Zennor £2 by the year.

In 1571 Henry Veuvyn was rated for goods at Lelant.

Soon after this date the family of Vivian became extinct, and the representation of it passed to Stevens of Bregia, with whose descendants Vivian is a frequent baptismal name.

Williams.

This is one of the original families of Saint Ives. John 'Wyllms' appears in the Subsidy Roll of *circa* 1520, having goods at Lelant to the yearly value of £8, an amount decidedly above the average. In the same year a person called John Williams 'Hicka' had lands in Saint Ives valued at 13*s*. 6*d*., and goods at Towednack at £4 per annum, while Noel Williams' goods at Saint Ives were valued at £3 a year. John Williams also had goods worth £8 yearly at Zennor.

In 1523 we again find John Williams at Lelant, where his goods are this time valued at £5, and at Towednack again £4. Noel Williams, of Saint Ives, again has goods value £7 there; and Simon Williams appears, his goods at Saint Ives being valued at £2 a year. John Williams, of Zennor, is this year rated at £4 for his goods there.

1524. This year John Williams still has goods at Lelant; also at Towednack, of the same value as before. Noel Williams's goods have now risen to £7 in value; Simon Williams's are still at £2.

In 1541 John Williams of Zennor is rated at £20 for goods.

In 1546 John Williams, of Saint Ives, is said to be worth £3 a year. Jenkyn Williams, John Williams, and Harry Williams, of Zennor, are put down at £3, £8, and £1 respectively.

In 1549 John Williams of Lelant paid 8*d*. to a subsidy.

In 1557 John Williams of Zennor was stated to be worth £6 a year in goods.

In 1571 John Williams of Saint Ives had goods there valued at £8 annually.

In 1585 Thomas Williams has goods to the yearly value of £3 at Saint Ives. In 1593 their value was £4, and in 1597 and 1599 £6.

In 1599 John Williams had goods at Zennor worth £5 a year.

In 1624 George Williams was rated at £3 for goods at Saint Ives.

Borough Accounts.

1573. John Williams, Capital Burgess.

'Rec. of John Wm for a grave tithe chese and the market-house rent, 14*s*. 10*d*.

'payd to John Wms for helling stones & lathe nayles for to drese the churche, 5*s*. 1*d*.

'payd to John Wms for things wch he delyueryd aboute the laste playe.'

1574. Thomas Williams, 'Wardon of the Eylde' (aisle); *i.e.*, sideman or churchwarden.

In 1578 Thomas Williams paid 2*d*. to a local rate, and was a burgess. He was a burgess again in 1580.

1586. 'Imprimis paid Thomas William for Christopher the mason of his Wages for workinge on the church wal, 13*s*.'

In 1592 Thomas Williams was again a burgess. About this time we find the following note, written in the margin of the list for a local rate, in which his name occurs: 'thomas wm xxd d: barell lyme of mony of the Reste in lime.' Also this entry: 'Itē paide to Thomas william ffor halfe pounde of matche, 4*d*.'

In 1596 Thomas Williams was a Capital Burgess. In 1597 he paid towards a local rate. In 1602 and 1603 he was again a Capital Burgess.

In 1603 we find George Williams among the burgesses of Saint Ives.

1604. 'Pd Thomas Willm for the residue of the 10li borrowed of him for the parrishes use, £1 19*s*. 4*d*.

Paide Thos William for vjc of latte nailes for the churche, 1*s*.'

In 1605 George Williams was chosen Porthrieve, and was succeeded in that office the following year by Thomas Williams, merchant.

In 1613 George Williams was a capital burgess, and again in 1615.

In 1620, among those paying towards the royal rate, we find George Williams (6*d*.), and Thomas Williams, residing on The Land, who paid 1*d*.

In 1631, among the burgesses is Henry Williams; he was an overseer of the poor in 1637.

1667. 'Recd of Jasper Willyams for his freedome, 10*s*.'

1715. 'To Richard Thomas for makeing the Cawsey by Jasper Williams, 2*s*.'

1768. 'Pd William Williams serjeant at mace one yrs. salary, £1.'

Parish Registers.

1651. Bapt[d] John s. of Francis Williams.
1656. Bapt[d] Thomas s. of Francis Williams.
1660. Bapt[d] William s. of William Williams.
1662. Bapt[d] Henry s. of William Williams.
1665. Bapt[d] Elinar d. of William Williams.
1668. Bapt[d] Joan d. of William Williams.
1669. Married Jasper Williams & Mary Howse.
1670. Bapt[d] John s. of Jasper Williams.
1671. Bapt[d] Wilmott d. of William Williams.
1672. Bapt[d] Thomas s. of Jasper Williams.
1674. Bapt[d] Anne d. of William Williams.
1675. Bapt[d] Edward s. of William Williams.
1677. Married Jasper Williams & Honor White.
1678. Bapt[d] Amy d. of Jasper Williams.
1681. Bapt[d] Margery d. of Jasper Williams.
1684. Bapt[d] Henry s. of Henry Williams.
1685. Bapt[d] Chrystian d. of Jasper Williams.
1687. Bapt[d] Christian d. of Thomas Williams.
1690. Bapt[d] Richard s. of Jasper Williams.
1701. Married John Williams & Mary Barbar.
1702. Bapt[d] John s. of John Williams.
1708. Bapt[d] Jasper s. of Thomas & Mary Williams.
1709. Married Henry Williams & Grace Teage.
1709. Bapt[d] Edward s. of William Williams.
1718. Married Bennett Rabnet & Tryphena Williams.
1722. Bapt[d] William s. of William & Mary Williams.
1725. Married William Williams & Anne Cogar.
1726. Bapt[d] William s. of William & Anne Williams.
1727. Married Richard Williams & Mary Legoe.
1728. Bapt[d] Richard s. of Richard & Mary Williams.
1730. Married Thomas Williams & Thomasine Middylton.
1730. Married John Williams *alias* Gillen & Mary Davy.
1731. Bapt[d] Florence d. of Jasper & Florence Williams.
1731. Bapt[d] the daughter of William & Ann Williams Shoorin.
1733. Bapt[d] Jasper s. of Jasper & Florence Williams.
1735. Married Honor d. of Jasper & Florence Williams.
1737. Bapt[d] John s. of Jasper & Florence Williams.
1738. Married M[r] William Hichens roper & Mary Williams.
1739. Bapt[d] John s. of Jasper & Florence Williams.
1741. Married Thomas Wall & Elizabeth Williams, a grass widow.
1744. Married William Williams & Margaret Lemall.

1745. Married Thomas Thomas & Margery Williams.
1760. Married Jasper Williams mariner & Mary Eustis spinster. Witness John Hichens & John Williams.
1764. Bapt[d] Jasper s. of Jasper & Mary Williams.
1765. Married Christopher Harvey mariner & Agnes Williams spinster. Witness William Williams and Leonard Humphreys.
1766. Married John Williams cordwainer & Frances Harry. Witness William Harry & Jasper Williams.
1771. Married Richard Harry and Christian Bryant (mariner & spinster). Witness Andrew Stevens and William Williams.

A List of old Saint Ives Wills, preserved at the Probate Registry at Bodmin:

1599. Thomas Saundry.
Lancellot Paul.
1600. Edmund Richards, *alias* Carniny.
William Mathew.
1601. Elizabeth Tailder.
William Berryman.
William Woolcock.
John Bosamoth.
John ....
1602. John Shapland.
George Goodall.
William Trenwith.
Richard Porthmere.
Edmund Richards.
Thomas James.
Jacob Wolcock.
John Allyn.
Chestine Barrett.
1603. Lawrence Sise.
Ambrose Creed.
1604. Alice James, *alias* Carndin.
1605. William Cock.
Robert Davy.
Roger Tackabur.
John Davy.
1606. Richard Walkey.
Richard Tucker.
Henry Trenwith.
John ....
1607. Richard Coffen.
Katherine Rundell.
Richard Gote.
1609. John Durant.
John Nawll.
Penticost Chapland.
Elizabeth Tailder.
1610. William Oats.
William Ellis.
1612. Thomas James.
Richard ....
Nicholas Bositheow.
John Toman.
Richard Hitchens.
Richard Harry.
Richard Bennett.
1613. John Brea.
1614. John Nance.
1615. Michael Pencaste.
1616. John Sterry.
Elizabeth Beard.
1617. Peter Johns.
John Nickell.
William Thomas.
George ....
1618. John ....
1619. John Hext, gent.
Mathew Trenwith.

Nicholas Carveith.
Thomas Geiles.
Edmund Player.
1620. Teage German.
1621. Martin Bishop.
Jane Jausling.
Walter Binnore.
1622. John Toman.
Thomas Toman.
Thomas Browne.
1623. Michael Potteribur.
1624. John Thomas.
William Hicks.
John Hicks.
1625. William Nickell.
Richard Hocken.
1626. Peter Jagow.
....
....
1627. George ....
1628. John ....
1629. Mary Champyon.
1631. Jacob Steary.
1633. John Steary.
Richard Hurley.
1634. .... Hicks.
1636. George Paynter.
Phillip Allen.
Elizabeth Christian Bennett.
.... Stephens.
.... Pears.
1639. .... Byshopp.
.... Tregeare.
.... Hicks.
1640. .... Thomas.
.... Bayley.
.... Nancothan.
Lewis Hendra.
1641. .... Bishop.
1642. Mary Williams.
1643. Grace Hurley.
.... Bishop.
John Carneny.
Thomas Newman.
1644. Lawrence ....
1645. Christopher Payne.
John James.
William Pitt.
Robert Bolitho.
1647. Florence Margaret Walker.
Richard Hicks.
1648. Dorothy Cubert.
John Mary, *alias* ....
Susanna Pears.
Alexander Bishop.
.... Tayler.
1660. .... White.
John Goodall.
1661. .... Bennett.
....
1669. ....
1711. John Mathews.
1752. Elizabeth Mathews.
1789. Thomas Mathews.

CHAPTER XXXI.

LOCAL NOTABILITIES WHO DO NOT FIGURE IN THE FOREGOING GENEALOGIES.

John Knill.

THIS celebrated man holds such a prominent position in the history of our town that his memory demands a separate chapter. The fullest biography of Knill is a scarce 8vo. pamphlet of 26 pages, entitled 'A Notice of John Knill of Gray's Inn, 1733—1811; by J. J. R. [John Jope Rogers.] Helston; R. Cunnack, 1871. Price sixpence.' From this, then, we shall gather our particulars of the life of this noteworthy mayor of Saint Ives.

John Knill was born at Callington, Cornwall, on January 1, 1733, and died at his chambers in Gray's Inn Square, London, on March 29, 1811, at the age of seventy-seven.

The Knill family were landowners at Callington, and seem to have been descended from Knill of that ilk in Herefordshire, to which place John Knill paid a visit of genealogical inquiry in 1792. His mother was a Pike of Plympton, and her mother an Edgcumbe of Edgcumbe.

John Knill was articled to Robert Hichens of Penzance, solicitor, and afterwards served with a London solicitor. He then became agent to the Earl of Buckinghamshire at Saint Ives. In 1762 he became collector of Customs of that port, and remained in that post until 1782, except during two short intervals of absence.

In November, 1767, John Knill was chosen Mayor of Saint Ives.

In 1773 the Government sent him to Jamaica to inspect the ports there. Knill remained in the West Indies one year, and received for his services, besides the warm thanks of the Board of Customs, the substantial sum of £1,500. Returning to Saint Ives in 1774, he resumed his duties as a collector of Customs, residing in a house of his own in Fore Street.

In 1777 Knill became private secretary to the Earl of Buckinghamshire, and, upon that nobleman being made Lord-Lieutenant of Ireland, had rooms in Dublin Castle; but he returned to Saint Ives after six months. Lord Buckinghamshire made Knill one of the trustees of his will.

In 1779 Mr. Knill wrote an account of the religious belief of the Coromantee negroes for Mr. Bryan Edwards' 'History of the West Indies.' In the same year he speculated in a bootless search for treasure which was supposed to have been hidden near the Lizard by a notorious pirate called Avery. Davies Gilbert says that Knill, after his return to Saint Ives from Jamaica, equipped some small vessels to act as privateers against smugglers.

In 1781 John Knill commanded a corps of volunteers at Saint Ives. After 1782 he was in the service of the Customs for two or three years as inspector of some of the western ports, making occasional tours of inspection from London, as appears from his journals and pocket-books.

In 1782 he went to London, and lived in Arundel Street, Strand. Already, on September 18, 1778, he had been admitted a member of Gray's Inn. In 1784 he purchased chambers in Coney Court, now called Gray's Inn Square. In 1787 he was called to the Bar, and in 1804 to the Bench of the Inn, of which he was treasurer in 1806. In London, Knill was a member of the Society of Arts and of the Cornish Club. In 1800 he became a magistrate for the county of Middlesex.

Amongst the Knill papers are journals of several tours which he took on horseback. One of these commenced at the Earl of Buckinghamshire's estate in Norfolk, whence Knill rode across to Wales and on to Saint Ives, returning to London through the southern counties. This was about the year 1785.

There still exists, in Knill's handwriting, the draft of a scheme for the suppression of wrecking, for which he received the thanks of Government. His near relation, Mr. Robert Hichens, stated that Knill drew the Income Tax Act for Pitt.

Mr. Knill was very fond of children, and liked to make them kind presents of toys. He was a very devout attendant at the services of the Established Church.

A Kit-cat portrait by Opie, painted in 1779, represents Knill very pleasingly, with bright, smiling, hazel eyes, well-arched eyebrows, and full, but not lofty, forehead; a resolute lip, dark, unpowdered hair, and close-shaven chin and cheek. He is dressed in a plain suit of blue, with frilled shirt and ruffles, and is depicted sitting in an easy attitude at table. Thus far the pamphlet.

In the year 1782 I find that John Knill took an active part in a scheme for the construction of a new road at Saint Ives. The following are copies of letters in the author's possession bearing on this subject:

'R^T^ WORSHIPFULL & DEAR SIR,

'I take the liberty to lay before you the two Reports respecting the Roads & the Streets which I send you herewith & after you have perused & considered them I will beg the favor of you to return them with this Note that I may send the same to the rest of the Justices according to their ranks.

'Mr Stephen's hath offered to make the whole second Hill for Five shillings ℘ Fathom. The whole does not exceed 276 Fathoms which will cost 69^li^. We shall I hope be able to raise enough from the Rate made & the Compositions to pay this & the other little repairs this year if it shall meet your expectation & the other Hill near the Town may be the object of another year. I am R^t^ Worshipfull & Dear Sir, Your dev^ted^ & m^t^ h'ble Servant.

'JOHN KNILL.

'Wedn' Even', 27 Feby 1782.'

Accompanying this letter is a report, which is endorsed:

'1782. Boro' of St Ives. Report of the Surveyors of the Highways as to making a new road into St Ives to avoid the Hills & Estimates of the Expence.'

The document begins thus:

'An Estimate of the Expence of making the Road from the Borough of St Ives from the corner of Mr Anthony's Cellar upon the Beach, & so through the Warren, & through the Ground beyond the new Stamping Mill so as to come out into the present Road at a small distance to the Northward of Wheal Margery Mine.

'From the Corner of Mr Anthony's Cellar to Porthnolver Cliff under James Hall's House is 360½ feet. . . .

'(Signed) JOHN KNILL.
'J^NO^ STEVENS.
'J^NO^ GRENFELL.
'R^D^ MAJOR.

'St Ives, 25 Febr^y^ 1782.'

'Tregenna 2^d^ March 1782.

'DEAR SIR,

'Being yesterday engaged in Buisness when your favor was brought me I could not look in to papers sent me till this morning. If the new Road thro my Lands is to be made I think with you that some sort of agreement should be reduced to writing for the satisfaction of all the concerned—an order must be made I presume for which I suppose there is a form. I have no Tenant that has any right to expect any advantage for cutting thro' any part of my Ground nor can I think that any Tenant or Lessee belonging to other gentlemen but must so plainly see the advantage of a new Road adjoining their holdings as to wave every pecuniary consideration for that reason. I have little doubt but by a half an hours conversation with you I could point out the saving of a considerable part of the expence alluded to in the estimate & am with great regard, Dear Sir, Your most obedient & very humble servant.

'S. STEPHENS.'

It was in the year 1782 that John Knill erected his mausoleum on Worvas Hill, on land purchased from Henry, Lord Arundel, for five guineas. The total cost of the monument was £226 1*s.* 6*d.* Sixpence a year is paid to the owner of Tregenna for a right of way to the obelisk. The following is an extract from Knill's will, dated 1809, the probate of which covers five skins of parchment:

'During a residence of upwards of 20 years at S[t] Ives, where I was Collector of the Customs and served all offices within the borough from constable to mayor, it was my unremitting endeavour to render all possible service to the town in general, and to every individual inhabitant; and I was so fortunate as to succeed in almost every endeavour I used for that purpose, particularly in respect to the building of their wall or pier, and in some other beneficial undertakings; and it was my wish to have further served the place by effecting other public works, which I proposed, and which will, I dare say, in time be carried into execution. It is natural to love those whom you have had opportunities of serving, and I confess I have real affection for S[t] Ives and its inhabitants, in whose memory I have an ardent desire to continue a little longer than the usual time those do of whom there is no ostensible memorial. To that end my vanity prompted me to erect a mausoleum and to institute certain periodical returns of a ceremony which will be found in a deed bearing date 29th May 1797, which hath been duly enrolled in his Majesty's High Court of Chancery, and now remains in a strong oaken box, placed in the Custom House at St. Ives, and an attested copy of which deed I shall leave for my executors hereinafter named.'

Amongst the numerous legacies bequeathed by this will were fifty-six five-guinea gold memorial-rings.

By a deed dated May 29, 1797 (drawn by Ritson, of Gray's Inn), Knill settled upon the mayor and capital burgesses of the borough of Saint Ives, and their successors for ever, an annuity of £10, as a rent charge, to be paid out of the manor of Glivian, in the parish of Mawgan, in the county of Cornwall, to the said mayor and burgesses, in the town hall, at twelve o'clock at noon, on the feast of the Nativity of St. John (Midsummer Day) in every year. The £10 then received are to be immediately paid by the mayor and burgesses to the mayor, collector of Customs, and the clergyman of the parish for the time being, to be by them deposited in a chest secured by three locks, of which each of them is to have a key, and the box is left in the custody of the mayor. Of this annuity a portion is directed to be applied to the repair and support of the mausoleum, another sum for the establishment of various ceremonies to be observed once every five years, and the remainder 'to the effectuating and establishing of certain charitable purposes.' In his will he directed that at the end of every five years, on the feast-day of St. James the Apostle, £25 shall be expended as follows: £10 in a dinner for the mayor, collector of Customs, and clergyman, and two friends to be invited by each of them, making a party of nine persons, to dine at some tavern in the borough; £5 to be equally divided amongst ten girls, natives of the borough and daughters of seamen, fishermen or tinners, each of them not exceeding ten years of age, who shall, between ten and twelve o'clock of the forenoon of that day, dance for a quarter of an hour at least, on the ground adjoining the mausoleum, and after the dance sing the 100th Psalm of the old version, 'to the fine old tune' to which the same was then sung in Saint Ives Church; £1 to a fiddler who shall play to the girls while dancing and singing at the mausoleum, and also before them on their return home therefrom; £2 to two widows of seamen, fishermen, or tinners of the borough, being sixty-four years old or upwards, who shall attend the dancing and singing of the girls, and walk before them immediately after the fiddler, and certify to the mayor, collector of Customs, and clergyman, that the ceremonies have been duly performed; £1 to be laid out in white ribbons for breast-knots for the girls and widows, and a cockade for the fiddler, to be worn by them respectively on that day and on the Sunday following; £1 to purchase account-books from time to time, and pay the clerk of the Customs for keeping the accounts. The remaining £5 to be paid to a man and his wife, widower or widow, sixty years of age or upwards, the man being an inhabitant of Saint Ives, and a seaman, fisherman, tinner, or labourer, who shall have bred up to the age of ten the greatest number of legitimate children by his or her own labour, care, and industry, without parochial assistance, or having become entitled to property in any other manner. Secondly, when a certain sum of money shall have been accumulated in the chest, over and above what may have been required for repairs of the mausoleum and the above payment, it is directed that on one of the forementioned days of the festival £50 shall be distributed, in addition to the £25 spent quinquennially, in the following manner: £10 to be given as a marriage portion of the woman between twenty-six and thirty-six years old, being a native of Saint Ives, who shall have been married to a seaman, fisherman, tinner, or labourer, residing in the borough between December 31 previously and the day following the said feast-day, that shall appear to the mayor, collector, and clergyman, to be the most worthy, 'regard being had to her duty and kindness to her parents, or to her friends who shall have brought her up'; £5 to be given to any woman, single or married, being an inhabitant of Saint Ives, who, in the opinion of the aforesaid gentlemen, shall be the best knitter of fishing nets; £5 to be paid to the woman, married or single, inhabitant of Saint Ives or otherwise, who shall by the same authorities be deemed to be the best curer and packer of pilchards for exportation; £5 to be given between two such follower-boys as shall by the same gentlemen be judged to have best conducted themselves of all the follower-boys in the several concerns in the preceding fishing season; and £25, the remainder of the said £50, to be divided among all the friendly societies in the borough, instituted for the support of the members in sickness or any other calamity, in equal shares; if there be no such society, the same to be distributed among ten poor persons, five men and five women, inhabitants of the borough, of the age of sixty-four years or upwards, and who have never received parochial relief.

The funds of the trust have not always admitted of several of these latter bequests being carried out; but the dancing around the mausoleum by ten children, accompanied by the fiddler and the two old women, has always been observed. The money, also, is regularly paid to the father or mother who has brought up the largest family without parish help; and the dinner, of course, has never been forgotten.

The first Knillian celebration took place in July, 1801, when, according to the will of the founder, a band of virgins, all dressed in white, with two widows and a company of musicians, commenced the ceremony by walking in pairs to the summit of the hill, where they danced, and sang a hymn composed for the purpose, round the mausoleum, in imitation of the Druids round the cromlechs of the departed brave.

Some idea of the joyous scene may be conceived from the following description of an imaginative spectator:

'Early in the morning the roads from Helston, Truro, and Penzance, were lined with horses and vehicles of every description. These were seen midst clouds of dust pouring down the sides of the mountains, while thousands of travellers on foot chose the more pleasant route through the winding passages of the vallies.

'At noon the assembly was formed. The wrestlers entered the ring; the troop of virgins, dressed all in white, advanced with solemn step, which was regulated by the notes of harmony. The spectators ranged themselves along the hills which inclose the extensive Bay, while the pyramid on the summit seemed pointing to the sun, who appeared in all the majesty of light, rejoicing at the scene.

'At length the Mayor of St. Ives appeared in his robes of state. The signal was given. The flags were displayed in waving splendour from the towers of the Castle.

'Here the wrestlers exerted their sinewy strength; there the rowers, in their various dresses of blue, white, and red, urged the gilded prows of their boats through the sparkling waves of the ocean; while the hills echoed to the mingled shouts of the victors, the dashing of the oars, the songs of the virgins, and the repeated plaudits of the admiring crowd, who stood so thick upon the crescent which is formed by the surrounding mountains as to appear one living amphitheatre.

'The ladies and gentlemen of Penzance returned to an elegant dinner, which they had ordered to be prepared at the Union Hotel, and a splendid ball concluded the entertainment of the evening.

'Hilarity and beauty danced to the most delicious notes of harmony, till the rosy finger of Aurora pointed to the hour at which the quinquennial festivities should close.'

These games were again celebrated in 1806 and 1811 with increased splendour and renewed admiration.

'This institution,' says the enthusiastic spectator already quoted, 'will go far to preserve the tone of the Cornish character, and can never be neglected while the Cornish men continue to be brave, and the Cornish women to be virtuous.'

The following chorus was sung by the virgins at the first celebration:

'Shun the bustle of the bay,
Hasten, virgins, come away;
Hasten to the mountain's brow,
Leave, oh leave, St. Ives below.
Haste to breathe a purer air,
Virgins fair, and pure as fair;
Fly St. Ives and all her treasures,
Fly her soft voluptuous pleasures;
Fly her sons and all the wiles,
Lurking in their wanton smiles.
Fly her splendid midnight halls,
Fly the revels of her balls;
Fly, oh fly, the chosen seat,
Where vanity and fashion meet.
Thither hasten, form the ring,
Round the tomb in chorus sing.
And on the loft mountain's brow—aptly dight,
Just as we should be, all in white,
Leave all our cowels and our cares below.'

Some appropriate verses were also sung by a minstrel adorned with ribbons.

In former years the custom had been for the dancers to walk in procession from the town to the mausoleum. But in 1881 the weather was so unfavourable that the old practice was departed from, and the actors were driven up in a waggonette. Then they marched inside the railings, where they danced round the monument, much to the merriment of the motley crowd of onlookers.

The names of the children were Annie Richards, Wilmot Chard, Nancy T. Bryant, Bessie Peters, Bessie Hollow, Margaret Dunn, Mary Ann Quick, Elizabeth J. Perkin, Mary Richards and Margaret W. Bryant, all under ten years of age.

The widows were Elizabeth Trevorrow, seventy-six, and Nancy Stoneman, seventy-four. These ancient crones, with their very much younger sisters, managed, at the end of their shambling, to quaver out the 'Old Hundredth,' and a 'fine old tune' they made of it. During the afternoon the money was paid to the recipients at the office of Mr. Hicks; and the sum of £5, for the man who had brought up the largest family of children up to ten years of age, was awarded to Andrew Noall, seventy-one, who had had sixteen children, nine of them being under the specified age. The fiddler received £1. In the evening the dinner was held at the Tregenna Castle Hotel. Mr. W. T. Tresidder, who acted as the mayor's deputy during the day, presided, Mr. Cogar being ill, and the other gentlemen being present were the Rev. J. Balmer Jones, vicar of Saint Ives; Mr. R. Minors, collector of Customs; Messrs. Tonkin Young and W. Kernick, the mayor's guests; Messrs. G. B. Pearse and G. Hicks, guests of the collector of Customs; and Mr. H. Hicks, of the Customs, who acts as clerk under Knill's bequest.

Previous to the day's ceremonies the mausoleum was repainted and generally restored. The coffin within was found to be full of water, a curious phenomenon, inasmuch as its huge 'casket' is supposed to be water-tight. On the occasion of re-opening the tomb some of the villagers became possessed of a curious desire to drink of this liquid.

The following were the persons who figured in the Knillian celebration of 1886:

Fiddler: Thomas Curnow.
Widows: Nancy Stoneman and Jane Bosanquet.
Virgins: Annie Perkins, Margaret Williams, Margaret Caredon, Lizzie Warren, Lizzie Jane Couch, Agnes Lang Harry, Catherine Ninnis Quick, Clarinda Noall, Harriet Bosanquet Noall, Lizzie Geen.
Controller of Customs: L. C. Reed, Esq.
Constable: Mr. Bennetts.

Jonathan Toup.

This talented man, the greatest Grecian of his time, was a native of Saint Ives, and spent much of his life there. His father, Jonathan Toup, was lecturer or Scripture-reader of this parish. He married Prudence, heiress of Busvargus, came to Saint Ives in 1712, and died there in 1721.

In the Corporation accounts we find the following entries, under the year 1712: 'more when we agreed with Mr. Toupe, 7*s.* 6*d.*'; and 'given Mr Toupe to come here, £1 1*s.* 6*d.*' His signature occurs both in the accounts and in the parish registers.

His son was born and baptised in 1713, as appears by an entry in the parish registers of that date: 'Baptised Jonathan son of Jonathan Toup minister.'

Another child of the same marriage was Mary, baptised in 1713. Jonathan Toup became a Commoner of Exeter College, Oxford, and took the degree of Bachelor of Arts. He was appointed curate of Philleigh, Cornwall, in 1736, and of Burian [Sennen and Saint Levan ?] in 1738. In 1750 he became rector of Saint Martin's, near Looe, and he received the degree of Master of Arts of Cambridge University in the year 1756. In 1774 he became vicar of Saint Merran and Prebend of Exeter. Mr. Toup was equally distinguished as a linguist and as a mathematician, an unusual combination. His chief work, first published in 1760, was his 'Emendationes in Suidam, in quibus plurima loca Veterum Græcorum, Sophoclis et Aristophanis in primis, tum explicuntur tum emaculantur,' which went through three editions. Toup is also remembered as the producer of the best edition of Longinus. He died unmarried in 1785, at Saint Martins, in the church of which parish there is a monument to his memory.

His sister, Mary Toup, was married to Charles Worth, Esq., of Saint Ives, in 1746. There are descendants of this marriage, both in the male line, and in the female line through Hicks and Kempthorne.

Henry Quick, the Zennor Poet.

Of Henry Quick there is not much to say. Mr. Millett, in his 'Penzance Past and Present,' writes: 'John Odger, Joe Elliott, Foolish Dick, Blind Dick, and Henry Quick—the Zennor poet, as he was called—will be familiar to many. The first three have been immortalized by the pencil of Pentreath, and the latter, if not immortalized, will be remembered by his rhymes, of which the following, referring to himself, is a specimen:

'In Zennor parish I was born,
On Cornwall's coast, remember;
My birthday was in Ninety-two,
The Fourth of December.'

It appears that this eccentric character was accustomed to hawk his rhymes about the streets of Penzance, as he tells us in another verse:

'Oftimes abroad I take my flight,
Take pity on poor Henny;
To sell my books 'tis my delight,
To gain an honest penny.'

In one of the earlier volumes of the *Western Antiquary* there is a rude wood-cut representing Henry Quick engaged in selling his ballads. He wears a tall hat and carries a bell.

A Pair of Nonagenarians.

Old Martha S., after she had reached her ninetieth year, received every Christmas a present of a bottle of brandy. One Christmas Dr. Stevens visited her, and found her in bed as usual (for she had been bed-ridden for years), with the bottle on a table near at hand. 'Is it good stuff, Martha?' enquired the Doctor. 'Oh, sir,' she replied, looking up solemnly in his face, and clasping the bottle to her bosom—'oh, sir, 'tes a blessed theng, a blessed theng!' Doctors Stevens and Rosewall did their utmost to assist this old lady to the honours of a centenarian; but she gave in a few weeks after her ninety-ninth birthday.

Another person who long enjoyed the distinction of being 'the oldest inhabitant' was Daniel Lander Ninnis, who was born on September 19, 1790, and died on March 31, 1888, aged ninety-seven. He was able to get about the street up to a few days before his death, and was often to be seen sitting in the sunlight in front of his house on the Wharf. He was frequently called upon by persons interested in local bygones, as he had a wonderfully clear recollection of things which happened when he was a boy. To the day of his death his sight and hearing were good, and his hair far from being white, though he was a great-great-grandfather.

In the summer of 1887 Daniel Ninnis, or 'Uncle Dall,' as he was familiarly styled, was visited by two gentlemen who were strongly opposed to alcohol and tobacco, as enemies of the human race. They were pleased to hear from Uncle Dall that he had been for the greater part of his long life an abstainer from strong drink; and they next asked whether the old man had not also avoided the pipe. Triumphant was the smile which played upon their features when he informed them that he had never smoked; but this smile died sadly away when the nonagenarian innocently added that he had always chewed, and would be glad of a 'quid' at that moment. He was, in fact, inveterately addicted to the use of plug tobacco.

CHAPTER XXXII.

PARLIAMENTARY HISTORY OF THE BOROUGH.

'THROUGH the bounty of Philip and Mary,' says Courtney ('Parliamentary History of Cornwall,' p. 61), 'Saint Ives was invested, in 1558, with the privilege of sending two members to the House of Commons, presumably through the interest of the supple Marquis of Winchester.'

'The borough was conterminous with the parish, and every person within its limits, paying scot and lot, was entitled to exercise the franchise, so that in 1820 the roll contained about three hundred and forty electors.'

The following is the list of members, with the dates of election:

1558. Thomas Randolph and William Chambre.

Randolph was a Commissioner of the Exchequer.

1559. John Harrington and William Glasioure.

Harrington was of a family seated in Rutland. He was chosen again in 1563, but being that year elected also for Carnarvon, he chose to sit for the Welsh constituency. The name of his successor in the Cornish borough is omitted from the roll, however. Glasioure belonged to Cheshire, and twice sat for the city of Chester, of which he eventually became the vice-chamberlain.

1563. John Harrington and William Glasioure.

1571. Thomas Clinton and J. Newman.

1572. E. Williams and Thomas Randolph.

1584. John James and Charles Blount.

These were expressed to be 'elected with the consent of William, Marquess of Winchester, and William, Lord Mountjoye, chief lords of the town and borough of St Ives.' John James was, in 1595, appointed physician to the Queen's household. Charles Blount, or Blunt, was afterwards created Earl of Devonshire and Lord Lieutenant of Ireland.

1586. Thomas Colby and John Morley.

Colby was of Banham, in Norfolk. Morley was a large landed proprietor in Sussex, one of whose descendants became allied with the Acklands.

1588. Mark Stewarde and Henry Hobart.

These also were declared 'returned with the consent of William, Marquess of Winchester, and Lord Mountjoy, lords of the port.' Stewarde was of Stuntney in the Isle of Ely. He was subsequently knighted, and his daughter was maid of honour to Queen Elizabeth. Hobart, who was ancestor of the Earls of Buckinghamshire, was afterwards made Chief Justice of the Common Pleas.

1593. Nowell Sotherton and Nicholas Saunders.

The former was, I believe, a Norwich man, and was, in 1606, created an extra Baron of the Court of Exchequer. The other member was at different times returned for other Cornish constituencies.

1597. V. Skinner and Nowell Sotherton.

1601. Thomas St. Aubyn and T. Breton.

The former Carew styles a man of 'ripe knowledge and sound judgment.'

1603. John Tregenna and W. Brook.

The first-named was the man returned to oppose the obnoxious Mr. Tregosse. (See *ante*, p. 468.)

1614. Sir Anthony Mayney and Sir Joseph Killigrew.

Mayney was a Kentish man. Killigrew was knighted at Newmarket in 1613, and died in 1616, aged only twenty-three.

1620. John, Lord Paulet, and Robert Bacon.

The latter was son of the premier baronet of England.

1622. Sir Francis Godolphin, knight, and W. Lake.

1625. Sir William Parkhurst and Sir Francis Godolphin.

Parkhurst was a Knight of the City of London.

1625. William Noye and Benjamin Tichborne.

The former, of an ancient family in West Cornwall, was made Attorney-General in 1631. The idea of levying ship-money is said to have originated with him. His colleague was a member of the old Hampshire family of Tichborne. Being chosen at the same time for Petersfield, he elected to sit for the latter borough, and his place at Saint Ives was taken by Mr. Edward Savage, who was a relative of the Marchioness of Winchester, and was knighted in 1639.

1627. John Payne and Francis Godolphin, esquire.

Payne is described as of Pallenswick, in Hammersmith; but Courtney seems to assume that he was of the same family with the Catholic portrieve put to death in 1549. At all events, a person of the same name is mentioned about this time in the borough records.

1640. William Dell and Sir Henry Marten, knight.

In this Parliament Dell got into trouble for stating 'that the churches beyond seas were about to fall from us because we were about to leave our religion.'

1640. (The Long Parliament.) Francis Godolphin and Lord Philip Lisle.

This Courtney presumes to have been Francis Godolphin, of Treveneage. The other member was eldest son of the Earl of Leicester, and one of the king's judges; but he chose to sit for Yarmouth, Isle of Wight, and was succeeded in his seat at Saint Ives by Edmund Waller, nephew of Hampden and cousin of Cromwell. Waller having entered into a conspiracy in favour of King Charles, was heavily fined and banished, his place for the borough of Saint Ives being taken by John Fielder, of Hampshire. Francis Godolphin also in the end seceded to the royal cause, and Carlyle says (but the authority is doubtful) that he was succeeded at Saint Ives by Henry Rainsford.

1659. John St. Aubyn and Peter Ceely.

The latter was of a distinguished Somersetshire family, branches of which settled at Plymouth and Saint Ives, and during the Commonwealth 'ruled the district from that town to the Land's End with undisputed sway.'

1660. John St. Aubyn and Edward Nosworthy.

The Nosworthys were a family who had acquired much property at Truro, and had also purchased some interest at Saint Ives. During the short period of their fortune they were strongly attached to the interests of the Kings Charles II. and James II.

A double return for the borough was made in the first Parliament of this year, but the extra return, that of James Praed and Peter Ceely, was voided. At the same time the franchise was declared to be vested in the residents at large, and not only in the capital burgesses.

1661. James Praed and Edward Nosworthy.

The latter was unseated, however, upon the usual election enquiry, and his place taken by John Basset, of Tehidy. 'The struggle,' says Courtney, 'was again between the capital burgesses and the inhabitants at large. Nineteen of the burgesses gave their support to Nosworthy, but the majority of the popular votes were this time cast for Basset. The committee reported, and the House accepted their view, that the right of voting was vested (as was determined by the last House) in the inhabitants at large, and Nosworthy was thereupon ejected. Before this decision had been given Mr. Basset had died, and another election was necessary. Nosworthy again contested the seat, and his opponent was a Mr. Daniel O'Neall, possibly the Irish Catholic who, through his position as groom of the bedchamber to Charles I., became a king's favourite, and was led on to take a share in Goring's plot to rescue the hapless Strafford.' Nosworthy was rejected for a second time. In May, 1663, several persons were summoned for breach of privilege in bringing ejectment actions against O'Neall in respect of his landed property. He died in 1664, and Nosworthy was at length returned for the borough of Saint Ives, although he was opposed by Sir William Godolphin, both at the poll and by petition.

1679 (March). Edward Nosworthy, senior, and Edward Nosworthy, junior.

1679 (October). Edward Nosworthy, senior, and Edward Nosworthy, junior.

The younger Nosworthy is spoken of by Courtney as the 'reckless son, who extinguished the fortunes of the family.'

1680. James Praed, junior, and Edward Nosworthy, junior.

This is the last time that a Nosworthy was elected.

The younger Nosworthy was a firm adherent of King James II., and was a Gentleman of the Privy Chamber to that monarch, whom he followed into exile.

'He died suddenly at Dunkirk, in 1701, and with his demise,' says Courtney, 'there ended a family which had risen in one generation and fallen in the next.'

1685. Charles Davenant and James St. Amand.

The former of these was a son of the poet laureate, and an industrious writer in favour of the Tory party.

1689. Walter Vincent and James Praed.

The former was a Truro man, and the latter was of Trevethow. From this date the Praeds long exercised the chief political power at Saint Ives.

1690. James Praed and W. Harris.

1695. James Praed and J. Michell.

1698. Sir Charles Wyndham, bart., and James Praed.

Wyndham became Praed's colleague through the refusal of the mayor to accept the votes for Sir Henry Hobart, 'on the ground,' as was alleged in the consequent petition, 'that the right of election was in the mayor, capital burgesses, and assistants only'; but the petitioners did not press the matter further.

1700. James Praed and Benjamin Overton.

Overton was the son of a 'fifth monarchy man,' who was hanged; but in 1690 he became Warden of the Mint.

[illegible] John Hawles, knight, and James Praed.
[illegible] had previously sat for Truro.
[Ja]mes Praed and Richard Chandler.
[illegible] was opposed by John Pitt, afterwards Lieutenant-[illegible] the Bermudas; but Chandler was returned by the [illegible] of course, petitioned; but the committee decided that Chandler had been duly elected, on the ground that the right of election belonged to the inhabitants not receiving alms. The House, however, supported Pitt, and declared that the franchise vested 'in the inhabitants of the borough paying scot and lot'; and the mayor, John Hicks, was ordered into custody for making a false return in opposition to the determination of 1661.

1705. Sir Bartholomew Gracedieu, knight, and John Borlase.

Gracedieu, of Huguenot descent, was Sheriff of London, and was knighted in the bedchamber at Kensington in 1697. Shortly after his election he became bankrupt.

1708. John Praed and John Borlase.

Christopher Harris and James Tregeare petitioned, but soon withdrew.

1710. John Hopkins and John Praed.

1713. Sir William Pendarves, knight, and John Hopkins.

John Elford and Lord Harry Pawlett, John Hichens and Paul Tremearne, petitioned 'for themselves and other unbribed burgesses,' as they significantly expressed it. 'Vulture Hopkins,' as he was nicknamed, is satirized by Pope. He was a miser, and accumulated an immense fortune.

1714. Lord Harry Pawlett and Sir John Hobart.

This election, the first after the accession of the Hanoverian line, marked the triumph of Whigism, and the consequent decline of the influence of the Tory Praeds. Lord Harry Pawlett was afterwards fourth Duke of Bolton.

1722. Sir John Hobart and H. Knollys.

Henry Waller and James Tregeare petitioned. The latter in 1718 was charged with murder, as to which we have written in a former chapter. (See *ante*, p. 301.)

'Most of the members for St. Ives at this period,' says the 'Parliamentary History of Cornwall,' 'were placemen who owed their preferments to the favour of the great Whig magnates, and their places in Parliament to the Hobart influence at St. Ives.'

1727. Sir Robert Rich and H. Knollys.

Rich, a Suffolk baronet, was successively a colonel of dragoons, a groom of the royal bedchamber, governor of Chelsea Hospital, and member of Parliament for the boroughs of Dunwich and Beer-Alston.

1738. Sir Robert Rich and 'William Mackworth, otherwise William Mackworth Praed.'

John Praed was the last male of his line. After his death in 1717 he was succeeded in his possessions by Sir Humphrey Mackworth of Glamorganshire, who, together with the estate of Trevethow, took the name and arms of Praed, and was father to William Mackworth Praed above mentioned.

1741. John Bristow and Gregory Beake.

Bristow, whose sister was married to Sir John Hobart, first Earl of Buckinghamshire, was Deputy-Governor of Southsea, and supplied money to the troops at Jamaica, at a profit of 14 per cent., which favouritism was one of the charges brought against the deposed Premier Walpole in 1742. Beake was a lieutenant-colonel in the Horse Guards.

1747. John Bristow and John Plumptree.

Lord Hobart was this year elected for both Saint Ives and Norwich, and chose the latter constituency. He thereupon offered the vacant seat to Plumptree, of Kent and Nottingham, sometime treasurer of the Ordnance.

1751. John Bristow and Samuel Stephens.

At this bye-election, caused by the death of Plumptree,

'when Mr. Samuel Stephens was returned, there first appeared,' says Courtney, 'prominently before the eyes of the public, a family which had hitherto been content to guide the feelings of the constituency in favour of others. For generations the bearers of the name had been acquiring wealth through the fisheries and mines of St. Ives, and their position in West Penwith was so marked even in 1603 that the then head of the house preferred the payment of the substantial sum of £16 to the receipt of the questionable honour of knighthood. [See *ante*, p. 451.] Up to 1751 the father of Mr. Samuel Stephens had acted as the agent to the Earl of Buckinghamshire in the management of the borough politics, but he broke off the connection in that year by procuring the election of his son.'

1754. Hon. George Hobart and James Whitshed.

George Hobart was afterwards third Earl of Buckinghamshire. This was the last time that a Hobart sat for Saint Ives.

'During the long reign of Farmer George, the representation of the borough was often the subject of dispute between the rival houses of Praed and Stephens,' says Courtney, in the work from which we are now drawing so largely.

1761. Humphrey Mackworth Praed and Charles Hotham.

The latter, a member of a Yorkshire family, had married Lady Dorothy Hobart. At the time of his election he was a captain of foot guards, and adjutant-general to the British forces in Germany. Soon afterwards he was made a groom of the bedchamber.

1768. Thomas Durrant and Adam Drummond.

'Durrant, a Norfolk squire, represented the Hobart interest, while Drummond was elected through the influence of the Duke of Bolton, whose sister he had married.'

1774. W. T. Praed and Sir Thomas Wynn.

Praed was unseated for bribery. Wynn was afterwards first Lord Newborough.

1775. Adam Drummond and Sir Thomas Wynn.

1778. Sir Thomas Wynn and P. Dehany.

The latter took the place of Drummond when he changed his seat for one in the north of Scotland.

1782. William Praed and Abel Smith.

Smith was of the renowned banking house, and was father of the first Lord Carrington. Praed was also a banker, founder of the Fleet Street firm.

1784. Abel Smith and Richard Barwell.

The latter Courtney calls 'that great spoiler of the natives of Hindostan.'

1790. William Praed and William Mills.

1796. William Praed and Sir Richard Carr Glyn.

Both these two colleagues of Praed were great bankers.

1802. William Praed and Jonathan Raine.

Raine was a renowned classical scholar and special pleader; he acted as auditor to the Duke of Northumberland's estates.

1806. Samuel Stephens and Francis Horner.

The latter was a clever political economist, and one of the founders of the *Edinburgh Review*. Courtney calls him 'one of the purest and cleverest politicians of the age.' The opponents of these members were two Indian colonels, Symes and Montgomery.

'Horner spent all the day in canvassing the town part of the constituency with his brother candidate, Samuel Stephens, the lord of Tregenna Castle. He entered every cellar in the place, "shook every individual voter by the hand, stinking with brine and pilchard juice, repeated the same smiles and cajoleries to every one of them," and (which was far more agreeable to him) found in those hovels a number "of pretty women, three or four of them quite beautiful," whom he religiously kissed.'

1807. Samuel Stephens and Sir Walter Stirling.

The name of Stirling is

'still familiar in Cornwall through the circumstance that Tregellas, the Cornish humourist, has written in his own racy style a description of the adventures in London of two of his constituents when summoned to give evidence before a Parliamentary Committee.'

Stirling was also a London banker.

1812. William Pole Tylney Long Wellesley and Sir Walter Stirling.

'The representation of St. Ives was about this date usually divided between the two great parties in the state. Wellesley was a supporter of the Whigs.'

1818. Samuel Stephens and Sir Walter Stirling.

1820. James Robert George Graham and Lyndon Evelyn.

'Graham, the keen politician, with as many changes of front as the weathercock,' was a Whig. The Tories were represented by Evelyn, who was of Keynsham Court, Herefordshire. Graham was unseated on petition, and his place taken by 'that election veteran Sir Christopher Hawkins.'

1826. Sir Christopher Hawkins and James Halse.

Mackinnon was a rejected candidate this year, but all three were Tories. Halse was greatly interested in mining, and built Halsetown, near Saint Ives.

1828. This year Hawkins retired to make room for Charles Arbuthnot, a friend of the Duke of Wellington, who had a place in the Ministry and a seat in the Cabinet.

1830. Pole Tylney Long Wellesley and James Morrison.

These were both Whigs; the latter a London merchant. Halse unsuccessfully opposed them.

1832. James Halse and Edward Lytton Bulwer.

These were Tory and Whig respectively. Halse was nothing more than a silent vote; but the latter became the renowned Lord Lytton, the author and (later in life) the Conservative politician.

This last election, turning as it did upon the great question of electoral reform, was regarded as of the highest importance, and was stubbornly fought. Praed was a defeated candidate. His brother, Winthrop Mackworth-Praed, the poet, contributed to the voluminous election-literature of this year what is now a very scarce little pamphlet of 32 pages: '*Trash*, dedicated, without respect, to James Halse Esq. M.P. Penzance. 1832.' From this brochure we select the following song:

THE LASSES OF THE BOROUGH.

I like to be drinking the health of the King.
And the health of the Queen is a very fine thing,
And the health of our sailors and soldiers, no doubt,
Is a health which no Briton is happy without;
  But the best of all healths is, 'the Maidens and Wives
  Who make the pot boil for the men of St Ives!'

There are dark curls and light, there are black eyes and blue,
But their hearts—bless their hearts!—are all honest and true;
There are some of them short, there are some of them tall,
But there's kindness and friendship and love in them all.
So the best of all healths is, 'the Maidens and Wives
Who make the pot boil for the men of St Ives!'

When a frank-hearted lad to their cottage rides up
They set on their table the loaf and the cup;
When the tyrant goes by who has trampled the poor
They fright him with frowns, as they ought, from the door;
Then the best of all healths is, 'the Maidens and Wives
Who make the bot boil for the men of St Ives!'

You cannot deceive them; they very well know,
The straight from the crooked, a friend from a foe,
The light from the darkness, the true from the false,
And, to cut short the matter—a Praed from a Halse!
And the best of all healths is, 'the Maidens and Wives
Who make the pot boil for the men of St Ives!'

The following is a list of the later members for Saint Ives, which since the Reform Bill has returned only one member to Parliament:

1833. James Halse.
1835. James Halse.
1837. James Halse (died 1838).
1838. William Tyringham Praed.
1839. William Tyringham Praed.
1846. Lord William Paulet.
1847. Lord William Paulet.
1852. Captain Robert M. Laffan, R.E.

'Captain Laffan is an Irish man,
He's got no business here;
Mr Paul es nothan' at all,
He wëant lev us have no beer.'
(*Local rhyme.*)

1857. Henry Paul.
1868. Charles Magniac.
1874. E. G. Davenport (died same year).
" Charles Praed; unseated on petition, but afterwards
1875. Charles Praed re-elected.
1880. Sir Charles Reed (died same year).
" Charles Campbell Ross.
" Sir John St. Aubyn (for the Saint Ives Division of West Cornwall. Raised to the peerage as Baron St. Levan in 1888).
1888. Thomas Bedford Bolitho (unopposed).

In consequence of the Parliamentary Redistribution Bill of 1884, the borough of Saint Ives was extended to include the whole Land's End district, including Penzance.

In the year 1874 occurred the memorable election in which Mr. Charles Praed was the Conservative candidate and Sir Francis Lycett the Liberal. Party feeling then ran very high. Mr. Praed having been elected, his opponent lodged a petition against the return, on the ground of bribery and corruption. Among the many persons of distinction in the world of law who came to Saint Ives to attend the inquiry into the alleged malpractices were Messrs. Lush and Hawkins, Q.C., afterwards Justices Lush and Hawkins. Mr. Praed was re-elected in the following year. The judicial examination of witnesses in the inquiry was held at the Town Hall.

'TRELOVHAN,' ST. IVES.

SILVANUS TREVAIL, ARCHITECT, 1891.

To face page 507.

CHAPTER XXXIII.

THE SAINT IVES ELECTION OF 1768.

In the year 1768 there was an election of two members of Parliament for the borough of Saint Ives, the candidates being Thomas Durrant, Adam Drummond, James Johnstone, and John Stevens.

Ever since Saint Ives became a borough, and especially since the election of 1660, there had been (as will be seen from our chapter on the Members of Parliament) much controversy as to the qualification for a voter in this town. One party claimed that all the inhabitants paying 'scot and lot' were entitled to vote; the other were for confining the privilege to the capital burgesses. This question was, in the year 1702, decided in favour of the larger franchise.

The important lawsuit of *Johnstone v. Hichens*, of which we will now give some interesting particulars, derived from the original documents used at the trial, in 1768, arose out of an attempt by the borough authorities to confine the ratepayers to their own supporters.

The issue was raised, according to the roundabout procedure of those times, in the form of a disputed gambling debt, the plaintiff claiming that he had bet the defendant ten pounds that the poor rate of 1767 was not a fair one—that it had proved to be not a fair one in fact, but that the defendant had, nevertheless, refused to pay up. In reply the defendant pleaded that the said rate had proved to be a fair one, and that plaintiff had therefore not won the bet. The question then to be decided was whether such poor rate was fair or not.

The following is an abridgment of the brief for the plaintiff

Kings Bench. Cornwall to wit.

The Plaintiffs Case.

The Plt & John Stevens of Lincolns Innfields in the County of Middsex Esqr, together with Adam Drummond & Thos Durant

Esq^{rs}, were candidates at the last gen^{l} Election for Burgesses to serve in Parliament for the Boro' of St. Ives in the County of Cornwall, wch came on at the Guildhall of the s^{d} Borough on Monday 21st day of March last.

That by a Resolution of the House of Commons, made the 8th day of Decr 1702, the right of election was declared to be in the Inhabit^{ts} of s^{d} Borough paying Lot & Scott.

That, there not having been for many years any regular or proper poors Rate for the s^{d} Borough, unjust Advantage being made thereof by the parish Officers to serve the purposes of Elections, sev^{l} of the Inhabitants of the s^{d} Borough paying Scott & bearing Lot did in or ab^{t} the Year 1766 apply to the Court of Kings Bench for and obtain a Mandamus directing the Church-Wardens & Overseers of the poor of the s^{d} Borough to make an equal poors Rate for the said Borough; in psūance whereof an equal poors rate for the s^{d} Borough was on the 16th Day of January 1767 made by the then Church Wardens and Overseers of the poor of s^{d} Borough in wch all the Inhabit^{ts} within the s^{d} Borough liable to be rated & assessed to the Church and poor were inserted; but as a great number of the persons so inserted were known to be in opposite Interest to the then Justices of the Peace for the s^{d} Borough, they at first refused to allow the s^{d} Rates & put the Inhabit^{ts} under the necessity of applying for and obtaining a Mandamus from the Court of Kings Bench, directing them to sign their Allowance to the s^{d} Rates; notwithstanding wch the s^{d} Justices still for some time refused to sign the s^{d} Rate for that purpose & absconded; but upon attachm^{t} being awarded by the Court of Kings Bench against them for their contempt, they at last on the 10th day of April 1767 signed & allowed the s^{d} Rate in due form; however they notwithstanding underwent the censure & punishment of the Court of Kings Bench & were fined 50^{li} each for their gross misbehaviour.

At Easter 1767 the Def^{t}, Wm Stevens, Thos Rosewall, Hugh Mulfra, Arnold Walters & *Henry Major were chosen Church Wardens and Overseers of the poor of the s^{d} Borough for the Year then next ensuing.

That an opposition being expected at the ensuing Election for members of parliament, the s^{d} Church Wardens & Overseers on the 5th day of June 1767, in a private manner without such publick notice as is usually given on those occasions, and, as pl^{t} is informed, under the influence and direction of John Knill Gent. the late returning Officer of said Borough, made a Rate or Assessment for the relief of the poor of the s^{d} Borough, from which they wilfully and unjustly omitted and left out the names of near 60 of the legal Inhabit^{ts} of s^{d} Borough who were in possession of messuages or Tenem^{ts} within the same, for wch they had been from time to time rated and Assessed to the Church and poor, in Order and with a view to deprive them of their Right of Voting at the then next Election for members to serve in parliam^{t} for the s^{d} Borough.

That several of the Inhabit^{s} so left out of the s^{d} Rate appealed therefrom to the next Quarter Sessions, when the said Rate was [illegible] of the sd Court quashed *pro tanto* for inequality. And when the sd parish Officers were asked what motive did Induce them to make such unjust illegal Rates, Henry Major & Arnold [illegible], two of the Overseers of the poor, answered, to the astonishment of all the Inhabitts of the sd Borough, that they wod omit or leave out of all the Rates they shod make the Names of all such persons as they thought wod Vote for or favour the Interest of the sd Stevens & his Friends who shd be proposed by him to be candidates for the said Borough at the then next ensuing general Election for Members to serve in parliament for the sd Borough. And that if Mr. Stephens or his friends should think themselves aggrieved, they might if they thought proper apply to parliament to seek redress. And the sd Defts Thos Hichens, who was one of the Church Wardens, on being asked by some of the Inhabitants who had been left off from the said Rate why they were treated with such Injustice and partiality & deprived of their respive Rights of Voting at the Election of Members to serve in parliament, answered that he was convinced that they had rateable property & shd have been added to the Rates, if they had not favoured the Interest of Mr. Stevens.

That in Michās Term last sevl of the Inhabits of the sd Boro' made an applicōn to the Ct of Kings Bench for a Writ of Mandamus to be directed to the parish officers of the said Borough to make an equal poors Rate for sd Borough; and a writ of mandamus issued accordingly directed to the Church Warden & Overseers of the poor of sd Borough and to every of them, commandg them to make or cause to be made an equal poors Rate upon the Inhabits & Occupiers of Estates, Lands Tenemts & other things rateable within the sd Borough for & towds the relief of the poor of the Borough accordg to the form of the Stāts in that case made & provided.

That on the 16th day of Nov. last the sd parish Officers by their Return to the sd Writ of Mandamus Certified that they had that Day according to the best of their Skill judgmt and Understanding made an equal poors Rate for the relief of the Poor of the sd Borough agreable to the form and tenor of the sd Writ.

That on the 29th Nov. last the sd poors Rate was published in the Church of St Ives aforesd, when to the Astonishmt of most of the Inhabitants of sd Borough it appeared that the Rate made on the 16th Day of Nov. was made on the same plan as that of the 5th June, without any one person being added thereto or taken therefrom, except one Mary Bryant Widow, of the sd Borough, who was added to the sd Rate made the 16th of Nov.

That the sd Rate made on the 16th Day of Nov. was appealed agst and quashed at the next Quarter Sessions held in and for the sd Borough *pro tanto* for inaequality.

That in Hilary Term last an application was made to the Court of Kings Bench by part of the Inhabitants of sd Borough for an Attachment agst the sd Parish Officers for their disobedience of the sd Writ of Mandamus in not making an equal poors Rate for the relief of the poor of the said Borough according to the tenor and exigency of the Writ, when a Rule nisi was granted agst them.

In Trinity Term last the s^{d} Parish Officers shewed Cause agst the s^{d} Rule, when the Court enlarg^{d} the Rule for shewing Cause ag^{t} the Attachm^{t}, & directed that in the mean time a feigned Issue should be tryed at the next assizes to be held in & for the s^{d} County of Cornwall, wherein the s^{d} James Johnstone Esqr sho^{d} be p^{lt} & the s^{d} Thos Hichens Def^{t}, in wc^{h} feigned Issue the Question should be :—

'Whether the Rate made on the 16th Day of Novr last past for the Borough of St Ives was a fair, equal and impartial Rate according to the tenor & Exigency of the Writ of Mandamus issued out of the s^{d} Court in Michas Term last past or not'; and if it should be found to have been otherwise, that the Postea shou'd be indorsed wherein and to what degree.

This Cause comes now on to be Tryed upon the above ment^{d} Issue; and in order to Shew that the Rate made on the 16th Day of Novr last was an unfair, unequal and partial Rate, there is a List subjoind of the Names of the persons left out of the s^{d} Rate who shou'd have been inserted therein, as being legal Inhabitants and having rateable property in the s^{d} Borough, and who from time to time had been rated to the Church and poor of s^{d} Borough, And also a List of the persons inserted in the Rate who shou'd not have been inserted therein, as being neither Inhabitants of the s^{d} Borough nor having rateable property therein.

The said parish Officers have admitted the Rate made the 16th Day of Novr last to be unfair & unequal; for in a Rate made on the 5th Day of March last for the Relief of the poor of the s^{d} Bor^{o} they have inserted 20 psons who were left out of the Rate made on the 16th Day of Nov^{r}, tho' there was no alteration in their Circumstances betw. these 2 periods; and every Circumstance attending the making the Rate of the 16th of Novr bears testimony of its partiality. And it's hoped the foll^{g} Decl^{ns} of some of the parish officers will fully establish that fact.

PROOFS FOR THE PLAINTIFF.

Richard Grenfell. Roger Renoden Mr. Thomas Michell. To prove that in a conversation between these Witnesses & Arnold Walters, one of the s^{d} parish officers, concern^{g} the s^{d} Rate made the 16th Day of Nov^{r}, the s^{d} Walters being asked how he & the other parish officers cou'd behave so basely as to treat the Inhabit^{ts} of the s^{d} Boro' in such a manner, the s^{d} Walters answ^{d} that they wo^{d} make Rates for the friends of Mr. Stevens to appeal agst and be at the expense of quashing till very near the gen^{l} Elect^{n} for members to serve in parliam^{t} when they wo^{d} make such a Rate as wo^{d} fav^{r} their Int^{t}; & as the Inhabit^{ts} wo^{d} have no opportunity to quash it (as no Q^{r} Sessions wo^{d} intervene) that wou^{d} be the Rate the returning officer, who was their friend, wou'd take the poll from.

Enoder Cock. To prove that Mr Knill, the returning officer of the s^{d} Boro', has frequently declared in the hearing of this Witness that he as Mayor wo^{d} with the parish officers cutt off from the Rates all such persons who shou'd oppose their Interest,

& only add to the same such persons as wou'd vote for their party. And when this Witness say'd it co[d] not be legally done, M[r] Knill replyd: 'You will certainly find it so, and we will by that means carry the Election.'

Richard Major. To prove that in Oct[r] last this Witness, having some conversation with Henry Major or one of the Overseers of the poor of the s[d] Borough, concerning the next gen[l] Elect[n] to be made for the s[d] Borough and how it was imagin'd Doct[r] Stevens wou'd be put off from being Elected a Member in the next Parliam[t] for the s[d] Borough, when s[d] Henry Major replyed: 'Thou ffool! don't you know better?—the Rate we have made already is of no signification, but we intend to make a Rate just before the next Election, and so poll by that Rate in defiance of Doctor Stevens.'

Roger Renoden. To prove that ab[t] the middle of Sept[r] last this Witness was in Comp[y] wth s[d] Henry Major, when this Witness asked him how he & the rest of parish officers cou[d] make such an unjust poors Rate for s[d] Boro', to which s[d] Major replied that he woo[d] cut off all the votes from the next poors Rate, excepting the four and twenty, (meaning the Mayor, Aldermen and Assist[ts] of s[d] Borough) & carry the next Election for members of Parliam[t] for s[d] Borough by them—and that he wou'd be damned if he did not do it, for that it was in his power now so to do, or used words to that effect.

A List of the persons left out of the Rate made for the Borough of S[t] Ives the 16th day of Nov[r] 1768. Shewing the nature of the property in respect of which they were liable to be rated, and the Witnesses to prove the same. [We leave out the particulars, save in a few cases]:—

Roger Renoden.
Thomas Richards, *alias* 'Hecka Bean.'
Francis Adams.
Robert Gear.
Anthony Couch.
Richard Bayley.
Thomas Cogar (freeholder).
William Cogar (blacksmith).
Jacob Care.
Hugh Ciceley.
Hugh Davis.
John Geen.
Ephraim Geen.
David Gyles.
Richard Grenfell.
Leonard Humphreys.
Patrick Hocking.
Robert Jennings Jun[r]
Richard Jennings.
Capt[n] Thomas Painter.
John Purfoy (freeholder). A messuage and cellars in S[t] Ives.
Michael Pearce.
William Purchase.
Stephen Pawley (freeholder). A dwellinghouse & cellar in S[t] Ives.
William Polmear.
Nicholas Row Jun[r]
Capt[n] Henry Row.
Paul Stevens Jun[r]
Christopher Trewhella; three messuages in S[t] Ives.
William Quick, mason.

Alexander James. A house in St Ives. [This name is crossed out.]
James Hall Junr
Garland Williams.
John Hodge.
Thomas Red.
Colan Pearce. A messuage in St Ives.
Paul Quick, of Brallan.
James Quick.
$Capt^n$ Edward Richards.
William Shugg.
Andrew Stevens. Offered to be admitted to poll. A messuage in St Ives; by lease. Rated for several years. Witness Sarah Harry.
William Sandow Junr A dwellinghouse in St Ives. Witness Jasper Williams.
John Tregarthen.
Thomas Richards Junr
Peter Thomas Junr
William Williams Junr, freeholder; a messuage in St Ives.
Thomas Wedge Senr
William Pearce.
Richard Quick, mason.
Job Stevens.
Robert Carne.
Nicholas Pearce.
Arthur Beriman; a messuage in St Ives, by lease; and a garden or orchard by assignment.
John Freeman, carpenter.
John Harry, cooper's son; an orchard & old walls, formerly a Dry-house, now a cooper's shop.
Benedict Wall.
Richard Michell.
James Trevorow; a mill & orchard in St Ives.
William Note.
Christopher Hodge.
William Williams, mariner. A messuage in St Ives. Witness William Harry.
Richard Thomas Senr
Richard Harry, cooper.
John Grenfell, shop-keeper.
John Wedge. A house and cellar in St Ives. Witness John Harry and Ann Lemall.
Thomas Bryant. A messuage in St Ives. Witness Hugh Edwards and John Thomas.
William Bryant. A messuage & linny in St Ives. Witness William Harry and Thomas Bryant.
Thomas Renowden.
George Jennings.
Edward Harry.
William Harry, ffooly.
William Minno.
William Barber.
James Berriman.
Richard Noall.
David Stevens Junr
Henry Carlyon. Freehold messuage. Witness Richard Lembrey and Elizabeth Lanyon.
Richard Stevens. Leasehold messuage. Witness Andrew Stevens.

A List of the persons inserted in the Raie made on the 16th day of November 1767 for the relief of the Poor of St Ives, who ought not to have been inserted therein.

Nathaniel Anthony. No estate or rateable property.

The Revd Jacob Bullock. Vicar of Zennor; obliged to residence in his parish. N.B. If it is pretended that Mr Bullock is rated for the house he farms of Mrs Worth, you'l observe she is charged and pays for it.

John Curnow. No estate or rateable property.

John Hawkings. No estate or rateable property.

Thomas Mathews. No estate or rateable property. N.B. If he pretends he is rated for the house he rents—he is rated too low, he paying 20li a year for it. The rate of 16 Novr 1768. John Stephens Senr

Captn Timothy Major. No estate or rateable property, nor ever rated before. Nor no inhabitant, he having served his time to Captain John James of the Mount.

Edward May. No estate or rateable property, nor ever rated before. N.B. He pretends to be rated for a smith's shop which is built on part of the Wastrell, of John Nance's estate in Hellesvear, which Nance is rated for.

John May.

John Michell.

William Pawley. He sold his estate to Anthony Couch before this rate was made.

Captn John Perkin. No resident, he living at Redrouth.

Mr William Pulkinghorne. No estate or rateable property.

George Toman.

Mr John Trengrouse, surgeon. No estate or rateable property, nor any inhabitant.

Henry Uren.

Thomas Wedge. Supposed to have a spurious Title and only made to answer the present purpose.

Captn Robert Watts.

Edward Paynter, joyner. No estate or rateable property. The house for which he is charged being the property of his sister, Catherine the wife of Vivian Stevens.

The Revd Thos Carlyon.

Matthew Clies.

Daniel Couch.

Captn William Hambly.

Captn Edward Kempthorne.

Thomas Paul Junr.

Andrew Noal.

This brief is marked 'Mr Mansfield; Mr Soll^{r} Genl; Mr Serg^{t} Davy.'

Accompanying it is an additional brief, from which we take the following particulars:

'Of those inserted in the Rate great inequality appears. Thus Samuel Stephens, one of the Aldermen, for an estate of 200^{li} per annum is rated at 2s. 6*d.*; while Thomas Mathews, for an estate worth 28^{li} per annum, is rated at 1s.

'The Revenue of the Town, the property of the Mayor, is not rated.

'The minister, one of the Aldermen, is not rated.

'Mr John's tenants of 45^{li} are not rated.

'Justice Veal's tenants are not rated.'

From these extracts it will be seen how the local landowners dominated public affairs at Saint Ives. The Town Council at this period was solely composed of men devoted to the interests of Stephens and his patron the Earl of Buckinghamshire. Nor did this political trial end, as had been hoped, in the overthrow of this predominating influence. Johnstone and Stevens, the popular candidates, were not able to make out their case, and the Stephens interest retained all its old ascendency in local politics.

Doctor John Stevens stood high in favour with a large section of Saint Ives people, and seems to have owed his political popularity largely to the fact that he was a native of the parish—he was born at Trowan. In our notice of the Lemal family we have seen how Doctor Stevens was substantially aided in the expenses of his campaign by Kitty Lemal's stocking-full of guineas. Colan Pearce (whose name will be found in the foregoing list of persons wrongfully deprived of a vote), at a later date came forward as a candidate, hoping to meet with the same support as had been accorded to the doctor. He seems to have applied to Kitty Lemal for a like subsidy, and to have met with a decided rebuff. The old song was:

'Kitty Lemal a stocking wound,
The Doctor soon the bottom found;
Colan Pearce tried the same,
But could not play the Doctor's game.'

John Knill, the mayor, was a most active and successful opponent of John Stevens; and there is a tradition to the effect that he said he 'would willingly suffer seven years in hell' for the damage he (Knill) had done to Stevens.

The votes at the election of 1768 were thus divided:

Durant, 107. Drummond, 106. Johnstone, 81. Stevens, 62.

Had the plaintiff made good his case, the voting would have stood thus:

Stevens, 107. Johnstone, 81. Durant, 26. Drummond, 25.

From a bundle of old letters in the possession of Mr. John Vyvyan Thomas, of Cardiff, I have been able to glean a few particulars as to the further history of Doctor Stevens. It would appear that after his unsuccessful contest at Saint Ives, he retired to the Continent, leaving his wife and family under the care of friends in Cornwall, and that he lived for some time, in more or less poverty, at Aix la Chapelle, under the name of Monsieur de Stephens, in the house of the Demoiselles Hendrickx de Schotz. The first letter contains direct reference to the election of 1768. It runs as follows:

'Lincoln's Inn Fields,
'Jan. 8th, 1767.

'DEAR BROTHER,

'I received yours of the 3rd instant, and as soon as I receive the one half of the expences from the Duke's friend, which I believe will be in a month, you shall have your money again if you want it. I will make up half of the tribute set in Penhale here, and perhaps some of our friends at St Ives will venture, ask them!—try if you can't make one gallon of brandy last 3 days, as nothing is got by drunkenness and rioting.—Hugh Edwards, the Parson, & all their friends have not 16 old houses, more than they live in to sell, and if we can only keep pace with them in the new votes we will beat them hollow in the old ones as there will be several double for me which even you do not know of.—Give the inclosed to Roger. Ld B. is now against the ministry, and all the officers must be for us, at the election, or turn out— Give as little into drinking as possible, and take care that you have no long alehouse scores. I have cash in the Banker's hands to pay all your bills as they become due, and in a few days will send some more.

'I remain,
'Your affectionate Brother,
'JNO. STEVENS.

'Mr Thomas Stevens, at Trowan near St Ives, Cornwall.'

In 1772 he writes from abroad: 'I never was better in my life, than I have been for a year past, owing to my being obliged to live upon new milk, Tea, etc. because I would not run in debt with any person. . . . As I am a Physician, all the people thought that I was useing such a diet for my health, and so all passed very well.' By the year 1795 Doctor Stevens' affairs had improved so far that he was able to send remittances to his relations in Cornwall. He says: 'I would not enter into such pick-pockett affairs as chances and shares in a Lottery Tickett, but I sent and bought a whole

Tickett; and resolved to give you and John the amount of the two small shares you mention'd; and to do some *great things* with the remainder. But I have just now received an answer that my *Tickett* was drawn a *Blank;* so you are like the butter milk boy.'

The following letter was written by the doctor's daughter, Miss Maria Stephens, to her uncle, Mr. John Stevens, of Saint Ives:

'Bower Hall Oct[r] 11th [1797.]

'MY DEAR SIR,

'I am very sorry to inform you of our lamentable loss, a loss for ever to be regretted by me, of a most beloved parent, and faithful Friend. He departed this painful life yesterday, I hope to everlasting happiness. I cannot at present enter into further particulars, except that my Father has left no Will, as for some time he has been incapable of making one. . . . I have a Miniature Picture of my Father, which was drawn about a year ago, and which he lately express'd a wish that your son should have one like it; and I will take the first opportunity to have one drawn the copy of it, and send it him, happy to do the smallest thing to express my gratitude to his memory. I shall be glad to hear from you of my aunt; and with hearty condolence for our irreparable loss, believe

'Your sincere Friend
'M. STEPHENS.'

The Bower Hall estate descended to the Doctor's son, Ellys Anderson Stephens, who was living in 1822. It has since gone into other hands.

The portrait referred to in the above letter is a tiny engraving in red tint, worked into a small pincushion, with an oval bit of glass over it. The pincushion is covered with silk, and has remains of tinsel embroidery and beading. The portrait represents an elderly man, side-face and bust. He wears a bag-wig and a court dress coat, with turn-down collar, and epaulet, and braiding in front, and frilled shirt-front. The forehead and chin are receding, the nose retroussé, the mouth small, and the cheeks full. The eyes are large, and the face expresses amiability without much strength of character.

Dr. John Stevens married the daughter and heir of Anthony Ellis, D.D., Bishop of Saint David's, 1752-61, of Bower Hall, Steeple Boumpstead, near Halstead, Essex.

CHAPTER XXXIV.

PUBLIC OFFICERS OF THE BOROUGH AND PARISH OF SAINT IVES.

Head Wardens and Portrieves.

1549. John Payne.
1573. William Trenwith.
1574. John Penhellack.
1575. Martin Trewinnard.
1576. George Hicks.
1577. Richard Peters.
1578. Henry Oates.
1579. John Carvoddres.
1580. Thomas James.
1582. Henry Sterry.
1583. Otes Merefield.
1584. John James.
1585. William Woolcock.
1586. Thomas Candrow.
1587. William Barratt.
1590. John Stephens.
1591. George Payne.
1592. Thomas Williams.
1593. John Cocking.
1594. Henry Hicks.
1595. Thomas Hicks.
1596. John James.
1597. John Tregenna.
1602. James Woolcock (died). John Rich.
1603. John Cocking senior.
1604. George Williams.
1605. George Payne.
1606. Thomas Williams.
1607. William Hichens. (Wm. Trenwith declined.)
1608. William Ceely.
1611. George Hicks.
1612. William Pitt.
1613. William Borthogge.
1614. Henry Hicks, senior.
1615. James Sterry.
1616. Thomas Purefoy.
1617. Richard Anne.
1618. John Sprigge.
1619. William Trenwith.
1620. Henry Hicks.
1621. William Borthogge.
1622. John Sterry.
1623. John Riche.
1624. George Hicks.
1625. Thomas Trenwith. (John Stevens declined.)
1626. John Trewinnard.
1627. Thomas Purefoy.
1628. Richard Hext.
1629. John Sprigge.
1630. John Payne.
1631. Henry Hicks.
1632. John Hicks.
1633. William Hichens.
1634. Stephen Barber.
1635. Edward Hammond. (James Praed declined.)
1636. Thomas Sise.
1637. John Sterry.
1638. Thomas Stevens.

Mayors.

1639. Richard Hext.
1640. Thomas Stevens.
1641. Henry Hickes.
1642. John Payne.
1643. Steven Barbar.
1644. Edward Hammond.
1645. Ephraim Sise.
1646. Thomas Sprigge.
1647. Thomas Noal.
1648. Alexander James.
1649. John Diggens.
1650. Peter Ceely.
1651. Thomas Purefoy.
1652. Nicholas Prigge.
1653. Richard Cowch.
1654. George Hammond.
1655. Henry Sterrie.
1656. Richard Hicks.
1657. Edward Hammond.
1658. Thomas Sprigge.
1659. Thomas Noal.
1660. Francis Robinson.
1661. William Diggens.
1662. Thomas Trenwith.
1663. Robert Spriggs.
1664. John Hichens.
1665. Richard Hichens.
1666. Thomas Sise.
1667. Hugh Harris.
1668. William Pearse.
1669. Francis Hammond.
1670. John Hichens, junior.
1671. George Hammond.
1672. Richard Hichens.
1673. Thomas Spriggs.
1674. Thomas Hicks.
1675. William Diggens.
1676. Hugh Harris (died).
1677. 15 Feb. William Hichens.
1 Nov. E. Nosworthy.
1678. Thomas Purefoy.
1679. Richard Pollard.
1680. Thomas Sprigges, junior.
1681. John Hawking.
1682. John Hichens.
1683. John Stevens.
1684. Thomas Trenwith.
1685. John Lanyon.
1686. Thomas Sprigg.
1687. John Stevens.
1688. John Hicks.
1689. John Hicks.
1690. John Lanyon.
1691. Thomas Sprigge.
1692. John Stevens.
1693. John James.
1694. Richard Hichens.
1695. John Hicks.
1696. John Lanyon.
1697. Thomas Sprigge.
1698. John Stevens.
1699. John James.
1700. John Hawking.
1701. John Hicks.
1702. Richard Pollard.
1703. Richard Hichens.
1704. John James.
1705. John Hawking.
1706. Richard Hichens.
1707. John Hicks.
1708. John James.
1709. Richard Pollard.
1710. John Hicks.
1711. John James.
1712. James Tregeare.
1713. John Hichens.
1714. Alexander James.
1715. John Hicks.
1716. Richard Pollard.
1717. John Hichens.
1718. Alexander James.
1719. Richard Pollard.

1720. Nathaniel Anthony.
1721. Thomas Anthony.
1722. Joseph Gubbs.
1723. John Ceely.
1724. Richard Harry.
1725. Thomas Spriggs.
1726. John Hichens.
1727. John Stevens.
1728. John Hichens, senior.
1729. John Noall.
1730. Nathaniel Anthony.
1731. Thomas Anthony.
1732. Joseph Gubbs.
1733. John Ceely.
1734. William Busvargus.
1735. Richard Harry.
1736. Thomas Sprigge.
1737. John Hichens.
1738. John King.
1739. Richard Harry.
1740. Michael Nicolls.
1741. Francis Ley.
1742. John Stephens.
1743. John Stevens.
1744. Francis Stevens.
1745. William Symond.
1746. William Harry.
1747. Michael Nicolls.
1748. John Hichens.
1749. John Edwards.
1750. Edward Stephens.
1751. John Stephens.
1752. John Stevens.
1753. John Stephens.
1754. Edward Stephens.
1755. William Harry.
1756. William Symond.
1757. William Harry.
1758. John Edwards.
1759. William Harry.
1760. John Stevens.
1761. Samuel Stephens.
1762. John Stevens.
1763. Samuel Stephens.
1764. John Stevens.
1765. Samuel Stephens.
1766. Hugh Edwards.
1767. John Knill.
1768. Hugh Edwards.
1769. John Stevens.
1770. Humphrey Mackworth Praed.
1771. John Stevens.
1772. Thomas Hichens.
1773. Edward Stephens.
1774. John Anthony.
1775. John Anthony.
1776. William Stephens.
1777. John Stevens, junior.
1778. Hugh Mulfra.
1779. Hugh Edwards.
1780. Thomas Trenwith.
1781. Thomas Hichens.
1782. John Anthony.
1783. William Stephens.
1784. Nathaniel Hicks.
1785. Thomas Hichens.
1786. John Stevens, junior.
1787. Timothy Wheelwright.
1788. John Stevens, junior.
1789. Francis Stephens.
1790. Thomas Wallis.
1791. Thomas Lane.
1792. James Anthony.
1793. Lewis Morgan.
1794. John Arthur.
1795. Nathaniel Hicks.
1796. John Stevens.
1797. Thomas Wallis.
1798. Paul Tremearne.
1799. James Anthony.
1800. Lewis Morgan.
1801. John Arthur.
1802. Vivian Stevens.
1803. Nathaniel Hicks.
1804. John Stevens.
1805. Thomas Wallis.
1806. Paul Tremearne, junior.

1807. James Halse.
1808. Thomas Tremearne.
1809. James Anthony.
1810. James Anthony.
1811. Thomas Tremearne.
1812. Thomas Wallis.
1813. James Halse.
1814. John Arthur.
1815. Thomas Tremearne.
1816. Augustus Stephens.
1817. William Bazeley.
1818. William Bazeley.
1819. Paul Tremearne.
1820. James Anthony.
1821. James Anthony.
1822. Paul Tremearne.
1823. Paul Tremearne.
1824. Paul Tremearne.
1825. Paul Tremearne.
1826. James Anthony.
1827. Samuel Stephens.
1828. Samuel Stephens.
1829. Richard Hichens.
1830. Richard Hichens.
1831. Walter Yonge.
1832. William Bazeley.
1833. William Bazeley, junior.
1834. Roger Wearne.
1835. William Bazeley.
1836. Daniel Bamfield.
1837. William Bazeley, junior.
1838. Roger Wearne.
1839. John Newman Tremearne.
1840. Samuel Hocking.
1841. Richard Kernick.
1842. William Bazeley.
1843. John Chellew (Walter Yonge refused).
1844. William Bazeley.
1845. Richard Kernick.
1846. William Bazeley.
1847. Matthew Trewhella.
1848. James Rosewall.
1849. Richard Kernick.
1850. William Bazeley.
1851. James Rosewall.
1852. John Newman Tremearne.
1853. John Newman Tremearne.
1854. Samuel Hocking (died).
1855. 13 April. Robert Hichens Bamfield.
9 Nov. Robert Hichens Bamfield.
1856. James Rosewall.
1857. William Bazeley.
1858. John Newman Tremearne.
1859. Richard Kernick.
1860. Robert Hichens Bamfield.
1861. William Bazeley.
1862. William Bazeley.
1863. Robert Hichens Bamfield.
1864. William Cade.
1865. Henry Major Harris.
1866. James Stevens Quick.
1867. Robert Snaith Hichens.
1868. 1 Nov. Robert Snaith Hichens (died).
19 Nov. William Mitchell Jennings.
1869. Tonkin Young.
1870. John May Kernick.
1871. William Docton.
1872. George Williams.
1873. George Williams.
1874. Charles Newman Tremearne.
1875. Charles Newman Tremearne.
1876. Thomas Cogar.
1877. William Craze.
1878. George Williams.
1879. George Williams.
1880. Thomas Cogar.
1881. John May Kernick.
1882. John May Kernick.
1883. John May Kernick.
1884. Edward Hain, junior.
1885. Edward Hain, junior.

1886. Edward Hain, junior.
1887. William Craze.
1888. William Craze.
1889. Edward Hain, junior.
1890. Joshua Daniel.
1891. Joshua Daniel.

The Protestant Clergy of Saint Ives.

The following is a list of the Vicars of Lelant, Saint Ives and Towednack, during the period when the three cures were served by one pastor. (The names in square brackets are those of their curates, ministers, lecturers, or readers, at Saint Ives.):

1547. George Mason.
1549. Gabriel Moreton.
1578. Robert Stopford.
1584. [Mr. Whisheker.]
1592. [Mr. Nickles.]
1596. 'Ye olde Vickar Stafford' is named in the Borough Accounts.
1597. John Bagwell.
1603. Thomas Masters.
1606. Robert Challacombe.
1608. [Mr. Jeffreys.]
1611. Nicodemus Pestell.
1617. [Mr. Whittinge.]
1618. [Alexander Harry; Messieurs Ingleton, Phippen and Morcumbe.]
1624. John South.
1629. [Messieurs Upcot, Symons and Sherwoode.
Joseph Sherwood, expelled from Saint Hilary under the Act of Uniformity, took up his abode at Saint Ives, where he preached and delivered weekly lectures.
Charles Morton, B.A., expelled from the rectory of Blisland, retired to Saint Ives, where he preached privately in neighbouring villages.]
1631. Thomas Corey. [Leonard Wellsteed, minister. Mr. Mitch, preacher. Wellsteed was ejected for nonconformity in 1648, but he returned as minister of Saint Ives under the Commonwealth.]
1638. Thomas Jackson.
1646. Benjamin Hugget. [John Whitworth.
1652. Mr. Land, in the absence of Mr. Wellsteed.
1653. Leonard Wellsteed, minister under the Commonwealth.
1655. Mr. Tucker.
1657. Thomas Tregosse; ejected for nonconformity.]
1660. Richard Fowler (afterwards vicar of Zennor).

1669. John Bullock (died 1676).
1677. [William Robinson, 'lecturer, deacon, and clerk.']
1693. John Hawkins.
1708. William Polkinghorne.
1712. [Jonathan Toup, lecturer.]
1726. John Keigwin.
1735. William Symonds. (In 1768 he became vicar of Saint Erth.)
1743. [Mr. Hoblyn.
1769. Thomas Lane.]
1775. George Rhodes. [Lewis Morgan.]
1786. Cornelius Cardew, D.D. [John Arthur.]
1808. [John Peters.
1813. Robert Peters.
1814. William Spry.]

The following were Perpetual Curates of Saint Ives:

1822. Charles Aldrich.
1833. William Malkin. [John C. Millett. Charles Jenkyn. John Bamfield. Francis Bazeley.]
1836. William James Havart. [Henry Batten]
1843. Samuel A. Ellis.
1850. David E. Domville.
1855. Franklin Tonkin.
1861. Richard Frederick Tyacke.
1869. John Balmer Jones (inducted as vicar).

Church Wardens of the Parish of Saint Ives.

1573. William Donnall and John Pawlye.
1574. John Androwe and Thomas Olver.
1575. Thomas James and Pearse Nole.
1576. John James and Thomas Cocke.
1580. Robert Luck and Richard Arde.
1581. Robert Luck and Richard Saundrie.
1584. John Richards and Roger Permantor.
1585. Thomas Watter and Thomas Kebarte.
1586. John Steven and John Davie.
1587. John Allen and John Thomas.
1590. Robert Davie and . . . .
1596. Harry Hendra and Henry Baylye.
1597. James Dyname and George Thomas.
1601. Peter Cloke and William Davye.
1602. John Hamblye and . . . .
1603. Richard Hocken and John Goodale.
1604. Henry James.

1605. George Webber and Alexander Pencaste.
1614. William Hechins and Humphry Anderdon.
1630. John Hicks and John James.
1631. John Rich and John Player.
1633. Thomas Purefey and Peter Goodale.
1634. Edward Hammand and Arthur Wescott.
1636. Stephen Barbar and Thomas Goode.
1637. Henry Hicks and George Hicks.
1638. Ephraim Syse.
1647. George Hicks.
1649. Thomas Stevens and William Nance.
1650. John Player and George Hammond.
1651. Alexander James and Richard Smith.
1653. Henry Hicks and Robert Cowch.
1656. Alexander James and Robert Cowch.
1672. William Pearse and John Treweeke.
1680. Thomas Sprig, junior, and John Hicks.
1726. Paul Tremearne and James Bennats.
1727. Wm Busvargus and Vivian Stevens gen^t^.
1728.
1729. John Hichens and Chas Worth.
1730. Richard Harry and Chas Worth.
1731. John Noall and Chas Worth.
1732. Hugh Edwards and John Noall.
1733. Hugh Edwards and John Noall.
1734. Wm Busvargus and Chas Worth.
1735. Timothy Wheelwright and Chas Worth.
1736. Richard Harry and Chas Worth.
1737. Richard Harry and Chas Worth.
1738. Thos Worth and John Edwards.
1739. Thos Pascoe and John Noall.
1740. Thos Pascoe and John Noall.
1741. Michael Nicolls and John Stephens.
1742. Timothy Wheelwright and Charles Worth.
1743. Timothy Wheelwright and Charles Worth.
1744. Timothy Wheelwright and Charles Worth.
1745. Michael Nicolls and Charles Worth.
1746. Timothy Wheelwright and Charles Worth.
1747. Timothy Wheelwright and Charles Worth.
1748. Michael Nicolls and Christopher Carpenter.
1749. Thomas Hichens and William Harry.
1750. Timothy Wheelwright and Charles Worth.
1751. Charles Worth and Timothy Wheelwright.
1752. Charles Worth and Christopher Carpenter.

1753. Christopher Carpenter and Charles Worth.
1754.
1755.
1756. Thomas Hichens, John Stephens, and John Daniel.
1757. Thomas Hichens, Hugh Mulfra, and John Noall.
1758. Thomas Hichens and Thomas Trenwith.
1767. Thomas Hichens, William Stephens, and Thomas Rosewall.
1768. Hugh Mulfra, John Nance, and Henry Major.
1769. Hugh Mulfra, John Nance, and Henry Major.
1770. Vivian Stevens, Hugh Mulfra, and Thomas Rosewall.
1771. Hugh Mulfra, William Hichens, and John Major.
1772. William Hichins, Richard Major, and John Major.
1773. Hugh Edwards, William Hichins, and Thomas Rosewall.
1774. Hugh Edwards, William Hichins, and Thomas Rosewall.
1775. William Stephens, Hugh Mulfra, and Richard Curnow.
1776. William Stephens, Thomas Hichins, and John Stevens.
1777. William Stephens, Hugh Mulfra, and John Stevens.
1778. Hugh Edwards, Thomas Hichins, jun^r^, Richard Curnow.
1779. John Thomas, William Worth, John Major.
1780. John Thomas, William Worth, and John Stevens.
1781. Hugh Edwards, ... Hickes, Matthew Stevens.
1782. Nathaniel Hickes, Timothy Wheelwright, John Major.
1783. Timothy Wheelwright, gen^t^, Thomas Hichins, jun^r^, gen^t^, John Major.
1784. Thomas Hichins, jun^r^, gen^t^, James Rosewall, Andrew Stevens.
1785. Thomas Hichins, jun^r^, gen^t^, James Rosewall, William Harry.
1786. James Rosewall, William Harry, John Stevens (in the Court). [*I.e.*, who lived at 'The Court,' Trevalgan.]
1787. Nathaniel Hickes, Thomas Hichens.
1788. Jacob Phillips, John Major, William Harry.
1789. Timothy Wheelwright, John Stevens, John Major.
1790. Thomas Wallis, John Stevens, Richard Major.
1791. Jacob Phillips, Richard Jenkins, John Stevens.
1792. Vivian Stevens, Paul Tremearne, John Stevens.
1793. Thomas Lane, William Worth, John Stevens.
1794. Nathaniel Hickes, Charles Richards, jun^r^, William Noall.
1795. Nathaniel Hickes, Charles Richards, jun^r^, William Noall.
1796. James Anthony, William Noall, John Hingston.
1797. James Anthony, John Hingston, William Noall.
1798. Vivian Stevens, John Stevens, John Paynter.
1799. Vivian Stevens, Jacob Phillips, John Stevens.
1800. Vivian Stevens, Jacob Phillips, John Stevens.

Wardens of the Market House, with the Sums paid for the Toll Farm.

1573. William Teage and Nicholas Rendall.
1574. John Goman and Nicholas Rendall.
1575. William Teage and Martin Goodall.
1576. Richard Peter and Roger Water, £15.
1579. Richard Corrye and Nicholas Randall.
1584. Henry Butsava.
1585. Richard Peter and Nicholas Randle.
1586. George Paine and Nicholas Rendall, £11.
1591. Richard Peter, £12.
1593. John Cockens.
1594. Richard Peter.
1596. Richard Peter, £11 10*s*.
1602. Thomas Watyer and Reis Elledon, £16 0*s*. 2*d*.
1605. Reis Eleydon, £18 10*s*.
1606. Richard Peter, £17 10*s*.
1607. Reis Ellydon, £17 12*s*.
1608. Reis Ellydon, £17.
1630. John Rich and Alexander James, £15 6*s*. 8*d*.
1631. Christopher Cocke, £16.
1632. Lewis Hendra, £16.
1633. John James, £18.
1634. John James, Lewis Hendra, and Peter Goodale, £19.
1635. Richard Peter.
1636. Richard Hockin, £20.
1637. William Thomas, £23 10*s*.
1638. Edward Hammande and Lewis Hendra, £22 10*s*.
1638. Peter Goodale, £22.
1639. John Payne, £40.
1640. Richard Peter, £40.
1644. Richard Hockin, £35.
1645. John Bosowe and Richard Pollard, £29.
1646. John Hechins, £40 10*s*.
1647. John Trewinnard, £33.
1648. John Bussow, £9 10*s*.
1650. John Sprye, £60.
1653. Morrish Dyer, £40.
1655. William Ackland and Thomas Painter, £49.
1656. William Thomas of Trethwall.
1657. William Ackland, £48 10*s*.
1658. George Hammond, £59.
1664. George Hammond and Walter Michell.
1665. Thomas Treunwith, £41.

1687. Enoder Cock and Mathew Gyles, £29.
1687. Edward Pryor and Thomas Harvy.
1690. Enoder Cock and Thomas Anthony.
1691. Matthew Gyles and John Stephens, £22.
1710. John Thomas, cooper.
1715. Thomas Stephens, junior.
1723. Abraham Mathews, £29 6*s*.
1764. Thomas Mathews and Nicholas Perce, £25 10*s*.
1774. Thomas Mathews and Thomas Quick, £37 10*s*.
1780. Thomas Mathews and James Bennats.
1783. Thomas Quick and Matthew Stevens.
1784. Thomas Quick and Thomas Mathews, £38.
1786. Abraham Cogar and Thomas Mathews, £47.
1789. Mathew Stevens.
1817. John Uren, John Daniell, and Philip Bennatts, £73 11*s*.
1821. John Quick.
1823. Benedict Quick (and partners).
1830. John Uren, £150.

Wardens of the Quay, with the Sums paid for the Toll Farm.

1573. Stephen Barboure and John Goman.
1574. Ralph Uryn and Thomas Manne.
1575. John Goman, George Goodall, and William Mathewe, £3 19*s*. 10*d*.
1576. Henry Bayliffe and Henry Davye.
1579. Richard Corrye and Nicholas Randall.
1584. James Jelbartt and James Hichen.
1585. George Hicks and John Sterrye.
1586. John Cossen and Nicholas Bossithioe.
1587. Thomas Watty and Jamss Sies.
1590. Henry Hicks.
1591. John Steeven, £2 13*s*. 4*d*.
1593. John Cockins.
1594. Joel Hicks.
1595. Richard Peter.
1596. William Ottes and Joel Hicks, £3 13*s*. 4*d*.
1601. Henry Tregerthen and Reynold Seneshen.
1602. John Barber and Stephen Luke.
1603. Giles Hauke and James James, £4 4*s*. 10*d*.
1605. John James and John Coosen, £4 17*s*.
1606. John Goman and Thomas Kyttowe, £5 2*s*. 10*d*.
1607. Richard Lynten and John Stephen.
1608. Richard Treyowe and Daniel Sprigge.
1610. George Williams, £5.
1612. John Barbar, £7 10*s*.

1614. John Barber, £4 12*s.*
1618. John Barber, £5.
1619. Richard Lynten, £5 5*s.*
1621. Richard Lynten.
1624. Richard Tregeowe, £6.
1625. Thomas Purefey and John Hicks, £6 10*s.*
1626. John Payne and John Cossen, £5.
1627. Stephen Barbar and Lewis Hendra.
1628. Edward Hicks and Henry Hamonde, £4 10*s.*
1629. Thomas Purefey, £6.
1630. John Hicks, £6.
1631. John Hicks, £8 10*s.*
1632. Edward Hammand, £11 10*s.*
1633. Richard Hext, £14.
1634. Edward Hamaund, £17.
1635. Thomas Goode, £14 10.
1636. Arthur Wescott and Thomas Goode, £12.
1637. Thomas Syse and John Hicks, £12 10*s.*
1638. Peter Ceely, £13.
1639. William Tregosse and Henry Stevens, £12 10*s.*
1640. William Phillips, £1.
1644. Peter Gibbs, £14.
1645. Alexander Bishoppe, £13 10*s.*
1646. Thomas Purefoy and Nicholas Sprigge, £20.
1647. Edward Hammond, £19 10*s.*
1650. Thomas Stevens, junior, £18 10*s.*
1651. George Hammond, £18.
1653. George Hammond, £15 10*s.*
1655. Peter Ceely, £19 10*s.*
1656. George Painter.
1657. George Hammond, £18.
1658. Edward Stevens, £20.
1664. Thomas Sise.
1665. Thomas Sise.
1684 (*circa*). Hector Taylor.
1687. John Stevens and Thomas Purefoy, junior.
1689. Thomas Collins and William Beriman.
1690. Richard Couch and Phillip Carlyon.
1700. Joel Bolitho and Paul Tremearne.
1701. Thomas Harvy and John Thomas.
1703. Patrick Hawking.
1712. John Trevascus.
1715. Thomas Stephens, junior.
1760. Thomas Mathews and John Stevens, junior.
1766. Thomas Mathews and Matthew Stevens, £47 7*s.* 6d.

Overseers of the Poor.

1581. Philip Cornwall and Cornwall Stephen.
1631. Richard Hext, Thomas Nancothan, William Nance, and Thomas Noale.
1632. Thomas Sise, William Dun, Andrew Phillipps, and William Trerie.
1633. John Sprigge, Henry Stevens, John Launton, and Francis Walker.
1634. Thomas Stevens, Christopher Cocke, John Hechins, and Timothy Maior.
1636. John Payne, Richard Hockin, William Thomas, and James Rosewall.
1637. John Sprigge, Henry Williams, John Launder, junior, and James Nenis.
1638. John Rich, Peter Goodale, Thomas Lynton, and Timothy Maior.
1651. William Diggens.
1653. Arthur Westcott and John Player.
1654. Thomas Purefoy, Richard Smith, George Paynter, and William Browne.
1656. Nicholas Prigge and Hugh Harris.
1672. Edward Hammond and John Hockin.
1679. Francis Stevens.
1681. John Stevens and John Treweek.
1693. Thomas Stephens.

Waywardens.

1633. John Denham and William Trerie.
1634. Alexander James and Thomas Browne.
1636. John Hechins and Charles Whyte.
1637. John Sterrie and John Nicholas, junior.
1638. John Sterrie and John Cocke, of Trevalgan.
1654. Lewis Cogar and William Ninnis.
1698. —— Sprigg and —— Hickes.

Recorders.

1652. John Seyntaubyne.
1680. James Praed.
16—. John, Earl of Bath.
1700. Charles, Duke of Bolton.
1723. James Cross.
1759. William Sandys.
1760. Corydon Carpenter.
1767. George Hobart.
1772. William Praed.

Constables.

1575. William Barett.
1590. William Barett.
1605 (*circa*). John Steven and George Hicks.

1614. .... Paynter.
1615. Thomas Toman and Edmund Player.
1620. Henry Hicks and John Browne.
1627. John Browne and Thomas Noale.
1637. John Hawke.
1646. George Hicks.
1648. John Thomas.
1651. Hugh Harris.
1653. John Thomas.
1654. Robert Sprigge.
1655. Richard Hichings.
1656. Hugh Harris.
1658. Thomas Syse.
1659. .... Couch and .... Player.
1660. Edward Wescoatt.
1671. John Hawking and Maurice Dyer.
1693. John Trevaskes and Humphry Tonkyn.
1723. Robert Nicholls, Abraham Matthews, and James Quick.
1776. Thomas Mathews and William Stevens, of Trevalgen.
1777. Thomas Mathews.
1778. Thomas Mathews.
1779. Thomas Mathews.
1781. Thomas Mathews, Richard Couch, and Christopher Trewhella.
1782. Richard Hichens Couch and Christopher Trewheela.
1787. Matthew Stevens.
1792. Andrew Stevens.
1798. Thomas Mathews and Joseph Williams.
1803. William Stevens and Mathew Daniel.
1805. James Quick Trenwith.
1821. John Quick.
1823. Benedict Quick.

Town Clerks.

1655. John Littleton.
1669. John Hicks.
1675—1683. Hugh Pawley.
1686—1690. John Newman.
1721—1729. John Penrose.
1762. John Stevens, junior.
1806. John Stevens.

Parish Clerks.

1637. Andrew Lawrie.
1650. Richard Fowler.
1655. Benjamin John.
1656—1669. John Thomas (and schoolmaster).
1672. .... Michell (and schoolmaster).
1677. William Robinson.
1704. Thomas Michell.
1727. Thomas (?) Mitchell.
1769. Patrick Hawking.
1797. Francis Stevens.
1816. Thomas Williams. (He held this office until his death in 1862.)

Wardens of the Aisle, or Sidesmen.

1573. John Paskowe.
1574. Stephen Barboure, William Lantone, and Thomas Williams.
1575. Pearse Goorge and William Mobe.

1630. John Bussithiow and Thomas Bereman.
1631. John Launder, senior, and Thomas Nicholas, *alias* James.
1633. James Barbar and John Cocke, of Trevalgan.
1634. Henry Treweeke and Henrie Steephen.
1636. Richard Peter and John Bussowe.
1637. Francis Walker and Henry Uren.
1638. Thomas Nancothan and James Rosewall.

Kings and Queens of the Summer Games.

1573. Henry Sterrie and Jane Walshe.
1574. John Oots and Margaret Hockin.
1575. James Huchin and Jenat Oots.
1576. John Holla and ....
1580. Thomas Eva and Elizabeth Amys.
1584. Gregor Polkenhorne and Mary Nancothan.
1585. Harry Hicks and Elizabeth Cockyn.
1588. .... Candrowe and ....
1590. .... James and ....
1591. William Stirrie and ....
1592. Joel Hicks and ....
1596. Nicholas Hicks and Jane Sterrye.
1597. Stephen Barbar and ....
1616. Henry Shapland and Elizabeth Taylor.
1634. John Stephens and Margery Hammande.

Collectors of the Port Farm.

1651. Richard Hicks.
1653. Richard Hicks.
1655. Renatus Treunwith and William Pearse.
1656. Richard Hoskings and Edward Wescoatte.
1657. John Thomas and Thomas Painter.
1658. William Pearse and John Treweeke.

LIST OF AUTHORITIES REFERRED TO IN COMPILING THIS WORK.

'Archæologia Cambrensis.'

Bannister's 'Glossary of Cornish Names'; London.

Blight's 'Ancient Crosses and other Antiquities in the West of Cornwall'; 3rd ed., Penzance, 1871.

Blight's 'Churches of West Cornwall'; 2nd ed., Oxford, 1885.

Blight's 'Week at the Land's End'; Truro, 1876.

Bloxam's 'Principles of Gothic Ecclesiastical Architecture'; 2 vols., 11th ed., London, 1882.

Borlase's 'History of Cornwall'; London, 1760.

Bottrell's 'Traditions and Hearthside Stories of West Cornwall'; 3 series, Penzance, 1873, etc.

Burke's 'General Armory'; London, 1878.

Burnet's 'History of the Reformation.'

Carew's 'Survey of Cornwall'; new ed., London, 1769.

Chambers' 'Book of Days'; 2 vols., London, 1881.

Colgan's 'Hiberniæ Sanctorum Acta'; 2 vols., Lovanij, 1645.

'Cornwall, its Mines and Miners'; London, 1855.

Courtenay's 'Parliamentary History of Cornwall.'

Courtney's 'Guide to Penzance'; 1845.

Cox's 'How to Write the History of a Parish'; 3rd ed., London, 1886.

Dunkin's 'Brasses of Cornwall.'

Dunkin's 'Church Bells of Cornwall.'

Evans' 'Ancient Bronze Implements of Great Britain.'

Gilbert's 'History of Cornwall.'

Green's 'Short History of the English People'; London, 1881.

Halliwell's 'Rambles in Western Cornwall'; London, 1861.

Hals' 'History of Cornwall.'

Hingeston-Randolph's Indices to the Exeter Episcopal Registers.

Hitchins' 'Sea-shore, and other Poems'; Sherborne, 1810.

Holinshed's Chronicle; London [1586].

Hunt's 'Popular Romances of the West of England'; London (1871).
Jago's Cornish Glossary; Truro, 1882.
Jago's 'English-Cornish Dictionary'; Plymouth, 1887.
Journal of the Royal Institution of Cornwall.
Leland's Itinerary.
Lysons' 'History of Cornwall'; 1814.
Mackworth-Praed's 'Trash'; Penzance, 1832. (An electioneering squib.)
Norden's Cornwall.
Norris' 'Sketch of Cornish Grammar'; Oxford, 1859.
'Notes and Queries.'
Oliver's 'Monasticon. Dioc. Exon.'
Penzance Natural History and Antiquarian Society's Transactions.
Rhŷs' 'Celtic Britain'; London, 1882.
Richards' Welsh-English Dictionary; Dolgelley, 1815.
Rogers' 'Notice of John Knill'; Helston, 1871.
'Route-Book of Cornwall'; Exeter.
Sikes' 'British Goblins'; London, 1880.
Stokes' 'Pascon' (Cornish poem on the Passion). Philological Society's Transactions.
Tonkin's 'History of Cornwall.'
Tregellas' 'Cornish Tales.'
Tregellas' 'Cornish Worthies'; 2 vols., London, 1884.
Tregellas' 'Haunts and Homes of the Rural Population of Cornwall'; Truro, 1879.
Tregellas' 'Tourist's Guide to Cornwall'; London, 1880.
Tregenna's 'Autobiography of a Cornish Rector'; London.
Valor Ecclesiasticus Hen. VIII.; Rolls Series.
Vivian's 'Heraldic Visitation of Cornwall, 1620.'
Wallis' 'Cornwall Register'; Exeter, 1847.
Wesley's Journal.
'Western Antiquary'; Plymouth.

CORRIGENDA ET ADDENDA.

Page 7. To the Ferns add, 'The Bracken, *Pteris aquilina*.'
" 7, line 34. For 'Great Britain,' read 'the British Isles.'
" 7, " 35. For 'the south-west of Cornwall,' read 'West Cornwall.'
" 10, " 3. Add also the '*Cyamium minutum*.'
" 16. Add, 'Within the Gurnard's Head vallum are several well-defined hut-circles, especially on the north-east slope, near the edge of the cliff, and not far from the vallum.'

Page 16, line 28. For 'rude-stone,' read 'rude stone.'
" 16, " 29. For 'country,' read 'county.'
" 27, " 26. Add, 'The church of Phillack is said to owe its origin to Saint Piala.'

Page 35. Add, 'On the west end of the roof of Saint Nicholas' Chapel there is a small sexagonal granite shaft, tapering towards the top, which must have originally terminated in a cross.'

Page 39, lines 16, 17. For 'This cross,' read 'It.'
" 39, Cross No. III. Add, 'The reverse side of the head is carved with a plain Latin cross.'

Page 39, Cross No. IV. Read, 'A crucifix, on a round-headed shaft, in Lelant cemetery; on the other side is carved a cross pattee fitchee.'

Page 40. *Holy Wells*. *Dele* the first line, and read, 'These were probably considered,' etc.

Page 40, Well No. II. Add, 'Almost certainly, "Venton Dovey" means "Saint David's Well," and "Nanjivvey," "Saint David's Stream," or "Valley."'

Page 45, line 27. For 'Domain,' read 'demesne.'
" 52, " 9. To the list of unexplained field-names, add, 'Park-an-creet, at the Stennack, above Nanjivvey.'

Page 54. On August 9, 1331, 'The parishioners of the Chapel of Porthya [Saint Ives], belonging to the Parish Church of Lanant, in Cornwall, obtained a license for the performance of Divine Service in the said Chapel, provided that by no means was any portion of the revenues arising within the boundaries of the Chapel District to be withdrawn from the Mother Church in Lanant.' The document was written at Clist, the manor at which Bishop Grandisson was staying. (Hingeston-Randolph; *Grandisson Register*, ii., 32.)

Page 57, line 5. For 'Church,' read 'church.'
" 58, " 55. Ditto.
" 58, " 43. For 'angels,' read 'demi-angel corbels.'
" 62, " 35. Add, 'There is, on the wall of the tower, a dial with a beehive painted on it.'

Page 66, line 13. For 'J. S.,' read '"I. S." on one side, and the letter "R." on the other.' And add, 'The old bench-ends by the west door bear the following devices: 1. Shield, with spear and sponge-rod crossed saltirewise. 2. Shield, with Saint Andrew's cross. 3. The letters "D. G." 4. A spread eagle. 5. A Tudor crowned rose. 6. The letters "I. S."' Add also, 'There is a fine slate credence-niche in the wall north of the site of the high altar.'

Page 69, line 36. For 'canons regular,' read 'Canons Regular.'
" 70, " 9. For 'fretwork,' read 'tracery.'
" 72, " 32. Add, 'In September, 1549, the bells of the parish churches of Devonshire and Cornwall having been rung to call the people together when they rose in defence of Catholicism, Cranmer and others of the Council

ordered all those bells to be taken down which had been rung, except one to be left in each church. (See Lee, "Edward VI.," App., p. 250.)'

Page 79, line 21. For 'John Halse,' read 'James Halse.'

" 90, " 24. Read, 'nichil.—The following is a translation of this document :—'

Page 94, line 21. For 'Valour,' read 'Valor.'
" 115, " 13. For 'ffrancor,' read 'ffrancor̄.'
" 117, " 38, b. For 'bonus,' read 'bonis.'
" 132. Add, 'In the year 1590, Richard Ferris, William Thomas and Andrew Hill, for a wager rowed in a Thames wherry from London to Bristol. They stayed a night at Saint Ives, and were hospitably entertained by Squire Arundell.'

Page 133, line 13. For 'Johe,' read 'Johē.'
" 133, " 23. For 'Willmo,' read 'Willmō.'
" 134, " 14. For 'Johes,' read 'Johēs.'
" 135, " 21, b. For 'Trernyke,' read 'Trerynke.'
" 135, " 22, b. For 'Ric,' read 'Ric :'
" 135, " 33, b. For 'Wyllm,' read 'Wyllm̄.'
" 136, " 26, a. For 'Thoms,' read 'Thom̄s.'
" 136, " 29, a. For 'Vyvya,' read 'Vyvyā.'
" 137, " 5, a. For 'Niwell,' read 'Nowell.'
" 137, " 15, a. For 'Stepho,' read 'Stephō.'
" 137, " 23, a. For 'Robto,' read 'Robtō.'
" 138, " 38. For 'Johes,' read 'Johēs.'
" 140, " 22, b. For 'Phélipus,' read 'Phelipus.'
" 140, " 24, b. For 'Johes,' read 'Johēs.'
" 141, " 11, b. For 'Johnes,' read 'Johnēs.'
" 141, " 36. For 'iñ,' read 'in.'
" 142, " 13. For 'Joeēs,' read 'Johēs.'
" 142, lines 31, 32, and 33. For 'subs.' read 'subs :'
" 144, line 23. For 'first,' read 'next.'

The accounts for the year marked [1576?] on p. 148 should have been marked [1595], and should have followed on from the bottom of p. 160.

Page 149, line 12. For 'or',' read 'o''
" 153, " 10. For 'exepted,' read 'excēpted.'
" 156, " 9. For 'Mouteioye,' read 'Moūteioye.'
" 164, " 12. For '[soldiers],' read '[marines].'
" 194, " 5. Add, 'C. S. Gilbert, quoting from Hicks' MS., says, "About the year 1634, the coast of Cornwall was much infested with Turkish pirates, and the fishermen of St. Ives met with two vessels on the main, whose crews were supposed to have been carried off. These vessels, which were ascertained to have come from Ireland, were laden with rum and staves, and being brought into St. Ives, were there seized by Sir John Arundell, who gave one of them to the fishermen who brought them in, and sent the other to Padstow. In 1635, a Turkish pirate of twelve guns, and about ninety men, was brought into the harbour. This ship had previously taken three small vessels belonging to Looe and Fowey, in which were twelve men and two boys, who were made prisoners, and the vessels turned adrift. Whilst the pirate was afterwards cruising in the channel, the captives conspired against the Turks, and being luckily all upon deck, a signal was no sooner given, than the captain was knocked down with the capstan bar, and thrown overboard. The other Turks were driven below deck, and the cabin and forecastle seized by the assailants, who immediately sailed for St. Ives. Fortunately the wind was south-west, whereby they reached that port in safety, although their enemies below continued to fire shot through the deck, during their perilous passage. She was immediately seized by the vice-admiral, who maintained the Turks in the town for some months, and is supposed to have afterwards sent them to their own country." N.B.—There is a family at Saint Ives, called Allen, who say they are descended from a "Saracen" who came to the town many generations back.'

Page 195, line 30. Add, 'After the Saint Ives Roundheads had been defeated at Longstone Downs, they successfully opposed the Royalist army, which, under Colonel Goring, was marching upon the town. "The inhabitants," says Gilbert, "stopped up the roads with hogsheads, filled with sand, and also kept a strong guard, which obliged the colonel and his men to march back into the country." It is said that barricades of pilchard-casks were put across the road in the Stennack.'

Page 196, line 17. Add, 'In 1653, on the proclamation of Cromwell's Protectorship, Hicks says "every soldier wore round his hat two yards of ribbon, one white, the other blue, and several hogsheads of beer were given to drink the old rebel's health."'

Page 297, line 8. Add the following, from Gilbert: 'In 1705, a Dutch ship, and the Expedition packet from Lisbon, commanded by captain Clies, were chased into St. Ives Bay, by a French privateer, which being fired on by the castle guns, tacked about, and on her departure, fired several shots into the town. One of these struck a young woman in the street, by which she died the following day.'

Page 325, line 21. Add, 'Bullan's Lane leads from the Stennack road northwards up the hill to Ayr.'

Page 327, line 8. Add, 'The Meadow is situate by the shore over the eastern end of Porthmeor.'

Page 357. Add the following extract from the *St. Ives Weekly Summary* of March 26, 1892: 'With reference to the St. Ives Fencibles, a correspondent writes:—I have interviewed an Old Salt upon the subject and he informs me that this body of volunteers was in existence during the French war, and was disbanded at "the Peace" in 1815; so that it is quite possible that Mr. Halse may have been the Lieutenant-Colonel in command. There was an earth-battery of fifteen guns on the Island, where the present battery now stands—"the two-gun battery" at the back of the Island, facing Porthmeor—and four guns were placed on "the Castle." The men assembled for drill on the quay every Sunday morning, each man receiving for his attendance the sum of one shilling, which was promptly spent for refreshment at the Ship Aground, or other favourite house, before going home to dinner. My Old Salt, who is now eighty-two, says that his father was one of the Fencibles, and that he can just remember "the Peace" in 1815, and the burning of Bonaparte in effigy on the Fore Sand. The fishermen, during the war, were allowed three months for the mackerel fishing, and three months for the Pilchard Sean fishery; but upon one occasion an English frigate took a number of men out of the boats when on the fishing-ground, the Captain remarking that "men he wanted, and men he must have!" So the fishermen, instead of returning to St. Ives with their catches, were taken away to fight the French.'

Page 361, line 7. For 'beech,' read 'beach.'

" 367. Add the following entry in Captain Short's Diary: '1842, June 21. A meeting of the parishioners was held yesterday in the Town Hall to take into consideration the propriety of making a church rate, when it was proposed to make a rate of one penny in the pound. This was refused by a majority of fourteen, in consequence of which the church clock was immediately stopped, the sexton, clerk, and the man who keeps the clock in repairs and winds it up weekly, being each three years in arrears of salary.'

Page 369, line 41. For 'Bloomfield,' read 'Blomefield.'

" 369. *Trevarrack.* Add, 'This huge boulder bears, in large letters deeply cut, the inscription, "I. R., 1730."'

Page 419, line 20. For 'under Edward William I., de Boteraus,' read 'under Edward I., William de Boteraus.'

Page 436, line 30. Thamsyn Lemal died *circa* 1780.

" 436, " 33. Ann Lemal was married to John Green 1770, and was living 1787.

Page 437, line 29. For '1773,' read '1780.'

" 441. Add, 'The last of the Pawleys was a Miss Jane Pawley, who died in the poorhouse early in the present century.'

Page 449, line 15. *Dele* 'the house was rebuilt about the year 1888.'

" 450, last line. For 'John son [*sic*],' read 'John [Joan] daughter.'

" 485. Add, 'The only representatives of the eldest line of the Williams family are Mrs. Hannah Grainger Vincent, and her sister, Miss Jessie Vivian Williams.'

Page 417, line 36. Add, 'The stream called Tye Shoot, flowing northwards down the hill into the Stennack.'

INDEX.

NOMINA PERSONUM.

INDEX II.

NOMINA LOCORUM.

INDEX III. (GENERAL).

TABULA RERUM.

Elliot Stock, 62, Paternoster Row, London, E.C.

Lightning Source UK Ltd.
Milton Keynes UK
11 April 2011

170747UK00001B/13/P